Communications in Computer and Information Science

2694

Series Editors

Gang Li ⓘ, *School of Information Technology, Deakin University, Burwood, VIC, Australia*
Joaquim Filipe ⓘ, *Polytechnic Institute of Setúbal, Setúbal, Portugal*
Zhiwei Xu, *Chinese Academy of Sciences, Beijing, China*

Rationale

The CCIS series is devoted to the publication of proceedings of computer science conferences. Its aim is to efficiently disseminate original research results in informatics in printed and electronic form. While the focus is on publication of peer-reviewed full papers presenting mature work, inclusion of reviewed short papers reporting on work in progress is welcome, too. Besides globally relevant meetings with internationally representative program committees guaranteeing a strict peer-reviewing and paper selection process, conferences run by societies or of high regional or national relevance are also considered for publication.

Topics

The topical scope of CCIS spans the entire spectrum of informatics ranging from foundational topics in the theory of computing to information and communications science and technology and a broad variety of interdisciplinary application fields.

Information for Volume Editors and Authors

Publication in CCIS is free of charge. No royalties are paid, however, we offer registered conference participants temporary free access to the online version of the conference proceedings on SpringerLink (http://link.springer.com) by means of an http referrer from the conference website and/or a number of complimentary printed copies, as specified in the official acceptance email of the event.

CCIS proceedings can be published in time for distribution at conferences or as post-proceedings, and delivered in the form of printed books and/or electronically as USBs and/or e-content licenses for accessing proceedings at SpringerLink. Furthermore, CCIS proceedings are included in the CCIS electronic book series hosted in the SpringerLink digital library at http://link.springer.com/bookseries/7899. Conferences publishing in CCIS are allowed to use our online conference service (Meteor) for managing the whole proceedings lifecycle (from submission and reviewing to preparing for publication) free of charge.

Publication process

The language of publication is exclusively English. Authors publishing in CCIS have to sign the Springer CCIS copyright transfer form, however, they are free to use their material published in CCIS for substantially changed, more elaborate subsequent publications elsewhere. For the preparation of the camera-ready papers/files, authors have to strictly adhere to the Springer CCIS Authors' Instructions and are strongly encouraged to use the CCIS LaTeX style files or templates.

Abstracting/Indexing

CCIS is abstracted/indexed in DBLP, Google Scholar, EI-Compendex, Mathematical Reviews, SCImago, Scopus. CCIS volumes are also submitted for the inclusion in ISI Proceedings.

How to start

To start the evaluation of your proposal for inclusion in the CCIS series, please send an e-mail to ccis@springer.com

Wolf-Tilo Balke · Koraljka Golub ·
Yannis Manolopoulos · Kostas Stefanidis ·
Zheying Zhang · Trond Aalberg · Paolo Manghi
Editors

New Trends in Theory and Practice of Digital Libraries

TPDL 2025 Short Papers and Workshops
Tampere, Finland, September 23–26, 2025
Proceedings

Editors
Wolf-Tilo Balke
Technical University Braunschweig
Braunschweig, Germany

Koraljka Golub
Linnaeus University
Kalmar, Sweden

Yannis Manolopoulos
University of Nicosia
Thessaloniki, Greece

Kostas Stefanidis
Tampere University
Tampere, Finland

Zheying Zhang
Tampere University
Tampere, Finland

Trond Aalberg
Norwegian University of Science
and Technology
Trondheim, Norway

Paolo Manghi
CNR
Pisa, Italy

ISSN 1865-0929   ISSN 1865-0937 (electronic)
Communications in Computer and Information Science
ISBN 978-3-032-06135-5   ISBN 978-3-032-06136-2 (eBook)
https://doi.org/10.1007/978-3-032-06136-2

© The Editor(s) (if applicable) and The Author(s), under exclusive license
to Springer Nature Switzerland AG 2026
Chapters "Cite Lens: An AI Tool for Detecting Out-of-Scope and Out-of-Context Citations" and "Flexible Metadata Harvesting for Ecology Using Large Language Models" are licensed under the terms of the Creative Commons Attribution 4.0 International License (http://creativecommons.org/licenses/by/4.0/). For further details see license information in the chapter.

This work is subject to copyright. All rights are solely and exclusively licensed by the Publisher, whether the whole or part of the material is concerned, specifically the rights of translation, reprinting, reuse of illustrations, recitation, broadcasting, reproduction on microfilms or in any other physical way, and transmission or information storage and retrieval, electronic adaptation, computer software, or by similar or dissimilar methodology now known or hereafter developed.
The use of general descriptive names, registered names, trademarks, service marks, etc. in this publication does not imply, even in the absence of a specific statement, that such names are exempt from the relevant protective laws and regulations and therefore free for general use.
The publisher, the authors and the editors are safe to assume that the advice and information in this book are believed to be true and accurate at the date of publication. Neither the publisher nor the authors or the editors give a warranty, expressed or implied, with respect to the material contained herein or for any errors or omissions that may have been made. The publisher remains neutral with regard to jurisdictional claims in published maps and institutional affiliations.

This Springer imprint is published by the registered company Springer Nature Switzerland AG
The registered company address is: Gewerbestrasse 11, 6330 Cham, Switzerland

If disposing of this product, please recycle the paper.

Preface

This CCIS volume includes research and demonstration papers presented at the 29th International Conference on Theory and Practice of Digital Libraries (TPDL) and research papers from the EcoDL workshop accompanying TPDL. The 29th TPDL conference was held in Tampere, Finland, on September 23–26, 2025, as a fully on-site event.

TPDL has been hosted in sixteen European countries during the previous twenty-eight years: Ljubljana, Slovenia (2024), Zadar, Croatia (2023), Padua, Italy (2022), virtual (2021), Lyon, France (2020), Oslo, Norway (2019), Porto, Portugal (2018), Thessaloniki, Greece (2017), Hannover, Germany (2016), Poznań, Poland (2015), London, UK (2014), Valletta, Malta (2013), Paphos, Cyprus (2012), Berlin, Germany (2011), Glasgow, UK (2010), Corfu, Greece (2009), Aarhus, Denmark (2008), Budapest, Hungary (2007), Alicante, Spain (2006), Vienna, Austria (2005), Bath, UK (2004), Trondheim, Norway (2003), Rome, Italy (2002), Darmstadt, Germany (2001), Lisbon, Portugal (2000), Paris, France (1999), Heraklion, Greece (1998), and Pisa, Italy (1997). Following this trip around Europe, TPDL 2025 was organized in Tampere, Finland, for the first time.

Over the years, TPDL has established itself as an important international forum focused on digital libraries and associated technical, practical, and social issues. TPDL encompasses the many meanings of the term "digital libraries", including new forms of information institutions; operational information systems with all manner of digital content; new means of selecting, collecting, organizing, and distributing digital content; and theoretical models of information media, including document genres and electronic publishing.

In 2025, TPDL expanded its scope to prominently include Document Analysis and Recognition, and Information Retrieval, acknowledging the vital role of those research areas in the creation (by means of digitization and information extraction from heterogeneous sources), access, discovery, and dissemination of digital content. This includes exploring innovative approaches to document image analysis and recognition, search algorithms, data retrieval, user engagement, and personalized content delivery within digital libraries, making these areas central themes for the conference.

Following a widespread CFP, 52 full papers were submitted, plus 40 short papers and 11 demo papers, thus making a total set of 103 submissions. All submissions were single-blindly reviewed by at least three members of the international Program Committee. 14 papers were accepted for a regular oral presentation, whereas another 11 were accepted for oral presentation as findings papers. Another 20 short papers and 8 demo papers were accepted for presentation as posters and inclusion in these proceedings.In conclusion, the acceptance ratio was 27% for full papers, 21% for findings papers and 50% for short papers. These four paper types present high-quality, original research relevant to the TPDL community.

Four keynote speakers covered a wide range of topics. In alphabetical order:

- Eero Hyvönen (Aalto University, Finland), who delivered a talk on "Digital Humanities on the Semantic Web: from Infrastructure to Practical Applications, AI-based Knowledge Discovery, and Web of Wisdom",
- Yannis Ioannidis (National and Kapodistrian University of Athens, Greece), who delivered a talk on "Interactive Digital Storytelling",
- Felix Naumann (University of Potsdam, Germany), who delivered a talk on "Data Quality in the Age of AI", and
- Evaggelia Pitoura (University of Ioannina, Greece), who delivered a lecture on "Explainability, Fairness, and Their Interplay".

In addition, three specialized workshops ran during the first day of the event, which were (in alphabetical order):

- BIRDS: Building Innovative Research Systems for Digital Libraries Workshop (thanks to Christin Katharina Kreutz and Hermann Kroll),
- EcoDL: 1st Workshop on Digital Libraries and AI-based Information Systems for Ecological Research and Practice (thanks to Jennifer D'Souza, Birgitta König-Ries, Tina Heger, and Marie I. Kaiser), and
- NKOS: Networked Knowledge Organization Systems and Services Workshop (thanks to Koraljka Golub, Claudio Gnoli, Douglas Tudhope, Joseph A. Busch, and Marcia L. Zeng)

This volume also includes the papers accepted at the EcoDL workshop, co-located with TPDL 2025. The workshop had its own international program committee, whose members served as the reviewers of the workshop papers included in this volume. 19 papers were submitted to the workshop, out of which 9 were selected for presentation at the conference and publication in this volume, giving an overall acceptance rate of 47%.

EcoDL 2025: 1st Workshop on Digital Libraries and AI-based Information Systems for Ecological Research and Practice, chaired by Jennifer D'Souza, Birgitta König-Ries, Tina Heger, and Marie I. Kaiser.

EcoDL 2025 explores the integration of AI, digital libraries, and FAIR data principles in ecological research to improve knowledge synthesis and predictive modeling. Ecology's complexity and the fragmentation of multi-scale data across diverse sources present challenges in generalization, requiring advanced computational tools for structured knowledge representation, search, and decision support. Recognizing the essential role of digital libraries in research infrastructure, we sought to explore AI-driven systems and FAIR data principles for enhancing ecological methodologies. This workshop invited researchers from ecology, AI, and digital information systems to discuss innovations in data synthesis, semantic search, causal inference, and machine learning applications in biodiversity and conservation. While interdisciplinary contributions from climate science, ecosystem restoration, and geography were welcome, our primary focus was on advancing ecological research through digital and computational tools. The EcoDL 2025 workshop sought to foster conversations around innovation in ecological informatics, supporting open science and advancing digital methods for ecological research and environmental sustainability.

We would like to thank our invited keynotes for their contribution to the success and sustainability of TPDL 2025. We would like to thank all authors for submitting their papers to TPDL 2025 and we hope they will submit their research papers again in the future. We express our gratitude to all the Program Committee members for their time and effort in ensuring the high quality of the TPDL 2025 program. Finally, we would like to thank our sponsors and supporters: Springer, Tampere University, the Municipality of Tampere and the Coalition for Networked Information. Last but not least, we would like to thank the local organizers for their precious help. We hope the conference attendees enjoyed the technical program, informal meetings, and interaction with colleagues from all over the world.

September 2025

Wolf-Tilo Balke
Koraljka Golub
Yannis Manolopoulos
Kostas Stefanidis
Zheying Zhang
Trond Aalberg
Paolo Manghi

Organization

General Chairs

Zheying Zhang — Tampere University, Finland
Kostas Stefanidis — Tampere University, Finland

Program Committee Chairs

Wolf-Tilo Balke — TU Braunschweig, Germany
Koraljka Golub — Linnaeus University, Sweden
Yannis Manolopoulos — University of Nicosia, Cyprus

Short Papers Chairs

Marcos Andre Goncalves — Federal University of Minas Gerais, Brazil
Christos Papatheodorou — National and Kapodistrian University of Athens, Greece

Demonstration Papers Chairs

Liana Ermakova — University of Western Brittany, France
Yannis Tzitzikas — University of Crete, Greece

Workshop Chairs

Trond Aalberg — Norwegian University of Science and Technology, Norway
Paolo Manghi — CNR, Italy

Doctoral Consortium Chairs

Nicola Ferro   University of Padua, Italy
Sanna Kumpulainen   Tampere University, Finland

Proceedings Chair

Michalis Mountantonakis   Foundation for Research and Technology Hellas, Greece

Web Chair

Tiago Brasileiro Araújo   Federal Institute of Paraíba, Brazil

Volunteers Chairs

Maria Stratigi   Tampere University, Finland
Toni Taipalus   Tampere University, Finland

Program Committee

Trond Aalberg   Norwegian University of Science and Technology, Norway
Robert Allen   Independent researcher
Vangelis Banos   International Hellenic University, Greece
Valentina Bartalesi   CNR, Italy
Uldis Bojars   National Library of Latvia, Latvia
José Borbinha   University of Lisbon, Portugal
George Buchanan   RMIT University, Australia
Ricardo Campos   University of Beira Interior, Portugal
Vittore Casarosa   CNR, Italy
Donatella Castelli   CNR, Italy
Songphan Choemprayong   Chulalongkorn University, Thailand
Florence Clavaud   Archives Nationales, France
Fabio Crestani   University of Lugano, Switzerland
Mickael Coustaty   University of La Rochelle, France
Boris Dobrov   Moscow State University, Russia
Fabien Duchateau   University of Lyon 1, France

Ingo Frommholz	University of Wolverhampton, UK
Maria Gäde	Humboldt University, Germany
Daniel Garijo	Polytechnic University of Madrid, Spain
Marcos André Gonçalves	Federal University of Minas Gerais, Brazil
Sergiu Gordea	Austrian Institute of Technology, Austria
Mark Hall	Open University, UK
Andreas Henrich	University of Bamberg, Germany
Nikos Houssos	Feel Therapeutics, Greece
Ying Hsang Liu	Uppsala University, Sweden
Isto Huvila	Uppsala University, Sweden
Ornella Irrera	University of Padua, Italy
Antoine Isaac	Europeana, France
Adam Jatowt	University of Innsbruck, Austria
Himarsha Jayanetti	Old Dominion University, USA
Jaap Kamps	University of Amsterdam, Netherlands
Sarantos Kapidakis	University of West Attica, Greece
Ioannis Karydis	Ionian University, Greece
Roman Kern	Graz University of Technology, Austria
Johannes Kiesel	Bauhaus University of Weimar, Germany
Péter Király	GWDG, Germany
Martin Klein	Los Alamos National Laboratory, USA
Petr Knoth	Open University, UK
Stefanos Kollias	National Technical University of Athens, Greece
László Kovács	HUN-REN SZTAKI, Hungary
C. Lee Giles	Pennsylvania State University, USA
Hyowon Lee	Dublin City University, Ireland
Elena Maceviciute	University of Borås, Sweden
Bruno Martins	University of Lisbon, Portugal
Robert McDonald	University of Colorado Boulder, USA
Yannis Manolopoulos	University of Nicosia, Cyprus
Cezary Mazurek	Poznań Supercomputing and Networking Center, Poland
Dora Melo	Polytechnic Institute of Coimbra, Portugal
András Micsik	HUN-REN SZTAKI, Hungary
Agnieszka Mykowiecka	Polish Academy of Sciences, Poland
Wolfgang Nejdl	Leibniz University Hannover, Germany
Clemens Neudecker	Berlin State Library, Germany
Erich Neuhold	University of Vienna, Austria
Jeppe Nicolaisen	University of Copenhagen, Denmark
Sérgio Nunes	University of Porto, Portugal
Dimitris Plexousakis	Foundation for Research and Technology Hellas, Greece

María Poveda-Villalón	Polytechnic University of Madrid, Spain
Jian Qin	Syracuse University, USA
Edie Rasmussen	University of British Columbia, Canada
Thomas Risse	University of Frankfurt, Germany
Irene Rodrigues	University of Évora, Portugal
Laurent Romary	INRIA, France
Seamus Ross	University of Toronto, Canada
Michalis Sfakakis	Ionian University, Greece
Gianmaria Silvello	University of Padua, Italy
Marc Spaniol	University of Caen Normandy, France
Cyrille Suire	University of La Rochelle, France
Hussein Suleman	University of Cape Town, South Africa
Douglas Tudhope	University of South Wales, UK
Vassilis Tzouvaras	National Technical University of Athens, Greece
Herbert Van de Sompel	DANS, Netherlands
Shenghui Wang	University of Twente, Netherlands
Michele Weigle	Old Dominion University, USA
Marcin Werla	Qatar National Library, Qatar
Maja Žumer	University of Ljubljana, Slovenia

TPDL Governance

Executive Board

Trond Aalberg	Norwegian University of Science and Technology, Norway
Antoine Doucet	University of La Rochelle, France
Gianmaria Silvello	University of Padua, Italy

Honorary Chairs

Constantino Thanos	ISTI, CNR, Italy
Ingeborg Solvberg	Norwegian University of Science and Technology, Norway

Steering Committee

Trond Aalberg	Norwegian University of Science and Technology, Norway
Gerd Berget	Oslo Metropolitan University, Norway
José Borbinha	University of Lisbon, Portugal
Daniel Brenn	Martin Luther University Halle-Wittenberg, Germany
George Buchanan	University of Melbourne, Australia
Vittore Casarosa	ISTI-CNR, Italy
Oscar Corcho	Polytechnic University of Madrid, Spain
Jérôme Darmont	University of Lyon 1, France
Antoine Doucet	University of La Rochelle, France
Fabien Duchateau	University of Lyon 1, France
Koraljka Golub	Linnæus University, Sweden
Mark Hall	Open University, UK
Antoine Isaac	Europeana, France
Adam Jatowt	University of Innsbruck, Austria
Sarantos Kapidakis	Ionian University, Greece
László Kovács	MTA SZTAKI, Hungary
Sanna Kumpulainen	Tampere University, Finland
Paolo Manghi	ISTI-CNR, Italy
Yannis Manolopoulos	University of Nicosia, Greece
Tanja Merčun	University of Ljubljana, Slovenia
Christos Papatheodorou	National and Kapodistrian University of Athens, Greece
Edie Rasmussen	University of British Columbia, Canada
Andreas Rauber	Technical University of Vienna, Austria
Cristina Ribeiro	University of Porto, Portugal
Thomas Risse	University of Frankfurt, Germany
Gianmaria Silvello	University of Padua, Italy
Marcin Werla	Poznań Supercomputing and Networking Center, Poland

Using LLMs for Improving the OCR Accuracy of Old Greek Handwritten
Documents 100
 Andreas Evangelatos, Konstantinos Palaiologos, Basilis Gatos,
 Panagiotis Kaddas, Aikaterini Christopoulou, Vassilis Katsouros,
 and Andreas Kakridis

Is Word2Vec Dead for Topic Modeling? A Case Study on Hospitality
Opinion Mining 110
 Marc-Alexis Azaïs, Jean-Loup Guillaume, and Mickaël Coustaty

DM-LP: A Large Arabic Script Languages Dataset for OCR
and Cataloguing Research 124
 Luca Sala, Riccardo Amerigo Vigliermo, Giovanni Sullutrone,
 and Sonia Bergamaschi

Sharing is Caring: A Text Alignment Approach for Sharing Annotations
of Copyrighted Texts 135
 Frederik Arnold and Robert Jäschke

Tracing the Evolution of Coastal Scientific Literature in Scopus
(1970–2023) 146
 Julien Delaunay, Marc-Alexis Azaïs, Dipendra Sharma Kafle,
 Nicolas Sidere, Antoine Doucet, and Olivier de Viron

On Recommending Fair Influential Scholars with Geographically Diverse
Impact 156
 Arpan Dam, Sayan Pathak, and Bivas Mitra

Ranking to Learn: Human Experts, Search Engines, or LLMs for Learning
Guidance 166
 Yasin Ghafourian, Allan Hanbury, and Petr Knoth

WCAG Compliance of Open Government Documents 176
 Gregory Slager and Maarten Marx

Semantic Enrichment in SQL Workflows Through Targeted LLM
Invocation 185
 Yannis Foufoulas, Eleni Zacharia, Harry Dimitropoulos,
 Natalia Manola, and Yannis Ioannidis

Design and Implementation of a Next-Generation OAIS-Compliant
Digital Preservation System for the NDPP 196
 Lu Wang, Beibei Kong, Zhenxin Wu, Qian Li, and Zhixiong Zhang

Contents

Short Papers

NERGL: Named Entity Recognition and Grounding with Large Language Models for Ukiyo-E Artworks 3
   Bohao Wu and Akira Maeda

A Study of Temporal Fusion Strategies for Named Entity Recognition in Historical Texts 14
   Emanuela Boros

Cite Lens: An AI Tool for Detecting Out-of-Scope and Out-of-Context Citations 25
   Jean-Baptiste de la Broise, Frank Sauerburger, Enric Sayas, Dan-Marin Tecu, Sanita Meijere, and Milos Cuculovic

Information Specialists' Perspectives on Research Data Management Support in Social Sciences and Humanities 35
   Anna Sendra, Minna Ahokas, and Sanna Kumpulainen

StoryNetworks: An Annotated Dataset of Event Dependencies from Short Descriptions 46
   Daisuke Machizawa, Naoki Sawahata, Ryohei Ikejiri, and Yasunobu Sumikawa

Evaluating Human-LLM Alignment in ETD Subject Classification 57
   Hajra Klair, Fausto German, Bipasha Banerjee, and William A. Ingram

Linking References to Documents in Parliamentary Debates 70
   Floris Bos, Marc van Opijnen, and Maarten Marx

From Notes to Models: Leveraging LLMs for Museum Closure Data 80
   George A. Wright, Andrea Ballatore, Alexandra Poulovassilis, and Peter T. Wood

LLM-Based Information Extraction to Support Scientific Literature Research and Publication Workflows 90
   Samy Ateia, Udo Kruschwitz, Melanie Scholz, Agnes Koschmider, and Moayad Almohaishi

Identification of Potential Co-citation Linkages via Context-Aware
Citation Network Embeddings 207
   Masaki Eto

Demo Papers

Mass Migration of Records: LRM-Factory, a Solution to Facilitate
the Transition to Linked Data for Bibliographic Agencies 219
   *Marie Bastien, Morgane Sedoud, Anne Dupiat, Gregory Cochin,
and Carole Bruno*

Drawio2Triples: Semantic Validation and RDF Transformation of CIDOC
CRM Example Diagrams 229
   Elias Tzortzakakis and Pavlos Fafalios

Interactive Association Map Creation from Documents Using Association
Rule Mining 238
   Efthimios Mitkousis and Yannis Tzitzikas

Interactive and Provenance-Aware Search and QA over Documents using
LLMs, RAG and Knowledge Graph Verbalization 248
   *Iordanis Sapidis, Valantis Zervos, Michalis Mountantonakis,
and Yannis Tzitzikas*

Demonstrating Narrative Pattern Discovery from Biomedical Literature 258
   *Hermann Kroll, Pascal Sackhoff, Bill Matthias Thang,
Christin Katharina Kreutz, and Wolf-Tilo Balke*

A Modern Open Source Integrated Library System by Invenio 267
   Karolina Przerwa and Salomé Rohr

LLM-Enhanced DETEXA Workflow Builder for Semantic Enrichment 276
   *Yannis Foufoulas, Eleni Zacharia, Harry Dimitropoulos,
Natalia Manola, and Yannis Ioannidis*

IILAP: Interactive Information Literacy Assessment Platform 287
   Petra Dadic and Liana Ermakova

EcoDL Workshop Papers

Assessing the Landscape of Digital Species Identifiers 299
   Ricardo A. Correia and Maxim C. Isaac

Validation Challenges in Large-Scale Tree Crown Segmentations
from Remote Sensing Imagery Using Deep Learning: A Case Study
in Germany 311
   *Taimur Khan, Jasmin Krebs, Sharad Kumar Gupta, Jonathan Renkel,
Caroline Arnold, and Nils Nölke*

Managing FAIR Research Products for Biodiversity and Ecosystems
Within the LifeWatch Italy Infrastructure 324
   *Andrea Tarallo, Cristina Di Muri, Martina Pulieri, Francesco De Leo,
Mariantonietta La Marra, Davide Raho, Alberto Basset, and Ilaria Rosati*

Flexible Metadata Harvesting for Ecology Using Large Language Models 338
   *Zehao Lu, Thijs L. van der Plas, Parinaz Rashidi, W Daniel Kissling,
and Ioannis N. Athanasiadis*

Ecolink: Towards a Knowledge Graph Schema for Complex Environmental
Systems 353
   *Tim Alamenciak, Carlos Alberto Arnillas, Harry Caufield,
Katherine Compton, Kian Drew, Robert Frühstückl, Tina Heger,
Birgitta König-Ries, Chris Mungall, Sierra Moxon, Justin Reese,
Jordan Tardif, and Lars Vogt*

Monitoring and Modeling the Dynamics of *Halophila Stipulacea*
Meadows Using Satellite Imagery and Machine Learning Techniques 367
   Tom Avikasis Cohen, Gil Rilov, Gidon Winters, and Anna Brook

Compressed Species Classification Models for Biodiversity Monitoring 382
   *Katriona Goldmann, Oliver Strickson, Tom A. August, Jonas Beuchert,
Dylan Carbone, Mariya Iqbal, Jenna L. Lawson, Grace Skinner,
and David Roy*

Creating Datasets of Moth Morphology and Behaviour from Textual
Sources with Large Language Models 392
   Bartolome Ortiz-Viso, Jenna L. Lawson, and Tom August

Augmenting Geospatial Data With Large Language Models Using
Compositional Attention for Improved Avian Mobility Tasks Prediction 407
   Kehinde Owoeye

Author Index 423

Short Papers

NERGL: Named Entity Recognition and Grounding with Large Language Models for Ukiyo-E Artworks

Bohao Wu[1](✉) and Akira Maeda[2]

[1] Graduate School of Information Science and Engineering, Ritsumeikan University, Osaka, Ibaraki 567-8570, Japan
gr0696fv@ed.ritsumei.ac.jp
[2] College of Information Science and Engineering, Ritsumeikan University, Osaka, Ibaraki 567-8570, Japan
amaeda@is.ritsumei.ac.jp

Abstract. The titles of ukiyo-e artworks often contain rich named entity information that closely corresponds to specific visual regions within the artwork. Effectively linking these entities across textual and visual modalities enables more accurate named entity recognition (NER) and facilitates deeper interpretation of historical materials. In this paper, we propose a multimodal NER method that integrates textual input, visual features from object detection, and external knowledge from large language models. Our method achieves state-of-the-art results in both NER for ukiyo-e titles and grounding of named entities to their corresponding image regions, thereby advancing the structured understanding and accessibility of ukiyo-e contents.

Keywords: Ukiyo-e · Named entity recognition · LLMs

1 Introduction

Ukiyo-e, a prominent art form originating in 17th-century Japan, vividly portrays everyday life during the Edo period. Artists often assigned titles to their works to convey themes, provide context, attract viewers, and preserve cultural heritage. With the rise of digital archives, resources such as the Japanese Prints (Ukiyo-e) and Paintings Portal Database [3], developed by the Art Research Center at Ritsumeikan University, now curate rich metadata–including titles, artists, seals, and publication details–laying a solid foundation for scholarly and computational research.

Among these metadata, titles are especially valuable as they frequently contain historical named entities that may correspond to specific regions in the images. Integrating textual and visual modalities offers the potential to enhance named entity recognition (NER) and to support deeper interpretation and dissemination of ukiyo-e. However, two key challenges remain: effectively leveraging multimodal data to improve NER, and accurately grounding entities within the visual regions of these stylistically complex Edo-period artworks.

1.1 Grammar of Ukiyo-E Titles

The Japanese writing system includes three main scripts: kanji, hiragana, and katakana. Kanji consists of thousands of characters representing words and ideas, while hiragana and katakana are phonetic scripts with 46 characters each. These scripts combine to convey meaning and sound. However, the grammar used in ukiyo-e titles often differs from modern Japanese, and classical grammar can also be challenging to interpret.

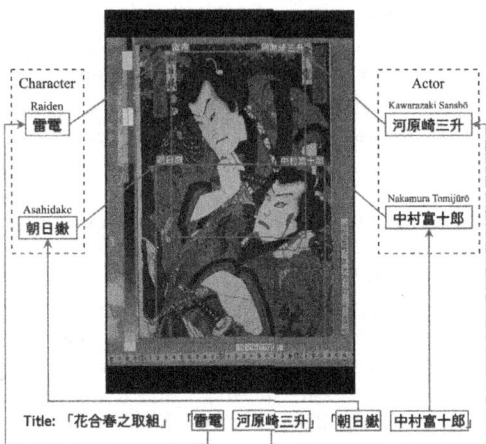

Fig. 1. Named entities in an ukiyo-e image and its title (Source: Japanese Prints (Ukiyo-e) and Paintings Portal Database, accession No.:NDL-106-00-065).

1.2 Images of Ukiyo-E

Figure 1 shows an example of an ukiyo-e print and named entities identified within it. This ukiyo-e artwork has a title (「花合春之取組」「雷電 河原崎三升」「朝日嶽 中村富十郎」 [1]) that depicts a theatrical performance staged as a flower comparison match in early spring. The scene features two kabuki actors assuming the roles of sumo wrestlers in dramatic confrontation. The character " 雷電 " (Raiden) is portrayed by the actor " 河原崎三升 (Kawarazaki Sanshō)", while " 朝日嶽 (Asahidake)" is performed by " 中村富十郎 (Nakamura Tomijūrō)". By illustrating both the actors and the characters they embody, the print conveys their commanding presence and charisma on stage. This composition exemplifies the yakusha-e, which is kabuki actors' dramatic poses and facial expressions.

---

[1] The title can be translated as "Spring Showdown of Courtesan Beauties, Raiden acted by Kawarazaki Sanshō, Asahidake acted by Nakamura Tomijūrō". It depicts a theatrical rivalry between two characters, symbolizing a contest of beauty and strength in a spring setting.

We propose a method named NERGL (**N**amed **E**ntity **R**ecognition and **G**rounding with **L**LMs) to address two key challenges. First, it improves the accuracy of NER in the analysis of ukiyo-e titles by combining textual information, visual features, and leveraging knowledge encoded in Large language models (LLMs). Second, it establishes explicit correspondences between the identified entities in the titles and their respective regions within the images. Our model is available online[2].

2 Related Work

2.1 Historical Named Entity Recognition

A wide range of studies have explored for historical named entity recognition (HNER) across various languages [7,10,12,15,20,24]. In modern-language NER task, transformer-based models [5,25] have achieved state-of-the-art performance. Building on those successes, transformer-based architectures have been increasingly adopted in HNER research [4,11]. Recent studies show that LLMs trained on modern corpora can be adapted to historical NER, especially with large-scale pretraining [6], but do not overpass the performance of fine-tuned NER neural models trained on historical corpora [8,9].

2.2 Multimodal Named Entity Recognition and Grounding

Multimodal Named Entity Recognition (MNER) is a task that enhances NER by incorporating images, alongside textual information. Early approaches integrated textual and visual modalities using modality attention mechanisms [19,21,30]. For multimodal task, BART [16] is proposed because its encoder-decoder structure can combine textual and visual features effectively. More recently, transformer-based architectures have also been applied to MNER, demonstrating their effectiveness in modeling complex relationships between text and images [26].

Although MNER integrates visual information into NER tasks, two major challenges remain. First, existing methods often fail to establish explicit correspondences between textual entities and their visual counterparts within images, limiting the resulting knowledge bases to the textual modality. Second, entity disambiguation remains problematic: even when named entities are correctly identified, homonymous expressions with identical surface forms may refer to distinct referents, leading to ambiguity in interpretation.

To address these limitations, the task of Multimodal Named Entity Recognition Grounding (MNERG) has been introduced. This task employs object detection techniques to extract visual regions and align them with textual named entities [27]. Recent work has further leveraged multimodal LLMs to integrate multi-granularity and multi-level information, enabling the construction of richer semantic associations between entities and visual contents [23]. In addition, visual grounding (VG) and visual entailment modules have been incorporated into LLMs to enhance entity grounding performance [17].

---

[2] Our dataset is available at https://huggingface.co/BohaoWu/Ukiyoe_MNERG.

2.3 NER for Ukiyo-E

Comparing with social media, ukiyo-e titles often contain more named entities and align closely with image content, posing challenges for existing methods. Prior studies have applied BERT-based models to perform NER on ukiyo-e titles [18,24]. To enrich metadata, ResNet-based visual features have been leveraged to identify visually similar prints, allowing complementary information to be shared across instances [14]. Additionally, object detection techniques have been applied to facilitate the automated identification of visual elements within ukiyo-e images [13,22].

Although text-based NER and image object detection have improved, current approaches still struggle to link entities in titles to visual regions. This limitation hinders deeper understanding and applications. To address these challenges, this paper proposes a method that not only improves the accuracy of named entity recognition in ukiyo-e titles by incorporating visual information, but also establishes correspondences between named entities and image regions.

3 Dataset

Table 1. Named entities in the ukiyo-e MNERG dataset.

Type	Character	Act	Actor	Location	Total
Training set	624	87	569	119	2049
Vaildation set	80	15	64	80	247
Test set	94	7	7	83	254
Total	798	109	640	932	2550

To support the MNERG task for ukiyo-e, we constructed a dataset of 1,082 randomly selected prints from meisho-e (famous place pictures) and yakusha-e (kabuki actor prints), each paired with its title and image. Titles were annotated with four named entity types: character, act, actor, and location. The dataset was split into training, validation, and test sets in an 8:1:1 ratio (Table 1). We also annotated image regions corresponding to entities in the titles using bounding boxes. Among the 1,082 prints, 788 (72.82%) contain at least one visually grounded entity.

4 Proposed Method

We propose a BART-based framework that integrates textual information, visual features, and knowledge from LLMs. By aligning bounding boxes with named entities and jointly optimizing NER and grounding losses, the model improves NER accuracy while enabling entity localization in images.

4.1 Integrating Multimodal Data

LLM Prompt. To incorporate external knowledge from LLMs, we design a task-specific prompt that presents the ukiyo-e title along with explicit instructions to identify four predefined types of named entities. The LLM is instructed to return NER results in a structured sequence format, including both entity spans and entity types, denoted as $l_s = (l_{s_1}, \ldots, l_{s_n})$. Through prompting, the LLMs will output an NER result l_{s_n} such as " 雷電 替名 ", which indicates that in the title shown in Fig. 1, " 雷電 (Raiden)" is labeled as a " 替名 (character)". These tokens are subsequently converted into word embeddings and used as part of the model input.

Textual Representation. Given an input ukiyo-e title sequence $U_s = (u_{s_1}, \ldots, u_{s_n})$, we encode both the title and the LLM output into the BART embedding layer. This produces a sequence of paired contextual representations $T = \{(t_{u_1}, t_{l_1}), \ldots, (t_{u_n}, t_{l_n})\}$, where $t_{u_i} \in \mathbb{R}^d$ and $t_{l_i} \in \mathbb{R}^d$ denote the embeddings of the i-th token from the title and the corresponding LLM-predicted token, respectively. These embeddings are processed jointly to facilitate downstream multimodal entity recognition and alignment.

Visual Representation. Given an input image v, we utilize VinVL [29], to extract candidate visual regions with detection scores above 0.5. Mean-pooled convolutional features of the top-K regions $B = \{b_1, \ldots, b_K\}$ are projected via a linear layer into the same space as text embeddings, yielding the final visual embeddings $V = \{v_1, \ldots, v_K\}$, where $v_i \in \mathbb{R}^d$.

Index Generation. Inspired by VG tasks [27,28], the model input is represented as $\text{Input}_i = [H_T, H_V] = \text{Encoder}([(t_{u_i}, t_{l_i}); v_i])$, where H_T and H_V are the text and visual embeddings. The triples $[(e_{\text{span}}, e_{\text{groundable}}, e_{\text{type}}), \text{Region}_{\text{pred}}]$ is the output of model. $e_{\text{groundable}}$ indicates whether the entity can be linked to a visual region. e_{type} is represented by dedicated label corresponding to predefined type. The remaining tokens in the output sequence refer to the positions of words in the input text. At the i-th time step, the decoder takes the encoded representation H_e and the previous output $y_{<i}$ as input to predict the output probability distribution $p(y_i)$:

$$p(y_i) = \text{Softmax}([C; \frac{(t_{U_i}, t_{L_i}) + \text{MLP}(H_T)}{2}] \cdot \text{Decoder}(Input_i; y_{<i})). \quad (1)$$

We use the cross-entropy loss to optimize the model, where N is the number of training samples and M is the length of the output sequence:

$$\mathcal{L}_T = -\frac{1}{NM} \sum_{j=1}^{N} \sum_{i=1}^{M} \log p(y_i^j). \quad (2)$$

4.2 Region Grounding

Lastly, for groundable entities, we stack an additional output layer to perform entity grounding. Specifically, let h_k denote the decoder hidden state at the time step where the predicted index corresponds to the *groundable* indicator (i.e., index 1). We compute a probability distribution over visual regions from VinVL, denoted as $p(z_k)$, as follows:

$$p(z_k) = \text{Softmax}(\frac{V + \text{MLP}(H_V)}{2} \cdot h_k). \tag{3}$$

Since regions extracted by VinVL may not perfectly match the ground-truth (GT) bounding boxes, we follow the standard VG protocol [28]. Specifically, we compute the Intersection over Union (IoU) between each detected region and all GT boxes associated with the current entity. For each visual region, the maximum IoU score across all GT boxes is retained as its alignment score. The resulting scores are then normalized to form a soft supervision distribution over the regions, denoted as $g(z_k)$.

To optimize entity grounding, we minimize the KullbackâĂŞLeibler divergence between the predicted region distribution $p(z_k)$ and the soft supervision $g(z_k)$:

$$\mathcal{L}_V = \frac{1}{NE} \sum_{j=1}^{N} \sum_{k=1}^{E} g(z_k^j) \log \frac{g(z_k^j)}{p(z_k^j)}, \tag{4}$$

where N denotes the number of training samples and E the number of groundable entities. During training, the overall loss function combines the standard NER loss $\mathcal{L}_T$ and the VG loss $\mathcal{L}_V$:

$$\mathcal{L} = \mathcal{L}_T + \lambda \mathcal{L}_V, \tag{5}$$

where λ is a weighting coefficient controlling the contribution of the VG loss, and is empirically set to 1 in our experiments. Given a i-th predicted sequence $u_{s_i} = [\hat{y}_1, \ldots, \hat{y}_l]$, where each token corresponds to either a vocabulary index or a special index from a predefined list (indicators, entity types, and special tokens), the sequence u_{s_i} is scaned sequentially to recover the predicted triples. It collects consecutive tokens into a candidate span until it encounters a special index indicating e_{type}. If the collected indexes in e_{span} are in ascending order and the next index matches a predefined type $e_{\text{groundable}}$, a triple will be added it to the result set E. The process continues until the end of the sequence, yielding a list of recovered entity-type triples for downstream use.

5 Experiments

Evaluation Metrics. We evaluate the performance of our proposed method using standard metrics for NER: precision, recall, and F1-score. The MNERG prediction is composed of entity, type, and visual region, whose correctness of each prediction is computed as follows [27]:

$$\frac{C_s}{C_t} = \begin{cases} 1, & p_s/p_t = g_e/g_t; \\ 0, & \text{otherwise.} \end{cases} \quad C_r = \begin{cases} 1, & p_v = g_v = \text{None}; \\ 1, & \max(\text{IoU}_1, \ldots, \text{IoU}_j) > 0.5; \\ 0, & \text{otherwise.} \end{cases} \quad (6)$$

$$\text{Correct} = \begin{cases} 1, & C_e = 1 \wedge C_t = 1 \wedge C_r = 1; \\ 0, & \text{otherwise.} \end{cases} \quad (7)$$

where C_s, C_t, and C_r denote the correctness of entity span, entity type, and region predictions. p_s, p_t, and p_r denote the predicted entity span, entity type, and region in the image, g_e, g_t, and g_r denote the gold entity span, entity type, and region. IoU_j denotes the IoU score between the predicted region p_r with the j-th GT bounding box $g_{r,j}$, which measures the overlap between two regions as the ratio of their intersection over their union. We then calculate precision, recall, and F1-score to measure the performance of NER and region grounding [27].

Experimental Setup. For NER methods, we use the BERT model published by Tohoku University [2]. For GMNER methods and NERGL methods, we use the BART model published by Kyoto University [1]. We select the top 18 bounding boxes extracted from VinVL, each with a score greater than 0.5. Both models are trained with batch size and epoch is 16 and 50.

Table 2. Experimental results of NER and MNERG metrics.

Methods	NER			MNERG		
	Precision	Recall	F1-score	Precision	Recall	F1-score
ChatGPT-4.1	72.71	38.21	49.69	-	-	-
BERT	75.70	76.77	76.07	-	-	-
BERT-CRF	79.76	79.53	79.40	-	-	-
MNER	84.32	83.32	83.82	-	-	-
GMNER	84.56	85.25	84.77	57.48	57.82	58.17
NERGL	**87.72**	**85.40**	**86.50**	**60.16**	**58.27**	**59.20**

5.1 Experimental Resutls

We compare ChatGPT-4.1, BERT [24], BERT-CRF [24], MNER [26], GMNER [27], and our proposed method NERGL. The results are shown in Table 2. NERGL, achieves the highest F1-scores in both evaluation settings, reaching 86.50% in standard NER metrics and 59.20% in MNERG metrics. Compared to traditional multimodal NER approaches, both MNERG and our method perform better on the ukiyo-e NER task. Although ChatGPT possesses recognition abilities, the lack of controllability in its output often leads to only 49.69%. Notably, by integrating outputs from LLMs, NERGL consistently outperforms all baselines in both settings. Since traditional NER methods do not provide mechanisms for predicting the grounding region of named entities, their results are not reported under the MNERG evaluation.

The performance across each named entity type is shown in Table 3. NERGL, achieves the best results on all four types, outperforming existing methods and resulting in the highest weighted average F1-score (W-F1-score).

Table 3. The F1-scores on four named entity types and W-F1-score.

Methods	Character	Act	Actor	Location	W-F1-score
ChatGPT-4.1	30.40	18.60	71.10	52.48	49.69
BERT	65.33	26.57	84.29	84.66	76.07
BERT-CRF	69.31	50.00	91.73	82.93	79.40
MNER	69.39	17.39	83.75	82.28	80.84
GMNER	75.79	50.91	92.12	85.48	84.27
NERGL	**80.76**	**66.67**	**94.09**	**86.85**	**86.50**

The results show that combining the BART model with multimodal data and outputs from LLMs improves performance. In particular, the accuracy of knowledge-dependent entities such as *Act* is greatly enhanced with support from LLMs.

6 Conclusion and Future Work

In this paper, we proposed NERGL for NER and grounding in ukiyo-e artworks by integrating textual information from titles, visual features extracted from images, and supplementary knowledge from LLMs. Our method demonstrated state-of-the-art performance in both NER and the more challenging MNERG task, effectively establishing correspondences between named entities and their visual representations in ukiyo-e artworks. Moreover, our approach addresses the challenge of unstable or unstructured outputs from LLMs by incorporating explicit decoding strategies and structure-aware processing. This also lays a foundation for constructing a multimodal knowledge graph for ukiyo-e artworks.

For future work, we plan to expand our dataset to include a broader range of artworks beyond ukiyo-e. We also aim to explore more advanced vision-language models and retrieval-augmented generation techniques to further improve accuracy. A user-interactive tool is planned to support the in-depth study of artworks, while promoting broader dissemination through digital archives.

Acknowledgments. This work was supported by JST SPRING, Grant Number JPMJSP2101 and JSPS KAKENHI Grant Number 23K11780. Sincere gratitude is extended to Prof. Ryo Akama of Ritsumeikan University for his invaluable insights and generous support for this paper.

References

1. BART Japanese Pretrained Model (2023). https://huggingface.co/ku-nlp/bart-large-japanese
2. BERT Models for Japanese Text. https://github.com/cl-tohoku/bert-japanese (2024). https://github.com/cl-tohoku/bert-japanese
3. Art Research Center, Japanese Prints (Ukiyo-e) and Paintings Portal Database, Ritsumeikan University (2025). https://www.dh-jac.net/db/nishikie
4. Boros, E., et al.: Robust named entity recognition and linking on historical multilingual documents. In: Cappellato, L., Eickhoff, C., Ferro, N., Névéol, A. (eds.) Working Notes of CLEF 2020 - Conference and Labs of the Evaluation Forum, Thessaloniki, Greece. CEUR Workshop Proceedings, vol. 2696. CEUR-WS.org (2020)
5. Devlin, J., Chang, M., Lee, K., Toutanova, K.: BERT: pre-training of deep bidirectional transformers for language understanding. In: Proceedings of the 2019 Conference of the North American Chapter of the Association for Computational Linguistics: Human Language Technologies, NAACL-HLT 2019, Minneapolis, MN, USA, vol. 1 (Long and Short Papers), pp. 4171–4186. Association for Computational Linguistics (2019). https://doi.org/10.18653/V1/N19-1423
6. Ehrmann, M., Hamdi, A., Pontes, E.L., Romanello, M., Doucet, A.: Named entity recognition and classification in historical documents: a survey. ACM Comput. Surv. **56**(2), 27:1–27:47 (2024). https://doi.org/10.1145/3604931
7. Fang, Z., Wu, L.C., Kong, X., Stewart, S.D.: A comparative analysis of word segmentation, part-of-speech tagging, and named entity recognition for historical Chinese sources, 1900-1950. In: Proceedings of the 5th International Conference on Natural Language Processing for Digital Humanities (2025). https://doi.org/10.18653/v1/2025.nlp4dh-1.1
8. González-Gallardo, C., Boros, E., Girdhar, N., Hamdi, A., Moreno, J.G., Doucet, A.: Yes but.. can chatGPT identify entities in historical documents? .In: ACM/IEEE Joint Conference on Digital Libraries, JCDL 2023, Santa Fe, NM, USA, pp. 184–189. IEEE (2023). https://doi.org/10.1109/JCDL57899.2023.00034
9. González-Gallardo, C., Hanh, T.T.H., Hamdi, A., Doucet, A.: Leveraging open large language models for historical named entity recognition. In: Linking Theory and Practice of Digital Libraries - 28th International Conference on Theory and Practice of Digital Libraries, TPDL 2024, Ljubljana, Slovenia. Lecture Notes in Computer Science, vol. 15177, pp. 379–395. Springer (2024). https://doi.org/10.1007/978-3-031-72437-4_22
10. Hamdi, A., et al.: A multilingual dataset for named entity recognition, entity linking and stance detection in historical newspapers. In: SIGIR '21: The 44th International ACM SIGIR Conference on Research and Development in Information Retrieval, Virtual Event, Canada, pp. 2328–2334. ACM (2021). https://doi.org/10.1145/3404835.3463255
11. Hanh, T.T.H., Doucet, A., Sidere, N., Moreno, J.G., Pollak, S.: Named entity recognition architecture combining contextual and global features. In: Ke, H.-R., Lee, C.S., Sugiyama, K. (eds.) ICADL 2021. LNCS, vol. 13133, pp. 264–276. Springer, Cham (2021). https://doi.org/10.1007/978-3-030-91669-5_21

12. Hubková, H., Král, P., Pettersson, E.: Czech historical named entity corpus v 1.0. In: Calzolari, N., (eds.) Proceedings of The 12th Language Resources and Evaluation Conference, LREC 2020, Marseille, France, pp. 4458–4465. European Language Resources Association (2020)
13. Khan, S., van Noord, N.: Context-infused visual grounding for art. In: Bue, A.D., Canton, C., Pont-Tuset, J., Tommasi, T. (eds.) Computer Vision - ECCV 2024 Workshops - Milan, Italy, September 29-October 4, 2024, Proceedings, Part VI. Lecture Notes in Computer Science, vol. 15628, pp. 118–136. Springer (2024). https://doi.org/10.1007/978-3-031-91572-7_8
14. Khan, S.J., van Noord, N.: Stylistic multi-task analysis of Ukiyo-e woodblock prints. In: 32nd British Machine Vision Conference 2021, BMVC 2021, Online, p. 213. BMVA Press (2021)
15. Labusch, K., Kulturbesitz, P., Neudecker, C., Zellhöfer, D.: BERT for named entity recognition in contemporary and historical German. In: Proceedings of the 15th Conference on Natural Language Processing, pp. 9–11 (2019)
16. Lewis, M., et al.: BART: denoising sequence-to-sequence pre-training for natural language generation, translation, and comprehension. In: Jurafsky, D., Chai, J., Schluter, N., Tetreault, J.R. (eds.) Proceedings of the 58th Annual Meeting of the Association for Computational Linguistics, ACL 2020, Online, pp. 7871–7880. Association for Computational Linguistics (202https://doi.org/10.18653/V1/2020.ACL-MAIN.703
17. Li, J., Li, H., Sun, D., Wang, J., Zhang, W., Wang, Z., Pan, G.: LLMs as bridges: reformulating grounded multimodal named entity recognition. In: Findings of the Association for Computational Linguistics, ACL 2024, Bangkok, Thailand and virtual meeting, August 11-16, 2024, pp. 1302–1318. Association for Computational Linguistics (2024).https://doi.org/10.18653/V1/2024.FINDINGS-ACL.76
18. Liagkou, K., Pavlopoulos, J., Machotka, E.: A study of distant viewing of Ukiyo-e prints. In: Calzolari, N., (eds.) Proceedings of the Thirteenth Language Resources and Evaluation Conference, LREC 2022, Marseille, France, pp. 5879–5888. European Language Resources Association (2022)
19. Lu, D., Neves, L., Carvalho, V., Zhang, N., Ji, H.: Visual attention model for name tagging in multimodal social media. In: Proceedings of the 56th Annual Meeting of the Association for Computational Linguistics (vol. 1: Long Papers), pp. 1990–1999 (2018)
20. Martin, L., et al.: Camembert: a tasty French language model. In: Proceedings of the 58th Annual Meeting of the Association for Computational Linguistics, ACL 2020, pp. 7203–7219. Association for Computational Linguistics (2020). https://doi.org/10.18653/V1/2020.ACL-MAIN.645
21. Moon, S., Neves, L., Carvalho, V.: Multimodal named entity recognition for short social media posts. In: Proceedings of the 2018 Conference of the North American Chapter of the Association for Computational Linguistics: Human Language Technologies, Volume 1 (Long Papers), pp. 852–860 (2018).https://doi.org/10.18653/V1/N18-1078
22. Ramos, P., Gonthier, N., Khan, S., Nakashima, Y., Garcia, N.: No annotations for object detection in art through stable diffusion. In: IEEE/CVF Winter Conference on Applications of Computer Vision, WACV 2025, Tucson, AZ, USA, February 26 - March 6, 2025, pp. 6228–6237. IEEE (2025). https://doi.org/10.1109/WACV61041.2025.00607
23. Wang, Z., et al.: Granular entity mapper: advancing fine-grained multimodal named entity recognition and grounding. In: Findings of the Association for Com-

putational Linguistics: EMNLP 2024, Miami, Florida, USA, pp. 3211–3226. Association for Computational Linguistics (2024). https://doi.org/10.18653/V1/2024.FINDINGS-EMNLP.183
24. Wu, B., Maeda, A.: A BERT-based method of named entity recognition for Ukiyo-e titles. In: Sustainability and Empowerment in the Context of Digital Libraries - 26th International Conference on Asia-Pacific Digital Libraries, ICADL 2024, Bandar Sunway, Malaysia, Proceedings, Part I, vol. 15493, pp. 3–17. Springer (2024). https://doi.org/10.1007/978-981-96-0865-2_1
25. Yang, Z., Dai, Z., Yang, Y., Carbonell, J.G., Salakhutdinov, R., Le, Q.V.: XLNet: generalized autoregressive pretraining for language understanding. In: Annual Conference on Neural Information Processing Systems 2019, Vancouver, Canada, pp. 5754–5764 (2019)
26. Yu, J., Jiang, J., Yang, L., Xia, R.: Improving multimodal named entity recognition via entity span detection with unified multimodal transformer. In: Proceedings of the 58th Annual Meeting of the Association for Computational Linguistics, pp. 3342–3352 (2020). https://doi.org/10.18653/V1/2020.ACL-MAIN.306
27. Yu, J., Li, Z., Wang, J., Xia, R.: Grounded multimodal named entity recognition on social media. In: Proceedings of the 61st Annual Meeting of the Association for Computational Linguistics (vol. 1: Long Papers), ACL 2023, Toronto, Canada, pp. 9141–9154. Association for Computational Linguistics (2023). https://doi.org/10.18653/V1/2023.ACL-LONG.508
28. Yu, Z., Yu, J., Xiang, C., Zhao, Z., Tian, Q., Tao, D.: Rethinking diversified and discriminative proposal generation for visual grounding. In: Lang, J. (ed.) Proceedings of the Twenty-Seventh International Joint Conference on Artificial Intelligence, IJCAI 2018, Stockholm, Sweden, pp. 1114–1120. ijcai.org (2018). https://doi.org/10.24963/IJCAI.2018/155
29. Zhang, P., et al.: VinVL: revisiting visual representations in vision-language models. In: IEEE Conference on Computer Vision and Pattern Recognition, CVPR 2021, virtual, pp. 5579–5588. Computer Vision Foundation / IEEE (2021). https://doi.org/10.1109/CVPR46437.2021.00553
30. Zhang, Q., Fu, J., Liu, X., Huang, X.: Adaptive co-attention network for named entity recognition in tweets. In: Proceedings of the AAAI Conference on Artificial Intelligence, vol. 32 (2018). https://doi.org/10.1609/AAAI.V32I1.11962

A Study of Temporal Fusion Strategies for Named Entity Recognition in Historical Texts

Emanuela Boros[✉][iD]

Digital Humanities Laboratory, EPFL, Lausanne, Switzerland
emanuela.boros@epfl.ch

Abstract. Temporal variation poses a unique challenge for named entity recognition (NER) in historical texts, where entities drift in surface form and salience across time. While language models (LMs) have made progress in various NLP tasks, their ability to reason about temporality, especially in diachronic contexts, remains limited or at least, questionable. In this paper, we systematically study how temporal metadata can be structurally embedded into NER models using a range of lightweight fusion strategies. We experiment with both absolute and relative temporal representations, injected into Transformer-based architectures via early or late fusion mechanisms such as cross-attention, adapters, and concatenation. Our evaluations on French and German historical datasets reveal that late fusion strategies yield more robust and temporally generalisable performance, particularly in early and noisy periods.

Keywords: Temporal NER · Historical NLP · Fusion strategies · Temporality · Transformer architectures

1 Introduction

Language is inherently temporal: its vocabulary, structures, and referents evolve across time. Yet LMs, despite their generalization power, still struggle with temporal reasoning [7,16,20,21,23,24,28,37,38,40]. Studies show that even advanced (generative) models like GPT-4 exhibit directionality biases [25], poor calibration over time [2], and difficulties retaining or reasoning over temporally anchored facts [6]. This limitation is particularly problematic in tasks such as named entity recognition (NER) over historical texts, where entities evolve, drift, or vanish entirely across time [3,8–10,26,29]. While temporality has been studied more commonly in video-based reasoning [18,21], in NLP tasks such as QA [1,4,13,17,31,34,38], or retrieval augmentation [11], historical NER remains comparatively underexplored.

Recent research has introduced temporal representations like time vectors [24], timestamp-aware pretraining [6], temporal graphs [19,22,30,33], and dynamic knowledge editing [39] to help models encode temporal signals. Yet these remain largely disconnected from token-level tasks like NER. Interpretability studies such as probing [14,35] and temporal diagnostic tests like TEMPLAMA [6] confirm that temporal information is often only weakly represented in model weights.

In the domain of NER, earlier efforts to address time drift focused on sampling or data augmentation in high-churn environments like different platforms of social media [5,29,36]. Meanwhile, historical NER introduces compounding challenges: diachronic drift, OCR degradation, and multilingual variation. Benchmarks such as HIPE [8–10] have laid the groundwork, and newer work has begun exploring temporally aware grounding through context retrieval [30], temporal knowledge graphs injection [12], or LLM-based inference [15]. While this is a good start, none have systematically compared architectural fusion strategies or directly assessed in practice whether models internalise temporal information.

In this paper, we (1) systematically inject temporal information into a Transformer architecture using explicit year embeddings, (2) design and compare a suite of modular, interpretable fusion strategies that incorporate time at different points in the model (e.g., early vs. late), and (3) benchmark their impact across decades and languages, while probing whether the models genuinely internalise temporal signals. We hope that this study will contribute to a clearer understanding of how time can be structurally integrated into token-level models and inform future work in (practical) historical NLP and temporally-aware sequence modeling.

2 Incorporating Temporality Into NER

Task Formulation. We treat historical named entity recognition (NER) as a straightforward token classification task, just with a temporal twist. Each input consists of a sequence of tokens $X = (x_1, x_2, ..., x_n)$, along with the document's publication year $year \in \mathbb{N}$. The goal is to assign each token x_i a label l_i, selecting from a standard entity taxonomy or marking it as non-entity. We use a Transformer-based architecture, where an encoder produces contextualized token representations $H = \text{Encoder}(X) \in \mathbb{R}^{T \times d}$, with T the number of tokens and d the hidden size. Each label l_i is then predicted from $h_i \in \mathbb{R}^d$, the contextualised representation of token x_i.

Temporal Fusion Strategies. To enable temporal adaptation of token classification models, we incorporate a temporal fusion module that integrates temporal context into token representations. This module fuses contextualised encoder outputs with a year-specific embedding using one of several strategies. We categorise them into *two fusion types*:

- `early fusion`, where temporal information is injected before or during encoding; and
- `late fusion`, where temporal information is applied to the encoder output.

We explore these strategies in *two modes of encoding temporal information*:

- `absolute` mode, the embedding index corresponds directly to the publication year (e.g., 1889); and
- `time-distance` mode, we instead compute the number of years between the document's publication date and a fixed reference year, namely 2025, assigning lower indices to more recent documents.

More specifically, let $y = \text{Emb}(year) \in \mathbb{R}^d$ denote the embedding of the document's publication year.

Baseline. This strategy skips temporal fusion entirely, i.e., $\tilde{H}_t = H_t$, and serves as a control condition.

Early Fusion

Cross-Attention Fusion (early-cross-attention). Temporal information is injected *before* encoding via cross-attention between the token embeddings and the year embedding:

$$\tilde{H} = H + \text{MultiHeadAttention}(Q = H, K = y, V = y),$$

where H denotes the input token embeddings and y is the year embedding, broadcast to match the input length. This mechanism allows each token to attend directly to the temporal context during encoding.

Late Fusion

Adapter Fusion (adapter). A lightweight MLP (adapter) processes the year embedding and adds the result to each token:

$$\tilde{H}_t = H_t + \text{MLP}(y), \quad \text{MLP}: \mathbb{R}^d \to \mathbb{R}^d.$$

Concatenation Fusion (concat). Generic fusion technique in many tasks, The year embedding is concatenated to each token vector and projected back to the original dimensionality:

$$\tilde{H}_t = W \cdot [H_t; y], \quad W \in \mathbb{R}^{2d \times d}.$$

Relative Temporal Fusion (relative). A nonlinear encoder transforms the year embedding into a relative temporal representation, which is used in a feature-wise linear modulation (FiLM)-like modulation [27]:

$$y' = \text{LayerNorm}(\text{SiLU}(Wy)), \tilde{H}_t = \gamma(y') \odot H_t + \beta(y'), \text{where:}$$

$\text{SiLU}(x) = x \cdot \sigma(x)$ is the sigmoid linear unit and $\sigma(x)$ is the logistic sigmoid.

Cross-Attention Fusion (late-cross-attention). Temporal information is fused with the encoder output using cross-attention, similar to the *early fusion* one but *after* encoding:

$$\tilde{H} = H + \text{MultiHeadAttention}(Q = H, K = y, V = y).$$

3 Experimental Setup

Datasets. Our experiments are based on the `hipe2020` dataset, as included in the HIPE-2022 shared task [10]. We focus exclusively on the French and German subsets, which include publication year metadata required for temporal modeling (the English subset was excluded due to missing training data). We use the coarse-grained entity taxonomy (*loc, org, pers, time, prod*) and retain all documents regardless of their temporal span. The French data comprises 10,923 annotated mentions across 1798–2018 with an average OCR noise rate of ≈33%, while the German subset contains 6,584 mentions spanning 1798–1950 with ≈43% OCR noise. While all splits cover wide temporal ranges, our goal is not to simulate chronological generalisation but to analyse the structural inclusion of time in the models.

Evaluation and Hyperparameters. We evaluate all models using micro-averaged F1 scores, computed at the entity level. All models are fine-tuned using the standard Transformer architecture, with the multilingual historical variant as base model[1] [32], with a maximum sequence length of 512 tokens. Models are trained using a batch size of 16, for 5 epochs, with a fixed seed (2025) for reproducibility.

NER Performance Across Temporal Strategies. To evaluate the effectiveness of temporal conditioning, we plot F1 scores across publication years for each fusion strategy under two temporal modes: `absolute` and `time-distance` in Fig. 1. At first glance, we might not be able to see big improvements, but we do observe several slight temporal patterns across both languages:

- **1800–1850**: Early periods exhibit high variability in F1 scores, likely due to OCR noise and sparse annotations. Late fusion strategies demonstrate notable gains in robustness, particularly under the `time-distance` mode, outperforming both baseline and early fusion.
- **1850–1900**: Performance stabilizes across models. While all strategies benefit from improved data quality, late fusion still maintains a slight edge, especially in French. Early fusion appears more sensitive to temporal encoding choices.
- **1900–1950**: F1 scores fluctuate again, particularly in German, with drops around 1940–1950. This may be attributed to document scarcity or inconsistencies in historical orthography. Late fusion again proves more resilient.
- **1950–2000**: Baseline models catch up, but late fusion strategies retain superiority, especially in the German subset. The performance gap narrows, suggesting a a a diminishing marginal benefit from temporal conditioning in modern decades.
- **2000–2018**: All models improve steadily due to better OCR and more standardised data. However, late fusion strategies still outperform slightly, reflecting their capacity to generalise across time even when temporal drift is lower.

---

[1] https://huggingface.co/dbmdz/bert-base-historic-multilingual-cased.

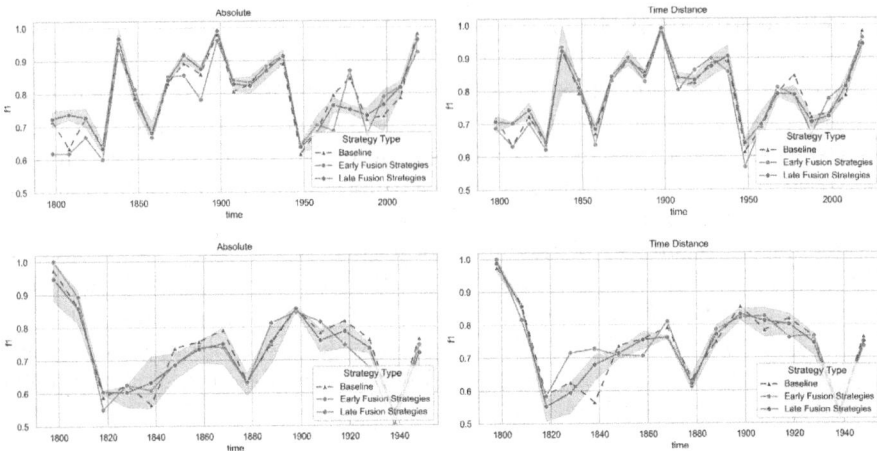

Fig. 1. F1 scores over time for French (top) and German (bottom) subsets of HIPE-2020 under two temporal modes: `absolute` (left) and `time-distance` (right).

Generally, we observe that all temporal fusion strategies, particularly late fusion ones, consistently improve NER performance across both languages with some benefits most pronounced in early or noisy periods, but before establishing the significance of these results, we analyse next other possible influencing factors.

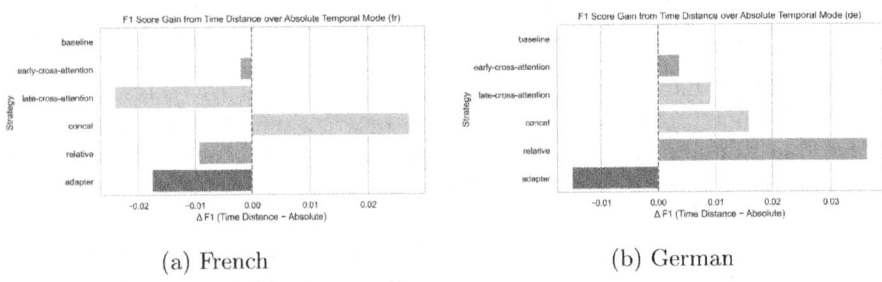

(a) French   (b) German

Fig. 2. Average F1 score difference between `time-distance` and `absolute` temporal modes, computed for each fusion strategy. Positive values indicate improved performance.

Absolute Time Versus Distance-Based Encoding. We compare the impact of `absolute` versus `time-distance` temporal encoding by computing the mean F1 score difference per strategy (Fig. 2). We see that, in German, strategies like `concat`, `relative`, and `adapter` benefit from `time-distance` encoding (up to +3 F1), suggesting improved temporal generalisation. In French, however, effects are less consistent: while `concat` gains slightly, others such as `adapter` and `late-cross-attention` perform better with `absolute` encoding. These results could imply that while the choice of temporal mode is secondary to the fusion strategy, it can still influence outcomes and should be tuned per language and setup.

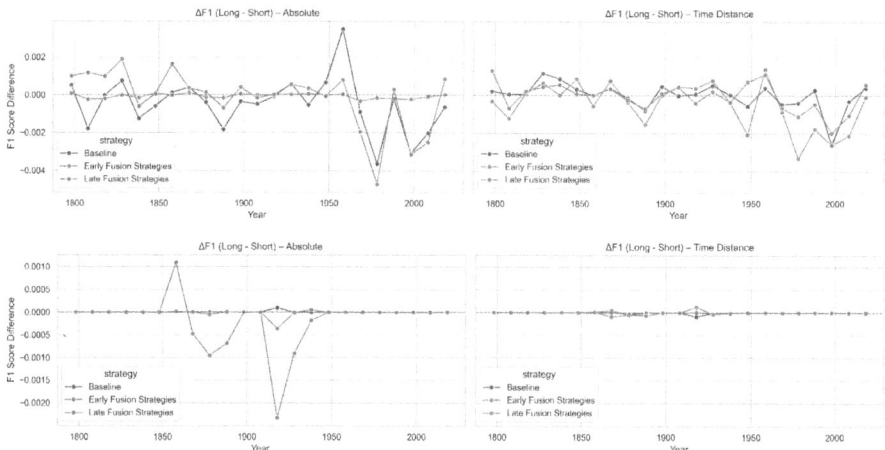

Fig. 3. Difference in F1 score for French (top) and German (bottom) between long and short entity mentions ($\Delta F1 = F1_{\text{long}} - F1_{\text{short}}$), across decades and fusion strategies for each temporal mode.

Entity Length Sensitivity. To explore whether temporal strategies differentially impact entity mentions of varying surface complexity, we categorize entities by their character length: those with 10 characters or fewer are considered *short*, those between 11 and 20 as *medium*, and those exceeding 20 characters as *long*. For each group, we compute average F1 scores and analyze the performance gap between long and short entities, denoted as $\Delta F1 = F1_{\text{long}} - F1_{\text{short}}$. Figure 3 presents the length sensitivity analysis across French (left) and German (right) subsets of the HIPE-2020 corpus. We observe that late fusion strategies tend to show a more stable or slightly positive gain for longer entities across both languages, particularly in earlier decades where surface forms tend to be longer or more structurally complex. The effect is more pronounced under the `time-distance` temporal mode, where relative temporal encoding appears to support generalisation over long spans. Baseline and early fusion strategies, by contrast, exhibit more unpredictability or minimal difference. These results suggest that injecting temporal signals at later stages of the model helps preserve surface-level distinctions critical for accurately identifying long entities.

Entity Type Gains from Temporal Fusion. To assess which entity types benefit most from temporal fusion, we compute the gain in prediction frequency for each surfaceâĂŞtype pair, defined as the increase in count compared to the baseline. Figure 4 shows that loc entities exhibit the highest variability and occasional large gains, suggesting that temporal conditioning improves their recall, likely due to historical drift and ambiguity. Other types such as org, pers, prod, and time show more modest and consistent distributions, indicating that improvements are generally limited in magnitude.

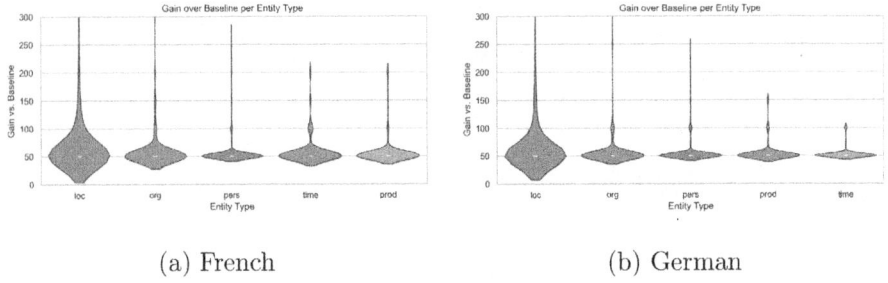

(a) French (b) German

Fig. 4. Distribution of gain over baseline for each entity type, measured as the difference in surface form frequency between temporal models and the baseline.

Do the Time-Based Models Really Learn Time?. To evaluate the extent to which our models encode temporal information internally, we adopt a linear probing strategy. Let $h_{\text{CLS}} \in \mathbb{R}^d$ denote the final hidden representation of the [CLS] token. We train a linear classifier of the form:

$$\hat{y} = \arg\max_i\ W_i^\top h_{\text{CLS}} + b_i,$$

where $W \in \mathbb{R}^{d \times Y}$, $b \in \mathbb{R}^Y$, and Y is the number of discrete publication years. To ensure that the probing task evaluates *latent* temporal knowledge rather than reflecting direct access to input metadata, we modify the forward pass by injecting a randomly sampled publication year $y \in \mathbb{N}$ during inference. This disables architectural conditioning on the true document year (whether absolute or time-distance). To account for randomness and obtain a more stable signal, we repeat the probing process five times and report the average accuracy across runs.

Figure 5 reports the average prediction accuracy, grouped by fusion type and strategy, and we notice that the late fusion strategies consistently yield higher accuracy than early fusion or baseline models, confirming that injecting temporal information after contextualization better preserves temporal signals in the latent space. Among them, late cross-attention, adapter, and concatenation lead to the best results. In contrast, the baseline and early-cross-attention models show minimal temporal encoding. We could even say that probing shows that time-aware architectures, especially late-fusion models, encode temporality even

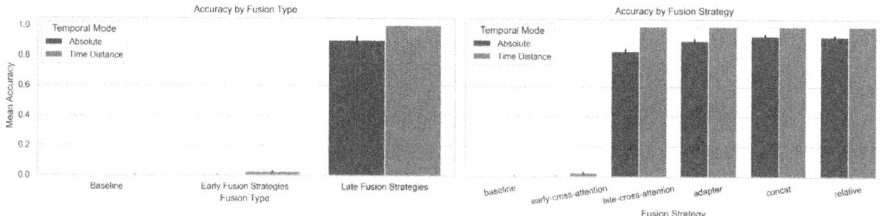

Fig. 5. Probing accuracy across models. Left: grouped by fusion type. Right: grouped by fusion strategy.

when gold-year metadata is removed. This suggests that structural fusion mechanisms lead to genuine internalisation of temporal context, rather than relying on surface-level cues.

Are the Improvements Really Significant?. To assess whether temporal fusion strategies offer statistically significant improvements over the baseline, we conducted paired t-tests across yearly F1 scores for each strategy and temporal mode. We noticed that most fusion strategies do not yield statistically significant gains at the $p < 0.05$ threshold with the exception of the `late-cross-attention` strategy under the `absolute` temporal mode demonstrates a significant difference compared to the baseline ($p = 0.041$). This could suggest that, while temporal fusion generally improves model performance, these improvements are often subtle and not uniformly consistent across years.

4 Insights and Conclusions

By structurally injecting time into Transformer-based architectures using modular fusion strategies, we demonstrate that temporal conditioning yields modest yet consistent gains for historical NER across languages, decades, and entity types. Late fusion strategies, particularly `late-cross-attention`, perform most robustly, especially in early, noisy periods, and help improve recognition of longer entities and temporally variable types like locations. Thus, based on our findings, we recommend: (1) adopting late fusion for integrating time; (2) testing both `absolute` and `time-distance` encodings, as their impact is context-dependent; and (3) using temporal fusion as a lightweight enhancement for diachronic or noisy corpora. While our approach is not novel and we acknowledge the growing utility of generative LLMs, we emphasize that real-world historical corpora often impose constraints: they may be large, private, or governed by restrictive policies. In such cases, structured methods that leverage metadata such as time or publication dates remain an important source of exploitable information for interpretable models.

Limitations

While our study presents a systematic comparison of temporal fusion strategies for historical NER, there still remian several limitations. First, we only consider year-level granularity, which may be insufficient for domains requiring finer temporal resolution. Second, our experiments are confined to the HIPE-2020 dataset's French and German subsets, results may not generalise to other languages or genres of historical text. Third, the probing analysis focuses solely on linear decodability of year embeddings and may underestimate more subtle forms of temporal encoding. Finally, our models are evaluated under controlled conditions using a single backbone architecture; real-world applications with noisy or missing metadata may yield different results.

Acknowledgments. This work has been supported by the Swiss National Science Foundation under grant No. CRSII5_213585 and by the Luxembourg National Research Fund under grant No. 17498891.

References

1. Agarwal, P., Strötgen, J., del Corro, L., Hoffart, J., Weikum, G.: DiaNED: time-aware named entity disambiguation for diachronic corpora (2018). https://www.aclweb.org/anthology/P18-2109/
2. Beniwal, H., Patel, D., D, K.N., Ladia, H., Yadav, A., Singh, M.: Remember this event that year? Assessing temporal information and reasoning in large language models (2024). https://arxiv.org/abs/2402.11997
3. Boros, E., et al.: Alleviating digitization errors in named entity recognition for historical documents. In: Proceedings of the 24th Conference on Computational Natural Language Learning, pp. 431–441 (2020)
4. Chang, H., et al.: A comprehensive evaluation of large language models on temporal event forecasting (2024). https://arxiv.org/abs/2407.11638
5. Chen, S., Neves, L., Solorio, T.: Mitigating temporal-drift: a simple approach to keep NER models crisp. In: Proceedings of the Ninth International Workshop on Natural Language Processing for Social Media, pp. 163–169. Association for Computational Linguistics, Online (2021). https://doi.org/10.18653/v1/2021.socialnlp-1.14
6. Cole, J.R.: Time-aware language models as temporal knowledge bases(2022)
7. Ding, X., Wang, L.: Do language models understand time? (2024). https://arxiv.org/abs/2412.13845
8. Ehrmann, M., Romanello, M., Bircher, S., Clematide, S.: Introducing the CLEF 2020 HIPE shared task: named entity recognition and linking on historical newspapers. (2020). https://doi.org/10.1007/978-3-030-45442-5_68
9. Ehrmann, M., Romanello, M., Doucet, A., Clematide, S.: Introducing the HIPE 2022 Shared Task: Named Entity Recognition and Linking in Multilingual Historical Documents (2022). https://doi.org/10.1007/978-3-030-99739-7_44

10. Ehrmann, M., Romanello, M., Najem-Meyer, S., Doucet, A., Clematide, S.: Extended overview of HIPE-2022: Named Entity Recognition and Linking in Multilingual Historical Documents. In: Faggioli, G., Ferro, N., Hanbury, A., Potthast, M. (eds.) Proceedings of the Working Notes of CLEF 2022 - Conference and Labs of the Evaluation Forum, vol. 3180. CEUR-WS (2022). https://doi.org/10.5281/zenodo.6979577, http://ceur-ws.org/Vol-3180/paper-83.pdf
11. Gade, A., Jetcheva, J.: It's about time: Incorporating temporality in retrieval augmented language models (2024). https://arxiv.org/abs/2401.13222
12. González-Gallardo, C.E., Boros, E., Giamphy, E., Hamdi, A., Moreno, J.G., Doucet, A.: Injecting temporal-aware knowledge in historical named entity recognition (2023). https://doi.org/10.1007/978-3-031-28244-7_24
13. Gruber, R., Abdallah, A., Färber, M., Jatowt, A.: ComplexTempQA: a large-scale dataset for complex temporal question answering (2024). https://arxiv.org/abs/2406.04866
14. Gurnee, W., Tegmark, M.: Language models represent space and time (2024). https://openreview.net/forum?id=jE8xbmvFin
15. Hiltmann, T., et al.: NER4all or context is all you need: using LLMs for low-effort, high-performance NER on historical texts. a humanities informed approach (2025). https://arxiv.org/abs/2502.04351
16. Jain, R., Sojitra, D., Acharya, A., Saha, S., Jatowt, A., Dandapat, S.: Do language models have a common sense regarding time? revisiting temporal commonsense reasoning in the era of large language models (2023). https://aclanthology.org/2023.emnlp-main.418/
17. Jia, Z., Abujabal, A., Roy, R.S., Strötgen, J., Weikum, G.: TempQuestions: a benchmark for temporal question answering (2018). https://doi.org/10.1145/3184558.3191536
18. Ko, D., Lee, J.S., Kang, W., Roh, B., Kim, H.J.: Large language models are temporal and causal reasoners for video question answering (2023). https://aclanthology.org/2023.emnlp-main.261/
19. Liang, K., et al.: A survey of knowledge graph reasoning on graph types: static. dynamic, and multimodal **46**(12), 9456–9478 (2022)
20. Liu, L., Yu, S., Wang, R., Ma, Z., Shen, Y.: How can large language models understand spatial-temporal data? (2024). https://arxiv.org/abs/2401.14192
21. Liu, R., Li, C., Tang, H., Ge, Y., Shan, Y., Li, G.: St-LLM: large language models are effective temporal learners (2024). https://www.ecva.net/papers/eccv_2024/papers_ECCV/html/7364_ECCV_2024_paper.php
22. Lu, Y., et al.: Knowledge editing with dynamic knowledge graphs for multi-hop question answering. In: Proceedings of the AAAI Conference on Artificial Intelligence, vol. 39, pp. 24741–24749 (2025)
23. Nako, P., Jatowt, A.: Navigating tomorrow: reliably assessing large language models performance on future event prediction (2025). https://arxiv.org/abs/2501.05925
24. Nylund, K., Gururangan, S., Smith, N.A.: Time is encoded in the weights of fine-tuned language models (2023). https://arxiv.org/abs/2312.13401
25. Papadopoulos, V., Wenger, J., Hongler, C.: Arrows of time for large language models (2024). https://openreview.net/forum?id=UpSe7ag34v
26. Pawłowski, A., Walkowiak, T.: NLP for digital humanities: processing chronological text corpora (2024). https://aclanthology.org/2024.nlp4dh-1.10/
27. Perez, E., Strub, F., De Vries, H., Dumoulin, V., Courville, A.: Film: visual reasoning with a general conditioning layer. In: Proceedings of the AAAI Conference on Artificial Intelligence, vol. 32 (2018)

28. Qiu, Y., Zhao, Z., Ziser, Y., Korhonen, A., Ponti, E.M., Cohen, S.B.: Are large language models temporally grounded? (2023). https://arxiv.org/abs/2311.08398
29. Rijhwani, S., Preotiuc-Pietro, D.: Temporally-informed analysis of named entity recognition (2020). https://www.aclweb.org/anthology/2020.acl-main.680/
30. Rosin, G.D., Guy, I., Radinsky, K.: Time masking for temporal language models. In: Proceedings of the Fifteenth ACM International Conference on Web Search and Data Mining, pp. 833–841 (2022)
31. Ruiz, A.G., de la Rosa, T., Borrajo, D.: On the temporal question-answering capabilities of large language models over anonymized data (2025). https://arxiv.org/abs/2504.07646
32. Schweter, S., März, L., Schmid, K., Çano, E.: HMBERT: historical multilingual language models for named entity recognition (2022). https://arxiv.org/abs/2205.15575
33. Song, R., et al.: Multilingual knowledge graph completion from pretrained language models with knowledge constraints. In: Rogers, A., Boyd-Graber, J., Okazaki, N. (eds.) Findings of the Association for Computational Linguistics: ACL 2023, pp. 7709–7721. Association for Computational Linguistics, Toronto, Canada (2023). https://doi.org/10.18653/v1/2023.findings-acl.488, https://aclanthology.org/2023.findings-acl.488/
34. Tan, Q., Ng, H.T., Bing, L.: Towards benchmarking and improving the temporal reasoning capability of large language models (2023). https://arxiv.org/abs/2306.08952
35. Thukral, S., Kukreja, K., Kavouras, C.: Probing language models for understanding of temporal expressions. In: Bastings, J., Belinkov, Y., Dupoux, E., Giulianelli, M., Hupkes, D., Pinter, Y., Sajjad, H. (eds.) Proceedings of the Fourth BlackboxNLP Workshop on Analyzing and Interpreting Neural Networks for NLP, pp. 396–406. Association for Computational Linguistics, Punta Cana, Dominican Republic (2021). https://doi.org/10.18653/v1/2021.blackboxnlp-1.31, https://aclanthology.org/2021.blackboxnlp-1.31/
36. Ushio, A., Barbieri, F., Sousa, V., Neves, L., Camacho-Collados, J.: Named entity recognition in twitter: a dataset and analysis on short-term temporal shifts (2022). https://aclanthology.org/2022.aacl-main.25/
37. Wallat, J., Jatowt, A., Anand, A.: Temporal blind spots in large language models (2024). https://arxiv.org/abs/2401.12078
38. Xiong, S., Payani, A., Kompella, R., Fekri, F.: Large language models can learn temporal reasoning (2024). https://aclanthology.org/2024.acl-long.563/
39. Yin, X., Jiang, J., Yang, L., Wan, X.: History matters: temporal knowledge editing in large language model (2023). https://arxiv.org/abs/2312.05497
40. Zheng, L.N., et al.: Understanding why large language models can be ineffective in time series analysis: the impact of modality alignment (2024). https://arxiv.org/abs/2410.12326

Cite Lens: An AI Tool for Detecting Out-of-Scope and Out-of-Context Citations

Jean-Baptiste de la Broise^(✉), Frank Sauerburger, Enric Sayas, Dan-Marin Tecu, Sanita Meijere, and Milos Cuculovic

MDPI, Grosspeteranlage 5, 4052 Basel, Switzerland
{jeanbaptiste.delabroise,ai-team}@mdpi.com
https://www.mdpi.com

Abstract. While citations are essential to scholarly communication, their role in assessing academic success has contributed to various forms of misuse. Citation cartels and citation padding are examples of such misuse, yielding irrelevant references and corrupting the academic record.

Here, we introduce a tool that we developed and use internally for detecting problematic citation behaviors, called *Cite Lens* (sample code available on GitHub: https://github.com/MDPI-AG/citelens.), which analyzes citations using vector (embedding) similarity. This tool can either detect misalignment between an article and its references (*article–reference similarity*), or the reference and the paragraph in which it is cited (*context–reference similarity*). We analyze the citation patterns across multiple publishers and topics and show the capability of this approach to detect problematic citations. This tool aims to support MDPI's editorial screening and help prevent unethical or manipulative citation behavior.

Keywords: research integrity · citation validation · citation analyis · semantic extraction · information retrieval · Natural Language Understanding · Artificial Intelligence

1 Introduction

Scientific progress inherently relies on building upon the work of others. In this context, citations in the scientific literature are used to credit the work of scholars whose foundations we build upon. Higher citation counts and publication in high-impact-factor journals are often perceived as direct reflections of the quality of a scientist's work and can often greatly influence career progression. Therefore, citations are a fundamental metric for assessing scientific quality [13]. However, as Goodhart's Law eloquently states, "When a measure becomes a target, it ceases to be a good measure". This over-reliance on citations exerts substantial pressure on the research community [12] (and publishers [9]) to inflate the number of citations, fostering the emergence of practices designed to increase citations. These practices include irrelevant citations, self-citation, citation padding [8], coercive citation [10], or even citation cartels [7]. These practices distort the scholarly record, weaken the credibility of academic metrics, and misalign them with their original purpose. In general, the onus of safeguarding against and detecting anomalies in the use of citations is placed on the publisher [4]. The detection of these misconducts presents different degrees of complexity. Although detecting author self-citation is trivial, detecting citation cartels is challenging and requires collaboration and communication between publishers, as these citation cartels can extend beyond a single journal or publisher [7]. One of the latest challenges is to detect the so-called irrelevant citations. These are references included in a scholarly work that do not contribute to the arguments or claims, and do not fit within the scope of the citing article [18].

We strongly believe in the use of modern Artificial Intelligence techniques towards increasing scientific integrity. Indeed, recent advances in Natural Language Processing (NLP) have revolutionized computational work on text documents. This paradigm shift was first apparent with Word2Vec [16], a model architecture that enabled a deeper understanding of semantics at the word level by learning meaningful vectors (embeddings) from words. However, Word2Vec's main limitation was its lack of understanding of context; this was later unlocked by attention-based models relying on the transformer architecture, such as BERT [6,19]. In this new paradigm, some initiatives have focused on training models specialized in representing academic text [2,3]; these models are smaller, more efficient to train and use, and perform similarly compared to foundational models in tasks involving academic text. The Specter [3] model is the main model used in this study. It is based on a novel pretraining objective that leverages the metadata contained in the academic citation network in place of the masked language modelling objective normally used to train BERT models. This new training objective uses contrastive loss: the model is trained to answer the question "Does article A cite article B?". Consequently, Specter embeddings should gather semantically related articles and isolate them from unrelated ones. Unfortunately, most of the current reference validation and ethics check tools [17] focus on metadata rather than the alignment in scope between the citing and referenced content. The sole use of AI in such tools is often a feature of generative AI detection, which is known to be unreliable [5,14]. We have noticed a gap in the research on methods for improving research ethics using AI solutions. In particular, tools are needed to evaluate the relevance of a citation based on semantic content to strengthen ethical oversight in scholarly publishing. To address this issue, we developed *Cite Lens*–an AI-powered tool used internally to screen for potentially out-of-scope references. It also analyzes the context in which citations appear.

2 Methodology

We define some key terms:
- **article embedding**: An embedding of the concatenated title and abstract of an article, computed using Specter.

- **citation context embedding**: Embedding of the context (usually a paragraph) in which a citation occurs. Computed using Specter.
- **similarity**: The cosine similarity between two embeddings.
- **article–reference similarity**: similarity between a reference embedding and the article embedding.
- **context–reference similarity**: similarity between a reference embedding and the citation context embedding.
- **article–same-topic-reference similarity**: Similarity between an article and a randomly selected reference from a different article within the same scientific topic, but published in a different journal.
- **article–different-topic-reference similarity**: Similarity between an article and a random reference from another journal and topic.

We aim to identify the general trends in the article–reference similarity and context–reference similarity across topics and publishers. We also want to confirm that the combination of low article–reference similarity and low context–reference similarity effectively indicates a potentially questionable reference.

As for the dataset, we select a set of open-access articles from three major publishers across four distinct research fields. For each combination of publisher and research field, we chose one journal indexed in Web of Science[1], resulting in a total of 12 journals; see Table 1. We randomly sample 100 peer-reviewed articles published from 2020 onward from each journal, resulting in a dataset of 1200 articles[2]. We process the PDF version of the articles using Grobid [15] to find the context in which each reference article is cited. We use Scilit[3] to extract the title and abstract of each reference. In order to improve the quality of the dataset, references not found in Scilit or with abstracts containing fewer than 100 characters are filtered out. The processing results in a dataset of 37 673 references (from 1168 articles in which we were able to find at least one reference), 10 980 in Oncology, 11 352 in Psychology, 9290 in Education and 6051 in AI. In the following sections, to ensure objectivity and avoid bias, the publishers will be named Publisher 1, 2, or 3. This approach aims to prevent any potential conflicts of interest.

We will compare the distribution of the article–reference similarity metrics in different cases using the Kolmogorov–Smirnov (KS) statistical test and the Wasserstein Distance (WD). Throughout the analysis, we use Specter [3] as an embedding model since we noticed that Specter2 and Specter2 proximity models have a higher uniform loss compared to Specter (Computed on a random sample of MDPI articles) making it more difficult to find useful thresholds on the embedding similarities. We also decided against using a more recent option, such as Qwen3 embeddings [20], as these models are heavier and would make the solution unscalable.

---

[1] https://www.webofscience.com/wos
[2] https://huggingface.co/datasets/mdpi-ai/citelens
[3] https://www.scilit.com

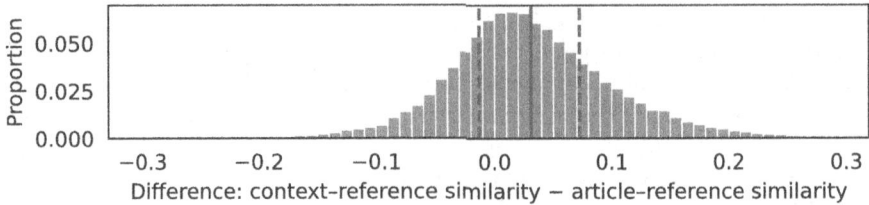

Fig. 1. Differences in contextual and regular similarity for each reference. The solid line represents the mean; dotted lines represent the 25th and 75th percentiles.

Table 1. Selection of journals for the analysis.

Journal	Publisher	Topic	EISSN	Impact Factor
EJIHPE	MDPI	Psychology	2254-9625	3.0
Cancers	MDPI	Oncology	2072-6694	4.5
AI	MDPI	AI	2673-2688	3.1
Education Sciences	MDPI	Education	2227-7102	2.5
Frontiers in Psychology	Frontiers	Psychology	1664-1078	2.6
Frontiers in Oncology	Frontiers	Oncology	2234-943X	3.5
Frontiers in AI	Frontiers	AI	2624-8212	3.0
Frontiers in Education	Frontiers	Education	2504-284X	1.9
BMC Psychology	Springer	Psychology	2050-7283	2.7
Journal of Cancer Research and Clinical Oncology	Springer	Oncology	1432-1335	2.7
International Journal of Computational Intelligent Systems	Springer	AI	1875-6883	2.5
International journal of STEM education	Springer	Education	2196-7822	5.6

3 Results

Unless otherwise stated, the difference between the distributions is statistically significant, with the p-value of the KS statistic (KS_s) below 0.05. The results are available in Table 2 and Table 3.

We first want to demonstrate that context–reference similarity and article–reference similarity are distinct enough to be useful metrics used in conjunction for analyzing out-of-scope referencing; see Fig. 1. We observe that the distributions of context–reference similarity and article–reference similarity differ, as we initially expected, with $KS_s = 1.7 \times 10^{-1}$ and $WD = 3.1 \times 10^{-2}$. This is a sizable difference compared to the ones we will discuss later.

A detailed comparison of the similarity metrics split by publisher and research field is presented in Fig. 2. When examining the most distinct citation patterns, Publisher 3 presents an interesting difference in citation patterns compared to Publisher 1 and Publisher 2 for the *Psychology* topic, with $KS_s \geq 7.8 \times 10^{-2}$, and for each combination of distributions, $WD \geq 1.0 \times 10^{-2}$. Publisher 3 is also distinct from Publisher 1 on the *Education* topic, with $WD = 1.4 \times 10^{-2}$; for each other topic, each publisher's citation patterns are similar, with $WD \leq 8.4 \times 10^{-3}$ and $KS_s \leq 6.0 \times 10^{-2}$. Note that on the topic of *AI* and *Oncology*,

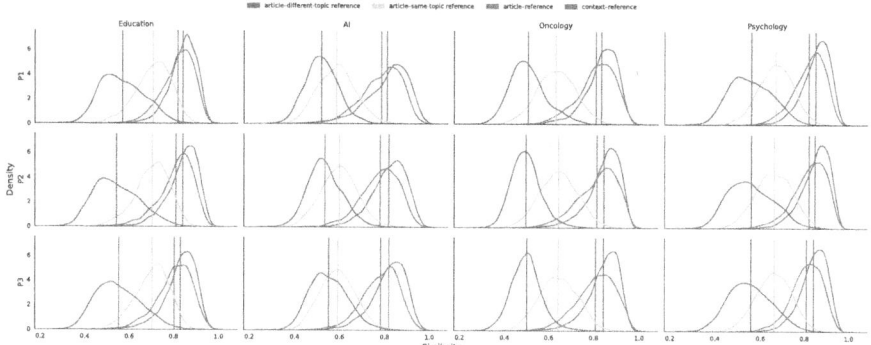

Fig. 2. Kernel density estimates and average represented as vertical lines for the article–different-topic-reference (leftmost in all figures), article–same-topic-reference, article–reference, and context–reference similarity (rightmost in all figures).

the distributions of article–reference similarity for different publishers are quite indistinguishable, with $WD \leq 8.13 \times 10^{-3}$. These results are reported in Table 2.

When comparing topics, each publisher has similar citation patterns in their *Psychology* and *Education* journals, with $KS_s \leq 7.8 \times 10^{-2}$ and $WD \leq 1.1 \times 10^{-2}$. These results are reported in Table 3. Our analysis show that the difference in article–reference citation similarity distribution between publishers are consistently less significant than the difference between topics. This means that by optimizing the tool based on topics, we can generalize and achieve consistent performance regardless of the journal or the publisher.

Table 2. Study of KS_s and WD for the article–reference similarity for each pair of publishers on each topic.

Topic	Publisher A	Publisher B	KS_s	p-Value	WD	Sample Sizes
Oncology	Publisher 3	Publisher 1	3.72×10^{-2}	4.95×10^{-2}	4.82×10^{-3}	4045, 1963
Oncology	Publisher 3	Publisher 2	5.74×10^{-2}	7.96×10^{-7}	7.99×10^{-3}	4045, 4972
Oncology	Publisher 1	Publisher 2	6.08×10^{-2}	5.81×10^{-5}	8.13×10^{-3}	1963, 4972
Education	Publisher 3	Publisher 1	8.36×10^{-2}	1.33×10^{-9}	1.36×10^{-2}	2406, 4023
Education	Publisher 3	Publisher 2	5.69×10^{-2}	4.01×10^{-4}	5.66×10^{-3}	2406, 2861
Education	Publisher 1	Publisher 2	3.56×10^{-2}	2.80×10^{-2}	8.48×10^{-3}	4023, 2861
AI	Publisher 3	Publisher 1	4.28×10^{-2}	7.39×10^{-2}	4.94×10^{-3}	2231, 1480
AI	Publisher 3	Publisher 2	4.42×10^{-2}	2.23×10^{-2}	5.52×10^{-3}	2231, 2340
AI	Publisher 1	Publisher 2	5.92×10^{-2}	3.33×10^{-3}	7.47×10^{-3}	1480, 2340
Psychology	Publisher 3	Publisher 1	7.76×10^{-2}	4.75×10^{-10}	1.00×10^{-2}	3850, 3503
Psychology	Publisher 3	Publisher 2	9.09×10^{-2}	1.52×10^{-14}	1.20×10^{-2}	3850, 3999
Psychology	Publisher 1	Publisher 2	3.32×10^{-2}	3.16×10^{-2}	3.62×10^{-3}	3503, 3999

Table 3. Study of KS_s and WD for the article–reference similarity distribution for each pair of topics for each publisher.

Publisher	Topic A	Topic B	KS_s	p-Value	WD	Sample Sizes
Publisher 1	Psychology	Oncology	6.69×10^{-2}	2.41×10^{-5}	1.16×10^{-2}	3503, 1963
Publisher 1	Psychology	Education	2.35×10^{-2}	2.48×10^{-1}	2.28×10^{-3}	3503, 4023
Publisher 1	Psychology	AI	1.77×10^{-1}	5.72×10^{-29}	3.57×10^{-2}	3503, 1480
Publisher 1	Oncology	Education	7.09×10^{-2}	3.23×10^{-6}	1.15×10^{-2}	1963, 4023
Publisher 1	Oncology	AI	1.30×10^{-1}	7.22×10^{-13}	2.56×10^{-2}	1963, 1480
Publisher 1	Education	AI	1.76×10^{-1}	1.30×10^{-29}	3.42×10^{-2}	4023, 1480
Publisher 2	Psychology	Oncology	5.71×10^{-2}	9.88×10^{-7}	1.06×10^{-2}	3999, 4972
Publisher 2	Psychology	Education	7.75×10^{-2}	3.60×10^{-9}	1.06×10^{-2}	3999, 2861
Publisher 2	Psychology	AI	2.27×10^{-1}	3.84×10^{-67}	4.19×10^{-2}	3999, 2340
Publisher 2	Oncology	Education	8.84×10^{-2}	8.32×10^{-13}	1.15×10^{-2}	4972, 2861
Publisher 2	Oncology	AI	2.10×10^{-1}	7.87×10^{-62}	3.64×10^{-2}	4972, 2340
Publisher 2	Education	AI	1.95×10^{-1}	4.26×10^{-43}	3.14×10^{-2}	2861, 2340
Publisher 3	Psychology	Oncology	6.61×10^{-2}	6.02×10^{-8}	1.31×10^{-2}	3850, 4045
Publisher 3	Psychology	Education	3.75×10^{-2}	2.99×10^{-2}	5.43×10^{-3}	3850, 2406
Publisher 3	Psychology	AI	1.40×10^{-1}	1.26×10^{-24}	2.59×10^{-2}	3850, 2231
Publisher 3	Oncology	Education	6.26×10^{-2}	1.37×10^{-5}	8.38×10^{-3}	4045, 2406
Publisher 3	Oncology	AI	1.31×10^{-1}	7.43×10^{-22}	2.33×10^{-2}	4045, 2231
Publisher 3	Education	AI	1.24×10^{-1}	4.30×10^{-16}	2.09×10^{-2}	2406, 2231

We study the performance of a classifier model at different values of thresholds. This model flags a reference as out-of-scope if the similarity is below a certain threshold, otherwise the reference is classified as in-scope.

We evaluate the model on two synthetic datasets of citations. Each dataset contains the full original dataset of references that we label as in-scope. For each such in-scope citation, we fabricate an out-of-scope alternative.

- **Dataset 1:** we sample a reference from another article in the dataset belonging to a different topic (on the left in Fig. 3).
- **Dataset 2:** we sample a reference from another article in the dataset published by a different publisher, but in the same topic (on the right in Fig. 3).

We assume that these methods of fabricating out-of-scope citations will yield actually out-of-scope citations in most cases, as it is highly unlikely that citing a random paper will yield an in-scope citation, even if we sample references from papers in the same topic.

As we believe context–reference similarity will not make much sense for this fabricated datasets, we will limit the study to the article–reference similarity. The Receiver Operating Characteristic (ROC) curve measures the true positive rate (TPR, the rate of correctly classifying a genuine citation as in-scope) against the false positive rate (FPR, the rate of incorrectly classifying a forged citation as in-scope) at different threshold values. The larger the area under the curve (AUC), the better the model's performance. For example, in Case 1 in Fig. 3, we observe that a threshold value exists such that TPR = 0.9 and FPR = 0.06. In Fig. 3, we measure the area under the ROC curve to assess the discriminative power of the similarity metric in the two cases mentioned above. Using Specter embedding with thresholding is a valid method with a high AUC of 0.98 when trying to spot forged references from different topics. As expected, the AUC is lower (0.89) when the forged reference originates from a paper on the same topic. $AUC = 0.98$ and $AUC = 0.89$ are considered, respectively, "excellent" and "considerable" scores for a classifier [11]. In Case 1, we achieve maximum $F_1 = 0.92$ at threshold $T = 0.68$. In case 2, we achieve maximum $F_1 = 0.81$ at threshold $T = 0.74$.

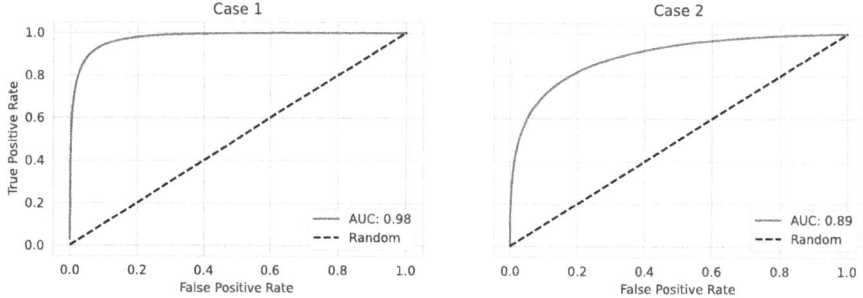

Fig. 3. ROC curves and AUC scores for the two cases. Case 1: article–reference (positives), article–different–topic-reference (negatives). Case 2: article–reference (positives), article–same–topic-reference (negatives).

4 Discussion

To summarize the findings, we first showed that the context–reference similarity is on average higher than the article–reference similarity. Secondly, while the difference in the citation behaviors observed between the publishers is negligible, the difference between topics is larger. The topic of *AI* is very different from the other three topics, with a lower observed article–reference similarity (mean = $0.78, \sigma = 8.4 \times 10^{-2}$) compared to the other topics (mean $\geq 0.81, \sigma \leq 8.6 \times 10^{-2}$). We hint that this difference may be explained by the recency, highly interdisciplinary nature, and fast-paced evolution of the field compared to the three others that are fields with established paradigms. In this regard *AI* can certainly be considered as a "pre-paradigm" field as defined by Thomas Kuhn [1].

On the other hand, the topics of *Education* and *Psychology* present very similar citation patterns. We suggest that this similarity can be explained by the inherent proximity of these two topics, given the existence of branches of psychology focused on education.

We also observed that a thresholding model using Specter embeddings is sufficient to detect forged references from different topics. Given the differences observed between topics, we expect that using specialized models for different topics could yield even better results. These observations show that the model can indeed be used for detecting out-of-scope references.

5 Conclusion

In a paradigm where the number of scientists–and consequently publications–is increasing, there is a growing need for AI-powered pre-check tools. Such tools can guide editors toward potentially problematic papers, improve publication quality, and filter out flawed manuscripts early, sparing reviewers' time.

In this context, by specifically detecting out-of-scope and out-of-context references, *Cite Lens* provides a novel mean of identifying potentially problematic citations. These results demonstrate that, in conjunction with other citation checking methods, such as self-citations, retracted references, etc., *Cite Lens* provides valuable insights that empower human editors in the manuscript evaluation process by highlighting potentially problematic citations that should be carefully evaluated. Ultimately, our objective is to discourage the use of these problematic citation patterns and improve the overall quality of the academic literature. It is important to note that we do not envision this tool as an independent decision-maker. We recognize that many complex cases require human expertise to ascertain the true legitimacy or problematic nature of a reference; this tool merely brings problematic cases to the editor's attention. Far from being a drawback, this characteristic reinforces our commitment to maintaining a human-centric editorial process.

6 Future Work

This study, while being an important milestone in our investigations, is limited by the size and breadth of the dataset, in the sense that it is difficult to find a comprehensive dataset of out-of-scope references, and this is even more difficult for out-of-context references. One potential future direction for this project is to construct a dedicated dataset and evaluate our method's performance on it. We also plan on training deep learning classification models specifically for this use case, which can certainly improve on the similarity thresholding method. Indeed, the current model is very useful to detect many egregious cases, but shows some limitations when references are semantically similar but out of scope e.g. when discussing a specific technique applied to a specific case and citing a paper using the same technique but in a completely different case. We also want to experiment using Large Language Models to bring some explainability in these edge cases that may not be obvious for non-experts.

As the citation behaviors change between topics, we also want to study whether training classification models specialized for different topics will yield more accurate results.

References

1. Bird, A.: Thomas Kuhn. In: Zalta, E.N. (ed.) The Stanford Encyclopedia of Philosophy. Metaphysics Research Lab, Stanford University, Spring 2022 Edn (2022)
2. de la Broise, J.B., Bernard, N., Dubuc, J.P., Perlato, A., Latard, B.: How to pre-train an efficient cross-disciplinary language model: the ScilitBERT use case. In: 2021 6th International Conference on Information Technology Research (ICITR), pp. 1–6 (2021). https://doi.org/10.1109/ICITR54349.2021.9657164
3. Cohan, A., Feldman, S., Beltagy, I., Downey, D., Weld, D.: SPECTER: document-level representation learning using citation-informed transformers. In: Jurafsky, D., Chai, J., Schluter, N., Tetreault, J. (eds.) Proceedings of the 58th Annual Meeting of the Association for Computational Linguistics. pp. 2270–2282. Association for Computational Linguistics, Online (2020). https://doi.org/10.18653/v1/2020.acl-main.207, https://aclanthology.org/2020.acl-main.207/
4. Council, C.: Cope discussion document: citation manipulation. COPE Council: Hampshire (2019). https://doi.org/10.24318/cope.2019.3.1
5. Dalalah, D., Dalalah, O.M.: The false positives and false negatives of generative ai detection tools in education and academic research: the case of chatgpt. Int. J. Manag. Educ. **21**(2), 100822 (2023). https://doi.org/10.1016/j.ijme.2023.100822
6. Devlin, J., Chang, M.W., Lee, K., Toutanova, K.: BERT: pre-training of deep bidirectional transformers for language understanding. In: Burstein, J., Doran, C., Solorio, T. (eds.) Proceedings of the 2019 Conference of the North American Chapter of the Association for Computational Linguistics: Human Language Technologies, Volume 1 (Long and Short Papers), pp. 4171–4186. Association for Computational Linguistics, Minneapolis, Minnesota (2019). https://doi.org/10.18653/v1/N19-1423
7. Fister, I., Fister, I., Perc, M.: Toward the discovery of citation cartels in citation networks. Front. Phys. **Volume 4 - 2016** (2016). https://doi.org/10.3389/fphy.2016.00049
8. Fong, E.A., Wilhite, A.W.: Authorship and citation manipulation in academic research. PLOS ONE **12**(12), 1–34 (2017). https://doi.org/10.1371/journal.pone.0187394
9. Frandsen, T.F., Nicolaisen, J.: Non-citable but not uncited: a large-scale citation analysis of editorials. In: Alonso, O., Cousijn, H., Silvello, G., Marrero, M., Teixeira Lopes, C., Marchesin, S. (eds.) Linking Theory and Practice of Digital Libraries. pp. 93–98. Springer Nature Switzerland, Cham (2023). https://doi.org/10.1007/978-3-031-43849-3_8
10. Ioannidis, J.P.: A generalized view of self-citation: direct, co-author, collaborative, and coercive induced self-citation. J. Psychosom. Res. **78**(1), 7–11 (2015). https://doi.org/10.1016/j.jpsychores.2014.11.008
11. Şeref Kerem Çorbacıoğlu, Aksel, G.: Receiver operating characteristic curve analysis in diagnostic accuracy studies: A guide to interpreting the area under the curve value. Turkish J. Emerg. Med. **23**(4), 195–198 (2023). https://doi.org/10.4103/tjem.tjem_182_23, eCollection 2023 Oct–Dec

12. Krauss, A., Danús, L., Sales-Pardo, M.: Early-career factors largely determine the future impact of prominent researchers: evidence across eight scientific fields. Sci. Rep. **13**(1), 18794 (2023). https://doi.org/10.1038/s41598-023-46050-x
13. Leydesdorff, L., Bornmann, L., Comins, J.A., Milojević, S.: Citations: indicators of quality? The impact fallacy. Fronti. Res. Met. Anal. **1 - 2016** (2016). https://doi.org/10.3389/frma.2016.00001, https://www.frontiersin.org/journals/research-metrics-and-analytics/articles/10.3389/frma.2016.00001
14. Liang, W., Yuksekgonul, M., Mao, Y., Wu, E., Zou, J.: GPT detectors are biased against non-native English writers. Patterns **4**(7), 100779 (2023). https://doi.org/10.1016/j.patter.2023.100779
15. Lopez, P.: GROBID: combining automatic bibliographic data recognition and term extraction for scholarship publications. In: Agosti, M., Borbinha, J., Kapidakis, S., Papatheodorou, C., Tsakonas, G. (eds.) Res. Adv. Technol. Digit. Lib., pp. 473–474. Springer, Berlin Heidelberg, Berlin, Heidelberg (2009)
16. Mikolov, T., Sutskever, I., Chen, K., Corrado, G., Dean, J.: Distributed representations of words and phrases and their compositionality. In: Proceedings of the 27th International Conference on Neural Information Processing Systems - ,vol. 2, p. 3111–3119. NIPS'13, Curran Associates Inc., Red Hook, NY, USA (2013)
17. Morressier: Morressier's guide to research integrity. https://www.morressier.com/company/morressiers-guide-to-research-integrity (2023). Accessed 04 June 2025
18. Pham, P., Le, H., Tam, N.T., Tran, Q.D.: A graph-based topic modeling approach to detection of irrelevant citations. Viet. J. Comput. Sci. **10**(02), 197–216 (2023). https://doi.org/10.1142/S2196888822500336
19. Vaswani, A., et al.: Attention is all you need. In: Proceedings of the 31st International Conference on Neural Information Processing Systems, pp. 6000–6010. NIPS'17, Curran Associates Inc., Red Hook, NY, USA (2017)
20. Zhang, Y, et al.: Qwen3 Embedding: advancing text embedding and reranking through foundation models. arXiv preprint arXiv:2506.05176 (2025)

Open Access This chapter is licensed under the terms of the Creative Commons Attribution 4.0 International License (http://creativecommons.org/licenses/by/4.0/), which permits use, sharing, adaptation, distribution and reproduction in any medium or format, as long as you give appropriate credit to the original author(s) and the source, provide a link to the Creative Commons license and indicate if changes were made.

The images or other third party material in this chapter are included in the chapter's Creative Commons license, unless indicated otherwise in a credit line to the material. If material is not included in the chapter's Creative Commons license and your intended use is not permitted by statutory regulation or exceeds the permitted use, you will need to obtain permission directly from the copyright holder.

Information Specialists' Perspectives on Research Data Management Support in Social Sciences and Humanities

Anna Sendra[1]((✉)) , Minna Ahokas[2] , and Sanna Kumpulainen[1]

[1] Tampere University, Kalevantie 4, 33014 Tampere, Finland
anna.sendratoset@tuni.fi
[2] CSC – IT Center for Science, Keilaranta 14, 02150 Espoo, Finland

Abstract. The increasing use of digital tools and materials in social sciences and humanities has generated a demand for research data management support. However, the provision of research data services for these disciplines remains underexplored. This study analyzes the implementation of research data management support for the social sciences and humanities from the perspective of academic libraries. Particularly, we explore existing research data services for these disciplines and investigate how research data management support for the social sciences and humanities could be improved. A participatory workshop with information specialists (n = 6) revealed three themes (research data services in practice, governance of the research data services, future of the research data services). Our findings contribute to understanding the current research data management support for the social sciences and humanities and increasing the maturity of research data services for these disciplines in academic libraries.

Keywords: Research Data Management · Academic Libraries · Social Sciences and Humanities

1 Introduction

Contemporary research processes are increasingly generating digital research data, requiring different actors "to develop policies, infrastructures, and services that support researchers in creating, storing, organizing, and preserving" this type of data [1, p. 4]. Accordingly, research data services (RDS) have become an integral part of many academic libraries over the last decade [2, 3]. Various factors respond to the widespread implementation of research data management (RDM) support in academic libraries, particularly the "policy changes among research funders" [4, p. 2182; 5, 6]. However, evidence suggests that the provision of RDS is convoluted due to elements such as insufficient librarian skills [7–9] and unclear responsibilities around RDM [10]. In this context, there is a growing body of literature that recognizes the need to increase the data literacy of librarians to improve the provision of RDM support [9, 11, 12].

A related issue in the provision of RDS is that not all academic libraries offer the same type of RDM support to their communities [7, 13]. Of particular concern is the provision of RDS for the social sciences and humanities (SSH). For example, a recent study found that RDM support for these disciplines is not in line with the support needs of researchers [14]. Moreover, universities have been observed to be more involved in digital research data from atmospheric science than in SSH digital research data [15]. RDM training for researchers also lacks discipline specificity, situation that is particularly affecting SSH-related fields [3]. Likewise, the infrastructure to support digital research data in these disciplines is almost non-existent [14, 16]. As Hagman and Bussell [17] explain, "the rationale for data management often exclude research data produced through qualitative, interpretive, and critical approaches".

As pointed out already in previous studies [18], there is a need to further understand the provision of RDS for the SSH. Nevertheless, most of the research to date has approached the implementation of RDM support in academic libraries without considering different disciplines. On this basis, the aim of this paper is to explore existing RDS for SSH scholars and identify how RDM support could be improved in these disciplines. Specifically, two research questions (RQ) are raised:

- RQ1: What is the state of RDS for the SSH?
- RQ2: How RDM support in SSH should be developed moving forward?

2 Literature Review

RDS are defined "as actions undertaken to provide researchers with support, advising, training, information, a technological infrastructure and a regulatory framework with respect to RDM throughout the lifecycle of the data" [19, Introduction section, para. 6]. Along with the development of infrastructure (e.g., to deposit data), several studies have previously indicated that the provision of RDM support and training is one of the key factors affecting the RDM practices of researchers [20, 21]. However, despite having a fundamental role in RDM, many of the available RDS have not yet reached the top level of development [13, 22]. Several studies have also reported that not all academic libraries currently offer RDM support as part of their service catalogue [8, 19, 23].

The need for RDS started to be prominent in the early 2010s, especially when national research data policies started to be implemented among funders and publishers both within and outside Europe amid increasing digitization processes [21]. These mandates were subsequently adopted by universities through institutional RDM policies [24]. Some academic libraries even had a leading role in the development of institutional RDM policies [25], task that these libraries have continued to exercise over time [13]. According to Andrikopoulou, Rowley, and Walton [26, p. 352], "policies are important for RDM". Overall, institutional RDM policies support the provision of RDS [19]. Nevertheless, evidence indicates that there are still universities that do not have an institutional RDM policy [13, 18].

Likewise, Tenopir et al. [8, 18] classify RDM support into consultative and technical RDS. Consultative or "advisory" [13, p. 1438] RDS are more of informational nature (e.g., helping with data management plans), whereas technical RDS involve more hands-on RDM support (e.g., preparing data for deposit) [18]. Both Tenopir et al. [8, 18] and others [13, 19] previously reported that academic libraries mostly provide consultative RDS. Moreover, academic libraries "have devoted a significant amount of attention in recent years to the final stage in the research process" [27, p. 479], thus overlooking its more active stages. Consequently, RDS do not always correspond with the desires of researchers, who increasingly demand support with data analysis [27, 28].

The misalignment between providers and users of RDS could lie on the fact that "[r]eassigning existing library staff is the most common tactic for offering" RDM support [6, p. 4]. Several studies have shown that academic librarians are not prepared to assume these new roles (e.g., helping with data analysis) without proper training [24, 25, 29]. The provision of RDS is also affected by the capacity for collaboration of academic libraries [18] and the number of financial resources available to implement RDM support in their service catalogue [30]. Cox, Kennan, Lyon, Pinfield, and Sbaffi [13, p. 1442] found, for instance, that RDS are usually better in academic libraries "with a specific team dedicated to RDM". Against this background, analyzing RDM support for the SSH becomes crucial, especially considering the growing digitalization of SSH research [31].

3 Research Setting

For this study, a participatory workshop with information specialists experienced in SSH RDM was conducted. Employing a participatory workshop research approach allows for the inclusion of stakeholder perspectives and focuses on research questions prioritized by communities, which are often overlooked by researchers [32]. The participatory workshop took place online during June 2024 and was conducted by the first and second authors in English. While a participatory workshop research approach challenges "traditional power dynamics in the research process" [32, p. 9], the engagement of participants during the workshop may influence the data collection process [33], especially in online settings [34, 35]. Additional challenges of conducting virtual participatory workshops include reduced interaction between participants [34] and decreased non-verbal communication cues [33]. The first and second authors tried to overcome these barriers by addressing questions to participants individually and encouraging discussion between them throughout the participatory workshop. The respondents (n = 6) were recruited via email. The call for participants was sent to several academic libraries, archives and services for the digital humanities and computational social sciences based in Finland. The call for participants was also sent to various SSH faculties at different Finnish universities. All respondents have a background in SSH (see Table 1).

Table 1. Profile of the participants.

Organization	Organization A (n = 3), Organization B (n = 1), Organization C (n = 1), Organization D (n = 1)
Position	Information specialist (n = 4), Senior specialist (n = 1), University lecturer (n = 1)
Main field	Humanities (n = 4), Social sciences (n = 2)
Main subfield	Arts (n = 2), Other social sciences (n = 2), History and archaeology (n = 1), Other humanities (n = 1)

The guide for conducting the participatory workshop included questions on (1) existing RDM support services for SSH scholars and (2) improvement of RDM support services for SSH scholars. A consent form and an information sheet (see Supplementary materials 1 and 2) with detailed information about the study (e.g., research purpose, voluntary participation) were sent to the respondents before the day of the participatory workshop. All respondents gave their informed consent to participate in the study. According to the guidelines of the Ethics Committee of the Tampere Region [36], which supervises non-medical research involving human subjects at Tampere University, no ethical review was required for the study. The participatory workshop was video recorded and lasted 83 min. The video recording was transcribed verbatim by a professional service for analysis. The first author cross-checked the transcript for consistency before pseudonymizing the data to protect the privacy of the respondents.

3.1 Data Analysis

An inductive (reflexive) thematic analysis [37, 38] was applied to the data collected. Reflexive thematic analysis is a suitable method for understanding the "views, perceptions, understandings, perspectives, needs, motivations of particular groups, about particular phenomena, in particular contexts" [39, p. 11], like the perspectives of information specialists on SSH RDM support analyzed in this study. Although the participant group was small, the development of themes was facilitated by their homogeneity in terms of position and field of study [39].

ATLAS.ti, version 24.2 was used to carry out the analysis. The study incorporated at least one method for increasing its reliability (cross-checking) and two methods for increasing its validity (reflexivity, peer debriefing) [40]. After getting familiar with the data collected, the first author generated the initial coding in several rounds. Then, the first author generated the preliminary list of themes using the initial coding. Both the initial coding and the preliminary list of themes were discussed with the research team until reaching agreement (cross-checking). Next, the first author generated the reviewed coding and list of themes, which were presented in a seminar to colleagues outside of the research team (peer-debriefing). The final coding consisted of 14 codes generated from 77 coded items (see Supplementary material 3). The research team, as specialists and researchers, tried to remain aware during the data analysis process of their personal experiences with SSH RDM (reflexivity). Three themes were identified in the data: (1) research data services in practice, (2) governance of the research data services, and (3) future of the research data services. Excerpts were selected to illustrate the themes.

4 Findings

4.1 Research Data Services in Practice

Codes (n = 8) included point of entry, types of data supported, types of training provided, types of services provided, relationship with the researchers, requested support, demanding tasks and complexities. In general, respondents described that SSH scholars typically get in touch with their RDS during the planning stage of the life of the data (e.g., when preparing documents related to ethical review processes). Moreover, requests for support usually revolve around data protection issues, especially regarding the use of digital tools to conduct research (e.g., ATLAS.ti). One respondent explained it as follows:

"I think many questions that we have been asked is about the data protection and the tools which can be used to collect the data, or can I use this tool to store the data, or can I use this survey tool or can I use this and that" (P4).

Likewise, most respondents reported that the types of data supported are varied both in terms of size and origin. That is, datasets can be both small and large in scale and come from different sources, such as interviews or photographs. The heterogeneity of data in SSH is precisely one of the complexities affecting the provision of RDS, along with the variation in interpreting data-related regulations between organizations and the timings to implement RDM training. Commenting on the variety of types of data supported, one of the respondents said:

"One of the things in my opinion that makes, for example, the humanities data challenging is that it is very versatile and the data that the humanists scholars use is not in all cases digital at all" (P1).

When talking about the types of services provided, respondents agree that they often provide general support without considering different disciplines, and delegate more specific requests (e.g., questions related to digital methods) to other units within the organization. Examples of RDS provided include data management planning support and data management training. Despite this approach to the provision of RDS, most respondents also described that some of their tasks remain demanding, especially if related to the initial (e.g., commenting on a data management plan, going through the ethical review documents) and final stages of the data lifecycle (e.g., supporting data sharing). Referring specifically to the final stages of the data lifecycle, one respondent commented:

"I could add to that that also... the end of the life cycle of the research, comes the question of how to open or publish or where to put the data then. We don't have that good advice on that" (P5).

As for the types of training provided, most respondents described that their educational opportunities include topics covering the whole data lifecycle. However, the focus of these trainings might be different between organizations, with some RDS devoting more time to data protection training than others. Similarly, while their educational opportunities are usually planned according to the calendar of the main funders, a common problem between the respondents is the lack of researcher engagement in data management training. As one respondent put it:

"We are also providing tailoring services, tailoring training sessions for research groups or students, groups doing their thesis, but [...] there have been not that many training sessions like that because nobody has asked" (P2).

4.2 Governance of the Research Data Services

Codes (n = 4) included responsibilities, start of the services, organization and importance of collaboration. In most cases, respondents described that the RDS in their organizations started in the mid-2010s, and only in one instance RDM support became available from the early 2010s. Most respondents also reported that the RDS in their organizations were not developed following any specific data lifecycle model. However, one respondent indicated that in their case RDM support is guided by the data policy of the organization.

"Something that guides our work here [...] is our data policy, which has now updated in 2021 and then we started the research data policy implementation work at the faculties and now faculties have written their implementation plans, and there it is said that the faculty is somehow responsible for giving training" (P6).

When further talking about the organization of the RDS, respondents overall described that RDM support is usually coordinated from the library with the help of other units of the organization, such as legal services. However, one aspect that remains unclear is the roles and responsibilities of those providing RDS. Commenting on requests related to digital tools and methods, one of the respondents said:

"These are very difficult for us because we are not the experts necessarily on specific tools and [...] on the methodologies. The methodological understanding and training should anyway come from the discipline" (P1).

Most respondents also find collaboration important in the provision of RDM support, both within and beyond their organization. For example, one respondent felt that "the better the connections you have, [...] the better the services" (P4). Particularly, the collaboration between organizations is perceived to complement each other's work. When discussing the joint development of social media guidelines, a respondent said:

"There's no point of doing just for us, or that we would tackle everything. [...] I think that national work is really something that we should do. And trying to find how we work together and who does the final work and where these guidelines would then be published" (P5).

4.3 Future of the Research Data Services

Codes (n = 2) included development of services and needs. Overall, respondents reported two needs related to the development of RDS. On the one hand, most respondents stated that RDS need more financial resources "to do things" (P3), such as maintaining internal collaborations to implement the data policy of the organization. On the other hand, one respondent also called for the development of RDM workflows according to different disciplines. As one respondent put it:

"We need more data or analysis on 'what does it mean?' to follow these guidelines in certain [...] research contexts, because we can say that 'okay, you can use interview data like this', but it's whole different thing to talk about interview data in historic research or in medicine" (P6).

When asked about the development of services, most respondents agreed that researchers should be more involved in the development of RDM support, as their participation would help with "figuring out what kind of services they [...] really need" (P5). One respondent also stated that the provision of RDS would benefit from having more information on the different places researchers obtain RDM support within the organization, while another respondent indicated that the learning outcomes of RDM training should be better defined:

"It should be more concentrated on one topic, such as data protection, [...] because researchers can know what to expect when they participate in research data protection

training, but when they participate in data management training it may not be that clear what to expect from the training" (P4).

5 Discussion and Conclusion

This study was designed to analyze current implementations of SSH RDM support in academic libraries and determine how RDS for these disciplines could be further developed. Overall, findings show that SSH RDM support is highly collaborative, far from being specialized and affected by unique challenges that complicate the provision of RDS for these disciplines. The findings are expected to contribute to the maturing [13] of SSH RDM support in academic libraries.

Regarding RQ1, results suggest that RDS for the SSH mostly provide advisory RDM support around data protection issues and in connection with the initial stages of the data lifecycle. These findings are consistent with previous studies indicating a general absence of technical RDS [8, 13, 18, 19]. Data protection is in fact a big challenge for the respondents. This could be related to the comprehensive data protection regulation present in the European Union [41], which tends to be more fragmented in other contexts [42]. Another interesting result is that respondents do not feel accountable for providing RDM support for data analysis, which confirms the non-engagement of academic libraries in the active stages of the research process [14, 27] and conflicts with the needs of researchers [14, 27, 28]. In fact, prior studies have reported that academic librarians perceive consultative RDS to be more valuable for researchers than technical RDS [43]. This finding may reflect the uncertainty regarding the responsibilities around RDM [10] and the lack of skills to provide this type of RDM support [4]. However, this result also raises questions in relation to contemplating the provision of RDS in academic libraries from a holistic perspective, especially when these libraries – like in Finland – do not have faculty status. In view of this, our analysis also highlights the importance of collaboration within and beyond the organization in the provision of RDM support, which according to Joo and Schmidt [43] can be an effective way for academic libraries to strengthen their offer of technical RDS.

Concerning RQ2, the most significant finding is the need for incorporating the researchers' viewpoint in the development of RDS for the SSH. This result is likely related to the variety of scholarly practices in SSH [44], which complicate the provision of SSH RDM support. Despite promising initiatives [45, 46], solutions to support the management of digital research data in these disciplines (and data-intensive research processes more generally) are usually developed without considering the needs and tasks of researchers [47]. Creating RDM workflows according to different disciplines, as one respondent suggested, could be a way to address the diversity of research processes within the SSH community. In this context, here it should be noted that Finnish academic libraries have been actively participating at the European level in the development of guidelines and best practices for providing RDM support. One example is the 6 Pillars of Engaging Researchers in Research Data Management (RDM) guide [48]. Another example is the guide How to Develop RDM Services - a Guide for HEIs [49], which already underlined that RDM training for researchers "is best developed in partnership with academic staff or disciplinary data experts" [49, p. 9]. Similarly, the need for more financial resources to develop RDM support services in academic libraires is in line with the findings of previous studies [41, 50]. As Reynolds and Richards [50, Resources & Funding section, para. 1] argue, financial resources "play a significant role in RDMS [research data management services] implementation, as it can determine how institutions provide services, if at all".

Despite its contributions, this study is limited by the low number of participants. Some of our questions were also particularly geared toward certain types of SSH digital research data (social media, visual materials). Therefore, the results might not be generalizable to all RDS providing SSH RDM support. A further study could include more respondents and consider SSH digital research data more generally. Notwithstanding these limitations, the study adds to our understanding of the provision of RDS for the SSH, which should become a priority for academic libraries and their organizations. As Tammaro [51, p. 1] reminds us, digital libraries "are networks of sociotechnical systems that bring together information and technologies with people and practices". To provide effective support for the management of digital research data, the practices of researchers and information specialists should be continuously evaluated to understand the specific tasks scholars and practitioners are engaged in. This is significant when considering that RDM support remains in its early stages of development and "can be expected to shift and grow both in meaning and substance as libraries and researchers understand how it can be used" [50, Current International Development of RDMS section, para. 1]. Altogether, the findings of this study have important implications for future provision of RDS, especially concerning policy development and librarian training. The provision of proper RDS for the SSH becomes crucial to attain better RDM practices from researchers. Only then will SSH scholars be more equipped to effectively perform their research work tasks, including the management of digital research data.

Acknowledgements. This project has received funding from the European Union – NextGenerationEU instrument and is funded by the Research Council of Finland, grant numbers 358723 and 358728. We would also like to thank the Information Studies seminar participants at Tampere University for their valuable comments and support.

Disclosure of Interests. The authors have no competing interests to declare that are relevant to the content of this article.

References

1. Lupu, V.: The role of the academic library in research data management [Doctoral dissertation, Moldova State University]. ANACEC (2025)
2. Hackett, C., Kim, J.: Planning, implementing and evaluating research data services in academic libraries: a model approach. J. Docum. **80**(1), 27–38 (2024). https://doi.org/10.1108/JD-01-2023-0007
3. Xu, Z.: Research data management practice in academic libraries. J. Libr. Schol. Commun. **10**(1), eP13700 (2022). https://doi.org/10.31274/jlsc.13700
4. Cox, A.M., Kennan, M.A., Lyon, L., Pinfield, S.: Developments in research data management in academic libraries: towards an understanding of research data service maturity. J. Assoc. Inf. Sci. Technol. **68**(9), 2182–2200 (2017). https://doi.org/10.1002/asi.23781

5. Antell, K., Foote, J.B., Turner, J., Shults, B.: Dealing with data: science librarians' participation in data management at Association of Research Libraries institutions. Coll. Res. Libr. **75**(4), 557–574 (2014). https://doi.org/10.5860/crl.75.4.557
6. Tenopir, C., Birch, B., Allard, S.: Academic libraries and research data services: current practices and plans for the future. Association of College & Research Libraries (2012)
7. Tang, R., Hu, Z.: Providing research data management (RDM) services in libraries: preparedness, roles, challenges, and training for RDM practice. Data Info. Manag. **3**(2), 84–101 (2019). https://doi.org/10.2478/dim-2019-0009
8. Tenopir, C., et al.: Research data services in academic libraries: data intensive roles for the future? J. eSci. Librariansh. **4**(2), e1085 (2015). https://doi.org/10.7191/jeslib.2015.1085
9. Igbinovia, M.O., Segun-Adeniran, C.D., Okuonghae, O.: Research data management in university libraries: the need for data literacy and technological revamp. IFLA J. **51**(1), 74–83 (2025). https://doi.org/10.1177/03400352241280902
10. Perrier, L., Blondal, E., MacDonald, H.: Exploring the experiences of academic libraries with research data management: a meta-ethnographic analysis of qualitative studies. Libr. Inf. Sci. Res. **40**(3–4), 173–183 (2018). https://doi.org/10.1016/j.lisr.2018.08.002
11. Adekoya, C.O., Nkemdilim, I.P., Ejovwokoghene, E.R., Olajide, O., Omolehin, J.R.: Data science: developing data-savvy librarians for effective research data management. Ref. Libr. **66**(1–2), 48–64 (2025). https://doi.org/10.1080/02763877.2025.2482086
12. Shah, N.U., Naeem, S.B., Bhatti, R.: Digital data sets management in university libraries: challenges and opportunities. Global Knowl. Mem. Commun. **74**(1–2), 446–462 (2025). https://doi.org/10.1108/GKMC-06-2022-0150
13. Cox, A.M., Kennan, M.A., Lyon, L., Pinfield, S., Sbaffi, L.: Maturing research data services and the transformation of academic libraries. J. Docum. **75**(6), 1432–1462 (2019). https://doi.org/10.1108/JD-12-2018-0211
14. Sendra, A., Late, E., Kumpulainen, S.: From data lifecycle to research activity model: research data management in data-intensive social sciences and humanities research. Aslib J. Inf. Manag. (2025). https://doi.org/10.1108/AJIM-12-2024-0959
15. Tenopir, C., et al.: Data sharing by scientists: practices and perceptions. PLoS ONE **6**(6), e21101 (2011). https://doi.org/10.1371/journal.pone.0021101
16. Strange, D., Gooch, M., Collinson, A.: Equality, findability, sustainability: the challenges and rewards of open digital humanities data. Int. J. Perform. Arts Digit. Med. **19**(3), 348–368 (2023). https://doi.org/10.1080/14794713.2023.2206286
17. Hagman, J., Bussell, H.: Assessing Data Services for Methodological Inclusiveness [Presentation slides]. University of Illinois Urbana-Champaign (2024)
18. Tenopir, C., et al.: Research data services in European academic research libraries. LIBER Q. **27**(1), 23–44 (2017). https://doi.org/10.18352/lq.10180
19. Martin-Melon, R., Hernández-Pérez, T., Martínez-Cardama, S.: Research data services (RDS) in Spanish academic libraries. J. Acad. Librariansh. **49**(4), 102732 (2023). https://doi.org/10.1016/j.acalib.2023.102732
20. Van den Eynden, V., et al.: Towards Open Research: practices, experiences, barriers and opportunities. Wellcome Trust (2016)
21. Van den Eynden, V., Corti, L.: The importance of managing and sharing research data. In: Corti, L., Van den Eynden, V., Bishop, L., Woollard, M. (eds.) Managing and sharing research data: A guide to good practice, pp. 2–32. SAGE Publications (2020)
22. Nahotko, M., Zych, M., Januszko-Szakiel, A., Jaskowska, M.: Big data-driven investigation into the maturity of library research data services (RDS). J. Acad. Librariansh. **49**(1), 102646 (2023). https://doi.org/10.1016/j.acalib.2022.102646
23. Si, L., Xing, W., Zhuang, X., Hua, X., Zhou, L.: Investigation and analysis of research data services in university libraries. Electron. Libr. **33**(3), 417–449 (2015). https://doi.org/10.1108/EL-07-2013-0130

24. Cox, A., Pinfield, S.: Research data management and libraries: current activities and future priorities. J. Librariansh. Inf. Sci. **46**(4), 299–316 (2014). https://doi.org/10.1177/0961000613492542
25. Pinfield, S., Cox, A.M., Smith, J.: Research data management and libraries: relationships, activities, drivers and influences. PLoS ONE **9**(12), e114734 (2014). https://doi.org/10.1371/journal.pone.0114734
26. Andrikopoulou, A., Rowley, J., Walton, G.: Research data management (RDM) and the evolving identity of academic libraries and librarians: a literature review. New Rev. Acad. Librariansh. **28**(4), 349–365 (2022). https://doi.org/10.1080/13614533.2021.1964549
27. Weller, T., Monroe-Gulick, A.: Understanding methodological and disciplinary differences in the data practices of academic researchers. Libr. Hi Tech **32**(3), 467–482 (2014). https://doi.org/10.1108/LHT-02-2014-0021
28. Xu, Q.: Modelling college faculty users' potential acceptance of library data services for research and teaching. Info. Discov. Deliv. **53**(1), 109–123 (2025). https://doi.org/10.1108/IDD-10-2023-0115
29. Carlson, J.R.: Opportunities and barriers for librarians in exploring data: observations from the data curation profile workshops. J. eSci. Librariansh. **2**(2), 17–33 (2013). https://doi.org/10.7191/jeslib.2013.1042
30. Oliver, J., Rios, F., Carini, K., Ly, C.: Data services at the academic library: a natural history of horses and unicorns. J. eSci. Librariansh. **13**(2), e780 (2024). https://doi.org/10.7191/jeslib.780
31. Sendra, A., Late, E., Kumpulainen, S.: Understanding researchers' perspectives on work tasks in digital humanities and computational social sciences. Digit. Hum. Nordic Baltic Count. Pub. **6**(1) (2024). https://doi.org/10.5617/dhnbpub.11488
32. Balazs, C.L., Morello-Frosch, R.: The three Rs: how community-based participatory research strengthens the rigor, relevance, and reach of science. Environ. Justice **6**(1), 9–16 (2013). https://doi.org/10.1089/env.2012.0017
33. Engler, J., et al.: Digital participatory workshops with patients and health professionals to develop an intervention for the management of polypharmacy: results from a mixed-methods evaluation and methodological conclusions. Res. Involv. Engag. **8**, 52 (2022). https://doi.org/10.1186/s40900-022-00387-1
34. Rushton, E.A.C., et al.: The challenges and affordances of online participatory workshops in the context of young people's everyday climate crisis activism: insights from facilitators. Child. Geograph. **21**(1), 137–146 (2023). https://doi.org/10.1080/14733285.2021.2007218
35. Lipton, B., et al.: Collaborating with young people: identifying the barriers and facilitators in co-designed research. Health Expect. **28**(3), e70308 (2025). https://doi.org/10.1111/hex.70308
36. Tampere Universities, https://www.tuni.fi/en/research/responsible-science-and-research/research-integrity/ethics-committee-of-the-tampere-region. Accessed 31 May 2025
37. Braun, V., Clarke, V.: Using thematic analysis in psychology. Qual. Res. Psychol. **3**(2), 77–101 (2006). https://doi.org/10.1191/1478088706qp063oa
38. Braun, V., Clarke, V.: One size fits all? What counts as quality practice in (reflexive) thematic analysis? Qual. Res. Psychol. **18**(3), 328–352 (2021). https://doi.org/10.1080/14780887.2020.1769238
39. Braun, V., Clarke, V.: Conceptual and design thinking for thematic analysis. Qualit. Psych. **9**(1), 3–26 (2022). https://doi.org/10.1037/qup0000196
40. Franklin, C.S., Cody, P.A., Ballan, M.: Reliability and validity in qualitative research. In: Thyer, B.A. (ed.) The Handbook of Social Work Research Methods (2nd ed.), pp. 355–374. SAGE Publications (2010). https://doi.org/10.4135/9781544364902.n19

41. Tóth-Czifra, E., et al.: Research data management for arts and humanities: integrating voices of the community. DARIAH-DE Working Papers, vol. 47 (2024). https://doi.org/10.47952/gro-publ-218
42. Fiero, A.W., Beier, E.: New global developments in data protection and privacy regulations: comparative analysis of European Union, United States, and Russian legislation. Stanford J. Int. Law **58**(2), 151–192 (2022)
43. Joo, S., Schmidt, G.M.: Research data services from the perspective of academic librarians. Digit. Libr. Perspect. **37**(3), 242–256 (2021). https://doi.org/10.1108/DLP-10-2020-0106
44. Given, L.M., Willson, R.: Information technology and the humanities scholar: documenting digital research practices. J. Assoc. Inf. Sci. Technol. **69**(6), 807–819 (2018). https://doi.org/10.1002/asi.24008
45. Candela, G., et al.: Promoting computational access to digital collections in the Nordic and Baltic countries: an Icelandic use case. J. Open Hum. Data **11**, 7 (2025). https://doi.org/10.5334/johd.261
46. De Paoli, S., Forbes, P., Andreini, G., Maryl, M., Błaszczyńska, M.: CoDesign for discovery in social sciences and humanities: addressing the heterogeneous needs of a community in digital scholarship. LIBER Q. **34**(1), 1–43 (2024). https://doi.org/10.53377/lq.14309
47. Van der Walt, A., Steyn, J., Trusler, A., Van Zaanen, M.: Challenges and opportunities of digital humanities training in South Africa: moving beyond the Silos. In: Estill, L., Guiliano, J. (eds.) Digital Humanities Workshops: Lessons Learned, pp. 56–66. Routledge (2023). https://doi.org/10.4324/9781003301097-7
48. Secretariat for the National Open Science and Research Coordination, https://avointiede.fi/en/news/six-pillars-data-management-marketing-researchers. Accessed 31 May 2025
49. Jones, S., Pryor, G., Whyte, A.: How to Develop Research Data Management Services – a guide for HEIs. DCC (2013)
50. Reynolds, C., Richards, K.: International perspectives on research data management services in academic libraries. School Info. Stud. Res. J. **15**(1) (2025). https://doi.org/10.55917/2575-2499.1514
51. Tammaro, A.M.: Editorial: digital libraries as sociotechnical systems. Digit. Libr. Perspect. **40**(1), 1–3 (2024). https://doi.org/10.1108/DLP-02-2024-144

StoryNetworks: An Annotated Dataset of Event Dependencies from Short Descriptions

Daisuke Machizawa[1]($\boxtimes$), Naoki Sawahata[1], Ryohei Ikejiri[2], and Yasunobu Sumikawa[1]

[1] Takushoku University, Tokyo, Japan
mczwdisk@gmail.com, sumikawa.lab@gmail.com
[2] Hiroshima University, Hiroshima, Japan
rikejiri@hiroshima-u.ac.jp

Abstract. Modeling real-world events as structured graphs is essential for advancing research in information retrieval, digital history, and narrative analysis. In this paper, we propose StoryNetworks, a novel dataset that transforms short event texts into annotated event networks. We curated 5,204 events from the Wikipedia Current Events Portal spanning 2016 and 2017, and manually annotated 2,494 directed dependencies between them. By bridging unstructured textual data with graph-based event modeling, StoryNetworks offers a valuable resource for computational social science and digital humanities. In addition, as creating dependency graph from short texts is a challenging task, this dataset should be useful for designing new models in event evolution modeling, narrative structure analysis, and information diffusion to obtain better accuracy. The dataset is publicly available at https://github.com/sumilab/dataset.

Keywords: Short event texts · event network · Wikipedia · structured dataset · timelines

1 Introduction

Events are fundamental units of information in digital libraries, news archives, and knowledge bases. Analyzing them in a structured manner, particularly by extracting dependencies between events, offers significant benefits. One such benefit is the enhanced ability to analogically apply historical knowledge to current societal issues. This ability is widely regarded as essential in education across many countries [2–4]. Structuring events into coherent datasets supports a range of applications, including temporal information retrieval [7,13,18,19,21], event detection and tracking [19], and event evolution graph creation [20,23]. However, the automatic organization of events remains a challenging task, especially when the source texts are short and lack clear narrative context.

This paper presents a dataset of events extracted from the Wikipedia Current Events Portal (WCEP)[1]. The WCEP is a community-maintained resource that captures notable daily events worldwide, presenting them as short summaries grouped by topic and date. Each entry is written concisely, often resembling a news headline, which makes it an ideal yet underutilized source for studying the structure and dynamics of short-form event texts.

The primary contribution of this study is the creation of StoryNetworks, a manually created dataset that transforms short real-world event texts into structured event networks based on dependency relationships. Unlike existing event graph datasets that often rely on long documents or narrative-rich content, StoryNetworks focuses on short texts, which are common in digital libraries and web-based collections but challenging for event understanding. By linking these minimal texts through dependencies, the dataset supports improved model creation for event detection, timeline generation [5], and event evolution graph creation from short descriptions. It also enables the development of information retrieval methods and educational tools that help users explore historical developments through structured, interpretable event relationships.

Related Work. Prior work has introduced event datasets with diverse domains and structures. Narrative-focused resources such as GLUCOSE [15] and CaTeRS [14] capture causal and temporal reasoning in fictional settings, while real-world datasets like DocRED [24], EventKG [6], GDELT [12], and TimeBank [17] provide factual relations, large-scale annotations, or temporal information, often derived through automated methods. However, these typically lack explicit, human-annotated dependency structures between events. Several datasets have been proposed for timeline summarization, including Timeline17 [1], Social Timeline [22], and TLS-Covid19 [16]. Timeline17 consists of 4,650 news articles retrieved via Google Search, aligned with 17 manually curated timelines. Social Timeline includes 5,788 articles from CNN, BBC, and The New York Times, with six timelines covering four major events. TLS-Covid19 contains 100,399 news articles in English and Portuguese, defining 178 timelines per language with detailed annotations of COVID-19-related developments. Our proposed dataset, StoryNetworks, differs in two key aspects. First, whereas existing datasets primarily consist of long-form, narrative-rich texts, StoryNetworks is constructed from short-form texts, specifically headline-like entries derived from the WCEP. Second, unlike prior datasets that organize events linearly, StoryNetworks models events as networks with dependency relations, enabling richer representations such as event threading and merging [23]. The W2E dataset [8] is closely related to our work, as it also collectes events from the WCEP and organizes them into topics for timeline construction and topic tracking. Yet, the topics in W2E are fundamentally presented as timelines and are not defined as network structures, as in the present study.

StoryNetworks introduces a directed event graph over 5,204 real-world events from 2016 and 2017, annotated with 2,494 dependencies. This enables structured

---

[1] https://en.wikipedia.org/wiki/Portal:Current_events.

analysis of event evolution, narrative flow, and information diffusion, offering a richer foundation for modeling how events relate and unfold over time.

2 Data Collection and Creation

Figure 1 illustrates the process of creating our dataset. We began by collecting event data from the WCEP. As shown in Fig. 1(a), WCEP provides a set of short textual descriptions for events, grouped by category. From these collected events, we then constructed timelines, as depicted in Fig. 1(b). Finally, as shown in Fig. 1(c), we connected the timelines to form a network structure.

Data Collection. We collected event descriptions as individual events, along with their allocated categories. We collected the following ten categories, which were manually assigned by Wikipedia editors and subsequently organized by [10]: Law and Crime (LC), Politics and Election (PE), Armed Conflict and Attack (AA), Art and Culture (AC), International Reations (IR), Disaster and Accident (DA), Business and Economy (BE), Sport (S), Health and Medi- cine (HM), and Science and Environment (SE).

Wikipedia's extensive repository of events, systematically organized by year and date, makes it a well-suited foundation for constructing the event networks central to our research. However, comprehensively covering all available data and manually constructing the network is a prohibitively labor-intensive task and therefore infeasible. Consequently, we decided that we focus on analyzing the period from January 1, 2016, to December 31, 2017 in this study. The rationale for selecting this specific timespan is twofold. First, regarding data quality: event records tend to decrease in number for earlier periods, while the most recent entries may suffer from inconsistent or incomplete documentation. In contrast, the data from this period is both well-documented and relatively stable in quality. Second, the chosen timespan encompasses a diverse range of global events, making it particularly suitable for our research objectives.

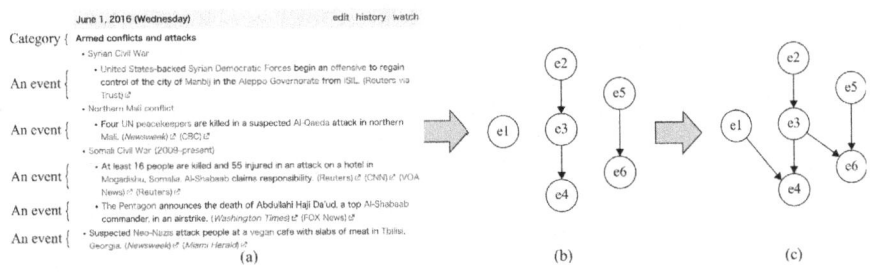

Fig. 1. Example events stored in the Wikipedia Current Events Portal. (a) Events of Wikipedia Current Events Portal. (b) Generated timeline example. (c) Timeline connection example

Timeline Creation. Timelines were manually constructed by four annotators. First, two annotators independently created timelines from the event data. A third validator then reviewed and revised them through discussion with the original annotators. Finally, a fourth inspector reviewed all revisions and removed any entries of questionable validity. We created 2,889 timelines as a result.

Network Creation. The same four annotators followed a similar procedure. Two annotators independently identified dependencies to connect timelines, which were reviewed and revised by a third annotator through discussion. The final inspector then checked all connections and removed any that were questionable. This entire process resulted in the construction of 2,494 dependency relationships.

3 Dataset Analysis

This section provides statistical insights into the events, timelines, and networks to characterize the properties of our dataset.

Fig. 2. Named entities extracted from all event texts

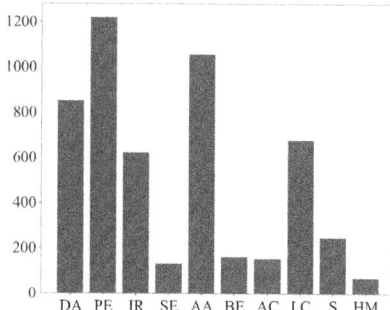

Fig. 3. Distribution of the number of occurrences per category

3.1 Event Analysis

We began by analyzing the entire event data to highlight two key characteristics: the brevity of the event texts and the diversity of event types. These analyses were conducted on 5,204 event descriptions stored in our dataset.

Text Analysis. We calculated the average number of tokens per description and found it to be just 12.5, highlighting the concise nature of the entries. To explore the range of subjects mentioned in these short texts, we analyzed the named entities appearing in the event descriptions using spaCy [9]. This analysis identified 26,815 entities, with an average of 5.1 entities per description. Figure 2 shows the word cloud of the collected entities. As larger words are more frequently mentioned in the dataset, we can see that most of events are related to countries such as the United States, Russia, Syria, China, North Korea, and

Turkey. These findings demonstrate that the dataset covers a broad geographical range and includes a wide variety of global actors.

Category Analysis. Next, we analyze the types of events included in the dataset. Figure 3 shows the number of occurrences per category. The results indicate that political and conflict-related events constitute the majority of the dataset, reflecting its primary thematic focus. Finally, we examined the temporal consistency of these category distributions. Figures 4 and 5 present stacked bar charts illustrating the number of categories per month for 2016 and 2017, respectively. These results confirm that political and conflict-related events consistently remain among the top categories; however, events from other categories are also recorded in each month.

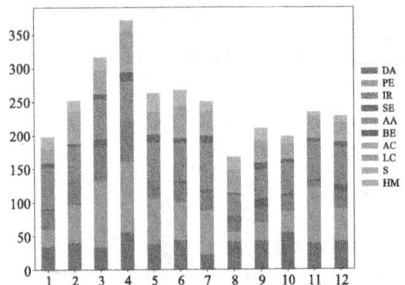

Fig. 4. Monthly distribution of event category occurrences in 2016

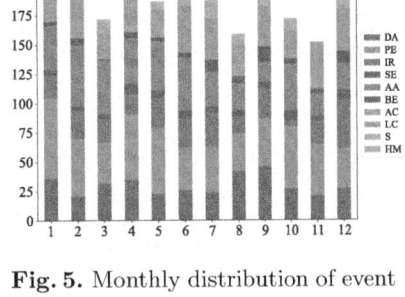

Fig. 5. Monthly distribution of event category occurrences in 2017

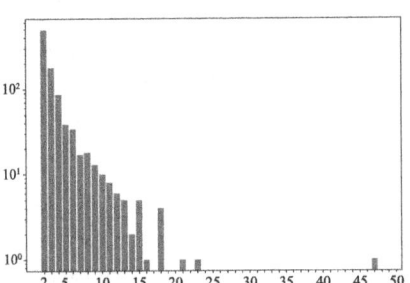

Fig. 6. Distribution of the number of events per timeline.

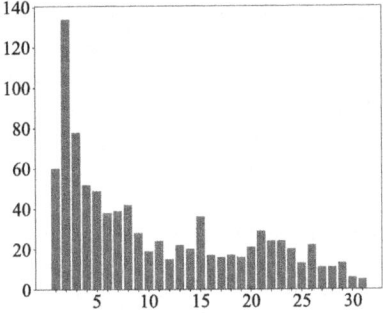

Fig. 7. Distribution of durations per timeline.

3.2 Timeline Analysis

We performed quantitative analyses on the timelines in our dataset to investigate their sizes and the degree of similarity between events within each timeline.

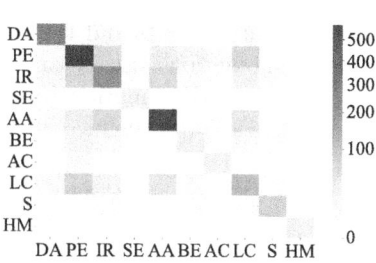

Fig. 8. Frequencies of category combinations within timelines

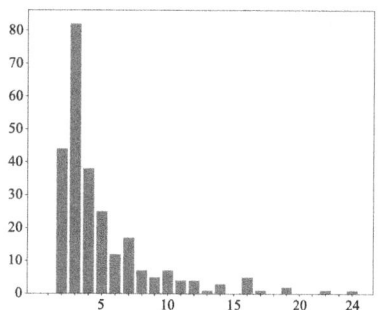

Fig. 9. Distribution of the number of events per network

Size Analysis. Figure 6 illustrates the distribution of timeline sizes. The size of a timeline is defined as the number of events it contains. The horizontal axis represents timeline size, while the vertical axis shows the count on a logarithmic scale. As shown in the figure, the most frequent timeline size is 2, and the number of timelines decreases as size increases. The largest timeline contains 47 events. We conducted a detailed examination of the results and found that timelines related to natural disasters and sports tend to be smaller in size, whereas those concerning conflicts and elections, especially, U.S. presidential election, tend to be larger.

We next analyzed the timespans of all timelines. For each timeline, we extracted the timestamps of the first and last events, then calculated the duration by subtracting the date of the first event from that of the last and adding one day. Figure 7 illustrates the distribution of timeline durations, with the horizontal axis indicating duration and the vertical axis showing the count. The results show that a substantial number of timelines span only a few days. Moreover, the number of timelines tends to decrease as the duration increases.

Similarity Analysis. Next, we analyzed the degree of similarity among events grouped within each timeline. This analysis focused on two aspects: the extent of shared vocabularies in the event texts within a timeline, and the combinations of event categories present in each timeline. In particular, the latter analysis aimed to examine whether events within the same timeline tend to share similar categories, reflecting the assumption that timelines typically group events with related content.

We computed two types of text similarity measures: (1) TF-IDF with cosine similarity based on all tokens, and (2) the Jaccard coefficient based on extracted entities. For every pair of events within each timeline, these similarity scores were calculated. The average values were 0.101 and 0.00044, respectively. These low scores indicate the difficulty of constructing timelines from short event texts, as shared tokens and entities are relatively uncommon. Consequently, simple text-based similarity models are insufficient for identifying coherent timelines. Incorporating contextual information from external sources is therefore essential for effective timeline construction.

We then counted the number of category combinations. For all defined dependencies within each timeline, we collected the associated events and their categories. Figure 8 plots the frequency of category combinations within timelines. We can see that for many categories, the most frequent combination was with the same category; in other words, many dependencies were defined between events of the same type.

3.3 Network Analysis

We conducted a final analysis focusing on the following three aspects of the networks: (1) the number of events contained in each network; (2) the number of combinations of event categories that serve as connection points between timelines; and (3) the contents represented across all networks.

Figure 9 shows the distribution of the number of events included in each network. We observe that the number of networks peaks at three events, with a subsequent decline as the number of events increases. This is a natural outcome, as the networks in this study are constructed by merging timelines, many of which are relatively small. Consequently, the number of events grouped into a single network tends not to be excessively large.

Next, Fig. 10 shows frequencies of category pairs for events connected between timelines. This result indicates that events within the same category often served as connection points across many categories. However, it is observed that the four categories IR, PE, AA, and LC exhibit high inter-connectivity with other categories. This suggests that, during the period from 2016 to 2017, numerous conflicts and policy developments involving multiple countries occurred, and events classified under AA and LC frequently acted as triggers for those in IR and PE, or vice versa. In contrast, S events had dependencies only on events within the same category; this is a distinctive characteristic of this category.

Finally, we analyzed the contents of the networks included in the dataset. To conduct this analysis, we assigned a name to each network and grouped networks with similar names. We then counted the number of networks belonging to each group. The initial naming and grouping were drafted by GPT-4, and the resulting assignments were reviewed and validated by two human annotators. Figure 11 presents the results of this analysis. The results indicate that many of the networks pertain to conflicts involving multiple countries, the policies of countries involved, and the 2016 U.S. presidential election. In addition, natural disasters constitute the sixth most frequent topic, while sports-related events, primarily associated with the 2016 Olympics, rank fifteenth in frequency.

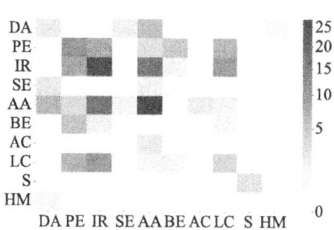

Fig. 10. Combination of event categories theta connect timelines

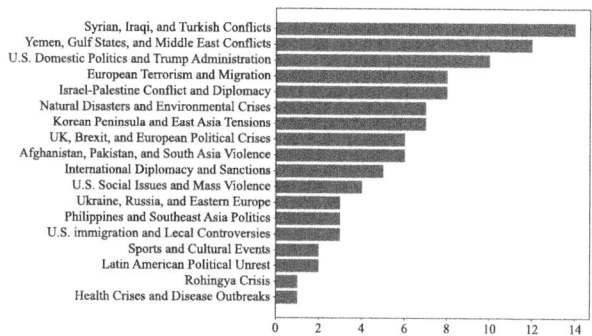

Fig. 11. The number of networks

4 Potential Use Cases

StoryNetworks enables structured analysis of over 5,000 short-form event descriptions by organizing them into dependency-based networks. This is especially valuable for studying short texts, which are prevalent in digital libraries and web archives but often difficult to interpret due to limited context and sparse information. A key use case is the development of machine learning models for tasks such as event detection, linking, and timeline construction from short texts, where models must determine whether multiple brief descriptions refer to the same underlying event. These tasks are particularly challenging when crucial details are missing or only indirectly referenced. StoryNetworks provides a realistic benchmark for advancing model performance in such low-context scenarios.

Beyond computational tasks, StoryNetworks also supports novel information retrieval methods, particularly in educational and social science contexts. Its network structure enables retrieval based on causal, temporal, or thematic relationships rather than simple keyword matching. In history education, this makes possible intelligent search interfaces that allow students and educators to trace the development of historical situations, understand cause-and-effect dynamics, and discover connections between past and present events [11]. Retrieval systems built on StoryNetworks can facilitate exploratory learning and narrative reconstruction by surfacing relevant event paths or clusters based on meaningful relationships [2,3]. Social scientists can also leverage the dataset to analyze the progression of political events, policy decisions, or international developments through structured dependencies that illustrate how actions lead to outcomes.

These use cases demonstrate how StoryNetworks serves both computational and interdisciplinary goals. By centering on short-form, real-world texts and explicitly modeling their interdependencies, the dataset supports robust event understanding and semantic access in information-sparse environments. This enables both automated systems and human users to reason effectively with minimal but richly connected data.

5 Conclusion

We introduced StoryNetworks, a novel dataset of over 5,000 short event texts from the WCEP, organized into structured networks via manually annotated dependencies. By targeting short-form content, it addresses challenges in event understanding and information retrieval under limited context. StoryNetworks supports applications such as event detection, timeline construction, and semantic enrichment, while enabling development of retrieval methods and educational tools for exploring historical narratives. Future work includes extending the dataset to additional years and exploring automatic dependency annotation for scalability.

Acknowledgements. This work was supported in part by MEXT Grant-in-Aids (#25K15357).

References

1. Binh Tran, G., Alrifai, M., Quoc Nguyen, D.: Predicting relevant news events for timeline summaries. In: Proceedings of the 22nd International Conference on World Wide Web, pp. 91–92. WWW '13 Companion, Association for Computing Machinery, New York, NY, USA (2013). https://doi.org/10.1145/2487788.2487829, https://doi.org/10.1145/2487788.2487829
2. Boix-Mansilla, V.: Historical understanding: Beyond the past and into the present. Knowing, Teaching, and Learning History: National and International Perspectives, pp. 390–418 (2000)
3. van Drie, J., van Boxtel, C.: Historical reasoning: towards a framework for analyzing students' reasoning about the past. Educ. Psychol. Rev. **20**(2), 87–110 (2008)
4. Ministry of Education, Culture, S.S., (MEXT), T.: Course of study for upper secondary schools (public notice of heisei 30) (2018). https://www.mext.go.jp/component/a_menu/education/micro_detail/__icsFiles/afieldfile/2019/11/22/1407073_03_2_2.pdf, [In Japanese]
5. Gholipour Ghalandari, D., Ifrim, G.: Examining the state-of-the-art in news timeline summarization. In: Jurafsky, D., Chai, J., Schluter, N., Tetreault, J. (eds.) Proceedings of the 58th Annual Meeting of the Association for Computational Linguistics, pp. 1322–1334. Association for Computational Linguistics, Online (2020). https://doi.org/10.18653/v1/2020.acl-main.122, https://aclanthology.org/2020.acl-main.122
6. Gottschalk, S., Demidova, E.: EventKG: a multilingual event-centric temporal knowledge graph. In: The Semantic Web: 15th International Conference, ESWC 2018, Heraklion, Crete, Greece, June 3–7, 2018, Proceedings, pp. 272–287. Springer-Verlag, Berlin, Heidelberg (2018). https://doi.org/10.1007/978-3-319-93417-4_18, https://doi.org/10.1007/978-3-319-93417-4_18
7. Hayashi, K., Maehara, T., Toyoda, M., Kawarabayashi, K.I.: Real-time top-R topic detection on twitter with topic hijack filtering. In: Proceedings of the 21th ACM SIGKDD International Conference on Knowledge Discovery and Data Mining, pp. 417–426. KDD '15, Association for Computing Machinery, New York, NY, USA (2015). https://doi.org/10.1145/2783258.2783402

8. Hoang, T.A., Vo, K.D., Nejdl, W.: W2e: a worldwide-event benchmark dataset for topic detection and tracking. In: Proceedings of the 27th ACM International Conference on Information and Knowledge Management, pp. 1847–1850. CIKM '18, Association for Computing Machinery, New York, NY, USA (2018). https://doi.org/10.1145/3269206.3269309
9. Honnibal, M., Montani, I.: spaCy 2: natural language understanding with bloom embeddings, convolutional neural networks and incremental parsing (2017)
10. Košmerlj, A., Belyaeva, E., Leban, G., Grobelnik, M., Fortuna, B.: Towards a complete event type taxonomy. In: Proceedings of the 24th International Conference on World Wide Web, pp. 899–902. WWW '15 Companion, Association for Computing Machinery, New York, NY, USA (2015). https://doi.org/10.1145/2740908.2742005
11. Lee, P.: Historical literacy: theory and research. Int. J. Hist. Learn. Teach. Res. **5**(1), 25–40 (2005)
12. Leetaru, K., Schrodt, P.A.: GDELT: global data on events, location, and tone. ISA Annual Convention (2013). http://citeseerx.ist.psu.edu/viewdoc/summary?doi=10.1.1.686.6605
13. Liu, W., et al.: A popular topic detection method based on microblog images and short text information. J. Web Sem. **81**, 100820 (2024). https://doi.org/10.1016/j.websem.2024.100820
14. Mostafazadeh, N., Grealish, A., Chambers, N., Allen, J., Vanderwende, L.: CaTeRS: causal and temporal relation scheme for semantic annotation of event structures. In: Palmer, M., Hovy, E., Mitamura, T., O'Gorman, T. (eds.) Proceedings of the Fourth Workshop on Events, pp. 51–61. Association for Computational Linguistics, San Diego, California (2016). https://doi.org/10.18653/v1/W16-1007, https://aclanthology.org/W16-1007/
15. Mostafazadeh, N., Kalyanpur, A., Moon, L., Buchanan, D., Berkowitz, L., Biran, O., Chu-Carroll, J.: GLUCOSE: generalized and contextualized story explanations. In: Webber, B., Cohn, T., He, Y., Liu, Y. (eds.) Proceedings of the 2020 Conference on Empirical Methods in Natural Language Processing (EMNLP), pp. 4569–4586. Association for Computational Linguistics, Online (Nov 2020https://doi.org/10.18653/v1/2020.emnlp-main.370
16. Pasquali, A., Campos, R., Ribeiro, A., Santana, B., Jorge, A., Jatowt, A.: TLS-Covid19: a new annotated corpus for timeline summarization. In: Advances in Information Retrieval: 43rd European Conference on IR Research, ECIR 2021, Virtual Event, March 28 – April 1, 2021, Proceedings, Part I. pp. 497–512. Springer-Verlag, Berlin, Heidelberg (2021). https://doi.org/10.1007/978-3-030-72113-8_33, https://doi.org/10.1007/978-3-030-72113-8_33
17. Pustejovsky, J., et al.: TimeBank: a corpus for annotating temporal information. In: Proceedings of the Corpus Linguistics Conference, pp. 647–656. Lancaster, UK (2003)
18. Qi, Y., Zhou, L., Si, H., Wan, J., Jin, T.: An approach to news event detection and tracking based on stream of online news. In: 2017 9th International Conference on Intelligent Human-Machine Systems and Cybernetics (IHMSC), vol. 2, pp. 193–196 (2017). https://doi.org/10.1109/IHMSC.2017.158
19. Radinsky, K., Horvitz, E.: Mining the web to predict future events. In: Proceedings of the Sixth ACM International Conference on Web Search and Data Mining, pp. 255–264. WSDM '13, Association for Computing Machinery, New York, NY, USA (2013). https://doi.org/10.1145/2433396.2433431, https://doi.org/10.1145/2433396.2433431

20. Sawahata, N., Machizawa, D., Ikejiri, R., Sumikawa, Y.: LLM-based dependency tracking for short event descriptions. In: The 29th International Conference on Theory and Practice of Digital Libraries. TPDL '25, Springer-Verlag, Berlin, Heidelberg (2025). https://sumilab.github.io/web/pdf/2025/tpdl2025_sawahata.pdf, accepted
21. Tan, Z., Zhang, P., Tan, J., Guo, L.: A multi-layer event detection algorithm for detecting global and local hot events in social networks. Proc. Comput. Sci. **29**, 2080–2089 (2014). https://doi.org/10.1016/j.procs.2014.05.192
22. Wang, L., Cardie, C., Marchetti, G.: Socially-informed timeline generation for complex events. In: Mihalcea, R., Chai, J., Sarkar, A. (eds.) Proceedings of the 2015 Conference of the North American Chapter of the Association for Computational Linguistics: Human Language Technologies, pp. 1055–1065. Association for Computational Linguistics, Denver, Colorado (2015). https://doi.org/10.3115/v1/N15-1112, https://aclanthology.org/N15-1112/
23. Yang, C.C., Shi, X., Wei, C.P.: Discovering event evolution graphs from news corpora. IEEE Trans. Syst. Man Cybern. Part A Syst. Hum. **39**(4), 850–863 (2009). https://doi.org/10.1109/TSMCA.2009.2015885
24. Yao, Y., et al.: DocRED: a large-scale document-level relation extraction dataset. In: Korhonen, A., Traum, D., Màrquez, L. (eds.) Proceedings of the 57th Annual Meeting of the Association for Computational Linguistics, pp. 764–777. Association for Computational Linguistics, Florence, Italy (2019). https://doi.org/10.18653/v1/P19-1074, https://aclanthology.org/P19-1074/

Evaluating Human-LLM Alignment in ETD Subject Classification

Hajra Klair[1](✉), Fausto German[1], Bipasha Banerjee[2], and William A. Ingram[2]

[1] Department of Computer Science Virginia Tech, Blacksburg, VA 24061, USA
khajra23@vt.edu
[2] University Libraries Virginia Tech, Blacksburg, VA 24061, USA

Abstract. Author-assigned subject labels in Electronic Theses and Dissertations (ETDs) are often inconsistent, overly broad, or misaligned with the research focus. This hampers discovery, aggregation, and analysis, especially for interdisciplinary research. LLMs offer a scalable alternative for automated classification, but their labeling rationale is opaque and introduces systematic biases. This study compares subject labels generated by LLMs with human-assigned labels for over 9,000 ETDs across 21 academic categories to assess the disagreement. We evaluate multiple prompt-based and fine-tuned LLM configurations and analyze areas of agreement and disagreement to identify patterns of misclassification. LLMs achieve competitive performance overall but frequently misclassify theoretical or interdisciplinary texts, often due to overweighting lexical cues and disregarding context. We show such errors are not random but reflect structured semantic divergences from human interpretation. These findings suggest a need for hybrid frameworks that combine LLM scalability with human contextual judgment to improve subject labeling in academic repositories.

Keywords: Classification · Large Language Models

1 Introduction

Electronic Theses and Dissertations (ETDs) form a global record of graduate research. To support discovery and analysis, authors are typically asked to assign subject labels at deposit, often without oversight. These labels are frequently inconsistent, overly broad, or misaligned with the work's actual content. A common issue is conflating departments with disciplines. For instance, labeling a thesis "Computer Science" when it may belong to "Human-Computer Interaction," "Computer Engineering," or "Computational Biology." Manual verification and reclassification are not feasible at scale. Labeling is subjective, especially in interdisciplinary cases, and the volume of submissions (often exceeding a thousand per year at large universities) makes human review impractical.

Automated classification, particularly with LLMs, offers a scalable and consistent alternative. LLMs can rapidly analyze text and apply uniform criteria, often detecting semantic cues missed or inconsistently applied by humans. However, they also introduce challenges, including systematic biases and difficulty with interdisciplinary content. These differences create recurring disagreement between human and automated labels.

Consider *The Impact of Psychoeducational Workshops on Self-Concept of Middle School Male Students* [10], classified by humans as "Educational Psychology," "Psychology," and "Middle School Education." A prompted LLM instead labeled it "Occupational Psychology." This misclassification seems to stem from overweighting intervention-related terms like "self-concept," "identity," and "group members," which are common in workplace psychology literature on organizational behavior and team dynamics. Despite the explicit reference to "middle school males," transformer models may underweight setting descriptors relative to methodological or lexical features. This raises questions about how LLMs interpret disciplinary boundaries and whether they can reliably substitute for human judgment in subject classification.

To investigate this misalignment more systematically, we evaluate LLM-based subject classification of ETDs using title and abstract text. We address four research questions:

- **RQ1**: Can automated methods, particularly LLMs, be reliably used to assign subject labels to ETDs?
- **RQ2**: Can human labeling and AI labeling on their own be considered consistent across various disciplines?
- **RQ3**: Do humans and LLMs exhibit systematic differences in how they assign subject labels? What semantic and contextual features explain these differences?
- **RQ4**: How can systematic biases be mitigated to improve the reliability and interpretability of automatic subject classification?

2 Related Work

Subject classification of scholarly documents has progressed from manual cataloging under MARC standards to automated techniques using supervised learning and deep neural networks. Medelyan et al. (2009) [11] showed that automated keyphrase extraction could support or outperform manual indexing in consistency and scalability.

Hierarchical and multi-label classification methods gained traction in the 2010s. Wu et al. (2015) [15] used multi-instance learning to identify areas of research expertise. Huang et al. (2017) [6] applied deep learning to large academic corpora, showing that neural models outperform bag-of-words approaches in capturing semantic structure. Park et al. (2022) [13] benchmarked transformer-based models for long-document classification, emphasizing the role of document length and architecture.

Recent work has applied LLMs to classification and analysis in digital libraries. Banerjee et al. (2024) [2] explored AI-driven chapter-level classification in ETDs, improving granularity and discovery. Garcia et al. (2025) [4] showed LLMs can model semantic distinctions critical for interdisciplinary classification. Grasso and Locci (2024) [5] found BERT variants outperformed generative LLMs like GPT-3.5 and LLaMA-2 on environmental research classification but noted that LLMs demonstrated consistent calibration.

Others have emphasized the limitations of LLM-based classification. Koo et al. (2024) [9] examined cognitive bias and transparency concerns. Ingram et al. (2024) demonstrate model disagreement in labeling research abstracts, raising concerns about variability and interpretability in LLM-based classification [7]. Chow, Kao, and Li (2024) [3] assessed ChatGPT's use for assigning Library of Congress Subject Headings (LCSH) to ETDs, finding that while LLMs reduced cataloging time, human catalogers were still essential for specificity and accuracy.

In our work, we explicitly analyze systematic differences between human-generated and AI-generated ETD classifications. By examining where and why discrepancies arise, we aim to improve the overall accuracy and trustworthiness of ETD classification. The study characterizes the patterns and causes of classification divergence between humans and AI systems on ETDs, with implications for subject labeling reliability in digital libraries.

3 Methodology

We frame ETD classification as a multi-class prediction task using a controlled vocabulary of 21 subject categories, derived from human-assigned metadata. The dataset includes over 9,000 ETDs, each with a title, abstract, and at least one subject label. Preprocessing and label normalization details appear in Sect. 4.

We evaluate three LLMs across six input and prompt configurations, varying by input length (title vs. abstract vs. title and abstract combined) and supervision type (zero-shot vs. few-shot). Few-shot prompts include four examples representative of the 21-class distribution, held fixed across experiments. Each model is prompted to assign exactly one label from the controlled vocabulary.

We also test the performance of supervised fine-tuning of models on the task using the same dataset. This is to provide a benchmark for evaluating whether zero-shot and few-shot LLM performance approaches or exceeds the accuracy of domain-adapted classifiers. All models are evaluated using standard multi-class metrics, including accuracy, precision, recall, and F1-score.

To assess the consistency and systematic differences between human-generated and AI-generated labels, we conduct a secondary analysis across all experimental runs. This includes pairwise agreement statistics, Chi-squared goodness-of-fit tests for label distributions and Kullback-Leibler (KL) divergence to quantify distributional shifts. This analysis allows us to isolate categories with high disagreement and examine whether classification errors are stochastic or exhibit structured semantic patterns.

4 Dataset

Our dataset comprises of over 9,000 electronic theses and dissertations (ETDs) from the Virginia Tech institutional repository, collected in 2020 [8]. Each ETD was linked to its subject category in the ProQuest Dissertations & Theses (PQTD) Global database via a combination of automated and manual checks using author, title, and date. Each ETD record contains a title, abstract, author, degree, and subject labels.

PQTD employs a four-level subject taxonomy, but for this study, we focused on the 432 leaf-level categories. These are *elemental*, directly reflecting the dissertation's disciplinary domain, and one of them must be chosen as the primary subject category by each author at submission, making them a reliable indication of scholarly focus.

To reduce class imbalance, we ranked all 432 categories by ETD count and selected the top 28. Of these, 8 containing "education" (e.g., "Higher Education," "Adult Education") were merged into one "Education" label to avoid overrepresentation. During this step, we randomly subsampled the Education group to match its size to other categories (as "Education" was not our main focus, our aim was fair cross-domain comparison, we chose this pragmatic approach). Remaining categories used their native PQTD assignments.

The resulting set of 21 subject categories was sufficiently balanced for comparative evaluation. We also performed some preprocessing including label normalization, removal of records with missing abstracts, and validation of mappings. The final dataset offers a controlled yet diverse benchmark for subject classification across academic domains. Appendix includes Category details.

5 Implementation

5.1 LLM Prompting

We experimented with three different LLMs using different prompt structures for the classification task: two proprietary models, GPT4.1-mini and GPT4.5-preview, and one open model, Mistral Instruct v0.3 from Hugging Face [12]. As described in Sect. 3, we tested each model with three input configurations: title only, abstract only, and title combined with abstract.

Each prompt consisted of a short task description instructing the model to classify a thesis into one of 21 predefined subject categories. The list of valid categories was included directly in the prompt. The model was instructed to output only the best-fitting category. Minimal temperature settings (0.01) were used to encourage deterministic output. Among the configurations tested, prompts using both title and abstract as input yielded the most accurate classifications across models.

5.2 Model Fine-Tuning

To compare against prompting-based classification, we fine-tuned several transformer-based models on the same dataset of 9,218 ETDs, using a

60%/20%/20% split for training, validation, and testing. Three models from Hugging Face were used as base encoders: LLaMA-3 (7B), GPT-2, and BERT-base-uncased. These were selected for their moderate computational requirements, enabling training within resource constraints. For all three models (BERT-base-uncased, GPT-2, and LLaMA-3), we adopted the Hugging Face `AutoModelForSequenceClassification` interface. This approach adds a single linear classification head to the model–on top of the [CLS] token for BERT-base-uncased and on the final hidden state of the last token for the decoder-only architectures, GPT-2 and LLaMA-3. The resulting logits are used for standard multi-class classification with cross-entropy loss. Unlike BERT, both GPT-2 and LLaMA-3 are decoder-only models, but the classification strategy remains consistent across all three, following Hugging Face guidelines. Fine-tuning was performed using the concatenated title and abstract as input. For efficient training given the computational constraints, we applied 4-bit quantization (using BitsAndBytes) and Low-Rank Adapter (LoRA) modules.

We tested batch sizes of 4, 8, and 16, and learning rates of 2^{-5}, 3^{-5}, and 5^{-5}. The best performance was achieved with a batch size of 8 and learning rate of 2^{-5}. To provide a non-neural baseline, we implemented a Support Vector Machine (SVM) classifier using TF-IDF features extracted from the title and abstract of each ETD.

6 Evaluation

We compared prompt-based, fine-tuned, and traditional machine learning models using macro-averaged accuracy, precision, recall, and F1 scores. Only the results using the combined title and abstract text as input are reported here, as this configuration consistently produced the highest scores across models.

Table 1. Subject Classification Performance of Prompted and Fine-Tuned Models

Group	Model	Accuracy	Precision	Recall	F1
Prompt-based	GPT-4.5-preview (Zero Shot)	68.43%	**72.95%**	**68.35%**	**68.15%**
	GPT-4.1-mini (Few Shot)	**76.15%**	70.93%	66.83%	66.86%
	GPT-4.1-mini (Zero Shot)	75.94%	70.71%	65.18%	65.47%
	Mistral v0.3 (Zero Shot)	58.74%	67.92%	58.48%	56.77%
Fine-tuned	BERT	72.07%	58.95%	61.71%	58.75%
	Llama-3	68.15%	66.81%	67.95%	65.95%
	GPT-2	51.34%	49.94%	51.19%	47.08%
Traditional ML	SVM	72.10%	59.43%	61.75%	59.49%

Table 1 summarizes the comparative performance of prompt-based LLMs, fine-tuned transformer models, and a traditional supervised baseline (SVM).

Among the prompt-based models, GPT-4.1-mini Few Shot achieved the highest accuracy (76.15%), but GPT-4.5-preview Zero Shot outperformed all others on precision (72.95%), recall (68.35%), and F1 score (68.15%), suggesting more balanced performance across classes. The zero-shot configuration of GPT-4.1-mini (75.94% accuracy, 65.47% F1) performed competitively but did not surpass the few-shot version. Mistral v0.3, in contrast, produced lower scores across all metrics.

Among the fine-tuned models, LLaMA-3 achieved the highest precision (66.81%), recall (67.95%), and F1 score (65.95%). BERT yielded slightly higher accuracy (72.07%) but a lower F1 score (58.75%). GPT-2 produced the weakest results (F1 = 47.08%), possibly due to its smaller size and older architecture. SVM performed comparably to BERT, with an accuracy of 72.10% and an F1 score of 59.49%.

Interestingly, GPT-4.1-mini (Few Shot) achieved the highest accuracy (76.15%) across all models, outperforming the newer GPT-4.5-preview (68.43%). However, its precision, recall, and F1 score were lower than GPT-4.5, and it only marginally outperformed its own zero-shot variant. This pattern suggests that the few-shot examples may have biased the model toward over-predicting high-frequency classes, boosting overall accuracy while reducing its ability to generalize across the full label set.

Category-level analysis revealed that misclassifications were most frequent between closely related disciplines. For example, the model often confounded "computer science" with "computer engineering," and "environmental engineering" with "ecology," likely due to overlapping terminology and interdisciplinary research themes. When the task was reframed to allow the model to select the top three most likely categories, the F1 score increased substantially to 91.83%. We give class-wise performance details in the appendix.

Table 2. Top-3 Classification Performance for GPT-4.5-preview

Model	Accuracy	Precision	Recall	F1 Score
GPT-4.5-preview (Top-3)	92.84%	95.45%	88.61%	91.83%

7 Discussion

We structure the discussion around our four research questions.

RQ1: Can automated methods, particularly LLMs, be reliably used to assign subject labels to ETDs?

LLMs and other AI models show moderate reliability in subject categorization, but they exhibit systematic bias when compared to human experts. Chi-squared tests indicate that nearly all tested models diverge significantly from human distributions ($p < 0.001$), suggesting these differences are not due to chance. To quantify alignment with human labels, we measured KL divergence; the results ranged from 0.3270 nats (Mistral) to 0.0658 nats (GPT-4.5), indicating variable levels of information loss across models. Human–AI agreement, measured by Cohen's kappa, ranged from 0.643 to 0.708, suggesting moderate but not high agreement.

LLMs perform best in applied domains such as biomedical engineering and education, which feature distinctive vocabulary and clear methodological markers, achieving accuracy rates above 85%. Performance in fields like ecology and marketing is moderate, likely due to lexical overlap with other neighboring disciplines. The poorest results, with accuracy below 60%, appear in theoretical or quantitative domains (e.g., statistics, mathematics, computer science), where models rely on methodological signals while overlooking application context. For instance, a thesis on riverbank restoration was misclassified by the LLM as "Ecology" due to biological keywords, while the human correctly classified it as "Environmental Science" (focusing on restoration management and environmental systems). Such misclassifications are most common at interdisciplinary boundaries, where models systematically overweight methodological language and underweight contextual framing.

LLMs are moderately reliable for ETD categorization, especially in applied fields with distinctive terminology. However, their performance declines in theoretical fields, where contextual grounding matters more.

RQ2: Can human labeling and AI labeling on their own be considered consistent across various disciplines?

TF-IDF vectorization and cosine similarity analysis revealed no statistically significant difference in labeling consistency between humans and AI (Wilcoxon $p > 0.05$; Cohen's $d < 0.5$). The two approaches exhibit complementary strengths rather than a systematic superiority of one over the other.

Humans showed greater consistency in social science domains, reflecting deeper contextual understanding. For example, in Education (30.3% higher human consistency), human labels aligned better with educational research frameworks while AI relied on surface-level terms. AI showed higher consistency in technical domains with specialized terminology, such as Occupational Psychology (28% higher AI consistency), where domain-specific vocabulary is more stable and predictive.

Neither method is uniformly more consistent. The distribution of strengths across domains supports the use of hybrid labeling approaches.

RQ3: Do humans and LLMs exhibit systematic differences in how they assign subject labels? What semantic and contextual features explain these differences?

Humans and AI systems demonstrate consistent differences in classification behavior. Human labelers prioritize institutional context and practical application, asking: "Where will this research be used?" and "Which community will benefit most?". In contrast, AI systems tend to focus on methodological cues and theoretical frameworks, asking: "What methods are used?" and "Which terms dominate?" Across all categories, LLMs systematically over-weight methodological terms and under-weight contextual terms. Approximately 40% of misclassifications occur at interdisciplinary boundaries, where research legitimately spans multiple domains. This is not a classification failure, but evidence that modern research increasingly transcends traditional disciplinary boundaries.

As an example, consider the thesis *An Exploratory Study of Urban Transportation and Air Quality Issues Using CO as an Indicator* [1]. It was labeled "Civil Engineering" by humans (focusing on transportation infrastructure) and "Environmental Science" by the LLM (focusing on pollution monitoring). This demonstrates how both perspectives are valid, but single-category systems force interdisciplinary research into artificial silos.

Humans and LLMs exhibit systematic differences in classification, especially on interdisciplinary and theoretical content. LLMs prioritize lexical signals, often missing contextual nuance leading to predictable biases. These patterns underscore the need for more context-aware models and multi-label classification systems.

RQ4: How can systematic biases be corrected to improve confidence in automatic labeling?

To improve the reliability of subject classification for ETDs, we believe practitioners can undertake a set of corrective strategies based on observed model behavior. First, hybrid pipelines combining AI-driven classification with human review in ambiguous domains, particularly in quantitative and theoretical fields like statistics and mathematics, may reduce error. Improving model sensitivity to domain-specific signal, while filtering misleading lexical features, could reduce systematic misclassification, particularly at disciplinary boundaries.

8 Conclusion and Future Work

This study shows that LLMs can match or exceed the performance of traditional and fine-tuned models in automating subject classification of ETDs, particularly in applied domains. However, our findings also reveal that LLMs exhibit systematic biases in theoretical and interdisciplinary fields, often favoring surface-level lexical cues over contextual or methodological grounding. Human and AI labeling show complementary strengths, suggesting that hybrid systems that combine LLM scalability with human contextual judgment may offer more reliable classification.

Future work should explore multi-label classification frameworks that better capture the complexity of interdisciplinary research. Additional domain-specific training and context-aware filtering could help reduce model biases. Expanding evaluation to include more institutions and subject taxonomies will test the generalizability of these findings.

Appendix

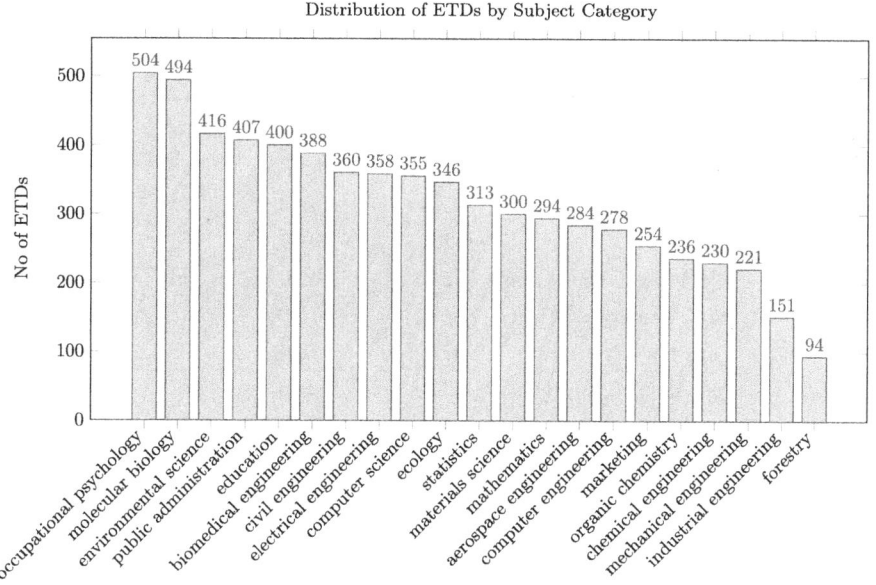

Fig. 1. Distribution of ETDs by Subject Category.

System Prompt
You are an expert academic paper classifier. Avoid these frequent confusions:
- Education vs Occupational Psychology
- Environmental Science vs Ecology
- Comp. Science vs Comp. Engineering
- Mechanical vs Aerospace Engineering

CATEGORIES: <LIST_OF_CATEGORIES>
Rules: Analyze title and abstract, choose **one** primary domain, respond with category name only.
Content Prompt
TITLE: <ETD_TITLE> ABSTRACT: <ETD_ABSTRACT>
CATEGORY:

Zero-shot prompt used in classification experiments.

Table 3. Class-wise Performance Metrics for GPT-4.5-preview (Zero Shot)

Class	Precision (%)	Recall (%)	F1 (%)
Aerospace Engineering	84.0	68.0	75.1
Biomedical Engineering	42.7	85.0	56.9
Chemical Engineering	52.9	46.0	49.2
Civil Engineering	87.0	60.0	71.0
Computer Engineering	43.4	53.0	47.7
Computer Science	44.9	61.0	51.7
Ecology	63.3	62.0	62.6
Education	62.8	91.0	74.3
Electrical Engineering	62.7	42.0	50.3
Environmental Science	37.5	75.0	50.0
Forestry	97.4	40.4	57.1
Industrial Engineering	70.0	49.0	57.6
Marketing	92.8	90.0	91.4
Materials Science	64.2	77.0	70.0
Mathematics	95.8	46.0	62.2
Mechanical Engineering	61.7	58.0	59.8
Molecular Biology	60.6	63.0	61.8
Occupational Psychology	82.8	82.0	82.4
Organic Chemistry	100.0	42.0	59.2
Public Administration	71.9	87.0	78.7
Statistics	91.1	51.0	65.4

System Prompt
You are an expert academic paper classifier.
Avoid these frequent confusions:
- Education vs Occupational Psychology
- Environmental Science vs Ecology
- Comp. Science vs Comp. Engineering
- Mechanical vs Aerospace Engineering

CATEGORIES: <LIST_OF_CATEGORIES>
Examples:

- 1: Title: Psychoeducational Workshops Self-concept.. Abstract: Effects.. Category: education
- 2: Title: Animated Word-Tracer Reading.. Abstract: Psychological Workp.. Category: occupational psychology
- 3: Title: Riverbank Impact Dragonflies.. Abstract: Pollution Environm.. Category: environmental science
- 4: Title: Cloud Security Computation.. Abstract: Algorithms Theory .. Category: computer science
- 5: Title: Reduced Order Modeling.. Abstract: Mechanical Systems ... Category: mechanical engineering
- 6: Title: Hippocampus Activity Patterns... Abstract: Engineering Neural.. Category: biomedical engineering
- 7: Title: Urban Transport Quality.. Abstract: Infrastructure Planning ... Category: civil engineering
- 8: Title: Microfluidic Granules Packing.. Abstract: Material Structure.. Category: materials science
- 9: Title: Polymers Excluded Volume.. Abstract: Statistical Data ..: statistics
- 10: Title: Home Automation System... Abstract: Electrical Circuit ..: electrical engineering
- 11: Title: Styryl Phosphonic Derivatives... Abstract: Chemical Molecular..: organic chemistry
- 12: Title: Free-Form Surfaces Maximization.. Abstract: Systems Optim..: industrial engineering
- 13: Title: Michigan Polling Accuracy.. Abstract: Market Analytics ..: marketing
- 14: Title: Fish Movement Alaska... Abstract: Species Population..: ecology

Instructions:

1. Focus on methodology, discipline, context.
2. Pick **one** best category from <LIST_OF_CATEGORIES>.
3. Respond only with the category name.

Content Prompt
TITLE: <ETD_TITLE> ABSTRACT: <ETD_ABSTRACT> CATEGORY:

Few-shot prompt used in classification experiments.

References

1. Albrinck, B.M.: An Exploratory Study of Urban Transportation and Air Quality Issues Using CO as an Indicator. Ph.D. thesis, ProQuest Dissertations and Theses, University of Cincinnati (2010). 176 pp. https://www.proquest.com/dissertations-theses/exploratory-study-urban-transportation-air/docview/866723558/se-2
2. Banerjee, B., et al.: Automating chapter-level classification for electronic theses and dissertations. arXiv preprint arXiv:2411.17614 (2024). https://arxiv.org/abs/2411.17614
3. Chow, E. H. C., Kao, T. J., Li, X.: An experiment with the use of ChatGPT for LCSH subject assignment on electronic theses and dissertations. arXiv preprint arXiv:2403.16424 (2024). https://arxiv.org/abs/2403.16424
4. Garcia, M. H., et al.: Exploring how LLMs capture and represent domain-specific knowledge. arXiv preprint arXiv:2504.16871 (2025). https://arxiv.org/abs/2504.16871
5. Grasso, F., Locci, S.: Assessing generative language models in classification tasks: performance and self-evaluation capabilities in the environmental and climate change domain. arXiv preprint arXiv:2408.17362 (2024). https://arxiv.org/abs/2408.17362
6. Huang, W., Wang, Z., Liu, X., Zeng, N., Liu, Y., Alsaadi, F.E.: A survey of deep neural network architectures and their applications. Neurocomputing 234, 11–26 (2017). https://doi.org/10.1016/j.neucom.2016.12.038
7. Ingram, W.A., Banerjee, B., Fox, E.A.: Agentic AI for improving precision in identifying contributions to sustainable development goals. In: Proceedings of the 2024 IEEE International Conference on Big Data (BigData 2024), Washington, DC, USA, pp. 8677–8679. IEEE (2024). https://doi.org/10.1109/BigData62323.2024.10825072
8. Jude, P.M.: Increasing accessibility of electronic theses and dissertations (ETDS) through chapter-level classification. Master's thesis, Virginia Tech (2020). http://hdl.handle.net/10919/99294
9. Koo, R., Lee, M., Raheja, V., Park, J. I., Kim, Z. M., Kang, D.: Benchmarking cognitive biases in large language models as evaluators. In: Proceedings of the 62nd Annual Meeting of the Association for Computational Linguistics (ACL 2024), pp. 1–29 (2024). https://arxiv.org/abs/2309.17012
10. Krugman, A.B.: The Impact of Psychoeducational Workshops on Self-Concept of Middle School Male Students. Ph.D. dissertation, Loyola University Chicago (2012). ProQuest Dissertations and Theses, Publication No. 3523417. https://www.proquest.com/dissertations-theses/impact-psychoeducational-workshops-on-self/docview/1027935212/se-2
11. Medelyan, O., Frank, E., Witten, I.H.: Human-competitive tagging using automatic keyphrase extraction. In: Proceedings of the 2009 Conference on Empirical Methods in Natural Language Processing, pp. 1318–1327 (2009). https://doi.org/10.3115/1699648.1699678
12. Mistral AI team: mistral-7B-instruct-v0.3. Hugging Face (2024). https://huggingface.co/mistralai/Mistral-7B-Instruct-v0.3
13. Park, H. H., Vyas, Y., Shah, K.: Efficient classification of long documents using transformers. arXiv preprint arXiv:2203.11258 (2022). https://arxiv.org/abs/2203.11258

14. Radford, A., Wu, J., Child, R., Luan, D., Amodei, D., Sutskever, I.: Language models are unsupervised multitask learners. OpenAI (2019). https://cdn.openai.com/better-language-models/language_models_are_unsupervised_multitask_learners.pdf
15. Wu, T., Wang, Q., Zhang, Z., Si, L.: Determining expert research areas with multi-instance learning of hierarchical multi-label classification model. In: Proceedings of the Twenty-Fourth International Joint Conference on Artificial Intelligence (IJCAI 2015), Buenos Aires, Argentina, pp. 2305–2311 (2015). https://www.ijcai.org/Proceedings/15/Papers/326.pdf

Linking References to Documents in Parliamentary Debates

Floris Bos[1], Marc van Opijnen[2], and Maarten Marx[1(✉)]

[1] IRLab, Informatics Institute, University of Amsterdam,
Amsterdam, The Netherlands
`maartenmarx@uva.nl`
[2] Publications Office of the Netherlands (Logius|Koop), The Hague, The Netherlands
`marc.opijnen@koop.overheid.nl`

Abstract. In Dutch parliamentary debates, over 95% of references to documents are implicit and non-standardized, hindering document accessibility and analysis. To address this challenge, we introduce a two-phase approach to automatically detect and link these references. The first phase uses a Large Language Model (LLM), specifically Gemini 2.5 Flash, for reference detection and semantic enrichment, extracting features like document type, a summary, and keywords. The second phase links these references to known documents using vector similarity search. Our large-scale analysis of 281 debates confirms the scale of the problem, revealing that nearly 74% of all detected references are implicit. Evaluation on a new, manually annotated gold-standard dataset of 191 references shows our detection method achieves an F1-score of 0.49, while the LLM classifies semantic features like document type with 92–97% accuracy. For the linking task, evaluated on 1,933 references, combining LLM-generated keywords with metadata filtering proves most effective. This approach correctly identifies the target document in 35% of cases (Hit@1) and places it in the top 10 candidates of 57% of the time (MRR 0.42). This work serves as a strong baseline for resolving complex, implicit references in a parliamentary proceedings. The methodology is inherently language-agnostic and shows significant promise for adaptation to other domains, such as legal case law or historical archives.

Keywords: Document Linking · Large Language Models · Known-item Search · Semantic Search

1 Introduction

"The meaning of a document is in its use", free after Witgenstein, is a statement librarians, archivists and IR scholars can relate to. Think of bibliometrics, the use of PageRank as a quality indicator, and anchor text as concise summaries as examples in which the use of a document, witnessed by a reference to it in another document, is employed to enrich the representation of the document, leading to improved performance in e.g., retrieval tasks.

We can access this use of documents in a corpus if the corpus is structured as a (weighted) directed network in which the links indicate references between documents. Hypertext, standardization (URLs), Web 2.0 techniques like WikiLinks, but also powerful parsing tools like GROBID [13] have made these links (almost) directly available in specific document collections. In other cases, the references are implicit and work has to be done to turn a document collection into a directed network.

This task is more generally known in NLP as Named Entity Recognition (NER) and Linking. Nowadays, NER can be performed with high accuracy by LLMs, needing no or only a few training examples [24]. Linking —finding out what a certain string is referring to—is usually treated as a known-item search task: there exists exactly one correct referent (although it may not be present in the use knowledge base). The difficulty of this task depends on the amount of homonimity (same string referring to multiple entities) and the synonymity (one entity having multiple "names"). For the traditional NER types, persons, organizations, locations, these aspects are usually handled using context and semantic embeddings [11].

Examples of corpora containing documents implicitly referring to other documents are court cases referring to laws and other court cases [15], scientific articles mentioning the use of datasets [17, 19] or containing archival references [21].

In this paper, we study references to parliamentary documents (legislative proposals, motions, amendments, letters by ministers, etc.) made in parliamentary debates. Examples of such references, with the reference to a parliamentary document in italics, are the following:

- "Hoe denkt mevrouw Hermann om te gaan met *de motie die zij in dit verband heeft ingediend?*" [1]
- "In november 2001 heeft de Kamer *een motie aanvaard waarin de regering werd gevraagd haar een notitie toe te sturen.*" [2]
- "In *de brief* heeft u ook aangetroffen dat er gewerkt wordt aan een structurele aanpak." [3]

For Dutch parliamentary proceedings, this is indeed a problem as less than 5% of these references are made explicit using a identifier [23]. We show how a multilingual LLM can solve the recognition task very well, while generating several disambiguation and retrieval features. These features are turned into semantic embeddings and matched against embeddings of the documents for linking the reference. Our best performing system successfully identifies 44% of the references with a precision of 55%. It accurately links 35% of references to the

---

[1] Translation: "How does Mrs. Hermann intend to deal with *the motion she has submitted in this regard?*"
[2] Translation: "On november 2001 the Parliament has accepted *a motion in which the government has asked her to send a memorandum*".
[3] Translation: "In *the letter* you also found that work is being done on a structural approach".

right document, with the correct document appearing in the top 10 candidates 57% of the time. We also release a manually curated dataset of 5 debates with 191 identified references from the Dutch House of Parliament, which serves as the gold standard for further evaluation.

Our approach is not novel, but can be seen as a strong baseline for the document linking task in a domain with novel challenging characteristics like 1) long references (log normally distributed, median = 1.39, max = 4.08), 2) anaphoric references ("my letter to the minister of last spring") and 3) vague and hard to resolve references.

We end this introduction with a motivation for this task based on the related case of references to datasets in scientific articles. Searching for datasets is difficult for humans [9], despite the fact that several well developed search systems [2] and an extensive body of research exists [3]. According to [9], this is due to the mismatch between the information need and the representation of the datasets. Users search for a dataset which is useful given a specific task. But the representation of the dataset is based on the metadata or the data it contains, and not on how the dataset is, or can be, used. The latter of course can be found in articles which mention the dataset. Enriching the representation of datasets with their use thus gives rise to the field of dataset mention detection [8].

2 Related Work

The detection and reconcilliation of dataset mentions in scientific articles is a task similar to ours, with similar features, in particular no standardized manner of referencing and thus a large variation in references to the same entity [17]. Several open benchmarks have been created [8,19]. Tested on the DMDD benchmark, a BERT embedding based classifier worked best for detection, followed by a CRF model from [8] using carefully chosen features (POS tags and dataset cue terms), which outperformed a BiLSTM classifier on fully learned features. An initial experiment testing entity linking showed little difference between lexical (BM25) and embedding (ColBERT, not fine-tuned) methods [19].

A problem which resembles our case because of the use of numerical identifiers in references to documents is linking in legal documents, to both case law and legislation. Several systems have been proposed, from rule-based to systems learned from examples [1,16,20,22].

An interesting case in which the representation of a document cannot be based on its content is described by Suzuki and Oard [21]. They want to enable search in huge archives of physical boxes with documents which for the sheer reason of size cannot be OCRed. References to these boxes in scientific articles are thus the only way to semantically enrich their representation. This resulted in the SUSHI shared task at NTCIR 2025 where participants must create a search system returning archival records based on a set of documents with detected references to them [14].

3 Methods

Our approach is a two-phase system: the first phase extracts candidate references from a Dutch parliamentary minute and enriches them with semantic features, and the second links them to known Dutch parliamentary documents using vector similarity search. We also introduce the annotated dataset used for development and evaluation.

3.1 Recognition, Description, and Improving Precision

The first stage of our system identifies, enriches, and validates the references. This recognition process uses a large language model (LLM), specifically Gemini 2.5 Flash [7]. This model allows us to process entire minutes in a single pass due to its high token limits (input = 1,048,576 tokens, output = 65,535 tokens). Using the LLM, we identify reference spans in the text. We also let the LLM extract several semantic features which are used later in the linking phase. These features include the full sentence containing the text span, a predicted document type (e.g., motion, letter, legislative proposal), the reference type as defined later in Table 1, a concise summary of the reference's content, and a set of thematic keywords, preferably aligned with the TOOI thematic thesaurus used across Dutch parliamentary documents [18].

To evaluate our approach, we use four prompting strategies based on the number of examples provided in the prompt (zero-shot vs. few-shot), and whether detection and validation are combined into a single prompt or separated into two prompts (single-pass vs. two-pass). A two-pass approach allows us to optimize for high recall first, then focus on precision after. In all prompts, we also let the LLM give a confidence score to each reference, using this score, we are able to filter out any vague, hypothetical, or future references.

3.2 Linking

Once candidate references are identified, the system attempts to link them to known parliamentary documents through semantic matching and narrowing down the vector search space by filtering. The problem is treated as known-item search, as each parliamentary document in our corpus is directly tied to a permanent identifier, often composed of a dossier number and a sequential document number (e.g., "34775-12"). Once an identifier can be linked to a reference, we have a match.

In this linking step we use the semantic features generated during recognition to create a query vector and/or filter the search space. This query vector is used to match against precomputed document vectors of known parliamentary documents using cosine similarity. The query vectors are built up in a modular way by concatenating them into a single string before embedding. This allows us to perform ablation experiments. For instance, we can assess the impact of using only the sentence and keywords, or the sentence and summary, or the sentence and summary with filtering on the publication year. This modular design supports extensibility.

The content of each parliamentary document in the search space (N = 14,027) is embedded using the gte-mulitlingual-base model [25], which is selected for its strong multilingual performance and 768-dimensional output vectors. Alongside the embedding the document type, date issued, and identifier are stored in an Elasticsearch index [5]. This allows us to filter the search space before performing vector similarity search using cosine similarity. As linking is performed offline and on a finite corpus of static parliamentary documents, speed is not a major issue in our current system.

3.3 Annotated Dataset

We created an annotated dataset from 5 recent debates from the Dutch Parliament consisting in total of 1.841 sentences and 30.142 words. 93 sentences (5.05%) contained one of more references to parliamentary documents. The annotation protocol was based on [12].

The following text strings were annotated as references: any sequence of words within the parliamentary minutes that refers to a parliamentary document or dossier. This includes explicit mentions of dossier or document numbers, as well as implicit references (e.g., by name, context, or document type). References to relevant third-party documents directly related to the parliamentary discussion were also annotated. For each identifier hit, annotators provided additional information. The most important information is the 'reference type', with definitions provided in Table 1. Depending on this reference type, annotators also provided additional metadata: the type of parliamentary document (e.g., letter, motion or legislative proposal), the correct external identifier (such as the dossier and/or document number), or an identifier linking to a previously annotated reference

Table 1. Definitions for each reference type in the annotation protocol.

Reference Type	Definition
explicit-dossier	Explicit mention of a dossier number
explicit-parl-doc	Explicit mention of a dossier number followed by a document number
impl-local	Reference to a document or dossier already mentioned, without an explicit number
impl-ext-dossier	Reference to an identifiable dossier without explicit mention of a dossier number
impl-ext-parl-doc	Reference to a specific parliamentary document without numbers
impl-third-party	Reference to materials not part of the parliamentary database but relevant to the meeting

(in case of a document reference making an anaphoric reference to an earlier (often explicit) document reference).

We evaluated inter-annotator agreement (IAA) on 194 matched references. We found substantial agreement for 'reference type' (Cohen's $\kappa = 0.87$) and 'document type' ($\kappa = 0.89$) [4]. Agreement for 'external identifier' was moderate ($\kappa = 0.59$), confirming the inherent difficulty of the linking task.

3.4 Evaluation Metrics

We evaluate detection of references using precision, recall and F1. As references can be long, exact match would be too strict. Instead, we follow [10], and state that a pair (t, p) of a true and a predicted string match iff the Jaccard similarity of the two sets of tokens is strictly larger than 0.5. This yields a one-to-one mapping. We use the same matching to produce Cohen's κ. We view recognition as a known item search task and evaluate it with mean $Hit@k$ (indicating whether the desired item is among the top k ranked results) and mean reciprocal rank (MRR).

4 Results

We present the evaluation of our system in two stages. First, we determine the best prompting strategy for reference detection using our annotated dataset. Second, we conduct a large-scale experiment on a full parliamentary year to demonstrate the system's performance on detection and linking in a real-world scenario.

4.1 Reference Detection

Table 3 contains the detection results for the four prompting strategies. The results show clearly that the agentic setup with two passes performs better and that providing a few examples is also beneficial. In the linking experiments, we will work with the correctly detected references by the fewshot-two-pass system.

We also asked the LLM to classify each detected reference along two dimensions: the document type (choice of 9) classes, like letter, motion, law, etc.) and the type of reference (implicit, explicit, in total 6 classes). These tasks were easy for the LLMs, with accuracies ranging between 92 and 97% except for document type prediction with the zero-shot-single-pass LLM which only scored 43%.

4.2 System in Action: A Large-Scale Experiment

To assess the practical applicability of our system, we applied our fewshot-two-pass strategy to 281 plenary debates from the 2019–2020 parliamentary year, totaling 3,318,439 words in 191,009 sentences. This large-scale analysis allows us to first understand the prevalence and nature of references in parliamentary proceedings and then to create a high-confidence dataset for the evaluation of

Table 2. Distribution of detected reference types in large-scale experiment (N = 14,976).

Reference Type	Count	Perc.
Implicit Local	6,432	42.3%
Explicit	3,825	26.2%
Implicit Parl. Doc.	2,618	17.5%
Implicit Dossier	1,084	7.0%
Third Party	1,014	7.0%

Table 3. Detection performance for each prompt strategy on the gold-standard dataset (N = 191).

Strategy	Precision	Recall	F1
zeroshot-single	0.47	0.38	0.42
fewshot-single	0.48	0.40	0.44
zeroshot-two-pass	0.53	0.37	0.44
fewshot-two-pass	**0.55**	**0.44**	**0.49**

our linking method. In these 281 min, the system detected 14,976 references. The detected references amount to an average of 53.3 references per minute (median = 49). On average every 13th sentence contains a reference to a document. The distribution of references over the 5 types, summarized in Table 2, shows that the vast majority (73.8%) is implicit, highlighting the need of a semantic approach next to simple rule-based methods. The length in number of words of the found references is lognormally distributed with a median of 3, a mean of 4, and a long tail of long (max is 58 words) and often linguistically complex references.

4.3 Reference Linking

We can use the 3,825 explicit references found in the large-scale detection experiment (see Sect. 4.2) to evaluate the performance of our linker. For these, we have the correct ground truth (the explicit link), which after removal creates a realistic implicit query. For example, the explicit reference "De motie-Moorlag (31532, nr. 248)" becomes the implicit query "De motie-Moorlag ()", with "31532-248" as the (correct) identifier. Of these 3,825 explicit references, 1,892 consisted of only a reference number and thus were not usable, leaving us with 1,933 test instances. The system had to find the correct document in a search space of 14,027 parliamentary documents sourced from the 2019–2020 parliamentary year.

The results of this linking experiment are shown Table 4. They demonstrate that enriching the query with LLM-generated semantic features is crucial. The best performing combination of an enriched query (text+sentence+keywords) and metadata filtering (year+doctype) correctly links the document 35% of the time and places it in the top 10 candidates 57% of the time.

When no filtering is applied, using keywords (text+sentence+keywords) is much more effective than using a summary (text+sentence+summary). Both the Hit@1 score and MRR nearly double from 0.14 to 0.26, and 0.19 to 0.34, respectively. We hypothesize that keywords provide a more discriminative and concise representation for known-item search. While a summary captures the general topic, it can introduce narrative language and noisy vocabulary, leading to topic-drift. In contrast, keywords, especially when aligned with the thesaurus,

Table 4. Linking performance for different feature combinations (N=1,933). The average 95% CI across all measurements is approximately ±0.03.

Features		Hit@1	Hit@10	MRR
Query	Filtering			
text+sentence	–	0.03	0.06	0.04
text+sentence+summary	–	0.14	0.30	0.19
text+sentence+keywords	–	0.26	0.51	0.34
text+sentence+keywords	doctype	0.30	0.55	0.39
text+sentence+keywords	year	0.30	0.55	0.38
text+sentence+keywords	year+doctype	**0.35**	**0.57**	**0.42**

function as key descriptors that are more likely to match the characteristics of the target document.

The data also highlights the significant benefit of metadata filtering. Applying a filter for document type or year to the keyword-based query leads to a clear improvement in scores. This shows that narrowing the search space is a critical step. By pre-filtering on metadata extracted by the LLM, the system can eliminate a large number of semantically similar but incorrect documents, which inherently improves the precision of the final vector search.

5 Conclusion and Future Work

We presented a two-phase approach for detecting and linking references to documents within Dutch parliamentary debates, moving beyond simple text matching to address the challenge of implicit, non-standardized references. Our method uses a large language model for the initial detection and semantic feature extraction, followed by vector similarity search for linking.

Evaluation against a manually created gold standard dataset of 191 references showed that few-shot, two-pass prompting strategy is most effective for reference detection. A subsequent large-scale experiment on 281 debates revealed that the vast majority of references (roughly 74%) are implicit. For the linking task, we demonstrated that enriching queries with LLM-generated semantic features and applying metadata filters is critical, achieving a Hit@1 of 35% and placing the correct document in the top 10 candidates 57% of the time.

Our approach shows strong potential for generalization. First, its core components being a multilingual LLM and a multilingual embedding model make the approach largely language-agnostic. Future work could validate performance across different languages using similar corpora, such as ParlaMint [6], which contains parliamentary debates from more than 20 European countries. Second, the task of resolving implicit, non-standardized references is not unique to parliamentary proceedings. The same implementations could be adapted to other domains like legal case law, corporate financial reports, or historical archives, where linking to supporting documents is useful for comprehension and analysis.

For future work, we plan to improve linking accuracy by adding a dedicated re-ranking step for the top candidates. We will also explore fine-tuning smaller, specialized models for the detection phase to create a more efficient and accurate system. Furthermore, we aim to investigate the robustness of our system by quantifying the impact of variance in the AI's non-deterministic outputs on overall performance. Finally, implementing a human-in-the-loop framework could support continuous improvement through active learning, creating a system that adapts over time.

Acknowledgments. Thanks to Wietske Boersma. This research was supported in part by the Netherlands Organization for Scientific Research (NWO) through the ACCESS project grant CISC.CC.016 and an Open Science Fund grant nr 01607400. Maarten Marx is partly funded by ICAI (AI for Open Government Lab). Views expressed in this paper are not necessarily shared or endorsed by those funding the research.

References

1. Agnoloni, T., Bacci, L., Peruginelli, G., van Opijnen, M., et al.: Linking european case law: BO-ECLI parser, an open framework for the automatic extraction of legal links. In: Proceedings of JURIX '17, pp. 113–118. IOS Press (2017)
2. Brickley, D., Burgess, M., Noy, N.: Google dataset search: building a search engine for datasets in an open Web ecosystem. In: Proceedings of WWW '19, pp. 1365–1375 (2019). https://doi.org/10.1145/3308558.3313685
3. Chapman, A., Simperl, E., Koesten, L., Konstantinidis, G., et al.: Dataset search: a survey. VLDB J. **29**(1), 251–272 (2020)
4. Cohen, J.: A coefficient of agreement for nominal scales. Educ. Psychol. Measur. **20**(1), 37–46 (1960)
5. Elasticsearch (2025). https://www.elastic.co/elasticsearch. Accessed 20 June 2025
6. Erjavec, T., Kopp, M., Ljubešić, N., Kuzman, T., et al.: Parlamint ii: advancing comparable parliamentary corpora across europe. Lang. Res. Eval. (2024). https://doi.org/10.1007/s10579-024-09798-w
7. Google Cloud: Gemini 2.5 Flash | Generative AI on Vertex AI (2025). https://cloud.google.com/vertex-ai/generative-ai/docs/models/gemini/2-5-flash. Accessed 27 May 2025
8. Heddes, J., Meerdink, P., Pieters, M., Marx, M.: The automatic detection of dataset names in scientific articles. Data **6**(8), 84 (2021)
9. Hulsebos, M., Lin, W., Shankar, S., et al.: It took longer than I was expecting: why is dataset search still so hard? In: Proceedings of HILDA 2024, pp. 1–4 (2024). https://doi.org/10.1145/3665939.3665959
10. Kirillov, A., He, K., Girshick, R., Rother, C., et al.: Panoptic segmentation. In: Proceedings of CVPR 2019, pp. 9404–9413. IEEE, Long Beach (2019)
11. Kolitsas, N., Ganea, O.E., Hofmann, T.: End-to-end neural entity linking. arXiv preprint arXiv:1808.07699 (2018)

12. Lee, S., DeLucia, A., Nangia, N., Ganedi, P., et al.: Common law annotations: investigating the stability of dialog system output annotations. In: Rogers, A., Boyd-Graber, J., Okazaki, N. (eds.) Findings of the ACL 2023, pp. 12315–12349 (2023). https://doi.org/10.18653/v1/2023.findings-acl.780. https://aclanthology.org/2023.findings-acl.780/
13. Lopez, P.: Grobid: combining automatic bibliographic data recognition and term extraction for scholarship publications. In: Agosti, M., Borbinha, J., Kapidakis, S., Papatheodorou, C., Tsakonas, G. (eds.) ECDL 2009. LNCS, vol. 5714, pp. 473–474. Springer, Heidelberg (2009). https://doi.org/10.1007/978-3-642-04346-8_62
14. Oard, D.W., Suzuki, T., Ishita, E., Kando, N.: Searching unseen sources for historical information: evaluation design for the NTCIR-18 SUSHI pilot task. In: Proceedings of EMTCIR 2024, vol. 3854 (2024)
15. van Opijnen, M.: Citation analysis and beyond: in search of indicators measuring case law importance. In: Proceedings of JURIX '12, pp. 95–104. IOS Press (2012)
16. van Opijnen, M., Verwer, N., Meijer, J.: Beyond the experiment: the eXtendable legal link eXtractor. In: Proceedings of Workshop on Automated Detection, Extraction and Analysis of Semantic Information in Legal Texts (ASAIL), ICAIL 2015 (2015)
17. Otto, W., Zloch, M., Gan, L., Karmakar, S., et al.: GSAP-NER: a novel task, corpus, and baseline for scholarly entity extraction focused on machine learning models and datasets. In: Proceedings of EMNLP 2023, pp. 8166–8176 (2023). https://aclanthology.org/2023.findings-emnlp.548/
18. Thema-indeling voor Officiële Publicaties (TOP-lijst). https://standaarden.overheid.nl/tooi/waardelijsten/work?work_uri=https%3A%2F%2Fidentifier.overheid.nl%2Ftooi%2Fset%2Fscw_toplijst. Accessed 20 June 2025
19. Pan, H., Zhang, Q., Dragut, E., Caragea, C., et al.: Dmdd: a large-scale dataset for dataset mentions detection. Trans. Assoc. Comput. Linguistics **11**, 1132–1146 (2023)
20. Savelka, J., Ashley, K.D.: Using conditional random fields to detect different functional types of content in decisions of united states courts with example application to sentence boundary detection. In: Proceedings of Workshop on Automated Semantic Analysis of Information in Legal Texts (ASAIL), ICAIL'17, vol. 10 (2017)
21. Suzuki, T., Oard, D.W., Ishita, E., Tomiura, Y.: Automatically detecting references from the scholarly literature to records in archives. In: Proceedings of International Conference on Asian Digital Libraries, pp. 100–107. Springer, Heidelberg (2023). https://doi.org/10.1007/978-981-99-8088-8_9
22. Varga, D., Gojdic, M., Szoplák, Z., Gurský, P., et al.: Extraction of legal references from court decisions. In: Proceedings of ITAT 2023, pp. 89–95 (2023)
23. Venema, P.L.P.: Improving Links to Referenced Documents in Dutch Parliamentary Meeting Notes. Bachelor's thesis, University of Amsterdam, Amsterdam, The Netherlands (2024). https://scripties.uba.uva.nl/search?id=record_54697
24. Wang, S., Sun, X., Li, X., Ouyang, R., et al.: GPT-NER: named entity recognition via large language models. arXiv preprint arXiv:2304.10428 (2023)
25. Zhang, X., Zhang, Y., Long, D., Xie, W., et al.: mGTE: generalized long-context text representation and reranking models for multilingual text retrieval. In: Proceedings of EMNLP (Industry Track) 2024, pp. 1393–1412 (2024)

From Notes to Models: Leveraging LLMs for Museum Closure Data

George A. Wright[1,2]($\boxtimes$), Andrea Ballatore[2], Alexandra Poulovassilis[1], and Peter T. Wood[1]

[1] Birkbeck, University of London, Malet Street, London WC1E 7HX, UK
{george.wright,a.poulovassilis,p.wood}@bbk.ac.uk
[2] Kings College London, The Strand, London WC2R 2LS, UK
{george.wright,andrea.ballatore}@kcl.ac.uk

Abstract. GLAM research often involves the collection of unstructured textual data which is semantically rich, but labour-intensive to handle and process. This paper explores the use of Large Language Models (LLMs) to support the transformation of such material into structured data that can be queried and quantitatively analysed. Focusing on a corpus of notes documenting the closure of over 500 UK museums between 2000 and 2025, we present a two-stage pipeline to automate the generation of data models. In the first stage, an LLM proposes schema fragments based on chunks of notes; in the second, the LLM collates these fragments into a coherent data model. As a preliminary evaluation, we introduce a method based on syntactic validity to assess the structure of the generated models in the absence of ground truth. Our experiments with Llama 3.1 show promising results using zero-shot prompting, though ensuring semantic consistency and model integration remain challenging.

Keywords: information extraction · Large Language Models · data modelling · museum data

1 Introduction

Research in the GLAM (Galleries, Libraries, Archives, and Museums) sector frequently involves the collection and analysis of unstructured textual data. In order to support rigorous analysis and querying, such data must often be transformed into more structured formats This transformation remains a significant bottleneck: While some elements of these datasets can be captured through manually designed data models, fully modelling the breadth and complexity of the information is often infeasible within project constraints.

In this context, Large Language Models (LLMs) such as GPT and Llama offer a promising, if imperfect, set of tools for automating aspects of data structuring [7,12]. Despite ongoing debates around their accuracy and generalizability, LLMs have demonstrated utility in tasks such as information extraction, ontology induction, and schema generation, especially in domains where training data is limited and where bespoke knowledge representations are required [1,14].

This article reports on our development of a semi-automated pipeline for data modelling, applied to a corpus of textual notes collected as part of a project on museum closures in the UK from 2000 to 2025.[1] The project team has gathered detailed records about the closure of some 500 museums, including the fate of their collections and their buildings [16]. As part of the project, we have constructed a graph-based data model to capture collection dispersal information, but, due to time constraints, parts of the data relating to reasons for closure and buidling use remain unstructured. We have therefore decided to trial approaches to automate data modelling. Museologists will then be able to quantify the types of event that lead to closure; the changing status, use, and ownership of ex-museum buildings; and how these vary according to museum attributes.

Our study here aims to explore the effectiveness of LLMs to assist in generating data models from such unstructured text. After reviewing related work (Sect. 2) and describing our museum closure data (Sect. 3), We present an LLM-based pipeline of two stages: a *model suggester*, which generates models for chunks of text; and a *model collator*, which merges them into one (Sect. 4). We investigate the impact of prompt design and chunking strategies on the syntactic correctness of outputs. (Sect. 5). Finally, we draw conclusions and discuss future work (Sect. 6).

2 Related Work

An LLM can be made to perform a task by providing it with a prompt that describes that task. *Prompt engineering* is the practice of altering prompts to improve performance. Adjustments include changing the way instructions are described, adding example input/output pairs (few-shot prompting [2]), and prepending the prompt with a role description which conditions the model to output tokens appropriate to the role, e.g., "you are a very serious professor" [10].

Progress has been made in reasoning tasks with *chain-of-thought* prompts: in a zero-shot setting, prompts are appended with the instruction "let's think step-by-step" [5]; in a few-shot setting, prompts are structured as worked examples [15]. This conditions an LLM to describe the steps leading to a solution.

With appropriate prompting, LLMs can be made to perform information extraction—to generate structured data such as a knowledge graph from a piece of text. Often, work on this task (see for example Polat *et al.* [12] and Papaluca *et al.* [11]) is tested on general knowledge text-to-triple datasets such as RED-FM [4] and NYT [13], which respectively align Wikipedia and New York Times text with Wikidata and Freebase triples. But the prevalence of similar content in LLMs' pre-training data makes these datasets perhaps less challenging than notes collected during novel academic research such as in our setting.

A finding by Papaluca *et al.* [11] is that high performance is possible with what they term a *0.5-shot* prompt. They found highest performance with 5-shot

---

[1] https://mapping-museums.bbk.ac.uk/museum-closure-in-the-uk-2000-2025/.

prompts—5 sentences alongside 5 sets of triples—but their 0.5-shot prompts contain only triples without matching sentences. For such prompts no pre-existing text/triple pairs are required. We have tested a similar approach.

As noted above, prompt engineering for information extraction often implicitly defines the ontology or data model by using a ground-truth ontology such as that of Wikidata, but we are automating the creation of a *new* ontology to record newly collected data. Frequently, ontology learning is separated into sub-tasks. These can include generating: lexical terms, types, a taxonomy, non-taxonomic relations, and additional constraints [1]. Lo *et al.* [7] in their *end-to-end* architecture only tackle the generation of taxonomies from text and use post-processing to combine them. We also separate tasks across a pipeline.

3 Museum Closure Data

The data collected by our project exists in three forms: (i) unstructured notes; (ii) a semi-structured spreadsheet (iii) a formal spreadsheet.

The unstructured notes consist of approximately 760,000 words including content from websites, newspaper clippings, email conversations with stakeholders and other information pertaining to closed museums and collections dispersal.

The semi-structured spreadsheet separates notes into three columns: the *collection* column describes what happened to each museum's collection post-closure; the *reasons* column describes what led to each closure; and the *building* column describes what happened to each museum's buildings post-closure.

To manually model the collection dispersal data, we created a formal spreadsheet with a controlled vocabulary. This is programmatically translated into a Neo4j graph database with 8 node and 13 relation types which serves as a basis for quantitative analysis of collection dispersal [16]. The formal spreadsheet and database do not however model data from the *reasons* or *buildings* columns.

4 Design of a Data Modelling Pipeline

We have designed a pipeline to automate modelling of the *buildings* and *reasons* data, partially inspired by our approach to modelling the collection data, but also influenced by the practical constraints of working with LLMs.

Our manual modelling of collection data was iterative. We first designed a model to describe dispersals from a sample of museums. As we sought to fit new data into the model, it needed adjustment with new features. Once the data model was changed, it was necessary to update representations of previously entered data. This continued until we had modelled all of the data [16].

Such gradual refinement was necessary because it is impossible for humans to read a large body of text and then produce a consistent model of its semantics in one step. A similar problem exists for LLMs: their input has a fixed limit[2] and their performance degrades with larger inputs within this limit [6]. But instead

---

[2] The LLM we use (Llama 3.1) has a context length of 128 thousand tokens.

of reproducing the cyclic process we followed when manually creating a data model, we have designed a pipeline with a hierarchical structure. This is easier to control and optimize. The pipeline consists of three main steps:

Data Model Suggestion. Text describing an aspect of the closure of a set of museums is broken into chunks. Each chunk is given to an LLM tasked with suggesting an appropriate data model of entity and relation types. This results in a collection of (not necessarily compatible) data models, one for each chunk.

Data Model Collation. Next, another LLM is tasked with combining these suggested data models into a single coherent model. The input to this LLM is the concatenation of models generated in the previous step.

Database Generation. Finally, an LLM uses the resulting data model to generate a graph database. This stage is left for future work.

5 Experiments

We have tested prompts for a data model suggester and have begun work on a model collator, so far using Meta's instruction-tuned 8 billion parameter Llama 3.1[3]. We will test other models in future. We ensure reproducibility by using a downloaded model[4] (and random seeds), not APIs to often updated models.

5.1 Data Set and Evaluation

As described in Sect. 3, we have text separated into *collection*, *building*, and *reasons* notes and a data model for the collection notes. We use the collection notes and data model as a support set to generate examples in n-shot prompts. We treat building notes as a development set for prompt optimization and the reasons notes as a test set. The building notes are shorter, so we assume that the reasons notes are more complex and a better test of the pipeline's generalizability.

Lacking a gold standard data model for buildings and reasons notes, we cannot directly measure correctness of a candidate data model. Automated evaluation at this stage is thus limited to syntactic correctness, which is important for gauging how well a relatively unconstrained process outputs models that conform to our JSON template for describing entities and relations (see Fig. 1a).

This is done by comparing the keys in a candidate data model with the keys in the template (see Fig. 1 for the template and an example model). The data models are represented with hierarchical JSON so must first be flattened into a list, where each element is the concatenation of the keys and array indices required to access the values in the leaves of the structure. Array indices are

---

[3] Downloaded from https://huggingface.co/meta-llama/Llama-3.1-8B-Instruct.
[4] The experiments were run on the King's College London HPC system [8].

```
{                                               {
    "entities": [                                   "entities": [
    {                                               {
        "name": "...",                                  "name": "Building",
        "properties": [                                 "properties": [
            {"name": "...", "data_type": "..."},            {"name": "Status", "data_type": "enumerated type"},
            ...                                             {"name": "Current use", "data_type": "string"},
        ]                                                   {"name": "Previous use","data_type": "string"},
    },                                                      ...
    ...                                             ]
    ],                                          },
    "relations": [                              ...
    {                                           ],
        "name": "...",                          "relations": [
        "source": entity_type,                  {
        "target": entity_type,                      "name": "USED_AS",
        "properties": [                             "source": "Building",
            {"name": "...", "data_type": "..."},    "target": "Current_use",
            ...                                     "properties": []
        ]                                       },
    },                                          ...
    ...                                         ],
    ],                                          "enumerated_types": [
    "enumerated_types": [                       {
    {                                               "name": "Status",
        "name": "...",                              "values": [
        "values": [                                     "open",
            "..."                                       "closed",
        ]                                               ...
    },                                              ]
    ...                                         },
    ]                                           ...
}                                               ]
                                            }
```

(a) The JSON template included in the LLM's prompt. (b) An extract from the model collator's output.

Fig. 1. The JSON template and an example output of an LLM that models building notes. All flattened keys in the candidate data model (e.g. "entities[0].name", "entities[0].properties[0].data_type") match with keys in the template.

replaced with 0 since order is unimportant. A similarity score is then calculated for each candidate/template key pair:

$$\text{Sim}(c,t) = 1 - \frac{L(c,t)}{\max(|c|,|t|)}$$

where $L(c,t)$ is the Levenshtein edit distance [9] between candidate and template keys. This is used for calculations of precision, recall, and F1 score (the harmonic mean of precision and recall), with:

$$\text{Prec}(C,T) = \frac{1}{|C|}\sum_{c\in C}\max_{t\in T}\text{Sim}(c,t) \qquad \text{Rec}(C,T) = \frac{1}{|T|}\sum_{t\in T}\max_{c\in C}\text{Sim}(t,c)$$

where C is the set of candidate keys and T the set of template keys.

5.2 The Data Model Suggester

The data model suggester must generate entity and relation types for modelling the semantics of a chunk of notes. In developing a model suggester, we varied the size of chunks and the text of the prompt. LLM temperature was fixed at 0 but future work will test other values. Table 1 sets out the parameters tested.

We tested prompts containing: an optional role description, a description of the input data, a task description, an optional example using the collection notes and data model, a chunk of notes with average lengths ranging between 1 and 4 thousand characters, and an optional "let's think step-by-step" instruction.

Roles included: *data modeller*, intended to condition the LLM to use terms used in data modelling; and *machine*, intended to encourage only JSON output.

We tested three task descriptions with accompanying JSON templates: *basic* requesting only entities and relations with a JSON template for representing them; *basic+hierarchy*, explicitly instructing the model to "include entities and relations necessary for making type hierarchies if appropriate"; and *basic+hierarchy+enums*, with a field for enumerated types in the JSON template. These test the need for and effect of explicitly requesting types and taxonomies.

Zero-shot prompts have no examples. 0.5-shot prompts (cf. [11]) have no example notes but do have our JSON-formatted collection data model as an example output. 1-shot prompts include a chunk of collection notes for five museums followed by our collection data model as an example output.

In addition to the different combinations of features described above, we tested a 1-shot chain-of-thought prompt which replaces the task description with steps of reasoning starting from a chunk of notes and showing how lists of entities, properties, and relations can be found and then used to assemble a data model.

Table 1. Parameters tested while developing the model suggester and their feature importance found by random forest regression.

Parameter	Options	Importance
Chunk size	1k, 2k, 3k, 4k	0.05
Role	none	0.25
You are a...	*data modeller interested in the aftermath of museum closure.*	
	machine which communicates only in JSON.	
Task	basic, basic+hierarchy, basic+hierarchy+enums	0.06
N-Shots	0, 0.5, 1	**0.55**
Chain-of-thought	none	0.09
	let's think step-by-step	
	worked through example (with 1-shot)	

Results. We instantiated 228 configurations of model suggester by combining different chunk sizes and prompting methods and ran them with the development set (building notes). A table of results is in our GitHub repository[5]. Some

---

[5] https://github.com/Birkbeck/museum-object-flows/tree/main/llm-data-modelling.

configurations performed well: the highest macro-averaged F1 score[6] was 0.95. Others output only English descriptions of the data, but no JSON, thus scoring 0. Using random forest regression to measure the importance of different prompt parameters, we found that the number of examples used in the prompt was the most important determiner of performance, followed by the role description, and then the presence or absence of chain-of-thought instructions (see Table 1).

On average, zero-shot prompts achieved higher F1 (0.79 for 0-shot, 0.71 for 0.5-shot, 0.28 for 1-shot), likely because examples of collection dispersal modelling are irrelevant to the task at hand. One would expect examples to improve performance, but that is often because they provide the LLM with vocabulary appropriate to the task (such as when Polat *et al.* [12] use semantic similarity to pick examples). Collection dispersal examples do not contain useful vocabulary beyond that found in the JSON template, but do significantly lengthen the context and thus hinder rather than help. They can also result in parts of the collection dispersal model being copied into the new building use model.

Role description was the second most important parameter: eight of the topten best performing configurations use the *data modeller* role and the other two use the *machine* role. The *machine* role, which instructs the LLM to output only JSON, did not prevent large blocks of English description being output.

Prompts with "let's think step-by-step" led to slightly higher performance (mean F1 of 0.62) compared with no chain-of-thought prompting (mean F1 of 0.59). Our one-shot chain-of-thought prompt resulted in very low performance (mean F1 of 0.06). Chain-of-thought prompts often led to long outputs stepping through incremental changes to the data model which were cut-off if they exceeded a maximum new tokens limit of 2000 (set for time-efficiency reasons). Differently worded prompts and looser output limits might improve performance.

The task description and chunk size had little effect on performance. Future tests will include larger chunk sizes to find when performance begins to decline.

The highest performing model suggester had a 0.5-shot prompt, the *data modeller* role, no chain-of-thought instruction, a task description with hierarchy and enums, and chunks of 4000 characters. Its F1 was 0.95 on the development set. We also ran it on the reasons test set where its F1 was 0.90.

5.3 The Data Model Collator

As a preliminary investigation into developing a data model collator, we used the suggested data models from the best model suggester as input to an LLM tasked with creating a single coherent data model. The prompt to the LLM was: "combine these suggested entity and relation models into a single model which incorporates characteristics from each of the suggestions" followed by a list of the data models output by the model suggester for each chunk of notes.

The F1 score for the development set was 0.98. The output model had five entity types including *museum* and *building*, 21 relation types, and 3 lists of enumerated types. An extract of this data model is shown in Fig. 1b and the

---

[6] The mean F1 for each of chunk calculated according to the method in Sect. 5.1.

full model is available in our GitHub repository (See footnote 5). Although the data model conforms to the JSON template (it has a precision of 1.0), it contains a number of inconsistencies. For example, *current use* and *previous use* are included as properties of the *building* type, but there are also *used as* relations from source *building* to target *current use/previous use* which would require current and previous use to be entities rather than properties. This indicates the need for a more robust automated evaluation to check that models are consistent. Another problem with the data model is that it contains a number of entities and relations copied from the collection dispersal model provided in the model suggester's 0.5-shot prompt. Additional evaluation of conciseness should check for the existence of such superfluous content in outputs.

We also ran this prompt with the outputs of the model suggester for the test set. But the prompt was about twice the length of the prompt for the development set and caused the GPU to run out of memory. This shows that a more generalizable pipeline will need to chunk the outputs of the data model suggester in a more gradual process of model collation.

6 Conclusions and Future Work

Our initial trial of an LLM-based data modelling pipeline shows that a data model can be produced by a sequence of two LLMs. This data model is not without errors, but is possible for a human to understand. Future work will investigate more robust automated evaluation that can detect these errors. In tests of the *data model suggester*, we found that use of examples and role descriptions had the largest effect on LLM performance with the highest performance achieved by 0- or 0.5-shot prompts and a data modeller role. We did not find that the chunk sizes tested had a significant impact on performance and will therefore test larger chunks in future, resulting in fewer suggestions for the model collator to process. Our initial test of the *model collator* shows some promise, with syntactically correct JSON (precision of 1.0 and recall of 0.96) being output for the development set. In ongoing work we are conducting more extensive tests of model collation, again considering different prompts. We will also test a more hierarchical approach to collation with small groups of data models being combined in a multi-step process. This will allow us to test whether including the English descriptions output by the model suggester aid the model collator.

For a more comprehensive study, we also plan to test a wider range of LLMs. Babaei Giglou *et al.* [1] found that LLMs with different architectures performed differently in their five ontology generation tasks: the best LLM at one task was not necessarily the best LLM for another. We will also test different temperatures and sampling strategies. Higher temperatures generally lead to more novel outputs and are appropriate for open-ended tasks (although it requires the accurate processing of factual information, our data modelling task is also quite open-ended). Different sampling strategies can also affect the overall coherence of the output [3], so will also be tested.

Once we have selected a configuration for data model generation, our next step will be to prompt another LLM with the data model and notes so that it can apply the data model to the notes and represent their semantics in a graph database. This is the final step in our pipeline from unstructured text to structured data. At this stage, we can further evaluate data models' conciseness by measuring the proportion of notes for which entity and relation types are instantiated. If we allow the LLM at the database generating stage to also suggest entities and relations which do not conform to a data model, we will also be able to evaluate model comprehensiveness by measuring the proportion of outputs that conform to the data model. We can then filter out data models that perform poorly on these metrics. We will then ask our museologist collaborators to carry out a human-led evaluation of the database, judging the degree to which it captures the information encoded in their notes and answers their research questions.

Disclosure of Interests. The authors have no competing interests to declare.

Acknowledgments. This work has been funded by the UKRI-AHRC project "Museum Closure in the UK 2000–2025", Grant No. AH/X012816/1, Oct. 2023–Sept. 2025. We thank the project's external Advisory Board and all members of the project team.

References

1. Babaei Giglou, H., D'Souza, J., Auer, S.: LLMs4OL: large language models for ontology learning. In: The Semantic Web " ISWC 2023: 22nd International Semantic Web Conference, Athens, Greece, November 6-10, 2023, Proceedings, Part I, p. 408–427. Springer, Heidelberg (2023). https://doi.org/10.1007/978-3-031-47240-4_22
2. Brown, T., et al.: Language models are few-shot learners. In: Larochelle, H., Ranzato, M., Hadsell, R., Balcan, M., Lin, H. (eds.) Advances in Neural Information Processing Systems, vol. 33, pp. 1877–1901. Curran Associates, Inc. (2020). https://doi.org/10.48550/arXiv.2005.14165
3. Holtzman, A., Buys, J., Du, L., Forbes, M., Choi, Y.: The curious case of neural text degeneration. In: Proceedings of the Eighth International Conference on Learning Representations (2020). https://arxiv.org/abs/1904.09751
4. Huguet Cabot, P.L., Tedeschi, S., Ngonga Ngomo, A.C., Navigli, R.: RED^{fm}: a filtered and multilingual relation extraction dataset. In: Rogers, A., Boyd-Graber, J., Okazaki, N. (eds.) Proceedings of the 61st Annual Meeting of the Association for Computational Linguistics, vol. 1: Long Papers, pp. 4326–4343. Association for Computational Linguistics, Toronto (2023). https://doi.org/10.18653/v1/2023.acl-long.237
5. Kojima, T., Gu, S.S., Reid, M., Matsuo, Y., Iwasawa, Y.: Large language models are zero-shot reasoners. In: Proceedings of the 36th International Conference on Neural Information Processing Systems, NIPS '22. Curran Associates Inc., Red Hook (2022). https://doi.org/10.48550/arXiv.2205.11916
6. Liu, N.F., et al.: Lost in the middle: How language models use long contexts (2023). https://arxiv.org/abs/2307.03172

7. Lo, A., Jiang, A.Q., Li, W., Jamnik, M.: End-to-end ontology learning with large language models (2024). https://arxiv.org/abs/2410.23584
8. London, K.C.: King's computational research, engineering and technology environment (create). https://doi.org/10.18742/rnvf-m076. Accessed 5 June 2025
9. Navarro, G.: A guided tour to approximate string matching. ACM Comput. Surv. **33**(1), 31–88 (2001). https://doi.org/10.1145/375360.375365
10. Ouyang, L., et al.: Training language models to follow instructions with human feedback (2022). https://arxiv.org/abs/2203.02155
11. Papaluca, A., Krefl, D., Rodríguez Méndez, S., Lensky, A., Suominen, H.: Zero- and few-shots knowledge graph triplet extraction with large language models. In: Biswas, R., Kaffee, L.A., Agarwal, O., Minervini, P., Singh, S., de Melo, G. (eds.) Proceedings of the 1st Workshop on Knowledge Graphs and Large Language Models (KaLLM 2024), pp. 12–23. Association for Computational Linguistics, Bangkok (2024).https://doi.org/10.18653/v1/2024.kallm-1.2
12. Polat, F., Tiddi, I., Groth, P.: Testing prompt engineering methods for knowledge extraction from text. Semant. Web **16**(2) (2025). https://doi.org/10.3233/SW-243719
13. Riedel, S., Yao, L., McCallum, A.: Modeling relations and their mentions without labeled text. In: Balcázar, J.L., Bonchi, F., Gionis, A., Sebag, M. (eds.) ECML PKDD 2010. LNCS (LNAI), vol. 6323, pp. 148–163. Springer, Heidelberg (2010). https://doi.org/10.1007/978-3-642-15939-8_10
14. Schaeffer, M., Sesboüé, M., Charbonnier, L., Delestre, N., Kotowicz, J.P., Zanni-Merk, C.: On the pertinence of LLMs for ontology learning. In: Proceedings of the 3rd International Workshop on Natural Language Processing for Knowledge Graph Creation (2024). https://ceur-ws.org/Vol-3874/paper1.pdf
15. Wei, J., et al.: Chain-of-thought prompting elicits reasoning in large language models. In: Proceedings of the 36th International Conference on Neural Information Processing Systems, NIPS '22. Curran Associates Inc., Red Hook (2022). https://doi.org/10.48550/arXiv.2201.11903
16. Wright, G.A., Ballatore, A., Poulovassilis, A., Wood, P.T.: Modelling and visualising flows of objects from museums. ACM J. Comput. Cult. Herit. (2025). in press

LLM-Based Information Extraction to Support Scientific Literature Research and Publication Workflows

Samy Ateia[1(✉)], Udo Kruschwitz[1], Melanie Scholz[2], Agnes Koschmider[2], and Moayad Almohaishi[2]

[1] University of Regensburg, Universitätsstraße 31, 93053 Regensburg, Germany
{samy.ateia,udo.kruschwitz}@ur.de
[2] University of Bayreuth, Universitätsstraße 30, 95447 Bayreuth, Germany
{melanie.scholz,agnes.koschmider,moayad.almohaishi}@uni-bayreuth.de

Abstract. The increasing volume of scholarly publications requires advanced tools for efficient knowledge discovery and management. This paper introduces ongoing work on an architecture using Large Language Models (LLMs) for the semantic extraction of key concepts from scientific documents. Our research, conducted within the German National Research Data Infrastructure for and with Computer Science (NFDIxCS) project, seeks to support FAIR (Findable, Accessible, Interoperable, and Reusable) principles in scientific publishing. We outline our explorative work, which uses in-context learning with various LLMs to extract concepts from papers, initially focusing on the Business Process Management (BPM) domain. A key advantage of this approach is its potential for rapid domain adaptation, often requiring few or even zero examples to define extraction targets for new scientific fields. We conducted technical evaluations to compare the performance of commercial and open-source LLMs and created an online demo application to collect feedback from an initial user-study. Additionally, we gathered insights from the computer science research community through user stories collected during a dedicated workshop, actively guiding the ongoing development of our future services. These services aim to support structured literature reviews, concept-based information retrieval, and integration of extracted knowledge into existing knowledge graphs.

Keywords: Large Language Models · Information Extraction · Scientific Publishing · Digital Libraries · FAIR Principles · Knowledge Graphs

1 Introduction

The scientific publication landscape is booming with global annual publication growing by 59% according to the NSF[1] and more than one million articles being

---

[1] https://web.archive.org/web/20250507134337 https://ncses.nsf.gov/pubs/nsb202333/executive-summary.

© The Author(s), under exclusive license to Springer Nature Switzerland AG 2026
W.-T. Balke et al. (Eds.): TPDL 2025, CCIS 2694, pp. 90–99, 2026.
https://doi.org/10.1007/978-3-032-06136-2_9

published per year in biomedicine and life sciences alone [6]. This rise in publications makes it harder for scientists to stay on top of their field, while also limiting the discoverability of their publications as they have to compete with others for visibility. Digital transformation and new tools such as LLMs can accelerate that problem, but also have the potential to assist scientists and publishing platforms in managing these challenges.

In computer science, publications are often accompanied by software artifacts and datasets for reproducibility, but their management frequently lacks standardization and fails to meet FAIR principles. The National Research Data Infrastructure for and with Computer Science (NFDIxCS) project[2] addresses this by creating an infrastructure to implement FAIR principles [21] for CS research outputs in Germany [5]. But to make these artifacts findable it is necessary to link them to relevant semantic information from the publication text itself, for example, research questions or methods so that they are discoverably as related work by other scientists.

Our project, situated within the NFDIxCS initiative, aims to develop tools to exactly address this problem. We leverage Large Language Models (LLMs) for the semantic analysis of scientific text, with the goal of enhancing the FAIR principles for scholarly literature. Specifically, we aim to:

- Develop robust methods for automatically extracting key semantic concepts (e.g., research questions, methodologies, findings) from scientific papers.
- Explore mechanisms for structuring these extracted concepts to improve the organization and distribution of digital content, potentially linking them to knowledge graphs.
- Design and prototype services, informed by community needs, that use this structured information to support researchers in their workflows.

This short paper presents our preliminary findings and outlines how user-driven requirements are shaping the trajectory of our research towards practical applications. We publish a demo system alongside its source code under a permissive license[3] alongside the results of our user workshops, and plan to maintain this practice for future services.

2 Related Work

In this work, we explore the use of LLMs for knowledge extraction to improve scientific workflows within digital libraries and beyond. We review related efforts in three key areas: platforms for scientific literature analysis, knowledge graphs for structuring scientific information, and the use of LLMs for information extraction.

---

[2] https://nfdixcs.org/.
[3] CC BY 4.0.

2.1 Platforms for Scientific Literature Analysis

Several platforms exist that use natural language processing (NLP) based on language models to highlight relevant information from scientific text, therefore assisting in navigating the considerable volume of publications. **Semantic Scholar** [2], for example, employs AI to provide summaries (TLDRs) and identify influential citations, while **Elicit** uses a systematic review inspired workflow, leveraging LLMs to synthesize findings from multiple papers in response to a user's query [20]. **Scite.ai** focuses specifically on citation context, classifying whether a citation supports, disputes, or merely mentions a claim [9]. While these platforms offer similar flexible LLM-based question answering tools, they do not currently offer the use of predefined domain-specific questions and mostly require a paid subscription to be fully utilized. With our approach, we want to potentially offer higher accuracy and user guidance through curated extraction targets and examples serving specialized communities.

2.2 Knowledge Graphs for Structuring Scientific Knowledge

Structuring scientific knowledge in a machine-readable format has long been a goal of the scientific community. The Open Research Knowledge Graph (ORKG) [8] is a prominent initiative aiming to represent the content of research papers as structured data. By describing papers through their contributions, methods, and findings, the ORKG facilitates systematic comparisons and reviews. Other notable examples are the discontinued Microsoft Academic Graph (MAG) [18] that was succeeded by OpenAlex [13] or SciKGraph [17]. However, curating such knowledge graphs often requires significant manual effort from researchers. Most recently, ORKG Ask was introduced, which offers the possibility to create ad-hoc comparison tables using information extraction with LLMs [11]. In our work, we want to build on that approach and take it a step further. Instead of just having users query questions on a set of retrieved papers, we explore how curated questions from domain-experts can be leveraged to prefill knowledge graph input templates for users. This complements the KG vision by lowering the barrier to entry and scaling up content acquisition. Embedding and indexing the extracted information in separate fields could lead to improved semantic search, by enabling users to search for papers with similar research questions or algorithms.

2.3 LLMs for Information Extraction in Science

In-context learning with LLMs describes the ability of these models to solve problems that they have not explicitly been trained on, by just giving the model an abstract description of the problem (**Zero-Shot**) or several examples (**Few-Shot**) in their input context. These approaches were first popularized with LLMs like GPT-3 [3] and enable their use in domains where limited, or no training data is available. Recent LLMs such as the Google Gemini series[4] or OpenAIs GPT-4.1[5] have pushed the size of the available context up to 1 million input tokens. Which makes it feasible to extract information from large text sources in a single step. These properties can be used in retrieval augmented generation (RAG) [16] systems that ground the knowledge of these models in relevant texts. Systems such as CORE-GPT have shown the usefulness of such approaches in questions answering across multiple scientific domains [12].

In our work, we explore both zero- and few-shot learning for extracting predefined semantic information from scientific texts, that can then be used to facilitate scientific knowledge discovery and publication workflows.

3 Methodology: LLM-Based Concept Extraction

Our system uses an LLM to extract semantic information from scientific documents. The demo UI allows a user to upload a paper and pose predefined or custom questions. The LLM then processes the document and a prompt to identify and return relevant information or synthesized answers (Fig. 1).

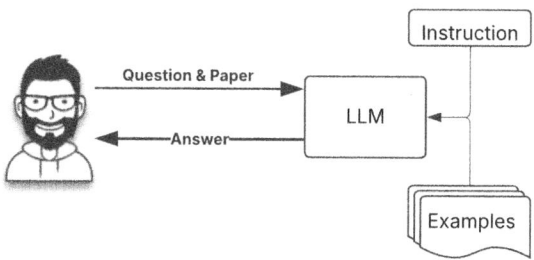

Fig. 1. LLM-based demo extraction pipeline.

3.1 In-context Learning for Rapid Domain Adaptation

We leverage the in-context learning of modern LLMs for rapid domain adaptation. By providing instructions and a few examples to guide extraction, our method avoids the need for the extensive, domain-specific datasets required by traditional supervised techniques.

In our evaluations we tested two modes: A **few-shot** mode where we supplied three in-domain examples each consisting of 1. the full text of the document; 2. the domain-specific information extraction questions, 3. the instructions, 4. the

---

[4] https://web.archive.org/web/20250607225206/https://blog.google/technology/ai/google-gemini-next-generation-model-february-2024/.
[5] https://web.archive.org/web/20250612080402/https://openai.com/index/gpt-4-1/.

manually crafted ideal answer from the document. In addition, we tested a **zero-shot** mode where we only supplied the instruction and the full text of the PDF.

The **zero-shot** mode formed our baseline for evaluation, but could also be used to offer the flexibility to the user to pose their own extraction questions against a document or a set of retrieved documents. The **few-shot** mode aligns the model with the style of the manual annotators, overcoming limited or missing instructions in the way the question was posed. This mode could be used in settings where predefined questions and predictable answer formats are important, for example when prefilling forms for later knowledge graph mapping.

We tested four different models: Qwen 2.5 72B instruct [14], Llama 3.3 70B instruct[6] [7], Gemini 1.5 Flash 002, Gemini 1.5 Flash 8B 001 [4]. Llama and Qwen were accessed via https://openrouter.ai while the Gemini models were accessed via the official Google API.

The instructions used chain of thought prompting [19] to generate a **reasoning** beside relevant **context** and the final **answer**.

The exact zero-shot prompt can be seen in Listing 1.1.

Listing 1.1. Zero-shot prompt example in Python

```
Extract the information answering the following question from
 the text:
Question: '''{question}'''
Text: '''{text}'''
Return a JSON object in the following format:
{{ "reasoning": "<think step by step and write down your
reasoning>",
"context": "<contains all relevant context from the text>",
"answer": "<one concise answer to the question for example:
yes/no/none, or a word or multiple words>"
}}
Try to be concise and limit your reasoning, answer, and the
extracted context to max 500 words.
```

3.2 Dataset and Domain

The initial development and a preliminary evaluation were carried out on a corpus of 122 scientific papers from the Business Process Management (BPM) conferences (20192023)[7]. This domain was selected due to the availability of domain experts who are actively constructing a knowledge graph in this area. Key concepts were manually annotated in the papers to establish a gold standard for evaluating extraction performance.

3.3 Extraction Example

An example of the extraction process is as follows:

---

[6] https://www.llama.com/docs/model-cards-and-prompt-formats/llama3_3/.
[7] https://bpm-conference.org/conferences/.

- **Target Concept:** Research Question
- **Query:** "What is the explicitly stated research question for the paper?"
- **Example Extracted Answer (from a paper):** "How to decide which processes need to be analyzed in detail to determine if changes are necessary."

This methodology provides a flexible framework, allowing us to target a wide array of semantic information within scientific texts with high adaptability, as only limited domain expert involvement is needed to create a few examples for each information item.

3.4 Demo System

To showcase the ability of the tool and collect initial user feedback, we built a demo UI using the Gradio framework [1] around our approach. The demo system is available online[8] (user:demo, pw:demo) and the source code for this system is available on GitHub[9].

3.5 User Feedback

In a pilot user study, we collected initial user-feedback with the demo system through a questionnaire after instructing a panel of users to choose one paper from a selection of business processing domain papers, upload it to the tool and select any questions that they were interested in.

At a separate workshop with around 30 participants from different computer-science fields, we collected user-stories that they would like to be solved by the offered and demonstrated technology.

4 Results

Model performance was evaluated by comparing LLM-generated extractions against a gold-standard dataset of 122 manually annotated papers. We partitioned extraction targets into three categories, each assessed with an appropriate metric. The metrics reported in Table 1 are defined as follows:

ExactAcc (Exact Accuracy): For categorical targets (e.g., "Keywords", "Type of Artefact"), we employed token-set accuracy. A prediction is considered correct if the Jaccard similarity [10,15] between its token set and the ground truth's token set exceeds a threshold of 0.8. This category contained 15 extraction targets with 1121 annotations in total.

BinF1 (Binary F1-Score): Targets with binary yes/no answers (e.g., "Formal concepts"), were treated as a binary classification problem. BinF1 is the macro-averaged F1-score. This category contained 13 extraction targets with 984 annotations in total.

---

[8] https://demo-d3.nfdixcs.org/.
[9] https://github.com/SamyAteia/nfdixcs-d3-knowledge-extraction-demo.

BERT_F1 (Semantic F1-Score): For free-text targets where phrasing varies (e.g., "Research question"), semantic equivalence was assessed using the F1-score from BERTScore [22]. This metric evaluates the similarity between the contextual embeddings of the predicted and reference answers. This category contained 4 extraction targets with 488 annotations in total.

The Overall score is the unweighted arithmetic mean of the three primary metrics (ExactAcc, BinF1, BERT_F1).

Table 1. Model comparison on the paper-coding benchmark

Model	ExactAcc	BinF1	BERT_F1	Overall
llama-3.3-70b (0-shot)	0.212	**0.556**	0.877	**0.548**
qwen-2.5-72b (0-shot)	0.219	0.514	0.887	0.540
gemini-1.5-flash-002 (3-shot)	**0.246**	0.330	0.893	0.490
gemini-1.5-flash-002 (0-shot)	0.183	0.390	0.883	0.486
gemini-1.5-flash-8b (0-shot)	0.171	0.345	0.881	0.466
gemini-1.5-flash-8b (3-shot)	0.180	0.148	**0.897**	0.408

BERT_F1 scores near 0.90 indicate strong semantic alignment on free-text fields, whereas binary indicators show moderate performance (best BinF1 = 0.56) and exact categorical extraction remains limited (ExactAcc < 0.25).

4.1 User Study and Workshop

Feedback from our pilot user study on the prototype demo UI was positive (88% satisfaction with extracted concepts), indicating the potential utility of the approach. While some feedback was UI related (hiding advanced configuration like few-shot examples, wanting more expert configuration), a main point was that the traceability of the extracted information should be improved.

In a separate workshop with around 30 computer-science researchers, we collected 56 user-stories. 38 of these focused on the task of literature research and comparison, 8 on assistance while writing papers, 3 on support in the review process, 3 were directed towards software development and 4 were unique. Overall, it became clear that the users want to go beyond just extracting concepts from one specific paper and compare the extracted information from multiple papers instead. The full categorized list is available in our repository (See footnote 9).

5 Discussion

The results of our technical evaluation and user-studies, while preliminary, provide valuable direction for the development of our future services.

Few-shot examples seemed to improve the performance of the models in tasks where specific categorial answers were needed and on the free-text extractions measured by BERTScore. But on the binary classification task, the performance decreased. This could be explained by a class bias introduced via the few-shot examples, while on the textual extractions the examples might have informed the model better about the expected format of the answers.

Using the full-text of documents in few-shot examples is costly and potentially increases noise. We are working on exploring the impact of more and shorter examples and selecting ideal examples for specific extraction target types.

The open-weight models Qwen 2.5-72B-Instruct and Llama 3.3-70B-Instruct seemed to perform better than the commercial models that we tested. For the Gemini 1.5-flash-8b model, this is most likely explained by the difference in size. The size of the normal Gemini 1.5-flash model is unknown but given our results and the cost and speed we suspect that it is also smaller than the 70 billion parameter models that we compared them to.

From the feedback that we collected through our pilot user study and the discussion in a later workshop, it became clear that there is a need for better transparency and traceability. Ideally, highlighting the text passages that inform an extracted information items in the source document.

Even though there are commercial services available that are similar to our tool, our contribution can inform researchers and professionals that want to offer customizable domain-specific services to their users. We demonstrate the feasibility of in-context learning and open-weights models for these use-cases and publish our code to boost independent development of transparent services.

6 Conclusion and Ongoing Work

We confirmed the potential of current LLMs to summarize and extract domain-specific information from scientific text. Through in-context learning, these models can be quickly adapted to specific scientific domains and facilitate the transfer of expert knowledge between researchers by highlighting and comparing key aspects of their work.

Through our user-centric approach, we collected valuable feedback and user-stories that can guide the development of current and future services. Notable transparency and the need that services enable the user to verify LLM generated output by tracing summarized information back to the source text.

Our ongoing work will focus on exploring embedding-based retrieval on the extracted structured information, therefore overcoming the arbitrary chunking issue that limits semantic relevance in vector search. We're also exploring how our approach can be integrated in the publishing process, prefilling templates for knowledge graph mapping e.g., for ORKG. Making it easier for authors to fill out forms that facilitate the discoverability of their work.

Overall, our work highlights the potential of LLMs to improve the publishing process and discoverability of scientific information in digital libraries and beyond.

Acknowledgments. This work is funded by the German Research Foundation (DFG) as part of the NFDIxCS consortium (Grant number: 501930651).

Disclosure of Interests. The authors have no competing interests to declare that are relevant to the content of this article.

References

1. Abid, A., Abdalla, A., Abid, A., Khan, D., Alfozan, A., Zou, J.: Gradio: hassle-free sharing and testing of ml models in the wild (2019). arxiv:1906.02569
2. Ammar, W., et al.: Construction of the literature graph in semantic scholar. arXiv preprint arXiv:1805.02262 (2018)
3. Brown, T., et al.: Language models are few-shot learners. Adv. Neural. Inf. Process. Syst. **33**, 1877–1901 (2020)
4. Georgiev, P., et al.: Gemini 1.5: unlocking multimodal understanding across millions of tokens of context (2024). arxiv:2403.05530
5. Goedicke, M., Lucke, U.: Research data management in computer science-NFDIxCS approach. In: INFORMATIK 2022, pp. 1317–1328. Gesellschaft für Informatik, Bonn (2022)
6. González-Márquez, R., Schmidt, L., Schmidt, B.M., Berens, P., Kobak, D.: The landscape of biomedical research. Patterns **5**(6), 100968 (2024). https://doi.org/10.1016/j.patter.2024.100968
7. Grattafiori, A., et al.: The llama 3 herd of models (2024). arxiv:2407.21783
8. Jaradeh, M.Y., Oelen, A., Prinz, M., Stocker, M., Auer, S.: Open research knowledge graph: a system walkthrough. In: Doucet, A., Isaac, A., Golub, K., Aalberg, T., Jatowt, A. (eds.) TPDL 2019. LNCS, vol. 11799, pp. 348–351. Springer, Cham (2019). https://doi.org/10.1007/978-3-030-30760-8_31
9. Lund, B., Shamsi, A.: Examining the use of supportive and contrasting citations in different disciplines: a brief study using Scite (scite. ai) data. Scientometrics **128**(8), 4895–4900 (2023)
10. Mann, W., Augsten, N., Bouros, P.: An empirical evaluation of set similarity join techniques. Proc. VLDB Endow. **9**(9), 636–647 (2016)
11. Oelen, A., Jaradeh, M.Y., Auer, S.: ORKG ASK: a neuro-symbolic scholarly search and exploration system. arXiv preprint arXiv:2412.04977 (2024)
12. Pride, D., Cancellieri, M., Knoth, P.: CORE-GPT: combining open access research and large language models for credible, trustworthy question answering. In: International Conference on Theory and Practice of Digital Libraries, pp. 146–159. Springer, Heidelberg (2023). https://doi.org/10.1007/978-3-031-43849-3_13
13. Priem, J., Piwowar, H., Orr, R.: OpenAlex: a fully-open index of scholarly works, authors, venues, institutions, and concepts. arXiv preprint arXiv:2205.01833 (2022)
14. Qwen, Yang, A., et al.: Qwen2.5 Technical Report (2025). arxiv:2412.15115
15. Schmidt, L., Mutlu, A.N.F., Elmore, R., Olorisade, B.K., Thomas, J., Higgins, J.P.: Data extraction methods for systematic review (semi) automation: Update of a living systematic review. F1000Research **10**, 401 (2025)
16. Shuster, K., Poff, S., Chen, M., Kiela, D., Weston, J.: Retrieval augmentation reduces hallucination in conversation. In: Findings of the Association for Computational Linguistics: EMNLP 2021, pp. 3784–3803 (2021)
17. Tosi, M.D.L., dos Reis, J.C.: SciKGraph: a knowledge graph approach to structure a scientific field. J. Informet. **15**(1), 101109 (2021). https://doi.org/10.1016/j.joi.2020.101109. https://www.sciencedirect.com/science/article/pii/S175115772030626X

18. Wang, K., Shen, Z., Huang, C., Wu, C.H., Dong, Y., Kanakia, A.: Microsoft academic graph: when experts are not enough. Quant. Sci. Stud. **1**(1), 396–413 (2020)
19. Wei, J., et al.: Chain-of-thought prompting elicits reasoning in large language models. In: Proceedings of the 36th International Conference on Neural Information Processing Systems, NIPS '22. Curran Associates Inc., Red Hook (2022)
20. Whitfield, S., Hofmann, M.A.: Elicit: ai literature review research assistant. Public Serv. Q. **19**(3), 201–207 (2023)
21. Wilkinson, M.D., et al.: The fair guiding principles for scientific data management and stewardship. Sci. Data **3**(1), 1–9 (2016)
22. Zhang, T., Kishore, V., Wu, F., Weinberger, K.Q., Artzi, Y.: Bertscore: evaluating text generation with bert. arXiv preprint arXiv:1904.09675 (2019)

Using LLMs for Improving the OCR Accuracy of Old Greek Handwritten Documents

Andreas Evangelatos[1,2(✉)], Konstantinos Palaiologos[1,2], Basilis Gatos[1,2], Panagiotis Kaddas[1,2], Aikaterini Christopoulou[1,2], Vassilis Katsouros[2,3], and Andreas Kakridis[4,5]

[1] National Centre for Scientific Research "Demokritos", Agia Paraskevi, Greece
{a.evangelatos,k.palaiologos,bgat,pkaddas, achristopoulou}@iit.demokritos.gr
[2] Athena Research Center, Athens, Greece
vsk@athenarc.gr
[3] Institute for Language and Speech Processing, Athens, Greece
[4] Bank of Greece, Athens, Greece
akakridis@econ.uoa.gr
[5] Panteion University, Athens, Greece

Abstract. OCR of historical handwritten documents is still a challenging task and an active research field due to the relatively low recognition accuracy achieved when processing manuscripts of different writing styles. In this work, we study the use of Large Language Models (LLMs) for correcting OCR in old Greek handwritten documents. We analyze two different old Greek datasets using a Deep Network based OCR along with several well-known and easy-to-use LLMs for correcting the output. Additionally, we generate synthetic erroneous texts and modify the LLM prompts to further investigate how LLMs perform in correcting noisy old Greek text. Experimental results show the potential of LLMs for OCR correction of old Greek handwritten documents, especially in cases where the recognition results are relatively poor.

Keywords: OCR Post-Correction · LLMs · Recognition of Historical Documents · HTR

1 Introduction

Handwritten text recognition (HTR) is an active research area for both language and computer scientists for at least the last twenty years. This is a rather challenging field of research as it involves the recognition of a great diversity of characters, writing styles, etc. The level of difficulty is raised even more when old and historic documents are involved. For the case of old Greek Documents, HTR has been proven to be a tedious and challenging task due to several unique characteristics of these documents. The use of multiple accents in old Greek Polytonic texts imposes the most significant difficulty for current processing and recognition tools. As a result, in most cases an OCR post-processing phase is essential in order to improve the recognition results.

Large Language Models (LLMs), like GPT-4 and Gemini 2.0, are in the spotlight when it comes to text transcription and correction, with several emerging applications. There are numerous examples of fast, accurate and cost-effective solutions for the OCR correction of old documents by using LLMs but this is an almost unexplored field of research when it comes to old Greek Handwritten Documents.

To this end, in this work we study the use of LLMs for the correction of the OCR of old Greek handwritten documents. To achieve this, we create two old Greek datasets, apply Deep Neural Network based OCR and, finally, we use several state of-the-art proprietary and open-source LLMs for OCR result correction.

2 Related Work

LLMs have been used with great success for the transcription of historical handwritten documents. In [1], LLMs are integrated into a software application and they achieve state-of-the-art recognition performance on historical handwritten English language documents without fine-tuning or extensive pre-processing. Recent literature suggests using LLMs for OCR post-correction in languages like English, German, Finnish, Brazilian Portuguese, and Bulgarian.

In [2], the authors assess open-weight LLMs for correcting OCR errors in historical English and Finnish data, examining parameter optimization, quantization, segment length, and text continuation. The authors of [3] explore GPT-3.5 and GPT-4 as Grammatical Error Correction tools for Brazilian Portuguese, comparing them to Microsoft Word and Google Docs. State-of-the-art LLMs are used in [4] for post-OCR text correction of historical Bulgarian documents. In [5], a prompt-based approach adapts generative LLMs to correct OCR in historical British newspaper articles. The work in [6] explores multimodal LLMs for OCR, post-correction, and named entity recognition on German Fraktur prints.

In [7], an explanatory study is presented regarding the post-correction of historical text transcripts using LLMs. This study assesses fourteen foundation language models using several post-correction benchmarks that include different languages, time periods, document types, transcription quality, and origins. Additionally, the study explores how different model sizes and prompts with increasing complexity perform in zero and few-shot settings.

In our work, we focus on the OCR post-correction of old Greek handwritten documents using several state-of-the-art proprietary and open-source LLMs.

3 Datasets

Our study utilizes two distinct handwritten datasets, each reflecting a different historical and linguistic context of Greek polytonic texts, along with unique scribal features.

The first dataset (Byzantine) includes digitized pages from Greek medieval manuscripts and early printed books dating from the 14th to the 16th centuries. These represent a wide range of handwriting styles from the Byzantine and post-Byzantine periods. It also includes pages from Robert Estienne's 1550 edition of the New Testament, printed in the *grecs du roi* typeface—designed to resemble medieval Greek handwriting and characterized by numerous ligatures and abbreviations.

A key feature of these manuscripts is the continuous script, often with no clear separation between words. This makes word segmentation and tokenization especially challenging. Ligatures—combinations of multiple letters into a single form—and abbreviations are frequent and vary significantly depending on the scribe, often requiring palaeographic expertise to interpret. The letterforms themselves often feature long ascenders and descenders, along with decorative flourishes that differ across manuscripts. Diacritical marks such as accents and breathings are sometimes joined or exaggerated, extending well above the accentuated characters and complicating line detection. Additionally, the lack of consistent ruling lines frequently results in light inclinations of the text lines, and the compressed, irregular spacing—used to conserve space or avoid splitting words—poses further difficulties for OCR systems trained on modern print.

The language of these texts reflects a deliberate combination of high Classical Greek and Koine, particularly used in biblical passages. Authors often showcase their education through complex syntax, rare vocabulary, and rhetorical flourishes. This display of linguistic command is further reinforced by the use of medieval orthography, reflecting both scholarly ambition and stylistic tradition.

From this dataset, we selected 10 pages: one from each of the following manuscripts—MS Eparchos, MS053, MS079, MS114 [8], MS Barocci 76, MS Paris. gr. 1293, BL Add. 34060, and MS Vat. Pal. 364—and two from Estienne's early printed edition [9].

The second dataset (HABoG) comes from a pilot project jointly developed by the Historical Archive of the Bank of Greece and the Document Image Analysis Group at the Institute of Informatics and Telecommunications, NCSR "Demokritos." This collection consists of the handwritten proceedings of the General Council of the Bank of Greece, covering the period from 1928 to 1988. These documents represent an invaluable historical and administrative record, reflecting nearly six decades of economic decision-making and institutional activity.

The minutes were written by various scribes, each responsible for formally recording the content of council meetings. Most scribes employed a calligraphic cursive script characterized by looped letters and smooth, connected strokes. Others favored a more slanted, faster cursive style, prioritizing speed over formality. This variation in handwriting styles introduces significant challenges for OCR systems, as letterforms often differ between scribes and can be easily confused—particularly when loops, flourishes, or quick strokes cause characters to resemble one another.

The language used in these texts is consistently formal, reflecting the official and procedural nature of the documents. Over the decades, evolving handwriting styles and the unique characteristics of each scribe call for additional training and customized OCR workflows to enable accurate transcription and consistent analysis.

From this dataset, we selected 10 handwritten pages dated between 1933–1987 selected from the proceedings of the General Council of the Bank of Greece.

The Byzantine dataset was divided into 10,807 training lines and 1,204 validation lines, corresponding to an approximate 90/10 split. In contrast, the dataset from the

HABoG dataset was split into 53,034 training lines and 12,770 validation lines, reflecting an 80/20 ratio. For the latter dataset, training was conducted using a version of the text without accents and breathings. This approach was chosen to simplify the transcription process and reduce inconsistencies in the historical encoding of diacritics. As a result, the OCR output for this dataset is also normalized and does not include polytonic accentuation. The model configuration was designed to improve performance across varying handwriting styles and to account for differences in textual conventions across the two datasets (Fig. 1).

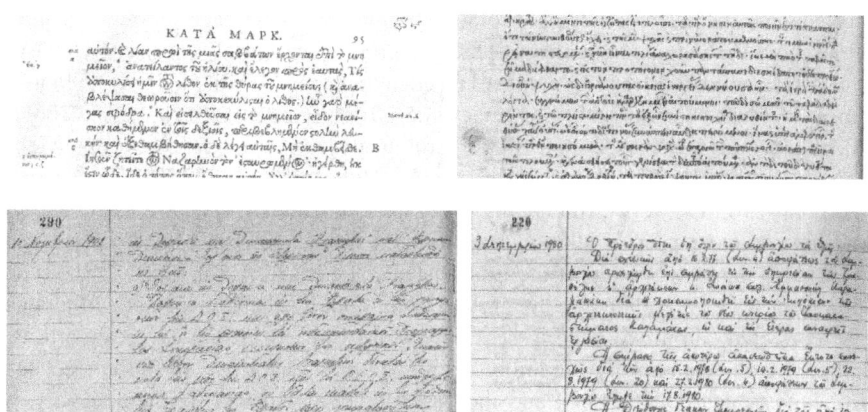

Fig. 1. Image samples from the Byzantine (top) and the HABoG (down) datasets.

4 Metholodology

Automatic text line segmentation is performed using a variation of the popular YOLOv5 Deep Neural Network model. This version is used for detecting oriented quadrilateral polygons (YOLOv5-OBB) [10]. The OCR model employed for prediction was trained with the open-source Calamari-OCR engine [11], and set up with the htr + network architecture. To improve performance, we extended its default architecture by incorporating an additional LSTM layer with 100 nodes and a dropout rate of 0.5.

To mitigate the errors present in OCR-generated text, we explore the use of LLMs as post-processing tools for automatic text correction (see Fig. 2). The OCR-generated text is given as input to the LLM which is prompted to return an enhanced version in its output correcting mistakes present in the input text. We design prompt templates customized for each dataset, incorporating detailed task instructions along with a concise overview of the relevant dialect and thematic content. We employ few-shot prompting [12] by incorporating k examples consisting of OCR-generated text paired with their corresponding corrected versions. For the Byzantine Dataset, we include 3 examples spanning 1 − 5 text lines, while for the HABoG Dataset we use 3 examples spanning 5 − 10 text lines. For both datasets, we preprocess the examples by joining lines into a single string. Also, we resolve incomplete words split across lines by hyphenation. This preprocessing is applied to both the OCR output and the corresponding ground truth text.

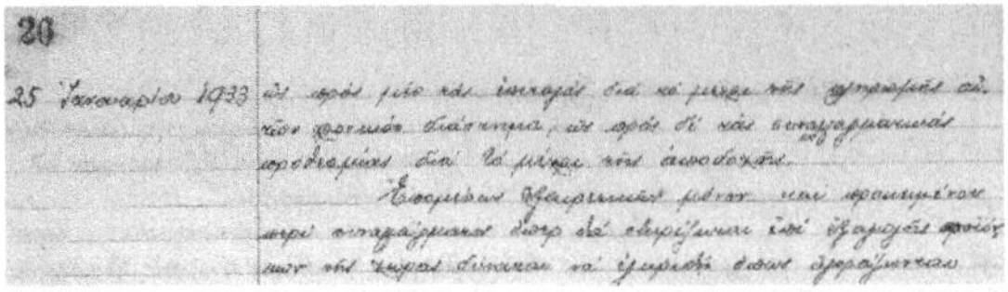

```
OCR:   20 25 Ιανουαριου 1933 ως προς μεν τας επικαγας δια το μεχρι της πληρωμης αυτων χρονικον διασκημα, ως προς δε νας
LLM:   20 25 Ιανουαριου 1933 ως προς μεν τας επιταγας δια το μεχρι της πληρωμης αυτων χρονικον διαστημα, ως προς δε τας
LABEL: 20 25 Ιανουαριου 1933 ως προς μεν τας επιταγας δια το μεχρι της πληρωμης αυτων χρονικον διαστημα, ως προς δε τας
```

Fig. 2. Example output of OCR, LLM, Label (ground truth) text (first 200 characters)

We assess the performance of several common Large Language Models, including both proprietary and open-source options. The proprietary models consist of OpenAI's ChatGPT-4o and GPT-4.1 [13], obtained through the OpenAI API, along with Google's Gemini 2.0 Flash, Gemini 2.5 Flash Preview (05/20), and Gemini 2.5 Pro Preview (06/05) [14], obtained through the Gemini API. Regarding open-source models, we utilize Meta's LLaMa 3.1-405B Instruct [15], accessed via Amazon Bedrock, and Mistral's DevStral-24B-Small-2505-Q4_K_M, run locally using the Ollama platform[1]. We use consistent sampling parameters across all models, setting the temperature to 0.2 and top-p to 0.9.

For both datasets, we report the Edit Distance, Character Error Rate (CER %) and Word Error Rate (%) relative to the ground truth, both for the OCR-generated text and LLM-corrected output. To better assess how well LLMs fix errors, we create artificial versions of our datasets by randomly changing some characters in the correct text, mimicking typical OCR errors, and then ask the best model to fix them. Lastly, we perform an ablation study to determine how different parts of the prompt affect results. In particular, we check how the performance changes when using detailed instructions versus short ones, the number of examples provided, and the length of those examples in text lines.

5 Experimental Results

The results for both the OCR-generated text and the LLM-corrected output for both datasets are presented in Table 1. We observe that almost all LLMs improve the OCR-generated text for the HABoG dataset, with the best performing model -Gemini-2.5-pro-reducing the CER by approximately 3.79% significantly improving on the performance of the OCR. In contrast, the Byzantine dataset appears to be a more challenging case for most LLMs as they have negative effect on enhancing the OCR output. This is likely due to the nature of Classical and Koine Greek, which are also likely under-represented in the web-sourced training data of most LLMs. The Gemini models in this case are the only ones improving on the OCR-generated text, with the best performing model -Gemini 2.5 pro- reducing the CER by approximately 0.67%.

Results on the synthetic versions of the Byzantine Dataset are presented in Table 2 and of the HABoG Dataset in Table 3. Those indicate that LLMs are generally ineffective at improving OCR-generated text when the OCR system performs well, but have a positive impact as OCR quality deteriorates. Specifically, The LLM has a negative effect when

[1] https://ollama.com/library/devstral

the OCR CER is less than 3% for the Byzantine Dataset and less than 2% for the HABoG Dataset. However, the LLM consistently improves text quality when CER is greater than 3% and 2% for the Byzantine and HABoG Datasets, respectively. This trend is further illustrated by the similar patterns observed in Figs. 3 and 4.

The results of our ablation study are presented in Table 4. They show that expert detailed task instructions are the most important factor in performance on all datasets. In addition, the inclusion of multiple in-context is also crucial as multiple examples lead to noticeable improvements even when detailed instructions are not available. When multiple examples are provided, the length of those examples has little to no significant impact and appears to be subject to the inherent variability of LLM output generation.

Table 1. Experimental Results using the Byzantine Dataset and the HABoG Dataset.

	Byzantine Dataset			HABoG Dataset		
	EditDist	CER(%)	WER(%)	EditDist	CER(%)	WER(%)
OCR	765	7.06	25.21	1350	7.98	31.16
OCR + devstral	915	8.45	24.39	1292	7.64	29.35
OCR + gpt-4.1	942	8.70	23.80	1072	6.34	18.63
OCR + chatgpt-4o	1033	9.54	25.79	1375	8.13	23.25
OCR + gemini-2.5-pro	692	6.39	17.23	708	4.19	14.10
OCR + meta.llama3-1	1027	9.48	24.44	1219	7.21	24.11
OCR + gemini-2.5-flash	756	6.98	17.94	947	5.60	17.44
OCR + gemini-2.0-flash	753	6.95	21.69	1042	6.16	19.66

Table 2. Experimental Results using the Byzantine Dataset and synthetically corrupted text (LLM = gemini-2.5-pro).

	w/o LLM			With LLM		
Text corruption rate	ED	CER(%)	WER(%)	ED	CER(%)	WER(%)
0.01	104	0.97	7.82	278	2.56	13.05
0.02	165	1.52	11.38	292	2.69	14.14
0.04	302	2.78	18.74	326	3.00	14.89
0.06	400	4.58	28.22	352	3.24	15.06
0.08	431	4.93	30.17	294	2.71	13.91
0.1	578	6.61	37.64	364	3.35	15.58
0.2	1157	13.24	59.02	550	5.49	19.66
0.3	1661	19.00	74.20	841	7.74	23.33
0.4	2111	24.14	81.95	953	8.77	25.63
0.5	3332	30.68	87.87	1541	14.18	31.84

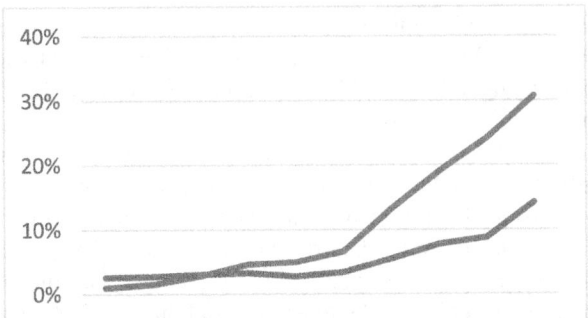

Fig. 3. CER using the Byzantine Dataset and synthetically corrupted text (blue line) as well as after applying LLM (red line) (LLM = gemini-2.5-pro).

Table 3. Experimental Results using the HABoG Dataset and synthetically corrupted text (LLM = gemini-2.5-pro).

Text corruption rate	w/o LLM			With LLM		
	ED	CER(%)	WER(%)	ED	CER(%)	WER(%)
0.01	117	0.70	5.24	304	1.80	5.03
0.02	255	1.51	10.39	345	2.04	5.73
0.04	431	2.55	16.90	415	2.45	6.76
0.06	614	3.64	23.83	520	3.07	7.87
0.08	866	5.12	31.20	467	2.76	8.99
0.1	1074	6.35	37.39	408	2.41	8.20
0.2	2174	12.86	60.18	647	3.82	12.82
0.3	3276	19.36	75.64	961	5.68	18.67
0.4	4245	25.09	83.06	1343	7.94	23.04
0.5	5305	31.36	89.65	2657	15.71	34.50

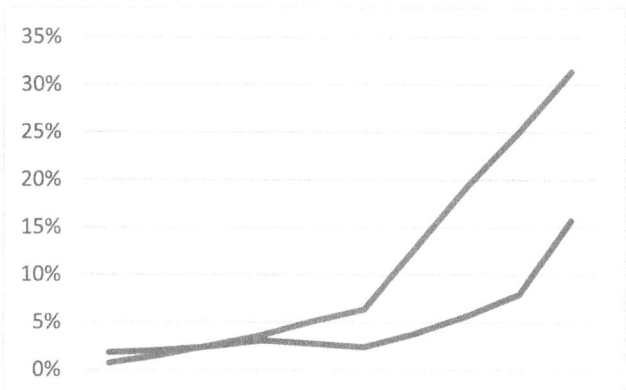

Fig. 4. CER using the HABoG Dataset and synthetically corrupted text (blue line) as well as after applying LLM (red line) (LLM = gemini-2.5-pro).

Table 4. Experimental Results using the Byzantine Dataset and the HABoG Dataset using several prompt configurations for the LLM (gemini-2.5-pro).

Full instruct.	# of exempl.	Exempl. Length	Byzantine Dataset			HABoG Dataset		
			EditDist	CER (%)	WER (%)	EditDist	CER (%)	WER (%)
no	0		15074	139,19	150,53	2724	16,10	73,25
no	1	1–5	4195	38,74	53,99	2166	12,80	61,58
no	1	5–10	1117	10,31	26,67	1849	10,93	49,55
no	3	1–5	1177	10,87	26,50	1625	9,61	44,15
no	3	5–10	1020	9,42	25,32	1367	8,08	34,54
yes	0		803	7,42	19,99	748	4,42	13,77
yes	1	1–5	987	9,11	22,04	696	4,11	13,85
yes	1	5–10	902	8,33	21,69	696	4,11	14,06
yes	3	1–5	692	6,39	17,23	696	4,11	14,72
yes	3	5–10	751	6,93	18,05	708	4,19	14,10

6 Conclusions

In this study, we explore the application of Large Language Models (LLMs) to correct OCR errors in old Greek handwritten documents, utilizing two old Greek datasets. The capability of LLMs for OCR correction of these documents is emphasized, particularly in cases where the recognition results are relatively poor. LLMs can be applied for OCR correction following inference from a system trained on a small or related dataset that yields relatively poor performance, particularly in cases where human correction is still ultimately required, thereby bypassing the time-consuming process of annotating a new dataset for OCR. In the future, we plan to extend our datasets, conduct tests on more LLMs, and incorporate portions of our datasets into the LLM training process.

Acknowledgments. This work is partially supported (a) by the Project "D-AI-LECT – Digital Analysis and Recognition of Handwritten Documents of Greek Dialects", Archimedes, Center for Research in Artificial Intelligence, Data Science and Algorithms, Athena Research Center, Greece, (b) by the Bank of Greece Historical Archive, as part of a pilot research study to investigate the use of AI in processing of large-scale digitised handwritten archives and (c) by project MIS 5154714 of the National Recovery and Resilience Plan Greece 2.0 funded by the European Union under the NextGenerationEU Program.

References

1. Humphries, M., et al.: Unlocking the archives: using large language models to transcribe handwritten historical documents. Comput. Vision Pattern Recogn. Hist. Methods J. Quant. Interdisc. Hist. **58**(3), 175–193 (2025). https://doi.org/10.1080/01615440.2025.2500309
2. Kanerva, J., Ledins, C., Käpyaho, S., Ginter F.: OCR error post-correction with LLMs in historical documents: no free lunches. In 3rd Workshop on Resources and Representations for Under-Resourced Languages and Domains (RESOURCEFUL-2025), pp. 38–47 (2025). https://doi.org/10.48550/arXiv.2502.01205
3. Penteado M. C., Perez, F.: Evaluating GPT-3.5 and GPT-4 on grammatical error correction for Brazilian Portuguese. In 40th International Conference on Machine Learning, Honolulu, Hawaii, USA (2023). https://doi.org/10.48550/arXiv.2306.15788
4. Beshirov, A., Dobreva, M., Dimitrov, D., Hardalov, M., Koychev I., Nakov, P.: Post-OCR text correction for Bulgarian historical documents. Int. J. Dig. Libr. **26**, 4 (2025). https://doi.org/10.48550/arXiv.2409.00527
5. Thomas, A., Gaizauskas R., Lu, H.: Leveraging LLMs for post-OCR correction of historical newspapers. In 3rd Workshop on Language Technologies for Historical and Ancient Languages (LT4HALA), pp. 116–121 (2024)
6. Greif, G., Griesshaber, N., Greif, R.: Multimodal LLMs for OCR, OCR post-correction, and named entity recognition in historical documents. (2025). https://doi.org/10.48550/arXiv.2504.00414
7. Boros, E., Ehrmann, M., Romanello, M., Najem-Meyer S., Kaplan, F.: Post-correction of historical text transcripts with large language models: an exploratory study. In Proceedings of the 8th Joint SIGHUM Workshop on Computational Linguistics for Cultural Heritage, Social Sciences, Humanities and Literature (LaTeCH-CLfL 2024), pp. 133–159 (2024)
8. Tsochatzidis, L., Symeonidis, S., Papazoglou, A., Pratikakis, I.: HTR for Greek historical handwritten documents. J. Imaging **7**, 260 (2021). https://doi.org/10.3390/jimaging7120260
9. Kaddas, P., Palaiologos, K., Gatos, B., Katsouros, V., Christopoulou, K.: A system for processing and recognition of Greek byzantine and post-byzantine documents. In: Document Analysis and Recognition (ICDAR 2023), LNCS, vol. 14190, pp 366–376 (2023). https://doi.org/10.1007/978-3-031-41685-9_23
10. Kaddas, P., Gatos, B., Palaiologos, K., Christopoulou, K., Kritsis, K.: Text line detection and recognition of GREEK polytonic documents. In: 17th International Conference on Document Analysis and Recognition (ICDAR 2023), International Workshop on Machine Learning (4th edition), LNCS, vol. 14194, pp. 213–225 (2023). https://doi.org/10.1007/978-3-031-41501-2_15

11. Wick, C., Reul, C., Puppe, F.: Calamari - a high-performance tensorflow-based deep learning package for optical character recognition. (2018). https://doi.org/10.48550/arXiv.1807.02004
12. Brown, T.B., Mann, B., Ryder, N., et al.: Language Models are Few-Shot Learners (2020). https://doi.org/10.48550/arXiv.2005.14165
13. OpenAI, Achiam, J., Adler, S., et al.: GPT-4 Technical Report (2024). https://doi.org/10.48550/arXiv.2303.08774
14. Team, G., Anil, R., Borgeaud, S., et al.: Gemini: a family of highly capable multimodal models (2025). https://doi.org/10.48550/arXiv.2312.11805
15. Grattafiori, A., Dubey, A., Jauhri, A., et al.: The Llama 3 herd of models (2024). https://doi.org/10.48550/arXiv.2407.21783

Is Word2Vec Dead for Topic Modeling? A Case Study on Hospitality Opinion Mining

Marc-Alexis Azaïs[1,2](✉) , Jean-Loup Guillaume[1] ,
and Mickaël Coustaty[1]

[1] L3i, Univ. La Rochelle, La Rochelle 17000, France
marc-alexis.azais@univ-lr.fr , jean-loup.guillaume@univ-lr.fr ,
mickael.coustaty@univ-lr.fr
[2] RMD Technologies, La Rochelle 17000, France

Abstract. Topic modeling plays a central role in social science research by uncovering thematic structures within textual data across diverse domains. It is particularly valuable in contexts where expert-annotated datasets are scarce and existing benchmarks rely on overly broad categories. Recent advances in dense embedding representations based on Sentence Transformer architectures offer new possibilities for scalable classification and interpretable analysis through embeddings comparison and visualization. This study compares the performance of recent embedding models derived from transformer-based language models with Word2Vec embeddings trained on domain large-scale corpora. Focusing on opinion mining in the hospitality sector, our case study shows that in scenarios involving large-scale unlabeled datasets, domain-specific Word2Vec embeddings remain an effective solution, and can even outperform more recent contextual embeddings. In addition, we provide an overview of the epistemic debate surrounding topic modeling research and highlight that the notion of a universally "*best*" topic model is meaningless.

Keywords: Topic Modeling · Opinion Mining · Text Embeddings · Corpus Analysis · Social Science

1 Introduction

Topic modeling refers to the task of discovering thematic structures within collections of textual documents. As emphasized by recent reviews of topic model applications, it has been primarily employed to support research in the social sciences by enabling the large-scale analysis of textual corpora [24,27]. Over time, its applications have expanded significantly, encompassing fields such as scientific literature analysis [45], political discourse [18], consumer opinion mining [31], or the study historical archives [32]. In this paper, we focus on the tourism sector, motivated by the comprehensive survey conducted by Ameur et al. [1], which examines more than 700 articles published over the past two decades on consumer opinion analysis in the hospitality reviews. A key insight from their work is the persistent scarcity of expert-annotated datasets, often constrained by a limited set of predefined categories. For example, the SemEval dataset for hotel reviews includes only 34 categories (five of which are labeled as miscellaneous) [43], whereas Booking.com employs a far more granular taxonomy comprising 239 distinct topics [59]. Another critical issue identified by Ameur et al. is the tendency of topic modeling methods to produce inaccurate classifications. All these limitations hamper the full exploitation of available corpora and are not unique to the hospitality domain; **they also reflects a broader challenge encountered in social science research**.

However, Ameur et al. do not take into account recent advances in topic modeling that leverage text embedding representations. In particular, methods based on Sentence Transformers [48] have significantly improved text representations across a wide range of semantic similarity benchmarks [36]. These dense embeddings can be clustered to derive topics, as implemented in frameworks such as BERTopic [19]. Thereby introducing a new paradigm for topic modeling grounded in semantic similarity rather than traditional word co-occurrence distribution [6]. In this paper, we investigate whether Sentence Transformers can be effectively leveraged for unsupervised opinion mining in the hospitality domain, and compare their performance with earlier approaches based on Word2Vec embeddings [34] trained on large-scale, domain-specific datasets. Specifically, we address the following research question: **Is Word2Vec becoming obsolete given recent developments in embedding representations?**

2 Experimental Settings

We evaluated the ability of various embedding models to retrieve all relevant sentences for a given query, representing Booking.com scenarios [59].[1]

2.1 Datasets

Selection. We selected three human-annotated english datasets from the hotel and restaurant domains: Rest14 [44], Rest16 [42], and HotelOATS [11]. These datasets provide sentence-level topic labels and their associated sentiments, along with annotation guidelines to clarify the assignment process. HotelOATS follows the Rest16 annotation guidelines, adapted for hotel reviews. In contrast, Rest14 does not include annotation guidelines but uses the same categories as Rest16.

Modifications. We made several modifications to these datasets, driven by the recognition that sentiment analysis is a highly subjective task [10, p. 7]. Indeed, all sentences are annotated using the ENTITY#ASPECT format. However, upon closer examination of the annotations, we identified several issues with this

---

[1] Dataset, evaluation pipeline and all embeddings visualizations available at: https://anonymous.4open.science/r/word2vec-topic-hospitality-tpdl2025-3FF4.

schema, many of which stem from arbitrary design choices. It remains unclear whether CLEANLINESS should be treated as an aspect tied to specific entities, such as in HOTEL#CLEANLINESS and ROOM#CLEANLINESS, or whether CLEANLINESS, HOTEL, and ROOM should instead be considered as three distinct entities. In addition, sentences such as "*I can't wait to go back*" and "*Will absolutely visit again*" labeled as RESTAURANT#GENERAL in Rest16, and "*I recommend this hotel*" labeled as HOTEL#GENERAL in HotelOATS, appear to express customer intent, a notion more appropriately studied in other research areas [31], rather than evaluating an overall experience. The distinction between GENERAL and MISCELLANEOUS labels also appears to be extremely ambiguous. Moreover, sentences such as "*Service was decent*" or "*Food was okay, nothing great*" are labeled as NEUTRAL, but linguistic research suggests that such formulations differ little from explicitly NEGATIVE statements, apart from their more polite tone [25]. There also appears to be confusion between the sentiment explicitly expressed by the author and the sentiment potentially perceived by readers. For example, "*Waited 35 min for a table for 8, which was ok for such a big crowd*" is labeled as NEUTRAL, but may reasonably be interpreted as NEGATIVE by readers. Consequently, we chose to remove sentences labeled with NEUTRAL or CONFLICTING sentiment, as well as those categorized under the MISCELLANEOUS aspect, since these labels introduce ambiguity and highly subjective interpretation. Following prior work [37], we excluded broad entity labels such as RESTAURANT and HOTEL, which are too general and could be more effectively divided into specific sub-entities and focused exclusively on retrieving topics at the entity level for a more interpretable assessment of model performance in an unsupervised setting.

2.2 Models

We selected several models from the Hugging Face Hub and categorized them according to their underlying architecture and training data: (i) static embeddings, (ii) opinion mining sentence transformers, (iii) general sentence transformers, and (iv) LLM-based sentence transformers.

Static Embeddings. We trained two static word embedding models using the Continuous Bag of Words (**CBOW**) and Skip-Gram (**SG**) architectures [34], leveraging large-scale in-domain datasets: *HotelRec* [2] for the hotel domain and *SixTripAdvisorReview* [7] for the restaurant domain. The text was preprocessed by removing stop words and punctuation. Sentence-level embeddings were computed by averaging the corresponding token embeddings. Additionally, we included *Potion-base-8M*, referred to as **Model2Vec** [57], which currently achieves state-of-the-art performance among static embedding models on MTEB [36].

Opinion Mining Sentence Transformers. We selected models that have been specifically fine-tuned for opinion mining tasks. Among them, **SentiCSE**

is based on the RoBERTa architecture and trained to capture sentiment representations directly within its embeddings [26]. Another model, **StanceSBERT**, is a variant of all-mpnet-base-v2 that has been fine-tuned on debate forum data, in the objective to suitable for social media opinion mining [15]. Finally, **TourBERT** is a BERT model fine-tuned on tourism review datasets [4].[2]

General Sentence Transformers. For general-purpose sentence representations, we included three representative families of models trained on large-scale, multidomain corpora. The first is the **E5** series developed by Microsoft and based on BERT [60]. Although the exact training data has not been disclosed, it is known to involve large-scale "web data". The second is the widely used **all** series from Hugging Face [47]. The third is the **GTE** series developed by Alibaba, which relies on the Transformers++ architecture and, for its more recent versions, on ModernBERT [28].

LLM Sentence Transformers. We also considered sentence embedding models built upon large language model backbones. These include **Sentence-T5-XXL** and **GTR-T5-XXL**, both based on Google's T5-XXL architecture [38,39]. In addition, we evaluated **E5-Mistral-7B-Instruct**, a model fine-tuned by Microsoft for embedding learning using the Mistral-7B-Instruct backbone [61].[3]

2.3 Details of Downstream Tasks

For each dataset, we generated two versions of the test set following ABSA terminology: (i) Aspect Category Detection (ACD) focuses on identifying aspects alone, (ii) Aspect Category Sentiment Analysis (ACSA), extends this by retrieving aspects with their associated sentiment. A single query is used for each aspect, derived from the annotation guidelines.[4] For ACD, the query is directly derived from these guidelines, while for ACSA, it is adjusted to include a sentiment representation within the description. Following Booking.com, we use the macro average precision score as an evaluation metric [59].[5]

3 Results

3.1 Quantitative Analysis

The results are provided in Table 1. Opinion mining sentence transformers perform worse than general-purpose sentence transformers such as the GTE series

---

[2] Unlike other Sentence Transformers, TourBERT was not trained with contrastive loss in a siamese network setup, but solely using a MLM objective.
[3] We use the prompt template web_search_query from the model card.
[4] https://alt.qcri.org/semeval2016/task5/data/uploads/absa2016_annotationguidelines.pdf.
[5] https://scikit-learn.org/stable/modules/generated/sklearn.metrics.average_precision_score.html.

and `Sentence-T5`, which achieve better performance on both ACD and ACSA tasks, despite being specifically designed for opinion mining. In particular, even `TourBERT` (fine tuned in hospitality data) performs poorly compared to the simpler and more efficient `all-MiniLM-L6-v2`, underscoring the importance of the siamese network architecture combined with contrastive learning. Surprisingly, the `CBOW` model achieves the best performance in the hotel domain for ACD tasks and remains highly competitive overall, with an average score only 1.85 points behind the top-performing model.

3.2 Qualitative Analysis

Embeddings for the hotel domain are provided in Fig. 1. Visualization of `StanceSBERT` shows signs of overfitting to sentiment representations, which may explain its poor performance despite being designed for Opinion Mining. Overall, topics such as HOTEL, SERVICE, LOCATION and FOOD & DRINKS are well separated across all models, whereas ROOMS, ROOM AMENITIES, and FACILITIES remain more challenging to distinguish. The sparsity observed in the embeddings across models underscores the importance of improved annotation quality. In the same way, general models have difficulties distinguishing topics when a negative opinion is expressed. Interestingly, the `CBOW` visualization aligns with its relatively strong performance on ACD.

4 Related Work

To address the question, *"Is Word2Vec becoming obsolete given recent developments in embedding representations?"*, our experimental results suggest that Word2Vec remains a promising approach to analyze hospitality reviews. However, determining whether Word2Vec is still the most suitable method requires a more nuanced perspective. Indeed, our literature review reveals a recent increase in criticism of topic modeling research, which may obscure ongoing progress in the field.

The Downfall of Neural Topic Models. Hoyle et al. [24] evaluate a variant of LDA [33] alongside more recent neural models, including those based on variational autoencoders [8] and their own earlier based on BERT [23]. They found that newer approaches do not produce substantial improvements compared to established ground truth. In addition, neural models tend to be less stable, exhibiting high variability across runs, and require more computational resources. The observation that simpler statistical models outperform neural methods is echoed in other works. For example, Harrando et al. reported similar findings in their systematic evaluation of topic models [20]. In the specific context of hospitality reviews, Airbnb's finds that ABAE, a neural topic model based on Word2Vec embeddings [21], does not significantly outperform basic Word2Vec embeddings clustering [35]. Tulkens et al. report similar findings, showing that a simple weighting algorithm applied to Word2Vec embeddings is effective for

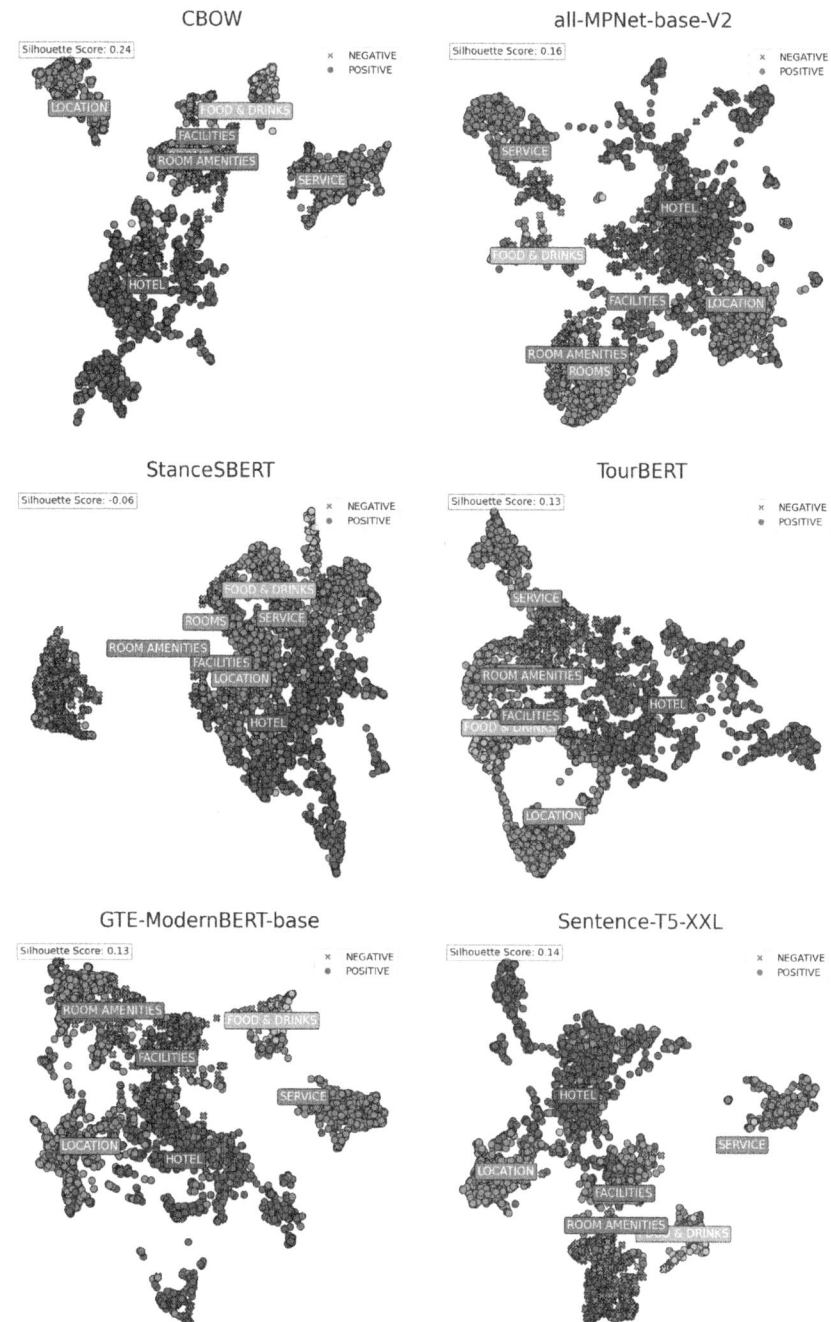

Fig. 1. UMAP visualization of embeddings in the hotel domain. General Sentence Transformer exhibit representational bias consistent with the findings of Nikolaev and Padó, with embeddings largely determined by nouns in sentence [40].

Table 1. Performance comparison of models across datasets for ACD and ACSA tasks. Underlined values represent the top models in each category, bolded values indicate the best models overall.

	ACD				ACSA			
	Hotel	Rest16	Rest14	Avg.	Hotel	Rest16	Rest14	Avg.
Static Embeddings								
CBOW	**65.11**	<u>60.41</u>	<u>72.66</u>	<u>66.06</u>	<u>38.67</u>	<u>38.19</u>	<u>52.79</u>	<u>43.22</u>
SG	60.87	53.44	64.87	59.72	34.74	36.48	48.87	40.03
Model2Vec	52.36	53.79	66.22	57.46	30.06	31.27	44.35	35.23
Opinion Mining Sentence Transformers								
SentiCSE	28.90	31.85	39.61	33.45	25.20	28.27	35.77	29.75
StanceSBERT	<u>37.56</u>	34.51	45.71	39.26	<u>30.17</u>	<u>30.82</u>	39.43	<u>33.47</u>
TourBERT	37.31	<u>35.46</u>	<u>47.92</u>	<u>40.23</u>	25.55	30.29	<u>41.98</u>	32.61
General Sentence Transformers								
all-MiniLM-L6-v2	55.49	55.88	71.42	60.93	32.04	40.18	47.23	39.82
all-MiniLM-L12-v2	56.29	53.66	68.34	59.43	31.21	38.89	45.85	38.65
all-MPNet-base-v2	49.78	48.84	60.91	53.17	31.84	36.06	43.31	37.07
E5-small-v2	50.76	43.09	59.33	51.06	37.36	40.69	51.32	43.12
E5-base-v2	55.20	46.63	60.64	54.16	37.39	40.55	51.90	43.28
E5-large-v2	52.36	43.57	60.39	52.11	38.35	39.29	50.79	42.81
GTE-base-en-v1.5	62.94	62.95	**77.23**	67.71	38.01	46.03	57.19	47.08
GTE-large-en-v1.5	<u>64.14</u>	<u>63.48</u>	76.13	<u>67.91</u>	<u>41.54</u>	46.32	<u>62.13</u>	<u>50.00</u>
GTE-ModernBert-base	60.33	61.49	75.12	65.64	40.60	<u>46.45</u>	58.18	48.41
LLM Sentence Transformers								
Sentence-T5-xxl	62.11	<u>62.57</u>	75.66	66.78	**45.30**	**48.56**	**65.89**	**53.25**
GTR-T5-xxl	55.96	52.91	71.15	60.01	31.38	37.61	47.16	38.72
E5-Mistral-7B-Instruct	<u>62.54</u>	62.16	<u>76.89</u>	<u>67.20</u>	37.63	40.48	55.36	44.49

implicit aspect extraction [56]. Finally, a systematic literature review of topic model applications on social media highlights that newer topic models are not adopted in practice by social scientists [27].[6]

The Promise and Pitfalls of LLM. Li et al. [29] compare an LLM-based topic model, TopicGPT [41], with LDA on a synthetic controlled dataset. They found that while LLM approaches incur substantially higher computational and financial costs, the extracted topics are not necessarily more informative than those

---

[6] For a practical guide to using LDA, see Antoniak's blog post [3].

generated by LDA.[7] Also, they underscore that incorporating human supervision can significantly enhance the pertinence of topics extracted with LLMs, and they emphasize the importance of software design that enables effective interaction. This conclusion is consistent with the perspective of Choi et al. [12], who argue that while LLMs can serve as effective tools to support human effort, generated topics still require expert refinement.[8]

The Evaluation Problem. Today, there is still no consensus on the best way to evaluate topic models [13]. For instance, early automatic evaluation methods that relied on extracted keywords were found to poorly correlate with human judgment. This discrepancy was first experimentally demonstrated at NeurIPS in 2009 [9], and these findings were later replicated in 2021 [22].[9] More recent automated evaluations have shifted towards comparing clusterings against established ground truth labels [24,30,41]. Nonetheless, this method also has notable limitations. As Grimmer et al. [18] emphasize, the objective of topic models is not necessarily to replicate a predefined ground truth, but rather to support the development of new ways to interpret data. Building on this idea, recent studies focus on human judgment to reassess claims about neural and LLMs topic models [29,30]. Similarly, Schofield et al. [52] highlight that expert topic modeling practitioners consistently revise their extracted topics to better align them with their own subjective domain knowledge.[10]

5 Conclusion

It has become clear that the NLP field is facing an evaluation crisis, as highlighted by the surge of position papers accepted at leading conferences addressing this issue [49,51,55,58], as well as the thoroughly documented malpractices in the evaluation of closed-source LLMs [5,54]. Topic modeling research exemplifies the persistent problem of evaluating tasks where interpretation is inherently subjective. As a way forward, Grimmer's position is particularly valuable: in the social sciences, the notion of a single "*best*" model is inapplicable, because the

---

[7] They report that processing 10,000 documents with LDA takes approximately 5 min, whereas clustering the same dataset using GPT-4o requires around 9 h and incurs an estimated cost of $65.

[8] The authors note that LLM predictions may become de facto ground truth due to anchoring bias. As the experiment was conducted in a single day, this effect might be reduced with clearer guidelines to limit task subjectivity [50].

[9] This replication was motivated by the findings of Doogan et al., who empirically demonstrate the inconsistency of topic model rankings across various keyword-based evaluation metrics and highlighted the challenges humans face in interpreting coherent themes associated with "*best*" extracted topics [14].

[10] For a more in-depth discussion of social science practices and requirements related to topic modeling, see Shadrova's position paper [53], Text as Data [17], the discussion by Hoyle et al. on Content Analysis [24], and Laureate et al. [27] who outlined requirements for future topic model development.

"*ground truth*" depends on the specific research objectives and individual interpretations of the text [16]. In our case study, Word2Vec may not be the most accurate method, but its learned embeddings serve as a useful aid for identifying patterns and organizing categories.[11] From this standpoint, we encourage computer scientists to remain open to "*traditional*" topic models like LDA, while placing greater emphasis on practical use cases over purely methodological innovations when designing new topic models.[12] To conclude, future research integrating LLM should prioritize human-centered evaluation, ensure computational efficiency to minimize delays in large-scale text exploration, and be supported by thoughtfully designed user interfaces to assist human interpretation - as demonstrated in works such as [29,46].

Acknowledgments. This work benefited from access to the computing resources of the "CALI 3" cluster. This cluster is operated and hosted by the University of Limoges. It is part of the HPC network in the Nouvelle-Aquitaine Region, financed by the State and the Region.

References

1. Ameur, A., Hamdi, S., Ben Yahia, S.: Sentiment analysis for hotel reviews: a systematic literature review. ACM Comput. Surv. **56**(2) (2023). https://doi.org/10.1145/3605152
2. Antognini, D., Faltings, B.: Hotelrec: a novel very large-scale hotel recommendation dataset. In: Proceedings of the 12th Language Resources and Evaluation Conference. pp. 4917–4923. European Language Resources Association, Marseille (2020). https://www.aclweb.org/anthology/2020.lrec-1.605
3. Antoniak, M.: Topic modeling for the people (2022). https://maria-antoniak.github.io/2022/07/27/topic-modeling-for-the-people.html. Accessed 02 June 2025
4. Arefieva, V., Egger, R.: Tourbert: a pretrained language model for the tourism industry. ArXiv arxiv:2201.07449 (2022). https://api.semanticscholar.org/CorpusID:246035422
5. Balloccu, S., Schmidtová, P., Lango, M., Dusek, O.: Leak, cheat, repeat: Data contamination and evaluation malpractices in closed-source LLMs. In: Graham, Y., Purver, M. (eds.) Proceedings of the 18th Conference of the European Chapter of the Association for Computational Linguistics, volume 1: Long Papers, pp. 67–93. Association for Computational Linguistics, St. Julian's (2024). https://aclanthology.org/2024.eacl-long.5/
6. Blei, D.M., Ng, A.Y., Jordan, M.I.: Latent dirichlet allocation. J. Mach. Learn. Res. **3**(Jan), 993–1022 (2003)
7. Botana, I.L.R., Bolón-Canedo, V., Guijarro-Berdiñas, B., Alonso-Betanzos, A.: Explain and conquer: personalised text-based reviews to achieve transparency (2022). https://arxiv.org/abs/2205.01759
8. Burkhardt, S., Kramer, S.: Decoupling sparsity and smoothness in the dirichlet variational autoencoder topic model. J. Mach. Learn. Res. **20**(131), 1–27 (2019)

---

[11] Echoing what Grimmer refers to as the discovery phase [16].
[12] This is notably emphasized in the conclusion of Hoyle et al. [24].

9. Chang, J., Gerrish, S., Wang, C., Boyd-Graber, J., Blei, D.: Reading tea leaves: how humans interpret topic models. Adv. Neural Inf. Process. Syst. **22** (2009)
10. Chebolu, S.U.S., Dernoncourt, F., Lipka, N., Solorio, T.: A review of datasets for aspect-based sentiment analysis. In: Park, J.C., et al. (eds.) Proceedings of the 13th International Joint Conference on Natural Language Processing and the 3rd Conference of the Asia-Pacific Chapter of the Association for Computational Linguistics, vol. 1: Long Papers, pp. 611–628. Association for Computational Linguistics, Nusa Dua (2023). https://doi.org/10.18653/v1/2023.ijcnlp-main.41. https://aclanthology.org/2023.ijcnlp-main.41/
11. Chebolu, S.U.S., Dernoncourt, F., Lipka, N., Solorio, T.: OATS: a challenge dataset for opinion aspect target sentiment joint detection for aspect-based sentiment analysis. In: Calzolari, N., Kan, M.Y., Hoste, V., Lenci, A., Sakti, S., Xue, N. (eds.) Proceedings of the 2024 Joint International Conference on Computational Linguistics, Language Resources and Evaluation (LREC-COLING 2024), pp. 12336–12347. ELRA and ICCL, Torino (2024). https://aclanthology.org/2024.lrec-main.1080/
12. Choi, A., Akter, S.S., Singh, J., Anastasopoulos, A.: The LLM effect: are humans truly using LLMs, or are they being influenced by them instead? In: Al-Onaizan, Y., Bansal, M., Chen, Y.N. (eds.) Proceedings of the 2024 Conference on Empirical Methods in Natural Language Processing, pp. 22032–22054. Association for Computational Linguistics, Miami (2024). https://doi.org/10.18653/v1/2024.emnlp-main.1230. https://aclanthology.org/2024.emnlp-main.1230/
13. Doogan, C.: A Topic is not a theme: towards a contextualised approach to topic modelling. Ph.D. thesis, Monash University, Australia (2022)
14. Doogan, C., Buntine, W.: Topic model or topic twaddle? Re-evaluating demantic interpretability measures. In: North American Association for Computational Linguistics 2021, pp. 3824–3848. Association for Computational Linguistics (ACL) (2021)
15. Ghafouri, V., Such, J., Suarez-Tangil, G.: I love pineapple on pizza != I hate pineapple on pizza: Stance-aware sentence transformers for opinion mining. In: Al-Onaizan, Y., Bansal, M., Chen, Y.N. (eds.) Proceedings of the 2024 Conference on Empirical Methods in Natural Language Processing, pp. 21046–21058. Association for Computational Linguistics, Miami (2024). https://doi.org/10.18653/v1/2024.emnlp-main.1171. https://aclanthology.org/2024.emnlp-main.1171/
16. Grimmer, J., Roberts, M.E., Stewart, B.M.: Machine learning for social science: an agnostic approach. Annu. Rev. Polit. Sci. **24**(1), 395–419 (2021)
17. Grimmer, J., Roberts, M.E., Stewart, B.M.: Text as Data: A New Framework for Machine Learning and the Social Sciences. Princeton University Press, Princeton (2022)
18. Grimmer, J., Stewart, B.M.: Text as data: the promise and pitfalls of automatic content analysis methods for political texts. Polit. Anal. **21**(3), 267–297 (2013)
19. Grootendorst, M.: Bertopic: neural topic modeling with a class-based tf-idf procedure (2022). https://arxiv.org/abs/2203.05794
20. Harrando, I., Lisena, P., Troncy, R.: Apples to apples: a systematic evaluation of topic models. In: Mitkov, R., Angelova, G. (eds.) Proceedings of the International Conference on Recent Advances in Natural Language Processing (RANLP 2021), pp. 483–493. INCOMA Ltd., Held Online (2021). https://aclanthology.org/2021.ranlp-1.55/
21. He, R., Lee, W.S., Ng, H.T., Dahlmeier, D.: An unsupervised neural attention model for aspect extraction. In: Barzilay, R., Kan, M.Y. (eds.) Proceedings of the 55th Annual Meeting of the Association for Computational Linguistics, vol. 1: Long

Papers, pp. 388–397. Association for Computational Linguistics, Vancouver (2017). https://doi.org/10.18653/v1/P17-1036. https://aclanthology.org/P17-1036/
22. Hoyle, A., Goel, P., Hian-Cheong, A., Peskov, D., Boyd-Graber, J., Resnik, P.: Is automated topic model evaluation broken? The incoherence of coherence. Adv. Neural. Inf. Process. Syst. **34**, 2018–2033 (2021)
23. Hoyle, A.M., Goel, P., Resnik, P.: Improving neural topic models using knowledge distillation. In: Webber, B., Cohn, T., He, Y., Liu, Y. (eds.) Proceedings of the 2020 Conference on Empirical Methods in Natural Language Processing (EMNLP), pp. 1752–1771. Association for Computational Linguistics, Online (2020). https://doi.org/10.18653/v1/2020.emnlp-main.137. https://aclanthology.org/2020.emnlp-main.137/
24. Hoyle, A.M., Sarkar, R., Goel, P., Resnik, P.: Are neural topic models broken? In: Goldberg, Y., Kozareva, Z., Zhang, Y. (eds.) Findings of the Association for Computational Linguistics: EMNLP 2022, pp. 5321–5344. Association for Computational Linguistics, Abu Dhabi (2022). https://doi.org/10.18653/v1/2022.findings-emnlp.390. https://aclanthology.org/2022.findings-emnlp.390/
25. Kamoen, N., Mos, M.B., Dekker (Robbin), W.F.: A hotel that is not bad isn't good. the effects of valence framing and expectation in online reviews on text, reviewer and product appreciation. J. Pragmat. **75**, 28–43 (2015). https://doi.org/10.1016/j.pragma.2014.10.007. https://www.sciencedirect.com/science/article/pii/S0378216614002112
26. Kim, J., Na, Y., Kim, K., Lee, S.R., Chae, D.K.: SentiCSE: a sentiment-aware contrastive sentence embedding framework with sentiment-guided textual similarity. In: Calzolari, N., Kan, M.Y., Hoste, V., Lenci, A., Sakti, S., Xue, N. (eds.) Proceedings of the 2024 Joint International Conference on Computational Linguistics, Language Resources and Evaluation (LREC-COLING 2024), pp. 14693–14704. ELRA and ICCL, Torino (2024). https://aclanthology.org/2024.lrec-main.1280/
27. Laureate, C.D., Poet, W.B., Linger, H.: A systematic review of the use of topic models for short text social media analysis. Artif. Intell. Rev. **56**(12), 14223–14255 (2023). https://doi.org/10.1007/s10462-023-10471-x
28. Li, Z., Zhang, X., Zhang, Y., Long, D., Xie, P., Zhang, M.: Towards general text embeddings with multi-stage contrastive learning (2023). https://arxiv.org/abs/2308.03281
29. Li, Z., et al.: Large language models struggle to describe the haystack without human help: human-in-the-loop evaluation of llms (2025). https://arxiv.org/abs/2502.14748
30. Li, Z., et al.: Improving the TENOR of labeling: Re-evaluating topic models for content analysis. In: Graham, Y., Purver, M. (eds.) Proceedings of the 18th Conference of the European Chapter of the Association for Computational Linguistics, vol. 1: Long Papers, pp. 840–859. Association for Computational Linguistics, St. Julian's (2024). https://aclanthology.org/2024.eacl-long.51/
31. Liu, B.: Sentiment Analysis and Opinion Mining. Springer, Cham (2022)
32. Marjanen, J., Zosa, E., Hengchen, S., Pivovarova, L., Tolonen, M.: Topic modelling discourse dynamics in historical newspapers. arXiv preprint arXiv:2011.10428 (2020)
33. McCallum, A.K.: Mallet: a machine learning for languagetoolkit (2002). http://mallet.cs.umass.edu
34. Mikolov, T., Chen, K., Corrado, G., Dean, J.: Efficient estimation of word representations in vector space (2013). https://arxiv.org/abs/1301.3781

35. Mitcheltree, C., Wharton, S., Saluja, A.: Using aspect extraction approaches to generate review summaries and user profiles. In: Bangalore, S., Chu-Carroll, J., Li, Y. (eds.) Proceedings of the 2018 Conference of the North American Chapter of the Association for Computational Linguistics: Human Language Technologies, vol. 3 (Industry Papers), pp. 68–75. Association for Computational Linguistics, New Orleans - Louisiana (2018). https://doi.org/10.18653/v1/N18-3009. https://aclanthology.org/N18-3009/
36. Muennighoff, N., Tazi, N., Magne, L., Reimers, N.: MTEB: massive text embedding benchmark. In: Vlachos, A., Augenstein, I. (eds.) Proceedings of the 17th Conference of the European Chapter of the Association for Computational Linguistics, pp. 2014–2037. Association for Computational Linguistics, Dubrovnik (2023). https://doi.org/10.18653/v1/2023.eacl-main.148. https://aclanthology.org/2023.eacl-main.148/
37. Nguyen, T.N., Ngo, H., Nguyen, K.H., Cao, T.D.: A self-enhancement multitask framework for unsupervised aspect category detection. In: Bouamor, H., Pino, J., Bali, K. (eds.) Proceedings of the 2023 Conference on Empirical Methods in Natural Language Processing, pp. 8043–8054. Association for Computational Linguistics, Singapore (2023). https://doi.org/10.18653/v1/2023.emnlp-main.500. https://aclanthology.org/2023.emnlp-main.500/
38. Ni, J., et al.: Large dual encoders are generalizable retrievers (2021). https://arxiv.org/abs/2112.07899
39. Ni, J., et al.: Sentence-t5: scalable sentence encoders from pre-trained text-to-text models (2021). https://arxiv.org/abs/2108.08877
40. Nikolaev, D., Padó, S.: Representation biases in sentence transformers. In: Vlachos, A., Augenstein, I. (eds.) Proceedings of the 17th Conference of the European Chapter of the Association for Computational Linguistics, pp. 3701–3716. Association for Computational Linguistics, Dubrovnik (2023). https://doi.org/10.18653/v1/2023.eacl-main.268. https://aclanthology.org/2023.eacl-main.268/
41. Pham, C.M., Hoyle, A., Sun, S., Resnik, P., Iyyer, M.: TopicGPT: a prompt-based topic modeling framework. In: Duh, K., Gomez, H., Bethard, S. (eds.) Proceedings of the 2024 Conference of the North American Chapter of the Association for Computational Linguistics: Human Language Technologies, vol. 1: Long Papers, pp. 2956–2984. Association for Computational Linguistics, Mexico City (2024). https://doi.org/10.18653/v1/2024.naacl-long.164. https://aclanthology.org/2024.naacl-long.164/
42. Pontiki, M., et al.: SemEval-2016 task 5: aspect based sentiment analysis. In: Bethard, S., Carpuat, M., Cer, D., Jurgens, D., Nakov, P., Zesch, T. (eds.) Proceedings of the 10th International Workshop on Semantic Evaluation (SemEval-2016), pp. 19–30. Association for Computational Linguistics, San Diego (2016). https://doi.org/10.18653/v1/S16-1002. https://aclanthology.org/S16-1002/
43. Pontiki, M., Galanis, D., Papageorgiou, H., Manandhar, S., Androutsopoulos, I.: Semeval-2015 task 12: aspect based sentiment analysis. In: International Workshop on Semantic Evaluation (2015). https://api.semanticscholar.org/CorpusID:61874237
44. Pontiki, M., Galanis, D., Pavlopoulos, J., Papageorgiou, H., Androutsopoulos, I., Manandhar, S.: SemEval-2014 task 4: aspect based sentiment analysis. In: Nakov, P., Zesch, T. (eds.) Proceedings of the 8th International Workshop on Semantic Evaluation (SemEval 2014), pp. 27–35. Association for Computational Linguistics, Dublin (2014). https://doi.org/10.3115/v1/S14-2004. https://aclanthology.org/S14-2004/

45. Raman, R., Pattnaik, D., Hughes, L., Nedungadi, P.: Unveiling the dynamics of ai applications: a review of reviews using scientometrics and bertopic modeling. J. Innov. Knowl. **9**(3), 100517 (2024)
46. Reif, E., Qian, C., Wexler, J., Kahng, M.: Automatic histograms: leveraging language models for text dataset exploration. In: Extended Abstracts of the CHI Conference on Human Factors in Computing Systems, pp. 1–9 (2024)
47. Reimers, N.: Train the best sentence embedding model ever with 1b training pairs (2021). https://discuss.huggingface.co/t/train-the-best-sentence-embedding-model-ever-with-1b-training-pairs/7354. hugging Face Forums
48. Reimers, N., Gurevych, I.: Sentence-bert: sentence embeddings using siamese bert-networks. In: Conference on Empirical Methods in Natural Language Processing (2019). https://api.semanticscholar.org/CorpusID:201646309
49. Rogers, A., Luccioni, A.S.: Position: key claims in llm research have a long tail of footnotes. arXiv preprint arXiv:2308.07120 (2023)
50. Röttger, P., Vidgen, B., Hovy, D., Pierrehumbert, J.: Two contrasting data annotation paradigms for subjective NLP tasks. In: Carpuat, M., de Marneffe, M.C., Meza Ruiz, I.V. (eds.) Proceedings of the 2022 Conference of the North American Chapter of the Association for Computational Linguistics: Human Language Technologies, pp. 175–190. Association for Computational Linguistics, Seattle (2022). https://doi.org/10.18653/v1/2022.naacl-main.13. https://aclanthology.org/2022.naacl-main.13/
51. Saxon, M., Holtzman, A., West, P., Wang, W.Y., Saphra, N.: Benchmarks as microscopes: a call for model metrology. arXiv preprint arXiv:2407.16711 (2024)
52. Schofield, A., Wu, S., Bayard de Volo, T., Kuze, T., Gomez, A., Sultana, S.: "my very subjective human interpretation": domain expert perspectives on navigating the text analysis loop for topic models. In: Proceedings of the ACM on Human-Computer Interaction, vol. 9, no. 1, pp. 1–30 (2025)
53. Shadrova, A.: Topic models do not model topics: epistemological remarks and steps towards best practices. J. Data Min. Dig. Human. **2021** (2021)
54. Singh, S., et al.: The leaderboard illusion. arXiv preprint arXiv:2504.20879 (2025)
55. Tedeschi, S., et al.: What's the meaning of superhuman performance in today's NLU? In: Rogers, A., Boyd-Graber, J., Okazaki, N. (eds.) Proceedings of the 61st Annual Meeting of the Association for Computational Linguistics, vol. 1: Long Papers, pp. 12471–12491. Association for Computational Linguistics, Toronto (2023). https://doi.org/10.18653/v1/2023.acl-long.697. https://aclanthology.org/2023.acl-long.697/
56. Tulkens, S., van Cranenburgh, A.: Embarrassingly simple unsupervised aspect extraction. In: Jurafsky, D., Chai, J., Schluter, N., Tetreault, J. (eds.) Proceedings of the 58th Annual Meeting of the Association for Computational Linguistics, pp. 3182–3187. Association for Computational Linguistics, Online (2020). https://doi.org/10.18653/v1/2020.acl-main.290. https://aclanthology.org/2020.acl-main.290/
57. Tulkens, S., van Dongen, T.: Model2vec: fast state-of-the-art static embeddings (2024). https://github.com/MinishLab/model2vec
58. Venkit, P., et al.: The sentiment problem: a critical survey towards deconstructing sentiment analysis. In: Bouamor, H., Pino, J., Bali, K. (eds.) Proceedings of the 2023 Conference on Empirical Methods in Natural Language Processing, pp. 13743–13763. Association for Computational Linguistics, Singapore (2023). https://doi.org/10.18653/v1/2023.emnlp-main.848. https://aclanthology.org/2023.emnlp-main.848/

59. Wang, F., et al.: Text2Topic: multi-label text classification system for efficient topic detection in user generated content with zero-shot capabilities. In: Wang, M., Zitouni, I. (eds.) Proceedings of the 2023 Conference on Empirical Methods in Natural Language Processing: Industry Track, pp. 93–103. Association for Computational Linguistics, Singapore (2023). https://doi.org/10.18653/v1/2023.emnlp-industry.10. https://aclanthology.org/2023.emnlp-industry.10/
60. Wang, L., et al.: Text embeddings by weakly-supervised contrastive pre-training. arXiv preprint arXiv:2212.03533 (2022)
61. Wang, L., Yang, N., Huang, X., Yang, L., Majumder, R., Wei, F.: Improving text embeddings with large language models. arXiv preprint arXiv:2401.00368 (2023)

DM-LP: A Large Arabic Script Languages Dataset for OCR and Cataloguing Research

Luca Sala[2]((✉)) [iD], Riccardo Amerigo Vigliermo[1] [iD], Giovanni Sullutrone[2] [iD], and Sonia Bergamaschi[2] [iD]

[1] Fondazione per le Scienze Religiose, Bologna, Italy
vigliermo@fscire.it
[2] Università di Modena e Reggio Emilia (UNIMORE), Modena, Italy
{luca.sala,giovanni.sullutrone,sonia.bergamaschi}@unimore.it

Abstract. We present the preliminary results of the work in building the DigitalMaktaba-LaPira-v1 (DM-LP-v1) dataset, a large-scale, openly available dataset aiming at advancing cataloguing and OCR research for multilingual Arabic script digital libraries. Derived from over 73,000 Arabic-script PDF volumes held by the FSCIRE "La Pira" Library, specialized in history and doctrines of Islam, the dataset includes frontispieces, indexes, and ISBN-bearing pages extracted as high-resolution images and structured OCR outputs. A reproducible pipeline combines Qwen-2VL-72B, a vision-language model for zero-shot page classification, with Google Vision AI for text extraction. Evaluation on a 100 books sample yields F1 scores above 94% across all tasks, confirming the pipeline's suitability for enriching bibliographic metadata. The dataset, comprising around 5 TB of images, structured text, and metadata, is released under a permissive license, along with scripts for PDF preprocessing and initial layout tagging; validation and quality control pipelines are in preparation. DM-LP-v1 aims to offer a scalable foundation for research in multilingual cataloguing, document layout analysis, and OCR fine-tuning, addressing a critical gap in multilingual Arabic script heritage in the context of digital libraries and cataloguing while supporting inclusive digital library development.

Keywords: Arabic Script Dataset · Digital Libraries · Visual Language Models · Arabic OCR · Title pages · Cataloguing pipeline

1 Introduction. The Importance of Digitizing Arabic Cultural Heritage

Within the Humanities, traditional libraries have long maintained the closest ties to informatics and technology. The natural overlap between computer science, information science, and library science has eased the transition from routine catalogue management to collaborative development of innovative digital tools

[8,19]. This synergy is especially evident in libraries and archives that steward historical and religious collections. Because religious-studies scholarship is inherently cross-disciplinary and rests on rich multi-linguistic, multi-alphabetic, and multi-confessional sources, such collections offer an ideal test-bed for digital innovation [1,8,37]. Against this backdrop, the present study draws on the extensive digital book holdings of the Giorgio La Pira Library in Palermo (Fondazione per le Scienze Religiose, FSCIRE), dedicated to Islamic history and doctrines. Two principal donors[1] supplied the core corpus for the *Digital Maktaba* project (hereafter DM), which proposes a state-of-the-art cataloguing methodology tailored to multilingual and multi-alphabetic resources, especially Arabic, Persian, and Azerbaijani, to support librarians with an integrated digital library [12,27,35]. By improving access to these sources, the project ultimately promotes inclusive library practice and helps mitigate the social costs of religious illiteracy [28]. Optical character recognition (OCR) is pivotal to DM and has been explored in our earlier work. Here we report first results from a pipeline that combines Vision-Language Models (VLMs) [10,23] with Google Vision AI to create a *silver-standard* dataset of Arabic-script title-page images and text. In this paper, **silver-standard** denotes OCR that is generated automatically via Google Vision AI after VLM page detection, while **gold-standard** refers to the same OCR after expert verification and correction. Our immediate goal is to assess how well the VLM classifies pages bearing key cataloguing data (frontispiece, index, ISBN), and to generate enriched metadata and OCR dataset that facilitate organisation and retrieval in digital libraries.[2] At present, VLM page classification and Google Vision AI text extraction are complete; a random subset of 500 documents is being manually reviewed to establish the gold-standard reference for future OCR refinement. The final phase will employ this dataset to train an open-source OCR engine such as Kraken [22] within the eScriptorium VRE [33], enabling automated extraction of cataloguing metadata from Arabic printed frontispieces.

1.1 Specific Arabic Script Challenges in the OCR and Title Pages Context

The Arabic script consists of twenty-eight graphemes and has the following marking characteristics: it proceeds from right to left (RtL); it is essentially consonantal as it only transcribes consonants and long vowels ($\bar{a}$, $\bar{\imath}$, $\bar{u}$); consonantal tension (doubling) is not indicated in unvoiced texts; it is cursive because twenty-two of the twenty-eight graphemes link to each other within the word, changing their form according to context (isolated, initial position, middle, final). Short vowels (a, i, u) are written with diacritical marks corresponding to short vowels: a (*fatḥa*), u (*ḍamma*), and i (*kasra*). To indicate that a given consonant is

---

[1] The Specialist Library on Islam and Iran in Qom, University of Religions and Denominations (https://historylib.com/about), and the Prince Ghazi Trust for Qur'ānic Thought (https://www.quranicthought.com/about-us/.)

[2] Code and Dataset can be found at: https://github.com/lucasala1997/DM-LP.

unvoiced, the symbol *sukūn* is placed on the grapheme. To indicate a double consonant the diacritic called *šadda* is used. Those marks are considered as not part of the alphabet [16]. Arabic has regularised the use of matres lectionis, whereby long vowels (ā, ī, ū) are systematically written with consonantal signs respectively *alif, yā', y* and *wāw, w*. Its consonantal system richness led to the adoption of diacritical dots to distinguish so-called homograph consonants (different but of the same sign or spelling) such as: *r* and *z* or *ḍ* and *ṣ*. Homography is one of the main issues with Arabic script [18].

Peculiarities of Arabic OCR in Digital Cataloging and Digital Libraries. OCR systems continue to struggle with non-digitally native texts, particularly in historical and religious domains. These texts often contain unstructured, noisy, and diverse data exposing limitations in current information extraction methods, especially for Arabic script [2,4]. The issue is even more relevant considering OCR's critical role in digitizing and preserving historical corpora [14,34]. Historical Arabic title pages present unique challenges in the OCR context, including varied layouts, vocalizations, calligraphic fonts (e.g., *Nasta'līq, Kūfī*), decorative elements, colored backgrounds, and multiscript content. Additional complications include Unicode inconsistencies (e.g., the *alif maqṣūra* in Arabic and Persian Unicode is encoded differently, though graphically identical), which can hinder accurate cataloging [21]. To address these issues, we treat the title page as part of a broader Frontispiece Pages Group (FPG), a cluster of initial pages containing metadata often presented in varying visual forms. While title pages often feature ornate designs that challenge standard OCR techniques, subsequent FPG pages typically adopt more standardized layouts, improving metadata extraction. From a document analysis perspective, these pages resemble Visually-rich Documents (VrDs), where layout complexity and noise (e.g., stamps, deterioration) complicate processing. Advances in VrD research, including graph-based models and layout-aware datasets [25,29,38], offer promising tools for addressing these challenges.

2 Related Works

Prior work underscores that relatively few digital library projects have tackled this kind of end-to-end automation for Arabic digital books cataloguing. Many earlier efforts to digitize Arabic corpora, such as the famous Shamela[3], ShiaOnline[4], the Open Islamicate Texts Initiative (OpenITI) [30], the KITAB project [3], or the Persian Digital library (PDL) [31] focused primarily on assembling large text corpora. Those projects were fundamental in demonstrating the value of making Arabic texts machine-readable employing OCR solutions such as Kraken for automatic character recognition. However, those projects were not focused primarily on developing a cataloguing tool or automate library cataloguing tasks. For what concerns proper OCR training datasets, in recent times

---

[3] https://shamela.ws/.

[4] http://shiaonlinelibrary.com/.

studies have made significant steps forward. Several dataset were published dealing with different features of both handwritten and printed Arabic text. Some datasets collected documents and Part of Arabic Words (PAWs) [7,11]. The Arabic Printed Text Imagex (APTI) [32] and the Printed Arabic Text Data Base (PATDB) [5] covered words and characters images. Some other datasets focused on segmentation and automatic font identification, such as the Arabic Printed Text Image Dataset/Multi-Font (APTID/MF) [20], the ALTID dataset [15], and the KAFD dataset [26]. More recently, the bilingual dataset with BPTI (Arabic/English) addressed the lack of bilingual datasets [40], the Quran Text Image Dataset (QTID) [9] and the Medina Qur'ān dataset [6]. At the time of writing, no specific dataset has been developed for the analysis of Arabic printed title pages OCR, as well as no attempt in this specific field combined VLMs, OCR and Arabic script in the context of digital libraries and cataloging. At the same time, research on Vision-Language Models (VLMs) has expanded across various fields, including image captioning, visual question answering (VQA), and object recognition [13]. By leveraging large-scale neural networks and extensive datasets, VLMs are capable of interpreting complex images that incorporate text, graphics, and other visual elements [24]. While their application in document analysis is still emerging, VLMs show strong potential for handling mixed-media layouts and intricate document structures. Unlike traditional OCR systems that focus solely on text recognition, VLMs adopt a holistic approach by jointly analyzing visual and textual content. For example, the Qwen2-VL-72B model [10,36,39,41] is designed for multimodal understanding and excels at tasks such as visual context interpretation, making it particularly suited for recognizing text within complex visual contexts, such as title page groups (FPGs). To the best of our knowledge, DM-LP will be the only dataset combining Arabic-script title pages with layout annotations, OCR geometries, and cataloguing-critical metadata (e.g., ISBN).

3 Dataset Creation Pipeline (DigitalMaktaba-Books-v1)

3.1 Data Source and Initial Preparation

The corpus employed in this study originates from a systematic digital acquisition campaign carried out by the Giorgio La Pira Library as part of its long-term commitment to preserve Arabic-script heritage. The 73 200 PDF volumes (around 616 GB) explored here represent the entirety of the second external hard disk (HD 2) donated by the Prince Ghazi Muhammad Trust for Qur'anic thought to the Giorgio La Pira Library (FSCIRE) and to the Digital Maktaba project. The material covers a broad chronological and thematic span from classical Islamic Jurisprudence (fiqh) to modern literature. Prior to any automated processing, incoming files were checked only for PDF structural integrity; no language or genre filters were applied so as to maintain maximal representativeness. Given the size of the collection and the heterogeneous server landscape available to the project, the PDFs were split into four size-balanced sub-corpora (chunk_1-chunk_4). Chunking allowed faster data transfer, parallel execution, simplifies checkpointing, and mitigates the risk of failure on multi-week jobs. Two execution back-ends were employed:

- Trinity–an on-premises NVIDIA DGX A100 appliance featuring 8 × A100-80 GB GPUs and a 64-core AMD EPYC host (FP16 compute, nearly 5 PFLOPS);
- Leonardo–the EuroHPC pre-exascale system at CINECA, Booster partition (4 × A100-64 GB + Intel Ice Lake CPU per node).[5]

Since bibliographical data and informative paratext useful for cataloging purposes are likely to be found in the first and last ten pages of a book, we decided after a check on 100 randomly chosen books, to focus on those groups of pages that hold the most informative content from a cataloguing perspective, i.e., title pages group (here FPG), Index, ISBN code and so on. It is worth noting that random selection may not ensure an equal distribution of data. Therefore, we plan to employ stratified sampling in future work to better capture rarer cases as well. Going back to the pipeline, it converts the PDF pages into PNG images (300 dpi) using a multi-process python script completing the process in 58 500 s (approximatively 16 h) on Trinity, sustaining 1419 pages min I/O throughput for a total amount of 1362160 images. The choice of 300 dpi for image extraction from PDFs reflects an empirical trade-off: it provided visually clear text while keeping image dimensions manageable for downstream processing. Although Qwen-2VL 72B can tokenize high-resolution images up to its 16,384-token visual limit (when enabled via vl_high_resolution_images=True), higher dpi values significantly increase image size and token count. To avoid excessive GPU memory usage and slowdowns, each image was subsequently resized to a maximum of 1024×1024 pixels before being passed to the model.

3.2 Page Classification with Qwen-2VL-72B

Recent advances in large vision-language models (VLMs) make them attractive zero-shot layout classifiers. We adopt Qwen-2VL-72B, the largest member of the Qwen-2VL family, which runs at full precision. In addition to its strong performance on public benchmarks, Qwen-2VL is available under a permissive license, facilitating academic reproducibility.

Prompt-Engineering Strategy. Three prompts were ultimately selected following an iterative design process conducted in collaboration with an Arabic language expert and a professional cataloguer, aimed at maximizing the accuracy of the results on a test subset of 100 books. The prompts were progressively refined based on layout and content considerations, as well as on the outcomes of multiple test iterations, in order to achieve performance improvements. The full prompt texts are provided on the associated GitHub page.

---

[5] See: https://www.hpc.cineca.it.

- **Frontispiece Page Group (FPG) identification**: the prompt is focused on the classification of the title pages, intended as the preferred source of information, building upon the International Standard for Bibliographic Description (ISBD) at its last update [17]. In the same prompt the FPG paradigm previously mentioned, as well as salient visual cues such as ornamental layouts or publisher logos and so forth are convoyed aiming to achieve the best performance possible.
- **Index**: the prompt is designed to search backward from the end of the volume, looking for Arabic and Persian keywords determining the beginning of the Index of contents. The keyword matching is coupled with other visual hints on the indexed layouts such as the presence of a two-column page layout with reading order from right to left with text, a dotted line and a numeral.
- **ISBN**: The script processes pages in an alternating sequence, starting from the first and last pages and progressively moving toward the center. This bidirectional approach continues until a valid ISBN-13 pattern is detected, at which point the execution halts to conserve computational resources.

Moreover, the generation of hyper-parameters were kept constant across clusters (temperature 0.0, top-p 1.0, top-k 50, max_tokens 128). At the same time, batch size was limited to 1000 images to fit within the 70 GB per-GPU memory budget.

3.3 Runtime, Hardware Footprint, and Effectiveness

Table 1 summarises wall-clock runtimes for the first processing chunk. The workflow was executed on *Trinity* and *Leonardo*, with compute-bound VLM stages scheduled on both and all network-bound steps handled on the former.

Table 1. Wall-clock runtimes for the workflow

Tasks	Runtimes
PDF→PNG rasterisation	0.12 s page
Frontispiece, index and ISBN tagging	0.4 s page
Google-Vision OCR	1.8 s page

Accuracy on the 100-book evaluation sample is high across all detection tasks (Table 2); ISBN extraction yielded an (F_1 of 99.5%), with minimal false positives. However, even such high accuracy may lead to cumulative errors at scale; further robustness tests are planned on the full corpus. The slightly lower precision for *Index* pages reflects a cautious bias toward recall: false positives introduce minimal noise, whereas false negatives would omit entire analytical indexes.

Table 2. Zero-shot classification accuracy on our 100-book sample.

Tasks	Precision	Recall	F-1
ISBN	99%	100%	99.5%
FPG	96.5%	93.8%	95.1%
Index	90.1%	97.4%	94%

3.4 OCR with Google Vision AI

For each page flagged as FPG, Index, or ISBN, we invoke Google Cloud Vision's Document OCR endpoint, which returns hierarchical text, bounding boxes' spatial coordinates, and confidence scores in JSON format. Vision AI was selected despite its cost because (i) it supports right-to-left scripts, (ii) it outperforms open-source engines on degraded half-tone scans, and (iii) it exposes bounding geometry critical for downstream layout studies. Batch size is capped at 100 images per request; an adaptive throttle maintains the sustained rate at 1800 images min to comply with quota limits. Each processed page yields four artefacts: the raw JSON, a plain-text dump, an XLSX with geometric metadata, and a PNG overlay for visual audit. Collectively these processing products occupy around 5 TB, hereafter referred to as the "silver-standard" layer, superior to naïve PDF text extraction yet still containing language-specific OCR errors that prevent gold-standard status. Future work will deploy human-in-the-loop correction and use the corrected subset to train an open-source Kraken OCR model through the e-scriptorium VrE to avoid the dependency on proprietary APIs.

3.5 Current Limitations

Several design decisions warrant brief comment. **(i) Duplicate volumes.** Volume-level deduplication has been postponed intentionally to avoid premature exclusion of variant editions. However, we plan to incorporate fuzzy hashing (e.g., SimHash[6]) and content-based clustering once OCR refinement is complete. This will allow us to group and de-duplicate volumes based on normalized textual content and metadata similarity, reducing redundancy in future training and retrieval tasks. **(ii) Vision-AI dependency.** The current reliance on Google Vision AI raises long-term sustainability concerns; the open-source KRAKEN roadmap described above is meant to address this. **(iii) Dissemination platform and licence.** The final hosting venue (Zenodo versus Hugging Face) and licence model (CC BY versus CC BY-NC) are under review and will be settled before submission.

---

[6] https://algonotes.readthedocs.io/en/latest/Simhash.html.

3.6 Reproducibility and Open Science

We will release a complete set of materials to support reproducibility, including: (i) the original PDFs; (ii) the processed outputs from Vision AI (including .xlsx, .json, raw .txt files, and images with annotated bounding boxes); (iii) a tagging file that marks the pages corresponding to each document type (i.e., cover pages, indexes, and ISBN pages); and (iv) the full codebase used to run the experiments.

4 Conclusion

In this paper we presented DigitalMaktaba-Books-v1, a 5-TB "silver-standard" corpus of Arabic front-matter, indexes and ISBN-bearing pages, extracted from more than 73 000 PDF volumes held by the Giorgio La Pira Library. In addition to making the dataset publicly available, we introduced a reproducible pipeline that couples a large vision-language model (Qwen-2VL-72B) with targeted prompt engineering and cloud-scale OCR. The resulting workflow achieves high-accuracy ISBN recognition on the sample set and high F1 scores for both frontispiece and index detection, while remaining practical on mixed GPU/CPU super-computing resources. Beyond the raw data, the contribution includes three domain-specific prompts, batch-parallel scripts for PDF conversion, empty-page filtering, and an ISBN-driven metadata linker that bridges born-digital scans with the library's catalogue. Each component is released under a permissive licence, enabling researchers to replicate, critique and extend our experiments without having to negotiate proprietary bottlenecks. Looking forward, we identify three immediate lines of work. First, we will deduplicate the corpus and curate a gold-standard subset for fine-tuning open-source character recognizers such as Kraken, thereby reducing reliance on commercial OCR. Second, we plan to expand coverage to the 72 417 volumes present in HD 1, applying the same methodology while benchmarking incremental prompt improvements. Third, we will investigate multilingual post-correction models that leverage the enriched MARC metadata to normalise bibliographic entities across scripts and transliteration schemes. Finally, the success of DigitalMaktaba-Books-v1 depends on community engagement. We therefore invite librarians, digital humanists and NLP researchers to contribute corrections, supply additional training data, and experiment with downstream tasks–from citation-index mining to layout-aware pre-training. Together, these collaborative efforts will accelerate progress in Arabic OCR, broaden access to under-digitised textual heritage, and move the field closer to the long-term goal of high-fidelity, open Arabic book corpora.

Acknowledgments. This work was supported by the PNRR project Italian Strengthening of ESFRI RI Resilience (ITSERR) funded by the European Union - NextGenerationEU (CUP:B53C22001770006). We also acknowledge ISCRA for awarding this project access to the LEONARDO supercomputer, owned by the EuroHPC Joint Undertaking, hosted by CINECA (Italy).

References

1. Adams, R.M.: Defining digital pedagogy in theological libraries. In: Anderson, C. (ed.) Digital Humanities and Libraries and Archives in Religious Studies: An Introduction, pp. 111–122. De Gruyter (2022). https://doi.org/10.1515/9783110536539-008
2. Adnan, K., Akbar, R.: Limitations of information extraction methods and techniques for heterogeneous unstructured big data. Int. J. Eng. Bus. Manag. **11**, 1–23 (2019). https://doi.org/10.1177/1847979019890771
3. Aga Khan University, C.: KITAB Project. https://kitab-project.org/blogs
4. Ahmed, M., Abidi, A.: Review on optical character recognition. Int. Res. J. Eng. Technol. (IRJET) **6**(6), 3666–3669 (2019)
5. Al-Hashim, A.G., Mahmoud, S.A.: Printed Arabic text database (PATDB) for research and benchmarking. In: Proceedings of the 9th WSEAS international conference on Applications of computer engineering, ACE'10, pp. 62–68. World Scientific and Engineering Academy and Society (WSEAS), Stevens Point, Wisconsin (2010)
6. Alsheikh, I., Mohd, M.: A quranic dataset for text recognition. In: Proceedings of the 1st International Conference on Informatics, Engineering, Science and Technology, Bandung, Indonesia (2019). https://doi.org/10.4108/eai.18-7-2019.2287842
7. Amara, N.E.B., Mazhoud, O., Bouzrara, N., Ellouze, N.: Arabase: a relational database for arabic ocr systems. Int. Arab J. Inf. Technol. **2**, 259–266 (2005)
8. Anderson, C.: Introduction. In: Anderson, C. (ed.) Digital Humanities and Libraries and Archives in Religious Studies: An Introduction, pp. 1–10. De Gruyter (2022). https://doi.org/10.1515/9783110536539. https://www.degruyter.com/document/doi/10.1515/9783110536539/html
9. Badry, M., Hassan, H., Bayomi, H., Oakasha, H.: QTID: quran text image dataset. Int. J. Adv. Comput. Sci. Appl. (IJACSA) **9**(3), 385–391 (2018). https://doi.org/10.14569/IJACSA.2018.090351. https://thesai.org/Publications/ViewPaper?Volume=9&Issue=3&Code=IJACSA&SerialNo=51
10. Bai, J., et al.: Qwen-VL: a versatile vision-language model for understanding, localization, text reading, and beyond (2023). https://doi.org/10.48550/arXiv.2308.12966. http://arxiv.org/abs/2308.12966
11. Bataineh, B.: A printed paw image database of Arabic language for document analysis and recognition. J. ICT Res. Appl. **11**, 199–211 (2017). https://doi.org/10.5614/itbj.ict.res.appl.2017.11.2.6
12. Bergamaschi, S., et al.: Preserving and conserving culture: first steps towards a knowledge extractor and cataloguer for multilingual and multi-alphabetic heritages. In: Proceedings of the Conference on Information Technology for Social Good, GoodIT '21, pp. 301–304. Association for Computing Machinery, New York (2021). https://doi.org/10.1145/3462203.3475927
13. Chen, Z., et al.: Intern vl: scaling up vision foundation models and aligning for generic visual-linguistic tasks. 2024 IEEE/CVF Conference on Computer Vision and Pattern Recognition (CVPR), pp. 24185–24198 (2023). https://api.semanticscholar.org/CorpusID:266521410
14. Chiron, G., Doucet, A., Coustaty, M., Visani, M., Moreux, J.P.: Impact of OCR errors on the use of digital libraries: towards a better access to information. In: 2017 ACM/IEEE Joint Conference on Digital Libraries (JCDL), pp. 1–4 (2017). https://doi.org/10.1109/JCDL.2017.7991582

15. Chtourou, I., Rouhou, A.C., Jaiem, F.K., Kanoun, S.: ALTID: Arabic/Latin text images database for recognition research. In: 2015 13th International Conference on Document Analysis and Recognition (ICDAR), pp. 836–840. IEEE Computer Society (2015). https://doi.org/10.1109/ICDAR.2015.7333879. https://www.computer.org/csdl/proceedings-article/icdar/2015/07333879/12OmNwB2dXI
16. Durand, O., Langone, A.D., Mion, G.: Corso di arabo contemporaneo. Hoepli, Milano (2010)
17. Escolano Rodríguez, E., et al.: ISBD International Standard Bibliographic Description: 2021 Update to the 2011 Consolidated Edition (2022). https://repository.ifla.org/handle/123456789/1939
18. Garbini, G., Durand, O.: Introduzione alle lingue semitiche. Studi sul Vicino Oriente antico, Paideia (1994)
19. Guerrini, M.: Verso nuovi principi e nuovi codici di catalogazione. Studi Bibliografici, Edizioni Sylvestre Bonnard, Milano (2005). http://archive.org/details/versonuoviprinci0000guer
20. Jaiem, F.K., Kanoun, S., Khemakhem, M., Abed, H., Kardoun, J.: Database for Arabic printed text recognition research. In: Petrosino, A. (ed.) ICIAP 2013. LNCS, vol. 8156, pp. 251–259. Springer, Heidelberg (2013). https://doi.org/10.1007/978-3-642-41181-6_26
21. Kew, J.: Notes on some Unicode Arabic characters: recommendations for usage. Draft 2, SIL (2005). https://static-scripts.sil.org/cms/sites/nrsi/download/arabicletterusagenotes/ArabicLetterUsageNotes.pdf
22. Kiessling, B., Kurin, G., Miller, M.T., Smail, K.: Advances and limitations in open source Arabic-script OCR: a case study. Dig. Stud./Le champ numérique **11**(1) (2021). https://doi.org/10.16995/dscn.8094. http://arxiv.org/abs/2402.10943
23. Liu, H., Li, C., Li, Y., Lee, Y.J.: Improved Baselines with Visual Instruction Tuning (2024). https://doi.org/10.48550/arXiv.2310.03744. http://arxiv.org/abs/2310.03744
24. Liu, H., Li, C., Li, Y., Lee, Y.J.: Improved baselines with visual instruction tuning. In: Proceedings of the IEEE/CVF Conference on Computer Vision and Pattern Recognition (CVPR), pp. 26296–26306 (2024)
25. Liu, X., Gao, F., Zhang, Q., Zhao, H.: Graph Convolution for Multimodal Information Extraction from Visually Rich Documents. In: Loukina, A., Morales, M., Kumar, R. (eds.) Proceedings of the 2019 Conference of the North American Chapter of the Association for Computational Linguistics: Human Language Technologies, vol. 2 (Industry Papers), pp. 32–39. Association for Computational Linguistics, Minneapolis (2019). https://doi.org/10.18653/v1/N19-2005. https://aclanthology.org/N19-2005
26. Luqman, H., Mahmoud, S.A., Awaida, S.: KAFD Arabic font database. Pattern Recogn. **47**(6), 2231–2240 (2014). https://doi.org/10.1016/j.patcog.2013.12.012
27. Martoglia, R., Bergamaschi, S., Ruozzi, F., Vanzini, M., Sala, L., Vigliermo, R.A.: Knowledge extraction, management and long-term preservation of non-Latin cultural heritages - Digital Maktaba project presentation. In: Alessia, B., Alex, F., Stefano, F., Stefano, M., Domenico, R. (eds.) Proceedings of the 19th Conference on Information and Research Science Connecting to Digital and Library Science. CEUR Workshop Proceedings, vol. 3365, pp. 153–161. CEUR, Bari (2023). https://ceur-ws.org/Vol-3365/#short11, iSSN: 1613-0073
28. Naso, P.: Rapporto sull'analfabetismo religioso in italia. In: Melloni, A. (ed.) I costi sociali dell'analfabetismo religioso, pp. 43–57. Il Mulino, Bologna (2014)

29. Nguyen, L., Piwowarski, B., Laborde, J., Moyse, G.: Learning reading order via document layout with Layout2Pos. In: Antonacopoulos, A., et al. (eds.) Linking Theory and Practice of Digital Libraries, pp. 3–19. Springer, Cham (2024). https://doi.org/10.1007/978-3-031-72437-4_1
30. Nigst, L., Romanov, M., Savant, S.B., Seydi, M., Verkinderen, P.: OpenITI: a Machine-Readable Corpus of Islamicate Texts (2023). https://doi.org/10.5281/zenodo.7687795. https://zenodo.org/record/7687795
31. for Persian Studies, R.I.: Persian Digital Library. https://launch.umd.edu/project/907
32. Slimane, F., Ingold, R., Kanoun, S., Alimi, A., Hennebert, J.: A new Arabic printed text image database and evaluation protocols. In: 10th International Conference on Document Analysis and Recognition, Barcelona, Spain, pp. 946–950 (2009). https://doi.org/10.1109/ICDAR.2009.155
33. Stokes, P., Kiessling, B., Stökl Ben Ezra, D., Tissot, R., Gargem, E.: The EScriptorium VRE for manuscript cultures. Classics@ J. Ancient Manus. Virt. Res. Environ. **18** (2021)
34. Sturgeon, D.: Chinese text project: a dynamic digital library of premodern Chinese. Dig. Scholarship Human. **36**(Supplement_1), 101–112 (2021). https://doi.org/10.1093/llc/fqz046. https://doi.org/10.1093/llc/fqz046
35. Sullutrone, G., Vigliermo, R.A., Sala, L., Bergamaschi, S.: Sensitive topics retrieval in digital libraries: a case study of ḥadī collections. In: Antonacopoulos, A., Hinze, A., Piwowarski, B., Coustaty, M., Di Nunzio, G.M., Gelati, F., Vanderschantz, N. (eds.) Linking Theory and Practice of Digital Libraries, pp. 51–62. Springer, Cham (2024). https://doi.org/10.1007/978-3-031-72440-4_5
36. Team, Q.: Qwen-2vl: Open multimodal large model (2024). https://qwen2.org/vl/. Accessed 12 June 2025
37. TheIliffSchoolof Theology, E.H.: Library as interface for digital humanities. In: Anderson, C.B. (ed.) Digital Humanities and Libraries and Archives in Religious Studies: An Introduction, pp. 147–164. De Gruyter (2022). https://doi.org/10.1515/9783110536539-010. https://www.degruyter.com/document/doi/10.1515/9783110536539-010/html
38. Wang, H., Wang, Q., Li, Y., Wang, C., Chu, C., Wang, R.: DocTrack: a visually-rich document dataset really aligned with human eye movement for machine reading (2023). https://doi.org/10.48550/arXiv.2310.14802. http://arxiv.org/abs/2310.14802
39. Wang, P., et al.: Qwen2-VL: enhancing vision-language model's perception of the world at any resolution (2024). https://doi.org/10.48550/arXiv.2409.12191. http://arxiv.org/abs/2409.12191
40. Yahia, M.H., Al-Muhtaseb, H.: Bpti: bilingual (Arabic/English) printed text images dataset for recognition research (2022). https://papers.ssrn.com/sol3/papers.cfm?abstract_id=4007916
41. Yang, A., et al.: Qwen2 Technical Report (2024). https://arxiv.org/abs/2407.10671v4

Sharing is Caring: A Text Alignment Approach for Sharing Annotations of Copyrighted Texts

Frederik Arnold(✉) and Robert Jäschke

Humboldt-Universität zu Berlin, Berlin, Germany
{frederik.arnold,robert.jaeschke}@hu-berlin.de

Abstract. Digital libraries are a crucial infrastructure for researchers to find and access resources. For example, researchers in the digital humanities and computational literary studies make frequent use of digital libraries to access relevant materials, such as text corpora, which they then annotate. These materials are often protected by copyright and are typically released under licensing terms that either prohibit redistribution entirely or impose significant limitations on how they can be shared. We present and evaluate an approach to separate annotations from the underlying text and create a fingerprint, which cannot be used on its own to recreate the original text and can therefore be shared. This fingerprint can be used to merge the separated annotations with another version of the original text. Our framework can easily be adapted to support different file formats and can be integrated into digital libraries to simplify sharing of annotations of copyrighted texts. The code is publicly available under the Apache License 2.0 at https://hu.berlin/sisc.

Keywords: annotation · sharing · open science · digital humanities

1 Introduction

Digital libraries are a vital infrastructure and integral part of modern research, providing platforms to find and access digital resources. In fields such as the digital humanities and (computational) literary studies, digital libraries serve as indispensable tools, granting scholars access to extensive corpora. However, these materials are often subject to copyright restrictions that do not allow redistribution, or only under rather restrictive conditions. This results in a number of complications. First, it makes it more difficult to acquire these materials in the first place, even for research purposes. Second, it makes it more difficult or even impossible to share the results of research efforts, for example, a corpus of annotated texts. The laws governing scholarly use of copyrighted material vary by country. In Germany, for instance, sharing of such material is difficult, even for research purposes. This results in situations where it is impossible to publish reproducible research because the underlying data cannot be shared.

Especially for annotations of textual data, one approach to work around these limitations is *stand-off markup* [7]. This describes the separate storage of content and markup, where the markup references the content by positions, for example, of characters or words. This separation has some advantages over inline markup: The original content is not manipulated, overlapping and multiple annotations are possible, and annotations can be shared without having to provide the underlying content. This is especially useful when copyright prohibits distribution. Although this simplifies sharing annotations of copyrighted content, the original text with the same character positions is needed for meaningful reconstruction. If the receiver of a standoff annotation has access to an identical version of the text, merging is easily possible (see, for example, [17]). Unfortunately, often an identical original is not available and acquisition of the exact same text can be hard or even impossible, since approaches for text extraction (e.g., from PDFs) like optical character recognition (OCR) still produce varying results.

In this work, we present *SisC* (**S**haring **is C**aring),[1] an approach to automatically separate annotations from the underlying text. SisC uses a *fingerprint*, that is, a masked version of the text, to merge stand-off annotations with another version of the original text, for example, extracted from a PDF file. The fingerprint cannot be used on its own to recreate (meaningful parts of) the original text and can therefore, to the best of our knowledge, be shared.

Digital libraries have long been battling with the legal and technical constraints that come with handling materials under copyright restrictions [3,8] and addressing these hurdles is essential for fostering collaboration and open science. With this work, we contribute our tool SisC to help alleviate some of the aforementioned issues. Our focus is not on a particular annotation methodology or format but to create a general framework which works with stand-off and inline annotations and can easily be adapted to different (textual) file formats.

This paper is organized as follows: In Sect. 2, we provide an overview on related work. We then introduce our method in Sect. 3, followed by an evaluation in Sect. 4. We conclude with a discussion in Sect. 5.

2 Related Work

Annotations for textual data can be stored in a variety of file formats (e.g., TXT, CSV, JSON, XML) which are not specific to annotations and only define an abstract structure of the content. To facilitate sharing and collaboration, different annotation formats were developed over time, build on top of the mentioned file formats. For example, CONLL, originally introduced as part of the CONLL-2000 Shared Task [9] grew into a widely used annotation format with a number of variants. TEI XML [15] is another popular format, developed by the Text Encoding Initiative, to provide a set of guidelines for annotating textual data.

Annotations are often realized as inline annotations which comes with the caveat that, without separation of data and annotation, sharing is difficult or

---

[1] The source code is available under the Apache License 2.0 at https://hu.berlin/sisc.

```
<TEI>
  <text>
    <body>
      <p>Some text with <q>an annotated quote</q>.</p>
    </body>
  </text>
</TEI>
```

Listing 1. Example TEI XML with an annotated quote.

impossible in cases where the annotated source is subject to copyright restrictions.

The terms *stand-off markup* and *stand-off annotation* are often used interchangeably and refer to the notion of storing content and markup separately. The idea dates back to the 1990s and an early mention of this concept can be found in [14]. Later, Thompson and McKelvie introduced semantics for hyperlinks for stand-off markup [16]. It is common to use the term stand-off markup to refer to the general concept of storing annotations and text separately, without any restrictions on the form the annotations can have. Sometimes, a stricter definition is used, in which stand-off markup only refers to the case where markup tags are separately stored but still conform to a context-free grammar with a strict hierarchical text structure, see, for example, [10]. Schmidt uses the term *stand-off properties* to refer to a type of stand-off annotation that allows for overlapping annotations. Burghardt and Wolff [4] give an overview over different formats and tools that implement stand-off concepts in various ways.

Derived text formats (DTF) are one approach to handling copyrighted material and sharing information [11,12]. Google N-Grams is an example for a dataset in such a format [5]. However, DTFs only work for cases where the exact text is not relevant, for example, when a term-document-matrix, n-gram counts, or word embeddings, are sufficient. Thus, they are unsuitable for sharing annotated texts.

3 Method

We introduce the overall idea of SisC using the example of the TEI XML file format which is widely used for annotating texts. Our approach works by creating an *exchange TEI XML file* that includes the annotations plus metadata for later alignment with (another version of) the text. Someone (e.g., a researcher or a digital library) who receives that file and has access to the original text can then reconstruct the annotated TEI/XML file.

3.1 Creating the Exchange File

From a TEI XML file with annotations (Listing 1), we create an intermediate TEI XML file (Listing 2) which consists of the original XML tags, but lacks the

```
<TEI>
  <text>
    <body sisc_start="0" sisc_end="36">
      <p sisc_start="1" sisc_end="35">
        <q sisc_start="16" sisc_end="34" />
      </p>
    </body>
  </text>
  <standoff>
  S___ _ex_ ___h __ __no_____ q_____.
  </standoff>
</TEI>
```

Listing 2. The annotated text from Listing 1 represented in our proposed TEI XML exchange format with *uniform* fingerprinting (for $n = 2$ and $d = 5$).

annotated text. Instead, it contains a *fingerprint* which *masks* the annotated text such that it cannot be reconstructed without additional information. During this process, the attributes `sisc_start` and `sisc_end` are added to the XML tags and refer to the start and end character positions of the text in the fingerprint, respectively, which is stored in the `standoff` tag. Prior to the fingerprint creation all XML tags are removed such that the resulting fingerprint only consists of text. This implementation decision was made to have a clear separation of the data handled in the different processing steps. For example, the masking step only works on strings without the need for additional information such as XML tags. This simplifies the addition of support for new file formats.

Properly handling whitespace in XML files is not trivial.[2] Currently, whitespace is preserved in the fingerprint, except around newlines. We plan to support further options in the future.

SisC implements two variants for handling page layout information during fingerprint creation. The first variant, *in-place*, is sufficient for works that consist of running text only. However, the page layout is often more complex and some elements do not follow a linear order. In particular, footnotes appear at the end of pages in a PDF file but might be moved to different positions in the TEI XML file, for example, their anchor positions. To handle such cases, SisC implements a second variant, *move-fn*, which moves footnotes to the end of the pages and makes the order of elements of the fingerprint match the order in the PDF file. This includes handling of footnotes that run over multiple pages. This variant requires that footnotes and page breaks are annotated in the TEI XML file. During processing, we introduce three additional attributes: `sisc_text_start` and `sisc_text_end` are added to the XML tags for footnotes and refer to the start and end character positions of the text in the fingerprint, respectively, after the text is moved to the new position. The attribute `sisc_skip` is added to the

---

[2] https://www.w3.org/TR/xml/#sec-white-space.

```
Running text at the end of a page some header text text on the next page
Ru_____ t___ _t ___ _nd __ _ p___ -----------------_ex_ __ th_ ___t ____
```

Listing 3. Alignment example with superfluous text (highlighted and aligned with a gap ('-') in the fingerprint). The first line shows the text that was extracted from the PDF file and the second line shows the fingerprint.

XML tags for page breaks to store the length of text that needs to be ignored during reconstruction. Specifically, for a footnote which starts on one page and ends on the next page, during fingerprinting that footnote is split and the length of the text between to the two parts needs to be known during reconstruction.

We propose uniform masking, that is to keep n characters every d-th character of the original text and replace characters at other positions. We only replace letter characters with '_' but keep all numbers and punctuation (see Listing 2).

Keeping the placeholder '_' instead of removing characters makes the process more comprehensible and can simplify debugging. When optimizing for (space) efficiency, the placeholder could be compressed (e.g., using run-length encoding).

3.2 Reconstruction of the Annotated Text

From this exchange format, we can reconstruct the original TEI XML if a version of the original text is available, for example, in a PDF file. To automatically extract the text from a PDF, we use pdf2image[3] and tesseract[4] and then align the fingerprint and the text with BioPython.[5] We then use the start and end positions (`sisc_start` and `sisc_end`) to merge the text and the TEI XML file.[6]

Text documents often contain segments, such as headers and footers, that are not necessarily included in their annotated versions. For our use case, such additional text segments need to be removed after alignment, in order to reconstruct the original TEI XML file as accurately as possible. Thus, we remove segments

Table 1. Statistics for the two corpora of annotated scholarly articles.

Literary work	Die Judenbuche	Michael Kohlhaas
Scholarly articles	44	49
Scholarly articles' characters	2 614 061	2 748 559
Footnotes	2 025	2 331
Footnotes' characters	471 027	482 099

---

[3] https://github.com/Belval/pdf2image.
[4] https://github.com/tesseract-ocr/tesseract.
[5] https://biopython.org.
[6] As described in Sect. 3.1, this is the simple case and more XML attributes are used for moved footnotes. More details are in the documentation and source code of SisC.

of text which are longer than 10 characters and are only present in the PDF file. An example is shown in Listing 3. The highlighted text is only present in the PDF file and aligned with a gap ('-') in the fingerprint.

4 Evaluation

4.1 Setup

We evaluate SisC on a dataset of 44 scholarly articles which interpret the novella *Die Judenbuche* by Annette von Droste Hülshoff, and 49 scholarly texts which interpret the novella *Michael Kohlhaas* by Heinrich von Kleist. The texts are in TEI XML format and all direct quotations were manually annotated (i.e., enclosed by <q>...</q>). Footnotes and page breaks are also annotated and the texts of footnotes are moved from the end of the page to their anchor positions. The texts were also manually corrected for OCR errors. The texts in both corpora contain many footnotes which make up around 18% of the text (see Table 1).[7]

These documents represent a typical research corpus for literary studies, with rich annotation of document structure, like paragraphs, section headings, page breaks, and footnotes. We use the corpus in our research project,[8] where we face the challenge of sharing copyrighted literary interpretations, which have been annotated, specifically, with citations to the two above-mentioned novellas.

We assume that the first page of PDF files contains the start of the main text. That is, author and title information may be present but the table of contents and other unrelated content has been removed.

We evaluate how faithfully SisC can reconstruct the original annotated document by measuring the average normalized Levenshtein similarity between the original and the reconstructed text. We set the number of kept characters to $n = 2$ and vary the distance d between 5 and 100 characters in steps of 5. Additionally, we evaluate two variants of our approach. In the first variant (*punct*), which resembles the setting $n = 0$ and $d = \infty$, only punctuation and whitespace characters are kept in the fingerprint but no additional characters. The second variant (*space*) further restricts this to only whitespace characters. All mentioned scenarios are evaluated with moved footnotes (*Move-fn*) and without moved footnotes (*In-place*). For the calculation of the Levenshtein similarity, we only take letter and number characters into account.

4.2 Results

The results in Fig. 1 show that the reconstruction of the TEI XML files works best when the positions of the footnotes in the fingerprint match the positions in the text extracted from a PDF (*Move-fn*). We get consistently high Levenshtein similarity between 0.949 and 0.963, independent of the distance

---

[7] One of the texts from the Judenbuche corpus is excluded from the evaluation, as it is over 200 000 characters long and thus took too long to process using BioPython.
[8] https://hu.berlin/keypassages.

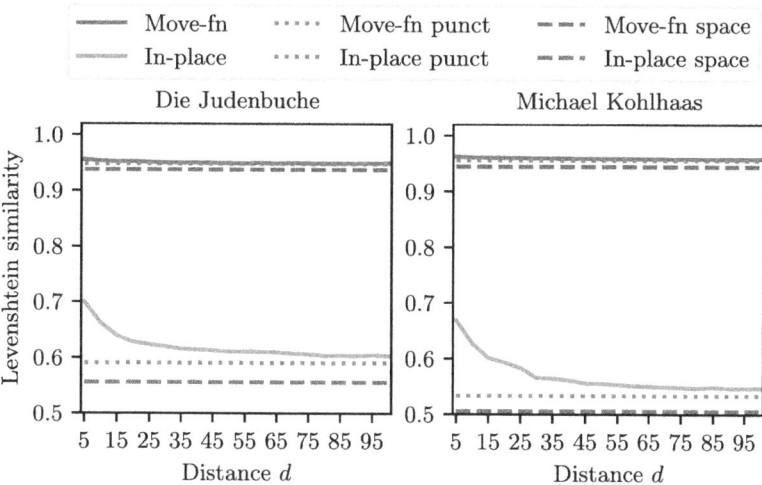

Fig. 1. Normalized Levenshtein similarity for *Die Judenbuche* and *Michael Kohlhaas* with (*Move-fn*) and without (*In-place*) moving footnotes for distances between 5 and 100 and two variants *punct* and *space*.

between unmasked characters. Even keeping only information about the positions of whitespace and punctuation (*punct*) or only whitespace (*space*) in the fingerprint is sufficient to achieve such a high similarity (between 0.938 and 0.956). That is, on average, only 5 characters every 100 characters are misaligned, equivalent to roughly 75 characters per page (assuming 1500 characters per page).

We identified three types of issues that remain. Firstly, general, smaller OCR errors. Secondly, variations between the fingerprint and OCR text due to tables and figures with descriptions. And thirdly, the first page of PDF files often contains a title, authors, date, affiliations, and so on. This can sometimes lead to alignment issues in the beginning of texts.

The results are worse when footnotes are not moved (*In-place*). With $d = 5$, we get a Levenshtein similarity of 0.70 for *Die Judenbuche*. With an increase in distance, the similarity gradually decreases to about 0.62 at $d = 35$, where it levels out and stays the same for larger d. We observe similar behavior for *Michael Kohlhaas*. This shows that there is a clear impact of the distance on the quality of the alignment. This observation is further supported by the performance of *punct* and *space* where we notice that the latter performs the worst.

We conclude that punctuation and whitespace alone already contain a lot of information which can be sufficient for good alignment, specifically in the case of moved footnotes. For the more difficult *In-place* case, we find that punctuation and whitespace characters only contain sufficient information for a certain level of quality of the alignment and that more information improves the alignment.

We also evaluated a second masking approach, where we keep text before and after annotations in a window of 10 characters on both sides and replace the remaining characters. The text of the annotations themselves is also masked. Our original hypothesis was that context masking might help in the *In-place* footnote case and that, even if the whole text cannot be reconstructed, reconstruction of certain annotations which are of special interest might be improved by this masking approach. This turned out not to be the case as this approach generally performed worse.

5 Discussion

We presented SisC, an approach for sharing of annotations of copyrighted texts. Our tool offers parameters to adjust the masking of text to fit personal preferences and specific legal requirements, which can vary by country.

Our evaluation shows that the approach works very well as long as footnotes appear at the same position in the fingerprint as in the PDF file. In our use-case of TEI XML files, which support rearranging the order of running text and footnotes, this is not an issue. But this could be a problem in other scenarios where rearrangement is not possible. The logical solution is to rearrange footnotes during alignment, but this needs information on the page layout of the PDF file.

Variations between the fingerprint and the OCR text due to figures and tables with captions can lead to alignment issues. This did not much impact our results as literary interpretations rarely contain tables or figures. We consider SisC most suitable for fields (like law or literary studies) that frequently annotate texts with infrequent use of tables and figures and whose licenses do not allow redistribution. Texts from other fields might need further development and testing.

Automatic layout detection of PDF files is a hard task in general [1] but recent approaches based on large language models show impressive results in OCR and layout detection tasks, even handling complex layouts [2,6,13,18]. We conducted tests with SpaCy Layout[9] and Mistral OCR[10] but found that both tools cannot reliably handle footnotes. For further details, see the appendix.

Our approach also assumes specific concepts for characters and words. Languages with variations of these concepts (e.g., non-Latin languages such as Chinese, Arabic, or Hindi) might require more sophisticated approaches.

To foster open science, we envision the integration of SisC into digital libraries and research data repositories. Scholars could then upload their annotations to repositories that create and publish exchange files. Repositories could then indicate to researchers that access an annotation, whether their local library has licensed the original work and forward them to its digital library. The digital library then retrieves the annotation from the repository and, using the licensed

---

[9] https://github.com/explosion/spacy-layout.
[10] https://docs.mistral.ai/capabilities/document/.

original text, reconstructs the annotated text. Digital libraries could also subscribe to repositories and show the availability of annotations for the licensed documents they provide and then allow their users to download annotated versions of the documents. Such integrations would take the burden from researchers to handle the processing of files and could foster the sharing of annotations.

Acknowledgments. Parts of this research were funded by the German Research Foundation (DFG) priority programme (SPP) 2207 *Computational Literary Studies* project *Is Expert Knowledge Key? Scholarly Interpretations as Resource for the Analysis of Literary Texts in Computational Literary Studies* (grant no. 424207720) (https://www.projekte.hu-berlin.de/en/schluesselstellen).

Disclosure of Interests. The authors have no competing interests to declare that are relevant to the content of this article.

Appendix: Layout Detection

SpaCy Layout can extract layout including headers, running text, tables, and footnotes but does not link footnotes to their anchor position in the main text. Mistral OCR has similar functionality but does not reliably link footnotes and their anchor positions. The resulting text format often contains an indication of the start of the footer section but no separation between individual footnotes or a link between a footnote's text and its anchor in the running text. Footnote numbers are often marked as superscript but are otherwise not distinguishable from other numbering.

We tested passing the resulting markdown from Mistral OCR to the large language model (LLM) GPT-4.1-mini to extract text from the markdown with the following prompt:

> This is pdf content in markdown:
> <BEGIN_IMAGE_OCR>
> {pdf_ocr_markdown}
> <END_IMAGE_OCR>.
> Convert this into plain text. Include the text of footnotes in the running text surrounded by triple brackets, for example, [[[Text of a footnote]]].

We found that this approach would sometimes work quite well and sometimes the LLM would combine multiple footnotes into one, include that combined footnote in triple brackets in the running text, and then later reference that earlier footnote instead of using the actual footnote text. Considering the recent developments, we conclude that it is only a matter of time until these tools can handle those cases, but at the current time this is beyond the scope of this work.

References

1. Binmakhashen, G.M., Mahmoud, S.A.: Document layout analysis: a comprehensive survey. ACM Comput. Surv. **52**(6) (2019). https://doi.org/10.1145/3355610
2. Blecher, L., Cucurull, G., Scialom, T., Stojnic, R.: Nougat: neural optical understanding for academic documents (2023). arXiv:2308.13418
3. Breemen, V.: Digital libraries under EU copyright law: a relationship set in stone? Eur. Pap. J. Law Integrat. **8**(2), 689–712 (2023)
4. Burghardt, M., Wolff, C.: Stand off-Annotation für Textdokumente: Vom Konzept zur Implementierung (zur Standardisierung?). In: Chiarcos, C., de Castillo, R.E., Stede, M. (eds.) Von der Form zur Bedeutung: Texte automatisch verarbeiten = from form to meaning: processing texts automatically: proceedings of the Biennial GSCL Conference 2009, pp. 53–59. Narr, Tübingen (2009). https://epub.uni-regensburg.de/14223/
5. Goldberg, Y., Orwant, J.: A dataset of syntactic-ngrams over time from a very large corpus of English books. In: Diab, M., Baldwin, T., Baroni, M. (eds.) Second Joint Conference on Lexical and Computational Semantics (*SEM), vol. 1: Proceedings of the Main Conference and the Shared Task: Semantic Textual Similarity, pp. 241–247. Association for Computational Linguistics, Atlanta (2013). https://aclanthology.org/S13-1035/
6. Kim, G., et al.: OCR-free document understanding transformer. In: European Conference on Computer Vision (ECCV). Lecture Notes in Computer Science, vol. 13688, pp. 498–517. Springer, Cham (2022). https://doi.org/10.1007/978-3-031-19815-1_29
7. Klug, H.W.: Stand-off-markup. In: Helmut W. Klug in collaboration with Selina Galka and Elisabeth Steiner in the HRSM project (ed.) KONDE Weißbuch, pp. 453–455 (2021). https://hdl.handle.net/11471/562.50.171
8. Samuelson, P.: Copyright and digital libraries. Commun. ACM **38**(3) (1995)
9. Sang, E.F.T.K., Buchholz, S.: Introduction to the CoNLL-2000 shared task chunking. In: Fourth Conference on Computational Natural Language Learning and the Second Learning Language in Logic Workshop (2000). https://aclanthology.org/W00-0726/
10. Schmidt, D.A.: Using standoff properties for marking-up historical documents in the humanities. it – Inf. Technol. **58**(2), 63–69 (2016). https://doi.org/10.1515/itit-2015-0030
11. Schöch, C., et al.: Abgeleitete Textformate: Prinzip und Beispiele. Recht und Zugang **1**(2) (2020). https://doi.org/10.5771/2699-1284-2020-2-160
12. Schöch, C., et al.: Abgeleitete Textformate: Text und Data Mining mit urheberrechtlich geschützten Textbeständen. Zeitschrift für digitale Geisteswissenschaften (2020). https://doi.org/10.17175/2020_006
13. Shehzadi, T., Stricker, D., Afzal, M.Z.: A hybrid approach for document layout analysis in document images. In: Barney Smith, E.H., Liwicki, M., Peng, L. (eds.) Document Analysis and Recognition - ICDAR 2024, pp. 21–39. Springer, Cham (2024). https://doi.org/10.1007/978-3-031-70546-5_2
14. Souter, C.: Towards a standard format for parsed corpora. Technical Report 93.5, University of Leeds, School of Computer Studies (1993)
15. TEI Consortium, eds.: TEI P5: Guidelines for electronic text encoding and interchange, version 4.4.0 (2022). https://www.tei-c.org/Guidelines/P5/
16. Thompson, H., McKelvie, D.: Hyperlink semantics for standoff markup of read-only documents. In: SGML Europe. Graphical Communications Association (1997)

17. Zehe, A., et al.: Shared task on scene segmentation@KONVENS 2021. In: Proceedings of the Shared Task on Scene Segmentation (2021)
18. Zhong, Z., et al.: A hybrid approach to document layout analysis for heterogeneous document images. In: Fink, G.A., Jain, R., Kise, K., Zanibbi, R. (eds.) Document Analysis and Recognition - ICDAR 2023, pp. 189–206. Springer, Cham (2023). https://doi.org/10.1007/978-3-031-41734-4_12

Tracing the Evolution of Coastal Scientific Literature in Scopus (1970–2023)

Julien Delaunay[1,2(✉)], Marc-Alexis Azaïs[1], Dipendra Sharma Kafle[1], Nicolas Sidere[1], Antoine Doucet[1], and Olivier de Viron[2]

[1] L3i, Univ. La Rochelle, 17000 La Rochelle, France
[2] LIENSs, Univ. La Rochelle, 17000 La Rochelle, France
{julien.delaunay,olivier.deviron}@univ-lr.fr

Abstract. This study examines the evolution of coastal research from 1970 to 2023 using bibliometric analysis of Scopus data. We analyzed publications with "coastal areas" or "littoral" in their titles or abstracts, focusing on trends in research themes. By combining traditional topic modeling with Large Language Models (LLMs), we identified key research domains and tracked their evolution. Our findings reveal a significant increase in publications, particularly since the 2000s. The field has become more interdisciplinary, integrating social sciences and humanities to address complex coastal challenges. This analysis underscores the value of scientometrics in informing policy and research agendas, supporting the development of sustainable coastal management strategies.

Keywords: Scientometrics · Large Language Models · Coastal areas

1 Introduction

The coastline, a dynamic and multifaceted interface encompassing approximately 8% of the Earth's surface, houses many of the world's major metropolises. Currently, over 2 billion individuals reside within 50 km of the coast, with 1 billion living within 10 km, and coastal populations are expanding at a faster rate than those inland [6]. Since the 1960s, coastal areas have evolved into centers of industrial relocation, maritime trade, and urban expansion [2,12]. Yet, this rapid transformation has generated spatial conflicts [9,18], intensified competition over natural resources, and accelerated environmental degradation [1,7,29]. Anthropogenic activities have disrupted natural coastal dynamics, while growing urbanization in hazard-prone zones has increased exposure to extreme events [17]. Global change exacerbates these vulnerabilities, underscoring the pressing need for sustainable coastal governance safeguarding both ecosystems and human communities [4,25].

Given the critical importance of coastal regions and the growing challenges they face, it is imperative to examine how scientific research has engaged with these issues over time. Bibliometrics, defined by Pritchard as "the application of mathematics and statistical methods to books and other media of communication" [20], offers a valuable methodological framework for this purpose. By analyzing the evolution of scientific publications in a multidisciplinary setting, it becomes possible to identify shifts in research priorities and emerging concepts. Such insights can support evidence-based policymaking, inform research agendas, and ultimately contribute to the formulation of more effective and sustainable coastal management strategies.

Scientometric studies on coastal research have covered environmental issues like eutrophication, pollution, blue carbon and climate impacts [8,13,15,23,24,32], as well as social topics such as tourism [22]. Some adopt multidisciplinary angles, focusing on specific ecosystems or national trends [21,26]. These studies remain thematically narrow; to our knowledge, this is the first to take a global, interdisciplinary approach and compare coastal research across domains.

On the other hand, Large Language Models (LLMs) have advanced topic modeling by improving interpretability over methods like Latent Dirichlet Allocation (LDA) [3] and BERTopic [11], generating more meaningful, human-aligned topics [16]. However, without guidance, they may produce generic results in specialized domains [14]. PromptTopic [30] and TopicGPT [19] address this by clustering sentences and using prompts for clearer, domain-relevant topics. These methods are effective in large-scale analyses, such as mapping research library collections [5].

This study examines the evolution of scientific publications from 1970 to 2023, analyzing trends in publication volume and research focus areas of the studies. The analysis utilizes data from Scopus and employs LLM-based topic modeling to identify key research domains.

2 Materials and Methods

2.1 Data Collection

The dataset includes titles, abstracts, ASJC subfields, and publication years of 66,240 articles from Scopus[1] published between 1970 and 2023 and mentioning "coastal area" or "littoral". Data were grouped by decade, with articles linked to ASJC fields and domains via their Scopus subfield keywords.

2.2 Predicting Custom Domains with LLMs

Although ASJC subfields offer high precision, their large number (over 200) makes them impractical for visualizing broad trends in topic evolution. ASJC fields, while fewer in number (70), lack the necessary specificity in environmental sciences to effectively illustrate topic evolution.

To align with our research focus, we defined a set of relevant domains: "Biology", "Ecology", "Geomorphology", "Geology (Others)", "Oceanography", "Sedimentology", "Hydrology", "Climatology/Atmosphere", "Engineering", "Chemistry", "Social Sciences & Humanities", "Policy and Governance",

---

[1] https://www.scopus.com/.

```
SYSTEM PROMPT
You are a highly skilled researcher specializing in oceanography, biology, and Earth sciences, with a strong focus on coastal areas.
Your task is to classify scientific articles into the most relevant predefined domains based on their content. I will provide you with the
list of domains and their definition, and the article title and abstract enclosed in triple backticks. I'll provide you with some examples
of well classified articles.
Your response should identify the domains that most accurately reflect the article's content. You should select the minimum number
of domains, the most precise and relevant. Base your classification strictly on the relevance of the article's title and abstract to the
domain descriptions, not on superficial mentions of terms like "coastal area" or "littoral". Do not prioritize domains or add extra
commentary—simply provide the selected domains in the expected output format. When I say "GO", proceed with the classification.
Domains: - Ecology : The natural science of the relationships among living organisms and their environment...
- Biology : Scientific study of life...
- Ecotoxicology : Study of the effects of toxic chemicals on biological organisms...
...
Output format: Domain 1 | Domain 2                                                          TASK DESCRIPTION
```

```
EXEMPLES:
Exemple 1:
Title:```Coastal paleolandscapes of southern Peru: Implications for Late Pleistocene human settlement```
Abstract: ```Archaeological evidence indicates that initial coastal settlement...```
Output: ```Social Sciences & Humanities```

Exemple 2:
...
                                                                        FEW-SHOT DEMONSTRATION
```

```
GO

Title:```Lidar visualization of the aerosol stratification and the internal boundary layer in the coastal area in case of breeze
circulation```
Abstract: ```This paper presents some results of an elastic-backscattering lidar experiment carried out in the Bulgarian Black
Sea...```
                                                                                 INPUT SENTENCE
```

Fig. 1. An example of a complete prompt without any predefined keywords or LDA-derived topics given.

"Public Health" and "Education", and manually annotated 150 examples in a multilabel setting (one article can have many labels). The annotation process was conducted by an expert in environmental sciences and a PhD student in computer science. A total of 100 examples were double-annotated, yielding Precision, Recall, and F1-score values of 82.33, 78.08, and 80.15, respectively, as measures of inter-annotator agreement. 50 more were then annotated by the PhD student.

Table 1. F1-Score of different strategies based on the number of examples in the prompt

Strategy	Number of examples			
	3	5	7	9
Title + Abstract	58.55	62.08	**62.72**	61.94
Title + LDA + Abstract	57.60	60.43	60.64	59.63
Title + ASJC subfields + Abstract	56.39	59.97	61.47	58.44
Title + LDA + ASJC subfields + Abstract	56.48	61.70	59.79	57.74

We used the Llama-3.1-8B model [10], via HuggingFace[2], to assign domain labels to articles based on titles and abstracts, guided by a few-shot prompt (see Fig. 1, inspired by [28]). To enhance the model's performance, we further experimented with enriching the input by including the ASJC subfields associated with each article, as well as the results of an LDA [3] applied to the combined title and abstract. We observed a relatively high recall (64.7% with no LDA nor ASJC subfields provided) and a low precision (44.01% with the same setting), indicating that while the model identifies relevant domains, it also generates a significant number of false positives. To mitigate this issue, we computed embeddings for the title, abstract, and associated LDA of each article using the all-MiniLM-L6-v2 [31] implementation from HuggingFace[3] and computed the cosine similarity between these embeddings and those of each predicted domain, removing domains with similarity scores below a threshold relative to the highest-scoring domain for the article. This approach significantly improved precision (61.94%), but also reduced recall (56.21%). Additionally, since some ASJC subfields and fields align with our domains, we employed a rule-based method to map potentially missed topics to our articles. Subsequent filtering further enhanced performances (Precision, Recall, and F1-score of 63.33, 62.12 and 62.71 respectively). Table 1 shows the final results for the different strategies, indicating that giving ASJC subfields and LDA actually harm the model performances, making it prone to introduce off-topic predictions coming from the provided ASJC subfields and LDA keywords. While the best performance ("*Title + Abstract*" with 7 examples) is still suboptimal, we further assess the coherence of the classified articles by generating a word cloud for each domain based on the LDA topics inferred from the abstracts. Each word cloud aligns well with the corresponding domain, supporting the validity of the classification. We therefore employed the configuration "*Title + Abstract*" with 7 examples to generate more relevant domains for our dataset.

3 Results

3.1 Publications General Evolution

In this section, we examine how the volume and focus of scientific publications related to coastal areas have evolved over time, to highlight the growing recognition of coastal challenges. We analysed the evolution of the publications throughout the decades, as shown in Fig. 2. Data for the total number of articles in Scopus comes from [27][4]. The analysis indicates an exponential increase in the number of publications over time, both in coastal scientific research and in the overall volume of scientific literature, with a marked surge during the 2000s and a pronounced acceleration throughout the 2010s.

---

[2] https://huggingface.co/meta-llama/Llama-3.1-8B.
[3] https://huggingface.co/sentence-transformers/all-MiniLM-L6-v2.
[4] Data previously made available at : https://figshare.com/articles/dataset/Scopus_1900-2020_Growth_in_articles_abstracts_countries_fields_and_journals/16834198.

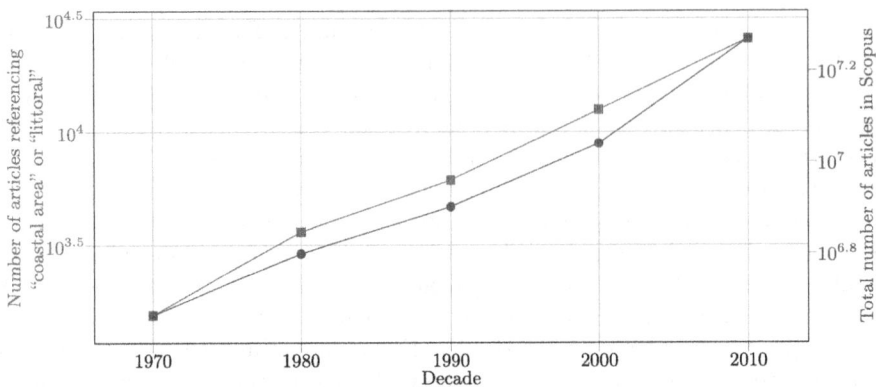

Fig. 2. Temporal evolution of Scopus publications referencing "coastal area" or "littoral" in titles or abstracts, compared to overall publication trends per decade

3.2 ASJC Domains and Fields Evolution

To evaluate the distribution of articles across various research areas and their evolution over time, we aligned the ASJC domains and fields with the subfields defined by Scopus. Subfields are grouped into fields, which are further grouped into top-level domains.

Figure 3 illustrates the temporal evolution of ASJC domains within the Scopus database. Notably, a single article may be linked to multiple ASJC domains or fields. The analysis indicates a marked rise in article numbers across all domains, with the Physical Sciences (PS) and Life Sciences (LS) domains exhibiting the most pronounced growth. The Social Sciences & Humanities (SSH) and Health Sciences (HS) domains also show consistent increases in publication numbers. However, and logically, the PS and LS domains have higher article counts than others. Remarkably, the intersection of PS and SSH is experiencing rapid growth, mirroring the overall trend in SSH, suggesting a growing emphasis on interdisciplinary research, as researchers increasingly recognize the value of integrating diverse perspectives to tackle intricate scientific challenges. While research at the intersection of PS and HS is expanding rapidly, the joint LS and HS intersection shows a less dramatic increase, though it remains substantial, following a trajectory similar to HS alone. Interdisciplinary collaboration is thus more pronounced in fields combining PS with other domains, rather than between LS and HS.

An analysis of the ASJC subject areas reveals that most of the fields common to the study of coastal areas fall within the PS domain. For readability issues, within the LS domain, we only retain the field of Agricultural and Biological Sciences and Immunology, since Pharmacology is very close to Chemical Engineering and knows a similar evolution. Given our focus on coastal areas, the majority of relevant articles are classified under Environmental Science and Earth and Planetary Sciences. This observation underscores the necessity of defining custom domains with a finer granularity, particularly within Environmental Science

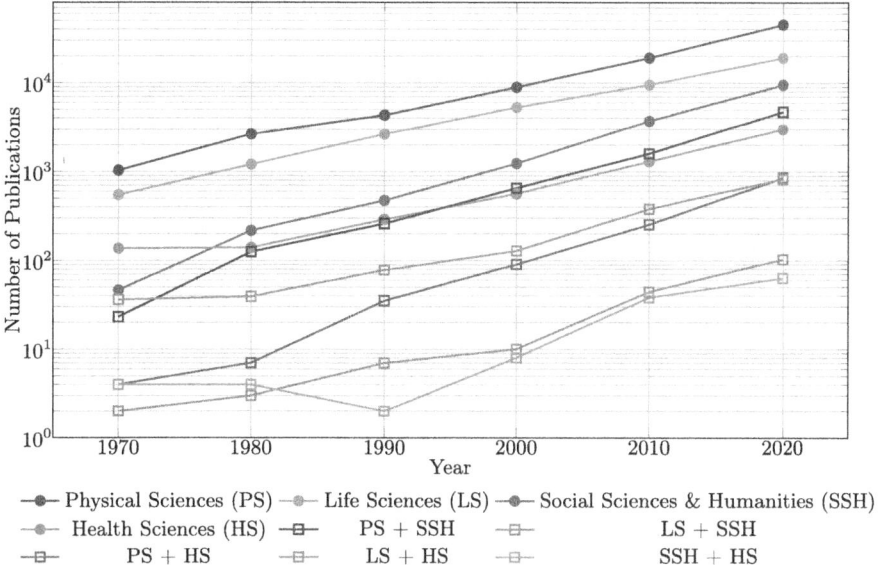

Fig. 3. Evolution of publications over time (log scale)

and Earth and Planetary Sciences, to better align with the specific scope of our research.

Figure 4 illustrates the temporal evolution of selected ASJC fields. All fields exhibit a general upward trend in publication volume, with Decision Sciences emerging in the 2000s, probably corresponding to its creation, and Business and Economics showing strong growth from the 1980s to the present. The corpus is predominantly composed of contributions from Environmental Science, Earth and Planetary Sciences, and Agricultural and Biological Sciences, followed by Engineering and Social Sciences. Notably, Social Sciences have demonstrated substantial growth, particularly during 1970–1980 and 2000–2010, with their publication output approaching that of traditionally dominant natural sciences by the 2010s. In contrast, Engineering has experienced a more modest increase. These trends indicate an interdisciplinary expansion of the research domain, supported by a strong foundation in environmental and earth sciences and increasing contributions from social and decision sciences. This evolution signals a broader shift toward integrating scientific, technical, and societal perspectives to address environmental challenges.

While PS and LS, remain predominant in coastal research, there is a growing trend among researchers to study coastal issues through the lens of social sciences and governance, combined with physical sciences. This shift toward interdisciplinarity, particularly between PS and SSH, reflects a recognition of the need to integrate diverse perspectives to address the complex challenges of coastal areas, signaling a move towards more holistic research methodologies.

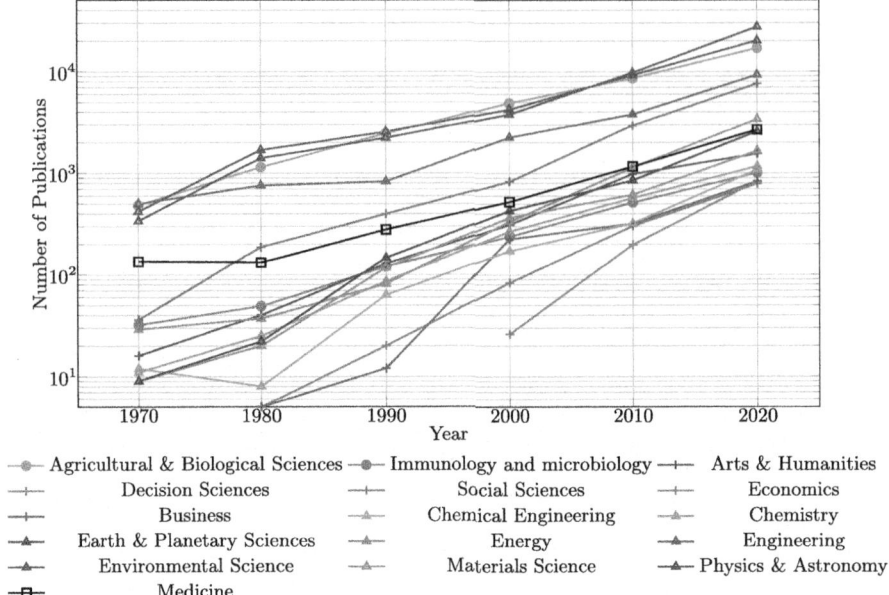

Fig. 4. Evolution of ASJC fields identified as relevant to our scope of study in Scopus database over time (log scale)

3.3 Custom Domains Evolution

Figure 5 shows the growth of publications per decade across hard and social science domains, based on Llama-3.1-8B predictions. All domains have steadily increased since the 1970s. In the formal and natural sciences, Ecology and Biology dominate, followed by Geology, Engineering, and Ecotoxicology. Climatology/Atmosphere shows the sharpest rise, reflecting growing concern over climate change. In the social sciences, Social Sciences & Humanities and Policy and Governance have seen marked growth, rivaling Biology and Geology by the 2010s and projected 2020s. Education has also increased. This convergence signals a notable rise in interdisciplinary research and a stronger integration of social dimensions within environmental studies. This shift highlights rising interdisciplinarity and greater attention to the socio-political aspects of environmental issues like coastal risks, climate adaptation, and sustainability.

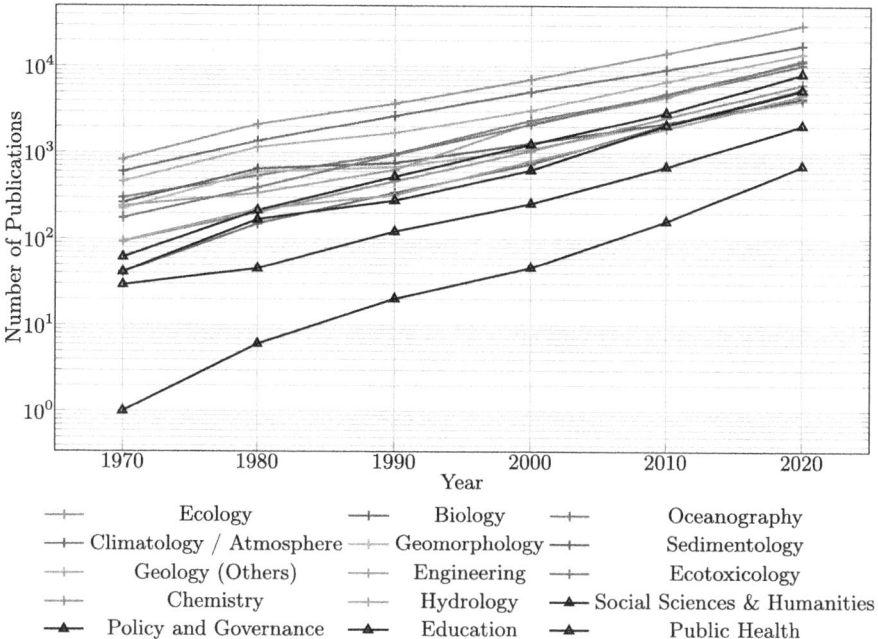

Fig. 5. Evolution of predicted Hard and Social Sciences domains per decade (log scale)

4 Conclusion

This study offers a scientometric analysis of coastal research publications from 1970 to the present, examining trends in publication volume and research themes.

Coastal research output has grown exponentially, especially since the 2000s, outpacing overall scientific publication growth and highlighting the increasing global importance of coastal issues. The field has undergone a notable interdisciplinary expansion, with increasing engagement from the social sciences and humanities. This evolution points to a broader recognition of the socio-political, cultural, and economic dimensions of coastal challenges, and the necessity of integrated, cross-sectoral approaches to address them. Methodologically, the study demonstrates the value of LLM-based topic modeling in revealing human readable research trends and thematic evolutions. However, limitations related to classification precision and recall highlight the need for continued refinement of these tools to enhance their applicability in domain-specific analyses.

Overall, the findings underscore the critical role of scientometric approaches in informing evidence-based policymaking and research prioritization. By tracing the trajectory of coastal research over time, this study contributes to a more informed understanding of the field's development and supports the advancement of more effective and sustainable coastal management strategies.

Acknowledgments. The first author was partly funded by the Nouvelle-Aquitaine Region. This work has also been supported by the TERMITRAD (AAPR2020-2019-8510010) project funded by the Nouvelle-Aquitaine Region, France

Disclosure of Interests. The authors have no competing interests to declare that are relevant to the content of this article.

References

1. Beatley, T.: Protecting biodiversity in coastal environments: introduction and overview. Coast. Manag. **19**(1), 1–19 (1991)
2. Bernhofen, D.M., El-Sahli, Z., Kneller, R.: Estimating the effects of the container revolution on world trade. J. Int. Econ. **98**, 36–50 (2016)
3. Blei, D.M., Ng, A.Y., Jordan, M.I.: Latent Dirichlet allocation. J. Mach. Learn. Res. **3**, 993–1022 (2003)
4. Bongarts Lebbe, T., et al.: Designing coastal adaptation strategies to tackle sea level rise. Front. Mar. Sci. **8**, 740602 (2021)
5. Casey, H.L., Adamou, A., Rodighiero, D.: Mapping techniques for an automated library classification: the case study of library loans at bibliotheca Hertziana. In: International Conference on Theory and Practice of Digital Libraries, pp. 127–143. Springer (2024)
6. Cosby, A., et al.: Accelerating growth of human coastal populations at the global and continent levels: 2000–2018. Sci. Rep. **14**(1), 22489 (2024)
7. Duarte, C.M., et al.: Global loss of coastal habitats: rates, causes and consequences. Fundación BBVA Madrid, Spain (2009)
8. Faiz, H., et al.: A scientometric analysis of heavy metals pollution in coastal areas (2003–2023). In: E3S Web of Conferences, vol. 527, p. 02011. EDP Sciences (2024)
9. Floerl, O., et al.: A global model to forecast coastal hardening and mitigate associated socioecological risks. Nat. Sustain. **4**(12), 1060–1067 (2021)
10. Grattafiori, A., et al.: The llama 3 herd of models. arXiv preprint arXiv:2407.21783 (2024)
11. Grootendorst, M.: BERTopic: neural topic modeling with a class-based TF-IDF procedure. arXiv preprint arXiv:2203.05794 (2022)
12. Hummels, D.: Transportation costs and international trade in the second era of globalization. J. Econ. Perspect. **21**(3), 131–154 (2007)
13. Laino, E., Iglesias, G.: Scientometric review of climate-change extreme impacts on coastal cities. Ocean Coast. Manag. **242**, 106709 (2023)
14. Lam, M.S., Teoh, J., Landay, J.A., Heer, J., Bernstein, M.S.: Concept induction: Analyzing unstructured text with high-level concepts using LLooM. In: Proceedings of the 2024 CHI Conference on Human Factors in Computing Systems, CHI 2024. Association for Computing Machinery, New York (2024). https://doi.org/10.1145/3613904.3642830
15. Leal, K.B., Robaina, L.E.d.S., De Lima, A.d.S.: Coastal impacts of storm surges on a changing climate: a global bibliometric analysis. Nat. Hazards **114**(2), 1455–1476 (2022)
16. Mu, Y., Dong, C., Bontcheva, K., Song, X.: Large language models offer an alternative to the traditional approach of topic modelling. In: Proceedings of the 2024 Joint International Conference on Computational Linguistics, Language Resources and Evaluation (LREC-COLING 2024), pp. 10160–10171 (2024)

17. Neumann, B., Vafeidis, A.T., Zimmermann, J., Nicholls, R.J.: Future coastal population growth and exposure to sea-level rise and coastal flooding - a global assessment. PLOS ONE **10**(3), 1–34 (2015). https://doi.org/10.1371/journal.pone.0118571
18. Notteboom, T., Pallis, A., Rodrigue, J.P.: Port Economics, Management and Policy. Routledge (2022)
19. Pham, C., Hoyle, A., Sun, S., Resnik, P., Iyyer, M.: TopicGPT: a prompt-based topic modeling framework. In: Proceedings of the 2024 Conference of the North American Chapter of the Association for Computational Linguistics: Human Language Technologies (Volume 1: Long Papers), pp. 2956–2984 (2024)
20. Pritchard, A.: Statistical bibliography or bibliometrics. J. Doc. **25**, 348 (1969)
21. Rhomad, H., Khalil, K., Elkalay, K.: Trends and hot spots of coastal science in moroccan atlantic coast: a bibliometric analysis. Environ. Dev. Sustain. **26**(6), 13807–13830 (2024)
22. Sharafuddin, M.A., Madhavan, M.: Thematic evolution of blue tourism: a scientometric analysis and systematic review. Glob. Bus. Rev. **25**(2), 533–554 (2024)
23. Sun, J., Ni, J., Ho, Y.S.: Scientometric analysis of coastal eutrophication research during the period of 1993 to 2008. Environ. Dev. Sustain. **13**, 353–366 (2011)
24. Sun, Y., Zhang, H., Lin, Q., Zhang, C., He, C., Zheng, H.: Exploring the international research landscape of blue carbon: based on scientometrics analysis. Ocean Coast. Manag. **252**, 107106 (2024)
25. Taherkhani, M., Vitousek, S., Barnard, P.L., Frazer, N., Anderson, T.R., Fletcher, C.H.: Sea-level rise exponentially increases coastal flood frequency. Sci. Rep. **10**(1), 6466 (2020)
26. Thattai, D., Rangarajan, S., Rajan, R.J., Rajan, L.J.: Mangrove literature from 2000 to 2019-a scientometric analysis of scopus records. J. Sci. Res. **11**(3), 458–468 (2023)
27. Thelwall, M., Sud, P.: Scopus 1900–2020: growth in articles, abstracts, countries, fields, and journals. Quant. Sci. Stud. **3**(1), 37–50 (2022)
28. Tran, H.T.H., González-Gallardo, C.E., Delaunay, J., Doucet, A., Pollak, S.: Is prompting what term extraction needs? In: International Conference on Text, Speech, and Dialogue, pp. 17–29. Springer (2024)
29. Virtanen, E.A., Kallio, N., Nurmi, M., Jernberg, S., Saikkonen, L., Forsblom, L.: Recreational land use contributes to the loss of marine biodiversity. People Nature **6**(5), 1758–1773 (2024)
30. Wang, H., Prakash, N., Hoang, N.K., Hee, M.S., Naseem, U., Lee, R.K.W.: Prompting large language models for topic modeling. In: 2023 IEEE International Conference on Big Data (BigData), pp. 1236–1241 (2023). https://doi.org/10.1109/BigData59044.2023.10386113
31. Wang, W., Wei, F., Dong, L., Bao, H., Yang, N., Zhou, M.: MiniLM: deep self-attention distillation for task-agnostic compression of pre-trained transformers. Adv. Neural. Inf. Process. Syst. **33**, 5776–5788 (2020)
32. Zhang, W., Qian, W., Ho, Y.S.: A bibliometric analysis of research related to ocean circulation. Scientometrics **80**, 305–316 (2009)

On Recommending Fair Influential Scholars with Geographically Diverse Impact

Arpan Dam[1](✉), Sayan Pathak[2], and Bivas Mitra[1]

[1] Indian Institute of Technology, Kharagpur, India
arpand@kgpian.iitkgp.ac.in, bivas@cse.iitkgp.ac.in
[2] Microsoft AI and Research, Redmond, WA, USA
sayanpa@microsoft.com

Abstract. Citation-based metrics dominate academic evaluation in scientometrics but often favor researchers from well-represented regions, reinforcing systemic biases in scientific recognition. To address this challenge, we introduce a fairness-aware influence maximization framework for scientometrics, identifying top-k influential authors in citation networks by considering both the number of distinct citing authors and the geographic diversity of these authors. We introduce a multi-task learning model, *Fair2Cite*, that jointly learns embeddings of influencers and followers, accurately estimating influence probabilities while capturing latent behavioral traits. These embeddings help in the construction of a bipartite graph, enabling the selection of fair and impactful influencers via the Independent Cascade model. Experiments on scientometric dataset demonstrate that our method outperforms state-of-the-art baselines in influence spread and achieves a more balanced citation distribution across global regions. Our framework promotes an inclusive academic ecosystem by recognizing diverse contributions beyond traditional metrics.

Keywords: Scientometrics · Influence · Fairness · Embeddings

1 Introduction

In scientometrics, influential authors are defined as the scholars, whose articles are cited by a large number of other researchers, indicating their intellectual impact and visibility within the academic community [2]. Identifying such authors is important for a variety of downstream applications, including expert recommendation, funding allocation, and shaping the direction of scientific research [22]. However, measuring influence of an author is challenging. First of all, not all citations carry equal importance. A citation from a high-prestige journal is arguably more impactful than one from a lesser-known venue. Thus, influence should depend not just on the number of citing authors (followers), but also on the prestige and quality of those citations. Secondly, the influence capacity of an influencer may vary widely among her followers [4], depending on the total number of (direct and indirect) citations she received from them. While prior works [5,23] have used metrics like PageRank or the h-index to identify influential authors, these approaches do not capture latent relationships between influencers and their diverse followers.

Close inspection of the scientometrics dataset reveals two classes of influencers (i) fair influencers, whose articles receive citations equitably distributed across diverse geographic regions (say, North America, Europe, China, Asia-Pacific etc.), in contrast to (ii) unfair influencers, whose impact remains concentrated within a few geographic regions only (say, in North America). These fair influencers are often interdisciplinary, as their work engages multiple fields and attracts attention from diverse geographic regions. However, our pilot study reveals that despite their vital role in connecting research communities and disciplines, fair influencers are consistently under-represented in leadership positions. Unfair influencers rely on their tightly-knit academic networks, often formed through highly concentrated citations within specific geographic regions, which in turn reinforce their leadership role. Unlike prior work that treated geographic bias [6,8,13,15,16] and leadership gaps [7,17] in isolation, we demonstrate that researchers with fair, geographically diverse influence face systematic exclusion from leadership roles, despite their comparable academic impact. This highlights the need to identify and recommend the fair influencers, so that their contributions can be appropriately rewarded and leveraged to strengthen the global research ecosystem. Although fairness-aware methods [11,12] have emerged, they often rely on historical citation logs and overlook the latent influence capacity among scholars.

In this paper, we propose *Fair2Cite*, a framework that recommends the top-k fair influential authors who can (i) maximize the total number of influenced scholars, and (ii) ensure a fair geographic distribution of these scholars across diverse geographical regions. At its core, *Fair2Cite* employs a multi layer neural model that learns embeddings for both influencers and their followers to accurately estimate influence capacity, while simultaneously preserving fairness aware properties, specifically the receipt of citations from a geographically diverse set of authors. Experimental results on a large-scale scientometrics dataset show that *Fair2Cite* outperforms existing baselines in terms of both influence spread (measured by the proportion of citing authors) and fairness (measured by the geographic diversity of citations).

2 Motivational Study and Problem Statement

We utilize a scientometrics dataset [1] comprising approximately 316,782 research articles, each annotated with the first and last authors along with their institutional affiliations. The country of origin for each article is determined based on the institutional affiliations of both the first and last authors [18]. The dataset includes around 200355 unique authors. Author name disambiguation has been achieved through OpenAlex. We focus our study on five geographic regions, defined based on citation volume, the number of contributing countries, and geographic location. These regions are: **North America** (including the United States and Canada), **Europe**, **China**, **Asia-Pacific** (excluding China), **South America**, and **Africa**.

2.1 Influential Authors in Scientometrics

We define influential authors as researchers who publish at the top journals and conferences (ranked by their Article Influence Score (AIS) [21])), and demonstrates high impact in terms of receiving direct and indirect citations (designated as *followers*). We construct a ranked list of authors U_C in terms of followers where each $u_i \in U_C$ is treated as a potential influencer. To capture the scope of influence for each u_i, we define their follower set as F_{u_i}, which includes all authors who have cited the work of u_i, either directly or indirectly through citation chains. Specifically, an author is considered a follower of u_i if they have cited at least one article authored by u_i, either themselves or through a transitive path in the citation network. For instance, if u_i is cited by u_2, and u_2's work is subsequently cited by u_3, then both u_2 and u_3 are included in F_{u_i}. Thus, in this example, $F_{u_i} = \{u_2, u_3\}$. By considering both direct and indirect citations, we aim to construct a more holistic representation of academic influence, as prior work has shown that scholarly ideas often propagate through extended citation chains [5,23]. In the following, we conduct a few pilot studies to demonstrate the challenges of detecting influential authors.

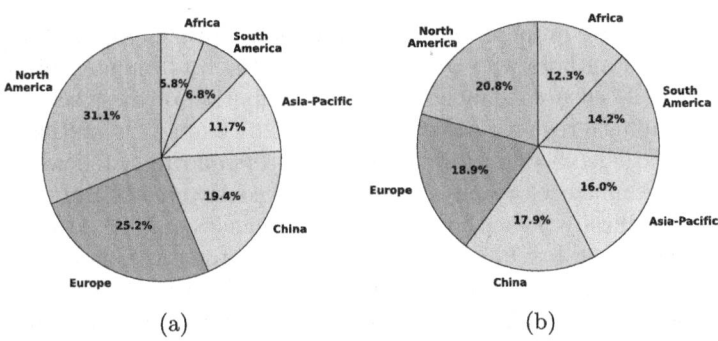

Fig. 1. Contrast in citation geography: Unfair influencers (left) exhibit concentrated citations from North America, Europe, and China (combined 75%) while Fair influencers (right) show balanced regional citation shares

2.2 Presence of Various Kinds of Influencers

We handpicked 20 influential authors exhibiting similar research proficiency (all publishing articles in top 15 journals, ranked by their Article Influence Score

(AIS) [21]), and demonstrating similar research impact in terms of followers. We examined the geographic distribution of citations received by articles published by each author, categorizing citations by region (e.g., North America, Europe, China, and others). In Fig 1, we show two categories of authors; the first category of authors receive citations proportionally across various geographic regions, reflecting equitable global engagement. On the other hand, the second category of authors exhibits concentrated citation, where over 75% of citations received from just three regions (North America, Europe, and China), with minimal representation from other parts of the world. We define the first category of authors as fair influencers, whose work is cited broadly across geographic boundaries, and the second category as unfair influencers whose impact is regionally constrained, despite comparable research impact.

2.3 Disparities in Academic Leadership Among Influential Authors

Next, we investigate how fair and unfair influential authors benefit from their roles in professional academic leadership. We define leadership roles as positions such as conference program chairs, journal editorial board members, and conference organizers. We collected data from the publicly available profiles of fair and unfair influencers and found that fair influencers held 3.7 positions on average, compared to 6.7 for unfair influencers. Our analysis reveals that unfair influential authors held nearly twice as many leadership roles on average compared to fair influencers ($p < 0.01$). A closer inspection suggests that this advantage arises from their tightly-knit academic networks, often formed through highly concentrated citations within specific geographic regions, which in turn reinforce their visibility and academic leadership. In contrast, fair influencers demonstrated significantly greater interdisciplinary reach, with 54% of their citations coming from blended articles spanning multiple research domains ($p < 0.01$), compared to only 32% for unfair influencers. However, despite publishing in top-tier journals and achieving broader interdisciplinary and geographic impact, fair influencers remain under-represented in formal academic leadership positions.

2.4 Problem Statement

Our pilot study highlights a critical gap in current academic reward systems, which tend to prioritize monolithic influence emphasizing localized and high-volume citations over geographically diverse scholarly engagement. Existing recommendation systems often overlook the equitable yet diverse impact of fair influential authors, unintentionally penalizing them in their career for their lower visibility within specific geographic regions. To address this imbalance, we aim to propose *Fair2Cite*, a novel framework designed to recommend the top-k fair influential authors, who can (i) maximize the total influenced scholars, and (ii) ensure fair distribution of influenced scholars across various geographic regions. It is important to recognize that an author's influence is not solely determined by the count of direct and indirect citations. Rather, the magnitude of influence depends on the (i) quality of the citing article, and (ii) it varies across different followers as well, making it crucial to accurately estimate the individual impact an author has on each follower. $Fair2Cite$ leverages these follower specific influence capacity estimations, while promoting geographic fairness, to generate more balanced and inclusive recommendations of influential authors.

3 Development of $Fair2Cite$

In the development of $Fair2Cite$, our first step is to identify potential influential authors (U_C) – those whose articles have received citations. We then construct their follower sets (F_{u_i}), capturing both direct and indirect citations, to reflect how their ideas propagate through the network. Next, we illustrate two important components of $Fair2Cite$ namely (i) quantifying fairness to characterize the fair influencers and (ii) quantifying the influence capacity that one influential author exerts on her followers. Details are provided below.

3.1 Quantifying Fairness of Each Potential Influencer

We compute a fairness score for each potential influencer $u_i \in U_C$ to assess how equitably their work is cited across major global regions. A higher score indicates broader geographic reach and more balanced international impact. Citations are categorized into five geo-regions based on geographic location and citation patterns, as defined in Sect. 2. For each region r, the fairness ratio is defined as $F_r = \frac{V_r}{E_r}$, where V_r is the number of citations to influencer u_i's articles from region r, and E_r is the total number of citations made by authors from that region. In case of collaborative articles, we assign 0.5 weight each to the first and last author's regions while computing V_r and E_r. An ideally fair influencer would have equal F_r values across all regions. We define fairness score of u_i as $f_{u_i} = \frac{2}{1+\exp\left(\frac{\sigma}{\mu}\right)}$ where σ and μ measures standard deviation and mean of $\{F_r\}$ across all regions r. A fairness score closer to 1 reflects a geographically balanced influence, while lower values indicate citation concentration in specific regions.

3.2 Quantifying Influence Capacity of Each Potential Influencer

We design a multi-task learning (MTL) model[1] to jointly learn embeddings of potential influencers and their followers while integrating fairness into the training process. To penalize citation unfairness, we down-sample each influencer's follower set F_{u_i} based on their fairness score f_{u_i}, retaining only $|F_{u_i}| \times f_{u_i}$ followers. This ensures that unfair influencers are assigned fewer influenced followers. Down-sampling prioritizes followers closer to influencer u_i by hop distance, as they are more likely to represent genuine influence. Let $F_{u_i}^s = \{y_1, y_2, \ldots, y_m\}$ denote the resulting sampled follower set of u_i. The MTL model is illustrated in Fig. 2. The MTL model takes as input a one-hot encoded vector x_{u_i} of the influencer u_i, where the input dimension is $|U_C|$, the total number of potential

---

[1] Code available at: https://github.com/ArpanDam/Citation_fair_influence.

influencers. The model consists of a shared embedding layer $\mathbf{M} \in \mathbb{R}^{|U_C| \times E}$, where E is the embedding dimension (set to 50), and two task-specific layers. The first task-specific layer, $\mathbf{I} \in \mathbb{R}^{E \times N}$, is responsible for predicting the followers of u_i, where N is the total number of authors in the dataset. The second task specific layer, $\mathbf{F} \in \mathbb{R}^{E \times 1}$, is used to predict the fairness score f_{u_i} of the influencer.

The embedding of influencer u_i is obtained from the shared layer $\mathbf{M}$, and the embedding of each follower y_j is derived from the follower-specific layer $\mathbf{I}$. To predict the followers $F^s_{u_i} = \{y_1, y_2, \ldots, y_m\}$, we apply the sigmoid activation function σ at the output layer and treat this as a multi-label classification problem. We use a weighted binary cross-entropy [20] loss L_e of influencer u_i for this task:

$$L_e = - \sum_{y_1 \in \text{all authors}} w_{u_i, y_1} [y_{u_i, y_1} \log(q_{u_i, y_1}) + (1 - y_{u_i, y_1}) \log(1 - q_{u_i, y_1})] \quad (1)$$

Here, q_{u_i, y_1} denotes the predicted probability output by the model during training. To reflect citation quality, we incorporate journal prestige into the weight w_{u_i, y_j} using the Article Influence Score (AIS) [21] of the citing journal. The weight is defined as:

$$w_{u_i, y_1} = \left(\frac{\sum_{c \in C_{y_1 \to u_i}} \frac{\text{AIS}(c)}{\text{AIS}_{\max}}}{T_{u_i}} \right) \cdot \log(1 + |C_{y_1 \to u_i}|)$$

where $C_{y_1 \to u_i}$ is the set of citations from y_1 to u_i, and T_{u_i} is the total number of articles by u_i. This formulation accounts for both proportional engagement and the quality of scholarly recognition. The log term reflects citation volume with diminishing returns. Additionally, by normalizing with the total number of publications T_{u_i}, it emphasizes influencers who achieve higher impact per article, assigning greater weight to those whose limited publications garner substantial recognition.

For fairness score regression, we use the Mean Squared Error (MSE) loss L_m. The overall loss function is defined as $L = L_e + L_m$. After training, we obtain embeddings for all influencers and their followers. We compute the probability of influence between influencer u_i and a follower y_j using the dot product of their embeddings followed by a sigmoid transformation. Let M_{u_i} denote the embedding of influencer u_i, and I_{y_j} denote the embedding of follower y_j. The influence capacity of u_i is then given by $p_{u_i, y_j} = \sigma(M_{u_i}^\top I_{y_j})$ where p_{u_i, y_j} represents the probability that u_i influences y_j. This formulation integrates both influence likelihood and fairness into a unified embedding space.

3.3 Recommending Top-k Fair Influencers

After computing the influence probabilities p_{u_i, y_j} between each potential influencer $u_i \in U_C$ and their respective followers $y_j \in F_{u_i}$, we construct a directed bipartite graph $G(U_C, F_{u_i}, E)$. The two partitions of this graph consist of the set of potential influencers U_C and their follower sets F_{u_i}. Directed edges are

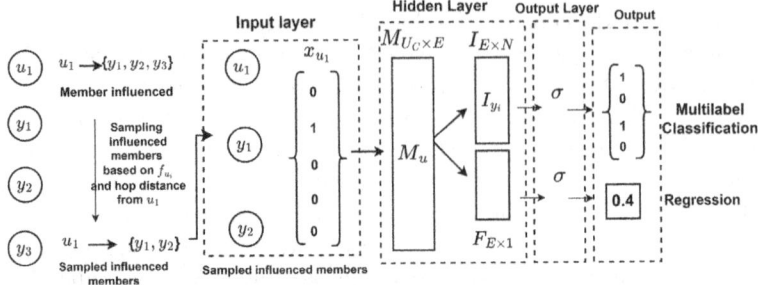

Fig. 2. Multi-Task Learning (MTL) Model for Predicting Influenced Population and Fairness Score. The model takes a potential influencer author u_1 and predicts both the set of influenced authors $F^s_{u_1} = \{y_1, y_2\}$, representing a subset of u_1's potential followers $\{y_1, y_2, y_3\}$, and the fairness score $f_{u_1} = 0.4$.

formed from each influencer $u_i \in U_C$ to their followers $y_j \in F_{u_i}$, with each edge weighted by the influence probability p_{u_i, y_j} obtained from the multi-task learning model. Since our MTL model explicitly penalizes unfair influencers during training by down-sampling their followers based on the fairness score, the resulting embeddings incorporate a fairness-aware characteristics. Consequently, unfair influencers are assigned lower influence probabilities, thereby reducing their potential to dominate influence selection based solely on raw connectivity. To identify the most impactful and fair influencers, we apply the Independent Cascade (IC) model [10] for 1000 simulations, on the bipartite graph G. For each influencer u_i, we simulate the influence spread over their follower set using the edge weights p_{u_i, y_j} as activation probabilities. We then recommend the top k influencers $I_k \subseteq U_C$ that yield the highest expected influence spread under the IC model. This approach ensures that the selected influencers not only have high reach but also demonstrate equitable citation visibility across regions. Thus, our framework promotes fairness without compromising on influence capacity.

4 Experimental Setup and Evaluation

4.1 Experiment Setup

We evaluated *Fair2Cite* on the scientometrics dataset [1] comprising approximately 316,782 research articles, each annotated with the first and last authors along with their institutional affiliations. The dataset includes the publication year of each article, allowing us to partition it into a training period (2000–2010) and a testing period (2010–2013). Using the training set, we compute influence probabilities between influencers and followers, and construct a bipartite graph to identify the top-k influencers. We then evaluated these top-k influencers on the test set. We evaluate the top-k influencers by counting the number of distinct authors in the test period who cite their articles, directly or through citation chains. This measures the real-world propagation of influence beyond the training window. We use the following performance metric to evaluate our algorithm:

(1) Quantifying Influence: This metric measures the percentage of authors who were influenced by recommended influencers, directly or indirectly. A higher influenced population indicates broader scholarly reach, reflecting multi-hop influence propagation.

(2) Quantifying Fairness: We measure fairness as $F = 1 - G$, where Gini index [9] G quantifies the inequality in the distribution of influence among geographic regions and is calculated as $G = 1 - \sum_{r=1}^{n}(X_r + X_{r-1})(W_r - W_{r-1})$. X_r denotes the cumulative proportion of citations (influenced population) up to region r, and W_r represents the corresponding cumulative proportion of the total number of citations from region r. Here, $X_0 = 0$ and $W_0 = 0$. A lower Gini index indicates a more equitable distribution of influence across regions while a higher index reflects concentration of influence in certain regions.

Baseline Algorithms: (a) *ABRIS-T* [14], which uses attribute-aware reverse sampling [3] for fairness. (b) *SetSOGWO* [19] a gray wolf optimization method maximizing minimax fairness and (c) *Crosswalk* [11], a random-walk approach that reweights edges for fairness.

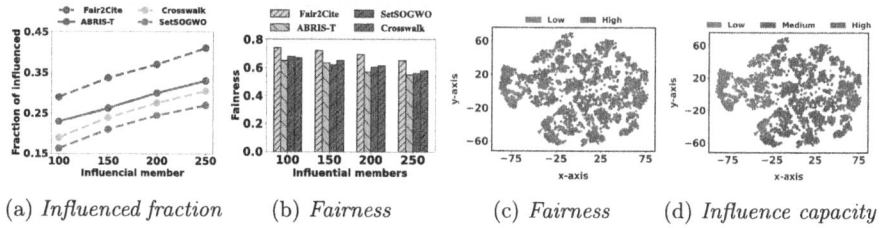

(a) *Influenced fraction* (b) *Fairness* (c) *Fairness* (d) *Influence capacity*

Fig. 3. (a)(b) *Fair2Cite* outperforms the baselines in terms of fraction of influenced and fairness. (c)(d) Plot showing *Fair2Cite* shows good clustering of embeddings in terms of fairness and influence spread.

4.2 Evaluation

(a) Evaluating Influence: Figure 3a plots the fraction of influenced population against the number of recommended influencers (k). As the number of influencers increases along the x-axis, the fraction of the influenced population representing the proportion of authors citing these influencers rises correspondingly.

(b) Evaluating Fairness: Figure 3b depicts the fairness, along the y-axis, compared to the number of recommended influencers (k). Figure 3a and Fig. 3b demonstrate that *Fair2cite* outperforms the baseline methods by achieving a higher fraction of the influenced population and promoting a more equitable distribution of influence across geographic regions.

Fair2Cite outperforms Crosswalk [11], which may miss critical bridge edges connecting communities due to its random walk approach, leading to lower-quality influencer selection. Similarly, *ABRIS-T* [14] focuses on covering attribute-grouped RR sets, overlooking structurally vital nodes, and its single scalar objective can overly penalize total influence for fairness. In contrast, $Fair2Cite$ balances these goals, selecting high-impact influencers while promoting fairness.

(c) Embedding Quality: Figure 3cd visualize the learned embeddings of influential authors. Figure 3c shows the clustering of influencer embeddings with respect to fairness scores (low: ≤ 0.5, high: > 0.5), confirming $Fair2Cite$ captures fairness-related traits of influencers. Figure 3d shows that embeddings of influencers with similar capacity are clustered together, demonstrating that embeddings also capture influence dynamics. These patterns confirm that our model learns representations that reflect both fairness and influence capacity.

5 Conclusion

This paper tackles the challenge of recommending fair influential authors in scientometrics, who may influence scholars from diverse geographical regions. We proposed $Fair2Cite$ which relies on a multi-task learning model to jointly learn embeddings of influencers and followers to correctly estimate the influence capacities, while ensuring fairness in citation across geographic regions. Experimental results show that $Fair2Cite$ achieves superior performance over baselines in terms of both influence spread and fairness, validating its ability to effectively learn meaningful embeddings and model influence dynamics.

Acknowledgement. This work has been partially supported by the DST-SERB funded project with grant number CRG/2021/005316.

References

1. Academic citation dataset. https://www.kaggle.com/datasets/kmader/aminer-academic-citation-dataset
2. Bibi, F., Khan, H.U., Iqbal, T., Farooq, M., Mehmood, I., Nam, Y.: Ranking authors in an academic network using social network measures. Appl. Sci. **8**(10), 1824 (2018)
3. Borgs, C., Brautbar, M., Chayes, J., Lucier, B.: Maximizing social influence in nearly optimal time. In: ACM-SIAM (2014)
4. Dam, A., Kumar, S., Bhattacharjee, D., Pathak, S., Mitra, B.: Topic aware influential member detection in meetup. In: ACM/SAC (2023)
5. Ding, Y., Yan, E., Frazho, A., Caverlee, J.: Pagerank for ranking authors in co-citation networks. J. Am. Soc. Inform. Sci. Technol. **60**(11), 2229–2243 (2009)
6. Fortunato, S., Bergstrom, C.T., et al.: Science of science. Science **359**(6379) (2018)
7. Girod, S., et al.: Reducing implicit gender leadership bias in academic medicine with an educational intervention. Acad. Med. **91**(8), 1143–1150 (2016)
8. Gomez, C.J., Herman, A.C., Parigi, P.: Leading countries in global science increasingly receive more citations than other countries doing similar research. Nat. Hum. Behav. **6**(7), 919–929 (2022)

9. Gong, H., Guo, C.: Influence maximization considering fairness: a multi-objective optimization approach with prior knowledge. Expert Syst. Appl. **214**, 119138 (2023)
10. Kempe, D., Kleinberg, J., Tardos, É.: Maximizing the spread of influence through a social network. In: ACM SIGKDD (2003)
11. Khajehnejad, A., Khajehnejad, M., Babaei, M., Gummadi, K.P., Weller, A., Mirzasoleiman, B.: Crosswalk: fairness-enhanced node representation learning. In: AAAI (2022)
12. Khajehnejad, M., Rezaei, A.A., Babaei, M., Hoffmann, J., Jalili, M., Weller, A.: Adversarial graph embeddings for fair influence maximization over social networks. arXiv preprint arXiv:2005.04074 (2020)
13. Larivière, V., Haustein, S., Mongeon, P.: The oligopoly of academic publishers in the digital era. PLoS ONE **10**(6), e0127502 (2015)
14. Lin, M., et al.: Fair influence maximization in large-scale social networks based on attribute-aware reverse influence sampling. J. Artif. Intell. Res. **76**, 925–957 (2023)
15. Nielsen, M.W., Andersen, J.P.: Global citation inequality is on the rise. Proc. Natl. Acad. Sci. **118**(7) (2021)
16. Pan, R.K., Kaski, K., Fortunato, S.: World citation and collaboration networks: uncovering the role of geography in science. Sci. Rep. **2**(1), 902 (2012)
17. Pingleton, S.K., Jones, E.V., Rosolowski, T.A., Zimmerman, M.K.: Silent bias: challenges, obstacles, and strategies for leadership development in academic medicine-lessons from oral histories of women professors at the university of kansas. Acad. Med. **91**(8), 1151–1157 (2016)
18. Ray, K.S., Zurn, P., Dworkin, J.D., Bassett, D.S., Resnik, D.B.: Citation bias, diversity, and ethics. Account. Res. **31**(2), 158–172 (2024)
19. Razaghi, B., Roayaei, M., Charkari, N.M.: On the group-fairness-aware influence maximization in social networks. TCSS (2022)
20. Wu, T., Huang, Q., Liu, Z., Wang, Yu., Lin, D.: Distribution-balanced loss for multi-label classification in long-tailed datasets. In: Vedaldi, A., Bischof, H., Brox, T., Frahm, J.-M. (eds.) ECCV 2020. LNCS, vol. 12349, pp. 162–178. Springer, Cham (2020). https://doi.org/10.1007/978-3-030-58548-8_10
21. Yan, E., Ding, Y.: Weighted citation: an indicator of an article's prestige. J. Am. Soc. Inform. Sci. Technol. **61**(8), 1635–1643 (2010)
22. Yan, E., Ding, Y.: Discovering author impact: a pagerank perspective. Inf. Process. Manage. **47**(1), 125–134 (2011)
23. Zhu, X., Turney, P., Lemire, D., Vellino, A.: Measuring academic influence: not all citations are equal. J. Am. Soc. Inf. Sci. **66**(2), 408–427 (2015)

Ranking to Learn: Human Experts, Search Engines, or LLMs for Learning Guidance

Yasin Ghafourian[1,2](✉) , Allan Hanbury[2] , and Petr Knoth[3]

[1] Research Studios Austria FG, 1090 Vienna, Austria
yasin.ghafourian@researchstudio.at
[2] Technische Universität Wien (TU Wien), 1040 Vienna, Austria
[3] Knowledge Media Institute, The Open University, Milton Keynes, UK

Abstract. Search engines and LLMs are increasingly being used in learning contexts to find and access learning resources. While conventional ranking mechanisms in general-purpose search engines are based on *topical relevance*, in learning contexts, *pedagogical suitability* plays a crucial role in addressing learners' information needs, i.e. how well a resource supports a learner in expanding their knowledge within a specific context. This paper conducts an empirical study, investigating how search engine rankings and LLM rankings compare to those of human experts and learners to determine which ranking approach best supports learning. Using statistical methods, we analyze agreement across rankings collected from seven experts, 60 learners, and five LLMs over four topics. Results show that LLM rankings align more closely with expert judgments than with search engines or learners. Both experts and LLMs exhibit moderate internal agreement but differ notably from search engine rankings, indicating that conventional search engines are not optimized for pedagogical effectiveness.

Keywords: Information Retrieval · User Study · Ranking · Large Language Models · Search Engines

1 Introduction

The internet offers vast learning resources—from scholarly articles and e-books to online courses and digital tools—which newer generations increasingly rely on for education [1]. General-purpose search engines have been the most used choice for students and researchers, thanks to their speed of retrieval and instant access to diverse learning materials [2–4]. However, selecting suitable materials remains challenging [5,6], as search engines typically rank by topical relevance, which does not always ensure pedagogical suitability for individual learners. This raises the question: How effectively do information retrieval systems assist learners in bringing pedagogically suitable resources to the top of the relevant ranked list?

Meanwhile, the emergence of Large Language Models (LLMs) has attracted researchers to study their potential to provide personalized learning experiences by analyzing learner knowledge and tailoring responses [7]. Jeon et al. [8] have investigated how LLMs can function as teaching assistants and evaluators in an educational setting. While both search engines and LLMs are widely used for learning, which offers better support in selecting the most suitable learning resources?

Furthermore, how do they compare to pedagogical rankings (which we define below) curated by human experts and learners themselves? Can we quantify these differences to understand their pedagogical impact?

To investigate these questions, in this paper, we focus on pedagogical ranking—the process of ordering educational resources based on their suitability for learning effectiveness, rather than purely on search relevance. Pedagogical ranking factors in content understandability and learner knowledge levels, ensuring that ranked content facilitates meaningful learning rather than just matching search intent. We call this task ranking to learn. More specifically, we look at:

Research Question. How do search engines, humans (experts & learners), and LLMs compare in terms of effectiveness with respect to pedagogical ranking of learning resources?

The study by Ghafourian et al. [9] has shown that search engine rankings have a limitation when ranking based on pedagogy. To investigate this in more detail our study involves obtaining rankings from human experts and LLMs, and comparing them with the rankings from Google and human learners for the same collection of web pages using a dataset from Ghafourian et al. [9]. This allows us to evaluate whether the LLMs and Google are suitable systems for customizing information presentations to learners with varying knowledge levels. We asked seven subject-matter experts—qualified professionals in COVID-19 and financial literacy that are the topics in the used dataset—to re-rank the web pages for each learner in descending order of pedagogical suitability, prioritizing those that best matched the learner's knowledge level. Details on expert backgrounds and recruitment appear in Sect. 2.2. In parallel, we hypothesized that LLMs could simulate expert judgment and instructed five LLMs to perform the same task.

2 Methodology

In this section, we describe our methodology used to evaluate and compare the pedagogical suitability of rankings provided by search engines, LLMs, human experts, and learners. We first present the dataset, followed by describing the process of involving human experts to provide pedagogically informed rankings for sampled learners. Finally, we explain how LLMs were prompted to simulate experts by modeling learner knowledge and ranking resources accordingly.

2.1 Dataset, Search Engine, and Learners

We use the dataset from Ghafourian et al. [9], which was created to evaluate how learners perceive resource relevance across multiple dimensions and how well general-purpose search engines support learning. Google, the most widely used search engine, was used in their study and serves as our representative. The authors conducted experiments in four learning domains—COVID-19, Financial Literacy, General Theory of Relativity, and World War 2—where online participants (referred to as learners) were shown 10 search result pages (SERP) and asked to rank them based on topical relevance, understandability, and engagement. The dataset includes both these learner-assigned rankings and the original Google rankings (from March 2023), enabling direct comparison. Learners also completed a short quiz beforehand to assess their subject knowledge. Both web resource content and learner knowledge were captured at the same point in time. Using these synchronized snapshots ensures that temporal dynamics do not compromise the validity of our findings. For the purposes of this study, we selected 60 learners from the four subject areas using stratified sampling, maintaining a balanced sample of 15 learners per subject with varying knowledge levels.

2.2 Human Experts

For our experiment with human experts, we could enlist the expertise of seven qualified professionals in two of the four subject areas: COVID-19 and Financial Literacy, whom we refer to as subject experts. Their participation has been on a voluntary basis. Yuan and Recker [10] have shown that individuals with advanced degrees will also develop evaluation skills comparable to those of trained educators through experience, indicating that non-teachers with sufficient expertise might assess educational resources similarly to teachers. Table 1 presents a summary of our experts' qualifications and the time spent by them on the task.

Table 1. Experts' Qualifications and Time Spent on Task by Subject Area

Expert Number	Subject Area	Degree	Time Spent (hours)
1	**Financial Literacy**	Post Doc (Economics)	1
2	**Financial Literacy**	Master's (Finance)	1.5
3	**Financial Literacy**	Master's (Economics)	2
4	**Financial Literacy**	MBA	2
5	**COVID-19**	Medical Doctor	2
6	**COVID-19**	Medical Doctor	2.5
7	**COVID-19**	Medical Doctor	3.5

In each subject, our experts studied the 15 sampled learners' quiz results and re-ranked the pages in descending order of pedagogical value, based on how well each page matched the learner's knowledge level and supported topic learning.

2.3 Large Language Models as Subject Experts

As the Large Language Models are being widely used by researchers and students, we have further progressed to evaluate whether LLMs can model learners' knowledge and recommend web resources in a ranking tailored to each learner's knowledge level. For this purpose, we have instructed five different LLMs to take on the role of an expert. These models are: Gemini 1.5 Flash and Gemini 1.5 Pro[1] from Google, as well as GPT-4, GPT-4o, and GPT-4o Mini from OpenAI[2].

We selected these models because, at the time of the experiment, they represented the latest advancements and supported web browsing, allowing them to access full webpage content—similar to how human experts viewed the linked pages. Although prompt design can affect LLM performance, we intentionally used a consistent, single prompt structure across all models. Our goal was not fine-tune prompts for performance but to assess how closely these models align with expert judgments when given identical instructions for pedagogical ranking.

Obtaining personalized rankings for the learners using each LLM model consisted of two phases: 1) learner profiling, through which learners' knowledge was

---

Instruction for knowledge model Generation

"You have designed the following test to assess people's general knowledge about COVID-19. Below is your "Test" and after that, under the section "Correct Answers for the questions in the test" you will see the correct answer to each question. Now users are going to give you their answers to the questions of the test. Based on their answers, assess the extent of their knowledge. Then create a knowledge model for each user that will represent their knowledge about COVID-19. This knowledge model should represent the user's strengths and areas that they need to improve"

Fig. 1. System instruction provided to the LLMs to generate a knowledge model based on learner test results given as a prompt.

Instruction for ranking according to the knowledge model

"You are a medical professor. You know the following list of webpages are useful for learners who want to expand their knowledge about COVID-19. First, read the webpages to get an understanding of what concepts and topics are covered in each webpage:
[Webpages number, title, and their links]
Now you will be presented with a learner's knowledge model. The knowledge model will give you an approximate assessment of how much the learner knows about Covid -19. For the learner, consider his\her knowledge model and rank the web pages from the most suitable webpage to the least suitable one for extending their knowledge about Covid-19. Print the ranking in the format " Rank X: Webpage number/web page title" "

Fig. 2. System instruction provided to the LLMs to re-rank web pages based on a learner's knowledge model, which is given as a prompt.

---

[1] https://aistudio.google.com/.
[2] https://platform.openai.com/.

assessed, and 2) reading the webpages and ranking each individual. A new LLM session was initiated in each phase and for each learner to avoid cross-user data bias in the LLM. In the first phase, the LLM was provided with quiz questions, correct answers, and each learner's responses to build a knowledge model representing the learner's extent of knowledge. Figure 1 shows the instruction used for this phase's prompts. We did not specify a particular structure for the output knowledge model, yet all the LLMs used followed a consistent pattern in most cases: (A) an analysis of the learner's test results, (B) identifying areas of strength, and (C) areas for improvement. Figure 3a presents an excerpt of the Knowledge Model output from Google Gemini for one of the sampled learners.

In the second phase, the LLM was prompted to assume the role of a domain expert and was provided with webpage links. Figure 2 shows the instruction given to LLMs for this phase's prompts. Using the knowledge model generated for each learner in the first phase, the LLM was then tasked with ranking the pages from most to least suitable for enhancing that learner's knowledge. Figure 3b presents an excerpt from Gemini's ranks for the same respondent of the first phase.

3 Results

This section presents our empirical results, starting with an analysis of internal agreement within the human expert and LLM groups to evaluate how their pedagogical rankings align across topics and learners. We then explore the degree of alignment across experts, LLMs, learners, and SERP, assessing the potential of LLMs and search engines to provide expert-level pedagogical rankings.

3.1 Agreement Among Human Experts and LLMs

As a first step, we have measured the level of agreement on pedagogical rankings for each topic among human experts and among LLMs. Although we only have expert rankings for COVID-19 and Financial Literacy topics, the strong connection and moderate agreement observed between human experts and between LLMs in these two domains prompted us to investigate whether similar patterns would emerge as well in the other two subject areas in experiments with LLMs.

To quantify this agreement across multiple rankings, we employed Kendall's Coefficient of Concordance (W) [11,12], and Spearman's Rank Correlation Coefficient (ρ) [13]. For each learner, the values W and ρ (since ρ is pairwise, its aggregated value is the average between pairs of experts or pairs of LLMs) are calculated and then averaged across all learners to obtain a representative indicator of agreement. We also calculated the p-value by comparing Kendall's W value to a chi-square distribution with 9 degrees of freedom (i.e. the number of web pages minus 1) to determine for how many learners the experts' rankings (or the LLMs' rankings) exhibit a statistically significant level of agreement. Tables 2 and 3 summarize the results for experts and the LLMs respectively. As observed in these tables, the human experts and LLMs have demonstrated a fair to moderate agreement among themselves in the subject areas.

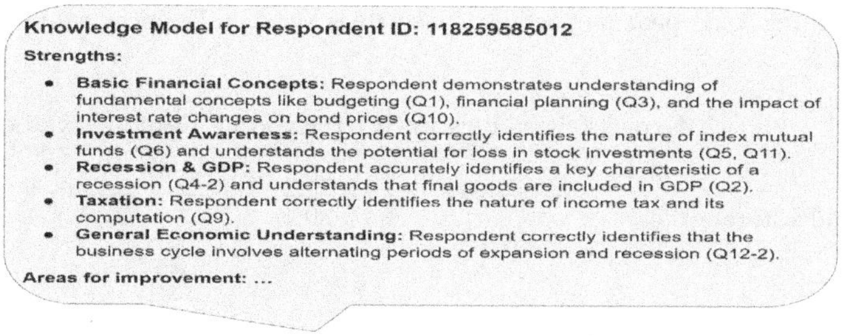

(a) A sample excerpt from phase 1: Knowledge model generation for a specific learner

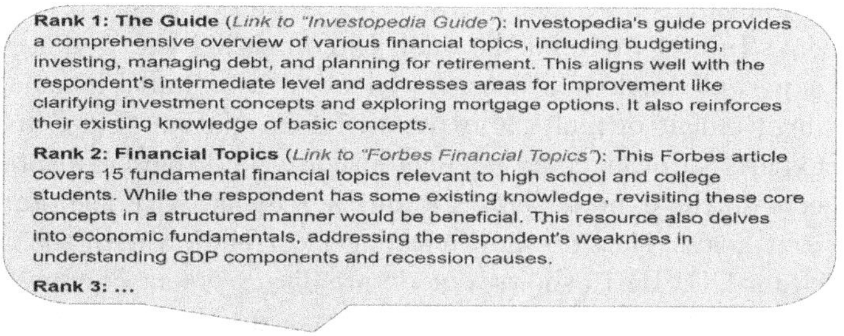

(b) A sample excerpt from phase 2: Ranking generation for the same learner

Fig. 3. An instance from LLMs' responses taken from Google Gemini

3.2 Comparative Analysis of Rankings Provided by Human Experts, LLMS, Search Engine and Learners

To address our research question, we analyzed the extent to which the rankings provided by different agents in this study—human experts, large language models (LLMs), Google, and the learners—align or differ from one another. This was done by calculating Spearman's rank correlation between the rankings assigned

Table 2. Quantification of experts' agreements using Kendall and Spearman Coefficients

Subject	Kendall's Concordance Coefficient	#Learners for whom experts' provided rankings have a statistically significant correlation	Spearman's Coefficient
COVID-19	0.67	11 (out of 15)	0.50
Financial Literacy	0.38	5 (out of 15)	0.18

Table 3. Quantification of LLMs' agreements using Kendall and Spearman Coefficients

Subject	Kendall's Concordance Coefficient	#Learners for whom LLMs' provided rankings have a statistically significant correlation	Spearman's Coefficient
COVID-19	0.58	14 (out of 15)	0.47
Financial Literacy	0.66	15 (out of 15)	0.59
Relativity	0.45	11 (out of 15)	0.32
World War 2	0.35	6 (out of 15)	0.19

Table 4. Aggregated Spearman correlations values between Experts' rankings, SERP's and learners'

Domain	Experts' Rankings vs SERP	Experts' Rankings vs Learners'
COVID-19	−0.45	0.14
Financial Literacy	0.4	0.1

by each pair of agents. Specifically, for each learner in the study, the Spearman coefficient was computed between the rankings provided by the agents, and these correlation values were then averaged across all learners to provide an overall assessment. Table 4 presents the analysis comparing the rankings provided by human experts, Google, and learners for COVID-19 and Financial Literacy. Given the involvement of multiple experts, the correlation values are averaged across the experts to produce an aggregate score. As Table 4 indicates, in none of the subjects do the experts show a strong agreement with the rankings from learners. Nevertheless, they do show a stronger correlation with the rankings of SERP, which for COVID-19 shows a moderate disagreement of experts with the rankings on the SERP and for financial literacy a moderate agreement.

Table 5. Comparison of alignment between LLMs, learners, and search engines using aggregated values of Spearman's correlation coefficient

Agents	COVID-19		Financial Literacy		Relativity		World War 2	
	Learners	SERP	Learners	SERP	Learners	SERP	Learners	SERP
Gemini Flash	0.05	0.07	0.13	0.70	0.0	−0.24	−0.28	0.33
Gemini Pro	−0.15	0.04	0.16	0.71	0.0	−0.35	−0.16	0.42
GPT4	−0.12	0.09	0.17	0.53	0.08	−0.33	−0.42	−0.21
GPT4Omni	−0.15	0.00	0.18	0.55	0.0	−0.17	−0.06	0.16
GPT4o-Mini	−0.24	0.17	0.19	0.54	0.0	−0.15	0.01	0.125

Similarly, we utilized Spearman's correlation to analyze how the web page rankings generated by LLMs in each subject area for each learner compare with rankings from Google, human experts (for COVID-19 and financial literacy), and the learners themselves. Table 5 shows the result of this analysis for Learners and SERP rankings compared to LLMs, and Table 6 presents the result for all rankings compared to human experts as the ground truth. By assuming that expert annotations represent the most accurate judgments among the available agents (Table 6), we can assess the effectiveness of large language models (LLMs), search engines, and learners in terms of their ranking performance. As we can see across Tables 5 and 6, LLMs tend to agree more with experts than with learners when they are prompted to re-rank according to learners' knowledge level. At the same time, we can see the effect of personalization by diverging more from SERP rankings in more complex and abstract topics such as COVID-19 or Relativity.

Table 6. Aggregated Spearman correlation values between rankings from SERP, learners, and LLMs, and those of human experts on COVID-19 and Financial Literacy.

		Learners	SERP	Gemini Flash	Gemini Pro	GPT4	GPT4 Omni	GPT4 o-Mini
Human Experts	COVID-19	0.14	−0.45	0.11	0.19	0.04	0.06	0.11
	Financial Literacy	0.1	0.4	0.24	0.29	0.21	0.22	0.29

In the domain of financial literacy, Ghafourian et al. [9] found that learners were relatively more knowledgeable in this area than in other domains. Additionally, Table 4 shows that experts moderately agree with SERP rankings in this topic ($\rho = 0.4$), suggesting that in this case the search engine's ranking was pedagogically sound, which may explain why learners' preferred rankings in this topic showed a moderate positive correlation with the SERP, with $\rho = 0.45$. Finally, as shown in Table 5, LLMs exhibit moderate to strong alignment with SERP in financial literacy. These findings suggest that when learners possess a baseline understanding of a topic and the SERP rankings are pedagogically appropriate (as demonstrated by high agreement with experts - Table 4), then LLMs tend to also be more aligned with search engine outputs.

4 Discussions and Limitations

Table 5 shows that LLM-generated rankings diverge from both learner and SERP rankings. This can be explained by the multidimensional nature of relevance [14,15]. When experts and LLMs prioritize suitability for learning based on knowledge levels in addition to the criteria used by SERP, the rankings shift. These observations don't provide enough evidence to conclude that experts and LLMs view general-purpose search engine rankings as suitable for the learners.

The lack of correlation between experts/LLMs rankings and those of learners can be traced to two patterns. In some cases, both learners and experts (LLMs) assign similar average rankings to specific web pages, suggesting agreement on web page's place in the ranking. However, for some other web pages, the average rankings by learners differ greatly from those of experts (LLMs). This may stem from limited subject knowledge, which makes it difficult for learners to identify appropriate resources. For example, a learner might favor oversimplified or overly complex material due to misjudging their learning needs. Experts, by contrast, would recommend resources that better support knowledge growth.

This behaviour can partly be attributed to confirmation bias in the learners [16,17], which is a form of cognitive bias [18]. In this context, confirmation bias manifests in learners' resource selection, where they may gravitate toward content that aligns with their existing perspectives or knowledge. This can reinforce prior knowledge, reduce exposure to new ideas, and give a false sense of mastery, undermining their ability to choose the most effective learning resources.

Our study does, however, have some limitations. We compare non-personalized search engine rankings (i.e., Google) with personalized LLM and expert rankings. Moreover, LLMs, being generative, may produce different knowledge model outputs for the same learner. We did not analyze how such variability influences subsequent rankings or how prompt variations affect performance. Our design fixed the prompts to isolate model behavior rather than optimize it, leaving this as a future research direction.

5 Conclusion

The objective of this research was to explore the effectiveness of different agents- human experts, LLMs, search engines, and learners- on the task of ranking learning content. To our knowledge, it is the first comparative study to evaluate these different agents in terms of pedagogical suitability. We have enlisted seven human experts who have collectively spent 14 h on a sample of 30 participants in the two subject areas of COVID-19 and Financial Literacy. We also evaluated five state-of-the-art LLMs simulating human expert judgments in all four subjects and for all 60 sampled participants. Our results showed that human experts and LLMs have a moderate degree of agreement across topics among themselves, while we know from the study that created the dataset that the agreement between human learners was not substantial. Our findings also showed that Google's rankings do not align well with expert judgments, indicating that general-purpose search engines are not optimized for pedagogical suitability. On the other hand LLMs, such as GPT-4 and Gemini, demonstrate a higher correlation in the provided rankings with human experts than human experts with learners. This shows promise for the use of LLMs as tutors and instructors in personalized education. Nevertheless, we have not seen evidence suggesting that the rankings provided by Google, LLMs nor the experts could mimic the rankings provided by the learners. Assuming that the rankings provided by human experts are of the best quality (given their time and diligence in ranking based on learners' knowledge as well as their internal consistency) it can be expected that LLMs cannot yet support the learners to the extent that a human expert can.

References

1. Szymkowiak, A., Melović, B., Dabić, M., Jeganathan, K., Kundi, G.S.: Information technology and gen Z: the role of teachers, the internet, and technology in the education of young people. Technol. Soc. **65**, 101565 (2021). https://doi.org/10.1016/j.techsoc.2021.101565. ISSN 0160-791X
2. Apuke, O.D., Iyendo, T.O.: University students' usage of the internet resources for research and learning: forms of access and perceptions of utility. Heliyon **4**(12), e01052 (2018)
3. Purdy, J.P.: Why first-year college students select online research resources as their favorite. First Monday (2012)

4. Salehi, S., Du, J.T., Ashman, H.: Use of web search engines and personalisation in information searching for educational purposes. Inf. Res. Int. Electron. J. **23**(2) (2018)
5. Head, A.J., Eisenberg, M.B.: What today's college students say about conducting research in the digital age. Proj. Inf. Lit. Progr. Rep. **4**(7) (2009)
6. Lee, S.S., Tay, S.M., Balakrishnan, A., Yeo, S.P., Samarasekera, D.D.: Mobile learning in clinical settings: unveiling the paradox. Korean J. Med. Educ. **33**(4), 349 (2021)
7. García-Méndez, S., de Arriba-Pérez, F., del Carmen Somoza-López, M.: A review on the use of large language models as virtual tutors. Sci. Educ., 1–16 (2024)
8. Jeon, J., Lee, S.: Large language models in education: a focus on the complementary relationship between human teachers and chatgpt. Educ. Inf. Technol. **28**(12), 15873–15892 (2023)
9. Ghafourian, Y., Hanbury, A., Knoth, P.: Ranking for learning: studying users' perceptions of relevance, understandability, and engagement. In: International Conference on Theory and Practice of Digital Libraries, pp. 284–291. Springer (2023)
10. Yuan, M., Recker, M.: Does audience matter? comparing teachers' and non-teachers' application and perception of quality rubrics for evaluating open educational resources. Educ. Tech. Res. Dev. **67**, 39–61 (2019)
11. Kendall, M.G., Smith, B.B.: The problem of m rankings. Ann. Math. Stat. **10**(3), 275–287 (1939)
12. Landis, J.R.: The measurement of observer agreement for categorical data. Biometrics (1977)
13. Spearman, C.: The proof and measurement of association between two things. Am. J. Psychol. **100**(3/4), 441–471 (1987)
14. Mao, J., et al.: When does relevance mean usefulness and user satisfaction in web search? In: Proceedings of the 39th International ACM SIGIR conference on Research and Development in Information Retrieval, pp. 463–472 (2016)
15. Cosijn, E., Ingwersen, P.: Dimensions of relevance. Inf. Process. Manage. **36**(4), 533–550 (2000)
16. Nickerson, R.S.: Confirmation bias: a ubiquitous phenomenon in many guises. Rev. Gen. Psychol. **2**(2), 175–220 (1998)
17. Wason, P.C.: On the failure to eliminate hypotheses in a conceptual task. Q. J. Exp. Psychol. **12**(3), 129–140 (1960)
18. Tversky, A., Kahneman, D.: Judgment under uncertainty: heuristics and biases: biases in judgments reveal some heuristics of thinking under uncertainty. Science **185**(4157), 1124–1131 (1974)

WCAG Compliance of Open Government Documents

Gregory Slager and Maarten Marx

IRLab, Informatics Institute, University of Amsterdam, Amsterdam, The Netherlands
gregory.slager@student.uva.nl, maartenmarx@uva.nl
https://irlab.science.uva.nl

Abstract. We study the WCAG compliancy and state of the metadata of PDF documents released under the Dutch Open Government Act (Woo). The results show that, in line with previous research on WCAG compliancy of PDF documents, only a fraction (0.2% of 31K) of the evaluated documents were WCAG compliant, with 160.407 WCAG related error instances in total. Five errors (out of 1.324) made up 68% of the total error instances, and 20 errors caused 95% of them. We have demonstrated that several of the errors in the top 20 can reliably be repaired with either existing Python packages or by using LLMs. We have automatically repaired six errors, reducing the total number of error instances in the dataset by 65K (40.5%). From the six defined essential metadata categories, the document language was least often missing in the documents (53.6% missing). Subject or description were most often missing, with a rate of 92.7%. Utilizing basic Python libraries and ChatGPT-4o for more complex metadata fields, our metadata field repairs had success rates between 69 and 92%. Repairing title metadata had a ROUGE-2 F1 score of .76.

Keywords: WCAG compliance · PDF · governmental publications

1 Introduction

We study compliance of PDF documents released by the Dutch government under its Open Government Act (Woo) with the Web Content Accessibility Guidelines (WCAG 2.2) [11]. By Dutch law these documents should be WCAG compliant and published as PDF/UA documents. We found that less than 0.2% complies. Compliance with these guidelines for documents released by a government is important for several reasons:

- compliance makes this information (more) accessible to (mostly visually) impaired persons;
- WCAG compliance causes these PDFs to be a lot closer to being FAIR scientific data as described in [13];
- and finally it improves transparency and thus potentially public trust in government.

© The Author(s), under exclusive license to Springer Nature Switzerland AG 2026
W.-T. Balke et al. (Eds.): TPDL 2025, CCIS 2694, pp. 176–184, 2026.
https://doi.org/10.1007/978-3-032-06136-2_17

Both verifying and ensuring compliance is difficult and often costly, because much of this work is still manual. Often, full compliance is not feasible for practical reasons. But this argument is too often used throw the hands up in the air and neglect accessibility completely, as "the guidelines are impossible to meet anyway". We believe this to be a fallacy. Every improvement is a step forward and many errors can be avoided or solved with the help of AI-powered assistants. Many of these avoidable errors do improve accessibility for visually impaired persons and do make documents better suitable for automatic information extraction or as training material for Large Language Models.

In this short note, we report on our measurements on both WCAG compliance and the state of the metadata of PDFs released by the Dutch government. We analyse the errors and indicate for a seizable portion how easily they can be avoided or repaired. Beyond these low hanging fruits there are exciting challenges in this field which are worthwhile to study both because of their real world benefits and of their scientific interest. Solving these challenges is truely cross-diciplinary, combining archival science, NLP, information extraction, AI, human computer interaction, and up to organizational science.

2 Related Work

WCAG compliance of e-government websites, not PDFs, has been studied for multiple countries, including the US [5], Northern Ireland [7], India [8], and several more. The findings of Lazar et al. [5] apply to most of these studies: websites do not comply, although some of the accessibility problems were minor and easy to fix. They consider two main causes: accessibility checking software does not work well, and requires a lot of manual work, and awareness of the issue is too low. Hackett et al. [2] study the relation between accessibility and complexity over time using the Internet Way Back Machine and find them strongly negatively correlated, but much less so for governmental websites. This latter finding is shared by another diachronic study: governmental websites do better than top traffic sites [3]. Ross et al. [9] use epidemiology as a tool to study inaccessibility of apps, noting co-occurrence of several errors. They notice how errors can spread through a population via copying of code.

Nganji [6] studies articles in PDF formats of four disability-related scientific journals and finds many of the same mistakes as we find here in our study. A positive point in his case was that there was always an HTML version of the article available as well. The importance of HTML as an alternative to a publication in PDF is felt strongly in the ArXiv community [1]. With only 2.4% of the ArXiv PDF papers being WCAG accessible, the need for software which transforms LaTeX source code into accessible HTML is felt strongly and an ongoing line of research and development. Researchers from the Allen Institute describe a system that directly transforms PDFs of scientific papers into high quality accessible HTML [12]. The PAVE accessibility remediation software described in [10] is a new initiative performing often much better than the industry standard Adobe Acrobat Pro. It aims to make it much easier to directly produce better accessible PDFs.

Table 1. Number of documents per Woo document category.

Advies: Beslisnota	19548
Advies	4506
Jaarplan/verslag	1310
Advies: Internetconsultatie	1007
Vergaderstuk Staten-Generaal	997
Beschikking	996
Vergaderstuk decentrale overheid	972
Onderzoek	870
Dossier na Woo/Wob-verzoek	829
Convenant	675
Agenda/besluitenlijst	259

Table 2. Number of documents per organisation category.

Ministerie	22936
Adviescollege	3601
Gemeente	2163
Hoog College van Staat	1276
Overheidsorganisatie	901
Agentschap	734
Provincie	284
Waterschap	53
Universiteit	16
Regionaal samenwerkingsorgaan	4
Inspectie	1

In summary, we see a lot of research on the accessibility of governmental websites, but not on the PDFs on these websites. Research on the accessibility of PDFs is concentrated on scientific journals, and several initiatives are working on providing HTML as an accessible alternative to PDF. Our study bridges these two streams of research, and shows that governmental PDFs are just as inaccessible as governmental websites and scientific PDFs and that also for these PDFs there is enough low hanging fruit which can be repaired using AI.

3 Methods

We describe the used dataset, the software used to extract metadata from PDFs and to check their WCAG compliance, and the methods we applied to repair some of the found errors.

3.1 Data

The dataset used in this paper consists of a selection of Dutch Freedom of Information Act (Woo) PDF documents indexed by the Woogle search engine [4] published before March 22, 2025. After filtering out duplicates and unusable documents, the dataset consisted of 31.969 documents that could be used for the WCAG analysis. Of the these, 31.150 were suitable for metadata analysis. The Dutch OpenGov Act contains 17 information categories whose publications should be made public. Our dataset covers 11 of these, see Table 1, released by 381 different publishing organizations, grouped in Table 2.

For the categories advies, agenda/besluitenlijst, beslisnota, convenant and jaarplan/verslag, all available documents were analyzed. Due to the large number of indexed documents belonging to the remaining categories, stratified sampling was used. The stratified sampling was done by calculating the ratio of documents per organization in the publishing category and maintaining the ratio of organizations per taken sample of approximately 1000 documents.

3.2 WCAG Compliance

The free, open source VeraPDF[1] software was used to investigate WCAG 2.2 compliance. It can be run in bulk and outputs in a convenient JSON format containing whether the document is WCAG compliant, the different error types and messages and the tags related to those error messages. The tags of the error messages contain an error severity level (critical, major, or minor) and the context of the error (e.g., metadata, language, figure, alt-text, etc.), see Fig. 1.

The output of the WCAG validation was combined with known Woogle metadata consisting of the date of publication, the publishing organization, the publishing organization's category and the Woo information category of the document. This enabled a fine-grained error analysis, seeing if errors are under- over over-represented in certain types of organizations or information categories.

3.3 Metadata Analysis

We applied the command line ExifTool by Phil Harvey[2] to extract all metadata from PDFs, using the -a -G1 options and write output to JSON. It outputs standard PDF metadata as well as user-defined XMP metadata. Exiftool gave an error on 819 of our 31K PDF files. We selected the following kind of metadata for analysis TaggedPDF, language, title, subject/description, publisher and various dates. Preliminary analysis showed that subject and description fields were often used interchangeably, therefore we grouped them into one category. We found a large number of metadata fields which could contain the value for the semantic tags. This lack of standardization makes information extraction difficult and hampers interoperability. The specific fields we used are listed below:

Tagging PDF:TaggedPDF

Language XMP-dcterms:Language, HTTP-equiv:ContentLanguage, PDF: Taal, XMP-pdfx:Taal, PDF:RapportTaal, XMP-pdfx:RapportTaal

Title PDF:Title, XMP-dc:Title, XMP-dc:Title-nl-NL, XMP-photoshop:Headline, XMP-OVERHEIDop:PublicationName, PDF:Titel and 12 others.

Description PDF:Subject, XMP-dc:Description, XMP-dc:Description-x-repair, PDF:Inhoudsindicatie, PDF:Onderwerp and 11 others.

Author PDF:Creator, PDF:Author, PDF:Producer, PDF:Publisher, PDF:Com-pany, PDF:OpgesteldDoor_Naam, PDF:Auteur and 37 others

Date PDF:CreateDate, XMP-dcterms:Issued, PDF:Date, PDF:Publicatiedatum, PDF:Created, XMP-pdfx:Datumvaststelling and 25 others.

For each tag, we concatenated all found values into a list. Dates were converted into iso-dates, and several ways of indicating "non-values" (like an empty string or the symbol "-") were normalized.

---

[1] https://verapdf.org/.
[2] https://exiftool.org.

Table 3. Top 20 PDF Error Types found on our dataset, together with (cumulative) incidence. Severity of the error is provided by VeraPDF.

ErrorMessage	Error Group	% of Errors	Cum. %	Severity
Content is neither marked as Artifact nor tagged as real content	User operation	17.2	17.2	Critical
ViewerPreferences dictionary is not present, or DisplayDocTitle key is set to false or is not present	Document set-up	15.2	32.4	Minor
StructTreeRoot entry is not present in the document catalog	System	14.1	46.5	Critical
Metadata stream does not contain dc:title	Document set-up	12.0	58.5	Major
Natural language for text in page content cannot be determined	Document set-up	9.5	68.0	Major
The font program is not embedded	System	4.5	72.5	Major
The document catalog dictionary doesn't contain metadata key	Document set-up	4.3	76.8	Critical
A CIDSet entry in the Font descriptor does not correctly identify all glyphs present in the embedded font subset	System	3.7	80.5	Minor
Link annotation whose hidden flag is not set and whose rectangle is not outside the crop-box has neither Contents key nor an Alt entry in the enclosing structure element	Document set-up	2.6	83.1	Major
Glyph widthin the embedded font program is not consistent with the Widths entry of the font dictionary	System	2.1	85.2	Major
Natural language for document metadata cannot be determined	Document set-up	2.0	87.2	Major
Figure structure element neither has an alternate description nor a replacement text	User operation	2.0	89.2	Major
Natural language in the Outline entries cannot be determined	User operation	1.1	90.3	Critical
A Link annotation is artifact or is nested within null tag (standard type = null) instead of Link or Reference	System	1.1	91.4	Major
ID key of the Note tag is not present	System	1.0	92.4	Major
A page with annotation(s) contains Tabs key with value null instead of S	System	0.8	93.2	Major
ViewerPreferences dictionary is not present, or DisplayDocTitle key is set to false or is not present	Document set-up	0.7	93.9	Minor
The glyph can not be mapped to Unicode	System	0.5	94.4	Critical
Table rows 1 and 2 span different number of columns	User operation	0.5	94.9	Major
A Type 2 CIDFont dictionary has missing or invalid CIDToGIDMap entry	System	0.4	95.3	Major

3.4 How We Repaired Errors

For repairing the WCAG errors and adding missing metadata, several different methods were used. The goal of repairing the errors was to keep the solution as simple and as cost effective as possible, whilst maintaining accurate results. Where possible, Python packages such as `Pypdf` for writing into the PDF's stream and `Langdetect` for language recognition were used. For writing metadata to PDF's, `ExifTool` was used. By using these packages, the fix would be robust and no input from the user would be necessary.

In case of semantic errors like missing titles in metadata, ChatGPT's 4o-mini Large Language Model (LLM) was used. An overview of repaired errors and the software used, can bee seen in Table 4. These repairs were done by feeding the PDF document to the LMM via the OpenAI API with custom prompts. The generated metadata gets written directly into the metadata of the document, also using `ExifTool`.

The following prompts were used:

- Title extraction: "Give the title of this document, no other tex".
- Subject/description extraction: "Summarize this document in one sentence
- Author extraction: "Give the publishing organization of this document"
- Date extraction: "Give the send date of this document, or the date of composition if there is not send date. If both are not present, return that no date was found".

To validate the repairing methods, a random sample of 23 PDFs from a set of PDFs which did not have any of the in 3.3 selected metadata was drawn and repaired. Prior to evaluation, reference metadata for all 23 documents were determined. The language of the documents was verified by manual inspection, the

Table 4. Automatically fixable errors and the software used to repair them.

ErrorMessage	Software used
ViewerPreferences dictionary is not present	Pypdf
Metadata stream does not contain dc:title	ChatGPT 4o-mini + Exiftool
Natural language for text in page content cannot be determined	Pypdf + Langdetect
Natural language for document metadata cannot be determined	Pypdf + Langdetect
Natural language in the Outline entries cannot be determined	Pypdf + Langdetect
ViewerPreferences dictionary DisplayDocTitle key is not present	Pypdf

author was retrieved from the Woogle dataset and the date was verified by manual inspection. For date selection, the composition date or send date was selected based on which one was present. The document titles were manually retrieved. Description/subject metadata could not be retrieved a priori.

For evaluation, the generated language, author and data metadata were compared to the reference metadata. If the generated and reference metadata matched, this was classed as a correct generation. Generated description/subject metadata was compared to the content of the document manually. If the generated data described the document fully, this was classed as a correct generation. For evaluation of the generated title metadata, the ROUGE-1 and ROUGE-2 metrics that measure the uni- and bi-gram overlap between the reference title and generated title were used.

4 Results

4.1 WCAG Compliance

In line with other research on WCAG compliance of PDFs we found that only a tiny subset of 79 files (0.2%) was fully compliant. In total we found 160.407 errors grouped into 1.302 error types. The top 20 types that occur the most, together covering 95% of all error instances, are listed in Table 3. We grouped these most occurring error types into three types; see Table 5.

VeraPDF has 14 error categories. Errors can belong to multiple categories and files can suffer from more than one error per category. Figure 1 shows for each category how many documents contain at least one error of that type.

4.2 Missing Metadata

We investigated for core semantic metadata whether the PDFs contained it. Table 6 contains the results. Note that we tried to find the required metadata in several fields, as listed in Sect. 3.3, and still found very high numbers of missing data. We see large variability over the different information categories. The outlier here is the author field, which appears to be always filled. However, the value

Table 5. Our grouping of the WCAG errors based on their origin, together with the number of error types belonging to each group and the percentage of all error instances.

Error group	Description	Number of error types	% of error instances
User operation	Errors from this error group occur while the user is composing the content of the PDF. These errors can arise multiple times per document.	3	19.7
Document set-up	Errors from this group occur whilst setting-up the document. The origin of these errors is often missing metadata or incorrect viewing options.	8	47.4
System	These errors often originate in the PDF software or the user's OS. These errors are often not fixable (automatically or by the user) and need workarounds.	9	28.2
Other	–	1282	4.7

Table 6. Percentage missing data per metadata field, and the macro averaged percentage and standard deviation over the 11 information types.

	missing	mean	std.
PDFtagged=Yes	68.9	46.3	27.4
Title	73.7	47.5	34.1
Subject/description	92.7	94.0	6.0
Author	0.0	0.0	0.0
Correct author	92.3	76.9	34.2
Date	94.3	81.1	34.1
Language	53.6	45.0	25.3

almost never corresponds to the normalized canonical name for that publisher which is present in our dataset, as indicated by the correct author field.

4.3 Reparation

For all 23 repaired documents the generated language, author and date matched the reference metadata. The language of the documents was verified by manually inspecting the documents. The author was verified by comparing the generated data to the data from the Woogle metadata. The generated date was compared to the given publication/send date in the respective document.

In 69.6% of cases, a correct description was provided. The generated description was compared to the content of the document. If the generated description was deemed as sufficiently covering the document, this was marked as correct.

The titles of the documents often consisted of multiple words. In order to measure the performance of our solution, the overlap between the generated title

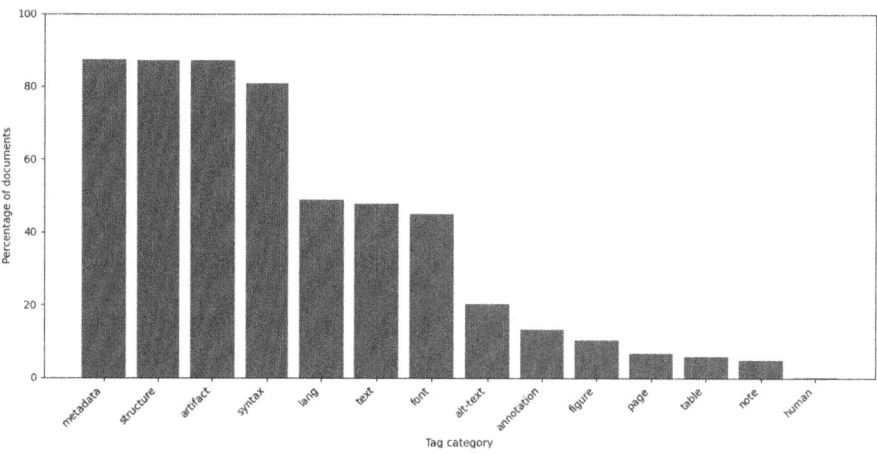

Fig. 1. Percentage of PDF files with at least one error within the given category (N=31.969).

and reference title was measured. The reference title was determined by manually inspecting the front page of the document. The mean ROUGE-1 F1 score was 0.81 and the mean ROUGE-2 F1 score was 0.76 By repairing the entire dataset, 65.018 WCAG errors were solvable. This is a decrease of 40.5%. By performing these repairs, the percentage of WCAG compliant documents increases from 0.2% to 3.1%.

5 Conclusion

We showed that WCAG compliance of PDFs released by the Dutch government is as bad as previously described for other corpora. This holds, even though the government is legally bound to WCAG compliance for its publications. It is not easy to produce compliant PDFs, we are aware of that. Still, we found many avoidable mistakes that could easily be repaired. The best way forward, also taken by ArXiv and the Allen institute for AI, seems to produce content-wise identical HTML versions of the PDFs. Of course, it is much better to do this at production time, than to use AI-based document-structure detection afterwards. It is encouraging, and a great example for the other Woo information categories, that this happens already with the Dutch parliamentary proceedings, which are available in PDF, HTML and even in their source XML format.

Acknowledgments. This research was supported in part by the Netherlands Organization for Scientific Research (NWO) through the ACCESS project grant CISC.CC.016 and an Open Science Fund grant nr 01607400. Maarten Marx is partly funded by ICAI (AI for Open Government Lab). Views expressed in this paper are not necessarily shared or endorsed by those funding the research.

References

1. Frankston, C., Godfrey, J., Brinn, S., Hofer, A., Nazzaro, M.: HTML papers on arXiv – why it is important, and how we made it happen (2024). https://arxiv.org/abs/2402.08954
2. Hackett, S., Parmanto, B., Zeng, X.: Accessibility of internet websites through time. In: Proc. SIGACCESS, pp. 32–39 (2003). https://doi.org/10.1145/1028630.1028638
3. Hanson, V.L., Richards, J.T.: Progress on website accessibility? ACM Trans. on the Web (TWEB) **7**(1), 1–30 (2013)
4. van Heusden, R., Larooij, M., Kamps, J., Marx, M.: A collection of FAIR Dutch freedom of information act documents. Sci. Data **12**(1), 795 (2025). https://doi.org/10.1038/s41597-025-05052-2
5. Lazar, J., Beere, P., Greenidge, K.D., Nagappa, Y.: Web accessibility in the mid-atlantic united states: a study of 50 homepages. Univ. Access Inf. Soc. **2**, 331–341 (2003)
6. Nganji, J.T.: An assessment of the accessibility of PDF versions of selected journal articles published in a WCAG 2.0 era (2014–2018). Learned Publishing **31**(4), 391–401 (2018)
7. Paris, M.: Website accessibility: a survey of local e-government websites and legislation in northern ireland. Univ. Access Inf. Soc. **4**, 292–299 (2006)
8. Paul, S.: Accessibility analysis using WCAG 2.1: evidence from Indian e-government websites. Universal Access inform. Soc. **22**(2), 663–669 (2023)
9. Ross, A.S., Zhang, X., Fogarty, J., Wobbrock, J.O.: Epidemiology as a framework for large-scale mobile application accessibility assessment. In: Proc. SIGACCESS, pp. 2–11 (2017)
10. Schmitt-Koopmann, F.M., huang, E.M., Hutter, H.P., Darvishy, A.: Towards more accessible scientific PDFs for people with visual impairments: step-by-step PDF remediation to improve tag accuracy. In: Proc. CHI 2025, pp. 1–16 (2025)
11. W3C: Web Content Accessibility Guidelines (WCAG) 2.1. Recommendation. Tech. rep., W3C (2005). https://www.w3.org/TR/WCAG21/
12. Wang, L.L., et al.: Improving the accessibility of scientific documents: Current state, user needs, and a system solution to enhance scientific PDF accessibility for blind and low vision users. arXiv:2105.00076 (2021)
13. Wilkinson, M.D., Dumontier, M., Aalbersberg, I.J.J.e.: The FAIR guiding principles for scientific data management and stewardship. Sci. Data **3**, 160018 (2016). https://doi.org/10.1038/sdata.2016.18

Semantic Enrichment in SQL Workflows Through Targeted LLM Invocation

Yannis Foufoulas[1(✉)], Eleni Zacharia[3], Harry Dimitropoulos[3], Natalia Manola[3], and Yannis Ioannidis[1,2]

[1] Athena Research Center, Athens, Greece
johnfouf@athenarc.gr
[2] National and Kapodistrian University of Athens, Athens, Greece
[3] OpenAIRE AMKE, Athens, Greece

Abstract. The growing need for scalable research resource discovery in digital libraries has motivated the development of frameworks that combine traditional processing with large language models (LLMs). Building upon DETEXA, a declarative and extensible SQL-based text analytics framework, we propose a key extension: the integration of LLMs through User-Defined Functions (UDFs). This architecture preserves the scalability and declarative nature of SQL workflows while selectively invoking LLMs for tasks that require deep semantic understanding. To balance the trade-off between efficiency and precision, we explore three processing alternatives: LLM-only pipeline, pattern-based approach, and a hybrid model with selective LLM invocation. As a running example, we focus on the extraction of Data and Software Availability Statements from research publications, demonstrating the benefits of hybrid semantic enrichment. Experimental results show that the proposed approach achieves significantly improved accuracy over pattern-based methods, while maintaining runtime performance compared to full LLM-based solutions. Our framework offers a path toward efficient, extensible, and semantically enhanced text analytics pipelines.

Keywords: SQL Workflows · LLMs · Data Availability Statements

1 Introduction

The exponential growth of open access publications has created opportunities for large-scale metadata enrichment in digital libraries, particularly in the area of research resource discovery. A critical challenge is extracting semantically rich information from scientific texts–an inherently challenging task due to the complexity, variability, and ambiguity of natural language in scholarly writing.

Existing solutions for large-scale text extraction typically prioritize either efficiency or semantic depth, but rarely both. Rule-based approaches scale well but struggle with linguistic variability [1], while machine learning approaches often demand substantial manual effort to achieve high accuracy [1–3]. In contrast,

LLM-based approaches provide richer semantic understanding but suffer from high computational costs, memory overhead, and limited scalability [4,5]. While commercial APIs such as OpenAI's ChatGPT offer strong performance, invoking them at scale becomes prohibitively expensive–especially for large corpora or real-time pipelines. This gap motivates the development of hybrid solutions that selectively combine the scalability of traditional methods with the semantic capabilities of lightweight, local, open-source, and cost-effective models.

To address this need, we build upon DETEXA [6,7], a scalable text analysis framework for digital library applications, implemented on top of YeSQL [8], which supports rich pipelines inside DBMSes through polymorphic, stateful, and dynamically typed UDFs. DETEXA enables fast experimentation and efficient processing by offloading heavy relational operations to the data engine while allowing procedural text transformations through in-process Python UDFs. By design, DETEXA strikes a balance between declarative expressiveness and scalable analytics, serving as the basis for the extensions we introduce in this work.

In this paper, we investigate a significant advancement to the DETEXA framework: scalar UDFs that integrate external Large Language Models (LLMs) into the SQL workflow. These functions enable deep semantic understanding and reasoning tasks beyond the reach of rule-based methods. Through this extension, we enable hybrid text mining workflows that combine the efficiency of database-driven processing with the inferential power of modern LLMs.

To demonstrate the potential of this hybrid architecture, we focus on a real-world use case: *the extraction of Data/Software Availability Statements (DAS)* from scientific publications. Recent studies have shown that publications containing DAS with links to data or software repositories are associated with higher citation impact, reinforcing the importance of accurately identifying and analyzing these statements [2]. DAS extraction is a challenging task, due to the diverse phrasing, implicit mentions, and heterogeneous structure of research articles (see explicit examples in next sections). LLMs help for resolving these ambiguities, but their computational cost prohibits their use at scale. Throughout the paper, we use the DAS extraction scenario as a running example to evaluate the performance and effectiveness of the proposed methodology. We describe the algorithm pipeline, detail the LLM-UDF integration into SQL, and provide experimental results highlighting the benefits of the approach. Our main contributions are summarized as follows:

- We extend DETEXA with a new class of **scalar UDFs that interface with external LLMs** inside SQL workflows.
- We propose a **hybrid SQL-LLM execution model** that selectively applies LLMs only where needed, combining efficiency with semantic depth.
- We present a detailed case study on **DAS extraction** from scientific publications to demonstrate the applicability and effectiveness of our approach.
- We show that the hybrid flow improves accuracy over pattern-based methods while maintaining scalability compared to LLM-only solutions.

2 Availability Statement Extraction Challenge

Automatically detecting and classifying DAS in research publications is essential for promoting open science and ensuring reproducibility. In this section, we present the problem and outline the associated challenges.

Problem Definition. Publications are classified into six categories according to their data/software availability[1]: *(1) Full and good* publicly accessible data/software via persistent links (e.g., Zenodo, GitHub); *(2) Supplementary* materials available as journal-hosted supplements without stable identifiers; *(3) On Request* access granted upon author request, with limited verifiability; *(4) No immediate access* mentioned but restricted due to legal, ethical, or embargo reasons; *(5) No Data* explicitly states no data/software were used; *(6) No DAS Statement* no availability statement present.

Individual DAS may contain multiple components–such as open access to software alongside restricted access to data–and were therefore assigned multiple category labels where appropriate to capture this granularity. For example, the following DAS includes both restricted data and openly shared code:

> "Data cannot be shared publicly because this is a Ministry of Defence funded project and data are subject to additional restrictions. All relevant code, and the pre-registration document is available online from: https://osf.io/mzxtn/" [10]

Challenges. The extraction and classification of DAS is complicated by a variety of factors. We organize these challenges into three main categories:

- **Structural Variation**: DAS content can appear in multiple locations within articles–including dedicated DAS sections, Acknowledgments, footnotes, or even supplementary materials. This heterogeneity complicates consistent detection. For example, in some cases, the "Data Availability" section may defer the actual statement to another part of the paper, requiring cross-referencing multiple sections to locate and interpret the full DAS:
  > "Data availability: A relevant statement is added in the Acknowledgement section." [11]
- **Linguistic Complexity**: DAS statements often use context-dependent or vague phrasing, or are embedded within long, multi-clause sentences:
  > "The datasets used and/or analysed during the current study are not publicly available due to IP restrictions. Part of the datasets used/analysed will be available after the publication of the article from the authors on reasonable request." [12]

Such statements raise uncertainty about which components are accessible and under what conditions. Additionally, DAS may combine multiple forms of availability (e.g., open code and restricted data), requiring nuanced interpretation of complex sentence structures.

---
[1] Based on the UKRN Open Research Indicators Pilot [9].

These challenges make surface-level text processing inadequate for accurate DAS extraction. Our approach combines SQL preprocessing with LLM semantic reasoning for more robust interpretation and classification.

3 Background and Related Work

In this section, we review related work across three key areas: recent advancements in in-database text mining; efforts to integrate LLMs directly within database systems; and research on the extraction and classification of DAS.

Text Mining with UDFs in Databases. In recent years, the integration of data science pipelines directly into data engines has gained popularity [13–15]. With UDFs, data engines can process and analyze text data efficiently, minimizing data transfer and leveraging the power of relational operations. YeSQL [8,16] extends SQL and supports seamless integration of polymorphic, stateful, and dynamically typed UDFs into existing DBMSes, facilitating fast experimentation and efficient pipelines directly inside a DBMS. DETEXA [6] is a framework with text mining capabilities built on top of YeSQL. Other UDF-centric works target the effective and efficient integration of UDFs to support scalable modern analytics and machine learning pipelines [17–21]. Several text analytics pipelines have been implemented inside DBMSes with UDF support [22–27].

Integrating LLMs with Database Engines. The integration of LLMs into databases for hybrid querying has garnered significant attention [28,29]. Production data engines have incorporated support for LLM UDFs [30]. In addition to the known UDF challenges discussed at [13,14], integration of LLMs poses new challenges: open-source, transformer-based LLMs require substantial memory to load and suffer from large invocation overheads [31]. If the UDF invoking the LLM is not stateful–which is common in existing UDF implementations, especially in tuple-at-a-time engines–or lacks global initialization capabilities, the model may be reloaded once per tuple, resulting in severe performance degradation. To mitigate this, our approach leverages YeSQL's stateful UDFs with global initialization, avoiding redundant loading and enabling efficient LLM invocation.

Research Resource Discovery. The extraction/classification of DAS is a critical task for research resource discovery. Researchers and practitioners often need to determine whether datasets or software used in a publication are accessible, and under what conditions. In this context, SoMeSci [32] has introduced a knowledge graph annotating software mentions in scientific articles, including metadata such as version and access URL, supporting more structured discovery and analysis of software resources. Colavizza et al. [2] systematically examined over 8,000 PLOS ONE articles and proposed a classification framework for DAS based on the location of the data, the presence of persistent identifiers, and the reusability of the shared resources. Their findings highlighted not only the diversity of DAS phrasings, but also the challenges of assessing actual accessibility and compliance with data sharing policies.

Early works on this topic focused on manually curated rules [1], while other efforts have employed ML methods but they typically operate over pre-extracted DAS sections and are proved inconsistent in this context. For example, Federer et al. [3] achieved only 68% classification accuracy on pre-identified DAS sections, with the remaining cases requiring manual labeling (see Fig. 2 of that work). These results underscore both the challenges of DAS classification and the limitations imposed by the lack of high-quality ground truth datasets.

Structured metadata initiatives have also supported DAS extraction. For example, Europe PMC has extended its section tagging pipeline to identify DAS by detecting <sec> elements with headings such as "Data Availability" [33]. Other studies have explored DAS across publication stages, including comparisons between medRxiv preprints and their published versions [34], as well as the automatic detection of dataset names within scientific papers to improve transparency and reuse [35, 36]. These efforts underscore the importance of flexible extraction techniques to support research resource discovery at scale.

Despite growing interest in DAS practices across disciplines, the general problem of DAS extraction remains unsolved [37]. Our work builds on these foundations by proposing a approach that combines efficient database processing with the semantic power of LLMs to address the extraction challenge at scale.

4 Hybrid DAS Extraction Workflow

To demonstrate the practical benefits of our approach, we apply it to the extraction of DAS from scientific publications. Our proposed workflow enhances the extraction of DAS from scientific publications by adding a classification step before invoking the LLM extraction process. This allows the system to first attempt to classify candidate contexts using a pattern based classification, reducing unnecessary LLM calls for contexts that can be classified with high confidence. If the classification confidence is below a certain threshold, the system proceeds to use the LLM for a more detailed extraction. This approach optimizes both accuracy and efficiency in the DAS extraction process.

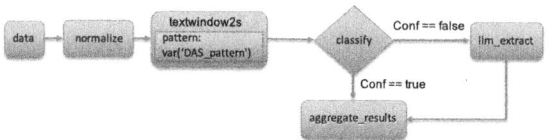

Fig. 1: DAS classification SQL algorithm flow

The overall DAS extraction procedure is illustrated in Fig. 1. It employs a series of User-Defined Functions (UDFs) to preprocess, extract, classify, and refine DAS contexts from research papers, combining traditional rule-based methods with large language model (LLM) assistance for improved accuracy[2].

---
[2] The generalization of the pipeline with support of various extraction tasks is demonstrated through our demo at [38].

Initially, the `normalize` UDF prepares the raw text by lowercasing, removing punctuation and newlines. The cleaned text is then scanned by `textwindow2s`, which uses regular expressions on predefined patterns (i.e., Appendix F at [39] lists patterns that indicate a DAS) to extract multiple candidate text snippets per document that likely contain DAS. These snippets are classified by the `classify` UDF using weighted, rule-based pattern matching tailored to the target DAS categories (Sect. 2). For example, *On Request* is linked to phrases like "reasonable request", while *No immediate access* relies on positive indicators such as "privacy restrictions" and excludes contradictory phrases like "is publicly available". The UDF outputs a predicted label and a confidence score. If the confidence surpasses a threshold (i.e., 0.5), the classification is accepted. Otherwise, the `llm_extract` UDF invokes an LLM to analyze the snippet, leveraging its semantic understanding to resolve ambiguous or complex statements and improve classification accuracy. Finally, since multiple snippets per document may yield different labels, the `aggregate_results` UDF applies rule-based prioritization to select the most informative final class. For instance, a generic *No DAS Statement* label would be superseded by a more specific, positive classification from another snippet within the same document. This hybrid approach balances efficiency with robust semantic interpretation, enabling scalable and accurate DAS extraction and classification.

Listing 1: DAS classification algorithm in DETEXA

```
select doi, aggregate_results(class, text_snippet)
    from (
select
    doi,
    case
        when classify_conf = true then class
        else llm_extract(text_snippet)
    end as class,
    text_snippet
from (
    select
        doi,
        classify(text_snippet) as classify_result
    from (
        select
            doi,
            textwindow2s(
                normalize(txt), 5, 2, 30,
                var('DAS_pattern')
            ) as text_snippet
        from data
    )
)
) as classify_result group by doi;
```

Listing 1 presents the algorithm's implementation. With DETEXA, relational operators such as `GROUP BY` and `CASE` statements are executed natively, allowing the computation to be performed directly on the data. Additionally, it becomes straightforward to apply filters, enabling SQL indexes to optimize query performance. This approach achieves notable performance through two main mechanisms: First, it significantly reduces reliance on LLMs by selectively invoking them only for ambiguous cases. Second, the stateful nature of UDFs in YeSQL allows for efficient integration of LLMs by enabling global-level initializations. This avoids row-level setup overheads, which would otherwise be prohibitively expensive given the heavy initialization costs of LLMs. Together, these optimizations make the proposed method both scalable and cost-effective.

5 Evaluation

System and Software Setup. The experiments are executed on a server equipped with dual Intel Xeon Gold 5318Y (96 cores, 192 threads, 2.10 GHz base, 3.4 GHz turbo) and 512 GB of RAM. Model inference is accelerated using two NVIDIA RTX A6000 GPUs, each with 48 GB of VRAM. The system runs CUDA Version 12.2, Python 3.10, and DETEXA [40]. For LLM-based classification and extraction, we use three models: Mistral-7B-Instruct-v0.3 (7B), Mistral-Nemo-Base-2407 (12B) and Llama-2-13b-chat-hf (13B). All models are hosted locally using HuggingFace's `transformers` library. For the interested reader, the LLM's UDF implementation is publicly available on GitHub [41].

Experimental Setup. We assess the effectiveness of our hybrid workflow, as described in Sect. 4, through experiments on real research publications. We use fulltexts from a dataset developed for Pilot 4 of the UKRN Open Research Indicators project [42], reflecting real-world phrasing and structural heterogeneity. In the absence of a sufficient public ground truth, our evaluation is based on manual validation of a random sample of 100 papers, of which 49 contain a DAS. This required a close reading of each paper's full text to locate dispersed and usually ambiguous DAS mentions (i.e., in a specific DAS section, or in a footnote, or elsewhere in the text)–a process that, while necessary, renders large-scale validation impractical in this context. We compare the following methods:

- **Pure SQL + UDFs:** A pattern-based method (i.e., generic DAS patterns from Appendix F at [39] and class specific patterns from spreadsheet at [9]) using DETEXA UDFs for normalization, contextual window extraction, and regex pattern classification.
- **LLM-Only (Full Text):** Prompting the entire document to a large language model (LLM) for DAS classification.
- **Hybrid (SQL + LLM):** A two-stage workflow: first, classify context windows using a weighted pattern-based classification; then, only when the classifier is uncertain, query the LLM with a focused window.

For context, we refer the reader to Sect. 3 for a discussion of related ML-based DAS classification efforts, which typically operate on pre-extracted DAS sections and suffer from limited effectiveness. Moreover, the lack of high-quality diverse training datasets makes ML methods unsuitable for experimentation in this domain. In contrast, our method processes the full text of publications–a

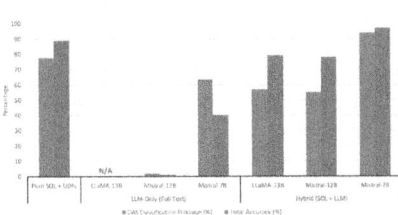 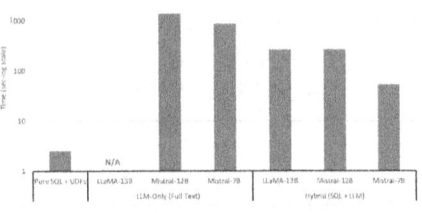
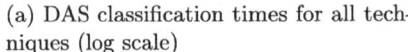

(a) DAS classification times for all techniques (log scale)

(b) Total Accuracy and precision in classifying the subset of texts that contain candidate text snippets

Fig. 2: Comparison of LLM and SQL pattern-based techniques for DAS classification on a sample of 100 documents

necessity here, as DAS statements are often scattered across different sections. For example, although this paper does not contain a dedicated DAS section, a statement appears at the first paragraph of Sect. 5, which is correctly extracted and classified by our algorithm in 20 msecs, without requiring an LLM call.

We report precision on documents that include DAS (49 total), total accuracy over the full dataset (100 documents), runtime, and error types.

As shown in Figs. 2a and 2b, the pure SQL+UDF approach is the fastest, completing in 2.5 s with 77.5% precision on the 49 DAS and 89% overall accuracy, with excellent performance in filtering out non-DAS documents. In contrast, full-document LLM inference is slower and less reliable: Mistral-7B takes 860 s and yields ill-structured output in over a third of cases, dropping precision to 40%. Larger models (e.g., LLaMA-13B) face memory and token limitations, while Mistral-12B classifies only two documents. Within the **hybrid workflow**, Mistral-7B achieves 93.8% precision and 97% accuracy in 53 s (2 papers/sec), outperforming Mistral-12B (270 sec, 78%) and LLaMA-13B (79%). These results show that small models may excel in targeted extraction in structured pipelines, and overall, the hybrid SQL+LLM pipeline offers high accuracy minimizing LLM overhead. Full-text LLMs are resource-intensive and error-prone, while larger models add cost without benefit. The pattern-based baseline is fast but less flexible for nuanced phrasing.

6 Conclusions and Future Work

We proposed a hybrid SQL+LLM workflow and its implementation for classifying DAS from scientific articles. By combining SQL-based preprocessing with selective LLM invocation, we balance both accuracy and efficiency. Using Mistral-7B, we achieved 93.8% classification precision and 97% total accuracy (compared to 77.5% and 89% respectively of the tuned pattern based approach), processing nearly 2 papers per second. These results show that small models, when guided by structured pipelines, can achieve excellent effectiveness in focused tasks. Our method is modular and scalable, making it suitable for real-time and high-volume processing. **Future Work** includes: (i) Deploying the pipeline in OpenAIRE for large-scale DAS indexing; (ii) Fine-tuning lightweight models on DAS-specific datasets; (iii) Automating LLM selection based on runtime input features; and, (iv) Generalization to related statements (e.g., CRediT, licensing).

Acknowledgements. This work was supported by the Horizon Europe projects EBRAINS 2.0 (GA.101147319) and EOSC Beyond (GA.101131875).

Disclosure of Interests. The authors have no competing interests to declare.

References

1. Krüger, F., Schindler, D.: A literature review on methods for the extraction of usage statements of software and data. Comput. Sci. Eng. **22**(1), 26–38 (2020)
2. Colavizza, G., et al.: The citation advantage of linking publications to research data. PLoS One **15**(4) (2020)
3. Federer, L.M., et al.: Data sharing in PLOS ONE: An analysis of Data Availability Statements. PLoS One, vol. 13, no. 5, 2018
4. Brown, T. B., et. al.: Language Models are Few-Shot Learners. arXiv preprint arXiv:2005.14165v4 (2020)
5. Rostam, Z.R.K., et.al.: Achieving peak performance for large language models: a systematic review. IEEE Access, 96017–96050 (2024)
6. Foufoulas, Y., et al.: Detexa: declarative extensible text exploration and analysis through sql. Int. J. Digit. Libr. **25**(3), 457–469 (2024)
7. Foufoulas, Y., et al.: Detexa: Declarative extensible text exploration and analysis. In: International Conference on Theory and Practice of Digital Libraries, pp. 107-119. Springer International Publishing (2022). https://doi.org/10.1007/978-3-031-16802-4_9
8. Foufoulas, Y., et al.: Yesql: you extend sql with rich and highly performant user-defined functions in relational databases. PVLDB **15**(10), 2270–2283 (2022)
9. McCutcheon, V., et al.: Ukrn data accessibility statement pilot classification discussion document. Zenodo (2025). https://doi.org/10.5281/zenodo.15223404
10. Harris, David J., et al. Can cognitive training capitalise on near transfer effects? Limited evidence of transfer following online inhibition training in a randomised-controlled trial. PLoS One **18**(11) (2023)
11. Ouderji, Z.H., et al.: Integration of anaerobic digestion with heat pump: machine learning-based technical and environmental assessment. Biores. Technol. **369**, 128485 (2023)
12. Karvelas, A., et al.: Investigating learning join order optimization strategies for rule-based data engines. Inform. Syst. Front. (2024). https://doi.org/10.1007/s10796-024-10555-1
13. Foufoulas, Y., Simitsis, A.: Efficient execution of user-defined functions in sql queries. PVLDB **16**(12), 3874–3877 (2023)
14. Foufoulas, Y., Simitsis, A. User-defined functions in modern data engines. In: IEEE ICDE, pp. 3593-3598 (2023)

15. Foufoulas, Y., Palaiologou, T., Simitsis, A.: UDFBench:ATool for Benchmarking UDF Queries on SQL Engines, SIGMOD (2025)
16. Foufoulas, Y., Simitsis, A., Ioannidis, Y.: Yesql: rich user-defined functions without the overhead. PVLDB **15**(12), 3730–3733 (2022)
17. Kläbe, S., et al.: Accelerating python udfs in vectorized query execution. In: CIDR (2022)
18. Spiegelberg, L., et al.: Tuplex: data science in python at native code speed. In: Proceedings of the 2021 International Conference on Management of Data, pp. 1718-1731 (2021)
19. Sichert, M., Neumann, T.: User-defined operators: efficiently integrating custom algorithms into modern databases. PVLDB **15**(5) (2022). https://doi.org/10.14778/3510397.3510408
20. Chasialis, K., et al.: QFusor: a UDF optimizer plugin for SQL databases. In: IEEE ICDE, pp. 5457-5460 (2024). https://doi.org/10.1109/ICDE60146.2024.00427
21. Blacher, M., et al.: Machine learning, linear algebra, and more: Is SQL all you need?. In: CIDR (2022)
22. Hellerstein, J.M., et al.: The MADlib analytics library. PVLDB **5**(12), 1700-1711 (2012).https://doi.org/10.14778/2367502.2367510
23. Giannakopoulos, T., et al.: Discovering and visualizing interdisciplinary content classes in scientific publications. D-Lib Mag. **20**(11/12) (2014). https://doi.org/10.1045/november14-giannakopoulos
24. Giannakopoulos, T., et.al.: Visual-based classification of figures from scientific literature. In: Proceedings of the 24th International Conference on World Wide Web, pp 1059-1060, (2015). https://doi.org/10.1145/2740908.2742024
25. Giannakopoulos, T., Stamatogiannakis, E., Foufoulas, I., Dimitropoulos, H., Manola, N., Ioannidis, Y.: Content visualization of scientific corpora using an extensible relational database implementation. In: Bolikowski, L, Casarosa, V., Goodale, P., Houssos, N., Manghi, P., Schirrwagen, J. (eds.) TPDL 2013. CCIS, vol. 416, pp. 101–112. Springer, Cham (2014). https://doi.org/10.1007/978-3-319-08425-1_10
26. Giannakopoulos, T., Foufoulas, Y., Dimitropoulos, H., Manola, N.: Interactive text analysis and information extraction. In: Manghi, P., Candela, L., Silvello, G. (eds.) IRCDL 2019. CCIS, vol. 988, pp. 340–350. Springer, Cham (2019). https://doi.org/10.1007/978-3-030-11226-4_27
27. Foufoulas, Y., Stamatogiannakis, L., Dimitropoulos, H., Ioannidis, Y.: High-pass text filtering for citation matching. In: Kamps, J., Tsakonas, G., Manolopoulos, Y., Iliadis, L., Karydis, I. (eds.) TPDL 2017. LNCS, vol. 10450, pp. 355–366. Springer, Cham (2017). https://doi.org/10.1007/978-3-319-67008-9_28
28. Zhao, F., et al.: Hybrid querying over relational databases and large language models. In: CIDR (2025)
29. Zhou, X., Sun, Z., Li, G.: Db-gpt Large language model meets database. Data Sci. Eng. **9**, 102–111 (2024)
30. Introducing the prompt() Function: Use the Power of LLMs with SQL. https://motherduck.com/blog/sql-llm-prompt-function-gpt-models
31. Liu, S., et al.: Optimizing LLM Queries in Relational Workloads. arXiv preprint arXiv:2403.05821v1 (2024)
32. Schindler, D., et al.: SoMeSci: a 5 star open data gold standard knowledge graph of software mentions in scientific articles. In: CIKM 2021, pp. 4574-458. https://doi.org/10.1145/3459637.3482017

33. Parkin, M.: How JATS supports data integration: extracting data availability statements and funding information from research articles in Europe PMC. In: JATS-Con (2019). https://doi.org/10.6084/m9.figshare.8159426.v1
34. McGuinness, L.A., Sheppard, A.S.: A descriptive analysis of the data availability statements accompanying medrxiv preprints and a comparison with their published counterparts. PLoS ONE **16**(5), e0250887 (2021)
35. Heddes, J., et al.: The automatic detection of dataset names in scientific articles. J. Inform. Sci. **6**(8) (2021)
36. Polak, M.P., Morgan, D.: Extracting accurate materials data from research papers with conversational language models and prompt engineering. Nat. Commun. **15**, 1569 (2024). https://doi.org/10.1038/s41467-024-45914-8
37. Kaggle. Make Data Count: Finding Data References. https://www.kaggle.com/competitions/make-data-count-finding-data-references (2024). Accessed June 2025
38. Yannis, F., et al.: LLM-Enhanced DETEXA Workflow Builder for Semantic Enrichment, TPDL (2025)
39. Etienne, V.-G., et al.: Annex A - Bibliometric Technical Report for the Study from Intent to Impact: Investigating the Effects of Open Sharing Commitments. Zenodo. https://zenodo.org/records/6643492
40. DETEXA source code. https://github.com/madgik/detexa
41. Implementation of the scalar UDF LLM_extract. https://github.com/madgik/detexa/blob/main/DETEXA/functions/row/llm.py
42. UK Reproducibility Network (UKRN), Open Research Indicators Project (2024). https://www.ukrn.org/open-research-indicators/

Design and Implementation of a Next-Generation OAIS-Compliant Digital Preservation System for the NDPP

Lu Wang[1,2]($^{\boxtimes}$), Beibei Kong[1], Zhenxin Wu[1,2], Qian Li[1,2], and Zhixiong Zhang[1,2]

[1] National Science Library, Chinese Academy of Sciences, Beijing 100190, China
wanglu2023@mail.las.ac.cn
[2] Department of Information Resources Management, University of Chinese Academy of Sciences, Beijing 100190, China

Abstract. The National Digital Preservation Program (NDPP) is China's largest "dark archive" network, dedicated to the long-term preservation of digital scholarly publications. To address the growing scale, diversity, and complexity of the scholarly record, NDPP has developed a next-generation in-house preservation system built on an open-source private cloud stack. The system offers a comprehensive suite of OAIS-compliant functions that support full life-cycle object management and routine archival operations. Archival Information Packages (AIPs) are structured using widely adopted standards—METS, PREMIS, Dublin Core, and OCFL—to ensure interoperability and self-descriptiveness. Dynamic scalability is achieved through containerized microservices, while high-performance processing of large-scale submissions is enabled by parallel processing mechanisms. Customizability is supported through a configurable preservation plan, dynamic plugin extensibility, and workflow orchestration. The system also integrates risk-aware, proactive preservation management. Currently, the platform supports seven categories of scholarly resources. Performance evaluations demonstrate a 5- to 15-fold increase in ingestion throughput on a Kubernetes cluster with 3 worker nodes.

Keywords: Digital Preservation · Scalability · Customization · Microservices · Cloud-based Infrastructure · High-throughput Ingestion

1 Introduction

The National Digital Preservation Program (NDPP) [1] is China's largest digital preservation network for scholarly publications. It federates six independent dark archive nodes to preserve over 14,000 e-journals, 150,000 e-books, and 100 million items, adding more than 10 million items annually. It ensures continued access to digital publications for eligible users from over 200 Chinese academic libraries upon trigger conditions [2] by maintaining OAIS-compliant digital archives [3].

Long-term digital preservation goes beyond simple collection, cataloging, and backup. An OAIS-compliant system must manage not only the data objects and their descriptive information but also the preservation metadata necessary to ensure authenticity, integrity, and long-term usability through ongoing preservation actions. At the NDPP scale, this requires a high-performance, extensible infrastructure to support full life-cycle object management and standards-based administrative operations. However, the current system—built on the Fedora 3 digital repository [4] with custom-developed monolithic services—faces critical limitations. Its sequential processing and static plugin loading restrict both throughput and flexibility. In addition, the use of a proprietary FOXMAL format for Archival Information Packages (AIPs) impedes interoperability. Finally, the system lacks several essential capabilities, including provenance tracking, risk-based object management, and comprehensive reporting.

These limitations motivate the following research questions:

Q1: How can ingestion be scaled for heterogeneous content?

Q2: How can the system remain extensible without downtime?

Q3: How can open, interoperable standards be adopted?

Q4: How can commercial-grade functionality and reliability be achieved while remaining sustainable and independent?

In response, we explore the design of a new cloud-native preservation system that aligns scalable technical implementation with domain standards and the long-term preservation needs of NDPP.

2 Related Work

Recent theoretical studies have identified critical capabilities and guiding principles for next-generation digital preservation infrastructures. Rieger et al. [5] evaluate existing digital preservation and curation systems in terms of their sustainability, technical effectiveness, and institutional compatibility, highlighting gaps between strategy and implementation. Abrams [6] reconceptualizes digital preservation by first envisioning an ideal, future-oriented system unconstrained by current technologies, and then deriving abstract functional models that treat preservation as a fundamentally communicative and experiential practice. Tallman [7] emphasizes the need for scalable, standards-based technical frameworks that can adapt to evolving preservation demands in the 21st century. Cramer et al. [8] focus on the future of the preserved digital scholarly record, advocating for resilient, distributed architectures that can accommodate the increasing diversity, interconnectivity, and evolving definition of scholarly outputs. While these works provide important conceptual guidance, many lack concrete implementations.

Several digital preservation systems have emerged as practical responses to recent theoretical advances. However, none fully meets the long-term preservation requirements of NDPP. Archivematica [9] lacks version control and essential post-ingest functions such as auditing and risk monitoring. Fedora 6 [10], a digital repository that supports versioning, fixity checking, and Linked Data, still requires substantial customization to meet NDPP's scale and complexity. Commercial platforms such as LABDrive [11] and Preservica [12] fall short of NDPP's principles of independence and sustainability. Although LOCKSS [13] is open-source and targets long-term preservation of digital publications, it assumes that distributed preservation nodes can share content across the network—a model fundamentally different from NDPP's independently operated node architecture.

To bridge these gaps, this paper presents a cloud-native, in-house preservation system designed specifically for the NDPP context. It combines customizable microservices, parallel workflows, state-of-the-art domain standards, and risk-informed preservation strategies to address the program's unique demands for scalability, extensibility, and interoperability, while supporting sustainable and standards-aligned operations.

3 Methodology

3.1 Core System Functions

In the new NDPP system, each preserved object (AIP) corresponds one-to-one with a **Submission Information Package (SIP),** representing a uniquely identified scholarly record such as a journal article, book chapter, or a dissertation. Publishers periodically submit source materials (PDFs, metadata, TOCs, etc.) as transfer packages, which are processed into SIPs. A **dataset** refers to a collection of AIPs that originate from the same source, follow a unified structure, and share a preservation plan.

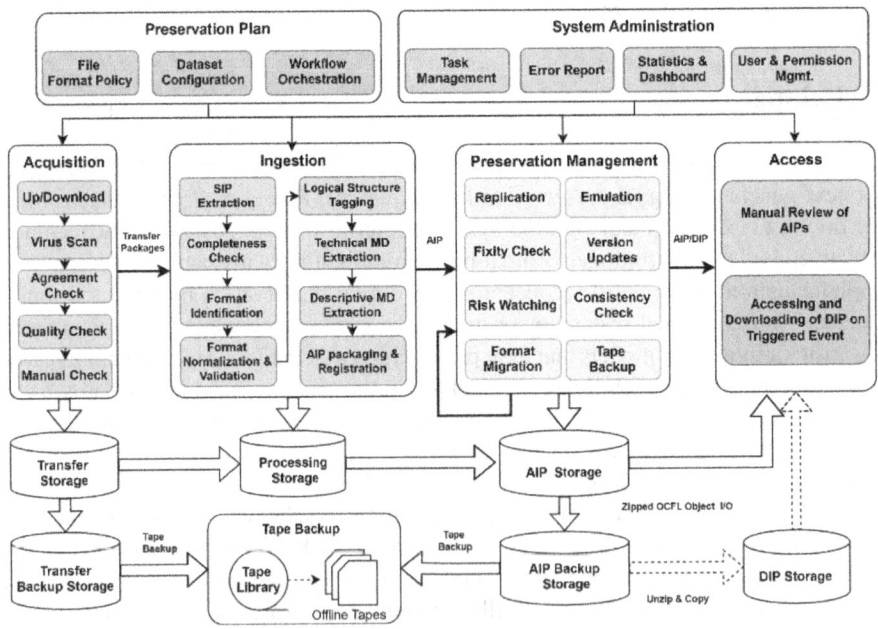

Fig. 1. Core Functions of the OAIS-Compliant NDPP Preservation System

As illustrated in Fig. 1, the system supports full life-cycle digital object management:

Acquisition collects, scans, and verifies transfer packages submitted by multiple publishers. **Ingestion** extracts and validates SIPs, enriches them with structural and technical metadata, and packages them into uniquely identified, standardized AIPs.

Preservation Management ensures long-term integrity through fixity checks, replication, format migration, and risk monitoring. **Access** enables browsing and full-text access of DIPs upon trigger events, and supports administrative review of AIPs as needed.

Preservation Plan manages format policies, dataset-level configurations, and workflow orchestration. **System Administration** provides access control, task management, monitoring, and statistical reporting—areas that are underdeveloped in the current-generation system.

3.2 The Logical Structure and Physical Storage of AIP

The system stores all AIP metadata in an XML file compliant with the METS2 schema [14], a widely adopted digital preservation standard. In the *mdSec* section, it records OAIS **Representation Information** and **Preservation Description Information** based on the PREMIS3 [15] metadata framework and its associated vocabularies [16], the de facto standard for preservation metadata. Key provenance events—such as data receipt, format migration, metadata extraction, and AIP creation—along with their execution environments and outputs, are logged using PREMIS Events, Objects, and Agents entities. The system captures descriptive metadata for both the preserved object and its related parent entities using an extended, multi-level Dublin Core schema. It represents logical and physical structures through the *structSec* section and provides an inventory and locations of the content files through the *fileSec* section.

The system organizes AIP directories following the OCFL (Oxford Common File Layout) specification [17], a best-practice standard in digital preservation. Using the OCFL library [18], it distributes AIPs under each dataset's root directory based on the SHA-512 hash of their UUID. This hashed identifier ensures even distribution and prevents filesystem bottlenecks. Within each OCFL object directory, the system stores multiple versions (e.g., v1, v2) in dedicated subdirectories to support versioned access. The OCFL library maintains an inventory.json file in each AIP directory, recording cryptographic digests, relative file paths, version metadata, and the object's logical structure. This inventory enables version tracking, deduplication across versions, automated fixity checks, and comprehensive audit trails.

Although the system partially records the above information in a relational database and an index engine, this design ensures that each AIP can be independently parsed and reindexed if detached from the system.

3.3 The Layered Software Architecture

The system adopts a layered architecture built on a fully open-source private cloud stack, as illustrated in Fig. 2.

The **Presentation Layer** consists of user interfaces developed using the Vue framework. The **Orchestration Layer** includes an external timed task manager and a custom pipeline scheduling engine, which together automate system operations.

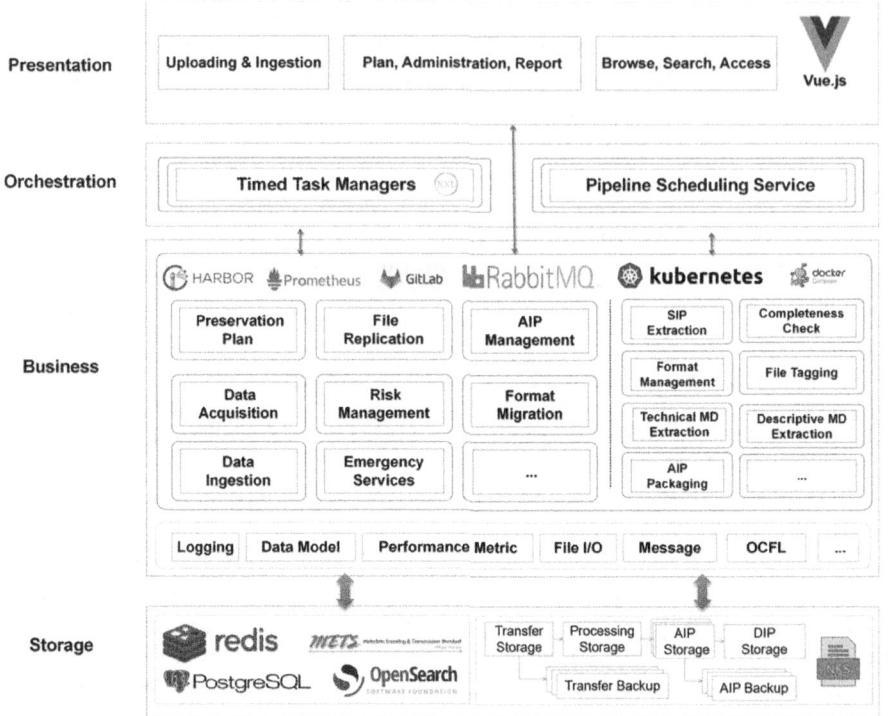

Fig. 2. Technical Architecture of the Next-Generation NDPP Digital Preservation System

The **Business Layer** comprises a set of self-developed web services and shared libraries that handle core data processing logic. Functional services (on the left) provide key capabilities such as Data Acquisition, Data Ingestion, and Emergency Services as monolithic web services, while pipeline microservices (on the right) collaboratively execute ingestion workflows under pipeline scheduling. Each service is built using the Spring Boot/Java framework and packaged into an independent JAR file (the green rectangle). These JARs are containerized via Dockerfiles into Docker images (the grey rectangle), which encapsulate not only the application but also its runtime dependencies. This containerization approach enables strong environment isolation, ensuring consistent behavior across development, testing, and production stages. Containers are deployed elastically on standalone machines or clusters via orchestration platforms (the blue rectangle) such as Kubernetes or Docker CE. As a result, each system function becomes a cloud-native service with elastic scalability, high availability, reliable environment consistency, and seamless support for Continuous Integration and Continuous Delivery (CI/CD).

The **Storage Layer** is entirely composed of external services, responsible for storing, managing, and backing up the data and metadata of digital objects.

3.4 High-Performance and Fault-Tolerant Data Ingestion Architecture

To support large-scale data submission with high throughput and fault resilience, the system implements the data ingestion function as a containerized, elastically scalable microservice pipeline. This architecture enables high-performance processing, dataset-specific workflow customization, fine-grained fault tolerance, and efficient resource utilization. For each dataset, a uniquely defined workflow—represented as an ordered sequence of ingestion microservices—is executed under the control of a central scheduler that communicates with services via a RabbitMQ message queue.

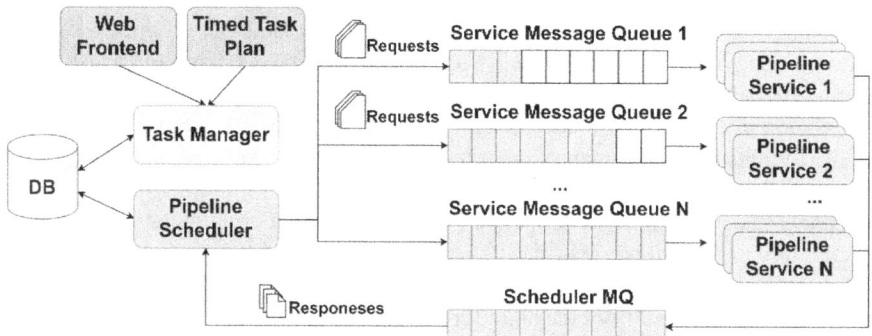

Fig. 3. The pipeline scheduling mechanism

As illustrated in Fig. 3, the scheduler periodically polls for pending tasks and dispatches them to the first microservice in the corresponding dataset's pipeline. Each microservice processes one task at a time and returns the result to the scheduler, which either forwards it to the next stage or marks it as failed. Execution control supports runtime commands such as cancel, resume, and retry. To reduce I/O overhead and prevent invalid tasks from blocking valid ones, intermediate outputs are stored in a distributed cache and processing file system. Fault isolation is further enhanced by enabling failed or paused tasks to resume from their last successful step, avoiding redundant computation.

To maximize performance under high-volume workloads, the system adopts parallelism at three levels:

Data Parallelism within Services. Utilizing the asynchronous thread pool provided by the Spring Boot framework, the system concurrently processes files, SIPs and AIPs within its custom services.

Pipeline-Level Parallelism. The ingestion pipeline is inherently parallelizable. With an average pipeline depth of N, any task volume exceeding N results in at least N tasks executing in parallel—even with only one instance per microservice.

Service Parallelism. Because microservices are deployed in containers, multiple instances of the same service can listen to a shared message queue. This allows concurrent processing of multiple tasks at the same pipeline step when workload increases.

Instance counts can be adjusted manually or automatically via Kubernetes Horizontal Pod Autoscaler (HPA) to ensure high throughput and responsiveness under varying loads.

3.5 Dynamic Plugin-Based Preservation Function Extension

To accommodate the diversity of SIPs submitted by different publishers—which may differ in directory structures and metadata formats—the system supports custom Business Plugins for tasks such as SIP directory parsing, metadata extraction, file labeling, and integrity verification. These plugins are uploaded and registered as JAR packages. Each plugin is associated with its corresponding service and dataset through a triplet rule composed of Service, Dataset, and Business Plugin. During runtime, the appropriate plugin is dynamically loaded and invoked within the service process.

To support the integration of various external tools required for processing different file formats (e.g., decompression or technical metadata extraction), the system also supports custom Format Plugins. These can be uploaded in multiple forms, including JAR packages, command-line scripts, or Python programs. Format Plugins are linked to specific services and file formats through triplets of Service, Format, and Format Plugin. Unlike Business Plugins, Format Plugins are executed as external processes, allowing them to remain isolated from the main service execution context.

These features, together with the static customization interfaces in the preservation plan module, form the functional extension mechanism to support the continuously emerging types of digital resources.

3.6 Risk-Informed Format Migration

To ensure the long-term accessibility of archived files, the system implements a risk-informed format migration strategy. Inspired by the NARA risk matrix [19], this strategy integrates a custom risk modeling approach that includes both a structured risk information model and a quantitative evaluation formula. When the system detects elevated risk levels for specific file formats, administrators can initiate migration tasks by submitting the corresponding AIPs and file lists to the Format Migration Service. Upon receiving a task, the service downloads the current version of the AIP to the temporary processing storage. It then invokes the appropriate format plugin, which encapsulates external migration tools, to perform file format conversion. Once migration is complete, the system updates the METS2 file to include technical metadata, documents provenance relationships between original and converted files, and revises both the physical and logical structure maps accordingly.

Finally, the updated AIP directory is re-submitted to the OCFL repository, replacing the previous version. This process ensures that format migration is both risk-responsive and preservation-compliant.

4 Results

The system currently ingests seven categories of scholarly resources from twelve datasets, including e-journals, e-books, conference proceedings, dissertations, numerical databases, product databases, and preprints. Hierarchical descriptive metadata is extracted and indexed, enabling structured browsing and auditing at levels such as journal, volume, serial, and conference. Full-text content is supported in PDF, HTML, and EPUB formats, while supplementary materials may include limited images, video, and audio. To scale up and support all 86 datasets across six NDPP nodes, additional processing plugins are under development.

We compared ingestion times between two system generations using real-world submission batches exceeding 100 GB and comprising hundreds of thousands of SIPs from four major publishers. The legacy system, limited to single-node deployment without parallel processing, was significantly outperformed by the new Kubernetes-based system, which ran 12 parallel processing instances across three worker nodes. As shown in Table 1, the new system achieved a 5 to 15 fold improvement in ingestion performance across diverse datasets.

Table 1. Ingestion Time Comparison Across Batches

Dataset Name	Batch Name	Old System (hrs)	New System (hrs)	Improvement
Springer Book	20250321_133952	69.36	4.6	15.1-fold
Springer Journal	20250324_091058	59.81	6.15	9.7-fold
IEEE Conference	20250612_154659	15.6	2.79	5.6-fold
WanFang Journal	20240418_151429	2.71	0.49	5.5-fold

In this comparison, each worker node in the new system was equipped with two 16-core Intel® Xeon® Silver 4314 CPUs, totaling 32 physical cores (64 threads), along with 256 GB of RAM and a 1 Gbit network connection to shared NFS storage. Resource monitoring indicated high CPU utilization and effective bandwidth usage during large-scale ingestion (see Fig. 4). In contrast, the ingestion service and Fedora 3 service of the legacy system were deployed on a single server configured with two 12-core Intel® Xeon® Silver 4214R CPUs, totaling 24 physical cores (48 threads), 1 TB RAM, and a directly attached disk array.

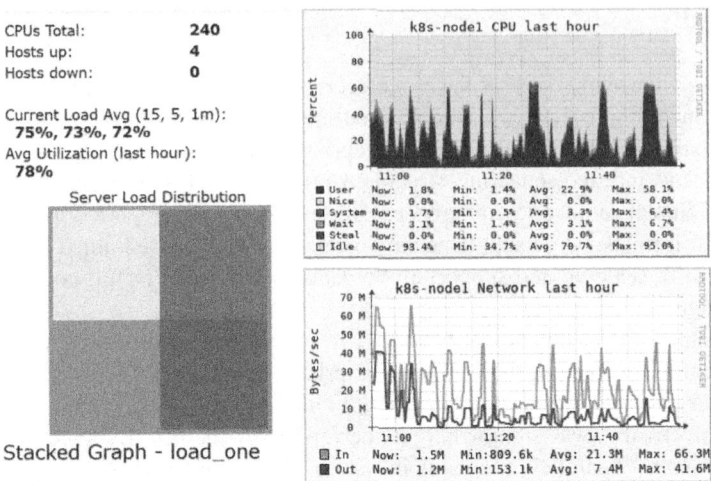

Fig. 4. Ingestion performance metrics during large-scale batch processing

5 Conclusions and Future Work

We have designed and implemented an OAIS-compliant long-term preservation system based on a private cloud infrastructure, with the specific goal of addressing the limitations of the NDPP legacy system in handling large-scale and diverse digital publishing resources. Validated through real-world ingestion scenarios, the system demonstrates good scalability, flexibility, and operational manageability. For new types of scholarly resources such as data papers, software papers, and executable papers, we are exploring strategies including the packaging of runtime environments and the integration of the Emulation-as-a-Service platform. External metadata and contextual information may be enriched via established open scholarly infrastructures such as OpenAlex [20], DataCite [21], and OpenAIRE [22].

In future work, we plan to enhance system stability, implement cross-node metadata aggregation via standardized protocols, and explore environment emulation strategies for the preservation of emerging scholarly resources. Ultimately, our objective is to provide a flexible, standards-aligned, and future-proof platform for preserving next-generation scholarly communication artifacts.

Acknowledgments. The authors gratefully acknowledge the support of the research program *"Research on Efficient Distributed Digital Preservation Repository"* (No. E4550901), funded by NSL, and the *Technical Support Talent Program 2023* (No. E4290902), funded by CAS.

References

1. Wu, Z., Zhang, X., Zheng, J., Zhang, D.: Collaborative mechanism for public digital preservation service in China. In: Proceedings of the International Conference on Digital Preservation (iPRES), pp. 1–10 (2021)

2. National Digital Preservation Program (NDPP): Emergency services. NDPP. https://ndpp.ac.cn/PreservationService_EmergencyService_en (Accessed 23 July 2025)
3. Consultative Committee for Space Data Systems: Reference Model for an Open Archival Information System (OAIS), Magenta Book, CCSDS 650.0-M-3 (2024). https://ccsds.org/wp-content/uploads/gravity_forms/5-448e85c647331d9cbaf66c096458bdd5/2025/01//650x0m3.pdf (Accessed 01 Jan 2025)
4. Fedora Development Team: Fedora Repository Architecture (Version 3). Fedora Commons (2009). https://wiki.lyrasis.org/display/FEDORA38/ (Accessed 23 July 2025)
5. Rieger, O., Schoenfeld, R., Sweeney, L.: The effectiveness and durability of digital preservation and curation systems. Ithaka S+R (2022). https://sr.ithaka.org/publications/the-effectiveness-and-durability-of-digital-preservation-and-curation-systems/ (Accessed 23 July 2025)
6. Abrams, S.: Rethinking digital preservation: Conceptual foundations. In: Proceedings of the 19th International Conference on Digital Preservation (iPRES), Urbana-Champaign, IL, USA (2023). https://hdl.handle.net/2142/121094 (Accessed 23 July 2025)
7. Tallman, N.: A 21st century technical infrastructure for digital preservation. Inf. Technol. Libr. **40**(4), 1–12 (2021). https://doi.org/10.6017/ital.v40i4.13355
8. Cramer, T., German, C., Jefferies, N., Wise, A.: A perpetual motion machine: the preserved digital scholarly record. Learned Publishing **36**(2), 312–318 (2023)
9. Archivematica Program: Archivematica: Open-source digital preservation system. Artefactual Systems, Tech. Rep. (2025). https://www.archivematica.org (Accessed 23 July 2025)
10. Fedora Project: Fedora Repository Architecture (Version 6). Fedora Commons (2023). https://docs.fedorarepository.org/en/latest/ (Accessed 23 July 2023)
11. Giaretta, D.L., Redondo, T.: Building LABDRIVE, a petabyte scale, OAIS/ISO 16363 conformant, environmentally sustainable archive. Inter. J. Digital Curat. **17**(1) (2022)
12. Smith, R.: Architectural changes for Preservica's future. Preservica Developers Blog (2022). https://developers.preservica.com/blog/architectural-changes-for-preservicas-future (Accessed 23 July 2023)
13. LOCKSS Program: Continuing to keep stuff safe with lots of copies: Communities and innovations. Stanford University Libraries, Tech. Rep. (2025). https://www.lockss.org (Accessed 23 July 2023)
14. Library of Congress: METS 2.0: Metadata Encoding and Transmission Standard. Library of Congress (2020). https://www.loc.gov/standards/mets/ (Accessed 23 July 2023)
15. PREMIS Editorial Committee: PREMIS: Preservation Metadata Implementation Strategies. PREMIS Working Group (2019). https://www.loc.gov/standards/premis/ (Accessed 23 July 2023)
16. Library of Congress: Preservation event types (PREMIS). Library of Congress Linked Data Service (2025). https://id.loc.gov/vocabulary/preservation/eventType.html (Accessed 23 July 2023)
17. Green, O.T., Lindh, T.D.: Oxford Common File Layout (OCFL) specification. Oxford University (2020). https://ocfl.io (Accessed 23 July 2023)
18. OCFL Community: ocfl-java: Java implementation of the Oxford Common File Layout (OCFL). GitHub (2024). https://github.com/OCFL/ocfl-java (Accessed 23 July 2023)
19. National Archives and Records Administration: Digital preservation framework for risk assessment and preservation planning. NARA (2024). https://www.archives.gov/preservation/digital-preservation/risk (Accessed 23 July 2023)
20. Priem, J., Piwowar, H., Orr, R.: OpenAlex: A fully open index of scholarly works, authors, venues, institutions, and concepts. arXiv preprint arXiv:2205.01833 (2022)

21. Robinson-Garcia, N., Mongeon, P., Jeng, W., Costas, R.: DataCite as a novel bibliometric source: coverage, strengths and limitations. arXiv preprint arXiv:1707.02665 (2017)
22. Artini, M., Manghi, P., Atzori, C., Houssos, N.: The OpenAIRE literature broker service for institutional repositories. D-Lib Mag. 21(11/12) (2015). https://doi.org/10.1045/november2015-artini

Identification of Potential Co-citation Linkages via Context-Aware Citation Network Embeddings

Masaki Eto

Gakushuin Women's College, Tokyo, Japan
masaki.eto@gakushuin.ac.jp

Abstract. Co-citation linkages are commonly used to measure implicit relationships between documents. Because traditional co-citation techniques have the drawback of treating the strengths of co-citation linkages equivalent within a single citing document, the analyses of citation contexts have proposed as solutions. Although an analysis that uses embeddings is one of the most promising techniques, such analysis has only been applied to co-citation linkages that are actually observed in citing documents. This study proposes a technique that identifies potential co-citation linkages via context-aware citation network embeddings. A potential co-citation linkage refers to a relationship between two documents of which one document is directly cited by a citing document, whereas the other is not; the uncited document is recommended to be cited in the same citing document based on the context-aware citation network embeddings. This study empirically evaluates the search performance of the proposed methods using potential co-citation linkages. The experimental results revealed that best-performing method outperforms baselines that target only co-citation linkages observed in the citing documents. Furthermore, the results indicated that the proposed method can appropriately incorporate potential co-citation linkages and can obtain relevant documents that are not identified by traditional co-citation searches.

Keywords: Co-citation · Citation Context · Network Embeddings

1 Introduction

In scientometrics and information retrieval, co-citation linkages are commonly used to measure the implicit relationships between documents. A co-citation refers to the linkage between a pair of documents that are concurrently cited by a third document. In the simplest retrieval method using co-citation linkages, documents are presented to the user based on the assumption that documents co-cited with a given seed document, which is known to be relevant, are likely to be topically similar to the seed document. However, traditional co-citation techniques treat the strengths of these linkages within a single citing document as equivalent, which presents a notable limitation. For example, all co-citation linkages are treated as binary; the strength of the co-citation linkages between two documents that are cited in the same sentence and the strength of co-citation linkages between two documents that are cited across paragraphs are treated as equal [1, 2].

Recently, techniques that use embeddings, such as bidirectional encoder representations from transformers (BERTs) [3], have enabled the sophisticated analyses of citation contexts and have offered a solution to this problem. For example, Eto [4] explored whether a technique using BERT could be used to accurately measure the strength of co-citation linkages within a single citing document. However, Eto's study focused only on applying the BERT technique to the co-citation linkages that were actually observed in the citing documents. Therefore, the study only contributed to improving the precision of search performance.

This study additionally focuses on applying the BERT-based technique to co-citation linkages that are not actually observed in the citing documents. In particular, this study proposes a technique that identifies potential co-citation linkages via context-aware citation network embeddings. A potential co-citation linkage refers to a relationship between two documents in which one document is directly cited by a citing document, whereas the other is not; the uncited document is recommended to be cited in the same citing document according to the context-aware citation network embeddings (Fig. 1). This proposed technique focuses on obtaining relevant documents that are not identified by traditional co-citation searches.

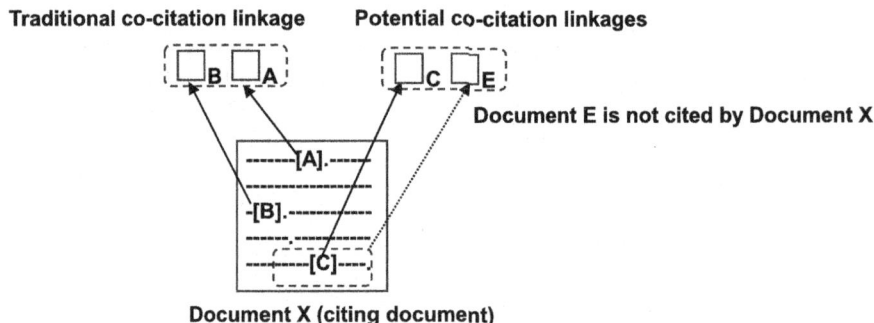

Fig. 1. Traditional co-citation linkages and potential co-citation linkages.

To evaluate the effects of using potential co-citation linkages, this study compares the search performance of the traditional co-citation-based method [4] and the proposed methods using both the traditional co-citation-based technique and potential co-citation linkages. The search performances are empirically evaluated through experiments.

2 Proposed Technique

2.1 Technique for Context-Aware Citation Network Embeddings

The proposed technique generates citation network embeddings that are aware of the citation context [5]. This technique fine-tunes the SciBERT model [6] in a masked paper prediction task. In this task, a cited document is masked (Fig. 2), and the SciBERT model is trained to predict the cited document using the citing document and the citation context.

In Fig. 2, document X is the document that originally cites documents A, B, C, and D. Document B is a masked document, and the SciBERT model outputs a list of ranked documents that may be suitable as replacements for the masked document B; documents D, C, E, A, and F are predicted.

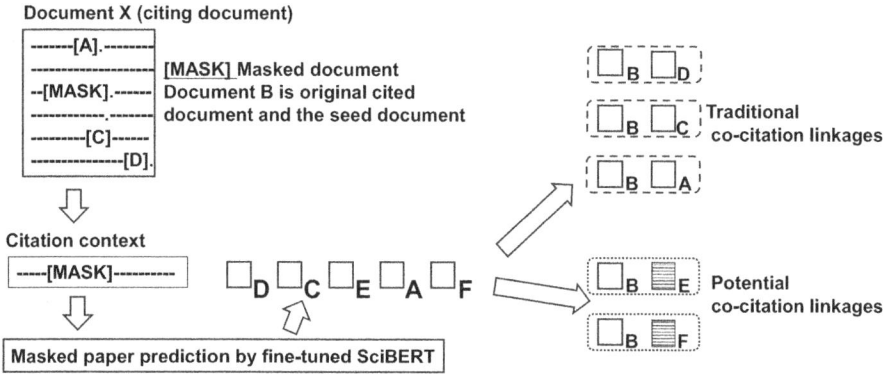

Fig. 2. Process of identifying potential co-citation linkages.

The proposed technique yields information about the co-citation linkages between the seed document (document B) and each of the predicted documents. Because the citation context for the masked document is originally written for citing document B and the SciBERT model predicts suitable documents for the context, document B and the predicted documents can be considered to be cited concurrently. In addition, the list of predicted documents includes a ranking that indicates the degree to which each of the documents is suitable for the context. This degree can be used as the strength of the co-citation linkage. The following co-citation linkages are yielded in Fig. 2: B-D, B-C, B-E, B-A, and B-F; the strongest linkage is between documents B and D.

The proposed technique yields two types of co-citation linkages: traditional and potential co-citation linkages. Traditional co-citation linkages are those observed between the seed document and each of the documents that were originally cited by the citing document, such as B-D, B-C, and B-A. Potential co-citation linkages are those observed between the seed document and each of documents that were not cited by the citing document, such as B-E and B-F.

2.2 Approaches for Ranking the Predicted Documents.

The proposed technique aims to identify a list of ranked documents with co-citation linkages using a masked document. To compile this list, this study uses the yielded co-citation information to measure the strength of co-citation linkages and to obtain relevant documents that go unidentified by traditional co-citation searches.

As described in Sect. 1, traditional co-citation search treats the strength of co-citation linkages as equivalent and cannot output a ranking from a single citing document. However, the proposed technique measures the strength of co-citation linkages from a single citing document and can output a ranking.

The proposed technique yields co-citation linkages between a seed document and the documents that are not cited by a citing document. These co-citation linkages are not included by traditional co-citation searches. Therefore, the list of co-citation linkages may include relevant documents that are not identified by traditional co-citation searches.

The proposed technique takes two approaches for identifying a list of co-citation linkages by incorporating two types of co-citation linkages. Figure 3 depicts an outline of the two approaches.

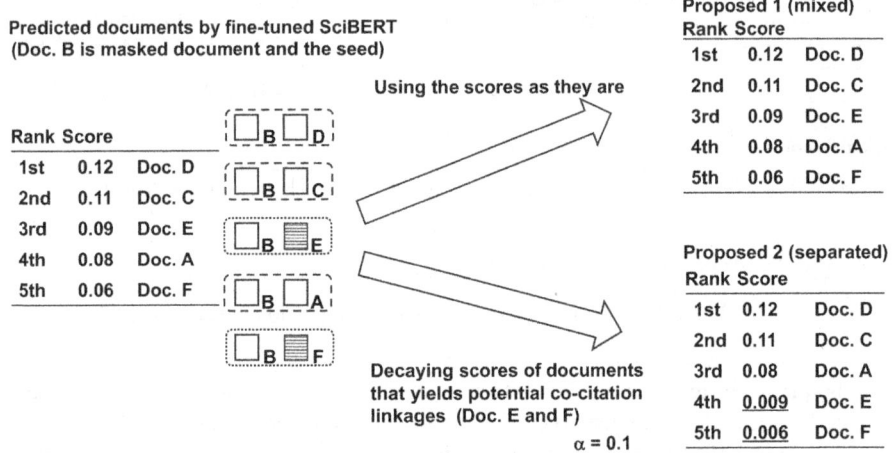

Fig. 3. Approaches for ranking the predicted documents.

Mixed Approach. This approach simply uses a ranked list predicted by the SciBERT. Alternaltively, the types of the co-citation linkages are ignored. In Fig. 3, the rank of document E, which is not cited by document X, is higher than the rank of document a, which is cited by document X. This approach means that the author of document X and the SciBERT model are equally capable of selecting documents that should be cited in document X.

Separated Approach. This approach separates the two types of co-citations During the process of ranking documents. In particular, this approach calculates scores as follows:

$$Score = \begin{cases} SciBERT\ Score (\text{if } type \text{ is traditional}) \\ \alpha \times SciBERT\ Score (\text{if } type \text{ is potential}) \end{cases} \quad (1)$$

where α is the decay factor and takes the value $0 < \alpha < 1$. This decay factor reduces the score of potential co-citation linkages because the predicted documents yielding potential co-citation linkages are not selected by the author of document X. This approach means that the author of document X is better than the SciBERT model for selecting documents that should be cited in document X. In Fig. 3, α is set as 0.01 and the scores of documents E and F are reduced. Therefore, the ranking using the separated approach shows that the top 3 documents are traditional co-citation linkages and the 4th and 5th documents are potential co-citation linkages.

3 Experimental Setup

3.1 Dataset

This study conducted experiments using the same dataset as was used in [4]. This dataset is based on the FullTextPeerRead dataset [7], and it comprises 16,669 citation contexts, where each context includes the texts preceding and following the citation position, the ID of the cited document, the title and abstract of the cited document, and the ID of the citing document. For each context, the texts were split into sentences using spaCy, which was loaded along with a biomedical text processing model (the en_core_sci_scibert model) [8]. This experiment used the two sentences preceding and following the citation position.

The aim of this experiment was to evaluate the effectiveness of the proposed technique. Rankings by the proposed methods are evaluated to determine whether each document in the rankings is relevant to the seed document. In this evaluation, a document was considered to be relevant if it shared one or more indexing terms with the seed document. As in a previous studies [4, 5], the names of the machine learning tasks defined in paperswithcode [9] were used as the indexing terms. These terms were searched for in the title and abstract of each cited document via string matching. In the search tasks, 1,362 citation contexts were used; they were extracted from the dataset in [4].

The parameters used to fine-tune the SciBERT model were identical to those employed in a previous study [4, 5]: a batch size of 16, a learning rate of $5e-5$, and 5 training epochs. The maximum length of the sub tokens preceding and following each citation position was set to 125. The sum of the token word/document, position, and token-type embeddings was used as the input representation. To fine-tune the model, we used 15,307 citation contexts obtained by excluding the 1,362 contexts that had been used for the ranking tasks from the 16,669 citation contexts.

3.2 Baselines and the Proposed Methods

This experiment evaluates the search performances of two baselines and two proposed methods. Table 1 presents the outlines of the four methods. Baseline 1 is based on the traditional co-citation search. This baseline method ranks documents randomly because traditional co-citation techniques treat the strength of co-citation linkages within a single citing document as equivalent. Moreover, the scores of documents that are not cited by the citing documents are 0 because such documents are outside the scope of Baseline 1. This baseline first randomly ranks documents that are identified by traditional co-citation linkages, and then randomly ranks the other documents, whose scores are 0.

Baseline 2 was proposed by a previous study [4]. This method targets only traditional co-citation linkages, and documents are ranked according to SciBERT scores. Because documents that are not cited by citing documents are also outside the scope of Baseline 2, the scores of such documents are 0. This baseline first ranks documents based on the SciBERT scores and then randomly ranks the other documents, whose scores are 0.

Proposed 1 targets traditional co-citation and potential co-citation. In addition, this method ranks documents based on the mixed approach (Fig. 3).

Proposed 2 targets traditional and potential co-citation linkages. In addition, this method ranks documents based on the separated approach (Eq. (1)). Because Eq. (1) has parameter α for decay, this experiment sets α to 0.01, 0.1, 0.5, and 0.9.

Table 1. Outlines of two baselines and two proposed methods.

Method	Co-citation type	Rank	Note
Baseline 1 (traditional)	Traditional	Unranked (randomly ranked) (documents whose scores are 0 are randomly ranked)	
Baseline 2 (ranked traditional)	Traditional	Ranked (documents whose scores are 0 are randomly ranked)	Eto[4]
Proposed 1 (mixed)	Traditional + Potential	Ranked by the SciBERT Score	
Proposed 2 (separated)	Traditional + Potential	Ranked by using Eq. (1)	Parameter α

4 Evaluation Results

4.1 Comparison of the Four Methods

This experiment evaluated the search performance of the baselines and the proposed methods by the average precision of the top-ranked k documents (AP@k), where k = 1, 5, 10, 15, 20, and 25.

Table 2 shows the mean scores for AP@k, and the maximum scores of the seven results at each k are shown in bold. As shown in this table, Proposed 2 (separated, α = 0.01) outperforms Baseline 2 in almost all cases; the paired t-test shows that there is a significant difference (p ≒ 0.000) between the two methods. Although Baseline 2 outperforms Proposed 2 (separated, α = 0.01) when k = 1, the paired t-test does not show that there is a significant difference (p ≒ 0.059) between the two methods.

Furthermore, the scores of Proposed 2 (separated) were higher than those of Proposed 1 (mixed). This suggests that the authors of the citing documents are superior to the SciBERT model in selecting documents that should be cited in the citing documents.

Table 2. Mean scores for AP@k.

	k					
	1	5	10	15	20	25
Baseline 1 (traditional)	0.466	0.265	0.181	0.138	0.114	0.102
Baseline 2 (ranked traditional)	**0.570**	0.305	0.200	0.152	0.126	0.113

(continued)

Table 2. (*continued*)

	k					
	1	5	10	15	20	25
Proposed 1 (mixed)	0.449	0.283	0.225	0.193	0.171	0.157
Proposed 2 (separated) $\alpha = 0.01$	0.563	**0.344**	**0.269**	**0.227**	**0.202**	**0.186**
Proposed 2 (separated) $\alpha = 0.1$	0.537	0.335	0.263	0.222	0.196	0.180
Proposed 2 (separated) $\alpha = 0.5$	0.477	0.303	0.240	0.204	0.181	0.166
Proposed 2 (separated) $\alpha = 0.9$	0.458	0.287	0.228	0.195	0.173	0.159

4.2 In-depth Evaluation of the Best-Performing Proposed Method

As discussed in Sect. 4.1, the best-performing proposed method is Proposed 2 (separated, $\alpha = 0.01$). This section presents an in-depth evaluation of the Proposed 2 (separated, $\alpha = 0.01$) method by comparing it with Baseline 2 (ranked traditional) to analyze the effects of the potential co-citation linkages.

Figure 4 shows the mean scores of AP@k, where k = 1, 2, 3…, 10. As shown in this figure, Proposed 2 outperforms Baseline 2 when k = 2 or more. In addition, as k increases in value, the difference between the two methods becomes greater. Because the scores of the proposed method are stable, this result suggests that the proposed method may appropriately incorporate potential co-citation linkages.

Table 3 presents the mean numbers of relevant documents at k. As described in Sect. 1, the aim of the proposed method is to obtain relevant documents that are not identified by traditional co-citation searches. This table suggests that users of the proposed method may obtain approximately one more relevant document when the users check the top 10 documents.

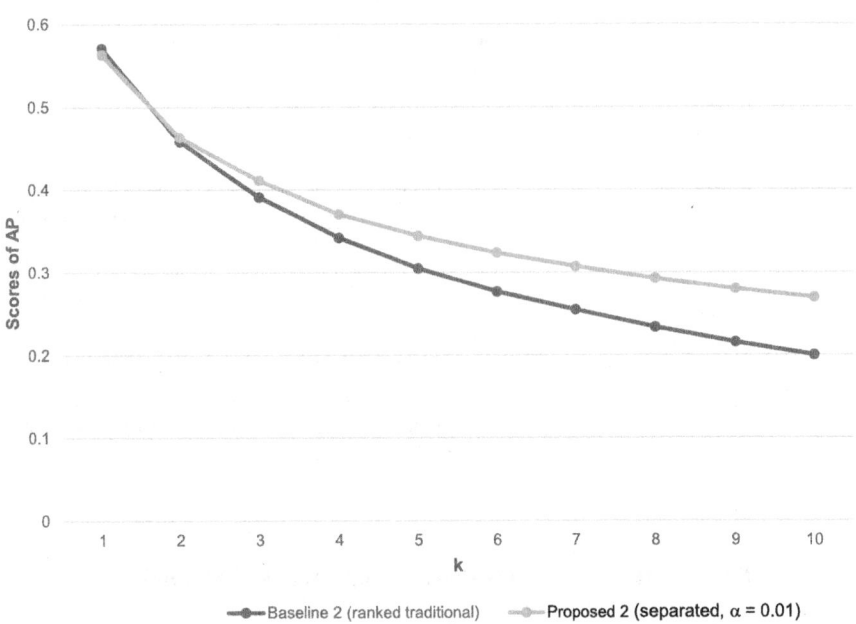

Fig. 4. Comparisons of Proposed 2 (separated) and Baseline 2 (ranked traditional).

Table 3. Mean numbers of relevant documents at k.

	k					
	1	5	10	15	20	25
Baseline 2 (ranked traditional)	0.570	1.872	2.506	2.812	3.040	3.343
Proposed 2 (separated, $\alpha = 0.01$)	0.537	2.070	3.521	4.612	5.499	6.317

5 Conclusion

This study proposes a technique that identifies potential co-citation linkages through context-aware citation network embeddings. This study empirically evaluated the search performance of the proposed methods. The experimental results revealed that the best-performing proposed method outperformed baseline methods that targeted only co-citations observed in the citing documents. Furthermore, the results indicated that the proposed method appropriately incorporated potential co-citation linkages and may have obtained relevant documents that were not identified by traditional co-citation searches.

Acknowledgments. This work was supported by JSPS KAKENHI Grant Number 23K11776.

References

1. Gipp, B., Beel, J.: Citation proximity analysis (CPA) - a new approach for identifying related work based on co-citation analysis. In: Proceedings of the 12th International Conference on Scientometrics and Informetrics, vol. 2, pp. 571–575 (2009)
2. Eto, M.: Evaluations of context-based co-citation searching. Scientometrics **94**(2), 651–673 (2013)
3. Devlin, J., Chang, M.-W., Lee, K., Toutanova, K..BERT: pre-training of deep bidirectional transformers for language understanding. In: Proceedings of the 2019 Conference of the North American Chapter of the Association for Computational Linguistics: Human Language Technologies, Volume 1 (Long and Short Papers), pp. 4171–4186 (2019)
4. Eto., M.: Can the strength of co-citation linkages be evaluated using context-aware citation network embeddings?. In: Proceedings of 2nd Workshop on Innovation Measurement for Scientific Communication (IMSC) in the Era of Big Data co-located with the ACM/IEEE Joint Conference on Digital Libraries 2024, Hong Kong and online (2024)
5. Ohagi, M., Aizawa, A.:. Pre-trained transformer-based citation context-aware citation network embeddings. In: The ACM/IEEE Joint Conference on Digital Libraries in 2022 (JCDL 2022), 20–24 June 2022, Cologne, Germany (2022)
6. Beltagy, I., Lo, K., Cohan, A.: SciBERT: A Pretrained language model for scientific text. In: Proceedings of the 2019 Conference on Empirical Methods in Natural Language Processing and the 9th International Joint Conference on Natural Language Processing (EMNLP-IJCNLP), Hong Kong, China. pp. 3615–3620, Association for Computational Linguistics (2019)
7. Jeong, C., Jang, S., Park, E.,: Choi S.: A context-aware citation recommendation model with BERT and graph convolutional networks. Scientometrics **124**, 1907–1922 (2020)
8. Neumann, M., King, D., Beltagy, I., Ammar, W.:. ScispaCy: fast and robust models for biomedical natural language processing. In: Proceedings of the 18th BioNLP Workshop and Shared Task, pp. 319–327 (2019)
9. paperswithcode, https://paperswithcode.com/sota, Accessed 20 June 2025

Demo Papers

Mass Migration of Records: LRM-Factory, a Solution to Facilitate the Transition to Linked Data for Bibliographic Agencies

Marie Bastien[1], Morgane Sedoud[1], Anne Dupiat[2]([✉]), Gregory Cochin[2]([✉]), and Carole Bruno[1]([✉])

[1] Hospices Civils de Lyon, Documentation centrale, Projet LRM-Factory, Lyon, France
{morgane.sedoud,carole.bruno}@chu-lyon.fr
[2] Tech'Advantage, Projet LRM-Factory, Lyon, France
{anne.dupiat,gregory.cochin}@tech-advantage.com

Abstract. Facilitating access to scientific bibliographic collections on the web of data is a major challenge for the sovereignty and scientific collaboration of European countries. The "LRM-Factory" project aims to create the first metadata factory to facilitate the transition to the semantic web for bibliographic agencies through the mass migration of collections to vocabularies such as RDA (Resource Description and Access). This demonstration paper will for through the full process of converting UNIMARC datasets into RDA compliant dataset through LRM-Factory.

Keywords: Bibliographic Collections · Mass Migration Tool · Web of Data · Semantic Web

1 Introduction

Early experiments of massive LRMisation showed that transformation processes cannot be achieved qualitatively by using only 1-1 correspondences between record fields and entity properties [1, 2]. The challenge is then to build a transformation model of thousands of complex rules that would still be readable by librarians during the process. The LRM-Factory project, piloted by the consortium ACASE (Access to Culture, Arts and Science through Entities), offers a solution to this challenge. There are two members of this consortium with specific missions. Tech'Advantage are the owner and developer of the integrated library system (ILS) Syrtis, capable of producing and receiving RDA records; they are also the owner and developer of CoM3T (Case-oriented MARC Metadata Migration Tool), the tool used to edit and configure mapping rules between two vocabularies based on the thesis of J. Decourselle [3]; finally, they also develop the platform called LRM-Factory giving its name to the project as it is the platform used to configure and launch conversions. The Documentation Center of the Hospices Civils de Lyon are the documentation experts of this projects: our mission in this project is to define and perfect the conversion rules for the tool CoM3T; one of our other missions is to produce documentation, as clear and reusable as possible for any documentation professional wishing to try this project available on the project's GitHub [4]. In this demonstration paper, we will present the conversion tool CoM3T and our methodology to pursue our conversion project before detailing our demonstration objectives and scenario.

2 CoM3T: A Pattern Level Migration Tool

In order to keep rules readable by non-IT people, we use an oriented graph of bibliographic patterns as a meta-model of rules [5, 6]. Each pattern, composed by entities and properties from the target model, must be a comprehensible piece of knowledge that is useful for the future users of the data. The LRM-Factory therefore calls the CoM3T engine which is capable of interacting with the transformation meta-model to reveal all the relevant patterns for each record processed, then consolidating the whole as a unified semantic graph (see Appendix 1). The validated RDF data produced can be directly reused into other tools. We also use APIs to be easily connected to third party systems (see Fig. 1).

Cataloguing structures, formats and rules are evolving quickly and it is important to be agile in the face of these changes. To remain flexible, a generic platform was created where both input and output vocabularies can be configured from external files, so the factory can be used with other formats (RDA-FR, BIBFRAME). In the current development of the project, we have been working on the conversion of UNIMARC record to RDA ontology using datasets given by the ABES' (*Higher Education Bibliographical Agency*).

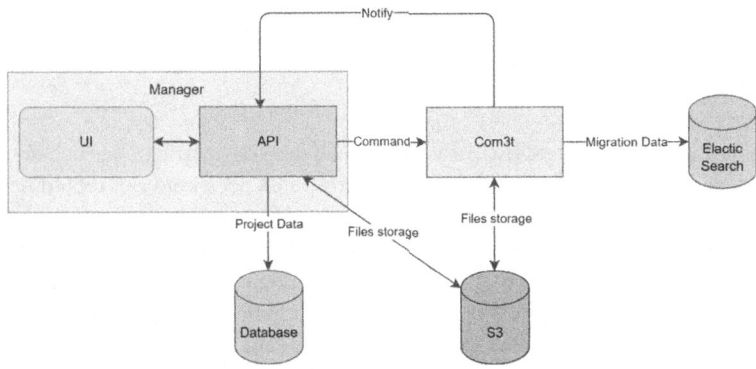

Fig. 1. Representation of the technical architecture of LRM-Factory.

3 Methodology: Working with Bibliographical Patterns

3.1 How to Work with Bibliographical Patterns

Bibliographic patterns are essential to create the mapping between UNIMARC and RDA and to develop the migration rules needed to convert ABES' dataset. As seen from our bibliographic research, no complete mapping already exists between UNIMARC and

RDA, so we decided to develop our mapping by setting up an excel mapping table expressing our rules in triplets (see Fig. 2).

tag unimarc	ind 1	Ind 2	code unimarc	position	valeur	commentaire / nom du champ F/O unimarc	exemple de valeur Unimarc Abes
200			a			Titre propre	Capitalisme et schizophrénie

Sujet	Prédicat	Objet
http://lrm-factory.fr/ressource/RDA/Manifestation#Key	http://rdaregistry.info/Elements/m/datatype/P30134	[Contenudu$a]^^xsd:string

Exemple

Sujet	Prédicat	Objet
http://lrm-factory.fr/ressource/RDA/Manifestation#Key	http://rdaregistry.info/Elements/m/datatype/P30134	"Capitalisme et schizophrénie"^^xsd:string

Fig. 2. This capture is an example taken from the work excel document for the project expressing our mapping in triplets. You can see the mapping for the title of the manifestation taken from the UNIMARC field 200$a using the property rdamd:P30134.

From the mapping table, we create and add rules to CoM3T as patterns. To create a pattern in CoM3T, we specify the position of the pattern in the global meta-migration model of patterns (by using unique references to entities to allow inheritance between patterns). For example, the supplement pattern in CoM3T's model is related to Creation encapsulating all the patterns related to RDA work entities. Then we describe any transformations to be done on input data (called "Views" in CoM3T), for example the UNIMARC field 305 "note on edition and bibliographical history" is transformed by a prefix view adding its UNIMARC title "note on edition and bibliographical history" to the object in the triplet. This enable us to keep the specificity of this field lost in RDA model since the property used is rdamd:P30137 "has note on manifestation". Finally, we add conditions to detect the targeted pattern from the UNIMARC records, for example the condition "if exist" is used for the mapping of the field 305 making explicit that this pattern will only be used if this field is present in the records.

3.2 Conversion Sprints

Being able to carry out a large number of tests in a short space of time is a key factor in guaranteeing agility and therefore the success of such migration project. In order to answer this objective, we aim to improve migration performances by leveraging macro-conditions and inheritance between bibliographic patterns. Hence, the latter can be ordered to prevent many useless computations of rules according to the librarian's principles. CoM3T also employs clustering algorithms that use specific combinations of data from the records to reduce the computing time performance of massive deduplication of created entities. Once the conversion and deduplication process are done, the results are exported and taken through a validation process.

3.3 Validation Tools

Various statistics are produced by CoM3T during the conversion process and give precise quantitative information. We also use three principal tools for validation control: Syrtis, GraphDB and SHACL (Shapes Constraints Language). The ILS Syrtis allows us to see our data in the perspective of a library catalog. It is a way for us to see the converted data in its target purpose. This enable us to see the context around our dataset and directly confront our mapping to the reality of usage. It helps us to find front-end errors or misfits. GraphDB is the triple store we use to have a direct view on the different patterns of our data. Its SPARQL endpoint is particularly useful to find specific patterns and entities but also to find and compare the RDA records from the conversion to those produced by hand. The graphs seen from the results enable us to compare old and new data easily. Finally, we have defined a SHACL specification of the expected target graph. This enables to formally validate the conformance of the RDF export's structure with the expected specification. It directly gives messages on the errors found on files and produces a report with examples. This level of precision makes the correction stage much more efficient and purposeful.

4 Demonstration: Conversion of UNIMARC Records to RDA

The tools developed for the LRM-Factory projects are still only used by the ACASE consortium members and haven't been shown to a wide audience. In order for us to showcase this part of our work and to get feedback from librarians interested in the conversion of catalog data, we present this demonstration paper. The objectives of the demonstration are: to demonstrate the complete process of a conversion starting from a simple UNIMARC record to an RDA catalog, to present all the functionalities of CoM3T, to demonstrate the process of managing a conversion sprint through LRM-Factory, to present the converted data in the ILS Syrtis and in the raw export RDF file.

Demonstration Scenarios

The silent video accompanying this paper is available at this link: https://youtu.be/HQc Fp96WTj0.

Presentation of the Chosen UNIMARC Record

For this demonstration, the chosen UNIMARC record (see Appendix 2) is a monograph titled "La mer et la vie" written by Yves Paccalet. The record is composed of basic elements: a title, an author, edition statements, general notes, subjects and identifiers. We will go through the conversion process of this record from UNIMARC to RDA using LRM-Factory and CoM3T. It will be modeled into a simple tree composed of a Work, an Expression and a Manifestation.

Presentation of CoM3T and its Parameters

CoM3T needs three configuration files to operate: incoming, outcoming and rules. The "incoming" is the file describing the input vocabulary we want to convert; in our demonstration it will be UNIMARC. The "outcoming" is the file describing the output vocabulary we want as the result of the conversion; in our demonstration it will be RDA. Those two files need to describe the vocabularies as much as needed for our conversion. The "rules" is the file containing all of the mapping rules we will create. In this demonstration, we will create a rules file from scratch in CoM3T.

Creating and Exporting Mapping Rules

CoM3T has its own vocabulary and parameters. To create a mapping there are four principal zones: cases, conditions, views and mappings. The case zone is where we will name our graph entity, the reference, and its parent (the entity it is attached to). To start our CoM3T graph, we need to create an entity connected to the root of the graph. We will create an entity referenced as Publication encapsulating all the mappings related to manifestations in RDA. The conditions zone enables the possibility to add specific treatment criteria to a mapping; for example, the mappings encapsulated in the Publication reference will only be treated if a 200$a field exists in the record with the condition "if exists". The views zone enables on the fly modification of the input data during the conversion. For example, we can add text prefixes to fields when specifications are needed; for the field UNIMARC 305 "note on edition and bibliographical history", we can choose to add the field's UNIMARC title as a prefix to keep its specificity as the RDA property chosen for this field's mapping is: rdamd:P30137 "has note on manifestation". The mappings zone is where all the mappings will be detailed, taking aspects from all the zones above and the incoming and outcoming files. This is where we will add a title to the manifestation from the 200$a field using the property rdamd:P30134 "has title of manifestation.

Mapping from to UNIMARC to RDA into CoM3T

Before mapping into CoM3T, we need to figure out how we want to map this record. Then, we will describe each of those mappings into CoM3T as presented above with the field 200$a example, going through all the entities, attributes and relations described in the RDA model. Once the mapping in CoM3T is finished, we export the final rules file and head onto LRM-Factory to manage the conversion.

Managing a Conversion in LRM-Factory

The UI of LRM-Factory enable the management of multiple conversions simultaneously. Each created conversion is called a project and is given a name and an identifier. For this demonstration, our project will be called "TPDL 2025 Demo". For each project, the UI shows a history of the actions done on the conversion. To conduct a conversion, there are steps to follow. The first step is to upload all the sources files to convert: the UNIMARC record; then the three main files used and created previously in CoM3T: incoming, outcoming and rules. Once all of those are uploaded, we will launch the analysis. The analysis gives statistics on the input dataset in UNIMARC and is the process during which CoM3T plans the conversion. After the analysis, the tool is ready to launch the conversion from UNIMARC to RDA. After the conversion, CoM3T will produce statistics on the output file in RDA. An important step after the conversion is the deduplication. Converting to RDA means creating a multitude of entities that are converted multiple times each in bigger input dataset. In our demonstration, we only create one work, manifestation and expression so we won't need this procedure. Once the conversion is done, we export it. There are two options: the first one is the export directly to the ILS Syrtis, and the second one is the export of the raw.xml file. We will now look at both of those exports.

Presentation of the Results in Syrtis and in the Raw File
For this verification, we will proceed as in any catalog and search according to the record's criteria; for example, title or author. We can then compare the entities information and the graph created within Syrtis to our first mapping description. In the raw file, we can explore the structure of the export, we then search for any structure mistakes; for example, URI coded as datatypes (text data).

Adding New Rules and Correcting the Errors Found
For this demonstration, we purposely inserted mistake into the conversion process. CoM3T is an agile tool enabling us to correct and change mappings as mistakes are found or vocabulary updated. We will go quickly through the previous process for the demonstration to show how corrections can be made and verified.

Comparing our Results
As done previously, we will search entities in CoM3T and in the raw export file to compare it to the previous results, showcasing the differences and correction made. This whole process is done as presented on bigger datasets enabling us to treat complex patterns and multitude of entities.

5 Conclusion

The software platform developed should enable millions of metadata to be processed in a simplified way. Such mass processing would be a European first. In this respect, it should be noted that the LRM-Factory project, winner of the 4th Programme d'investissements d'avenir (PIA), is supported by the State as part of the "Digitisation of heritage and architecture" scheme of the France 2030 cultural and creative industries (CCI) sector, operated by the Caisse des Dépôts. It is also worth highlighting the potential for future development. Therefore, our goal is to allow libraries to reproduce the project themselves, and so one of our missions is to produce documentation, as clear and reusable as possible and available on GitHub [4] for any documentation professional wishing to try this project.

Appendixes

Appendix 1. Representation of CoM3T's semantic graph.

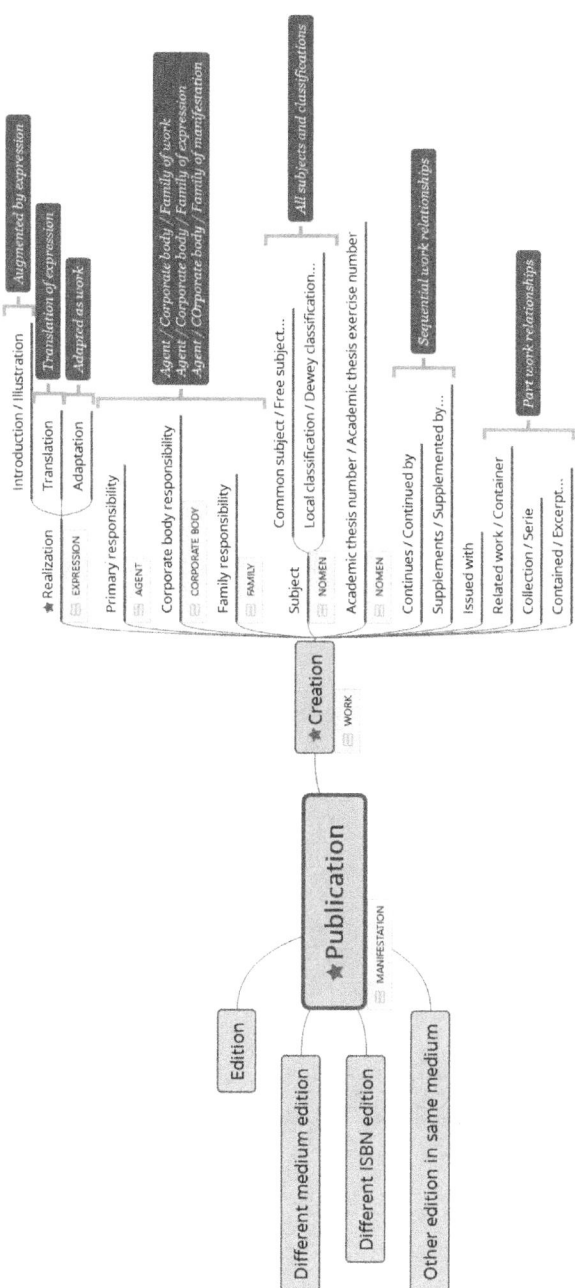

Appendix 2. The UNIMARC record chosen for this demonstration both in front office view (www.sudoc.fr) and back office view.

Identifiant pérenne de la notice :	https://www.sudoc.fr/003448738
Type(s) de contenu (modes de consultation) :	Texte
Type de support matériel :	Volume
Titre :	La mer et la vie : chronique de la mer des origines au XXe siècle / Yves Paccalet
Alphabet du titre :	Latin
Auteur(s) :	Paccalet, Yves (1945-... ; biologiste). Auteur
Date(s) :	1994
Langue(s) :	français
Pays :	France
Publication :	Paris : Larousse, 1994
Description :	1 vol. (224 p.) : ill. en noir et en coul ; 37 cm
ISBN :	2-03-505103-7 (rel.) : 300 FRF
EAN :	9782035051035
Annexes :	Bibliogr. p. 223. Index
Sujets :	Évolution (biologie) -- Ouvrages de vulgarisation
	Mer -- Ouvrages de vulgarisation
	Origine de la vie
	Écologie marine -- Ouvrages de vulgarisation
	Biologie marine -- Ouvrages de vulgarisation
	Paléo-océanographie
	Océanographie
	Animaux marins
	Ressources marines
Origine de la notice :	BN SF
Liens externes	
Catalogue Général de la BnF :	Voir la notice BnF

```
001 003448738
003 https://www.sudoc.fr/003448738
010 .. $a 2-03-505103-7 $b rel. $d 300 FRF
020 .. $a FR $b 09515212
033 .. $a http://catalogue.bnf.fr/ark:/12148/cb357324892
073 .. $a 9782035051035
100 .. $a 19950123d1994 m y0frey50 ba
101 0. $a fre
102 .. $a FR
105 .. $a a z 00|y|
106 .. $a r
181 .0 $6 01 $a i $b xxxe $a b $b xb2e
181 .. $6 02 $c txt $c sti $2 rdacontent
182 .0 $6 01 $a n
182 .. $6 02 $c n $2 rdamedia
200 1. $a La mer et la vie $b Texte imprimé $e chronique de la mer des origines au XXe siècle $f Yves Paccalet
210 .. $a Paris $c Larousse $d 1994
215 .. $a 1 vol. (224 p.) $c ill. en noir et en coul. $d 37 cm
300 .. $a Bibliogr. p. 223. Index
606 .. $3 12423905 $a Évolution (biologie) $2 rameau
606 .. $3 11932881 $a Mer $2 rameau
606 .. $3 11931063 $a Biologie marine $2 rameau
608 .. $3 12061363 $a Ouvrages de vulgarisation $2 rameau
606 .. $3 11971143 $a Écologie marine $2 rameau
700 .| $3 11918349 $o ISNI0000000121302620 $a Paccalet $b Yves $f 1945-.... $4 070
```

References

1. Aalberg, T., Merčun, T., Žumer, M.: Coding FRBR-structured bibliographic information in MARC. In: Xing, C., Crestani, F., Rauber, A. (eds.) Digital Libraries: For Cultural Heritage, Knowledge Dissemination, and Future Creation. ICADL 2011. Lecture Notes in Computer Science, vol. 7008, pp. 128–137, Springer, Heidelberg (2011)
2. Aalberg, T., Žumer, M.: The value of MARC data, or, challenges of frbrisation. J. Doc. **69**(6), 851–872 (2013)

3. Decourselle, J.: Migration et enrichissement sémantique d'entités culturelles. Thèse de doctorat, École doctorale en Informatique et Mathématiques de Lyon, Université Claude Bernard, Lyon (2018). https://theses.hal.science/tel-01919806/file/TH2018DECOURSELLEJOFFREY.pdf. Accessed 25 July 2024
4. GitHub LRM-Factory. https://github.com/LRM-Factory, last accessed 2024/07/25
5. Nuzzolese, A.G., Gangemi, A., Presutti, V., Ciancarini, P.: Encyclopedic knowledge patterns from Wikipedia links. In: Aroyo et al. (eds.) ISWC 2011, Part I, Lecture Notes in Computer Science, vol. 7031, pp. 520–536. Springer, Heidelberg (2011)
6. Aalberg, T., Duchateau, F., Takhirov, N., Decourselle, J., Lumineau, N.: Benchmarking and evaluating the interpretation of bibliographic records. Int. J. Digit. Libr. **20**(2), 143–165 (2018)
7. Tillett, B.B.: Bibliographic relationships. In: Bean, C.A., Green, R. (eds.) Relationships in the Organization of Knowledge. Information Science and Knowledge Management, vol. 2, pp. 19–35. Springer, Dordrecht (2001)
8. Tillett, B.B.: What is FRBR? A conceptual model for the bibliographic universe. Aust. Libr. J. **54**(1), 24–30 (2005)
9. Aalberg, T., Merčun, T., Žumer, M.: Interactive displays for the next generation of entity-centric bibliographic models. In: Choemprayong, S., Crestani, F., Cunningham, S. (eds.) Digital libraries: Data, information, and knowledge for digital lives, ICADL 2017. Lecture Notes in Computer Science, vol. 10647, pp. 199–211. Springer, Heidelberg (2017)
10. Aliverti, C., Behrens, R., Schaffner, V.: RDA in Germany, Austria, and German-speaking Switzerland – a new standard not only for libraries. JLIS.it. **7**(2), 253–278 (2016)
11. Arastoopoor, S., Fattahi, R.: Mapping UNIMARC fields to FRBR entities and user tasks. Int. J. Inf. Sci. Manag. **11**(1), 43–56 (2013)
12. Cross, E., Andrews, S., Grover, T., Oliver, C., Riva, P.: In the company of my peers: implementation of RDA in Canada. Cataloging Classif. Q. **52**(6–7), 747–774 (2014)
13. Delsey, T.: Functional Analysis of the MARC 21 Bibliographic and Holdings. https://www.loc.gov/marc/marc-functional-analysis/original_source/analysis.pdf. Accessed 25 July 2024
14. Lee, S., Jacob, E.K.: An integrated approach to metadata interoperability. Libr. Resour. Tech. Serv. **55**(1), 17–32 (2011)
15. Morris, S.R., Wiggins, B.: Implementing RDA at the library of congress. JLIS.it **7**(2), 199–228 (2016)
16. Parent, M.: Implementing RDA in a time of change: RDA and system migration at RMIT university. Cataloging Classif. Q. **52**(6–7), 775–796 (2014)
17. Riva, P.: Mapping MARC 21 linking entry fields to FRBR and Tillett's taxonomy of bibliographic relationships. Libr. Resour. Tech. Serv. **48**(2), 130–14 (2004)
18. Seppälä, M.-L.: Mapping from RDA to BIBFRAME. In: EURIG 2024 Open Session. https://www.rdatoolkit.org/sites/default/files/uploads/MappingRDABIBFRAME_Eurig2024.pdf. Accessed 25 July 2024
19. Young, T.: RDA implementation at the British Library. https://www.slideshare.net/CILIPCIG/rda-implementation-at-the-british-library-thurstan-young-british-library. Accessed 25 July 2024
20. Wennerlund, B., Berggren A.: Leaving comfort behind: a National Union Catalogue Transition to linked data. https://library.ifla.org/id/eprint/2745/1/s15-2019-wennerlund-en.pdf. Accessed 25 July 2024
21. Zapounidou, S., Ioannidis, L., Gerolimos, M., Koufakou, E., Bratsas, C.: Entity management using RDA and wiki base: a case study at the national library of Greece. J. Libr. Metadata **24**(40), 1–21 (2024)

22. Bibliographic Framework Initiative. https://www.loc.gov/bibframe. Accessed 25 July 2024
23. Bibliographic Transition in France Homepage. https://www.transition-bibliographique.fr. Accessed 25 July 2024
24. Joint Steering Committee for Development of RDA Homepage. https://www.rdatoolkit.org/archivedsite. Accessed 25 July 2024

Drawio2Triples: Semantic Validation and RDF Transformation of CIDOC CRM Example Diagrams

Elias Tzortzakakis[1] and Pavlos Fafalios[1,2]

[1] Information Systems Laboratory, FORTH-ICS, Heraklion, Greece
[2] Technical University of Crete, Chania, Greece
{tzortzak,fafalios}@ics.forth.gr

Abstract. Drawing diagrams is a common practice in ontology documentation, used either to better communicate and explain the context of specific functional units of a model or to demonstrate use cases through examples based on well-known, meaningful stories and events. Drawio2Triples is a tool tailored for CIDOC CRM, a formal ontology widely used in the cultural heritage domain for documenting museum collections, historical archives, and other cultural resources. The tool supports the validation of ontology example diagrams created with diagrams.net (a.k.a. draw.io) and their transformation into RDF triples, suitable for storage in triplestore databases or use with RDF data management and ontology development tools. The validation process can detect semantic errors, such as invalid domain or range specifications of properties, incorrect use of property direction, or simple typos in the names of classes and properties. The tool is especially useful for pedagogical purposes, such as ontology learning, and is currently being extended to support any formal ontology.

Keywords: CIDOC CRM · Semantic Validation · Diagram Transformation · Ontology Learning · Draw.io · RDF

1 Introduction

Drawing diagrams is a common and long-established practice in ontology documentation and communication. Diagrams are often used to explain the structure and semantics of a model, to focus on specific functional units, or to illustrate practical use cases through examples. They support better understanding by providing a visual context that complements the formal definition of the ontology, can facilitate its communication with domain experts who are less familiar with formal notations, and can be particularly helpful in pedagogical settings, such as ontology learning and training activities, where diagrams of ontology instances facilitate the comprehension of the ontology concepts.

An example of a formal ontology is the CIDOC Conceptual Reference Model (CIDOC CRM) which is an ISO standard (ISO 2117:2023) and has been extensively used for information integration in the field of cultural heritage [3]. Due to its event-centric nature and complex hierarchy of classes and properties, diagrams can greatly facilitate the understanding of the semantics of core classes and properties, clarify modeling patterns, and provide users with intuitive entry points to the ontology.

In recent years, the diagrams.net tool (also known as draw.io) has become widely used for creating such visual representations, due to its ease of use, browser-based interface, and support for collaborative editing. It allows ontology engineers and practitioners to manually construct diagrams that refer to ontology elements (instances, classes, properties), either for conceptual design, examples depiction, teaching, or documentation purposes.

However, the process of manually creating ontology instantiation diagrams inevitably introduces the possibility of semantic errors. Common mistakes include assigning properties to instances with incorrect domain or range classes, using inverse directions unintentionally, or including invalid or mistyped class and property names. These issues can lead to confusion, misinterpretation, or inconsistency between the diagram and the formal ontology, especially in cases where the diagram is used as a basis for further modeling or implementation.

To address this need, we introduce Drawio2Triples, a tool tailored for the CIDOC CRM ontology that supports the semantic validation and transformation of ontology instances diagrams created with draw.io. The tool parses the diagram content and checks for logical consistency with respect to the latest official version of CIDOC CRM. It reports semantic issues such as invalid domain-range usage, directionality errors, and unrecognized elements. Furthermore, it transforms the content of the diagram into RDF triples, enabling its use in triplestore databases or related RDF data management or ontology development applications. The tool also supports embedding of one or more images within a diagram. Each image is extracted and encoded in base64, allowing it to be included directly in the resulting RDF representation.

The tool is publicly available through the web[1]. While it has been initially designed for diagrams based on CIDOC CRM use cases, it is currently being extended to support any formal ontology.

The rest of this paper is organised as follows. Section 2 provides the required background and discusses related works. Section 3 details the functionality of the application. Finally, Sect. 4 concludes the paper and discusses future work.

2 Background and Related Work

2.1 Draw.io

The diagrams.net tool (also known as draw.io)[2] is a graph drawing software application used to create diagrams such as flowcharts, process diagrams, UML diagrams, network diagrams, and others. It is available both as a web application (for online use) and desktop application (for offline use), and has been

---

[1] https://isl.ics.forth.gr/cidoc_services/drawioXMLToTriples/.

[2] https://diagrams.net/.

widely used for creating visual representations of ontologies due to its ease of use, intuitive interface, and support for both online and offline editing.

One of its core features is the use of a structured XML format for serializing and storing diagrams. Each diagram created in draw.io is represented as an XML document that encodes the layout, shapes, labels, styles, and interconnections of the graphical elements. This XML structure enables programmatic access to the contents of a diagram, making it suitable for automated processing, transformation, or validation. In the context of ontology documentation, this format allows for the extraction of semantic elements from the visual layer, such as classes, properties, and instances, which can then be interpreted and converted into machine-readable formats.

2.2 Use Case: CIDOC CRM

The CIDOC Conceptual Reference Model (CIDOC CRM)[3] is a formal ontology developed for the cultural heritage domain, aiming to facilitate the integration, mediation, and exchange of heterogeneous documentation about museum collections and other cultural objects [3]. It has been an ISO standard since 2006 (ISO 21127) and has since undergone two official (ISO) revisions, in 2014 and 2023.[4] The latest stable community version is 7.1.3 (February 2024).[5]

The ontology is fundamentally event-centric, modeling the world in terms of events and spatiotemporal processes that connect actors, objects, places, and concepts. This approach enables the representation of rich contextual information and the dynamic aspects of cultural heritage data. It is extensively used by cultural institutions, research projects, and heritage information systems as a semantic framework for data integration and semantic interoperability. However, its expressive power comes with considerable complexity, as it includes a deep class hierarchy, a rich network of properties, and a variety of modeling constructs that require careful application. Indicatively, its latest release (7.1.3) consists of 81 classes, 160 properties, and a class hierarchy with a depth of nine levels.

To support understanding and adoption, diagrams play a key role in CIDOC CRM documentation. They are used to illustrate modeling examples, demonstrate use cases, and explain core notions of the ontology in a visual and pedagogically effective manner. To facilitate the creation of diagrams, a dedicated CIDOC CRM library for draw.io has been developed by the Canadian Heritage Information Network (CHIN).[6] The library contains the shapes of all the classes as well as the connectors for the properties of each ontology, while the colour scheme is the one adopted by the Special Interest Group (SIG) of CIDOC CRM.[7]

---

[3] https://cidoc-crm.org/.
[4] https://www.iso.org/standard/85100.html.
[5] https://cidoc-crm.org/versions-of-the-cidoc-crm (accessed on June 2, 2025).
[6] https://github.com/chin-rcip/diagrams.net_libraries.
[7] More in: https://cidoc-crm.org/Resources/cidoc-crm-graphical-representation-templates.

2.3 Related Work

A wide range of tools have been developed for visualizing RDF data [1]. These tools typically focus on graph-based representations of semantic data to support navigation, exploration, and understanding. Examples include LodLive [2], VOWL [10], and WebVOWL [9]. While effective for presenting data that already exists in RDF form, these tools operate in the opposite direction of our approach: they take RDF as input and produce visual representations, whereas Drawio2Triples starts from visual diagrams and produces RDF data as output.

Closer to our work are tools and approaches that support the construction of ontology instances (RDF content) through graphical interfaces or diagrammatic input. For example, Graffoo [5] allows users to create diagrams that represent OWL ontologies and provides mappings to OWL constructs, although it is mainly used for ontology design rather than instantiation. Similarly, tools like WebProtégé [7] and VocBench [11] provide form-based interfaces for entering RDF/OWL content, but they lack support for free-form diagrammatic modeling. Finally, some research prototypes have explored template/form-based and sketch-driven ontology population, but these are often limited in scope or lack semantic validation capabilities. Examples include Populus [8] (providing a spreadsheet-like interface), and OntoCAD [6] (tailored to CAD drawings and buildings-related ontologies).

To our knowledge, Drawio2Triples is the first tool that combines support for free-form ontology instantiation diagrams (via draw.io), semantic validation against an underlying ontology, and transformation into RDF triples. This makes it particularly suitable for documentation, teaching, and rapid prototyping of data using a very familiar (to end users) visual paradigm.

3 The Drawio2Triples Application

3.1 Input and Output

The application takes as input one `.drawio` file, which is an XML file used to save and store the data of a draw.io diagram. The output of the application includes:

- statistics: number of classes and number of properties (in plain text format),
- ontology validation issues along with information on how to fix them (in plain text format),
- the generated RDF data in two formats: Turtle (.ttl) and RDF/XML (.rdf).

For the transformation to RDF, we consider the RDFS generation policies adopted by CIDOC CRM.[8] For example, when an instance of the class `E62 String` is detected, it is not represented as a separate resource; instead, its value is assigned directly as a literal. The same is followed for the classes `E59 Primitive Value`, `E60 Number`, `E61 Time Primitive`, `E94 Space Primitive`, and `E95 Spacetime Primitive`.

---

[8] https://gitlab.isl.ics.forth.gr/cidoc-crm/cidoc_crm_rdf/-/tree/master/7.1.3.

The URIs of the class instances in the two RDF files consist of a constant prefix and a unique ID. The ID is the same as that of the shape in the draw.io file. In addition to the RDF triples that describe the instances depicted in the diagram, the generated RDF files include three supplementary triples: one that represents the entire diagram as an instance of rdfs:Resource, one that assigns a label (rdfs:label) to this resource, and one that provides a comment (rdfs:comment). The label follows the format: "CIDOC-CRM v7.1.3 example produced by input file: <filename.drawio>". The comment includes the statistics and any validation errors that were detected (more below). A related future task is to make all the above configurable through the user interface.

3.2 Diagram Design Requirements

For the creation of a class instance, the "List" shape from the general library should be used. The name of the class must be written in the upper section of the shape and the name of the class instance in the lower section, as illustrated in Fig. 1a. Optionally, an image can be included at the bottom of the shape (Fig. 1b). The image must be embedded within the shape (by dragging and dropping it onto the shape). During data transformation, the image is automatically encoded in base64 and embedded in the resulting RDF file.

For the properties connecting class instances, any of the arrows can be selected. The name of the ontology property should be entered in the textbox that appears after double-clicking the arrow, and the arrow's source and target endpoints must be correctly attached to the class instances (see Fig. 1c).

If syntactic errors are detected in the diagram, such as a property whose source or target endpoint is not property attached, the application displays an error message to the user and does not proceed to the validation and transformation processes.

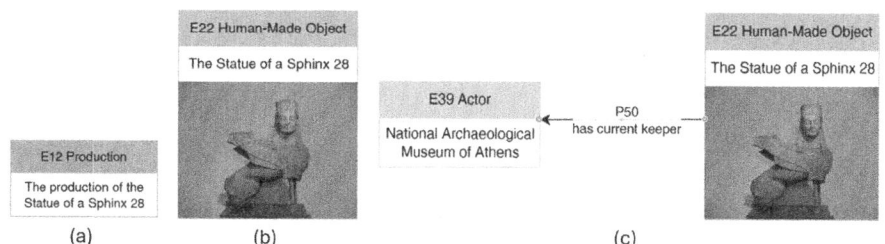

Fig. 1. Example of drawing (a) a class instance, (b) a class instance together with an image, and (c) a property instance connecting two class instances, in draw.io.

An alternative (and more convenient) way for adding CIDOC CRM class and property instances into the draw.io diagram is to use a ready-made library[9] which

---

[9] https://isl.ics.forth.gr/cidoc_services/files/examples/diagrams_to_triples/CIDOC-CRM_7.1.3_examples_library.xml.

contains all classes and properties of the latest official CIDOC CRM version (7.1.3) and which follows the colour scheme adopted by CIDOC CRM. The library can be quickly imported from the draw.io menu (File → Open Library From: → URL). The examples of Fig. 1 make use of this library.

Properties of Properties. CIDOC CRM contains properties that have their own properties (called .1 properties). In this case, the domain of the property is a property and the range a class. An example is the property *P14 carried out by: E39 Actor* (of E7 Activity) which has the property *P14.1 in the role of: E55 Type*. This .1 property allows specifying the role that the actor had while carrying out the activity.

Since RDF does not provide a direct way to express properties of properties, there have been different approaches on how to implement them, including standard RDF reification, named graphs, singleton properties, N-ary relations, and RDF-star (see Sect. 3.3 in [4] for more details). CIDOC CRM SIG recommends to implement them using *property classes* and provides a supplementary RDFS file for this.[10] Drawio2Triples follows this approach for validating and transforming .1 properties existing in the drawing. Such properties are defined similarly to simple property arrows by specifying the target endpoint of the arrow to a class instance and grouping together the .1 and the parent property arrows. An example is shown in Fig. 2.

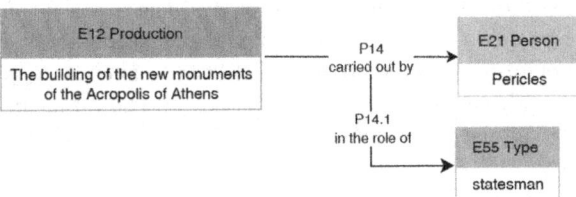

Fig. 2. Example of drawing a property of property (.1 property) in draw.io.

3.3 Validation

The application performs the following ontology consistency checks and provide feedback on how to resolve them:

– *Invalid domain or range class*: Each CIDOC CRM property has a specific domain and range class. However, valid domain or range classes include not only the explicitly defined ones, but also all their subclasses, as determined

---

[10] See the file CIDOC_CRM_v7.1.3_PC.rdf at: https://gitlab.isl.ics.forth.gr/cidoc-crm/cidoc_crm_rdf/-/tree/master/7.1.3.

by the transitive closure of subclass relationships in the ontology. When such an error is detected, the application suggests the correct set of domain or range classes associated with the property.
- *Wrong property direction*: Most CIDOC CRM properties have inverse properties. For example, the property *P2 has type: E55 Type* (of E1 CRM Entity) has the inverse property *P2i is type of: E1 CRM Entity*. A common mistake is using the property in the wrong direction when linking an instance of the domain class to an instance of the range class. When such an error is detected, the application suggests using the appropriate inverse property.
- *Unknown class or property name*: This occurs when the name of a class or property does not match any class or property in CIDOC CRM, typically due to a typo or the use of a deprecated term. When such an error is detected, the application suggests renaming the class or property name.

If one or more of the above errors are detected, the application continues generating the RDF files and embeds error descriptions as a comment using the rdfs:comment property.

3.4 Web Interface

The application is accessible online at: https://isl.ics.forth.gr/cidoc_services/drawioXMLToTriples/. Figure 3 displays the home page. Users can either upload their own draw.io diagram or choose from twenty preloaded examples.[11]

Figure 4 shows the resulting webpage after validation and RDF transformation have been completed. In this example, the validation process identified two issues and provides guidance on how to correct them. The entire validation and transformation process takes only a few seconds.

3.5 Demonstration Scenarios

Apart from experimenting with the twenty preloaded example diagrams, users can interact with the application through the following scenarios:

- **Scenario 1**: Create a simple diagram in draw.io, save it locally, and upload it to the Drawio2Triples application for validation and transformation into RDF. Then, examine the generated statistics and inspect the RDF triples.
- **Scenario 2**: Introduce a syntactic error in the diagram such as a property whose source or target endpoint is not properly attached to the corresponding class shape. Identify the error through validation, correct it, and retry.
- **Scenario 3**: Introduce a semantic error, such as assigning a property to a class with an invalid domain or range. Use the feedback provided by the application to identify the issue, make the necessary corrections, and retry.

---

[11] Developed as part of a MSc thesis at the University of West Attica, Greece.

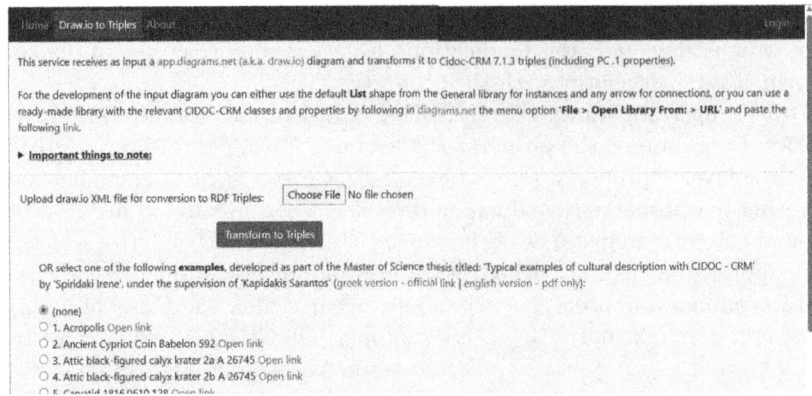

Fig. 3. The web interface of the Drawio2triples application.

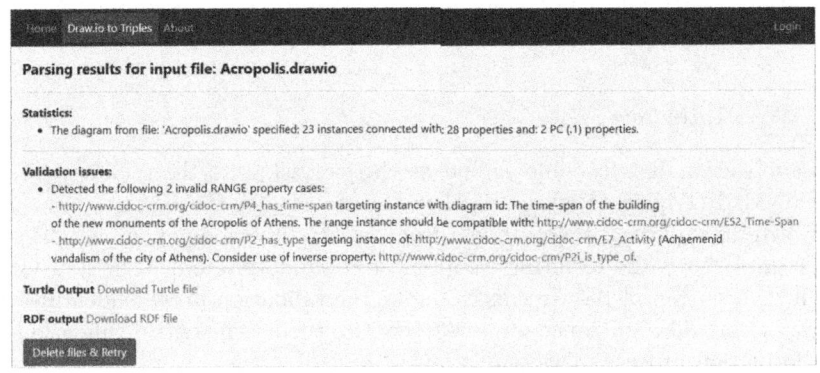

Fig. 4. The webpage after validation and transformation have been completed.

4   Conclusion and Future Work

We have presented Drawio2Triples, an application that validates and transforms ontology instantiation diagrams created with draw.io. The validation concerns the detection of semantic errors, such as the use of invalid domain or range classes for properties. The output includes statistics, description of the validation issues along with information on how to correct them, and RDF files of the ontology instances in Turtle and RDF/XML formats.

We are currently working on generalizing the application to support any input ontology. We also plan to extend it to enable the validation and transformation of diagrams representing ontologies or ontology extensions. This will facilitate the graphical construction of new ontologies and their rapid serialization.

Acknowledgments. The authors sincerely thank Martin Doerr for motivating the development of the application, as well as Irene Spiridaki and Sarantos Kapidakis (Univ. of West Attica, Greece) for their extensive use of the application, their feedback, and for contributing the examples included in the web application. This work has received funding from the European Union under Grant Agreement No. 101157364 – ECHOES.

References

1. Antoniazzi, F., Viola, F.: RDF graph visualization tools: a survey. In: 2018 23rd Conference of Open Innovations Association (FRUCT), pp. 25–36. IEEE (2018)
2. Camarda, D.V., Mazzini, S., Antonuccio, A.: Lodlive, exploring the web of data. In: Proceedings of the 8th International Conference on Semantic Systems, pp. 197–200 (2012)
3. Doerr, M.: The CIDOC conceptual reference module: an ontological approach to semantic interoperability of metadata. AI Mag. **24**(3), 75 (2003)
4. Fakih, G., Serrano-Alvarado, P.: A survey on sparql query relaxation under the lens of rdf reification. Semantic Web **15**(6), 2507–2554 (2024)
5. Falco, R., Gangemi, A., Peroni, S., Shotton, D., Vitali, F.: Modelling owl ontologies with Graffoo. In: Presutti, V., Blomqvist, E., Troncy, R., Sack, H., Papadakis, I., Tordai, A. (eds.) ESWC 2014. LNCS, vol. 8798, pp. 320–325. Springer, Cham (2014). https://doi.org/10.1007/978-3-319-11955-7_42
6. Häfner, P., Häfner, V., Wicaksono, H., Ovtcharova, J.: Semi-automated ontology population from building construction drawings. In: KEOD, pp. 379–386 (2013)
7. Horridge, M., Gonçalves, R.S., Nyulas, C.I., Tudorache, T., Musen, M.A.: Webprotégé: a cloud-based ontology editor. In: Companion Proceedings of The 2019 World Wide Web Conference, pp. 686–689 (2019)
8. Jupp, S., et al.: Populous: a tool for building owl ontologies from templates. BMC Bioinform. **13**, 1–12 (2012)
9. Lohmann, S., Link, V., Marbach, E., Negru, S.: Webvowl: web-based visualization of ontologies. In: Lambrix, P., et al. (eds.) EKAW 2014. LNCS (LNAI), vol. 8982, pp. 154–158. Springer, Cham (2015). https://doi.org/10.1007/978-3-319-17966-7_21
10. Lohmann, S., Negru, S., Haag, F., Ertl, T.: Visualizing ontologies with vowl. Semantic Web **7**(4), 399–419 (2016)
11. Stellato, A., et al.: Vocbench 3: a collaborative semantic web editor for ontologies, thesauri and lexicons. Semantic Web **11**(5), 855–881 (2020)

Interactive Association Map Creation from Documents Using Association Rule Mining

Efthimios Mitkousis[1] and Yannis Tzitzikas[1,2](✉)

[1] Computer Science Department, University of Crete, Heraklion, Greece
tzitzik@ics.forth.gr
[2] Information Systems Laboratory, FORTH-ICS, Heraklion, Greece

Abstract. One method to aid the understanding of a document corpus is to try constructing *automatically* a word/term/knowledge map for that corpus by analyzing the contents of the documents. Several methods have been proposed in the literature for this task. In this paper we investigate a novel method that is based on *Association Rule Mining (ARM)*. ARM was proposed for databases, for structured data in general, as a method for data mining, e.g. for market basket analysis. Here we investigate its application over documents. In particular, we leverage association rule mining, through the *Apriori* algorithm, to find pairs of terms that co-occur in documents and their association. Each rule is characterized by its *confidence* and *support*. Then we map these rules to graphical elements. A key merit of the approach is that the user can interactively change the *confidence* and *support* threshold and obtain a different visualization. The evaluation over small datasets, up to datasets with 125.654 distinct words, showed that this approach is feasible and can produce maps that show the dominating words and connections.

Source code: https://github.com/EfthimisM/AssociationMaps
Video: https://youtu.be/eN9VrmmS6Ls.

Keywords: Taxonomy Creation · Topic Extraction · Association Rule Mining

1 Introduction

MOTIVATION. In many cases we have to construct a taxonomy/map of words or phrases or entities from a particular corpus of documents, as a means to facilitate the *understanding* of the domain, the understanding of the contents of the corpus, as well as for other tasks including *key topics detection*, production of *summaries and overviews*, detection of *unexpected associations*, etc.

APPROACH. We reduce the problem of map construction to *association rule mining*, and investigate and experimentally analyze various options concerning the words to select, as well as the effect of *confidence* and *support*. The process is illustrated in Fig. 1.

Interactive Association Map Creation from Documents Using ARM

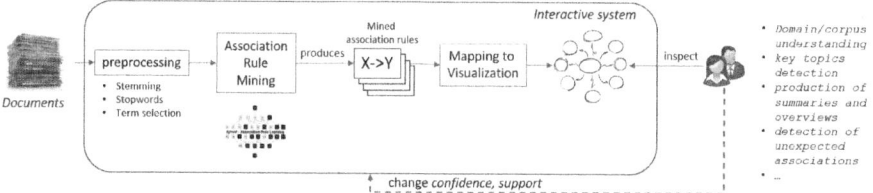

Fig. 1. Overview of Association Rule mining over documents

RELATED WORK and NOVELTY. The problem of automatic construction of lexicons, taxonomies, ontologies, and knowledge graphs is subject of research for many years. Related work include clustering [9,20], taxonomy creation [12,13,16], automated creation of faceted taxonomies [4], methods for automatic *ontology* construction from text (e.g. see the review [2] that captures shallow and deep learning methods), as well as recent methods that use LLMs (Large Language Models) for automatically producing ontologies, e.g. [3]. To the best of our knowledge this is the *first work* that reduces the problem of topic/taxonomy/map creation to association rule mining. We call the produced maps **Association-Maps**. If applied without any preprocessing or restriction we get an *association word map*. If applied after entity mining, we get an *association knowledge graph*. If applied over a predefined terminology we get an *association taxonomy*. Key emphasis is given on *transparency*, i.e. on enabling the user to interactively change the values of confidence/support, as a means to aid understanding. Another merit is that all the produced edges have a clear interpretation, and the efficiency of this method in comparison to methods based on embeddings.

DEMONSTRATION. We shall demonstrate a system that offers this functionality over various datasets and we shall see how confidence and support affects the results. Finally, the paper reports various measurements and findings by testing this method over various datasets and settings.

2 Background: Association Rule Mining

Association Rule Mining (ARM) is a rule-based machine learning method for discovering interesting relations between variables in large databases. Such processes involve detecting frequent itemsets, which are groups of items that commonly appear together, and then creating rules based on these itemsets. Let U be the set of all *objects* (e.g. all products). A *transaction* (e.g. a market basket) is any subset of U. An *association rule* has the form $A \to B$ where A and B are two disjoint sets of objects ($A, B \subseteq U$, and $A \cap B = \emptyset$). A rule $A \to B$ is characterized by its *support* and *confidence* which are metrics to calculate the importance of the given rule. If T is the set of transactions, $I(S)$ denotes the transactions that contain the set of objects in S ($S \subseteq U$), then the support and confidence of a rule $A \to B$ is defined as: $support(A \to B) = \frac{|I(A) \cap I(B)|}{|T|}$, i.e. it is the proportion of T that contain both A and B, while $confidence(A \rightarrow B) = \frac{|I(A) \cap I(B)|}{|I(A)|}$, i.e. it is the proportion of the transactions in $I(A)$ that also contain B. The end goal is to find all possible rules that have high enough $confidence$ and $support$. There are many algorithms for mining association rules, however the most commonly used, and the one we used in our work, is the *Apriori* Algorithm [1]. It works by identifying the frequent individual items in the database and extending them to larger and larger item sets as long as those item sets appear sufficiently often in the database. The frequent item sets determined by Apriori can be used to determine association rules which highlight general trends in the database, and this has various applications in domains such as market basket analysis.

3 Mapping to Association Rule Mining

In our case, the notion of item(s) correspond to word(s), and the notion of transaction corresponds to the notion of document. Therefore through ARM we can create rules for words and phrases that commonly occur in the same documents. The configuration parameters, *support* and *confidence*, are also useful in our setting: the *support* can be used to filter out rules that occur too few times (note that in documents in most of the cases we have a lot of words that occur too few times), while the *confidence* can be used to infer words with high co-occurence as well as taxonomic relationships.

Let $D = \{d_1, \ldots, d_n\}$ be the collection of documents. For a $d \in D$ we shall use $words(d)$ to denote the set of distinct words that appear in d. Let $Words = \cup \{words(d) \mid d \in D\}$. If S is a set, we shall use $P(S)$ to denote the powerset of S, e.g. if $S = \{a, b\}$, then $P(S) = \{\{a, b\}, \{a\}, \{b\}, \emptyset\}$. Let us include a small example to grasp the idea of ARM. Consider the following toy collection of documents:

TID	Items
T1	An apple is a fruit
T2	Apples are red
T3	Red is a color
T4	Apples are either green or red
T5	Apples are red fruits

At first we remove the *stopwords*, and we perform word *stemming*, ending up with the itemset $U = \{appl, fruit, red, green, color\}$. Their document frequency and occurrences are:

appl (4): T1, T2, T4, T5
fruit (2): T1, T5
red (4): T2, T3, T4, T5
green (1): T4

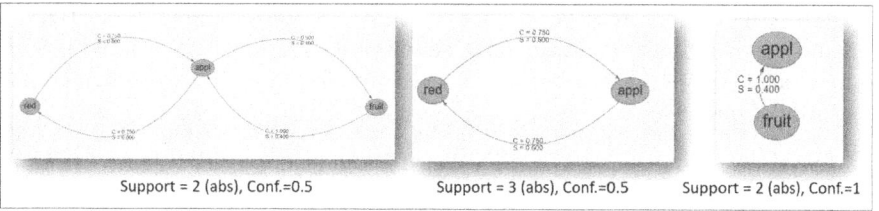

Fig. 2. Mined rules for various support and confidence values.

color (1): T3

If we set the following thresholds: $support = 2$ (as an absolute value, not as a percentage), and $confidence = 0.5$, then we get the following four rules:
- $\{appl\} \to \{fruit\}$ with confidence $= 0.5$. This holds because the number of documents where apple and fruit appear together is 2 (T1, T5) and the number of documents that we find apple is 4 (T1, T2, T4, T5), therefore $conf = 2/4 = 0.5$.
- $\{fruit\} \to \{appl\}$ with $confidence = 1$.

This time, since the number of documents where apple and fruit appear together is 2 (T1, T5) and the number of documents that we find fruit is 2 (T1, T5), the confidence formula that we showed in Sect. 2 yields $conf = 2/2 = 1$.
- $\{appl\} \to \{red\}$ with confidence $= 0.75$.
- $\{red\} \to \{appl\}$ with confidence $= 0.75$.

We can visualize these rules as a network where each term is represented as a node and the rules correspond to edges that connect the terms/nodes, as shown in Fig. 2 (left). If we increase the support threshold to 3 and keep the confidence to 0.5 we get different results, i.e. the only rules that satisfy these thresholds are:
- $\{appl\} \to \{red\}$ with confidence $= 0.75$.
- $\{red\} \to \{appl\}$ with confidence $= 0.75$.

as shown in Fig. 2 (middle). In general, the more we increase the support and the confidence, the less rules are mined. If we set the support back to 2, and increase the confidence threshold to 1, we get only $\{fruit\} \to \{appl\}$ with confidence $= 1$, and thus the network shown in Fig. 2 (right).

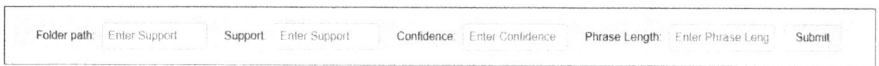

Fig. 3. User input for interactive association maps

4 The Workflow

The process is illustrated in Fig. 1. We take as input a set of documents, and we perform the following steps.

⟦1⟧. We tokenize, we remove stopwords, and apply stemming. Note that on demand one could also perform *term selection*, i.e. define criteria for the words to be considered (either on statistical measures or through a predefined list of keywords of interest).

⟦2⟧. The system takes as input from the user (from a simple GUI shown in Fig. 3): (a) a *support* threshold (absolute or percentage), (b) a *confidence* threshold, and (c) the desired *phrase length*. The latter determines what the program considers as terms for indexing and rule extraction. For phrase length of 1, the system treats every individual word as a term. For a phrase length of 2, it considers consecutive pairs of words as terms, and so on.

⟦3⟧. The A-priori algorithm [11] is applied. It is a widely used method for association rule mining. It takes a collection of items and uses specified values for *support* and *confidence* to identify the largest possible subsets that meet these criteria. However, Apriori is known to be resource-intensive in terms of memory usage. To mitigate potential memory issues, our tool first calculates the number of possible subsets that would need to be stored at each step (powerset). If the number is too large for the available system resources, the process ends and the program returns all the rules that it has extracted up to that point, and the user is prompted to increase the *support* value. This is not problematic for the problem at hand, in the sense that only rules with considerable support value make sense and are useful to mine and visualize.

⟦4⟧. After having identified the subsets of terms that meet our specified parameters, we extract all possible association rules from these subsets and calculate the confidence value for each rule. Any duplicate rules generated during this process are identified and removed to ensure uniqueness.

⟦5⟧. The rules that we found from the extraction should be now stored in a way so every subset found is stored only once with all the associated words and their given *confidence* value.

⟦6⟧. We produce a graph visualization that illustrates the connections between different nodes derived from the previous steps. Each term that has passed all filtering stages and is involved in at least one rule is displayed in the main panel of the screen. This representation provides an intuitive way to explore the associations and hierarchical relationships among the terms.

5 Application Examples

Efficiency. In general, the worst case time complexity depends on the number of distinct words (which is bounded, recall the Heap's Law [7]) and not on the size of the collection. However, the practical runtime is much lower due to the selective generation of subsets of length k and the early termination of the recursive process when subsets fail to meet the *support* threshold. To check efficiency we performed a number of experiments over a laptop equipped with an AMD Ryzen 7 2700X CPU and 32 GB of RAM. However, the program was restricted to using a maximum of 10 GB of memory to simulate constrained computational environments. A few indicative results are shown in Table 1. The first column shows the number of documents, the second the number of unique words, the third the Support, the fourth the Confidence, then the Execution time, the main memory used, MD stands for max depth (it refers to the maximum number of iterations the algorithm needs for finding valid subsets given the support threshold), and the number of extracted rules.

Table 1. Experimental results about execution time, main memory and extracted rules

#Docs	Uniq. words	Support	Confidence	Exec. time	Memory	MD	# Rules
40	3.690	0.7	1	0.8"	380 MB	7	3
40	3.690	0.7	0.5	0.8"	441 MB	7	30
40	3.690	0.55	1	1"	516 MB	12	32
40	3.690	0.55	0.5	1"	517 MB	12	190
453	125.654	0.93	1	38"	1.2 GB	8	1
453	125.654	0.93	0.5	38"	1.2 GB	8	112
453	125.654	0.8	1	82"	5.7 GB	4	44
453	125.654	0.8	0.5	84"	6 GB	4	5400

The first 4 rows correspond to a *small dataset* that comprises 40 AI-generated descriptions of movies, each having approximately 600 words, in total 3.690 unique words. The last 4 rows, correspond to a *corpus of scientific papers* about *ecosystem restoration* selected by FAO UN, that contains more than 125K unique words (the number of unique words is quite high, the Oxford dictionary has around 500K words, recall Heap's Law). We can see how the confidence/support values determine the number of rules extracted: from 1 to 5400 rules. With regards to efficiency, we observe (see the last row) that the maximum time required (without any special optimization or special hardware) is only 84 s for mining 5400 rules. (this includes the time for reading the documents).

Examples of Maps Produced. Two examples of maps created over the small dataset are shown in Fig. 4(left). Over the bigger dataset, with the scientific papers, if we use support = 0.93 and confidence 1.0, we get only one rule: $\{area\} \rightarrow \{restoration\}$ which is actually the theme of this collection. If we set support = 0.65 and confidence: 0.5 we get the map shown in Fig. 4(right). which provides more detailed view of the topics of this collection and has an hierarchical structure (the upper level contains general terms like: ecosystem, restoration, effects).

Rule Mining Over Predefined Terms. Over the dataset with the scientific papers, we tested association rule mining restricted on a particular vocabulary. In brief, we used a vocabulary that comprises 272 terms in total: it contains (a) 205 terms that describe *ecosystems*, and (b) 66 terms that describe *restoration*

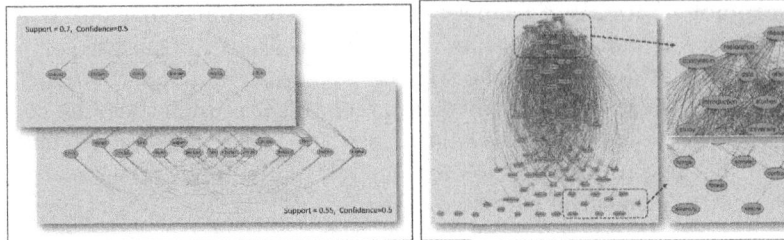

Fig. 4. Left: Examples of the small dataset, Right: Examples over the bigger dataset

types. Concerning (a), this set of terms is constructed from the IUCN global ecosystem typology [8]. It is a hierarchical classification system that in its upper levels, defines ecosystems by their convergent ecological functions and in its lower levels, distinguishes ecosystems with contradicting assemblages of species engaged in those functions. With regards to (b), i.e. *ecosystem restoration types*, this list has been based on a glossary of terms[1], prepared by the Society for Ecological Restoration (SER) [19]. The final version of the vocabulary underwent various edits and refinements from people from FAO. The current version of this vocabulary consists of 67 distinct terms. Figure 5 shows two screenshots of the mined rules. The first enables us to understand which are the main topics, while the second provides a very detailed view of the terms.

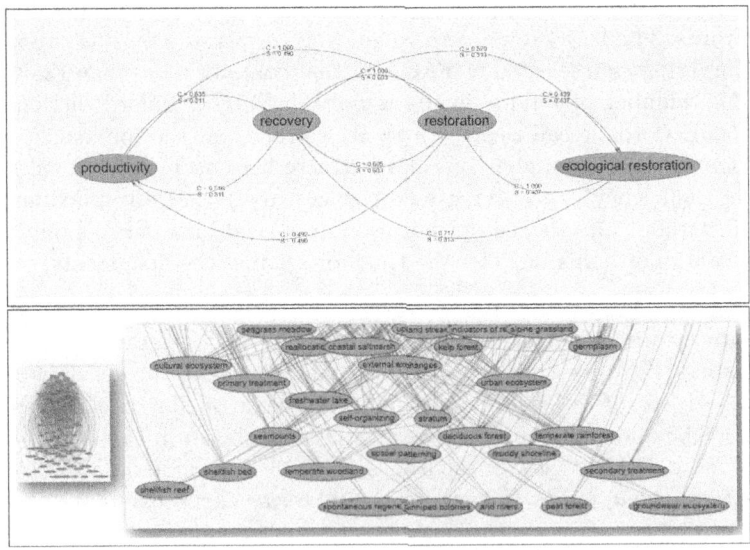

Fig. 5. Examples over the bigger dataset using a controlled vocabulary

---

[1] https://www.seraustralasia.com/standards/glossary.html.

Analysis. To understand how confidence and support affect the number of mined rules, Fig. 6 shows a plot that shows how many rules (in logscale) are mined for support = 0.6, 0.65 and 0.725 and various confidence levels. In these experiments we kept only noun words and we did not apply stemming.

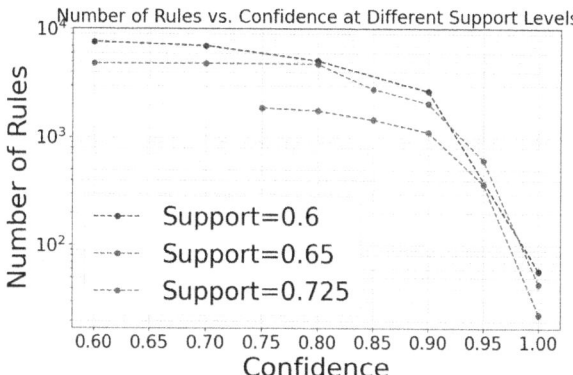

Fig. 6. Number of mined rules for various support and confidence pairs

6 Conclusion and Potential

We have proposed a method for creating what we call *AssociationMaps*, from document collections using association rule mining. A key feature is its interactivity, allowing users to dynamically adjust the *support* and *confidence* thresholds as well as *phrase size*, to tailor the results to their needs. We showcased the feasibility of this approach over various datasets. The *value* of such maps is that they could aid users in understanding a set of documents and getting various overviews of variable granularity. Therefore such maps could be added to any digital library system.

There are several directions that are worth further research. One concerns *visualization and abstraction*, i.e. (i) investigate novel *visualization methods* (none of the current visualization methods [5] seem appropriate for our task), (ii) apply link analysis over the rules (if they are numerous) in order to be able *to reveal the more important* ones (as in [17]).

Another direction is to elaborate on the *granularity of analysis*, i.e. one could consider as transaction not an entire document but smaller units such as sentences or *paragraphs* (like the chunks of RAGs [6]) and then investigate how such a choice affects computational complexity and rule relevance.

The last direction concerns *real-time efficiency*. Note that such maps could enrich *faceted search* interfaces [15,18], and just like [10] offers geographic maps during the faceted interaction, AssociationMaps could summarize the contents of the current set of documents during the interaction. In such scenario, we need an effective *caching scheme*: A plain cache could be enough if the corpus is stable, however if the corpus is dynamic (e.g. in the context of interactive search), then a more sophisticated caching scheme is required that can exploit cached *partial results*, analogous to the case of [14].

Acknowledgments. This work has received funding from the projects: Blue-Cloud 2026 (A federated European FAIR and Open Research Ecosystem for oceans, seas, coastal and inland waters, HORIZON.1.3 Research infrastructures Grant ID 101094227), and SemantyFish (Advancing the visibility, interoperability and exploitability of FishBase, TPPA OSCARS 2024-2025).

References

1. Agrawal, R.: Fast algorithms for mining association rules. VLDB (1994)
2. Al-Aswadi, F.N., Chan, H.Y., Gan, K.H.: Automatic ontology construction from text: a review from shallow to deep learning trend. Artif. Intell. Rev. **53**(6), 3901–3928 (2020)
3. Babaei Giglou, H., D'Souza, J., Auer, S.: LLMs4OL: large language models for ontology learning. In: International Semantic Web Conference, pp. 408–427. Springer (2023)
4. Dakka, W., Ipeirotis, P.G., Wood, K.R.: Automatic construction of multifaceted browsing interfaces. In: Proceedings of the 14th ACM International Conference on Information and Knowledge Management, pp. 768–775 (2005)
5. Fister, I., Jr., Fister, I., Fister, D., Podgorelec, V., Salcedo-Sanz, S.: A comprehensive review of visualization methods for association rule mining: taxonomy, challenges, open problems and future ideas. Expert Syst. Appl. **233**, 120901 (2023)
6. Gao, Y., et al.: Retrieval-augmented generation language models: a survey. arXiv preprint arXiv:2312.10997, vol. 2, no. 1 (2023)
7. Heaps, H.S.: Information Retrieval: Computational and Theoretical Aspects. Academic Press, Inc. (1978)
8. Keith, D.A., Ferrer-Paris, J.R., Nicholson, E., Kingsford, R.T.: IUCN global ecosystem typology 2.0. Descriptive profiles for biomes and ecosystem functional groups. IUCN, Gland (2020)
9. Kopidaki, S., Papadakos, P., Tzitzikas, Y.: STC+ and NM-STC: two novel online results clustering methods for web searching. In: Vossen, G., Long, D.D.E., Yu, J.X. (eds.) WISE 2009. LNCS, vol. 5802, pp. 523–537. Springer, Heidelberg (2009). https://doi.org/10.1007/978-3-642-04409-0_51
10. Lionakis, P., Tzitzikas, Y.: PFSgeo: preference-enriched faceted search for geographical data. In: Panetto, H., et al. (eds.) OTM 2017. LNCS, vol. 10574, pp. 125–143. Springer, Cham (2017). https://doi.org/10.1007/978-3-319-69459-7_9
11. Liu, Y.: Study on application of apriori algorithm in data mining. In: 2010 Second International Conference on Computer Modeling and Simulation, vol. 3, pp. 111–114. IEEE (2010)
12. Luu, A.T.: Automatic taxonomy construction from textual documents. Ph.D. thesis (2017)
13. Medelyan, O., Witten, I.H., Divoli, A., Broekstra, J.: Automatic construction of lexicons, taxonomies, ontologies, and other knowledge structures. Wiley Interdisc. Rev. Data Mining Knowl. Discov. **3**(4), 257–279 (2013)

14. Papadakis, M., Tzitzikas, Y.: Answering keyword queries through cached subqueries in best match retrieval models. J. Intell. Inf. Syst. **44**, 67–106 (2015)
15. Sacco, G.M., Tzitzikas, Y.: Dynamic taxonomies and faceted search: theory, practice, and experience, vol. 25. Springer (2009)
16. Sanderson, M., Croft, B.: Deriving concept hierarchies from text. In: Proceedings of the 22nd Annual International ACM SIGIR Conference on Research and Development in Information Retrieval, pp. 206–213 (1999)
17. Tzitzikas, Y., Hainaut, J.-L.: How to tame a very large ER diagram (using link analysis and force-directed drawing algorithms). In: Delcambre, L., Kop, C., Mayr, H.C., Mylopoulos, J., Pastor, O. (eds.) ER 2005. LNCS, vol. 3716, pp. 144–159. Springer, Heidelberg (2005). https://doi.org/10.1007/11568322_10
18. Tzitzikas, Y., Manolis, N., Papadakos, P.: Faceted exploration of RDF/S datasets: a survey. J. Intell. Inf. Syst. **48**, 329–364 (2017)
19. Whisenant, S.: The society for ecological restoration. Ecol. Restor. **29**(3), 207–208 (2011)
20. Zamir, O., Etzioni, O.: Web document clustering: a feasibility demonstration. In: Proceedings of the 21st Annual International ACM SIGIR Conference on Research and Development in Information Retrieval, pp. 46–54 (1998)

Interactive and Provenance-Aware Search and QA over Documents Using LLMs, RAG and Knowledge Graph Verbalization

Iordanis Sapidis[1,2](✉), Valantis Zervos[1,2], Michalis Mountantonakis[1,2], and Yannis Tzitzikas[1,2]

[1] Information Systems Laboratory, FORTH-ICS, Heraklion, Greece
{sapidis,vzervos,mountant,tzitzik}@ics.forth.gr
[2] Computer Science Department, University of Crete, Heraklion, Greece

Abstract. When working with a corpus of documents (e.g. in the context of a digital library), various access services are offered such as browsing, keyword search, and faceted search. Recently, Retrieval Augmented Generation (RAG) approaches have been proposed that can leverage LLMs to offer *Question Answering* (QA) services while addressing the hallucination problem of LLMs. In this direction, this paper investigates an approach for offering QA over *document corpora* and related *Knowledge Graphs* that exploits LLMs, RAG, and RAG enhanced with information from Knowledge Graphs. To address the challenge of black-box interaction, we present an interactive system called `SemanticRAG`. which enables users to ask questions, view the answer generated by each method, and obtain the provenance of each answer. We showcase the feasibility and value of this approach by deploying it over a corpus of scientific papers collected by the FAO UN for ecosystem restoration.
Online Demo: https://demos.isl.ics.forth.gr/SemanticRAG/.

Keywords: QA · RAG · Knowledge Graph · User Interaction

1 Introduction

To aid users in exploiting a collection of documents, various access services are usually offered, such as *browsing*, *keyword search*, and *faceted search*. Recently, *Retrieval Augmented Generation* approaches have been proposed (see [5,16] for a survey), that leverage information retrieval and recent advances in AI, particularly Large Language Models (LLMs), to offer *Question Answering (QA)* services that can address the weaknesses of LLMs (i.e. the problem of hallucinations, and the recency of information). Since Knowledge Graphs (KGs) [8] also provide a valuable source of background information as well as terminology, in this paper, we investigate an approach that leverages information derived from KGs.

To tackle the problem of black-box interaction, we demonstrate an interactive system, called `SemanticRAG`. This system enables users to ask questions, view the answer generated by each method, and access the provenance of each answer. Specifically, it provides links to the relevant source—either the *paragraph* from which the answer was derived (in the case of document chunks) or the *specific lines* used from the data file verbalization. We showcase the feasibility and value of this approach by deploying it over a corpus of scientific papers collected by the FAO (Food and Agriculture Organization of the United Nations) for ecosystem restoration.

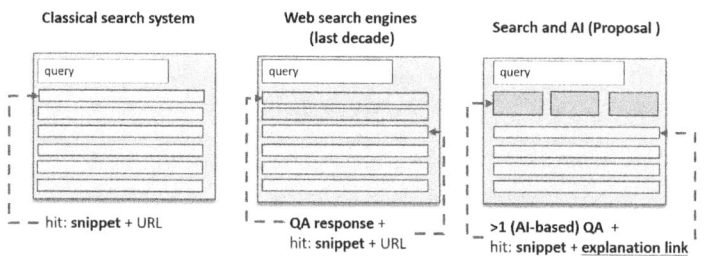

Fig. 1. The proposed interaction.

The main idea regarding interaction is shown in Fig. 1. On the left we can see the layout of a classical search system; in the middle, the recent layout of search engines that also include the response of a QA/AI service for some queries; while at the right side, we illustrate our proposed layout, which includes multiple answers with explanation links.

Figure 2 shows a screenshot of the running system SemanticRAG.. The underlying dataset comprises 453 scientific papers in PDF, selected from FAO UN as a means to detect possible biases of the scientific community regarding ecosystem restoration, and a CSV dataset containing 13,603 entries, generated from related Knowledge Graphs (KGs) in that domain. The user has submitted the query "Did tigers ever exist in Bali?". The system provides three responses: one from the LLM alone, one using RAG, and one using KG-enhanced RAG. The first response from the standalone LLM claims there is "no recorded evidence of tigers existing in Bali". However, the second and third responses, which leverage information from the PDF documents, yield the correct answer: tigers did exist in Bali but are now extinct.

At the bottom of the screen, the user can view the *related chunks* from the PDFs—specifically, those identified by the RAG system as most relevant and supplied to the LLM for answer generation. For each chunk the user receives a *snippet* with the query terms highlighted. Moreover, an important usability feature is that by clicking on such a chunk the user can navigate directly to the corresponding paragraph in the PDF enabling them to read and verify that paragraph as well as its surrounding context (see the bottom right side of Fig. 2). This functionality provides *explainability and context* which are essential for validation and trust. In summary, this interface not only leverages the capabilities of LLMs, but also utilizes the content of the specific papers, as well as background knowledge (from Knowledge Graphs), enabling users to understand how each answer is derived.

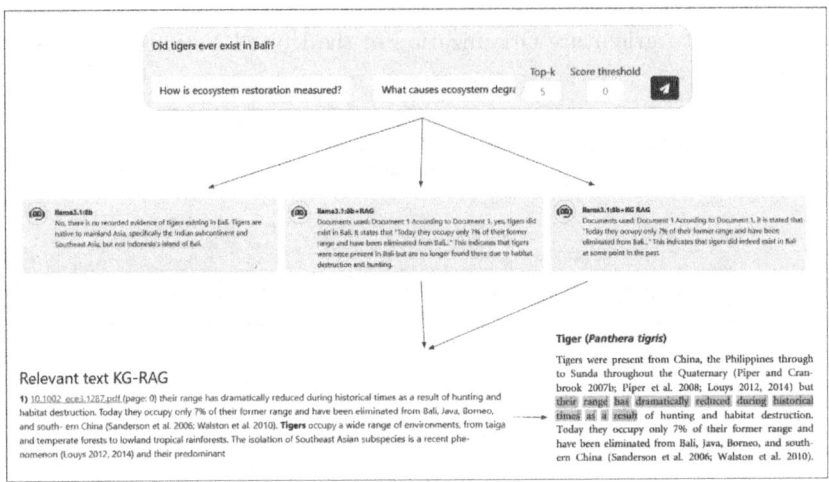

Fig. 2. Running example of `SemanticRAG`.

In a nutshell, the contributions of this demo paper are: (a) it presents a publicly deployed interactive research prototype, `SemanticRAG.`, which enables users to inspect answers obtained from *different* techniques (LLM, RAG, RAG+KG), (b) it demonstrates how such services can leverage *various types of resources* (documents, vocabularies, thesauri, and knowledge graphs) by *verbalizing* them, (c) it provides a solution to the *black-box* interaction of LLMs, by providing users with the provenance of each answer (either document excerpts or data file entries), (d) it reports our experience (and efficiency results) from evaluating this system on a collection of scientific papers gathered by FAO UN for a given task.

The rest of the paper is organized as follows, Sect. 2 describes in brief related work and the positioning of this work, Sect. 3 presents the pipeline of *SemanticRAG* and Sect. 4 shows results concerning the efficiency. Section 5 presents demonstration scenarios and finally Sect. 6 concludes the paper and describes directions for future work.

2 Related Work and Positioning

Retrieval-Augmented Generation (RAG) systems [5,16] enhance AI-generated responses by combining external knowledge retrieval with language models, improving accuracy and reducing hallucinations through context-aware outputs. This allows for up-to-date, domain-specific answers and mitigates reliance on static training data. However, RAG requires significant computational resources for real-time retrieval, and its performance depends on the quality and relevance of the sourced data. Below we first discuss RAG and KG approaches, then relevant applications, and finally the positioning of this work.

RAG Systems and KGs. There have been recently several RAG and KG approaches [10]; indicatively the KG-RAG pipeline [12] aims to reduce information hallucinations by constructing a KG, whereas GraphRAG [4] introduces a new approach that constructs a knowledge graph and generates multi-level summaries which improves the generated answers in summarization tasks. Furthermore, the Quasar system [3] is based on a pipeline of 4 stages, including Question Understanding, Evidence Retrieval where KGs, web tables, and texts are used (from Wikipedia and Wikidata [14]) for retrieving relevant data, Re-ranking and filtering based on graph neural networks (GNNs) and Answer Generation.

Relevant Applications. Here, we discuss the most relevant applications. First, RAGonite [11] is a conversational QA system that combines heterogeneous data elements such as passages, lists, tables, and KGs. Moreover, Self-RAG [2] is a framework that retrieves documents on demand, generates segments in parallel, and finally criticizes its own generations and selects the best segment. Furthermore, Auto-RAG [15] offers a multi-turn dialogue to interact between the LLM and the document retriever. Finally, regarding live demos, *deepset.ai* [1] provides a comparison between a baseline RAG and a RAG+KG approach for a set of preloaded documents. Stanford STORM [6] and Co-STORM [13] are tools designed to enhance knowledge curation by leveraging LLMs to generate structured, citation-rich content. Their primary focus lies in identifying relevant web pages to support question answering and assisting users in exploring information. In contrast, our approach is focused on QA over a specific dataset and incorporates knowledge graphs.

Positioning. In comparison to the above approaches, we introduce a configurable online application for domain-specific QA that enables the comparison of answers from different techniques (plain LLM, document RAG, document and KG RAG). The application provides the *provenance* of every answer returned, thereby offering greater *transparency*. This enables users to address the *black-box interaction*, *verify the responses* of the system, and see their context. Furthermore, we provide examples that showcase the value of the KG and of its verbalization.

3 The Pipeline of `SemanticRAG`.

An overview of the process is illustrated in Fig. 3. We can see that parallel indexing steps are performed to enable hybrid retrieval and fusion. The pipeline is implemented using Langchain[1] to facilitate integration with LLMs.

---

[1] https://python.langchain.com/.

1 Document Indexing. SemanticRAG. takes as input any number of documents in PDF or CSV format. The textual content is first extracted and then automatically split into *chunks* of up to 500 characters, with a 50-character *overlap* between consecutive chunks to preserve context continuity. The chunks are then processed for vector and lexical indexing. For *vector indexing* each chunk is encoded as *a dense vector* using nomic-embed-text[2], a general-purpose open weights embedding model with 137M parameters. We chose nomic-embed-text due to its competitive performance and compact size [9], making it well-suited for local deployment.

The vector of each chunk is then stored in a Chroma database, an open-source and lightweight embeddings database, along with metadata for identifying the source document. For *lexical indexing* we employed the BM25 retrieval model, implemented using the BM25s library [7].

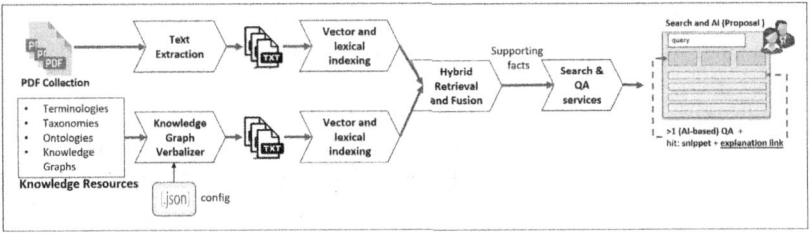

Fig. 3. The pipeline of SemanticRAG.

2 Knowledge Resource Verbalizer. Since we want to be able to leverage in the process any kind of related knowledge resource (either terminology, ontology, knowledge graph, or any structured data in general), we have developed KGverbalizer, a tool that takes as input such artifacts and generates an enhanced output text file that can contribute to the QA process, analogously to the approach of [3]. To grasp the idea, suppose that we have a terminology that contains terms like "Yellow Fin Tuna". If we know that this terminology is about fish species, we produce textual descriptions like "Yellow Fin Tuna is a fish species". The latter can indeed contribute to the QA process, the single term cannot. For this reason, KGverbalizer supports a configuration, expressed as a single JSON file, that specifies the *text generation rules* to be applied to each term of an input file. These rules include simple ones, such as ADD_PREFIX (e.g., adding a prefix to a specific type of ecosystem terms) or ADD_SEPARATORS (e.g., formatting a knowledge graph into human-readable text by adding separator text between the entities). All parameters and specifications are fully customizable through the configuration file. At the end, the tool generates as an output a .csv file containing each term along with its ID and the final human-readable, verbalized text after applying all rules.

---

[2] https://ollama.com/library/nomic-embed-text

`KGverbalizer` can be used both manually and programmatically, as it includes an API (`KGverbalizer` API) that allows for integration into external codebases.

3 **Hybrid Retrieval and Fusion.** `SemanticRAG`. enables the user to perform two key functions: **(a) Document Search**. The user submits a question/query and the system retrieves the most relevant chunks based on *cosine similarity*, enabling users to explore the content of the collection. Furthermore, the user can click on a hit and the system directly opens a window that shows the corresponding part of the PDF. **(b) Chatbot Interaction:** The user interacts with an integrated chatbot powered by Llama-3.1-8B. The chatbot leverages the RAG pipeline to retrieve relevant document chunks in response to user queries. The retrieval process includes configurable parameters such as top-k and a score threshold for filtering the retrieved data that the chatbot incorporates into its responses. A small cross encoder model is used to rerank retrieved snippets. To ensure that the responses are aligned with the retrieved chunks, we provide the following prompt to the LLM:

```
Carefully examine all the provided data and answer based solely on the given information.
If the data is  entirely irrelevant, you must explicitly state that  no relevant data has
been found and respond based on your own knowledge.
You are given the following data: ...
```

4 Efficiency

Efficiency of Interaction. We have deployed our system to a machine with an RTX3090 GPU and an AMD EPYC 7232P CPU. Overall, it takes around 4 to 6 s to answer a question using RAG or KG RAG, depending on the value of top-k. The time is spent as follows: (i) 0.55 s (9%) to load the indexes, (ii) 0.9 s for retrieval (0.82 for vector and 0.02 for lexical) (16%), (iii) 1.2 s for reranking (21%), and finally (iv) 3.1 s (54%) to generate the answer for a top-k value of 10. In general lower top-k values reduce the time spent for generation.

Assuming a top-k value of 10, around 12 s are needed for the 3 responses (plain LLM, RAG, and KG-RAG) to be generated, as RAG and KG-RAG take approximately 5 s each, while the plain LLM takes approximately 2 s due to having only a generation phase. It is worth noting that generation time largely depends on the number of output tokens (i.e. the size of the response) as well.

KG Verbalization. The verbalization of two files—one with plain terms and another from GRSF containing 9 attributes—that together contain approximately ~13.500 terms, takes around 2 s and is performed once.

Indexing. This is also performed once, and its speed depends on the data. In our use case, the FAO PDFs contain 7,616 pages, split into 66,413 chunks, and a CSV derived from the verbalized GRSF KG contains 13,602 lines split into 13,602 chunks. For the verbalized GRSF, the time required to load the CSV is negligible (~0.24 s). Since each row is sufficiently small, no chunk splitting was necessary. Converting all rows into vectors and indexing them took 158 s in total, resulting in a processing rate of approximately 86 rows per second. Indexing the 7,616 FAO PDF pages took a total of 1,778 s or 29.6 min. Of this, 939 s (53%) were spent loading the PDFs and converting their contents to plain text, 1 s (0.06%) was required to split the corpus into smaller chunks, and 839 s (47%) were used to convert each chunk into a vector and index it. In total, 1,936 s (32 min) were needed for the entire indexing phase of the FAO and GRSF datasets combined.

Query Capabilities. Without the knowledge resources and the corresponding KG verbalization task, the query capabilities of the system would be lower. We can approximately quantify the extra query capabilities that the KG verbalization offers, by analyzing the occurrences of the KG resources in the document corpus, in the sense that if a scientific term is not present in any of the documents, then the queries that include that term cannot be answered by the plain RAG. In our case (FAO use case), we measured the occurrences of the KG resources and found that the documents contain 133,509 distinct terms, the KG contains 34,844 distinct terms, and the terms in common are 8,034. It means that 76% ($\frac{34,844-8,034}{34,844}$) of the KG terms do not appear at the docs.

5 Demonstration Scenarios

The SemanticRAG. web application[3] and a tutorial video[4] can be accessed online. Here, we demonstrate the system over various collections and questions with emphasis on cases where SemanticRAG. provides superior answers. Apart from the example described in Sect. 1, and Fig. 2, consider the following scenario:

```
Question: Is Coenonympha tullia endangered?
LLM Answer:  "No, Coenonympha tullia is not considered an endangered species."
```

However, this species is actually listed as "Least Concern" on the IUCN Red List. The answer using RAG is:

```
According to the provided data from the IUCN Red List of Threatened Species (2010),
Coenonympha tullia is listed as "Vulnerable". However, it is also mentioned that it is
considered the most threatened of the British subspecies and has undergone numerous local
population losses. Additionally, it is described as being in international decline primarily
due to habitat degradation and destruction. Therefore, while not explicitly stated as
"endangered", the data suggests that Coenonympha tullia is indeed at risk and vulnerable
to extinction.
```

This example shows how even with a relatively small collection of scientific articles, the user can obtain the correct answer. In this case, the answers from RAG and KG RAG are similar, as the KG does not provide any additional information about the question and no relevant chunks from the KG are retrieved.

We can see an example where the KG RAG provides a better answer by asking the question "Is the freshwater sculpin protected by the EU Habitats Directive?":

---

[3] https://demos.isl.ics.forth.gr/SemanticRAG/.
[4] https://www.youtube.com/watch?v=bBQ73jvAH8U.

```
LLM Answer: No, the Freshwater Sculpin is not listed as a protected species under the EU
Habitats Directive. However, its habitat, the freshwater habitats of the European eel
(Anguilla anguilla), are protected under the directive.
```

```
RAG Answer:
To answer this question, I will examine the provided documents...
The EU Habitats Directive (Document 11) lists several species that are protected, including
some fish species, but the freshwater sculpin is not among them.
```

Both the plain LLM and RAG provide a wrong answer but the KG RAG correctly answers the question as shown in Fig. 4. It uses data from both the document for identifying protected species and the verbalized KG for finding the scientific name of the freshwater sculpin mentioned in the previous snippet.

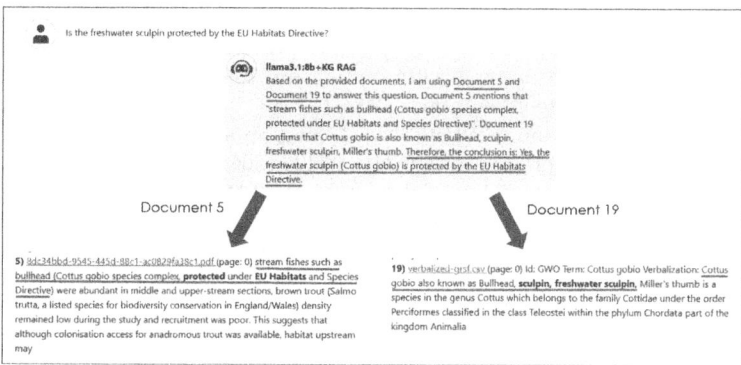

Fig. 4. Response where the KG RAG performs better.

6 Conclusion

Answering questions based on a specific set of documents and KGs and providing the paragraphs that explain the answer is very useful for verifying the response; however, it is quite challenging. We investigate a method that requires no specialized training, and can leverage formally expressed knowledge (in the form of terminologies, taxonomies, ontologies), which may prove useful for specialized questions. For transparency and expandability, we enable users to view the distinct answers generated by (a) LLM, (b) RAG, and (c) KG-RAG. We have showcase SemanticRAG., which demonstrates the feasibility of this approach, and it has been deployed over a corpus of PDF documents related to the FAO UN. The indexing of 7,616 PDF pages, and the verbalized KG that contains approximately 13,000 terms takes 32 min in total. The interactive QA, takes from 8 to 12 s depending on the size of the answer.

There are various directions for further work and research including (a) converting the retrieved chunks to RDF triples, harmonizing them, and then investigating whether this method positively affects the quality of answers, and (b) performing a task-based evaluation with experts of FAO UN to assess the usability and value of the `SemanticRAG` system.

Acknowledgements. This work has received funding from the projects: Blue-Cloud 2026 (A federated European FAIR and Open Research Ecosystem for oceans, seas, coastal and inland waters, HORIZON.1.3 Research infrastructures Grant ID: 101094227), and VeriFish (Stimulating sustainable seafood consumption through a verifiable indicator framework, HORIZON-MISS-2023-OCEAN-01, Grant ID 101156426).

References

1. deepset.ai (2025). https://graphrag-demo.deepset.ai/. Accessed June 2025
2. Asai, A., Wu, Z., Wang, Y., Sil, A., Hajishirzi, H.: Self-RAG: learning to retrieve, generate, and critique through self-reflection. In: The Twelfth International Conference on Learning Representations (2023)
3. Christmann, P., Weikum, G.: RAG-based question answering over heterogeneous data and text. arXiv preprint arXiv:2412.07420 (2024)
4. Edge, D., et al.: From local to global: a graph RAG approach to query-focused summarization. arXiv preprint arXiv:2404.16130 (2024)
5. Fan, W., et al.: A survey on RAG meeting LLMs: towards retrieval-augmented large language models. In: Proceedings of the 30th ACM SIGKDD Conference, pp. 6491–6501 (2024)
6. Jiang, Y., Shao, Y., Ma, D., Semnani, S.J., Lam, M.S.: Into the unknown unknowns: engaged human learning through participation in language model agent conversations. arXiv preprint arXiv:2408.15232 (2024)
7. Lù, X.H.: BM25S: orders of magnitude faster lexical search via eager sparse scoring (2024). https://arxiv.org/abs/2407.03618
8. Mountantonakis, M., Tzitzikas, Y.: Large-scale semantic integration of linked data: a survey. ACM Comput. Surv. (CSUR) **52**(5), 1–40 (2019)
9. Nussbaum, Z., Morris, J.X., Duderstadt, B., Mulyar, A.: Nomic embed: training a reproducible long context text embedder (2025). https://arxiv.org/abs/2402.01613
10. Procko, T.T., Ochoa, O.: Graph retrieval-augmented generation for large language models: a survey. In: 2024 Conference on AI, Science, Engineering, and Technology (AIxSET), pp. 166–169. IEEE (2024)
11. Saha Roy, R., et al.: RAGONITE: iterative retrieval on induced databases and verbalized RDF for conversational QA over KGs with RAG. In: Datenbanksysteme für Business, Technologie und Web (BTW 2025), pp. 787–794. Gesellschaft für Informatik, Bonn (2025)
12. Sanmartin, D.: KG-RAG: bridging the gap between knowledge and creativity. arXiv preprint arXiv:2405.12035 (2024)
13. Shao, Y., Jiang, Y., Kanell, T.A., Xu, P., Khattab, O., Lam, M.S.: Assisting in writing wikipedia-like articles from scratch with large language models. arXiv preprint arXiv:2402.14207 (2024)
14. Vrandečić, D., Krötzsch, M.: Wikidata: a free collaborative knowledgebase. Commun. ACM **57**(10), 78–85 (2014)

15. Yu, T., Zhang, S., Feng, Y.: Auto-RAG: autonomous retrieval-augmented generation for large language models. arXiv preprint arXiv:2411.19443 (2024)
16. Zhao, P., et al.: Retrieval-augmented generation for AI-generated content: a survey. arXiv preprint arXiv:2402.19473 (2024)

Demonstrating Narrative Pattern Discovery from Biomedical Literature

Hermann Kroll[1(✉)], Pascal Sackhoff[1], Bill Matthias Thang[1], Christin Katharina Kreutz[2,3], and Wolf-Tilo Balke[1]

[1] TU Braunschweig, Braunschweig, Germany
krollh@acm.org, balke@ifis.cs.tu-bs.de
[2] TH Mittelhessen - University of Applied Sciences, Gießen, Germany
ckreutz@acm.org
[3] Herder Institute, Marburg, Germany

Abstract. Digital libraries maintain extensive collections of knowledge and need to provide effective access paths for their users. For instance, PubPharm, the specialized information service for Pharmacy in Germany, provides and develops access paths to their underlying biomedical document collection. In brief, PubPharm supports traditional keyword-based search, search for chemical structures, as well as novel graph-based discovery workflows, e.g., listing or searching for interactions between different pharmaceutical entities. This paper introduces a new search functionality, called narrative pattern mining, allowing users to explore context-relevant entities and entity interactions. We performed interviews with five domain experts to verify the usefulness of our prototype.

Keywords: Digital Libraries · Narrative Information Access · Graph-based Discovery · Pattern Mining · Entity Search

1 Introduction

Digital libraries maintain extensive collections of knowledge and need to provide effective access paths for their users. Ideally, two types of searches should be supported: precise search for relevant material and exploratory search [7]. In this paper, we focus on exploratory search to allow users to find new and interesting ideas for their own work. For instance, the connected papers service[1] allows users to explore the connection between different research articles, e.g., who cites whom or what is adjacent to a certain paper. This way users may find new and interesting articles for their own work.

We, as the specialized service for Pharmacy in Germany, build upon that idea. The biomedical/pharmaceutical domain is an entity-centric one, e.g., research focuses around certain drugs, diseases, targets, methods and more; see for instance a PubMed query log analysis [1] or entity-centric services like PubTator [12]. That is why we developed a new entity-centric search functionality

---

[1] https://connectedpapers.com.

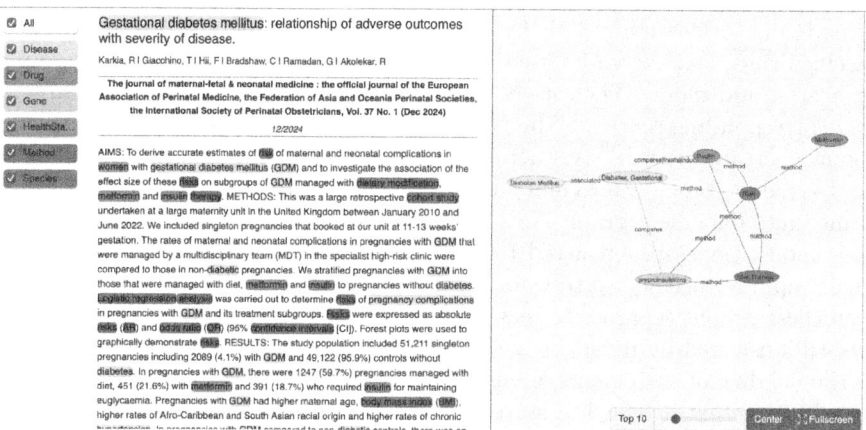

Fig. 1. Document Visualization: The left side shows the document text. Detected entities are highlighted in corresponding colors. A UI selection box on the left side allows to show or hide certain entity types. The right side depicts extracted interactions between entities as a labeled and colored graph.

for our platform, which we are describing in the following. The main idea is that users start their search with a set of relevant entities for their own work. Then, the service first retrieves documents that include these entities and second, mines patterns between the given and other context-relevant entities. All information is then visualized as a network so that users can explore context-relevant entities and entity interactions, so called *narrative patterns*. A click on a network's edge forwards users to corresponding literature supporting the selected entity-entity interaction. While our Narrative Discovery System has been published [7], this paper introduces our *narrative pattern*-driven discovery method and prototye.

2 Narrative Discovery System

PubPharm[2], the specialized information service for Pharmacy in Germany, aims to provide effective and innovative access paths to the pharmaceutical literature for our research community. In the past, we proposed and implemented a discovery system for narrative information access [7]. The system called the Narrative Service[3] allows users to formulate their information needs as graph patterns, i.e., interaction patterns between entities. This way, users may search for literature stating that *Metformin is used to treat diabetes mellitus in adult patients*. In addition, variables can be used to explore the literature, e.g., *any drugs* used to treat diabetes mellitus in adult patients. The service is capable of answering these queries through graph pattern matching. The Drug Overviews[4] service

---

[2] https://www.pubpharm.de.
[3] https://narrative.pubpharm.de.
[4] https://narrative.pubpharm.de/drug_overview.

extends our discovery system by allowing users to generate overviews about specific drugs, i.e., known interactions like therapies, target interactions, administrations, and more. When users click on some information, they are directed to a corresponding search in the Narrative Service, e.g., searching for literature about a certain drug-disease therapy.

To enable graph pattern matching, the relevant biomedical literature is transformed into document graphs, i.e., relevant biomedical entities are detected, and their interactions are extracted from texts. Instead of building a single knowledge graph, we decided to transform each text into a small document graph and keep these graphs separated. Reasons for this decision were that 1) user queries are still answered by retrieving relevant literature instead of short answers and 2) the validity of statements is ensured [3], i.e., the system retrieves the corresponding context in which a statement is valid. A visualization of an enriched document in our system is shown in Fig. 1 or online[5]. Entities were detected by performing a dictionary-based entity linking against existing vocabularies and by using existing biomedical annotation tools like GNormPlus [13], TaggerOne [10], and PubTator Central [12]. Statements were extracted by deploying PathIE, a method for extracting statements via the grammatical structure of sentences, and by extracting association statements if two entities co-occur within the same sentences. These methods are part of our extraction toolbox [6], which we described [2] and analyzed [8] comprehensively. In brief, most of our self-developed methods do not rely on supervision and thus bypass the need for training data, but they only come with a moderate extraction quality. The code for our discovery platform and the extension for this paper is available at GitHub[6] and SoftwareHeritage[7]. Our system (as of May 2025) includes 38M PubMed/Medline articles.

The Narrative Service itself provides precise literature searches due to graph-based queries and, thus, entity-interaction-aware searches [7]. A keyword-based search functionality assists users in formulating graph queries [4]. Exploratory searches are, as of now, supported by using variables in queries or using the Drug Overview functionality. This paper contributes a new access path for our service that allows users to discover entity interactions in contexts.

3 Mining Narrative Patterns

Entity interactions play a central role within the biomedical literature. The goal of our narrative pattern mining here is to allow an exploration of the literature, i.e., visualizing and thus summarizing what is known and often described between a set of searched entities. With that, the system can shed light on context-relevant entities and interactions between them, so that users can explore

---

[5] https://narrative.pubpharm.de/document/?document_id=38844413&data_source=PubMed.

[6] https://github.com/HermannKroll/NarrativeIntelligence/.

[7] SoftwareHeritage ID: swh:1:dir:5b87566505d9f3ad0837cc91f105ee163515ec3d.

the entities' neighborhood. This kind of exploration should assists users in understanding the relationships between biomedical entities and possibly discover new relevant entities to the users' information needs.

System Architecture. In brief, our service expects a list of searched entities as its input. The output is a graph pattern that 1) puts the searched entities in relation and 2) adds more entities that play a central role in the searched entities' contexts. Therefore, we first identify relevant documents, retrieve the document graphs, score the graphs' edges, and sort these edges by their final score. Users can then select how many edges shall be displayed.

Identifying Relevant Documents. Our goal is to support users in exploring the literature by showing what is written about the set of searched entities. We, therefore, decided to extract these patterns from documents that include all of the searched entities. This way, only information appearing in a context (a document) that includes all searched entities is considered.

Users enter a list of strings. Each string represents a search for entities in our system. Each of these strings has to be translated into entities from our vocabulary. Therefore, we use the following translation paradigm: Suppose a user types the string *diabetes melli* in the search but does not complete their string insertion yet. All entities that include both the terms *diabetes* and *melli* in one of their synonyms are valid translations, e.g., *diabetes mellitus, diabetes mellitus type 1, diabetes mellitus type 2*, and many more. These valid translations are then suggested to users during the input as keywords. A user can pick one of the suggestions, e.g., *diabetes mellitus* as keyword[8] or finish their typing and lock in their inserted string as a keyword. With that, we can translate the user's input keyword into a set of entities. Next, we use an inverted index to retrieve document IDs in which a particular entity has been detected. This gives us the set of documents relevant for a specific keyword.

If a user enters multiple keywords, the translation is conducted for all keywords. Then we compute the intersection between those sets of documents relevant for *single* keywords to identify documents fitting *all* entered keywords.

Scoring Edges. Next, we retrieve the document graphs for the retrieved document IDs fitting all keywords and mine the actual narrative pattern. Combining all graphs and showing the resulting one to the user would likely to be overstraining them. For instance, when searching for entities like *diabetes mellitus* and *metformin*, thousands of documents are retrieved. The resulting graph would then also include hundreds of different statements. We tackled this problem in two ways: 1) We score each graph edge so that only the most important ones are shown to the users. Users can control how many edges should be visualized at once. 2) We only show edges that are incoming or outgoing from one of the user's searched entities so that these entities are put into the focus of the generated narrative pattern. We score graph edges as follows, which proved to be

---

[8] Note that selecting *diabetes mellitus* as keyword will still also translate the keyword to *diabetes mellitus type 1* etc.

Algorithm 1. Mining Narrative Patterns from Document Graphs

1: **Input**: list(set(entities translated from each keyword)) **Output**: a ranked list of documents
2: $relDocPerKeyword$ = list()
3: **for** $entitiesForKeyword \in$ listOfEntitiesPerKeyword **do**
4: $\quad relDocPerKeyword$.append(getRelevantDocs($entitiesForKeyword$))
5: $intersectRelDocs$ = set.intersection(*relDocPerKeyword)
6: edge2score = dict()
7: docs = retrieveDocumentData($intersectRelDocs$)
8: **for** $d \in$ docs **do**
9: $\quad$ **for** $e \in$ d.edges **do**
10: $\quad\quad$ **if** $e.subject \in$ entities $\vee$ $e.object \in$ entities **then**
11: $\quad\quad\quad$ edge2score[s] += score(e, d)
12: edge2score = sortByScoreDescending(edge2score)
13: **return** edge2score

effective for ranking and recommending documents in our discovery system [5,9]:
$score(e, d) = \textit{tf-idf}(e, d) * coverage(e, d) * confidence(e, d)$

The scoring function takes a graph edge e and its corresponding document d as its input and returns a numeric score. In brief, tf-idf stands for term-frequency inverse-document-frequency and prefers edges that appear often within d but rarely within the whole collection. Coverage favors edges that include entities used across the document (and not just at the beginning or end of some text). Confidence boosts edges with high extraction confidence, i.e., the extraction method extracted the edge with high confidence. For more details we refer the reader to our prior works [5,9] or our actual implementation.

The score function allows us to score each document graph edge. For the narrative pattern, we compute the union of all retrieved graphs. Then, we score each of its edges as follows. Let D be the set of retrieved documents relevant for all keywords and e be an edge of the narrative pattern, we sum the scores for this edge in every document from D for our final score: $fscore(e) = \sum_{d \in D} score(e, d)$. $score$ returns 0 if the edge e is not present in document d.

Our final Algorithm is shown in Algorithm 1. First, it retrieves relevant documents and then sums up the scores for each edge in every retrieved document. The edges are then sorted in descending order with regard to their scores.

4 Demonstration

Our new narrative pattern discovery component has been integrated into our main discovery system[9], and a tutorial video is available at[10]. In the following, we first describe the user interface and explain our design decisions. We then describe a preliminary user evaluation that we intend to extend in the future.

---

[9] https://beta.narrative.pubpharm.de, tab *Pattern Discovery (Beta)*.
[10] https://pharmrxiv.de/receive/pharmrxiv_mods_00026752.

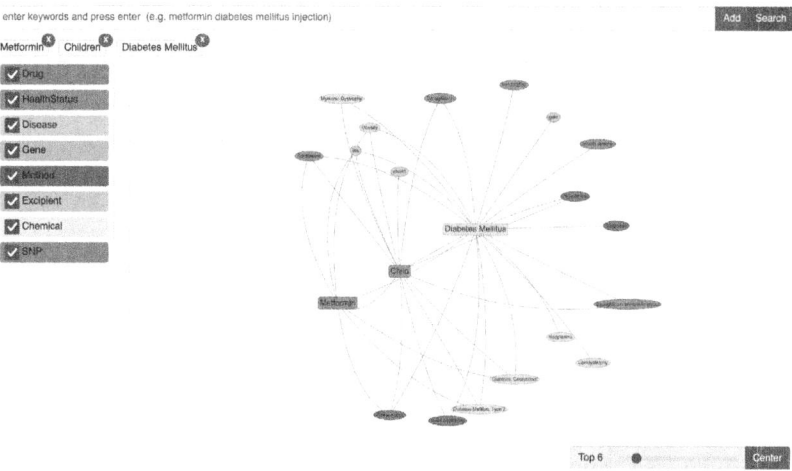

Fig. 2. Pattern Visualization: The extracted pattern is shown in the center of the screen. Nodes are colored depending on their entity type. The searched entities are depicted as rectangle nodes with a larger font. Users may hide certain entity types or select how many edges are visualized at once.

4.1 User Interface

Users can enter a list of searched entities by typing into a search bar. They are assisted with an autocompletion functionality that proposes known entity terms. They can then add entity terms to their search by pressing `enter` or clicking the `add` button on the right. Entities are then added to a list below the search bar. They can be removed by clicking on a red cancel sign. Next, users may start the search by pressing `enter` or clicking the `search` button.

The system replies with a color-coded graph representation. The searched entities are highlighted in the center of the visualization as rectangle nodes with a larger font. Every other node is a rounded oval. Nodes' colors depend on their entity types, e.g., red for drugs. A unified entity-type coloring is used across the whole discovery system. We decided to keep the representation simple, so we removed edge labels. Suppose users want more details on a certain interaction (edge) between two entities. In that case, they can click on an edge and are forwarded to a corresponding search in our discovery system, i.e., literature is shown that supports the clicked interaction between two entities. Entity types can be hidden or made visible via clicking the colored boxes on the left side of the screen. This way, users can narrow down the pattern to show only certain entity types, such as drugs, diseases, and targets. Our document graph representation has already established a similar feature; see Fig. 1. At the bottom, users may select how many edges should be visualized simultaneously. By default, this is set to five edges per concept. If users scroll further down, they see a list of documents that contain the searched entities. This feature delivers Provenance, which allows users to screen the literature used to generate the pattern. In addi-

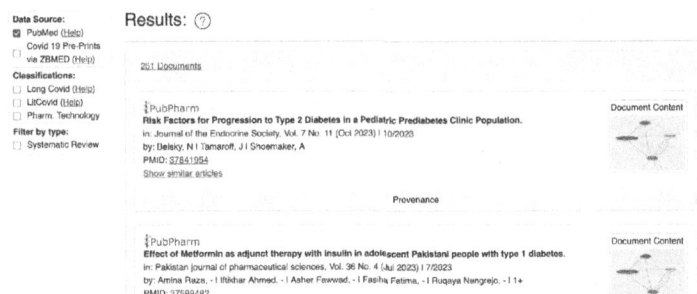

Fig. 3. Result Lists: The system shows the document lists used to generate the narrative pattern. Filter options are available to further narrow down searches.

tion, a source selection filter is shown on the left side. Here, users can select which data sources are used for the pattern mining step. They can narrow down their searches to specific collections or certain document classes, e.g., articles relevant to Pharmaceutical Technology or published within a specified time span. Screenshots of our user interface are shown in Fig. 2 and Fig. 3.

4.2 User Evaluation

Setup. For our small-scale user evaluation, we conducted one on one interviews taking around thirty minutes with five participants in German. Participants were familiar with PubPharm and the Narrative Service as they already took part in earlier studies. Participants were able to access the tool via Zoom and remote desktop control. Two experienced interviewers lead the participants through the three-part study: **1. Introduction.** (5 min) Participants were informed on the purpose and terms of the study before they consented to take part in the study. Afterwards, the interviewer gave a brief overview of the tool. One of the interviewers took notes while the other interviewer lead the participant through the study. **2. Usage of the system with thinking aloud.** (15 min) Participants used the whole system freely while thinking aloud [11] to work on one of their research questions. **3. Semi-structured interview.** (10 min) We followed an earlier evaluation on parts of the system [4] for the semi-structured interview and asked participants the same questions on general thoughts regarding the tool, encountered problems, liked components, changes required for them to consider using the tool and if they had any other comments.

Results. Participants **encountered problems** related to the *search bar*: they did not immediately understand how keywords were supposed to be entered with one participant noting *you need to first understand what it wants then you are able to do it.* They had trouble with selecting keywords the system had in the vocabulary. The two buttons `search` and `add` were not descriptive enough. When *clicking edges* in the displayed graph, participants were surprised that the triggered search would lose the context of the graph and only look for the entities associated with the edge (and not all entities that were searched in the first place). The click opened the results in a new tab leading to some difficulty to navigate back to the original graph. Participants identified some *interface problems* which are easy to correct from a technical point of view: cryptic error messages, small-sized symbols, similar colors used in the graph and uncertainty which fields can be clicked. We made some *additional observations*: in general it seemed to have been unclear what the additional values was, that the new tool brought. Participants would have required more time. They often did not scroll to see the documents resulting the search but only checked out the graph, sometimes they did not interact with the graph, they did not use the `top x` functionality or the possibility to restrict the depicted concept types.

As for **liked components** participants mentioned the fitting results for precise queries, the tool's power to provide a good overview of a topic, its intuitive and logical handling as well as the possibility to evaluate the results while searching which makes the tool stand out against using LLMs. The *interface* was praised: its visualization of relations and keywords, the possible interactions as well as opening clicked edges in a new tab. For participants, the tool and especially the interaction with the graph was behaving *according to their expectations*, clicking on an edge focuses on this specific part of the graph and shows literature backing the edge. We *observed* users clicking edges, deleting keywords and modifying or restricting their queries, using the `top x` functionality, restrict the depicted concept types in the graph, and recovering from involuntary clicks.

Participants mentioned some **required changes** or potential future features: Some participants were unsure how to express some technical terms in English which hints towards a language-independent query option. In terms of *search* there are many ideas: exclusion of edges, inclusion of terms which are not part of the tool's vocabulary, the option to query with variables, a `clear all` button for queries, an improved sorting for suggested keywords, typo resistance, and enabling the search between three interconnected components. Participants wished to *export or save* their searches, networks and interesting works. In terms of *visualization* they wished for seeing the pattern search and result list in one view. One participant asked for the inclusion of cross-references. *Other* wishes were video tutorials, better explanations and an extension of the data source to also incorporate news articles.

5 Conclusion

In brief, this paper introduces a novel access path for PubPharm's Narrative Discovery System. Our narrative pattern mining approach assists users with entity-driven exploratory search. This way users can explore the neighborhood of searched entities. The conducted interviews verified the usefulness of our system and the entity-driven and network-based visualization.

Future work will tackle described problems and improve the search. We intend to provide users with the option to enter keywords similar to a Google search before employing, e.g., an LLM to suggested potential interesting patterns.

References

1. Herskovic, J.R., Tanaka, L.Y., Hersh, W., Bernstam, E.V.: A day in the life of PubMed: analysis of a typical day's query log. J. Am. Med. Inform. Assoc. **14**(2), 212–220 (2007). https://doi.org/10.1197/jamia.M2191
2. Kroll, H.: Narrative Information Access - A new Paradigm for Digital Libraries (Narrativer Informationszugriff - Ein neues Paradigma für Digitale Bibliotheken). Ph.D. thesis, TU Braunschweig, Germany (2023). https://doi.org/10.24355/DBBS.084-202401171145-1
3. Kroll, H., Kalo, J.-C., Nagel, D., Mennicke, S., Balke, W.-T.: Context-compatible information fusion for scientific knowledge graphs. In: Hall, M., Merčun, T., Risse, T., Duchateau, F. (eds.) TPDL 2020. LNCS, vol. 12246, pp. 33–47. Springer, Cham (2020). https://doi.org/10.1007/978-3-030-54956-5_3
4. Kroll, H., Kreutz, C.K., Sackhoff, P., Balke, W.: Enriching simple keyword queries for domain-aware narrative retrieval. In: ACM/IEEE Joint Conference on Digital Libraries, JCDL 2023, Santa Fe, NM, USA, 26–30 June 2023, pp. 143–154. IEEE (2023). https://doi.org/10.1109/JCDL57899.2023.00029
5. Kroll, H., Kreutz, C.K., Thang, B.M., Schaer, P., Balke, W.: Building an explainable graph-based biomedical paper recommendation system (technical report). CoRR abs/2412.15229 (2024). https://doi.org/10.48550/ARXIV.2412.15229
6. Kroll, H., Pirklbauer, J., Balke, W.: A toolbox for the nearly-unsupervised construction of digital library knowledge graphs. In: ACM/IEEE Joint Conference on Digital Libraries, JCDL 2021, Champaign, IL, USA, 27–30 September 2021, pp. 21–30. IEEE (2021). https://doi.org/10.1109/JCDL52503.2021.00014
7. Kroll, H., Pirklbauer, J., Kalo, J., Kunz, M., Ruthmann, J., Balke, W.: A discovery system for narrative query graphs: entity-interaction-aware document retrieval. Int. J. Digit. Libr. **25**(1), 3–24 (2024). https://doi.org/10.1007/S00799-023-00356-3
8. Kroll, H., Pirklbauer, J., Plötzky, F., Balke, W.: A detailed library perspective on nearly unsupervised information extraction workflows in digital libraries. Int. J. Digit. Libr. **25**(2), 401–425 (2024). https://doi.org/10.1007/S00799-023-00368-Z
9. Kroll, H., Sackhoff, P., Breuer, T., Schenkel, R., Balke, W.: Ranking narrative query graphs for biomedical document retrieval (technical report). CoRR abs/2412.15232 (2024). https://doi.org/10.48550/ARXIV.2412.15232
10. Leaman, R., Lu, Z.: TaggerOne: joint named entity recognition and normalization with semi-Markov models. Bioinformatics **32**(18), 2839–2846 (2016). https://doi.org/10.1093/bioinformatics/btw343
11. Lewis, C.: Using the "thinking Aloud;; Method in Cognitive Interface Design. https://books.google.de/books?id=F5AKHQAACAAJ
12. Wei, C.H., Allot, A., Leaman, R., Lu, Z.: PubTator central: automated concept annotation for biomedical full text articles. Nucleic Acids Res. **47**(W1), W587–W593 (2019). https://doi.org/10.1093/nar/gkz389
13. Wei, C.H., Kao, H.Y., Lu, Z.: GNormPlus: an integrative approach for tagging genes, gene families, and protein domains. BioMed Res. Int. **2015**, 918710 (2015). https://doi.org/10.1155/2015/918710

A Modern Open Source Integrated Library System by Invenio

Karolina Przerwa[✉] [iD] and Salomé Rohr [iD]

CERN, Meyrin, Switzerland
karolina.zdzislawa.przerwa@cern.ch
https://home.cern

Abstract. This paper presents key features of InvenioILS (Integrated Library System), using the CERN Library Catalogue as a primary example. The demonstration targets researchers, librarians, and developers in academic or research settings interested in open-source library infrastructure. It outlines the motivation for developing a new ILS, along with its main features, architecture, and deployment options - offering a high-level view of how InvenioILS supports research-focused environments. Core functions like loan management, cataloging, acquisitions, and user services will be shown within a modular, flexible system. The session will also highlight customization options, collaborative development efforts, and the practical impact and adaptability of the Invenio framework for a broad range of library types.

Keywords: integrated library system · open source · catalogue

1 Motivation

The CERN Library [8] serves a diverse research community, including physicists, students, engineers, IT staff, and administrators. It manages a catalogue of **250,000** records covering both digital and physical resources, and handles around **3,800** loans and **1,000** purchase orders annually.

Before InvenioILS, the CERN Library managed its holdings in the CERN Document Server. To focus that platform on institutional content, the catalogue was moved to a separate system. CERN's IT department [15] began modernizing the software with an emphasis on usability and a scalable, maintainable data model. Given the limitations of existing open-source ILS options and the need for flexibility, InvenioILS was built from scratch using the Invenio [1] framework - also powering Zenodo [13] and the CERN Document Server.

Today, the CERN Library Catalogue runs on InvenioILS, while the CERN Document Server uses InvenioRDM, developed with global partners, including RERO [7], who contributed to invenio-circulation module for handling loans. The systems are interoperable, linking digital and physical records. Since 2021, the CERN Library has used InvenioILS for cataloguing, imports, circulation, acquisitions, ILL, and public access. Continuous collaboration between librarians and developers has resulted in a reliable, feature-rich platform now available to other libraries.

InvenioILS is fully **open source** [4] and can be tailored to meet the needs of different library types (Fig. 1).

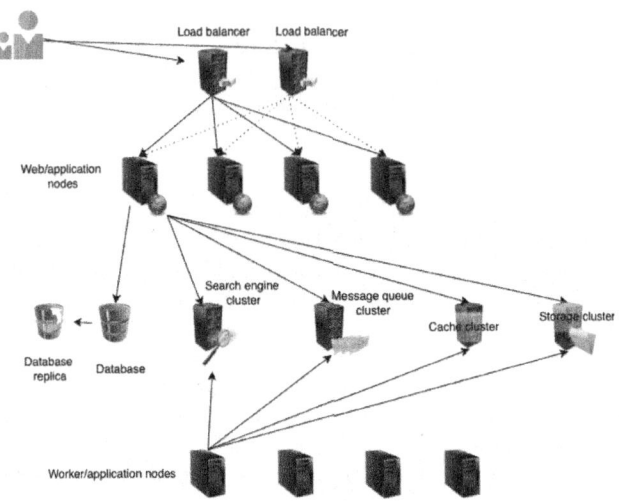

Fig. 1. Application architecture diagram

2 System Overview

2.1 Architecture

InvenioILS is built on a modular architecture designed for scalability, flexibility, and easy integration. It uses the Invenio framework, also employed in digital repositories and research data platforms. The backend is written in **Python with Flask** [9] and provides a **REST API** [10] that separates services from the user interface. Data is stored in a relational database, with **OpenSearch** [11] handling indexing and fast search. Background tasks like overdue notices and bulk imports run through Celery workers. The frontend is a textbfReact-based web app that communicates via the API, making it easy to build custom interfaces without changing backend logic. The system is highly customizable, with extension points across the stack. Its modular setup lets administrators enable only the components they need - such as Single Sign-On or OAI-PMH support.

2.2 Data Model

The metadata schema of InvenioILS is based on DataCite [2] and adapted to fit cataloguing needs. It uses a flexible, schema-driven approach where key data

- such as items, patrons, loans, and orders - are stored in JSON format within a relational database (typically PostgreSQL [12]). Libraries can describe items using standard fields like document type, title, authors, edition, language, publication year, imprint, and identifiers (ISBN, DOI, report number). Additional fields include abstract, table of contents, free-text subjects, and relations to series, translations, or other editions. Schema validation ensures that metadata input follows required formats and includes mandatory fields, helping maintain consistent data quality across records.

2.3 Scalability

The Invenio framework - the base of InvenioILS - has been designed with scalability in mind, making it well-suited for repositories and library catalogues expecting sustained growth. Its proven performance is demonstrated by large-scale deployments such as Zenodo, which currently hosts over **4.5 million** records without any noticeable degradation in responsiveness or system stability (Fig. 2).

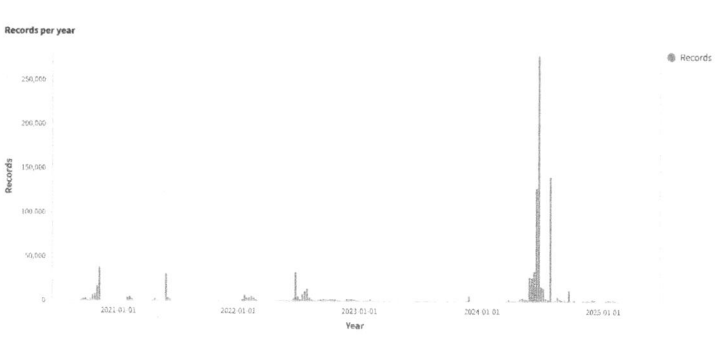

Fig. 2. Histogram of record additions in Zenodo in last 5 years

3 Key Features and Innovations

3.1 Circulation Management

Literature Requests. InvenioILS offers standard circulation features - loans, returns, renewals, reservations, and reminders - along with a literature request workflow. Users can submit a blank form with a reference or request an electronic version from an existing record. Librarians then manage the request: linking it to a record, triggering an interlibrary loan or acquisition, fulfilling it, or declining if needed. This simplifies the process, as users don't need to choose the service - librarians handle it. All actions are tracked within the system.

At CERN, users can also choose to pick up reserved items at the library or have them delivered to their office - an appreciated option on a large campus.

Self-Checkout with a Mobile Device. Provided with a QR code to scan and their own mobile device, a patron can check out any book from the library on their own. The software is integrated with a barcode reader, so that any device with a camera can read the code and automatically create a loan on the user's account. The feature helps to make the shelves more accessible and open to patrons - it is used in approximately **10%** of loans.

3.2 Acquisitions and Interlibrary Loans

InvenioILS allows libraries to register vendors and purchase orders, enabling full tracking of acquisitions. Each acquisition is linked to a document, making it easy to see what was bought, when, from whom, and at what price - helping manage annual budgets. Acquisitions can have statuses such as pending, ordered, received, or cancelled. Filters and CSV export support tasks like provider-based reporting (Fig. 3).

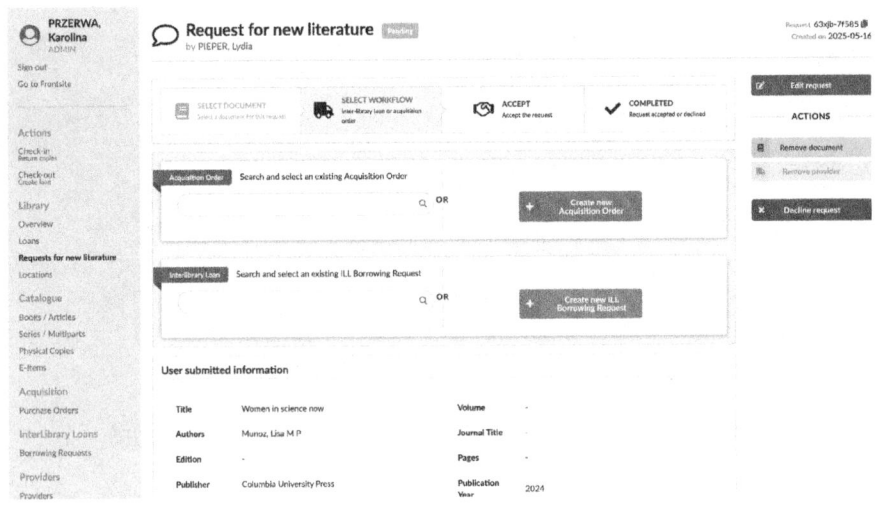

Fig. 3. Literature request workflow: Create/Select Document, Create/Select Workflow (Acquisition or Interlibrary Loan), Accept/Decline, Completed

For interlibrary loans, article requests follow the same workflow as acquisitions, since the article is received and sent to the patrons - which is an innovative approach. Physical interlibrary loans include a loan and return step, managed within the system.

Another example of an innovation is that a patron receiving an interlibrary loan sees it as a regular loan in their account - the underlying library operations are transparent, what provides the patron with an improved user experience. They can request extensions like any other loan, but these are handled manually by librarians, who confirm or decline based on availability.

3.3 Library Management

InvenioILS supports multiple locations and sub-locations ("internal locations"), making it suitable for multi-site setups. Each location can include contact details and opening hours, including exceptions for holidays. This information is shown to users and used in calculating loan due dates. Librarians can manage all of this directly from the back office.

Patron accounts are synced via CERN's LDAP [14] and anonymized when someone leaves the institution to comply with data privacy rules. All metadata, including loan history, is searchable both in the user interface and in the back office, allowing easy extraction of statistics like the number of loans over a given period (Fig. 4).

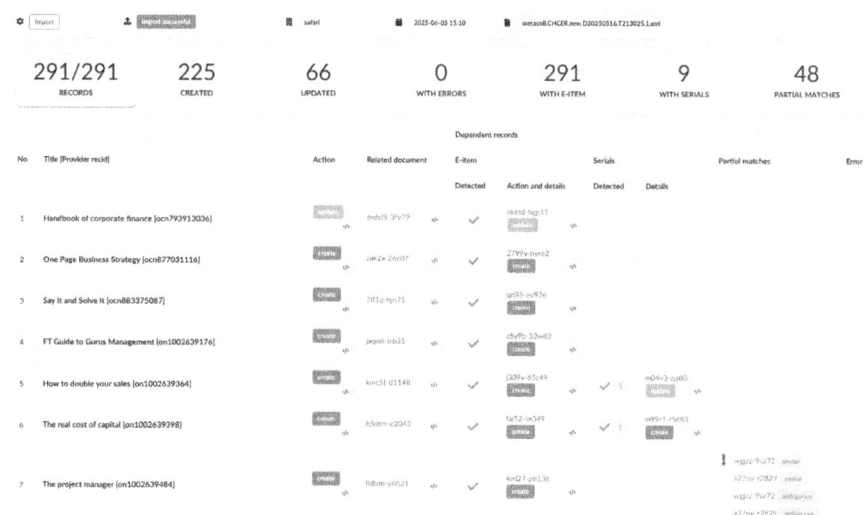

Fig. 4. Customized bulk import interface

3.4 Cataloguing and Importation of Records

InvenioILS supports both manual cataloguing and adding a customized bulk import of records. The importer must be configured per provider, based on the source format. Once mapping rules are defined, uploading an XML file triggers two actions: (1) the file is converted into InvenioILS's JSON schema, with validation errors reported for correction; (2) the system checks for existing records - creating new ones, updating full matches, or flagging partial matches for review. The importer also creates or updates linked e-items. Two modes are available: 'preview' for reviewing the file and 'import' for applying changes (Fig. 5).

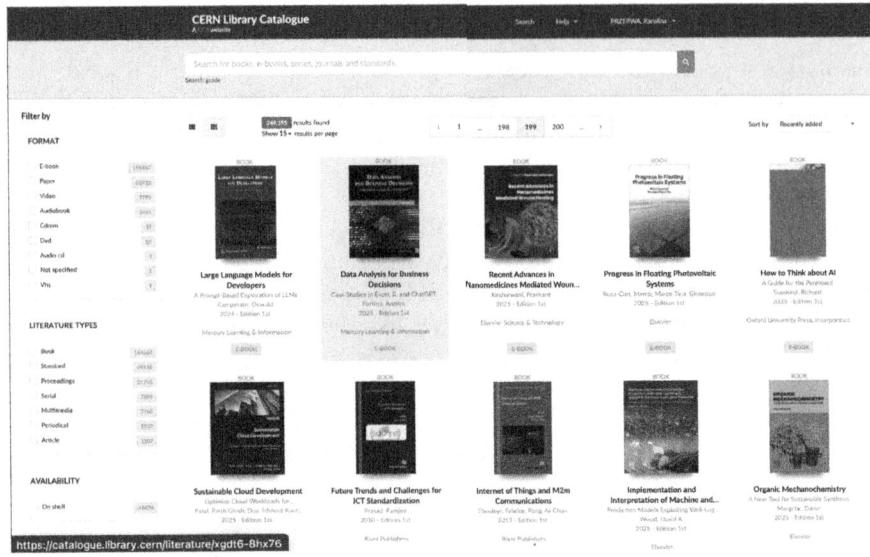

Fig. 5. User search interface

3.5 User Interface

The user interface allows patrons to search the library catalogue through a general search bar, with an optional guide for building advanced queries. Filters help to narrow search results - and are configurable per instance. Once a record is found, users can:

- Click "Access online" if the item is electronic; labels indicate if it's open access or login-protected.
- Select "Find it on shelf" to view a map showing the book's physical location (requires an integration with a map application)
- Use "Request loan" with options for pickup, delivery, or urgency ("require before" date).
- Request the e-book version, which librarians will review.
- Submit a request form if the item is not in the catalogue.

Each patron has an account under "Your loans" menu item, where they can view and extend current loans, track literature requests, and review loan history.

The same web interface provides access to both the front and back office, allowing librarians to easily switch views - even at the record level - improving efficiency and saving time.

4 Demonstration Scenario

The demonstration [3] will be interactive to ensure the audience engagement and well targeted content - the audience will be asked to vote for features they would like to see live. To meet the time limitations of the demonstration (20 min), we will present only the most voted features (3 to 4 out of 6), choosing between

1. Patron check-out and interface
2. Loan management
3. Acquisitions and interlibrary loans
4. Library management
5. Cataloguing
6. Bulk importation of records

For example: If "Loan Management" is selected, we will show the real-time patron check-out flow, how due dates are calculated using the calendar configuration. The detailed description of each feature is provided in Sect. 4. Link to a demo website [6] will be given for people who would like to explore further InvenioILS.

5 Deployment and Customization

5.1 Deployment

InvenioILS supports modern deployment using Docker [16], with starter Docker Compose files bundling core services - server, task queue, and frontend - into reproducible units. It can be deployed on-premise or in the cloud using tools like Kubernetes [17] or OKD [18]. Configuration through environment variables allows easy setup without modifying the code.

At CERN, both the Library Catalogue and the InvenioILS Demo run reliably. While deployment needs some DevOps knowledge, the Invenio community offers documentation [5], templates, and active support to help new adopters.

5.2 Customization

Running an on-premise ILS often comes with the need to tailor the system to institutional needs. From experience, we know adopters may want to customize their instance - f.e., by adjusting colors and logos to match institutional branding or based on personal preference.

InvenioILS supports many types of customization, from simple visual changes to replacing the user interface entirely. Librarians can define loan policies and circulation rules, while the modular design allows developers to add new features as needed.

Whether it's adding a document type, changing the homepage, or implementing complex workflows like authority control or inter-library circulation, InvenioILS gives developers the tools to adapt the system to their specific requirements (Fig. 6).

Fig. 6. An example of front page customization - CERN Library Catalogue on the left, ILS Demonstration website on the right

6 Lessons Learned and Challenges

The Invenio framework and its two main products - InvenioILS and InvenioRDM - have had a clear impact in academic and research communities. From our experience, we have learned close collaboration between domain experts and IT specialists is essential to create high quality features and research institutions often share similar needs, and working together benefits all.

These insights came through challenges, especially in dealing with complex bibliographic standards and turning them into a smooth, user-friendly experience for both librarians and patrons.

7 Conclusions and Future Work

InvenioILS already offers many features for managing library catalogues. As an extensible system, it continues to evolve based on user needs. Areas under consideration for improvement include interface accessibility, expanded data extraction for KPIs and statistics, and integration with RFID readers to support bulk cataloguing and inventory. Invenio framework developers are also exploring the use of AI to support curation workflows and are gathering input from the community on future needs.

Though originally developed for the CERN Library, InvenioILS is suitable for all types of libraries - public, school, or special. Libraries interested in adopting the system, contributing to its development, or providing feedback are encouraged to contact the authors.

References

1. CERN and contributors. Invenio Software. https://inveniosoftware.org/. Accessed 2025/06/15

2. DataCite. DataCite Metadata Schema. https://schema.datacite.org/. Accessed 2025/06/15
3. Pieper L., Przerwa K.: InvenioILS, An Open-source integrated library system - live demo with the CERN library catalogue. https://www.youtube.com/watch?v=C82rhhHJQfU. Accessed 2025/06/15
4. CERN and contributors. InvenioILS. https://github.com/inveniosoftware/invenio-app-ils. Accessed 2025/06/15
5. CERN and contributors. InvenioILS developer documentation. https://invenioils.docs.cern.ch/. Accessed 2025/06/15
6. CERN and contributors. InvenioILS demonstration instance. https://invenioils.web.cern.ch/. Accessed 2025/06/15
7. Réseau des bibliothèques de Suisse occidentale. RERO. https://www.rero.ch/en
8. CERN Scientific Information Service. https://sis.web.cern.ch/
9. Flask framework. https://flask.palletsprojects.com/en/stable/
10. Representational state transfer (REST). https://restfulapi.net/
11. Opensearch. https://opensearch.org/
12. PostgreSQL. https://www.postgresql.org/
13. Zenodo, General-purpose repository. https://zenodo.org
14. Lightweight Directory Access Protocol (LDAP). https://ldap.com/
15. CERN information technology department. https://information-technology.web.cern.ch/
16. Docker. https://www.docker.com/
17. Kubernetes. https://kubernetes.io/
18. OKD. https://okd.io/

LLM-Enhanced DETEXA Workflow Builder for Semantic Enrichment

Yannis Foufoulas[1], Eleni Zacharia[3], Harry Dimitropoulos[3(✉)], Natalia Manola[3], and Yannis Ioannidis[1,2]

[1] Athena Research Center, Athens, Greece
[2] National and Kapodistrian University of Athens, Athens, Greece
[3] OpenAIRE AMKE, Athens, Greece
harryd@athenarc.gr

Abstract. The increasing demand for accurate and scalable semantic enrichment of scientific publications has driven the need for hybrid frameworks that combine database-centric processing with the semantic power of Large Language Models (LLMs). We present the DETEXA+LLM Semantic Enrichment Workflow Builder, an extension of the DETEXA framework, which allows users to define, execute, and visualize hybrid text analysis workflows over relational backends. Our system supports declarative construction of pipelines that integrate regex-based pattern matching, classification, and selective LLM invocation via automatically generated Python UDFs and YeSQL queries. A visual web interface enables users to configure metadata enrichment workflows with minimal programming effort. We demonstrate the utility of our approach through three diverse and essential use cases for digital libraries: (i) classification of Data and Software Availability Statements (DAS), (ii) extraction of Protein Data Bank (PDB) codes, and (iii) mining of funding source mentions. Our results show that combining rule-based logic with targeted LLM calls improves both accuracy and efficiency, making the system suitable for large-scale scholarly metadata extraction tasks.

Keywords: Metadata enrichment · LLMs · User Defined Functions

1 Introduction

Extracting structured semantic metadata from unstructured scientific publications remains a persistent challenge in the development of scholarly infrastructures. Tasks such as identifying Data and Software Availability Statements (DAS), linking to software repositories, or extracting funding acknowledgements are essential for fostering transparency, compliance monitoring, and discoverability in the open science ecosystem. Accurate and scalable automation of these tasks is vital for organizations like OpenAIRE, EOSC, and national funding bodies, which rely on timely and machine-readable metadata to index research outputs, assess policy adoption, and support cross-repository integration.

Manual curation is infeasible at scale, while existing automated approaches face trade-offs between interpretability, performance, and flexibility. Traditional rule-based methods, while scalable, are often brittle and difficult to maintain due to linguistic variability. Conversely, full-document LLM pipelines are computationally costly and susceptible to hallucination. Moreover, unified and user-friendly tools integrating both paradigms are lacking.

To address this gap, we present the *DETEXA+LLM Semantic Enrichment Workflow Builder*, a visual and declarative interface for designing hybrid text analytics workflows over relational data backends. Built as an extension to DETEXA [1,2]—a rich declarative text analytics system for digital libraries applications—our system enables users to combine pattern-based matching, rule-based classification, and selective LLM invocation using automatically generated Python UDFs and YeSQL queries. The web-based interface offers modular configuration of preprocessing, context extraction, classification logic, aggregation rules, and LLM prompts, requiring minimal programming effort. To enable this hybrid functionality, we extend DETEXA by integrating LLMs as *stateful, dynamically typed scalar UDFs*, leveraging YeSQL's polymorphic UDF support. This allows efficient and selective invocation of external language models without incurring repeated initialization overheads, and facilitates smooth embedding of semantic reasoning within declarative SQL workflows.

We demonstrate the flexibility and power of this architecture through three representative use cases: (i) single-label classification of DAS categories, (ii) multi-mention extraction of Protein Data Bank (PDB) codes, and (iii) identification of funding sources. These cases illustrate how hybrid workflows can achieve high precision and efficiency by leveraging traditional methods where appropriate and selectively invoking LLMs only when necessary.

Our contributions are: (i) an extension to DETEXA with a new class of stateful scalar UDFs that interface with external LLMs inside SQL workflows; (ii) a hybrid declarative workflow for research metadata enrichment which combines rule-based approaches with LLMs; (iii) a declarative and visual interface for constructing end-to-end enrichment pipelines with configurable preprocessing, extraction, classification, LLM invocation, and aggregation logic; and (iv) a demonstration in three real-world scenarios: DAS classification, PDB code extraction, and funding source identification. A video presentation of the main demonstration features is available at [3].

2 Related Work

We briefly review related research across three key areas pertinent to our demonstration scenarios: text mining in database systems, integration of large language models (LLMs) in databases, and scholarly metadata extraction.

In recent years, the integration of data science pipelines into data management systems has gained popularity [4–6]. Text mining within database systems leverages User-Defined Functions (UDFs) to efficiently process text data, minimizing data movement overheads. Frameworks such as YeSQL [7,8] have facilitated seamless integration of polymorphic, stateful, and dynamically typed UDFs, accelerating in-database text analytics. DETEXA [1,2] is built on top of YeSQL and provides declarative text exploration capabilities for digital library applications. Other UDF-centric works target the effective and efficient integration of UDFs in a data engine to support scalable modern analytics and machine learning pipelines [9–13]. Several text analytics pipelines have been implemented inside DBMSes with UDF support [14–19].

Integrating LLMs within data engines has attracted attention [20–22]. Transformer based LLMs have high memory requirements and invocation costs [23]. Non-stateful LLM UDFs reload models per call, severely degrading performance, while stateful implementations (e.g., YeSQL) allow persistent initialization.

In scholarly metadata extraction, automated approaches face various linguistic and structural complexities [24]. DAS extraction, critical for research reproducibility and transparency, is notably challenging due to diverse phrasings, implicit references, and heterogeneous structures [25–27]. Machine Learning approaches have shown limited effectiveness, correctly classifying only 68% of DAS, with the remainder requiring manual labelling [28]. Similarly, extracting Protein Data Bank (PDB)[1] codes is complex due to their potential confusion with other entities such as antibody identifiers, dates, and scientific notation [1,29]. Context-aware disambiguation techniques are crucial to achieving high precision [30,31]. Funding/project information mining also poses unique challenges, as mentions are typically scattered throughout publication texts and can vary significantly in phrasing and specificity. Efficient extraction requires both targeted pattern-based searches and semantic disambiguation to correctly identify funding sources, project identifiers, and associated metadata [1].

Our demonstration scenarios highlight these diverse extraction challenges and illustrate how the proposed visual interface can be used to implement and run hybrid pipelines integrating pattern-based classification, targeted LLM invocation, and relational database optimizations, effectively addressing the limitations observed in existing techniques.

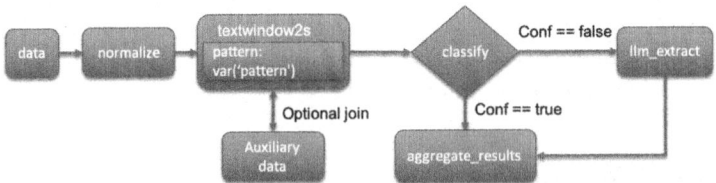

Fig. 1. Hybrid SQL+LLM semantic enrichment pipeline.

---

[1] https://www.rcsb.org.

3 Demonstrable Components

3.1 Hybrid Text Analytics + LLM Pipeline

The proposed pipeline comprises several components—some mandatory, others optional—as illustrated in Fig. 1. It leverages a series of User-Defined Functions (UDFs) to preprocess text, extract potential matches (optionally via join operations), and classify context snippets from research papers by combining traditional methods with the support of a large language model (LLM).

The process begins with the `normalize` UDF, which prepares the raw text through a series of selected preprocessing steps, such as lowercasing, punctuation and newline removal, stopword elimination, and more. The cleaned text is then passed to `textwindow2s`, which uses regular expressions to extract snippets based on predefined patterns. After this step, an optional `JOIN` can be performed—for example, when searching for project identifiers, the extracted text snippets can be joined with a reference list of known project identifiers (e.g., from CORDA datasets) to filter out false matches.

The resulting snippets are classified by the `classify` UDF through weighted, and optionally distance based pattern matching. Each snippet receives a predicted label and a confidence score. If the confidence exceeds a defined threshold (e.g., 0.5), the classification is accepted. Otherwise, the `llm_extract` UDF is invoked to engage an LLM, which analyzes the snippet using its semantic capabilities to handle ambiguous or complex statements and improve accuracy.

Finally, since a single document may produce multiple snippet-level predictions, the `aggregate_results` UDF applies user defined logic to prioritize and select the most informative final label. This step is necessary for use cases such as classifying a paper's overall data availability. However, in other cases—e.g., when identifying links to funding projects—aggregation may not be applicable or required, as multiple valid labels may coexist.

3.2 Workflow Configuration Interface

The *DETEXA+LLM Semantic Enrichment Workflow Builder* is a web-based interface enabling hybrid text mining workflows without requiring programming expertise. Users define pattern-based extractors, normalization, classification and aggregation rules, and selective LLM invocation within structured SQL pipelines. Figure 2 presents the modular user interface guiding workflow creation. The interface is implemented in JavaScript.

Pattern Definition and Text Preprocessing. The user selects a dataset and using *Define Regex Pattern* form, enters a primary regular expression pattern to detect semantically meaningful anchor phrases. An optional checkbox allows users to indicate whether the pattern typically appears within lists or tables (e.g., a table with PDB codes). *Normalization options* include lowercasing, punctuation removal, stopword elimination, stemming, lemmatization, and Unicode normalization.

Text Window Configuration. The user specifies the *text window parameters* selecting how much textual context to extract around each pattern match by configuring the number of tokens before and after the match, and the maximum length of the match window. This contextual window is passed to downstream UDFs, including classifiers and LLMs.

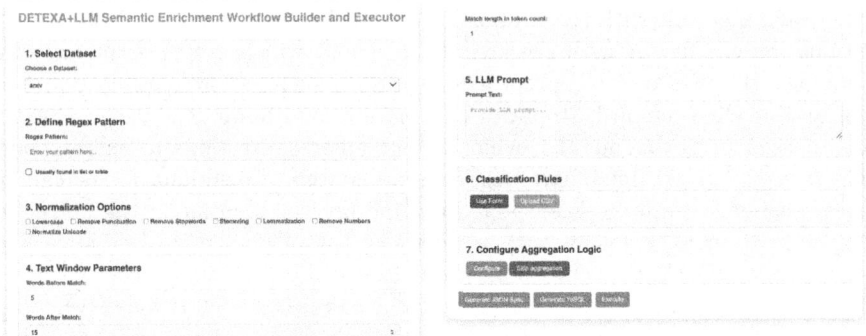

Fig. 2. Main DETEXA+LLM interface for workflow configuration.

LLM Prompt Specification. The interface offers a natural *LLM prompt* that is provided to the external LLM when invoked. This prompt is used only in low-confidence classification cases, based on scores from pattern-based classifiers. This selective invocation ensures both speed and interpretability.

Classification Rules via Form or CSV. Each class is defined by positive and negative regex patterns, optionally weighted and configured with distance-based scoring. Users may define classes manually via the form interface or upload a CSV file containing class names, patterns, weights, and polarities. Figure 3 presents an abridged example of patterns appropriate for DAS classification.

Aggregation Logic. After individual classification outputs are produced (per match window), users optionally select aggregation strategies to consolidate multiple predictions per document as shown in Fig. 4. They may choose between frequency-based, confidence-based, or priority-based aggregation. A drag-and-drop list allows defining class priority, and additional rule-based overrides can be added (e.g., "If class A is present, always choose B"). This logic is compiled into a Python UDF and included in the generated pipeline.

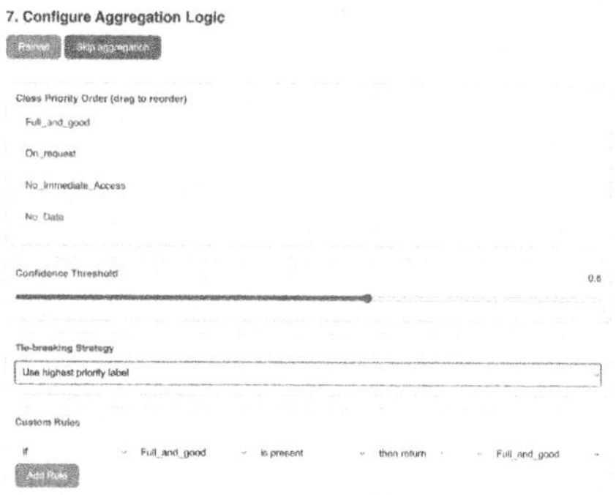

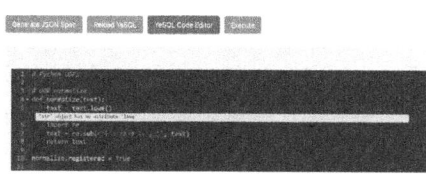

Fig. 4. Aggregation rules setup (example abridged; categories include *Full and good, Supplementary, On Request, No immediate access, No Data, No DAS Statement*) [32].

Fig. 3. Classification rule builder using positive/negative patterns (example abridged).

Code Generation and Execution. The interface supports exporting and sharing of the complete configuration in JSON format enhancing reproducibility and portability via the *Generate JSON Spec* button. Users may press *generate YeSQL* to produce just in time code according to their parameters. Advanced users can view, edit, and execute the generated pipeline directly in the browser, with the ability to add custom Python functions and SQL queries to extend the

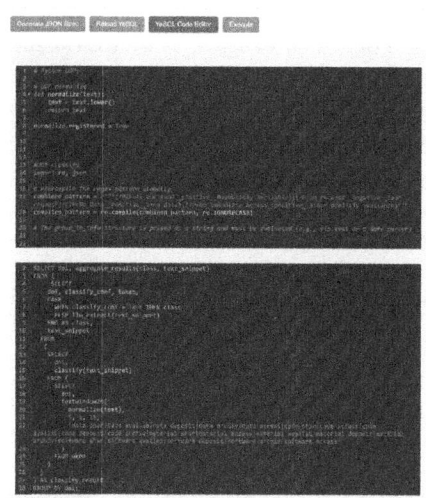

Fig. 6. Error handling.

Fig. 5. Generated YeSQL and Python UDFs editable via integrated editor.

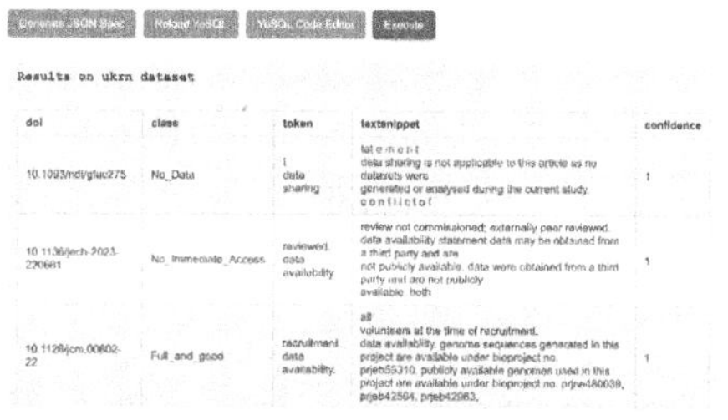

Fig. 7. Results.

workflow builder's capabilities. The interface supports query editing with syntax high lighting, and real-time feedback (Fig. 5). If the edited code (UDF code or the YeSQL query) contains an error, the backend returns a detailed message to the frontend, and the corresponding line is automatically highlighted to assist in rapid debugging and iterative refinement (Fig. 6). Users can run the complete workflow by selecting a dataset and pressing the *Execute* button. The backend compiles the YeSQL query just in time, registers the UDFs, runs on the selected data sources and returns structured results (e.g., DAS classification results). Execution results are shown in a table as shown in Fig. 7.

4 Demo Scenarios

We demonstrate the capabilities of the DETEXA+LLM interface through three representative scenarios, each highlighting different usage patterns, rule configurations, and levels of LLM involvement. For each scenario, we construct and execute workflows to showcase performance efficiency, scalability across datasets of varying sizes, and ease of development. We present the precision and performance of the proposed pipeline. The experiments are executed on a server equipped with dual Intel Xeon Gold 5318Y (96 cores, 192 threads, 2.10 GHz base, 3.4 GHz turbo) and 512 GB of RAM. The system runs CUDA Version 12.2, Python 3.10, and DETEXA Workflow Builder [33]. The query engine runs in single-threaded mode on a single CPU, while the LLM component[2] is accelerated using two NVIDIA RTX A6000 GPUs, each with 48 GB of VRAM.

4.1 Scenario 1: Data and Software Availability Statement (DAS) Classification

The goal is classifying DAS presence into one of six categories, evaluated using representative metadata records from UK institutions as part of the UKRN Open Research Indicators project [34], with selected examples publicly available via FigShare[3]. The users follow the steps below within the demonstrated interface:

- Define a pattern (e.g., `available at, data is stored`) to anchor the search.
- Preprocessing steps like lower case conversion.
- Classification rules using domain-specific positive and negative patterns.
- A fallback prompt for LLM invocation in ambiguous cases.
- An aggregation logic to combine multiple window-based predictions into a single label per document.

This hybrid configuration ensures accurate classification while minimizing unnecessary LLM calls. The output is a single DAS label per article, accompanied by a confidence score. Based on manual evaluation of a random sample of 100 documents—49 of which contained relevant information—the classification achieved 93.8% accurate classification of existing statements (overall precision over 100 documents: 97%). The pipeline achieves a throughput of 2 papers per second, with performance primarily limited by the latency of LLM inference.

---

[2] `Mistral-7B-Instruct-v0.3` from HuggingFace's `transformers` library.
[3] https://doi.org/10.25392/leicester.data.28675934.

4.2 Scenario 2: Protein Data Bank (PDB) Code Extraction

In this scenario, the interface is used to extract Protein Data Bank (PDB) codes mentioned in biomedical publications. These codes follow a well-defined format (e.g., `1ABC`, `2XYZ`), making them well-suited for pattern-based recognition. Here, we are using open access publications from PubMed. Extraction steps:

- A pattern with a digit and 3 alphanumerics is defined to match PDB codes.
- Lower case conversion and punctuation removal are applied to the texts.
- Classification is based on positive distance-weighted patterns such as `protein data bank`, `pdb`, and negative patterns such as `antibody`, to disambiguate similarly formatted strings.
- No LLM is needed, as precision is already high using pattern-based methods.
- Aggregation is skipped; multiple PDB codes per document are expected.

The system returns all PDB codes along with positional context, facilitating downstream indexing or linking to external protein repositories. Based on rigorous testing with samples from PubMed publications (1K links validated), the current precision and recall rates for PDB code extraction are both approximately 98%, with processing speeds around 80 papers per second.

4.3 Scenario 3: Funding Information Mining

This scenario targets the extraction of funding project mentions in publications, often found in acknowledgements or scattered in the text. We use open access publications from ArXiv. The configuration includes:

- Define anchoring patterns to match project identifiers, such as 9-digit (e.g., Horizon Europe) or 6-digit (e.g., FP7) numbers.
- Normalization: lowercasing, stopword removal, and Unicode normalization.
- Join with a reference list of known project identifiers (e.g., from the CORDA dataset) to eliminate false matches.
- Use distance-weighted patterns for classification (e.g., `funded by`, `supported`, `grant agreement`).
- Skip LLM and aggregation steps, as multiple valid identifiers may co-occur.

The output includes matched snippets enriched with publication and project identifiers (e.g., Horizon 2020 codes). The system processes approximately 100 full-texts per second, achieving 99.5% precision for European project codes based on manual validation of 1K links.

User Interaction. Attendees can actively engage with the demo, refining results, modifying UI parameters or code, and rerunning the workflow accordingly.

5 Conclusions and Future Work

This demonstration introduced a hybrid workflow builder combining rule-based, database-centric analytics with selective LLM-based enrichment. The demonstration includes three real-world digital library use cases. In the future, we plan to integrate features that support task-based evaluation, collaborative editing, sharing, reusability of workflows, and integration with knowledge graphs and external APIs. Enhancements for real-time multi-user workflow design and support for explainability auditing are also under consideration.

Acknowledgements. This work was supported by the Horizon Europe projects EBRAINS 2.0 (GA.101147319) and EOSC Beyond (GA.101131875).

Disclosure of Interests. The authors have no competing interests to declare.

References

1. Foufoulas, Y., et al.: Detexa: declarative extensible text exploration and analysis through SQL. Int. J. Digit. Libr. **25**(3), 457–469 (2024)
2. Foufoulas, Y., et al.: DETEXA: declarative extensible text exploration and analysis. In: International Conference on Theory and Practice of Digital Libraries. Springer, Cham (2022)
3. Foufoulas, Y., et al.: Accompanying video for the TPDL 2025 demo: "LLM-Enhanced DETEXA Workflow Builder for Semantic Enrichment". https://doi.org/10.5281/zenodo.16450765
4. Foufoulas, Y., Simitsis, A.: Efficient execution of user-defined functions in SQL queries. PVLDB **16**(12), 3874–3877 (2023)
5. Foufoulas, Y., Simitsis, A.: User-defined functions in modern data engines. In: IEEE ICDE, pp. 3593–3598 (2023)
6. Foufoulas, Y., Palaiologou, T., Simitsis, A.: UDFBench: A tool for benchmarking UDF queries on SQL engines. SIGMOD (2025)
7. Foufoulas, Y., et al.: YeSQL: you extend SQL with rich and highly performant user-defined functions in relational databases. PVLDB **15**(10), 2270–2283 (2022)
8. Foufoulas, Y., Simitsis, A., Ioannidis, Y.: YeSQL: rich user-defined functions without the overhead. PVLDB **15**(12), 3730–3733 (2022)
9. Kläbe, S., et al.: Accelerating python UDFs in vectorized query execution. CIDR (2022)
10. Spiegelberg, L., et al. Tuplex: data science in python at native code speed. In: Proceedings of the 2021 International Conference on Management of Data, pp. 1718–1731 (2021)
11. Sichert, M., Neumann, T.: User-defined operators: efficiently integrating custom algorithms into modern databases. PVLDB, vol. 15, no. 5 (2022). https://doi.org/10.14778/3510397.3510408
12. Chasialis, K., et al.: QFusor: a UDF optimizer plugin for SQL databases. IEEE ICDE, pp. 5457–5460 (2024). https://doi.org/10.1109/ICDE60146.2024.00427
13. Blacher, M., et al.: Machine learning, linear algebra, and more: is SQL all you need? CIDR (2022)

14. Hellerstein, J.M., et al.: The MADlib analytics library. PVLDB **5**(12), 1700–1711 (2012). https://doi.org/10.14778/2367502.2367510
15. Giannakopoulos, T., et al.: Discovering and visualizing interdisciplinary content classes in scientific publications. D-Lib Mag. **20**(11/12) (2014). https://doi.org/10.1045/november14-giannakopoulos
16. Giannakopoulos, T., et al.: Visual-based classification of figures from scientific literature. In: Proceedings of the 24th International Conference on World Wide Web, pp. 1059–1060 (2015). https://doi.org/10.1145/2740908.2742024
17. Giannakopoulos, T., Stamatogiannakis, E., Foufoulas, I., Dimitropoulos, H., Manola, N., Ioannidis, Y.: Content visualization of scientific corpora using an extensible relational database implementation. In: Bolikowski, Ł, Casarosa, V., Goodale, P., Houssos, N., Manghi, P., Schirrwagen, J. (eds.) TPDL 2013. CCIS, vol. 416, pp. 101–112. Springer, Cham (2014). https://doi.org/10.1007/978-3-319-08425-1_10
18. Giannakopoulos, T., Foufoulas, Y., Dimitropoulos, H., Manola, N.: Interactive text analysis and information extraction. In: Manghi, P., Candela, L., Silvello, G. (eds.) IRCDL 2019. CCIS, vol. 988, pp. 340–350. Springer, Cham (2019). https://doi.org/10.1007/978-3-030-11226-4_27
19. Foufoulas, Y., Stamatogiannakis, L., Dimitropoulos, H., Ioannidis, Y.: High-pass text filtering for citation matching. In: Kamps, J., Tsakonas, G., Manolopoulos, Y., Iliadis, L., Karydis, I. (eds.) TPDL 2017. LNCS, vol. 10450, pp. 355–366. Springer, Cham (2017). https://doi.org/10.1007/978-3-319-67008-9_28
20. Zhao, F., et al.: Hybrid querying over relational databases and large language models. CIDR (2025)
21. Zhou, X., Sun, Z., Li, G.: DB-GPT: large language model meets database. Data Sci. Eng. **9**(1), 102–111 (2024)
22. Introducing the prompt() Function: Use the Power of LLMs with SQL. https://motherduck.com/blog/sql-llm-prompt-function-gpt-models
23. Liu, S., et al.: Optimizing LLM Queries in Relational Workloads. arXiv preprint arXiv:2403.05821v1 (2024)
24. Schindler, D., et al.: SoMeSci: a 5 star open data gold standard knowledge graph of software mentions in scientific articles. In: CIKM 2021, pp. 4574–4583 (2021). https://doi.org/10.1145/3459637.3482017
25. Colavizza, G., et al.: The citation advantage of linking publications to research data. PLoS One **15**(4) (2020)
26. Krüger, F., Schindler, D.: A literature review on methods for the extraction of usage statements of software and data. Comput. Sci. Eng. **22**(1), 26–38 (2020)
27. Parkin, M.: How JATS supports data integration: extracting data availability statements and funding information from research articles in Europe PMC. JATS-Con (2019). https://doi.org/10.6084/m9.figshare.8159426.v1
28. Federer, L.M., et al.: Data sharing in PLOS ONE: an analysis of data availability statements. PLoS One **13**(5) (2018)
29. Yannis, F., Anna, G., Lefteris, S., Harry, D., Natalia, M., Yannis, I.: Extracting biological knowledge from literature using SQL. Poster presented at the 5th International Workshop on Mining Scientific Publications (WOSP 2016) (2016)
30. Cole, C., Ott, C., Valdes, D., Valafar, H.: PDBMine: A Reformulation of the Protein Data Bank to Facilitate Structural Data Mining. arXiv:1911.08614 (2019)
31. Garda, S., Leser, U.: BELHD: Improving Biomedical Entity Linking with Homonym Disambiguation. arXiv:2401.05125 (2024)

32. McCutcheon, V., Eadie, M., Williamson, L., Pajor, R.: UKRN Data Accessibility Statement Pilot Classification Discussion Document. Zenodo (2025). https://doi.org/10.5281/zenodo.15223404
33. DETEXA source code. https://github.com/madgik/detexa
34. UK Reproducibility Network (UKRN), Open Research Indicators Project (2024). https://www.ukrn.org/open-research-indicators/

IILAP: Interactive Information Literacy Assessment Platform

Petra Dadic(✉) and Liana Ermakova

Université de Bretagne Occidentale, HCTI, Brest, France
{petra.dadic,liana.ermakova}@univ-brest.fr

Abstract. As digital competence becomes a core priority for lifelong learning in Europe, the need to teach AI literacy grows increasingly urgent. To address this, we present IILAP, a browser-based Interactive Information Literacy Assessment Platform, designed to support the teaching and assessment of critical reading of AI-generated content. IILAP includes a Teacher Tool for curating chatbot QA datasets with truth labels and sources, and a Student Interface that provides responses enriched with citations and trust indicators. The system logs interaction data—such as time on task, source clicks, verification attempts, and error detection—to help educators identify gaps in students' critical reading skills. After each session, automated Excel reports summarize these measures for easy assessment. Developed through an initial user study, IILAP enables classroom deployment of controlled chatbot interactions and provides structured analytics aligned with indicators of critical thinking. This demo showcases how the system bridges user behavior and educational evaluation to fostering AI literacy in education.

Keywords: Academic Information Access · Information literacy · Educational technology · AI literacy

1 Introduction

As digital libraries become AI-enhanced, they shift from static archives to active participants in knowledge creation. Large Language Models (LLMs) are increasingly embedded in scholarly systems, transforming how users search, summarize, and interact with academic content [6,17,29]. This evolution heightens the need for digital literacy, particularly the ability to critically assess authoritative-sounding but potentially inaccurate information. Despite their fluency, LLMs often generate false or misleading statements, known as "hallucinations". These hallucinations [2,3,7,10,12,14,16,25,27,28,30] can be particularly problematic in domains where precision is critical, such as scientific research, journalism, or public policy. Several studies showed that even advanced models like GPT-4 and LLaMA-2 often produce incorrect citations, misinterpreted data, or false claims [7,8,11,13,23,28]. These tools ease access to information but blur the line between fact and AI guesswork. Their errors often sound convincing, making them hard for many users to spot [5,15,17,20,24,29]. Although model-level approaches such as retrieval-augmented generation (RAG) aim to reduce hallucinations by grounding outputs in external sources [19], they often overlook the end user role and offer limited transparency in how content is selected, cited, or attributed [21,26]. At the same time, the design of user interfaces surrounding these systems has received limited attention, despite their potential [18,22].

To address these gaps, we present the Interactive Information Literacy Assessment Platform (IILAP)—a browser-based tool designed to teach and assess critical reading of LLM-generated content. Its web-based format aligns with students' digital habits, ensures accessibility across devices, and supports both classroom and self-directed learning. IILAP includes a Teacher Tool for annotating chatbot question-answer (QA) datasets, adjusting source credibility, launching Student Interface, and evaluating performance at individual and class levels. Student Interface presents curated responses with trust indicators and citations to foster critical engagement. The platform logs student interactions and generates reports to help educators address specific difficulties. As many students overrely on AI tools like ChatGPT, often neglecting fact-checking [4,29], IILAP supports digital library evolution and aligns with the European Commission's focus on digital skills as essential competencies for lifelong learning [9].

2 System Architecture and Design

The platform uses the open-source Python web framework Gradio [1], enabling interaction tracking, flexible interface customization, and rapid deployment. The system consists of Teacher Tool (Fig. 1) and Student Interface (Fig. 2).

Teacher Tool is a browser-based control panel that allows educators to manage chatbot QA datasets, configure source settings, and track student performance. New entries can be added and annotated via the "Add New Annotation" button, while the "Existing Data" button provides access to, and control over, previously created entries. Each entry contains labeled True/False claims and source metadata, with annotation streamlined through configurable checkboxes. Source credibility can be adjusted using the "Source Credibility" button, which defines how trustworthy each source appears in Student Interface. Once the dataset is prepared, the "Launch Student Interface" button starts a Python subprocess and generates a shareable Gradio URL for student access in classroom or self-directed settings. After student sessions, the "Evaluation" button produces XLSX reports with interaction logs and behavioral metrics (e.g., conversation length, verification attempts, and error detection rates) to assess critical thinking at both the individual and class level.

Educator Workflow: Dataset Configuration → Misinformation Calibration → Interface Customization → Session Deployment → Post-session Analysis

Student Interface is a web chatbot that accepts natural language input and returns responses enriched with educator-defined metadata like trust indicators, claim highlights, and source citations. Queries are matched by semantic similarity to the most relevant teacher-authored response from a 21-entry dataset of

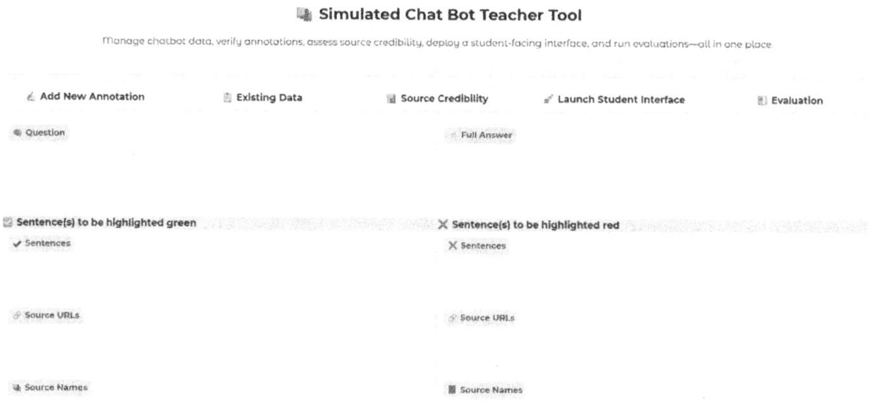

Fig. 1. Teacher Tool Interface.

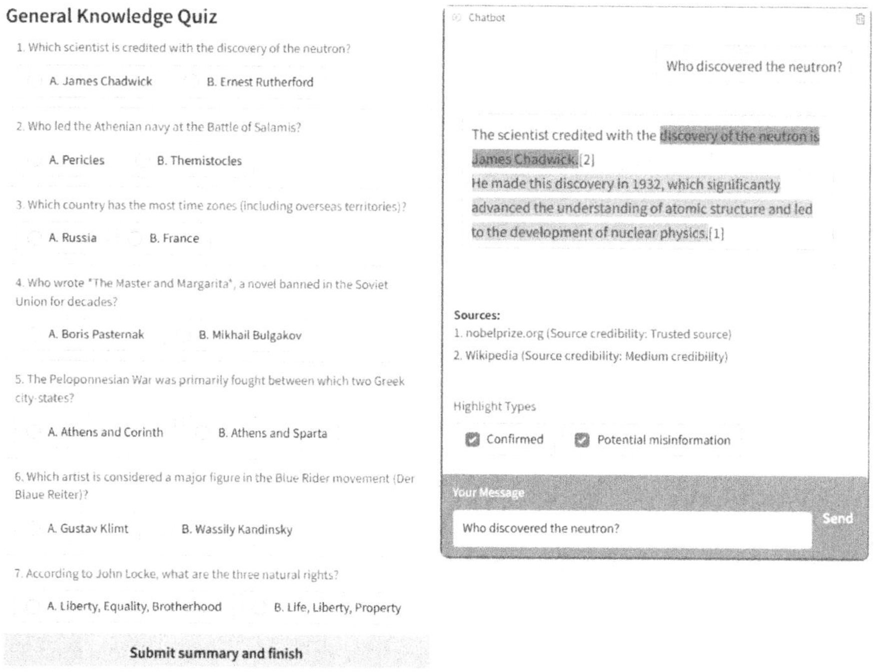

Fig. 2. Student Interface.

multiple-choice questions and related queries. The dataset is intentionally seeded with errors such as incorrect highlights, source misattributions, and factual inaccuracies. Responses are visually annotated (see Fig. 2) based on educator configurations. The interface logs detailed interaction data—submitted queries, time spent, citation clicks, verification attempts, and follow-ups—for later analysis.

Student Workflow: User Input → Question Matching → Database Lookup → Response Augmentation (e.g., trust indicators, claim markers) → Gradio Display

3 Demonstration Scenario

Instructors use IILAP to support units on AI literacy and misinformation, tasking students with evaluating the credibility of AI-generated content across real-world domains such as health, history, and current events. The controlled simulation offers safe, structured exposure to information quality challenges in AI-driven search, while generating measurable insights into students' development of critical evaluation skills—essential for navigating AI-integrated digital libraries.

Before the session, instructors use Teacher Tool to prepare prompts with annotated chatbot responses mixing accurate, misleading, and fabricated claims, each labeled and supported by real or pseudo-citations. Trust indicators and highlights guide critical engagement. As shown in Fig. 1, educators label claims, assign trust levels, and add source metadata, which appear in Student Interface with green highlights for accurate and red for false information (Fig. 2).

Students access Student Interface through their browsers, engaging in natural language dialogue with the chatbot. They can click on sources and flag suspicious claims (e.g., Wikipedia or NobelPrize.org in Fig. 2). The system logs key behaviors—verification, time on task, follow-ups, and misinformation detection—without disrupting the conversation.

After the session, the instructor reviews a detailed IILAP report showing how students engaged with the material, which misinformation types went undetected, and where support is needed. Multiple-choice questions assessed students' ability to identify errors such as incorrect highlights, source misattributions, and factual inaccuracies. This data guides follow-up discussions on common trust traps, citation patterns, and AI-generated text's persuasive tone, informing future assignments and assessment criteria for digital source evaluation.

4 Evaluation

We conducted three studies to evaluate our system. The first gathered user perceptions and system usefulness via surveys, behavioral metrics, and open feedback. The second involved 5 volunteers in a simulated classroom using Student Interface, sharing their views on its support for critical source evaluation. The third focused on Teacher Tool, with participants acting as instructors to create content, deploy the system, and review student data. Teacher feedback assessed the system's educational viability and tool usability.

Initial Study. The study comprised three parts. In the pre-study, participants answered a set of demographic and experience-based questions (7 drop-downs, 3 open-ended, 1 single-select, and 1 multi-select) to provide context for later interactions. In the main study, users wrote a brief summary on the topic "Do AI systems make more accurate decisions compared to humans?" while interacting with a simulated RAG chatbot. Suggested questions and prewritten responses guided exploration; user inputs were matched to the closest available answer. The 60 question-answer pairs were created using a combination of researcher-designed questions and those generated with the help of ChatGPT, based on an effort to anticipate the full range of questions users might ask. Some chatbot answers contained manually inserted errors. The interface was manipulated across 12 experimental conditions, varying response content (e.g., factual errors) and presentation elements (e.g., highlight color, source visibility, and credibility scores). These variations included unhighlighted misinformation, misrepresented sources, and inconsistently labeled accuracy, allowing analysis of how users respond not only to content accuracy but also to its framing. Finally, a post-study survey collected feedback through 12 Likert-scale and 5 open-ended questions.

We collected data via behavioral tracking, free-form user inputs (e.g., summaries and feedback), and responses to multiple-choice and Likert-scale questions (from -2 very dissatisfied to 2 very satisfied). Behavioral data from the AI chatbot interaction phase included time-stamped logs of user actions (clicks, typing, question count, time on task, use of highlighting, source engagement, summary length). Since all chatbot responses were predefined, each was labeled by key characteristics stored in a lookup table for later analysis. Free-form data, including summaries and open-ended feedback, was manually reviewed and sorted based on what they described such as "likes", "dislikes," "user behavior," "verification preferences," and "suggested improvements." This process ensured nuanced interpretation, including feedback given in the wrong fields or spread across multiple responses. For example, a comment like "I was taking into account the colors but also my own opinion" was categorized as "Combination of suggestions and personal experience" within "verification preferences". Finally, user summaries and questions were evaluated alongside chatbot responses to assess interaction quality, with special attention to whether users were misled, skeptical, or actively fact-checking—patterns that were logged for further analysis.

Student Interface Usability Study Setup. The second study also had three parts. First, participants answered demographic and experience questions. In the main phase, they completed a short quiz using the simulated RAG chatbot. Quiz questions produced chatbot responses with key information highlighted—some highlights were accurate, others misleading or incorrect. Source attribution was also manipulated: some answers had correct sources, others had misattributed sources, and some included unrelated sources. This setup tested participants' ability to detect factual errors, misleading highlights, and issues with sources. After the quiz, participants reflected on whether they noticed any errors in the chatbot's answers. The final phase collected feedback via Likert-scale and open-ended questions on their experience, trust, and error detection strategies. Data included behavioral logs (e.g., response time, highlight use, source engagement) and participants' error identifications based on multiple-choice questions.

Teacher Tool Usability Study Setup. To evaluate Teacher Tool, participants in this study had to interact with all of the system functionalities and fill out a survey upon completion. Tasks that the users had to complete were: creating a new data entry, deleting existing entries, adding, modifying and deleting information on source credibility, launching Student Interface, and running automatic evaluation on already existing student data. To prove that they managed to complete all the tasks, participants had to submit status messages that only appear upon completion of the task.

5 Results and Findings

Initial Study Results. 80 participants (18+, English-proficient, internet access) gave informed consent. They were recruited via social media platforms and university mailing lists, reflecting typical scholarly information system users—individuals with advanced educational and professional backgrounds. Most were aged 18-34 (68.75%) with near gender parity. They were primarily from France (47.5%) and Croatia (28.75%), with only 2 native English speakers. Most were digitally experienced (88.75%), and 45% had used AI in academic/pro settings. For search, 93.75% use search engines, AI chats (76.25%) and online databases (70%), with less use of books, peers, forums, and social media.

Most users reported a positive experience interacting with the system, with 63.75% finding the interface easy to use and 83.75% agreeing that AI responses were clear. Highlighting was particularly well-received, with 67.5% preferring it for clarity. Half of the participants mentioned aspects they liked—highlighting (13), ease of interaction (11), and source attribution (10) were most frequently cited. However, concerns were raised about interface design (12 users), response clarity (7), and hallucinated or inaccurate content (4), aligning with the study's aim to test user responses to deliberately embedded errors. Some users also noted issues with source diversity and credibility scoring. The suggested improvements included a broader question handling (19 users), a history feature (7), tutorials (7), and sourcing only scientific content (5). Overall, feedback was largely favorable, although users expressed a clear desire for greater transparency, contextual information, and flexibility to verify or interact with source material.

Critical thinking was assessed via behaviors like correcting errors, questioning sources, and probing further; 46 of 80 participants showed such engagement. These users showed significantly different behaviors—they interacted with the chatbot longer (6 m 21 s vs. 2 m 14 s), asked more questions (4.5 vs. 2.3), and were more likely to click and spend time on sources (0.85 clicks and 4.5 s vs. 0.03 clicks and near-zero time). This behavioral contrast suggests that metrics such as interaction duration, question frequency, and source engagement can serve as practical proxies to identify critical engagement.

However, overall source engagement was low. Only 8 participants clicked on the sources, and 35 failed to notice attribution errors. Some users showed misplaced trust—9 relied solely on the names of the sources, while 7 attempted to verify information through follow-up questions rather than checking the sources directly. This pattern highlights the risk of error when source attribution is inaccurate and users do not independently verify the content.

Usability Results of Student Interface. 6 student participants took part in the second study, representing varying levels of AI experience: 1 very experienced, 1 beginner, and 4 moderately experienced. Most used AI occasionally, except for 2 participants who used it regularly. 4 out of 6 participants were satisfied with their prior AI experience, 2 felt neutral. Regarding the tool, 3 strongly agreed that it was easy to use, 1 agreed, and 2 were neutral. Responses about clarity were generally positive, with 4 agreeing and one strongly agreeing that the responses were clear. The highlighted information feature was appreciated by most, with 2 strongly agreeing and 2 agreeing it helped, although 1 participant disagreed. The tool helped critically evaluate information for 3 participants (2 strongly agreed and 1 agreed), while 2 disagreed and 1 remained neutral. Notably, participants generally did not notice errors or ask follow-up questions. 2 participants strongly agreed that the tool would be useful in school, 2 agreed, and 2 disagreed. Overall, 2 participants strongly agreed that their experience interacting with the system was good, 2 agreed, 1 remained neutral, and 1 disagreed. In terms of their quiz performance, all participants, except 1, managed to get all answers correctly, indicating that they were not misled by incorrect claims presented by the chatbot. 2 participants clicked on the sources to verify claims while others just looked at the source name.

Ability to spot errors varied between participants. 2 participants correctly recognized incorrect credibility scores, 1 identified misinformation in unhighlighted text, and none correctly flagged the green-highlighted wrong information. 2 instances of source misattribution were noted. Additionally, 4 users were able to correctly identify red-highlighted correct information, with 2 spotting it on more than one occasion. Overall, while error recognition was not consistent across all participants or types of misinformation, most were able to detect at least 1 type of issue during the task.

Participants provided diverse suggestions for improving the AI tool. Some emphasized the need for better handling of semantically similar questions, noting that different phrasings often confused the system. Others requested richer, more contextual answers rather than just direct facts, preferring broader explanations or comparisons between perspectives. 1 participant highlighted the lack of meaningful follow-up in conversations. While 1 participant felt no changes were necessary, another recommended a fully open AI setting with open-ended questions. In terms of what users liked, responses highlighted the clean and easy-to-use interface, the helpfulness of the highlights, and the visibility of citations. Overall, while the interface and clarity were well-received, participants expressed a desire for deeper, more nuanced interactions and better semantic flexibility.

Teacher Tool Usability Results. 5 participants took on the role of teachers and evaluated Teacher Tool. Although 2 of 5 participants self-identified as not very skilled with technology, and one identified as not skilled at all, all successfully completed all assigned tasks. Overall, the tool was considered user-friendly: 3 participants described it as somewhat easy to use, while one rated it as very easy and one as somewhat difficult. 4 participants agreed that inputting data into the system was very easy, and 2 found it somewhat difficult. However, deleting rows from the data table posed some challenges, with 2 participants finding it somewhat difficult, one finding it neutral, and 2 finding it very easy. Managing sources in the sources table was very easy for 2 participants, somewhat easy for one and somewhat difficult for 2. Launching Student Interface was considered very easy by 4 participants and somewhat easy by one. Feedback on creating reports varied: 2 participant found it somewhat easy, one very easy, and 2 remained neutral. Adding new entries was unanimously the participants' favorite feature. One participant suggested improving the deletion process by enabling row-click deletion and adding an undo button for greater ease of use.

6 Conclusion

In this demo paper, we introduced the Information Literacy Assessment Platform IILAP[1] designed to support the teaching and assessment of critical reading in AI-mediated academic search. It contains Teacher Tool and Student Interface. Across three evaluation studies, users engaged meaningfully with the system's features and provided largely positive feedback on its usability and value.

The first study exposed 80 participants to realistic misinformation scenarios, measuring their responses through behavioral indicators and error analysis. Results showed that critically engaged users exhibited distinct interaction patterns, such as longer engagement time, more frequent questioning, and greater source interaction, validating the system's core design assumptions. However, the low overall rate of source verification and the varied ability to detect subtle misinformation highlight the continued need for explicit instruction and better interface support to foster robust evaluative habits.

With that in mind, we expanded the system and evaluated its deployment in classroom settings, allowing students to interact with the platform as part of structured learning sessions. These deployments demonstrated the platform's effectiveness in stimulating reflection, prompting verification attempts, and exposing gaps in students' information literacy strategies, particularly in response to manipulated or misleading AI-generated content. Participants found Teacher Tool intuitive and functional for configuring content, annotating responses, and analyzing student data, highlighting its potential for deployment in schools. The generated report can be used directly to assess students' critical engagement.

Overall, IILAP offers a robust, research-based solution for fostering digital literacy and critical thinking. Its flexible design, data-driven feedback, and realistic AI search simulations make it a valuable resource for educators preparing students to engage critically with AI-generated content. Ongoing refinement, guided by user feedback, will support the continued development of IILAP as a versatile, real-world-tested tool for teaching information literacy in the AI era.

Acknowledgments. This project was funded by the National Research Agency under the program "Investissements d'avenir" (France 2030), referenced ANR-19-GURE-0001. The authors declare no competing interests related to this article.

---

[1] Demo, code, data, and documentation at: https://simpletext-project.com/enable/.

References

1. Abid, A., Abdalla, A., Abid, A., Khan, D., Alfozan, A., Zou, J.: Gradio: hassle-free sharing and testing of ml models in the wild (2019), https://arxiv.org/abs/1906.02569
2. Ateia, S., Kruschwitz, U.: Is ChatGPT a biomedical expert? – Exploring the Zero-Shot performance of current GPT models in biomedical tasks, July 2023. https://doi.org/10.48550/arXiv.2306.16108, http://arxiv.org/abs/2306.16108, arXiv:2306.16108 [cs]
3. Barros, S.: I think, therefore i hallucinate: minds, machines, and the art of being wrong (2025), https://arxiv.org/abs/2503.05806
4. Bastani, H., Bastani, O., Sungu, A., Ge, H., Kabakcı, O., Mariman, R.: Generative AI can harm learning. https://doi.org/10.2139/ssrn.4895486, https://papers.ssrn.com/abstract=4895486
5. Buçinca, Z., Malaya, M.B., Gajos, K.Z.: To trust or to think: cognitive forcing functions can reduce overreliance on AI in AI-assisted decision-making. Proc. ACM on Hum.-Comput. Interact. **5**, 1–21 (2021)
6. Capra, R., Arguello, J.: How does AI chat change search behaviors? (2023). https://doi.org/10.48550/arXiv.2307.03826, http://arxiv.org/abs/2307.03826
7. Ermakova, L., et al.: Overview of the CLEF 2024 simpletext track: improving access to scientific texts for everyone. In: Goeuriot, L., et al. (eds.) Experimental IR Meets Multilinguality, Multimodality, and Interaction. Proceedings of the Fifteenth International Conference of the CLEF Association (CLEF 2024), LNCS, Springer (2024)
8. Espinha Gasiba, T., Iosif, A.C., Kessba, I., Amburi, S., Lechner, U., Pinto-Albuquerque, M.: May the source be with you: on chatgpt, cybersecurity, and secure coding. Information **15**(9), 572 (2024)
9. European commission: digital: the confident, critical and responsible engagement with digital technologies for learning, working and participating in society (2025), https://education.ec.europa.eu/education-levels/school-education/basic-skills, Accessed 22 June 2025
10. Galitsky, B.A.: Truth-o-meter: collaborating with llm in fighting its hallucinations. Preprints, July 2023. https://doi.org/10.20944/preprints202307.1723.v1, https://doi.org/10.20944/preprints202307.1723.v1
11. Ghanem, D., Zhu, A.R., Kagabo, W., Osgood, G., Shafiq, B.: Chatgpt-4 knows its abcde but cannot cite its source. JBJS Open Access **9**(3), e24 (2024)
12. Guerreiro, N.M., et al.: Hallucinations in large multilingual translation models (2023), https://arxiv.org/abs/2303.16104
13. Huang, B., Chen, C., Shu, K.: Authorship attribution in the era of llms: problems, methodologies, and challenges (2025), https://arxiv.org/abs/2408.08946
14. Huang, L., et al.: A survey on hallucination in large language models: Principles, taxonomy, challenges, and open questions. ACM Trans. Inf. Syst. **43**(2), 1–55 (2025)
15. Islam, I., Islam, M.N.: Exploring the opportunities and challenges of ChatGPT in academia. Disc. Educ. **3**(1), 31 (2024)
16. Ji, Z., et al.: Survey of hallucination in natural language generation. ACM Comput. Surv. **55**(12), 1–38 (2023)
17. Klarin, J., Hoff, E., Larsson, A., Daukantaitė, D.: Adolescents' use and perceived usefulness of generative AI for schoolwork: exploring their relationships with executive functioning and academic achievement. Front. Artif. Intell. **7**, 1415782 (2024)

18. Leiser, F., et al.: Hill: a hallucination identifier for large language models. In: Proceedings of the 2024 CHI Conference on Human Factors in Computing Systems. CHI 2024, ACM, New York, NY, USA (2024). https://doi.org/10.1145/3613904.3642428
19. Lewis, P., et al.: Retrieval-augmented generation for knowledge-intensive nlp tasks. In: Proceedings of the 34th International Conference on Neural Information Processing Systems. NIPS 2020, Curran Associates Inc., Red Hook, NY, USA (2020)
20. Manakul, P., Liusie, A., Gales, M.J.F.: SelfCheckGPT: zero-resource blackbox hallucination detection for generative large language models, October 2023. https://doi.org/10.48550/arXiv.2303.08896, http://arxiv.org/abs/2303.08896, arXiv:2303.08896 [cs]
21. Mialon, G., et al.: Augmented language models: a survey (2023), https://arxiv.org/abs/2302.07842
22. Papenmeier, A., Kern, D., Englebienne, G., Seifert, C.: It's complicated: the relationship between user trust, model accuracy and explanations in ai. ACM Trans. Comput.-Hum. Interact. **29**(4) (2022). https://doi.org/10.1145/3495013
23. Press, O., Hochlehnert, A., Prabhu, A., Udandarao, V., Press, O., Bethge, M.: Citeme: can language models accurately cite scientific claims? Adv. Neural. Inf. Process. Syst. **37**, 7847–7877 (2024)
24. Pride, D., Cancellieri, M., Knoth, P.: Core-gpt: combining open access research and large language models for credible, trustworthy question answering, July 2023
25. Rawte, V., Sheth, A., Das, A.: A survey of hallucination in large foundation models (2023). https://doi.org/10.48550/arXiv.2309.05922, http://arxiv.org/abs/2309.05922
26. Shuster, K., Poff, S., Chen, M., Kiela, D., Weston, J.: Retrieval augmentation reduces hallucination in conversation (2021), https://arxiv.org/abs/2104.07567
27. Tonmoy, S.M.T.I., et al.: A comprehensive survey of hallucination mitigation techniques in large language models (2024), https://arxiv.org/abs/2401.01313
28. Vendeville, B., Ermakova, L., Loor, P.D.: Resource for error analysis in text simplification: new taxonomy and test collection. In: Ferro, N., Maistro, M., Pasi, G., Alonso, O., Trotman, A., Verberne, S. (eds.) Proceedings of the 48th International ACM SIGIR Conference on Research and Development in Information Retrieval, SIGIR 2025, Padua, Italy, 13–17 July 2025. ACM (2025). https://doi.org/10.1145/3726302.3730304
29. Xu, R., Feng, Y., Chen, H.: ChatGPT vs. google: a comparative study of search performance and user experience (2023). https://doi.org/10.48550/arXiv.2307.01135, http://arxiv.org/abs/2307.01135
30. Zhao, Z., Cohen, S.B., Webber, B.: Reducing quantity hallucinations in abstractive summarization (2020), https://arxiv.org/abs/2009.13312

EcoDL Workshop Papers

Assessing the Landscape of Digital Species Identifiers

Ricardo A. Correia[1,2,3](✉) and Maxim C. Isaac[1,2]

[1] Biodiversity Unit, University of Turku, 20014 Turku, Finland
{raheco,mcisaa}@utu.fi
[2] Helsinki Lab of Interdisciplinary Conservation Science (HELICS), Department of Geosciences and Geography, University of Helsinki, 00014 Helsinki, Finland
[3] Helsinki Institute of Sustainability Science (HELSUS), University of Helsinki, 00014 Helsinki, Finland

Abstract. The potential of leveraging digital data to support biodiversity conservation is widely recognized, yet data retrieval from digital platforms is not straightforward. Species-level digital identifiers, which are unique representations of species in digital platforms, can help to structure, retrieve, and integrate relevant information but their availability across digital platforms remains unclear. We examined digital species identifiers from over 500 digital platforms linked to multiple knowledge domains and assessed their availability for more than 1.5 million species across all major taxonomic groups. Our analysis revealed substantial variation in species representation across platforms. While many species are recognized in digital platforms linked with the life sciences and general knowledge, only a minority is featured in platforms associated with the social sciences, arts and humanities, or technology. Species coverage is also highly uneven between taxonomic groups. Birds, mammals, and flowering plants are relatively well represented, but other taxonomic groups tend to be represented in very few platforms which limits the potential for cross-platform data integration. These findings highlight major gaps in the representation of global biodiversity on digital platforms. Addressing these disparities will enable a more comprehensive, automated, and integrated use of digital data for conservation.

Keywords: Biodiversity data integration · digital species representation · taxonomic biases · Wikidata

1 Introduction

In the midst of a global biodiversity crisis [1], there is growing evidence that carefully planned, targeted conservation actions can help to prevent species extinctions [2, 3]. Only a limited number of species seem to currently benefit from a robust set of conservation actions [4], so expanding conservation efforts to a broader range of taxa in need of support will be essential to avert further species extinctions and achieve global conservation targets [5]. Yet, our capacity to develop and implement conservation interventions for a broader set of species is limited by several factors. For example, conservation resources are generally scarce, and often unequally distributed among taxa [6–8], which restricts the possibility of developing targeted conservation actions for many species. Lack of adequate knowledge to develop targeted actions for many species can be another limiting factor [9, 10]. Developing detailed conservation plans requires a solid and up-to-date evidence basis, but current knowledge of global biodiversity suffers from several important shortfalls [11]. Our understanding of species' taxonomies, distributions, population trends, evolutionary histories and other relevant ecological aspects is incomplete, and most existing information is biassed towards more popular species and taxa [9, 12]. Similar gaps in knowledge exist for threats to biodiversity [13] and the societal factors that drive these threats along with conservation efforts [14]. Filling these knowledge gaps is therefore an essential step towards the development of tailored and successful conservation actions.

One option to increase the knowledge available for biodiversity conservation and minimize existing information gaps is to take advantage of the large amounts of data available online [15]. More than half of the world's population has access to the internet nowadays [16], and increasing use of these technologies has also spurred the availability of information about biodiversity online, either as the primary focus of available content or in the form of secondary information that is captured and shared unintentionally [17]. New research areas have emerged in recent years with a focus on mobilizing this information to generate ecological [18] and socio-cultural [19] insights that can inform biodiversity conservation. Indeed, data obtained from the internet are increasingly used in a diverse range of conservation applications [20]. Examples include improving spatial conservation planning [21], monitoring wildlife trade [22], tracking shifts in species distributions [23], understanding sentiments towards protected areas [24], and assessing trends of public interest in biodiversity conservation topics [25].

Despite its great potential, using data obtained from the internet for conservation applications is not without difficulties [20]. Harnessing such data involves a detailed process of data collection, filtering, information extraction, validation and harmonization before it can be integrated with other sources and used for conservation applications [15]. Each step in this process presents specific challenges. In the context of data collection, beyond issues related to data access, there are also complications in identifying and capturing relevant content due to the complexities of language [26, 27]. For instance, many vernacular species names have multiple meanings - a classic example is the word 'Jaguar' referring to both the animal and the car brand - and thus not all content where they feature will be of relevance to conservation. One possible alternative is to use scientific species names [26, 28]; the use of a binomial nomenclature system and Latin language decreases the limitations associated with vernacular species names. However, not all relevant content available online will refer to species using their scientific names and not accounting for species with scientific name synonyms will further restrict the content captured [29].

Another possibility is to leverage pre-existing species representations in online systems that can facilitate access to relevant content. Indeed, many online databases, semantic networks, and other digital systems already recognize species and their associated content through specific identifiers that link to relevant information. One example of this approach often found in the scientific literature is the use of Google Knowledge Graph identifiers associated with a topic, which leverage a semantic network of concepts related to the topic of interest to capture relevant internet search data from the Google Trends platform [30, 31]. As an example, the topic that pertains to the animal 'Jaguar' will recognize relevant mentions in other languages (e.g. 'Jaguaari' in Finnish) while distinguishing mentions related to the car brand. Yet, the usefulness of this approach to gather online data about multiple taxonomic groups and knowledge areas remains unclear. Here, we fill this gap by providing an assessment of available digital species identifiers for over 1.5 million species and over 500 digital platforms. Our aim is to evaluate the degree to which existing digital systems can facilitate automated, large-scale extraction and integration of online information about biodiversity by exploring how existing digital species identifiers link to different taxonomic groups and knowledge areas.

2 Methods

2.1 Collecting Digital Species Identifiers

We used the Wikidata platform (https://www.wikidata.org) to collect information about existing digital species identifiers. Wikidata is a freely accessible and open knowledge base that acts as a repository of structured data for other Wikimedia projects such as Wikipedia and Wiktionary. Wikidata represents an ideal source of information for this assessment because it already compiles existing digital identifiers linking to external platforms as a means to boost data quality and identify missing items and information. For example, Wikidata compiles species identifiers from several authoritative biodiversity compilation efforts such as the Global Biodiversity Information Facility (GBIF), the Catalogue of Life (CoL), the Encyclopedia of Life (EoL), and others, which facilitate the validation of the species represented. Also, it can be edited freely by both human users and machine systems, thus streamlining the inclusion of relevant information in their database from several sources and ensuring its representativeness and comprehensiveness. Some authors have argued that Wikidata could act as a central repository for species information [32], and other platforms such as GBIF already leverage information about digital identifiers from Wikidata in their systems, making this an ideal platform for this work.

We collected information about digital species identifiers from Wikidata using the Wikidata Query Service, which we accessed programmatically using the *WikidataQueryServiceR* R package [33]. For this, we first obtained a list of species represented in Wikidata by querying its database for any entries which have the *taxon rank* property (P105) matching a species (Q7432). We also inquired whether these entries had an associated GBIF taxon ID (P846). This query returned a list of 2 905 067 Wikidata species entries, with their unique Wikidata entity and GBIF taxon identifiers. This list of species was validated against the GBIF backbone taxonomy to identify those with accepted status, resulting in a total of 1 501 508 valid species. While we acknowledge this excludes from the analysis several species synonyms for which digital identifiers may be available, reconciling all synonyms and validating their associated digital identifiers was outside the scope of this work and we adopted the more conservative approach of including taxonomically valid species only. We then used the same service to extract from Wikidata all the properties with an assigned external identifier associated with each species in our list, keeping information about the property name (e.g. OpenAlex ID) and the identifier itself (e.g. C2781255694). Digital identifiers associated with either Wikidata or GBIF were however excluded form the analysis as they were used to generate and validate the species list for data extraction and all species therefore featured both. The resulting dataset included a list of 9 276 031 unique species identifiers which were used for further analysis.

Based on this list of digital identifiers and their associated platforms, we then compiled a list of the digital platforms featured in our sample. Each of the 506 digital platforms in our list was validated and classified as either a generalist knowledge platform (e.g. digital encyclopaedias) or associated with a more specific knowledge area among Arts & Humanities, Life Sciences & Biomedicine, Physical Sciences, Social Sciences or Technology following the list of Web of Science Research Areas. We also characterized the taxonomic coverage (general or taxa-specific), geographical focus (global or regional) and language availability (English only, other language only, multiple languages, or not specified) of each platform.

2.2 Data Analysis

Our analysis of the available digital species identifiers focused on evaluating their taxonomic and knowledge area coverage with the intent to assess if the existing landscape of digital identifiers can support information integration across different taxa and knowledge areas. Specifically, we used descriptive statistics to assess the distribution of digital platforms with available digital species identifiers in relation to their associated knowledge areas, taxonomic and geographical coverage and language representation, and the distribution of digital identifiers across individual species and taxonomic kingdoms. We also used Kruskal-Wallis rank tests to assess differences in species representation among digital platforms associated with the various knowledge areas, and Wilcox rank sum tests for pairwise comparisons between knowledge areas. We opted for a non-parametric test due to the highly skewed nature of the data. Finally, we used UpSet plots to explore the intersection in the availability of digital species identifiers between different knowledge areas. All analysis were implemented in R software version 4.3.3.

3 Results

Over eighty percent of these digital platforms have a general (97, 19.2%) or life sciences (304, 60.1%) scope, but we also found species indexed in platforms with a social (44, 8.7%), arts and humanities (26, 5.1%), physical sciences (9, 1.8%) or technology (26, 5.1%) focus. The geographical focus of these platforms was almost evenly split between global (271, 53.6%) and regional content (235, 46.4%). About one third of all platforms (180, 35.6%) had a specific taxonomic focus but these included only platforms associated with the life sciences; the remaining two-thirds were not taxonomically restricted (326, 64.4%). Among those that targeted specific taxonomic groups, the majority focused on either animals (84, 16.6%) or plants (n = 83, 16.4%) and only a few targeted fungi (7, 1.4%) or a combination of these groups (6, 1.2%), mostly plants and fungi. Most of the digital platforms are reportedly available in one language only (354, 70.0%) but some are multilingual (54, 10.7%), whereas the remainder do not specify any language (98, 19.4%). Among the single-language platforms, English was by far the most frequent language (252, 49.8%) but other well represented languages include French (19, 3.8%), Spanish (11, 2.2%) and German (11, 2.2%). The distribution of the various digital platforms across knowledge areas, and taxonomic, geographical and language features is represented in Fig. 1.

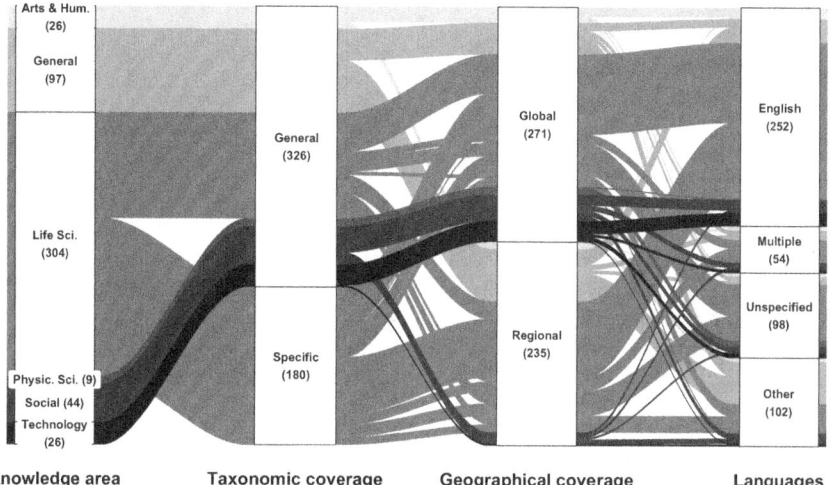

Fig. 1. Flow diagram representing the distribution and connections of the sampled digital platforms across knowledge areas, taxonomic coverage, geographical coverage and language dimensions.

The median number of digital identifiers available for valid species per digital platform is approximately fifty (median = 50.5, IQR ± 2207.5), but this varies widely between platforms (see Fig. 2). Indeed, more than one third of platforms assessed feature ten or less species only (187, 30.0%) and only a small fraction of them recognizes more than one hundred thousand species (24, 4.7%). These differences in species representation among platforms were also reflected across their knowledge areas. We observed significant differences in the number of species represented per platform in each knowledge area (Kruskal-Wallis test; chi-squared = 149.87, d.f. = 5, p-value < 0.001), with platforms associated with the life sciences (median = 744, IQR ± 7256) showing a significantly higher number of species represented than those related to other knowledge areas (Fig. 2). General digital platforms (median = 9, IQR ± 64) feature a significantly higher number of species than platforms connected to the arts and humanities (median = 1, IQR ± 1), whereas there were no statistical differences in species representation between platforms associated either of these knowledge areas and those with a physical sciences (median = 2, IQR ± 3), social (median = 6, IQR ± 11) or technology focus (median = 5, IQR ± 321).

There is also wide variation in the distribution of digital identifiers across taxonomic groups (see Fig. 3). Approximately half of the species in our sample (803 617, 54.2%)

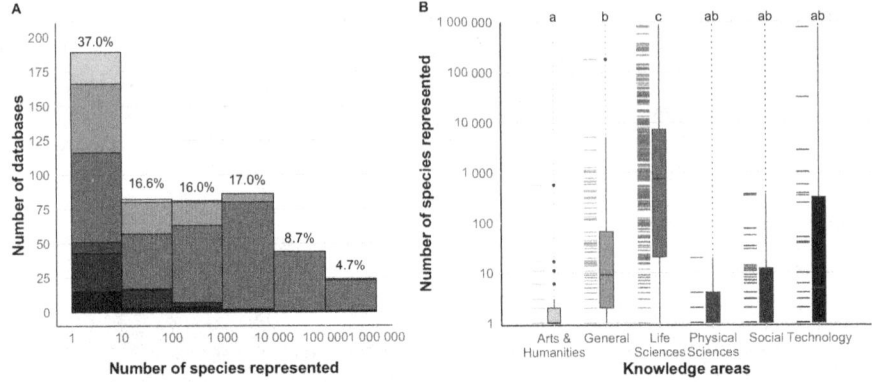

Fig. 2. Overview of species representation across digital platforms, including the distribution of the number of species represented across all assessed platforms (A) and within the platforms affiliated with each knowledge area (B). The values annotated in panel A represent the proportion of all databases represented in each bar. Different letters annotated in panel B represent statistical differences (p-value < 0.05) between the number of species represented in databases associated with each knowledge area. The colour scale represents different knowledge areas: Arts & Humanities (yellow), General (orange), Life Sciences (red), Physical sciences (pink), Social sciences (purple), and Technology (dark blue). Please note the x-axis in panel A and y-axis in panel B are represented in logarithmic scale.

are represented by five or less digital identifiers, and the large majority of species (1 428 192, 96.4%) are represented by no more than fifteen (see Fig. 3A). Given that each identifier is unique to a specific database, most species are therefore represented in only approximately 3% of the over 500 databases assessed. At the other end, 722 species (~0.05%) were associated with fifty or more digital identifiers and are thus represented in at least 10% of the databases assessed. Most digital identifiers are associated with either animal (57.1%), plant (35.8%) or Fungi (6.3%) species. In contrast, Archaea, Bacteria, Chromista and Protozoa combined gather less than one percent of the digital identifiers in our dataset (see Fig. 3B). The number of digital identifiers associated with each species also varied widely within taxonomic groups (see Fig. 4). For example, over three million digital identifiers in our dataset are associated with insect species but this is a highly specious group, so each species is linked with approximately five digital identifiers. In contrast, amphibians, mammals and flowering plants (Liliopsida and Magnoliopsida) are represented by a smaller total number of digital identifiers, but each species is linked on average to ten or more digital identifiers.

The large variation in species representation across digital platforms inevitably leads to an unequal species representation across platforms linked with different knowledge areas (see Fig. 5). Nearly all species (98.5%, 1 459 130) in our dataset are represented in at least one digital platform linked with the Life Sciences, and over half (54.7%, 811 139) are also represented in digital platforms linked with the Technology area. In contrast, very few species are represented in digital platforms associated with the Arts and Humanities (<0.1%, 496), Physical Science (<0.1%, 27) or Social science (0.1%, 1285) areas. Given the wide representation of species in some knowledge areas, most species (62.4%; 936

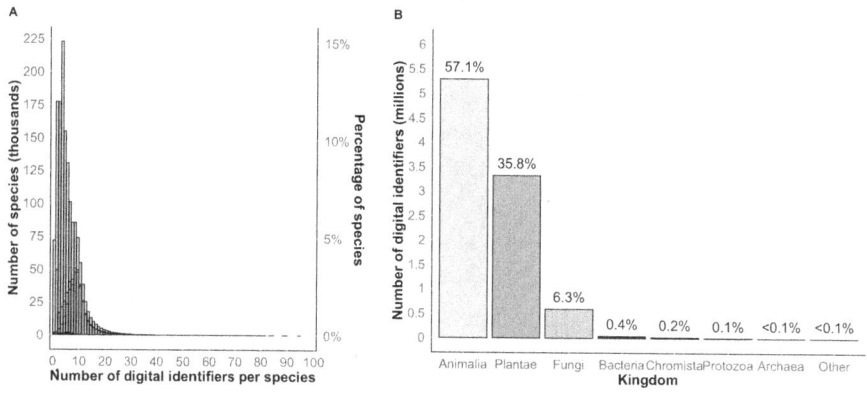

Fig. 3. Distribution of digital identifiers across all species (A) and across the taxonomic kingdoms (B).

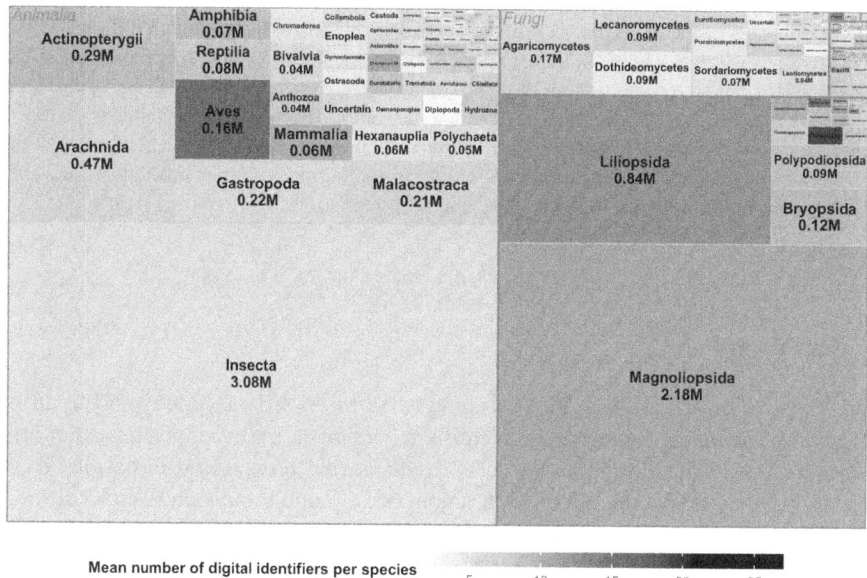

Fig. 4. Treemap chart of the distribution of digital identifiers across taxonomic groups. Each coloured box represents a taxonomic class within a taxonomic kingdom (grey frame). The size of each box represents the proportion of digital indicators associated with the respective taxonomic group, and the number inside each box represents the number of identifiers in millions available for that group. The colour of each box represents the mean number of digital identifiers available per species.

463) have digital identifiers linked with two or more knowledge areas. The most common representation of species between knowledge was across the Life Sciences, Technology, or generalist platforms, but combinations with other knowledge areas are also present.

No species were represented only by digital identifiers associated with platforms linked with the Arts and Humanities, Physical sciences or Social sciences.

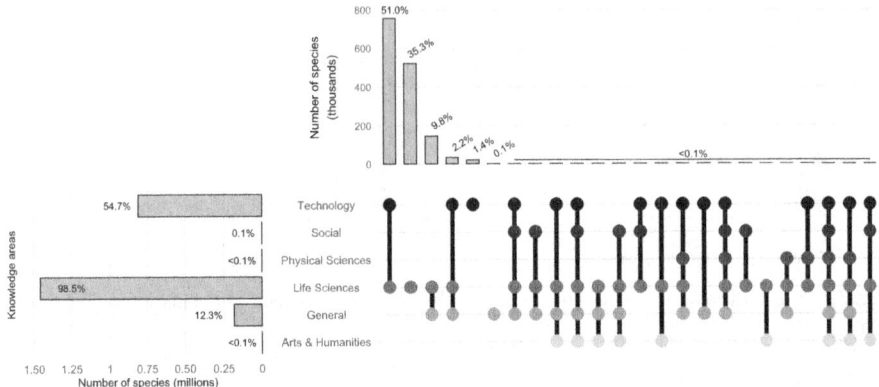

Fig. 5. Analysis of the occurrence of digital species identifiers associated with different knowledge areas at the species level. In the UpSet plot (bottom right), coloured dots linked by vertical black lines indicate the combinations of digital identifiers for different knowledge areas available for at least one species. The horizontal bar plot (bottom left) represents the number of species with at least one digital identifier associated with each knowledge area. The vertical bar plot (top right) represents the number of species with at least one digital identifier linked the knowledge areas represented in the respective knowledge area combination.

4 Discussion

This study offers what is to our best knowledge the first large-scale analysis of the landscape of available digital species identifiers, encompassing over 500 online platforms and more than 1.5 million species. Our results reveal pronounced disparities in the availability of species identifiers, both among taxonomic groups and across different knowledge domains. This uneven digital representation of biodiversity highlights both substantial opportunities and persistent challenges associated with leveraging digital data in support of biodiversity research.

Most available digital species identifiers are linked to either general knowledge platforms or those associated with the life sciences. Digital platforms associated with the life sciences remain by far the most taxonomically comprehensive, containing far more species indicators per platform than platforms linked to other knowledge domains. Nevertheless, a small but notable proportion of identifiers is linked with platforms that intersect with other knowledge areas, such as the social sciences, arts and humanities, physical sciences, and technology. This representation is promising, as it suggests the potential for broader integration of biodiversity data available in different knowledge domains [15, 34]. While the dominance of digital species identifiers in the life sciences domain is to be expected, ensuring the integration between different knowledge areas will require that platforms associated with other knowledge domains increase their digital systems to better capture and integrate species-related content. Similarly, the prominence of species representation in digital platforms available in English language only limits inclusive access and the integration of regionally or culturally specific knowledge. Language biases can lead to the underutilization of valuable non-English sources and may skew global understanding of biodiversity trends [35]. The development of multilingual and locally grounded platforms would be another important stop towards more equitable representation and consideration of relevant biodiversity knowledge in different languages.

Our analysis also exposes strong taxonomic differences in digital identifier availability. Over 90% of identifiers pertain to animal and plant species, while microbes and other lesser-known taxa including Archaea, Bacteria, Chromista, and Protozoa are dramatically underrepresented. This mirrors longstanding biases in biodiversity interest and knowledge, where charismatic or well-studied taxa receive disproportionate attention, and less visible groups are overlooked [9]. Another critical finding is the limited overlap in species representation across platforms. Most species are associated with five or fewer digital identifiers, and only a tiny fraction (0.05%) appear in 10% or more of the databases surveyed. This fragmentation restricts the potential for automated or large-scale information retrieval about individual species using digital identifiers, reducing their visibility and limiting cross-platform data integration. Indeed, although digital identifiers have the potential to improve biodiversity data discoverability, their current deployment is highly inconsistent and the lack of standardization, limited potential for interoperability, and inconsistent maintenance of species representation in digital platforms further diminish their effectiveness. Developing digital systems that can identify complex relationships between species concepts and other species-related material in an era of 'big-data' will be essential to achieve progress [36]. For example, boosting the representation of species in digital platforms could contribute towards a Globally Integrated Structure of Taxonomy supporting biodiversity science and conservation [37]. This could expand the integration of biodiversity data beyond taxonomic, genetic, physical, spatial and functional aspects to include also technological applications and socio-cultural dimensions.

These results provide important clues about areas for further development of biodiversity-inclusive digital systems, but some limitations of our study also need to be acknowledged. Our analysis is based on the availability of identifiers rather than their practical performance in data retrieval, so their usability has not been assessed in detail. We also relied on publicly accessible metadata, which may not fully reflect available internal or proprietary identifiers in certain platforms. Furthermore, using identifier counts as a proxy for digital representation does not necessarily capture the richness or quality of information available for each species. In this study, we have not assessed the accuracy of the data retrieved using digital identifiers and this should be a focus of further research. Finally, the number of species assessed in this work are only a fraction of the over 2 million species that have so far been scientifically described [38] and we also did not assess other taxonomic levels (e.g. Genus, Order, etc.), so our work does not reflect the overall availability of digital identifiers for all known biodiversity and across all taxonomic levels.

Despite these limitations, our results stress that it is crucial to work with digital platforms towards expanding the taxonomic and geographic coverage of digital species identifiers, particularly for underrepresented groups and regions. Enhanced collaboration across digital platforms and knowledge areas can help bridge the gap between life sciences and other knowledge domains, especially the social sciences and humanities, which are vital for understanding the human dimensions of biodiversity loss. Finally, the adoption of common standards and the promotion of open, multilingual infrastructures will improve the discoverability and utility of online species data. Building a more coordinated, inclusive, and interoperable digital infrastructure will help ensure our capacity to fully harness the value of online data in addressing the global biodiversity crisis.

Acknowledgments. This work was funded by the Academy of Finland (grant agreements #348352 and #353785) and the KONE Foundation (grant agreement #202101976).

Disclosure of Interests. The authors have no competing interests to declare that are relevant to the content of this article.

References

1. IPBES: Summary for policymakers of the global assessment report on biodiversity and ecosystem services. IPBES Secretariat, Bonn, Germany (2019)
2. Bolam, F.C., et al.: How many bird and mammal extinctions has recent conservation action prevented? Conserv. Lett. **14**, e12762 (2021). https://doi.org/10.1111/conl.12762
3. Langhammer, P.F., et al.: The positive impact of conservation action. Science **384**, 453–458 (2024). https://doi.org/10.1126/science.adj6598
4. Senior, R.A., Bagwyn, R., Leng, D., Killion, A.K., Jetz, W., Wilcove, D.S.: Global shortfalls in documented actions to conserve biodiversity. Nature. 1–5 (2024). https://doi.org/10.1038/s41586-024-07498-7
5. CBD: Kunming-Montreal global biodiversity framework (2022)
6. Adamo, M., et al.: Dimension and impact of biases in funding for species and habitat conservation. Biol. Cons. **272**, 109636 (2022). https://doi.org/10.1016/j.biocon.2022.109636
7. Davies, T., et al.: Popular interest in vertebrates does not reflect extinction risk and is associated with bias in conservation investment. PLoS ONE **13**, e0203694 (2018). https://doi.org/10.1371/journal.pone.0203694
8. Mammola, S., et al.: Towards a taxonomically unbiased European union biodiversity strategy for 2030. Proc. R. Soc. B **287**, 20202166 (2020). https://doi.org/10.1098/rspb.2020.2166
9. Mammola, S., et al.: Drivers of species knowledge across the tree of life. eLife. **12**, RP88251 (2023). https://doi.org/10.7554/eLife.88251
10. Correia, R.A., et al.: Conservation needs and opportunities drive LIFE funding allocation for European birds. Biol. Cons. **300**, 110833 (2024). https://doi.org/10.1016/j.biocon.2024.110833
11. Hortal, J., de Bello, F., Diniz-Filho, J.A.F., Lewinsohn, T.M., Lobo, J.M., Ladle, R.J.: Seven shortfalls that beset large-scale knowledge of biodiversity. Annu. Rev. Ecol. Evol. Syst. **46**, 523–549 (2015). https://doi.org/10.1146/annurev-ecolsys-112414-054400
12. Troudet, J., Grandcolas, P., Blin, A., Vignes-Lebbe, R., Legendre, F.: Taxonomic bias in biodiversity data and societal preferences. Sci. Rep. **7**, 9132 (2017). https://doi.org/10.1038/s41598-017-09084-6
13. Joppa, L.N., et al.: Filling in biodiversity threat gaps. Science **352**, 416–418 (2016). https://doi.org/10.1126/science.aaf3565

14. Mascia, M.B., et al.: Conservation and the Social Sciences. Conserv. Biol. **17**, 649–650 (2003). https://doi.org/10.1046/j.1523-1739.2003.01738.x
15. Soriano-Redondo, A., et al.: Harnessing online digital data in biodiversity monitoring. PLoS Biol. **22**, e3002497 (2024). https://doi.org/10.1371/journal.pbio.3002497
16. International communication union: measuring digital development, Facts and figures 2022. International communication union, Geneva (2022)
17. Pernat, N., et al.: Overcoming biodiversity blindness: Secondary data in primary citizen science observations. Ecol. Solut. Evid. **5**, e12295 (2024). https://doi.org/10.1002/2688-8319.12295
18. Jarić, I., et al.: iEcology: harnessing large online resources to generate ecological insights. Trends Ecol. Evol. S016953472030077X (2020). https://doi.org/10.1016/j.tree.2020.03.003
19. Ladle, R.J., et al.: Conservation culturomics. Front. Ecol. Environ. **14**, 269–275 (2016). https://doi.org/10.1002/fee.1260
20. Correia, R.A., et al.: Digital data sources and methods for conservation culturomics. Conserv. Biol. **35**, 398–411 (2021). https://doi.org/10.1111/cobi.13706
21. Chowdhury, S., et al.: Using social media records to inform conservation planning. Conserv. Biol. **38**, e14161 (2024). https://doi.org/10.1111/cobi.14161
22. Soriano-Redondo, A., et al.: Online wildlife trade in species of conservation concern. Conserv. Lett. **16**, e12985 (2023). https://doi.org/10.1111/conl.12985
23. Sbragaglia, V., Espasandín, L., Jarić, I., Vardi, R., Ramírez, F., Coll, M.: Tracking ongoing transboundary marine distributional range shifts in the digital era. Marine Ecology Progress Series. SHIFT (2023). https://doi.org/10.3354/meps14309
24. Souza, C.N., et al.: Using social media and machine learning to understand sentiments towards Brazilian national parks. Biol. Cons. **293**, 110557 (2024). https://doi.org/10.1016/j.biocon.2024.110557
25. de Oliveira Caetano, G.H., Vardi, R., Jarić, I., Correia, R.A., Roll, U., Veríssimo, D.: Evaluating global interest in biodiversity and conservation. Conserv. Biol. **37**, e14100 (2023). https://doi.org/10.1111/cobi.14100
26. Correia, R.A., Jepson, P., Malhado, A.C.M., Ladle, R.J.: Internet scientific name frequency as an indicator of cultural salience of biodiversity. Ecol. Ind. **78**, 549–555 (2017). https://doi.org/10.1016/j.ecolind.2017.03.052
27. Patterson, D., Mozzherin, D., Shorthouse, D., Thessen, A.: Challenges with using names to link digital biodiversity information. Biodivers. Data Journal. **4**, e8080 (2016). https://doi.org/10.3897/BDJ.4.e8080
28. Jarić, I., Courchamp, F., Gessner, J., Roberts, D.L.: Data mining in conservation research using Latin and vernacular species names. PeerJ **4**, e2202 (2016). https://doi.org/10.7717/peerj.2202
29. Correia, R.A., Jarić, I., Jepson, P., Malhado, A.C.M., Alves, J.A., Ladle, R.J.: Nomenclature instability in species culturomic assessments: why synonyms matter. Ecol. Ind. **90**, 74–78 (2018). https://doi.org/10.1016/j.ecolind.2018.02.059
30. Correia, R.A., Mammola, S.: The searchscape of fear: a global analysis of internet search trends for biophobias. People Nature. (2023). https://doi.org/10.1002/pan3.10497
31. Wang, W., Sant, S.-L., King, E.: Examining audiences' information-seeking behavior surrounding the super bowl and sex trafficking: insights from google trends data (2024). https://doi.org/10.1123/ijsc.2024-0017
32. Page, R.D.M.: Wikidata and the bibliography of life. PeerJ **10**, e13712 (2022). https://doi.org/10.7717/peerj.13712
33. Popov, M.: WikidataQueryServiceR: API client library for "Wikidata query service". R package version 1.0.0, https://CRAN.R-project.org/package=WikidataQueryServiceR, (2020)

34. Heberling, J.M., Miller, J.T., Noesgaard, D., Weingart, S.B., Schigel, D.: Data integration enables global biodiversity synthesis. Proc. Natl. Acad. Sci. **118**, e2018093118 (2021). https://doi.org/10.1073/pnas.2018093118
35. Amano, T., et al.: Tapping into non-English-language science for the conservation of global biodiversity. PLoS Biol. **19**, e3001296 (2021)
36. Patterson, D.J., Cooper, J., Kirk, P.M., Pyle, R.L., Remsen, D.P.: Names are key to the big new biology. Trends Ecol. Evol. **25**, 686–691 (2010). https://doi.org/10.1016/j.tree.2010.09.004
37. Sandall, E.L., et al.: A globally integrated structure of taxonomy to support biodiversity science and conservation. Trends Ecol. Evol. **38**, 1143–1153 (2023). https://doi.org/10.1016/j.tree.2023.08.004
38. IUCN: The IUCN red list of threatened species. Version 2025-1, http://www.iucnredlist.org, (2025)

Validation Challenges in Large-Scale Tree Crown Segmentations from Remote Sensing Imagery Using Deep Learning: A Case Study in Germany

Taimur Khan[1(✉)], Jasmin Krebs[2], Sharad Kumar Gupta[1,3], Jonathan Renkel[4], Caroline Arnold[5], and Nils Nölke[6]

[1] Helmholtz Centre for Environmental Research (UFZ), Theodor-Lieser-Street 4, 06120 Halle (Saale), Germany
taimur.khan@ufz.de, sharad.gupta@ufz.de

[2] Leipzig University, Augustusplatz 10, 04109 Leipzig, Germany
jk21byxu@studserv.uni-leipzig.de

[3] HZDR - Centre for Advanced System Understanding (CASUS), Untermarkt 20, 02826 Görlitz, Germany

[4] Martin Luther University Halle-Wittenberg, Von-Seckendorff-Platz 4, 06120 Halle (Saale), Germany
jonathan.renkel@geo.uni-halle.de

[5] Helmholtz-Zentrum Hereon, Max-Planck-Straße 1, 21502 Geesthacht, Germany
caroline.arnold@hereon.de

[6] Forest Inventory and Remote Sensing, University of Göttingen, Büsgenweg 5, 37077 Göttingen, Germany
nils.noelke@forst.uni-goettingen.de

Abstract. Deep-learning–based individual tree-crown (ITC) mapping has become increasingly prominent in remote sensing, yet rigorous validation of these predictions at large spatial scales remains challenging. Using data from an extensive case study involving the mapping of approximately 218.7 million trees across the German federal states of Sachsen and Sachsen-Anhalt from multispectral aerial imagery, we demonstrate that scaling such models beyond controlled environments significantly exacerbates validation difficulties. Minor inaccuracies in tree crown segmentation can critically affect practical applications, including forestry management and urban planning. Our findings highlight validation complexities arising specifically from tree allometry, seasonal variability, shadow effects, and annotation characteristics within training datasets. Consequently, achieving reliable model performance requires deliberate design of training data and potentially leveraging task-specific pre-training through Foundation Models. We emphasize the importance of rigorous validation procedures to ensure the reliability and practical utility of large-scale deep-learning models in ecological and urban management contexts.

Supplementary Information The online version contains supplementary material available at https://doi.org/10.1007/978-3-032-06136-2_30.

Keywords: Deep Learning · Ecology · Forestry · Remote Sensing

1 Introduction

The urgency of climate change and biodiversity loss significantly heightens the importance of large-scale tree crown segmentation. Forests act as crucial carbon sinks and biodiversity reservoirs [18], while urban trees offer vital ecosystem services [20]. To generate comprehensive assessments of forest health, carbon stocks, and urban greenery, we need to accurately map tree crowns over vast areas, including trees both within forests and outside of them. These trees outside forests, often found in agricultural or urban settings, must be part of our inventories, making their detection and mapping a key priority for scaling local observations to a global context. Large-scale segmentation enables consistent, detailed monitoring of these vital resources, informing sustainable forest management, urban planning, and policy development. The ambition to create national and global inventories, such as those envisioned in [25], hinges on the reliability of such foundational segmentation data. In an era marked by rapid environmental change, comprehensive mapping efforts are indispensable. Tree crown segmentation is a cornerstone task for these objectives, as the size and structure of a tree crown—shaped by species-specific branching patterns, site conditions, and competition for light—directly influences primary production.

While recent advances in deep learning offer unprecedented capabilities for automated segmentation, their robust validation at scale presents a critical, unaddressed hurdle. The integration of deep learning into remote sensing has opened new ways in how we monitor and analyse ecological systems [29,30]. Tree crown segmentation has especially benefited from advances in convolutional neural networks (CNNs) and transformer-based architectures. Latter was used by [8], for single tree detection. Approaches leveraging high-resolution imagery have demonstrated remarkable capabilities in delineating individual tree crowns [5,24,26], illustrating the potential for scalable and automated tree mapping.

However, while these deep learning models demonstrate impressive performance in controlled environments or with limited-scale datasets, their deployment at expansive spatial extents, such as regional or national scales, exposes a distinct spectrum of challenges that remain largely unaddressed. Foremost among these is validation—a critical yet underexplored hurdle in ensuring the reliability and generalizability of model outputs. As recent studies have shown, the performance of tree crown segmentation models is highly sensitive to the characteristics of the training data, such as tree size, species diversity, seasonal variations, vitality conditions, and image quality [2,16], a fact that directly reflects the profound complexity of how tree crowns appear in real-world conditions. To enable scalable validation frameworks, it is therefore necessary to accurately characterize and account for this complexity.

A key metric in this context is the Crown Projection Area (CPA), defined as the vertical projection of the crown onto a horizontal plane. Deriving CPA provides essential insights both at the individual tree level—where it provides predictions of diameter, volume, and growth rates—and at the stand level, supporting models of competition and canopy gap dynamics [10,21]. However, inaccuracies inherent in the segmentation process, particularly when applied at large scales, can lead to biased estimations of these critical tree variables, underscoring the urgent need to address robust validation challenges in large-scale tree crown segmentation.

Among the available crown metrics, crown spread is particularly valuable as an independent variable for validating segmentation results, as it captures essential information about tree size and structure. However, accurate estimation of crown spread is complex in both field and remote sensing contexts. Errors can arise not only during the segmentation process but also from the methods used to derive crown spread from segmented polygons, especially for irregularly shaped crowns. The choice of calculation method strongly influences the quality of crown spread estimates and, consequently, the reliability of validation metrics. Furthermore, the accuracy of validation is fundamentally dependent on the quality of reference data; coarse or inconsistent ground-truth datasets can substantially limit the precision of assessment.

Building on our extensive experience in applying deep learning models to large-scale tree crown segmentation across Germany at the federal-state level, this paper (1) identifies and characterizes the key challenges involved in assessing segmentation accuracy over expansive, heterogeneous terrains–including variability in canopy structure, imaging conditions, and regional ecological gradients–and (2) provides concrete methodological recommendations to address these challenges. By coupling a rigorous evaluation of terrain-specific segmentation limitations with these targeted recommendations, we aim to foster a dialogue on the methodological innovations required to ensure that deep learning advancements in remote sensing translate into actionable insights at the scales required by global environmental challenges.

2 Case Study: Tree Crown Segmentation in Saxony And Saxony-Anhalt, Germany

To evaluate the performance and limitations of large-scale crown segmentation and its validation, the DeepTrees model [24] was applied in a one-shot prediction approach (i.e. trained model used to make a single prediction on an input without additonal training) using pretrained model weights provided by Freudenberg et al. [5] as well as model weights trained in DeepTrees [24], applied to high-resolution multispectral Digital Orthophoto Imagery (DOP20) covering the German federal states of Saxony (SN) and Saxony-Anhalt (ST) [11,12]. SN, covering approximately $18,450\,km^2$, and Saxony-Anhalt, spanning around $20,452\,km^2$, represent diverse ecological and urban landscapes, ideal for assessing large-scale segmentation model performance (Fig. 3 in Appendices). The 4-channel (RGBi) DOP20 imagery, with a spatial resolution of 20 cm per pixel, enables precise tree crown delineation. The DeepTrees model identified approximately 218.7 million individual tree crowns—137.3 million in SN and 81.4 million in ST (Fig. 1a). The resulting segmentation dataset has been made available upon request on Zenodo (https://doi.org/10.5281/zenodo.15638573).

Despite optimized methods, exact matches between predicted and ground-truth crown spreads were low (32%), though expanding the margin of error to ±5 m increased accuracy significantly (89%), highlighting validation challenges. The segmentation model systematically overestimated small crowns (<6 m) and underestimated large crowns (>16 m), yet the crown area versus spread relationship remained stable (Fig. 1b), indicating consistent segmentations. Validation quality proved crucial; notably, the local inventory ('Baumkataster' Halle/Saale) provided broad intervals (5 m), limiting validation precision but still achieving an overall IOU of ~70%. The segmented tree crowns show substantial regional variability in tree distribution, reflecting ecological, topographical, and land-use gradients (Fig. 3).

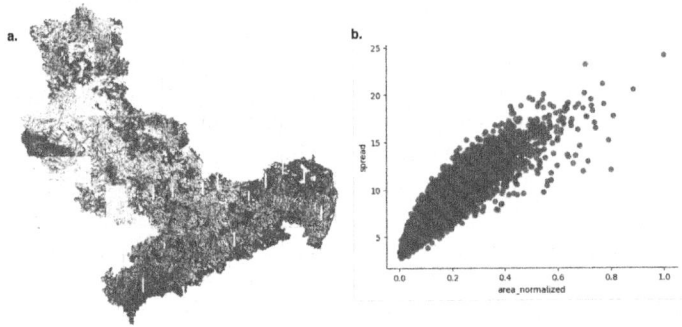

Fig. 1. (a) Spatial distribution of individual tree crown segmentation polygons derived from multispectral DOP20 imagery across the German federal states of Sachsen (SN, green) and Sachsen-Anhalt (ST, blue), totaling 218.7 million predicted crowns. (b) Relationship between normalized crown area (x-axis) and estimated crown spread (y-axis) for a subset of the segmented trees from Halle (Saale), ST. (Color figure online)

3 Challenges

Validating large-scale tree crown segmentation models reveals a web of interrelated challenges. Among these challenges is phenology, a moving target: the same forest can look drastically different between leaf-on summer imagery and leaf-off winter scenes. Models trained on a single phenological period often struggle in another, yielding inconsistent segmentation accuracy across the year [6,13,19]. For example, a canopy delineation that performs well on lush summer foliage may under-segment sparse autumn crowns or miss bare branches in winter (Fig. 3a). Such season-driven variability not only degrades model performance but also complicates validation – a one-shot model might appear accurate in one season and fail in the next, raising questions about how and when accuracy should be assessed. Incorporating multi-season data including the key phenological stages: leaf emergence, flowering, fruiting, autumn coloring and leaf fall, during both training and validation is essential, as phenological dynamics have been shown to strongly influence model generalizability [2,16].

Spatial and illumination heterogeneity of landscapes, driven by terrain and illumination differences, poses a major hurdle for both segmentation and its validation. An algorithm that segments tree crowns flawlessly in a flat, well-lit park may struggle in a shadow-drenched valley or on a steep mountainside. Variations in ground elevation and slope alter the angle of solar illumination, leading to uneven lighting and shadows that can confuse models. In mountainous or rugged terrains, trees on north-facing slopes might appear darker or partially occluded compared to those on south-facing slopes with direct sun, even if they are the same species and healthy. Such effects result in site-specific performance: accuracy drops when moving to new topographies or sensor angles. Weinstein et al. (2020) observed this kind of cross-site performance gap, where a tree detection model trained in one region underperformed when applied to a different region's imagery without adaptation, underscoring how terrain and context influence outcomes [27]. Fine-tuning can increase accuracy, but requires additional data and computational resources. For validation, this means that accuracy estimates from one area may not transfer to another – a critical issue when assessments at national or global scales are required.

A further fundamental challenge lies in the scarcity of accurate ground-truth data at scale. Reliable validation hinges on high-quality reference data (the "ground truth"), yet collecting detailed crown delineations over large regions is logistically difficult and expensive. For instance, field surveys can map individual trees with great precision, providing highly accurate tree position information (e.g., through GPS measurements of trunk location or detailed canopy spread on the ground) [23]. However, doing this over thousands of square kilometers is infeasible. Conversely, while aerial and satellite imagery offer broad coverage, even at high resolutions, they present significant challenges for unequivocally labeling each tree crown for validation purposes. This is due to factors like canopy overlap, varied lighting conditions, complex tree morphologies, and the sheer scale of the areas to be annotated, which introduce ambiguities and make consistent manual delineation impractical or prohibitively expensive across large regions. UAV (drone) campaigns can bridge the gap by capturing very high-resolution images or LiDAR of sample areas, but they are limited in flight range and still require extensive human annotation to turn imagery into usable ground truth. The net result is a mismatch of scales: our models aspire to map every tree across entire countries, but our ground truth typically covers only small plots or scattered samples []. This mismatch means that validating a "wall-to-wall" tree map (i.e. predictions or classifications are made across an entire spatial extent) often involves extrapolating from a tiny fraction of ground-referenced trees, introducing uncertainty. Moreover, ground-reference datasets may not capture the full diversity of conditions (species, canopy shapes, management regimes, etc.) present in the larger mapping area, biasing the validation. Expanding ground-truth collection – through automated methods or crowdsourcing – is thus not just a recommendation but a necessity to overcome this validation bottleneck (as we discuss later).

Compounding the issue of limited data is the inconsistency in reference annotations and evaluation metrics. Even when ground-reference data exist, their format can differ – sometimes reference trees are marked by a single GPS point (e.g., trunk location), sometimes by a hand-drawn polygon outlining the single crown. This creates a challenge in validation: how do we decide if a predicted crown polygon "matches" a ground-truth point, or how to handle cases where one field-mapped tree corresponds to multiple overlapping crown segments in the image? (Fig. 2c) Conversely, field crews might delineate a broad canopy as one crown while an automated model splits it into two segments (or vice versa), especially in dense stands where crowns merge. These ambiguities in one-to-one correspondence make it hard to define what a "correct" segmentation is. Traditional pixel-wise accuracy metrics like Intersection-over-Union (IoU) treat segmentation purely as an image overlap problem, which may not reflect the ecological reality of counting individual trees. IoU penalizes differences in shape or area but doesn't account for whether the count of tree objects is correct. In an extreme case, a model could slightly over-segment every tree (splitting each true crown into two smaller polygons) and still achieve a reasonable IoU, despite doubling the perceived tree count – a significant error for applications. On the other hand, object-centric metrics such as panoptic segmentation quality attempt to consider both detection and delineation of objects [9]. Panoptic metrics combine aspects of object detection (was each tree detected?) with segmentation quality (was each crown correctly outlined?), which can be more appropriate for tree mapping. However, even these require well-defined ground-truth objects to compare against. When the ground truth itself is inconsistent (e.g., how to count a clumped cluster of stems with overlapping crowns), validation metrics struggle to fully capture model performance. The choice of evaluation metric thus becomes non-trivial: depending on whether one prioritizes exact crown shape, tree count, or canopy cover, the "best" metric may differ. Establishing consensus on evaluation protocols is part of the challenge – without it, different studies may report accuracy in incompatible ways.

There is also the issue of scale and resolution in validation reporting. A model's accuracy can appear to vary depending on the spatial scale at which it is evaluated. For instance, a segmentation model might achieve high overall accuracy when averaged over an entire large region, yet if one zooms into a small test area (say a single city park or forest stand), the error rate might be much higher or lower. This can happen if errors are not evenly distributed: the model could perform very well in one type of landscape (e.g., neat urban street trees) and poorly in another (dense natural forest), and a coarse regional average could mask these extremes. Consequently, a user working on a local conservation project might experience worse performance than the "headline" accuracy suggests, because that headline number was diluted by many easier cases elsewhere. Ensuring that validation is robust across scales is tricky – one must balance broad coverage with local detail. It calls for multi-scale validation approaches, where accuracy is reported at multiple grain sizes or stratified by landscape or habitat type.

The above challenges reflect the multifaceted difficulties of validating tree crown segmentation at scale. For an at-a-glance overview of these issues and recommendations, see Table 1 in the Appendix.

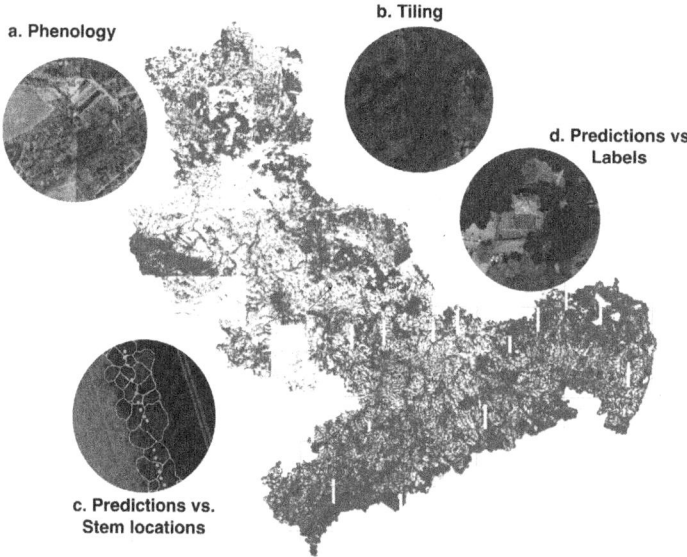

Fig. 2. Illustration of key validation challenges in large-scale tree crown segmentation across two federal states (Sachsen-Anhalt; in blue & Sachsen; in green) in Germany. Insets highlight specific issues: (a) seasonal variation (phenology) affecting appearance, (b) tiling artifacts in image preprocessing, (c) misalignment between predicted crowns and known tree stem locations, and (d) discrepancies between predicted crowns (blue) and labeled ground truth (red), emphasizing model performance gaps. Blue (Sachsen-Anhalt) and green (Sachsen) overlays represent modelled individual tree crowns across different Federal States in Germany. (Color figure online)

4 Recommendations

Validating large-scale tree segmentation models is challenging due to seasonal variability, diverse terrain (Fig. 3b,c) [3] and illumination conditions, inconsistent ground truth data, ambiguous evaluation criteria, and scale-dependent performance. These factors significantly affect the reliability and practical value of AI-generated tree maps for forestry, ecology, and urban planning.

Addressing these challenges necessitates a multi-faceted approach that integrates advanced modeling techniques, improved validation methods, and robust data collection. Recommended strategies include enhancing model robustness through sophisticated training approaches and developing standardized evaluation frameworks to assess real-world performance accurately. These efforts aim to ensure that advances in deep learning yield reliable, actionable insights for large-scale tree mapping.

Leveraging self-supervised learning (SSL) enhances the generalizability of segmentation models by utilizing abundant unlabeled remote sensing data. Unlike traditional supervised methods constrained by limited annotations, SSL enables models to derive meaningful representations through tasks such as predicting missing image parts or distinguishing augmented views of scenes. Pre-training models with extensive unlabeled geospatial imagery allows them to internalize intrinsic landscape patterns—textures, shapes, and seasonal variations—which can be efficiently fine-tuned with fewer labeled samples for specific tasks like tree crown segmentation. Recent research underscores the effectiveness of SSL-based geospatial foundation models. PhilEO Bench demonstrated improved performance across multiple remote sensing applications, such as building footprint extraction and road mapping, compared to training models from scratch [4]. SSL-trained models inherently recognize basic vegetation structures, shadows, and seasonal dynamics, facilitating accurate segmentation under varying conditions. For example, a model trained on seasonal satellite imagery implicitly distinguishes between a tree's winter and summer appearances, significantly reducing the required fine-tuning. Expanding this approach, Mendieta et al. (2023) employed continual SSL training, integrating new data distributions to develop a robust Geospatial Foundation Model (GFM) proficient across diverse remote sensing tasks [15]. This continual learning paradigm ensures segmentation models remain current with evolving landscapes and sensor technologies. Thus, SSL effectively addresses challenges associated with limited labeled data and dataset biases, improving adaptability and performance of large-scale segmentation models.

Integrating multi-view and multi-temporal data enhances model consistency by training with diverse imagery of the same trees captured from varying angles, sensors, or times. Multi-view data encompass multi-angle (nadir and oblique aerial images), multi-platform (satellite and drone imagery), and multi-temporal (images from different seasons or years) perspectives, enabling models to learn robust invariances for reliable segmentation under varying conditions. Combining leaf-on and leaf-off images, compels the model to recognize structural features beyond mere greenness, thus improving seasonal generalization. Self-supervised learning (SSL) techniques, such as masked autoencoders and contrastive learning, effectively utilize multi-view datasets by encouraging models to generate consistent representations across different views without manual labels. Studies utilizing masked image modeling and contrastive SSL on multi-view satellite imagery have demonstrated significant performance improvements in segmentation and detection tasks [4,17]. Employing multi-view consistency training directly mitigates challenges associated with phenological and illumination variations, thereby enhancing model robustness and facilitating validation.

For example, discrepancies in model predictions between leaf-on and leaf-off imagery could flag areas requiring further examination. Thus, multi-view and multi-temporal training provide models with contextual understanding of the dynamic and three-dimensional nature of trees, stabilizing segmentation results across real-world variability.

Integrating terrain data into tree segmentation models addresses image variability caused by uneven topography. Fusing Digital Elevation Models (DEMs) or LiDAR-derived terrain data with imagery during model training can enhance segmentation accuracy. This can involve providing elevation/slope as an additional input channel or designing models to process terrain context separately. Self-supervised pre-training can leverage elevation data to improve feature representations. By differentiating between bare earth and above-ground structures, models learn to distinguish actual objects from illumination differences caused by slope and aspect. For instance, a terrain-informed model can differentiate shaded hillsides from canopy gaps or recognize a single tree crown on a steep slope despite perspective distortion [7]. Incorporating terrain data directly addresses spatial heterogeneity, providing a reference frame to normalize variability and improve validation. This allows for error analysis stratified by terrain class, ensuring consistent performance across diverse topographies. We recommend that future segmentation models, particularly for regions with varied topography, adopt terrain-aware training strategies. Even with limited DEM availability, approximating slope from imagery or using coarse global elevation data can be beneficial. Ultimately, integrating real-world topography with pixel appearance enhances model understanding and generalizability, leading to more robust deployment in new landscapes.

Focus Model Attention on Domain-specific Features. Advancements in model architecture and training objectives, such as feature-guided masked autoencoders, can enhance segmentation reliability by directing learning toward high-level, domain-relevant features rather than pixel-level noise. In remote sensing, specific spectral and textural cues (e.g., high near-infrared reflectance in healthy canopies) distinguish tree crowns from other land covers. Feature-guided methods train models to reconstruct meaningful feature representations—such as vegetation indices or edge maps—instead of raw pixels. For example, FG-MAE (Feature Guided Masked Autoencoder) tasks the model with predicting domain-specific features (e.g., NDVI or engineered representations) for masked image regions, promoting semantic understanding rather than texture replication [17]. Applied to tree segmentation, such pre-training focuses internal representations on vegetation structure (e.g., crown edges or canopy height), improving delineation of complex canopies and separation from backgrounds. Early studies in multispectral and SAR imagery confirm improved segmentation in challenging environments [1]. Integrating feature-guidance is thus recommended for large-scale tree mapping, particularly in complex landscapes, as it not only increases accuracy but may also yield more interpretable outputs and uncertainties to support validation and error diagnosis.

Expand Validation Beyond Pixel Agreement – Use Ecological Consistency Checks. Traditional segmentation validation relies on geometric overlap with ground truth, but tree mapping can benefit from leveraging ecological allometric relationships as an additional check. Allometry—well-established links between tree dimensions such as trunk diameter, height, and crown width—provides expected bounds for tree size relationships. Applying allometric equations to segmentation outputs serves as a "sanity check": for example, predictions where crown sizes and tree heights deviate significantly from field-based distributions may indicate model errors or missing trees. Overly large predicted crowns in a region without tall trees, or consistently small crowns in old-growth forests, can reveal segmentation artifacts. Recent studies, such as Song et al. (2023), have used statistical models to connect remote sensing outputs to allometric expectations, highlighting ecological validation as a valuable approach [22]. Implementing such checks requires integrating ancillary data, such as LiDAR-derived heights or species-specific formulas, to cross-validate AI-generated tree maps. This recommendation shifts validation from a purely computer-vision perspective to an application-oriented perspective: after all, if the ultimate goal is to use these maps for carbon accounting, biodiversity, or forestry, then passing an ecological reality check is as important as scoring well on IoU.

Establish Community Benchmarks and Evaluation Frameworks. The field of geospatial AI is recognizing the value of standard benchmarks – datasets and metrics on which different methods can be compared in a reproducible way. Standard datasets and metrics like ImageNet and COCO have significantly impacted computer vision, inspiring geospatial counterparts such as GEO-Bench and PANGAEA [14]. We propose developing specific benchmarks for tree crown segmentation and mapping, covering diverse landscapes, seasons, and remote sensing sources. Standardized evaluation metrics, such as IoU for segmentation and detection accuracy, would ensure comparability and transparency in results. Additionally, benchmarks should require multi-scale assessments, evaluating not only overall accuracy but also performance in challenging subsets (e.g., dense forests vs. isolated trees), incorporating auxiliary criteria like allometric consistency. Regular competitive challenges using standardized large-scale tree mapping tasks can accelerate method improvement and robustness. Ultimately, these community-driven benchmarks facilitate transparent, credible model evaluations and iterative progress in geospatial AI.

Innovate in Ground-Truth Data Collection and Labeling. Advances in modeling alone cannot eliminate the need for enhanced validation datasets. We recommend expanding ground-truth collection through automation, crowdsourcing, and active learning. Automated techniques using drones or AI-equipped aircraft can rapidly generate tree crown annotations, minimizing expert involvement. Crowdsourcing allows non-experts to efficiently label straightforward cases, supported by redundancy and quality controls, proven effective in urban tree mapping. Active learning strategies prioritize uncertain or conflicting model predictions for expert review, significantly optimizing annotation efforts [28]. Additionally, promoting open data practices and sharing existing inventories and LiDAR datasets from public agencies can provide critical validation resources. Integrating these approaches—automation, crowdsourcing, active learning, and open data—will effectively bridge validation data gaps and enhance model robustness and generalizability.

5 Conclusion

Deep learning has opened a new frontier for tree crown segmentation from remote sensing imagery, yet its promise is contingent on our ability to validate these models reliably and at scale. As this paper has outlined, the challenges are not merely technical—they are epistemological. They force us to ask: what does it mean to "know" a tree from above, when the canopy is a moving target shaped by phenology, terrain, land cover and image artifacts?

The comprehensive case study in Sachsen and Sachsen-Anhalt exemplifies how substantial regional variability in ecology, topography, and land use affects model performance. Validation challenges identified—including phenological dynamics, spatial heterogeneity, and scale-dependent accuracy—highlight the need for robust validation frameworks tailored to large spatial extents.

Emerging methods such as self-supervised learning, geospatial foundation models, and multi-view fusion offer a compelling pathway forward. These approaches not only reduce reliance on costly annotations but also capture the underlying structure of complex and dynamic landscapes. Equally, validation must evolve beyond static benchmarks. Indirect metrics—like allometric plausibility checks— must be brought into the fold. Validation, in this context, becomes less about binary correctness and more about probabilistic trust.

Pursuing the recommendations, the field can significantly advance accurate and trustworthy large-scale tree mapping by integrating robust, self-supervised, multi-view, and terrain-aware models with continuous validation against classical metrics and real-world plausibility, using feedback for active learning and expanded training data. The real frontier is integration: aligning spatial, temporal, and ecological knowledge through a fusion of data-driven and domain-aware models. As these systems are deployed across continents, cities, and seasons, the imperative is not just to scale algorithms, but to scale insight. Only then can tree segmentation models become dependable instruments for managing the living infrastructure of our planet.

Acknowledgments. DeepTrees is part of the DeepTrees: Deep-Learning based spatiotemporal tree inventorying and monitoring from public orthoimages project, funded by the Integration Platform "Sustainable Future Land Use" at Helmholtz-Centre for Environmental Research – UFZ within the Programme oriented Funding (PoF) period IV of the Helmholtz Program "Changing Earth – Sustaining our Future", Topic 5 "Landscapes of the Future. This repository is based on the work described in Freudenberg et al. (2022). This work was supported by Helmholtz Association's Initiative and Networking Fund through Helmholtz AI [grant number: ZT-I-PF-5-01]. This work used resources of the Deutsches Klimarechenzentrum (DKRZ) granted by its Scientific Steering Committee (WLA) under project ID AIM.

Disclosure of Interests. The authors have no competing interests to declare that are relevant to the content of this article.

References

1. Allen, M.J., Owen, H.J., Grieve, S.W., Lines, E.R.: Manual labelling artificially inflates deep learning-based segmentation performance on rgb images of closed canopy: validation using tls. arXiv preprint arXiv:2503.14273 (2025)
2. Cong, P., Zhou, J., Li, S., Lv, K., Feng, H.: Citrus tree crown segmentation of orchard spraying robot based on rgb-d image and improved mask r-cnn. Appl. Sci. **13**(1), 164 (2022)
3. European Space Agency (ESA): Copernicus DEM GLO-30 - Global Digital Elevation Model (30 m). Copernicus Open Access Hub (2020), https://spacedata.copernicus.eu/collections/copernicus-digital-elevation-model, version: GLO-30, Public Release
4. Fibaek, M., et al.: Phileo bench: evaluating geospatial foundation models. IEEE Trans. Geosci. Remote Sens. (2024)
5. Freudenberg, M., Magdon, P., Nölke, N.: Individual tree crown delineation in high-resolution remote sensing images based on u-net. Neural Comput. Appl. **34**(24), 22197–22207 (2022)
6. Garnot, V.S.F., et al.: Deep learning meets tree phenology modelling: Phenoformer versus process-based models. Methods Ecol. Evol. (2025)
7. Han, X., et al.: ms-gfm: multisensor geospatial foundation models. IEEE Trans. Geosci. Remote Sens. (2024)
8. Jiang, T., Freudenberg, M., Kleinn, C., Lüddecke, T., Ecker, A., Nölke, N.: Detection transformer-based approach for mapping trees outside forests on high resolution satellite imagery. Ecol. Inf. **87**, 103114 (2025). https://doi.org/10.1016/j.ecoinf.2025.103114, https://www.sciencedirect.com/science/article/pii/S1574954125001232
9. Kirillov, A., He, K., Girshick, R., Rother, C., Dollár, P.: Panoptic segmentation (2019), https://arxiv.org/abs/1801.00868
10. Krajicek, J.E., Brinkman, K.A., Gingrich, S.F.: Crown competition—a measure of density. Forest Sci. **7**(1), 35–42 (1961)
11. Landesamt für Geobasisinformation Sachsen (GeoSN): DOP20 - Digitale Orthophotos (RGBI, 20cm), Freistaat Sachsen. GeoBasis-DE / GeoSN (2022), https://www.landesvermessung.sachsen.de/digitale-orthophotos-bildflug-2022-8995.html, rGB and Color-Infrared orthophotos, National data license (DL-DE-BY-2.0)
12. Landesamt für Vermessung und Geoinformation Sachsen-Anhalt (LVermGeo): DOP20 - Digitale Orthophotos 20 cm, Sachsen-Anhalt. GeoBasis-DE / LVermGeo ST (2020), https://www.lvermgeo.sachsen-anhalt.de, licensed under Datenlizenz Deutschland - Namensnennung - Version 2.0
13. Liu, G., et al.: Deepphenomem v1. 0: deep learning modelling of canopy greenness dynamics accounting for multi-variate meteorological memory effects on vegetation phenology. Geosci. Model Dev. **17**(17), 6683–6701 (2024)
14. Marsocci, V., et al.: PANGAEA: a global and inclusive benchmark for geospatial foundation models (2024). https://doi.org/10.48550/arXiv.2412.04204, https://arxiv.org/abs/2412.04204

15. Mendieta, M., Han, B., Shi, X., Zhu, Y., Chen, C., Li, M.: GFM: building geospatial foundation models via continual pretraining. In: Proceedings of the IEEE/CVF International Conference on Computer Vision (ICCV) (2023). https://doi.org/10.1109/ICCV.2023.12345, https://arxiv.org/abs/2302.04476
16. Moussaid, A., Fkihi, S.E., Zennayi, Y.: Tree crowns segmentation and classification in overlapping orchards based on satellite images and unsupervised learning algorithms. J. Imaging **7**(11), 241 (2021)
17. Mukkavilli, K., et al.: Foundation models for generalist geospatial artificial intelligence (2023). https://doi.org/10.48550/arXiv.2310.18660, https://arxiv.org/abs/2310.18660
18. Pan, Y., et al.: The enduring world forest carbon sink. Nature **631**(8021), 563–569 (2024)
19. Sapkota, R., Karkee, M.: Integrating yolo11 and convolution block attention module for multi-season segmentation of tree trunks and branches in commercial apple orchards. arXiv preprint arXiv:2412.05728 (2024)
20. Sharma, S., Hussain, S., Kumar, P., Singh, A.N.: Urban trees' potential for regulatory services in the urban environment: an exploration of carbon sequestration. Environ. Monit. Assess. **196**(6), 1–27 (2024)
21. Shimano, K.: Analysis of the relationship between dbh and crown projection area using a new model. J. For. Res. **2**(4), 237–242 (1997)
22. Song, Q., Albrecht, C.M., Xiong, Z., Zhu, X.X.: Biomass estimation and uncertainty quantification from tree height. arXiv preprint arXiv:2305.09555 (2023). https://doi.org/10.48550/arXiv.2305.09555, https://arxiv.org/abs/2305.09555
23. Steier, J., Goebel, M., Iwaszczuk, D.: Is your training data really ground truth? a quality assessment of manual annotation for individual tree crown delineation. Remote Sens. **16**(15), 2786 (2024)
24. Taimur Khan, Arnold, C., Grover, H.: Deeptrees: tree crown segmentation and analysis in remote sensing imagery with pytorch. Preprint (2025). https://doi.org/10.13140/RG.2.2.32837.36329, https://rgdoi.net/10.13140/RG.2.2.32837.36329
25. Tolan, J., et al.: Very high resolution canopy height maps from rgb imagery using self-supervised vision transformer and convolutional decoder trained on aerial lidar. Remote Sens. Environ. **300**, 113888 (2024)
26. Weinstein, B.G., Marconi, S., Bohlman, S., Zare, A., White, E.: Individual tree-crown detection in rgb imagery using semi-supervised deep learning neural networks. Remote Sens. **11**(11), 1309 (2019)
27. Weinstein, B.G., Marconi, S., Bohlman, S.A., Zare, A., White, E.P.: Cross-site learning in deep learning rgb tree crown detection. Eco. Inform. **56**, 101061 (2020)
28. Wu, J., Chen, J., Huang, D.: Entropy-based active learning for object detection with progressive diversity constraint. In: Proceedings of the IEEE/CVF Conference on Computer Vision and Pattern Recognition (CVPR), pp. 9397–9406, June 2022
29. Zhao, H., Morgenroth, J., Pearse, G., Schindler, J.: A systematic review of individual tree crown detection and delineation with convolutional neural networks (cnn). Current Forestry Rep. **9**(3), 149–170 (2023)
30. Zheng, J., Yuan, S., Li, W., Fu, H., Yu, L., Huang, J.: A review of individual tree crown detection and delineation from optical remote sensing images: Current progress and future. IEEE Geosci. Remote Sens. Mag. (2024)

Managing FAIR Research Products for Biodiversity and Ecosystems Within the LifeWatch Italy Infrastructure

Andrea Tarallo[1](✉) 📵, Cristina Di Muri[1] 📵, Martina Pulieri[2] 📵, Francesco De Leo[1,3] 📵, Mariantonietta La Marra[2] 📵, Davide Raho[1] 📵, Alberto Basset[1,2,3,4] 📵, and Ilaria Rosati[1,3] 📵

[1] Institute of Research on Terrestrial Ecosystems (IRET), National Research Council (CNR), SP Lecce-Monteroni, 73100 Lecce, Italy
andrea.tarallo@cnr.it
[2] Department of Biological and Environmental Sciences and Technologies, University of Salento, SP Lecce-Monteroni, 73100 Lecce, Italy
[3] NBFC, National Biodiversity Future Center, Piazza Marina 61, 90133 Palermo, Italy
[4] LifeWatch ERIC Service Centre, 73100 Lecce, Italy

Abstract. Biodiversity and ecosystem services are declining at an alarming rate, a trend expected to intensify due to human-induced climate change. Addressing this crisis requires comprehensive data collection and integration. However, the digital outputs resulting from the research lifecycle are often fragmented and heterogeneous. Combining these research products can yield new insights, but only if they are made Findable, Accessible, Interoperable, and Reusable, i.e. FAIR. Adherence to FAIR principles ensures that data and digital outputs can be integrated and reused by both humans and machines. In this context, national infrastructures are key in supporting the generation and management of FAIR digital outputs. This paper presents the LifeWatch Italy digital infrastructure, a national initiative developed to support the FAIR management of digital research products within the ecology domain. LifeWatch Italy aims to provide services and platforms that address key stages of the research data lifecycle, including data collection, curation, annotation, publication, and reuse. A suite of integrated platforms enables structured data ingestion, semantic annotation using controlled vocabularies and ontologies, taxonomic validation via national and international backbones, and publication in standardised, open formats. Interoperability is achieved through the adoption of widely accepted community standards, persistent identifiers, and automated workflows that ease the burden on individual researchers, ensuring that all the digital products meet FAIR principles by default. The infrastructure aspires to have a key role as national hub for biodiversity and ecosystem research in Italy, supporting the scientific community, and ensuring long-term usability of research outputs.

Keywords: National research infrastructure · Interoperability · FAIR Principles

1 Introduction

Biodiversity and related ecosystem services are declining worldwide, with this trend expected to be exacerbated over the next decades by human-induced climate change acting under different scenarios [1]. Addressing the current and predicted biodiversity crisis requires intensive data collection to monitor changes in biodiversity across geographical and temporal scales and to develop effective knowledge-based conservation strategies [2]. Biodiversity monitoring and data collection are usually performed by different actors, including environmental agencies, research institutions, museums, NGOs, lays and specialised volunteers acting through a variety of monitoring programmes, often limited in their spatiotemporal and taxonomic coverage [3].

Thanks to a growing awareness of Open practices (Access, Science, Research, Source), the volume of available biodiversity data is growing at an unprecedented rate [4]. However, in many instances, they still lack fit for use, integration and reuse because of structural and technological challenges [5]. Although notable examples of global repositories for biodiversity data exist, such as the Global Biodiversity Information Facility (GBIF) [6], most of the digital products of the research pipeline are often fragmented and dispersed across different sources, including scholarly literature, databases of public research institutes, government agencies, and generalist data archives [3, 7]. In addition, research products are highly diverse in nature, encompassing everything from raw and processed data to scripts and services, training materials, and they can be available in different structures and formats, limiting their interoperability across systems [8]. By combining different research products, e.g. datasets and analytical pipelines or web-services, scientists can aggregate and build on existing knowledge to generate novel findings or address different scientific challenges [9]. The use of standards and semantic artefacts provides an opportunity to overcome this challenge and integrate these digital products, yet their adoption is still inadequate, especially in some specific scientific domains [10]. To ensure the long-term value and reusability both by humans and machines, though, biodiversity data and related digital research products must adhere to the FAIR principles, which provide guidelines for their Findability, Accessibility, Interoperability, and Reusability [11].

In this context, national initiatives and infrastructures can play a crucial role in supporting scientific communities to generate FAIR digital research outputs that can be efficiently managed and integrated within different distributed information systems [5, 12, 13]. It is important to acknowledge that the FAIR principles should not be interpreted as a binary attribute of data. FAIRness exists along a spectrum, and its assessment remains a complex and evolving challenge. Notwithstanding, when developing national infrastructural solutions for managing ecological information, all the challenges described above must be addressed. This paper introduces the LifeWatch Italy digital infrastructure, the result of a series of coordinated efforts to establish a national hub supporting the management of digital research products in ecology. LifeWatch Italy [14] is the Italian node of the LifeWatch European Research Infrastructure Consortium (LifeWatch ERIC) [15], the e-Science infrastructure dedicated to biodiversity and ecosystem research. In response to the growing variety and complexity of digital research products, LifeWatch Italy has significantly enhanced its infrastructure by envisioning a model that integrates services and platforms to support scientists throughout the entire research cycle, promoting best practices in data management and ensuring that research products are aligned with the principles of FAIR and Open Science. In addition to bringing openness, reusability and long-term value to different research outputs, the LifeWatch Italy research lifecycle ensures interoperability between systems to overcome fragmentation and research silos. By facilitating data collection, curation, annotation, discovery, analysis and reuse through different interconnected components, this management model accelerates research progress and avoids time and effort consuming towards data wrangling for different purposes.

The following sections present the main components of the LifeWatch Italy infrastructure (see Fig. 1), illustrating how each platform and service supports the implementation of FAIR principles along the entire research lifecycle, from data collection to curation and validation, annotation, analysis and reuse. It should be noted, however, that individual platforms and services are not limited to a single purpose. They are designed to be flexible and to address multiple needs simultaneously, reflecting an integrated approach to research data management.

2 The Research Lifecycle in LifeWatch Italy

2.1 Collection

The LifeWatch infrastructure focuses on supporting the management and integration of research data. It usually does not directly engage in data collection activities such as field campaigns or monitoring schemes. Data collection is, however, increasingly becoming a multifaceted process, involving a wider range of contributors, including citizens and specialised volunteers, and leveraging emerging methods and technologies to support the on-site activities of these actors [16]. In response to this evolving landscape and accounting for the need to standardise these data and facilitate their ingestion into data management systems, two platforms have been developed: the Citizen Science Platform [17], designed to assist researchers in launching and managing citizen science projects; and the Bioacoustic Platform [18], aimed at collecting biodiversity data from recorded soundscapes. Both platforms are briefly introduced below.

Citizen Science Platform. Citizen science has emerged as an effective approach to involve the public in scientific research, particularly in biodiversity and ecosystem monitoring [19]. Citizen science activities often rely on user-friendly digital applications offering simplified data collection, facilitating participation and networking opportunities [16]. However, the maintenance, and management of digital applications for data collection present several challenges such as the need for specialised Information and Communication Technology (ICT) skills for data management and safety storage, the infrastructural costs associated with large volumes of data, and the increasing demand for structured and rich metadata. In this context, the Citizen Science Platform has been developed to enable the creation of customisable web applications for data collection by the public. The platform supports various levels of user authorisation, allowing registered users to create and manage their own projects. Upon review and approval by the platform administrators, project leads can configure a dedicated project webpage for dissemination and customise a data collection web application. The web application

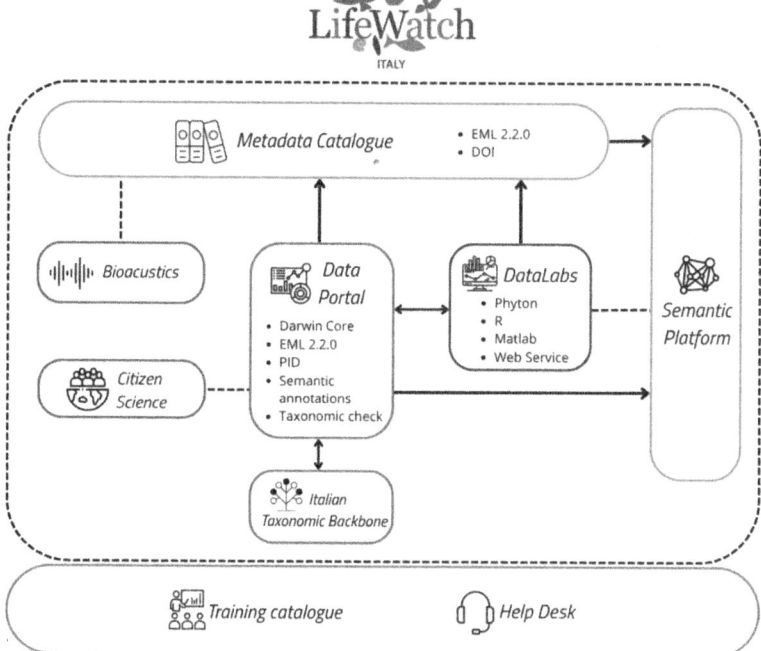

Fig. 1. LifeWatch Italy platforms and services to support the research lifecycle in the biodiversity and ecosystem domain. The figure shows the platforms developed for collection (green circles), curation and validation (dark orange circles), discovery (light orange circles), analysis (blue circle), and reuse (blue sky circle) of digital research products. Existing interconnections between platforms are represented with arrows. Dotted lines show future connections. Icons: Flaticon.com.

allows for flexible configuration of observation parameters, including the collection of video and audio files, and automatically records the geolocation of each submission. The application is accessible via smartphones, facilitating widespread participation. Project administrators can access, validate, and analyse the submitted data, generating reports and enabling open access to validated records, which can be visualised on a map. The dataset can be downloaded into structured and interoperable formats to enable a facilitated ingestion by other LifeWatch services and platforms, e.g. the Data Portal. This solution offers a sustainable, cost-effective and scalable way for setting up and managing citizen science activities and their associated data.

The platform offers additional functionalities, including a) a section dedicated to fundamental knowledge about citizen science, including its history, methodologies, and key principles; b) a practical guide for developing and managing citizen science projects supporting users through the essential steps of project formulation, community engagement, data management, and communication; c) a searchable repository of training materials to support skills uptake in citizen science methodologies and management; d) a comprehensive directory of citizen science projects, visualised on an interactive map.

Bioacoustic Platform. Non-destructive methods, such as camera traps, environmental DNA, bioacoustic monitoring, and remote sensing, in conjunction with technological advancements are considered game changers for biodiversity monitoring as they economise on human and natural capital [20]. Among these methods, acoustic monitoring has emerged as a particularly effective approach, especially when combined with artificial intelligence [21]. The integration of animal sounds with ecological information enables the extraction of valuable insights into ecosystems and species behaviour. The Bioacoustic Platform has been developed to support the recognition of species acoustic signals through the processing of spectral signatures. Registered users can upload audio recordings accompanied by relevant metadata. The platform analyses each recording and generates five visual representations of the sound: Time Fourier Transform, Spectrogram, Mel Spectrogram, Mel-Frequency Cepstral Coefficients, and Waveform. A machine learning model trained to identify species provides a ranked list of probable matches by comparing the uploaded sound with existing recordings in the platform. Users can review these results and select the most appropriate match. This system facilitates the collection and management of audio recordings and associated metadata, such as geolocation. The platform provides a user-friendly solution for mapping species distributions, making it an optimal solution for initiatives that wish to engage both specialists and lay people.

2.2 Curation and Validation

The scope of the curation and validation phase is to increase the quality of data by structuring and harmonising it to expected values and accepted semantic rules [22]. This phase encompasses syntactic validation, semantic annotation, and taxonomic alignment and, in the LifeWatch Italy infrastructure, it is enabled through the integration of multiple services and platforms. The LifeWatch approach maximises the reuse of existing technical solutions and standards, including (meta)data schema, semantic artefacts, and taxonomies, with the aim of aligning national efforts to community-accepted FAIR practices already in use within the community of ecologists.

Data Portal. Data curation and validation in the LifeWatch Italy infrastructure is mainly performed through a number of services embedded in the Data Portal [23]. The Data Portal serves as the primary access point to biodiversity data, including species lists and associated biological/ecological traits and/or co-occurring ecosystems and environmental data. In addition to data access, the platform has been developed and customised to support comprehensive data management, from curation and validation to publication and discovery of semantically annotated data and metadata. Accessibility is facilitated through the adoption of open formats, whereby the XML is used for metadata, following the Ecological Metadata Language (EML) 2.2.0 [24], and the CSV for datasets. The use of flat CSV files meets the needs of the scientific community, who usually prefer to record their data in spreadsheets. Nonetheless, the Data Portal is designed to accommodate a wide range of data formats, including geospatial file formats. Data interoperability is supported by the utilisation of the Darwin Core (DwC) standard as data model [25]. The DwC is a widely recognised and adopted standard to share biological and ecological information. In addition to the DwC standard, other community-accepted controlled vocabularies and coding standards are used depending on the specific requirements and scopes of the datasets. Preferentially, data are annotated using semantic artefacts stored in EcoPortal [26], e.g. EnvThes [27]. This annotation process is carried out via the EML attribute list associated to a data table. In particular, each attribute, corresponding to a column header in dataset, is defined by a property URI (e.g. oboe:containsMeasurementsOf) and a value URI, i.e. the URI of a concept from a controlled vocabulary (e.g. traitsThesaurus:bodyLength). Alignment with DwC and other discipline-specific standards supports data harvesting, aggregation and integration into other international biodiversity data initiatives. Prior to publication, datasets undergo a review and validation process via a structured data curation workflow, which includes the taxonomic validation of biological records and checks on the submitted metadata. In particular, taxonomic data are cross-referenced and aligned against national and international taxonomic backbones, including the Italian backbone (see Italian Taxonomic Backbone section) and three Global Species Databases, i.e. the Catalogue of Life [28], the World Register of Marine Species [29], and the World Flora Online [30]. Regarding the metadata check, the submitted metadata records are subject to an automated validation of EML records using XSD (XML Schema Definition) that guarantees that metadata conforms to expected values, ensuring their syntactic accuracy. A final editorial review is carried out by the portal's data managers prior to ap-proval, who assure that only well-curated digital products are uploaded on the Data Portal. Once approved by the portal's data managers, datasets and associated metadata are published, and a Persistent Identifier (PID) is assigned. By default, (meta)data records are granted with a Handle ID, while DOIs are provided upon request. Additionally, other PIDs are embedded into the metadata to ensure stable and persistent referencing among digital objects, supporting cross-system integration. These include ROR for institutional affiliations and ORCID for individuals. This approach improves traceability, citation, and discoverability of datasets and related resources, aligning with best practices in FAIR data publishing [5].

Semantic Annotation. Following the FAIR Principles, the primary objective of LifeWatch is to achieve standardised and interoperable data, both internally and across external infrastructures, within the domains of ecology, ecosystems, and biodiversity. Semantic artefacts play a pivotal role in enabling semantic interoperability, thus facilitating data integration and machine-readability [10]. To support this, dataset's metadata is semantically enriched using controlled vocabularies and ontologies. Users can annotate metadata using concepts/classes recalled via API from EcoPortal [26], the LifeWatch ERIC repository of semantic artefacts, or by using URIs from semantic artefacts available in other catalogues. By linking metadata attributes to concepts and relationships from ontologies or controlled vocabularies, it becomes easier to understand the content and context of data, enabling alignment across heterogeneous sources [31]. This approach helps overcome linguistic and structural ambiguities, ultimately fostering semantic interoperability.

Italian Taxonomic Backbone. Taxonomy is far from being a static science, it is rather a highly dynamic and investigative process [32]. As noted by [33], this dynamicity is captured within multiple independent initiatives, each with different aims and scopes (e.g. taxon-specific or limited to specific areas) instead of converging over a single authoritative list of the world's taxa [34, 35]. As a result, curated taxonomic information remains fragmented across numerous repositories [36].

With the rapid growth of biological data, accurately identifying taxa in datasets is a key requirement for ensuring data interoperability. In Italy, several research groups have been collecting taxonomic records of species occurring in the Country within different systems, from simple checklists to relational databases [37–39]. In this regard, LifeWatch Italy aim to provide a unified access point to all such taxonomic information and to align it with international standards, i.e. DwC. The Italian Taxonomic Backbone [40] currently includes:

- The complete Checklist of the Fauna of Italy, comprising approximately 27,000 animal species and subspecies provided by the Comitato Fauna d'Italia.
- The complete Checklist of the Flora of Italy, with nomenclature provided by the FlorItaly [38], which includes the most recent national checklists for native and alien vascular plants. Accepted names and synonyms comprise approximately 25,000 records.
- The complete Checklist of the Lichens of Italy, provided by ITALIC 8.0 [39] online database (https://italic.units.it), which includes around 17,000 records covering accepted names, basionyms, and synonyms for lichens.

For each species concept, the Backbone assigns a persistent identifier (PID). When a one-to-one match exists between a taxon in the Italian Taxonomic Backbone and a global species database, such as the Catalogue of Life, this correspondence is made explicit by linking the respective PIDs (e.g. [41]). These harmonised taxonomic references are then reused across datasets.

The Italian Taxonomic Backbone is accessible through a web interface with the following features:

- Searching for one or more taxa;
- Viewing and downloading search results into CSV;
- Requesting modifications to existing taxa information or the addition of new ones. Each submission initiates a review process managed by an expert taxonomist for the interested group.
- Adding new checklists or updating existing ones, either manually or via API.

In addition, this service is recalled through API within the Data Portal and can be used for the taxonomic validation. The availability of these checklists, maintained and continuously updated by the national scientific community, along with the support of the LifeWatch Italy infrastructure facilitates the establishment of a robust and reliable centre for the aggregation and dissemination of biodiversity data in Italy, making it a key node for the sharing of accurate biodiversity information to international systems.

2.3 Discovery

Over the last decade, the field of e-Science has grown enormously to face the need of Big Data analysis and management. LifeWatch is deeply rooted in this context to develop an infrastructure that provides services to support the scientific community of ecologists in exploiting such data. However, "Small Data", i.e. data with few observations, in ecology are significant as they represent the greatest part of scientific activities, often focusing on manipulative or observational experiments on specific taxa or habitats [42]. Hence, data discovery and integration are key for such an ecosystem of "Small Data" allowing them to resemble Big Data especially when further manipulated and reused to address big scientific questions and challenges.

Semantic Platform. The use of ontologies for the integration of heterogeneous data sources is a common practice in information technology applications to achieve semantic interoperability within a data infrastructure, and across different infrastructures [43, 44]. LifeWatch Italy has developed an ontology-based approach for data discovery and integration by merging existing semantic artefacts, namely the SOSA Ontology [45], PROV Ontology [46] and DCAT vocabulary [47]. The resulting model was extended to include temporal, geospatial, ecological, and taxonomic information (e.g. classes TemporalEntity, GeoPoint, ObservationCollection, Taxon and TaxonRank). Moreover, concepts related to measurements and observations are used as instances of the class ObservableProperty and selected from controlled vocabularies stored in EcoPortal [26], such as EnvThes [27] and the Traits Thesaurus [48]. Data and metadata are mapped against the ontology to produce RDF triples organised into knowledge graphs, networks of entities and relationships among them. Knowledge graphs are accessible and searchable through the web interface of the Semantic Platform [49], which offers a powerful and intuitive way to explore and interact with a wide range of interconnected data. The platform provides extensive search capabilities across multiple variables, people and organisations, geo-temporal contexts, taxonomies and measurements, up to single observations, i.e. single data points within a dataset. Users can integrate heterogeneous data sources through semantically enriched queries (SPARQL), generating custom datasets that can be exported and reused within external systems and services.

Metadata Catalogue. All the research products can be discovered within the LifeWatch Italy Metadata Catalogue [50], a unique access point to data, workflows, Virtual Research Environments (VREs), services, scripts, and training resources. Metadata can be searched through a web interface with simple and advanced searching options, allowing users to refine criteria using facets and search boxes. Records are available through structured and descriptive metadata based on international standards, Ecological Metadata Language (EML 2.2.0) and ISO 19139, thus promoting metadata sharing and exchange across organisations and infrastructures [31]. In addition to these standards, users can request additional metadata schemas or profiles to the platform's admins providing a certain level of flexibility based on users' needs.

The catalogue includes the F-UJI tool [51], a service to evaluate the FAIRness of metadata using the assessment metrics defined by the FAIRsFAIR project [52]. The service performs evaluations on individual metadata records and the catalogue as a whole, delivering detailed reports with scores for each FAIR metric. Prior publication, users can check the FAIR assessment report, enabling them to enhance the FAIR score by supplying additional metadata descriptions. Digital Object Identifiers (DOIs) can be assigned upon request to ensure the persistent identification and citation of metadata records.

2.4 Analysis

DataLabs. Computational analysis is crucial to discover meaningful patterns, especially in the current era characterised by high volume, velocity and variety of data [53]. In this context, analytical scripts and services should have immediate access to the most up-to-date data and metadata and they should as well be described through structured metadata and with compatible encodings based on community-accepted standards [54]. In essence, cloud computation and connections between (meta)data management systems and computational systems are pivotal to ensure reliable, repeatable and reproducible analyses. To this aim, LifeWatch Italy has developed DataLabs [55], a coding platform designed to support collaborative and documented data analysis within a multi-user environment. Powered by JupyterHub, it enables the scalable and secure deployment of personalised JupyterLab instances [56], facilitating access to reproducible workflows across research teams.

The platform integrates three different programming languages, commonly used in the field of environmental science: R, Python, and MATLAB [57]. The platform also offers an innovative feature: analytical scripts can be translated into web services, significantly enhancing their long-term reproducibility. Once published, these services can be accessed either through a graphical user interface, or via RESTful API calls for machine-to-machine interactions.

The interaction between DataLabs and the Data Portal is bidirectional: users can import datasets into their research projects, and they can also upload both local files used as input within their scripts and the output generated by the resulting services or scripts. All these actions are automatically reflected in the Metadata Catalogue, helping researchers build complete, well-documented, and highly reproducible analytics, while ensuring full provenance and traceability across the entire data lifecycle.

Scripts and services created within DataLabs can be utilised as building blocks to develop new workflows and VREs, supporting dynamic, repeatable, and scalable scientific investigations [58].

2.5 Reuse

To ensure widespread and effective adoption of the LifeWatch Italy infrastructure, key platforms have been integrated with two essential support services: the e-Training Platform [59] and the Help Desk [60].

e-Training Platform. The e-Training Platform provides a dedicated online space for capacity building. It hosts a wide range of guidelines, tutorials, and educational content aimed at facilitating the effective use of the infrastructure and its various components.

Helpdesk. The Help Desk offers user support via a ticketing system, enabling users to receive technical assistance and guidance on using the infrastructure's platforms and services. It is designed to streamline troubleshooting and improve user experience across the digital ecosystem.

3 Future Developments and Considerations

The LifeWatch Italy infrastructure, while already fully operational, is also in continuous development (see Fig. 1). The vision is to create a unified and interconnected ecosystem of services and platforms, where all digital research products, i.e. datasets, metadata, analytical scripts, web services, semantic artefacts, etc. are all accessible through a single infrastructure. To anticipate this interconnection, the platforms of the Infrastructure are already accessible through a Single Sign-On system, allowing users to move across platforms and services using a unique account.

One of the primary goals for future development is the consolidation of platform interconnection. While platforms such as the Data Portal, Metadata Catalogue, DataLabs, Bioacoustic Platform, and Citizen Science Platform already serve distinct purposes, their full integration is still in progress (see dotted lines in Fig. 1). The ambition is to ensure that research products generated or submitted within one platform are automatically referenced or shared to other platforms or services wherever meaningful connections are established. For instance, when a user uploads an audio file to the Bioacoustic Platform or data is collected through citizen science initiatives, (meta)data should become discoverable through the Data Portal and Metadata Catalogue, ultimately linked to taxonomic references and eventually reused for downstream analyses.

Achieving such interoperability requires standardised data and metadata flows, persistent identifiers, and shared vocabularies across all services. Furthermore, interfaces and APIs are under continuous development to support real-time synchronisation and automated cross-referencing among services.

There are also strategic considerations related to long-term sustainability and user engagement.

Usage statistics are systematically collected across all platforms through backend systems, capturing metrics such as number of users and session duration. In addition, selected indicators, such as the number of digital objects available, are displayed on the front end of the platforms. Current figures indicate a positive trend in both usage and content availability. Over the past year, more than 600 new users have registered and interacted with LifeWatch Italy services, which now provide access to several hundred digital objects. While some platforms have only recently been released and remain in the early stages of adoption, a significant increase in usage is anticipated in the coming years. This growth is expected to be driven by ongoing and upcoming dissemination activities aimed at promoting awareness and adoption of the Infrastructure across the ecological and biodiversity research communities, especially at National level.

As the infrastructure evolves, maintaining coherence and usability will require a structured governance, continuous feedback from users, coordination with the broader LifeWatch ERIC infrastructure, and alignment with emerging FAIR practices and standards to facilitate the generation of research outputs that are as FAIR as possible. It is also important to acknowledge that building and maintaining such an infrastructure is not solely a technical challenge. Scientists often face significant barriers to data FAIRification, including lack of time, expertise, or institutional support [61]. To address these challenges, LifeWatch Italy currently benefits from national funding that supports dedicated data stewards. These professionals play a key role in assisting the scientific community with data mobilisation and effective platform usage, helping to mitigate some of the obstacles to data sharing and reuse. Future financial investments are crucial to ensure the long-term viability and usability of the platforms, their underlying services, and the storage and computational resources required to support them. Equally critical is the availability of skilled personnel. Technical (ICT specialists, data stewards) and scientific (data scientists, informaticians) staff who can manage editorial workflows, provide user support, develop new features, and ensure alignment with international standards and community needs. The value of the infrastructure lies not only in its technology but in the human capacity to curate, validate, and promote the effective use of available research products.

In the coming years, efforts will be directed toward closing remaining technical and operational gaps, fostering full platform integration, and enhancing the overall user experience. The ultimate aim is to offer a robust, open, and FAIR-compliant hub for biodiversity and ecosystem data in Italy, capable of supporting cutting-edge research, policy, and conservation efforts.

Acknowledgments. The authors thank the two anonymous referees who helped improving the clarity and quality of the article. This work has been supported by the PON-IR "LifeWatchPLUS" (CIR01_00028; PIR01_00028) and Next Generation EU Mission 4 "Education and Research" - Component 2: "From research to business" - Investment 3.1: "Fund for the realisation of an integrated system of research and innovation infrastructures" - Project IR0000032 - ITINERIS - Italian Integrated Environmental Research Infrastructures System - CUP B53C22002150006.

Disclosure of Interests. The authors have no competing interests to declare that are relevant to the content of this article.

References

1. Pereira, H.M., Martins, I.S., Rosa, I.M.D., Kim, H., Leadley, P., Popp, A., et al.: Global trends and scenarios for terrestrial biodiversity and ecosystem services from 1900 to 2050. Science **384**, 458–465 (2024). https://doi.org/10.1126/science.adn3441
2. Navarro, L.M., Fernandez, N., Guerra, C., Guralnick, R., Kissling, W.D., Londoño, M.C., et al.: Monitoring biodiversity change through effective global coordination. Curr. Opin. Environ. Sustain. **29**, 158–169 (2017). https://doi.org/10.1016/j.cosust.2018.02.005
3. Kühl, H.S., Bowler, D.E., Bösch, L., Bruelheide, H., Dauber, J., Eichenberg, D., et al.: Effective biodiversity monitoring needs a culture of integration. One Earth **3**(4), 462–474 (2020). https://doi.org/10.1016/j.oneear.2020.09.010
4. Chen, X., Jagerhorn, M.: Implementing FAIR Workflows along the research lifecycle. Procedia Comput. Sci. **211**, 83–92 (2022). https://doi.org/10.1016/j.procs.2022.10.179
5. Güntsch, A., Overmann, J., Ebert, B., Bonn, A., Le Bras, Y., Engel, T., et al.: National biodiversity data infrastructures: ten essential functions for science, policy, and practice. Bioscience **75**(2), 139–151 (2025). https://doi.org/10.1093/biosci/biae109
6. Global Biodiversity Information Facility, GBIF Homepage, https://www.gbif.org/, Accessed 11 June 2025
7. Sweet, F. S. T., Apfelbeck, B., Hanusch, M., Garland Monteagudo, C., Weisser, W. W.: Data from public and governmental databases show that a large proportion of the regional animal species pool occur in cities in Germany. Journal of Urban Ecology, **8**(1), juac002 (2022), https://doi.org/10.1093/jue/juac002

8. Reichman, O. J., Jones, M. B., Schildhauer, M. P.: Challenges and opportunities of open data in ecology. Science, 331(6018), 703–705 (2011). https://escholarship.org/uc/item/7627s45z
9. McCleery, R., Guralnick, R., Beatty, M., Belitz, M., Campbell, C.J., Idec, J., et al.: Uniting experiments and big data to advance ecology and conservation. Trends Ecol. Evol. 38(10), 970–979 (2023). https://www.sciencedirect.com/science/article/pii/S0169534723001337
10. Di Muri, C., Pulieri, M., Raho, D., Muresan, A.N., Tarallo, A., Titocci, J., et al.: Assessing semantic interoperability in environmental sciences: variety of approaches and semantic artefacts. Sci. Data 11, 1055 (2024). https://doi.org/10.1038/s41597-024-03669-3
11. Wilkinson, M., Dumontier, M., Aalbersberg, I., Appleton, G., Axton, M., Baak, A., et al.: The FAIR Guiding Principles for scientific data management and stewardship. Sci. Data 3, 160018 (2016). https://doi.org/10.1038/sdata.2016.18
12. Peterson, J.D., Kasperowski, D., van der Wal, R.: Bringing together species observations: a case story of Sweden's biodiversity informatics infrastructures. Minerva 61, 265–289 (2023). https://doi.org/10.1007/s11024-023-09491-2
13. Schulman, L., Lahti, K., Piirainen, E., Heikkinen, M., Raitio, O., Juslén, A.: The Finnish biodiversity information facility as a best-practice model for biodiversity data infrastructures. Sci. Data 8, 137 (2021). https://doi.org/10.1038/s41597-021-00919-6
14. LifeWatch Italy Homepage, https://www.lifewatchitaly.eu/, Accessed 11 Jun 2025
15. LifeWatch ERIC Homepage, https://www.lifewatch.eu/, Accessed 11 Jun 2025
16. Hognogi, G.G., Meltzer, M., Alexandrescu, F., Stefanescu, L.: The role of citizen science mobile apps in facilitating a contemporary digital agora. Hum. Soc. Sci. Commun. 10, 863 (2023). https://doi.org/10.1057/s41599-023-02358-7
17. LifeWatch Italy citizen science homepage, https://citizenscience.lifewatchitaly.eu/, Accessed 11 Jun 2025
18. BioAcoustic homepage, https://bioacoustics.lifewatchitaly.eu/, Accessed 11 Jun 2025
19. Cheung, S.Y., Leung, Y.F., Larson, L.R.: Citizen science as a tool for enhancing recreation research in protected areas: applications and opportunities. J. Environ. Manage. 305, 114353 (2022). https://doi.org/10.1016/j.jenvman.2021.114353
20. Stephenson, P.J.: Technological advances in biodiversity monitoring: applicability, opportunities and challenges. Curr. Opin. Environ. Sustain. 45, 36–41 (2020). https://doi.org/10.1016/j.cosust.2020.08.005
21. Znidersic, E., Towsey, M., Roy, W.K., Darling, S.E., Truskinger, A., Roe, P., et al.: Using visualization and machine learning methods to monitor low detectability species - the least bittern as a case study. Eco. Inform. 55, 101014 (2020). https://doi.org/10.1016/j.ecoinf.2019.101014
22. Sinaci, A.A., Núñez-Benjumea, F.J., Gencturk, M., Jauer, M.L., Deserno, T., Chronaki, C., et al.: From raw data to FAIR data: the FAIRification workflow for health research. Methods Inf. Med. b59(S01), e21–e32 (2020). https://doi.org/10.1055/s-0040-1713684
23. LifeWatch Italy DataPortal. https://data.lifewatchitaly.eu/, Accessed 11 Jun 2025
24. Jones, M.B., O'Brien, M., Mecum, B., Boettiger, C., Schildhauer, M., Maier, M., et al.: Ecological metadata language version 2.2.0. KNB data repository. https://doi.org/10.5063/F11834T2
25. Darwin core maintenance group. List of Darwin core terms. biodiversity information standards (TDWG) (2021). http://rs.tdwg.org/dwc/doc/list/, Accessed 11 Jun 2025
26. EcoPortal, https://ecoportal.lifewatch.eu/, Accessed 11 Jun 2025
27. EnvThes, https://doi.org/10.48373/0PWD-C575, Accessed 23 Jul 2025
28. Catalogue of life homepage, https://www.catalogueoflife.org/, Accessed 11 Jul 2025
29. World register of marine species homepage, https://www.marinespecies.org/, Accessed 11 Jun 2025
30. World flora online, https://www.worldfloraonline.org/, Accessed 11 Jun 2025

31. Chong, S.S., Schildhauer, M., O'Brien, M., Mecum, B., Jones, M.B.: Enhancing the FAIRness of arctic research data through semantic annotation. Data Sci. J. **23**(1), 2 (2024). https://doi.org/10.5334/dsj-2024-002
32. Kennedy, J. B., Kukla, R., Paterson, T.: Scientific names are ambiguous as identifiers for biological taxa: their context and definition are required for accurate data integration. In: Ludäscher, B., Raschid, L. (eds) Data Integration in the Life Sciences. DILS 2005. Lecture Notes in Computer Science (2005), vol 3615. Springer, Berlin, Heidelberg. https://doi.org/10.1007/11530084_8
33. Grenié, M., Berti, E., Carvajal-Quintero, J., Dädlow, G.M., Sagouis, A., Winter, M.: Harmonizing taxon names in biodiversity data: a review of tools, databases and best practices. Methods Ecol. Evol. **14**, 12–25 (2005). https://doi.org/10.1111/2041-210X.13802
34. Costello, M. J.: Taxonomy as the key to life. Megataxa, **001**(2), 105–113 (2020). https://doi.org/10.11646/megataxa.1.2.1
35. Garnett, S.T., Christidis, L., Conix, S., Costello, M.J., Zachos, F.E., Bánki, O.S., et al.: Principles for creating a single authoritative list of the world's species. PLoS Biol. **18**(7), e3000736 (2020). https://doi.org/10.1371/journal.pbio.3000736
36. König, C., Weigelt, P., Schrader, J., Taylor, A., Kattge, J., Kreft, H.: Biodiversity data integration - the significance of data resolution and domain. PLoS Biol. **17**(3), e3000183 (2019). https://doi.org/10.1371/journal.pbio.3000183
37. Bologna, M.A., Zapparoli, M., Olivero, M., Minelli, A., Bonato, L., Cianferoni, F.: Italian fauna checklist. LifeWatch Italy Data Portal (2021). https://data.lifewatchitaly.eu/handle/123456789/129792
38. Portal to the Flora of Italy, http://dryades.units.it/floritaly, Accessed 11 Jun 2025
39. Martellos, S., Conti, M., Nimis, P.L.: Aggregation of Italian lichen data in ITALIC 7.0. J. Fungi **9**(5), 556 (2023). https://doi.org/10.3390/jof9050556
40. LifeWatch Italy Italian taxonomic backbone https://taxonomicbackbone.lifewatchitaly.eu/, Accessed 11 Jun 2025
41. Psilota atra (Fallen, 1817), https://taxonomicbackbone.lifewatchitaly.eu/taxon/206661, Accessed 23 Jul 2025
42. Todman, L.C., Bush, A., Hood, A.S.: 'Small data' for big insights in ecology. Trends Ecol. Evol. **38**(7), 615–622 (2023). https://doi.org/10.1016/j.tree.2023.01.015
43. Falster, D., Gallagher, R., Wenk, E.H., Wright, I.J., Indiarto, D., Andrew, S.C., et al.: AusTraits, a curated plant trait database for the Australian flora. Sci. Data **8**, 254 (2021). https://doi.org/10.1038/s41597-021-01006-6
44. Le Guillarme, N., Hedde, M., Potapov, A.M., Martínez-Muñoz, C.A., Berg, M.P., Briones, M.J., et al.: The soil food web ontology: aligning trophic groups, processes, resources, and dietary traits to support food-web research. Eco. Inform. **78**, 102360 (2023). https://doi.org/10.1016/j.ecoinf.2023.102360
45. Semantic sensor network ontology, SOSA, https://www.w3.org/TR/2017/REC-vocab-ssn-20171019/, Accessed 11 Jun 2025
46. PROV-O: The PROV ontology, http://www.w3.org/TR/prov-o/, Accessed 11 Jun 2025
47. Data Catalog Vocabulary (DCAT) - Version 3, https://www.w3.org/TR/vocab-dcat-3/, Accessed 11 Jun 2025
48. Traits Thesaurus (TRAITS_THES), https://doi.org/10.48373/sa6p-ta25, Accessed 23 Jul 2025
49. LifeWatch Italy semantic platform, https://semantics.lifewatchitaly.eu/, Accessed 11 Jun 2025
50. LifeWatch Italy metadata catalogue, https://metadatacatalogue.lifewatchitaly.eu/, Accessed 11 Jun 2025
51. F-UJI automated FAIR data assessment tool, https://www.f-uji.net, Accessed 11 Jun 2025
52. Huber, R.: FAIRsFAIR data object assessment metrics (0.8). Zenodo (2025). https://doi.org/10.5281/zenodo.15045911

53. Farley, S.S., Dawson, A., Goring, S.J., Williams, J.W.: Situating ecology as a big-data science: current advances, challenges, and solutions. BioScience **68**(8), 563–576 (2018). https://www.jstor.org/stable/90023897
54. Tanhua, T., Pouliquen, S., Hausman, J., O'brien, K., Bricher, P., De Bruin, T., et al.: Ocean FAIR data services. Front. Mar. Sci. **6**, 440 (2019). https://doi.org/10.3389/fmars.2019.00440
55. LifeWatch Italy DataLabs. https://datalabs.lifewatchitaly.eu/, Accessed 11 Jun 2025
56. Kluyver, T., Ragan-Kelley, B., Pérez, F., Granger, B., Bussonnier, M., Frederic, J., et al.: Jupyter notebooks – a publishing format for reproducible computational workflows. In: F. Loizides & B. Schmidt (eds.), Positioning and Power in Academic Publishing: Players, Agents and Agendas, pp. 87–90. IOS Press (2016)
57. Kambouris, S., Wilkinson, D.P., Smith, E.T., Fidler, F.: Computationally reproducing results from meta-analyses in ecology and evolutionary biology using shared code and data. PLoS ONE **19**(3), e0300333 (2024). https://doi.org/10.1371/journal.pone.0300333
58. Zhao, Z., Koulouzis, S., Bianchi, R, Farshidi, S., Shi, Z., Xin, R. et al.: Notebook-as-a-VRE (NaaVRE): from private notebooks to a collaborative cloud virtual research environment. Softw. Pract. Exp. **52**(9), 1947–1966 (2022). https://doi.org/10.1002/spe.3098
59. LifeWatch Italy Training Platform. https://training.lifewatchitaly.eu/, Accessed 11 Jun 2025
60. LifeWatch Italy Help-Desk, https://helpdesk.lifewatchitaly.eu/, Accessed 11 Jun 2025
61. Hughes, L.D., Tsueng, G., Di Giovanna, J., Horvath, T.D., Rasmussen, L.V., Savidge, T.C., et al.: Addressing barriers in FAIR data practices for biomedical data. Sci. Data **98**, 10–11 (2023). https://doi.org/10.1038/s41597-023-01969-8

Flexible Metadata Harvesting for Ecology Using Large Language Models

Zehao Lu[1], Thijs L. van der Plas[1]($\boxtimes$), Parinaz Rashidi[2],
W Daniel Kissling[2], and Ioannis N. Athanasiadis[1]

[1] Wageningen University and Research, 6708 Wageningen, PB, The Netherlands
{zehao.lu,thijs.vanderplas,ioannis.athanasiadis}@wur.nl
[2] University of Amsterdam, 1090 Amsterdam, GE, The Netherlands

Abstract. Large, open datasets can accelerate ecological research, particularly by enabling researchers to develop new insights by reusing datasets from multiple sources. However, to find the most suitable datasets to combine and integrate, researchers must navigate diverse ecological and environmental data provider platforms with varying metadata availability and standards. To overcome this obstacle, we have developed a large language model (LLM)-based metadata harvester that flexibly extracts metadata from any dataset's landing page, and converts these to a user-defined, unified format using existing metadata standards. We validate that our tool is able to extract both structured and unstructured metadata with equal accuracy, aided by our LLM post-processing protocol. Furthermore, we utilise LLMs to identify links between datasets, both by calculating embedding similarity and by unifying the formats of extracted metadata to enable rule-based processing. Our tool, which flexibly links the metadata of different datasets, can therefore be used for ontology creation or graph-based queries, for example, to find relevant ecological and environmental datasets in a virtual research environment.

Keywords: Metadata · Ecological data · FAIR data · Large language models (LLM)

1 Introduction

Ecological and environmental sciences are vital to addressing the global biodiversity crisis, for example, by monitoring species diversity and ecosystem health, and by quantifying the effects of climate change, human interventions and conservation action [11,12,14]. Increasingly, the scientific community has advocated that these challenges can only be met by integrating different data streams, including Earth observation, citizen science records, sensor networks, long-term ecological monitoring surveys and environmental DNA [3,4,8,13,18,22,26]. Essential to this mission are best practices in the large-scale collection, sharing and re-analysis of environmental and ecological data [4,8,13].

Z. Lu and T. L. van der Plas—These authors contributed equally.

© The Author(s) 2026
W.-T. Balke et al. (Eds.): TPDL 2025, CCIS 2694, pp. 338–352, 2026.
https://doi.org/10.1007/978-3-032-06136-2_32

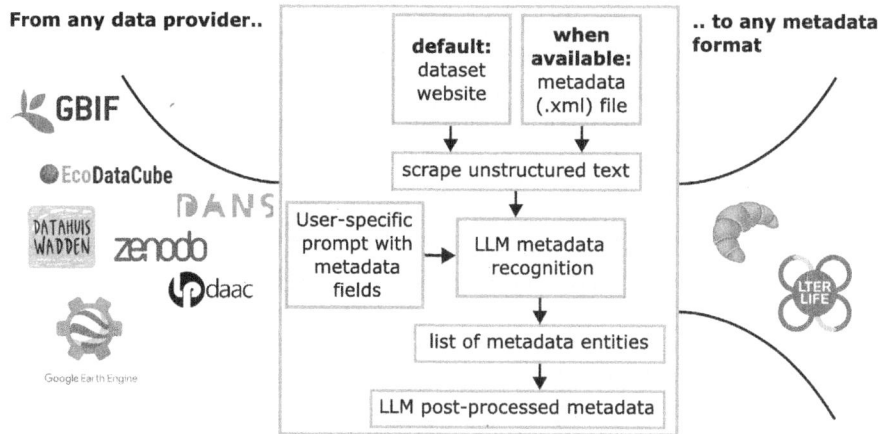

Fig. 1. Diagram of our LLM-based metadata harvester that retrieves and converts metadata from any data provider to any metadata format.

For example, FAIR (findable, accessible, interoperable and reproducible) data facilitate efficient re-analysis [30], stored either by individual researchers at data archival providers such as GBIF (Global Biodiversity Information Facility) and Zenodo, or at organisational repositories such as Google Earth Engine.

Metadata that describe the key data properties are critical to (using) FAIR data [13,16,30]. With metadata, researchers can determine the relevance of a dataset for their research purposes prior to analysing it, enabling them to efficiently search across a large set of datasets. However, while data providers often enable users to access or search across metadata from their catalogue, there is no unified way of retrieving and querying metadata across different data providers, hindered by differences in metadata availability and formatting (but note that catalogues of multiple data repositories exist [3,19]). For example, interpreting metadata remains a key challenge for reusing FAIR data [21]. Such obstacles are especially challenging in ecology, where a wide range of data can be of relevance, distributed across different data repositories, involving several scientific disciplines [3,16]. While, in contrast, searching for scientific articles across different journals has become an anchor point of modern scientific research, searching for scientific datasets remains a challenge for most researchers [6].

Metadata standards (or schemas) that unify metadata formats of different datasets (and data providers) are therefore crucial. However, different metadata standards are not always intercompatible due to differences in which metadata fields are used and how they are formatted, even if they are considered FAIR [16]. Importantly, there is no one-size-fits-all solution: data providers and researchers from different communities may need to prioritise different metadata (*i.e.* different fields or different standards), just as academic journals vary in citation style and lay-out. Instead, a flexible solution is required that can retrieve metadata from any data provider and convert these to any user-defined metadata format.

Large language models (LLMs) have been suggested to improve the accessibility of ecological datasets [23]. Indeed, LLMs have been used successfully to annotate textual, descriptive metadata such as title, description, keywords and domain [9,29,31], and to convert text input into ontologies [2]. Yet, to maximise usability, an integrated, open-source LLM tool is needed that harvests metadata directly from dataset source web pages, including exact (numeric) metadata such as spatial resolution or license information, and returns these in a unified format.

Here, we introduce an LLM-based metadata harvester that scrapes metadata from any data provider and converts these to a user-specified format (Fig. 1). We evaluate our tool on an annotated set of datasets across seven providers and two output formats, and show that our LLM metadata harvester successfully retrieves both structured and unstructured metadata. Finally, we demonstrate how these retrieved metadata can be used to construct a metadata knowledge base that establishes links between datasets across providers. With this, our tool enables researchers to create user-specific knowledge bases of datasets that are designed for efficient data discovery, thereby facilitating 'big data' ecology [4,26].

2 Methods

Named Entity Recognition. We have developed an LLM-based approach that, when given an URL, automatically scrapes all metadata from any machine-readable text format, and converts these to any metadata format using an LLM that performs named entity recognition (Fig. 1). First, all text is scraped from a dataset landing page, and if available, from structured metadata files (such as .xml files). Next, the user specifies what metadata *entity types* (*i.e.*, fields that specify metadata types such as *Title, Publication date*, etc.) should be retrieved, including their definitions. This is integrated into a prompt (adapted from [7]) that asks the LLM to retrieve all *entities* of these entity types. Because LLMs sometimes deviate from predefined schemas when generating structured outputs [28], we use a second LLM call to post-process the extracted metadata entities and improve the formatting of the final output. Here, we task the LLM to constrain the output such that for each dataset, only 1 entity per entity type is retrieved. While this is generally applicable for most metadata entities (*e.g.*, there can only be a single 'publication date'), this forces other entity types to return an enumeration of (sub-)entities in a single text string (*e.g.*, multiple authors are returned as as single entity).

Metadata Field Descriptions. Users specify which metadata the LLM should extract, by inserting the metadata fields (entity types) and definitions (entity descriptions, *e.g.*, using existing metadata standards and vocabularies) in the prompt. To demonstrate this, we considered two different metadata standards: the LTER-LIFE[1] metadata format and Croissant, which are used by the ecology

---

[1] LTER-LIFE is a research infrastructure project to develop Digital Twins of ecosystems (https://lter-life.nl/en). As part of this, a metadata standard (currently version 0.0.1) has been developed, which we will refer to here as 'LTER-LIFE'.

Table 1. Metadata fields considered for harvesting, using two different formats (LTER-LIFE and Croissant) with partial overlap. Notably, even where metadata fields overlap, their definitions (*e.g.* standards and vocabularies) still differ: Croissant uses Croissant definitions, while LTER-LIFE definitions used here originate from DCAT-AP or ISO 19115, see table.

Group	Metadata field	Croissant?	LTER-LIFE?
Metadata on metadata	Metadata date	–	Yes - ISO 19115
	Metadata language	Yes - Croissant	Yes - ISO 19115
	Responsible organization	–	Yes - ISO 19115
Identification	Title	Yes - Croissant	Yes - DCAT-AP
	Description	Yes - Croissant	Yes - DCAT-AP
	Unique Identifier	–	Yes - DCAT-AP
	Resource type	–	Yes - DCAT-AP
	Keywords	Yes - Croissant	Yes - DCAT-AP
Data contact information	Data creator	Yes - Croissant	Yes - DCAT-AP
	Data contact point	–	Yes - DCAT-AP
	Data publisher	Yes - Croissant	Yes - DCAT-AP
Spatial properties	Spatial coverage	–	Yes - DCAT-AP
	Spatial resolution	–	Yes - DCAT-AP
	Spatial reference system	–	Yes - ISO 19115
Temporal properties	Temporal coverage	–	Yes - DCAT-AP
	Temporal resolution	–	Yes - DCAT-AP
Intellectual rights	License	Yes - Croissant	Yes - DCAT-AP
	Access rights	–	Yes - DCAT-AP
Distribution	Distribution access URL	–	Yes - DCAT-AP
	Distribution format	–	Yes - DCAT-AP
	Distribution byte size	–	Yes - DCAT-AP
	Same as	Yes - Croissant	–
	Date published	Yes - Croissant	–
	Date last modified	Yes - Croissant	–

and machine learning research communities, respectively. Firstly, we used the LTER-LIFE metadata format, consisting of a community-developed minimum set of 21 metadata fields across 7 categories (see Table 1). LTER-LIFE metadata definitions make use of the Dutch ISO19115-based geography metadata profile[2] and the DCAT3 (Data Catalog Vocabulary version 3) standard vocabulary[3]. We translated Dutch definitions to English and manually supplemented entity descriptions where the standard definitions were insufficient. Secondly, Croissant

---

[2] https://geonovum.github.io/Metadata-ISO19115/.
[3] https://www.w3.org/TR/2024/REC-vocab-dcat-3-20240822/.

is a metadata format designed to make datasets 'machine learning ready' [1]. We used Croissant metadata definitions as listed under the 'Required' and 'Recommended' fields from 'Dataset-level Information'[4]. Croissant fields partially overlap with the LTER-LIFE metadata format (both require a title, license, etc.), but their metadata field definitions still differ.

Software Implementation. We used Python packages `BeautifulSoup` and `Playwright` to scrape website landing pages, and `BeautifulSoup` to parse .xml files. LLM calls and subsequent analysis and visualisation were performed in Python 3. We used and compared the OpenAI GPT-4 [20] and Google Gemini 2.5 Flash-05-20 [5] LLMs. We adapted our prompt from LightRAG [7], with the critical difference that we specify which entity types should be extracted (as defined by the desired metadata format), whereas the default LightRAG implementation extracts entities of any type. We calculated description embeddings using SBERT all-MiniLM-L6-v2 [24], which creates same-length embeddings regardless of the input text length, allowing us to compute the cosine similarity between pairs of embeddings. All code is available at https://github.com/LTER-LIFE/llm-metadata-harvester.

Evaluation Datasets. We evaluated our metadata harvester on 24 metadata fields, across 16 datasets from 7 data providers (see Tables 1,2). This set of datasets was selected to cover terrestrial and aquatic datasets, from both ecological and environmental domains, including *in situ* observations (*e.g.*, forest inventories, GBIF occurrence records) and Earth observation datasets (*e.g.*, from MODIS, Landsat, Sentinel-2). One dataset ('Ecotopenkaart 2016', from Datahuis Wadden) also provided a metadata (.xml) file. Metadata varied in completeness across datasets, and was written in English for most datasets, except for the three datasets from Datahuis Wadden that were largely written in Dutch. (LLMs were prompted to return metadata fields in English.) We created a ground-truth dataset by manually annotating all metadata fields of both the LTER-LIFE and Croissant metadata formats for all 16 datasets. We annotated 'N/A' when a metadata field was absent in the original source. In addition, we distinguished between unavailable metadata, present *structured* metadata and present *unstructured* metadata (Fig. 2). We considered metadata to be structured if it was clearly labelled as metadata (*e.g.*, a table with entry 'Spatial resolution: 30 m'), and to be unstructured if the information was only present in free-form text (*e.g.*, if the spatial resolution would only be mentioned in a description that said 'The data was aggregated yearly from 30-m bi-monthly Landsat data').

Evaluation Metrics. We distinguish between metadata fields that require a fuzzy match (*Description* and *Keywords*) and fields that require an exact semantic match (all other fields). Exact match fields enable us to use deterministic string-matching metrics, while fuzzy matches require LLM-based metrics. We use ROUGE-L F1 score, which compares string-to-string similarity, to test exact

---

[4] https://docs.mlcommons.org/croissant/docs/croissant-spec.html.

Table 2. Overview of datasets used in the evaluation, separated by seven (meta)data providers.

Name	Provider	URL	Abbreviation
Dutch forest reserves database and network	DANS	page	Dutch forest database
Ecotopenkaart 2016	Datahuis Wadden	page, xml	Ecotope map 2016
Ecotopenkaart 2017	Datahuis Wadden	page	Ecotope map 2017
Waddenbalans 2024	Datahuis Wadden	page	Wadden balance 2024
Actual probability distribution for Quercus robur	EcoDataCube	page	Oak distribution
Cloud-free reconstructed Landsat bimonthly NDVI	EcoDataCube	page	Landsat NDVI
Cloud-free reconstructed Landsat yearly blue band	EcoDataCube	page	Landsat blue
Cloud-free reconstructed Landsat yearly green band	EcoDataCube	page	Landsat green
Waterleidingduinen camera trap P1	GBIF	page	Camera trap P1
Waterleidingduinen camera trap P2	GBIF	page	Camera trap P2
Waterleidingduinen camera trap P3	GBIF	page	Camera trap P3
eBird observation dataset	GBIF	page	eBird
Harmonized Landsat Sentinel-2	Google Earth Engine	page	HLS
MODIS Terra MOD09A1 Version 6.1	LP DAAC	page	MODIS
Downscaled LUH2 land use scenarios for Belgium	Zenodo	page	LUH2 Belgium
Waterleidingduinen camera trap P1-3	Zenodo	page	Camera trap P1-3

matches [15], and Faithfulness and Response Relevancy to test fuzzy matches. Faithfulness and Response Relevancy were originally designed for evaluating retrieval augmented generation (RAG) systems, which is conceptually similar to retrieving metadata from dataset landing pages. We assessed Faithfulness (fraction of claims in the metadata field that are supported by the dataset landing page) and Response Relevancy (similarity between generated questions that would yield the metadata as answer and the question "What is the <FIELD> of this dataset?", where <FIELD> is 'description' or 'keywords') using Python package Ragas and the OpenAI GPT-3.5 Turbo LLM.

Statistics. All scores are indexed between 0 (no match) and 1 (perfect match). Unless denoted otherwise, scores are presented with error bars as mean ± standard error of the mean (SEM). We only evaluate post-processed results unless specifically mentioned otherwise. We use the likelihood-ratio test to test the effect of one variable while controlling for another. Specifically, we fit a mixed effects model using a fixed effect (variable) while controlling for a random effect (variable) and acquire the maximum log likelihood. We then obtain the maximum log likelihood of a second model using the random effect variable only, and test their log likelihood difference using the χ^2-distribution to quantify the effect of the fixed effect variable [17].

3 Results

3.1 Retrieving and Converting Metadata from Any Provider to Any Format

Our metadata harvester successfully retrieved metadata from all 7 data providers and converted these into 2 different metadata formats (independently), with varying accuracy across data providers (Fig. 3). Note that the two different metadata formats (LTER-LIFE and Croissant) extract different metadata fields (Table 1), which largely explains the differences between their accuracy levels. Metadata retrieval accuracy varies significantly across data providers ($p = 3 \cdot 10^{-6}$ for GPT-4, $p = 9 \cdot 10^{-5}$ for Gemini 2.5 Flash, two-way likelihood-ratio test controlling for the random effect of metadata field), which is caused by differences across the datasets they host (Table 2).

Our post-processing procedure - where a second LLM is prompted to adjust the extracted metadata if necessary to follow formatting guidelines - strongly

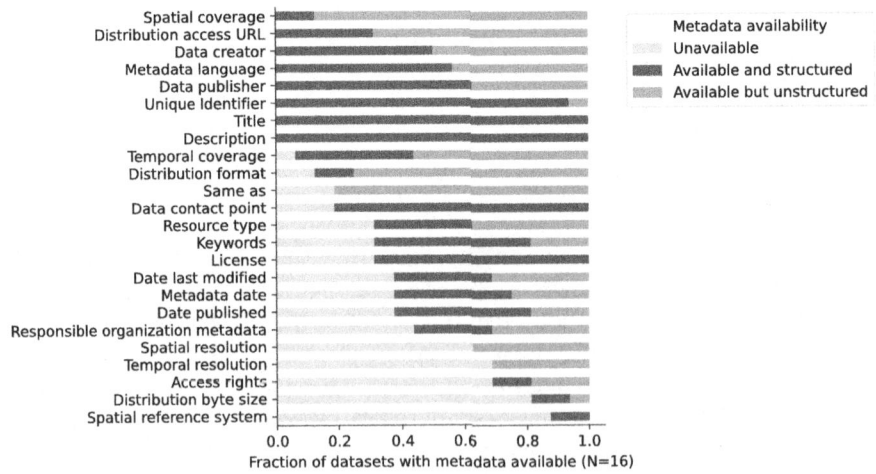

Fig. 2. Overview of the manually annotated metadata for $N = 16$ datasets (Table 1), which was either unavailable, available and structured, or available but unstructured.

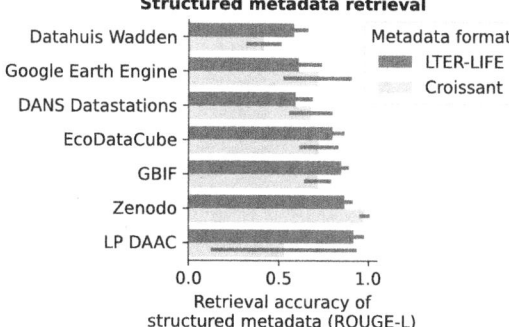

Fig. 3. Retrieval accuracy of post-processed, structured, present metadata per provider and metadata format (averaged across LLMs). Note that because the Croissant metadata format contains fewer fields, its uncertainty estimates are generally higher, especially for LP DAAC where N=2 for Croissant.

improves accuracy across all metadata fields (Fig. 4a, $p = 4 \cdot 10^{-62}$, two-way likelihood-ratio test controlling for the random effect of metadata field). LLM choice had a smaller effect, with Gemini 2.5 Flash outperforming GPT-4 (Fig. 4b, $p = 7 \cdot 10^{-5}$, two-way likelihood-ratio test controlling for the random effect of metadata field). We observed that this difference occurred because GPT-4 occasionally failed to follow output instructions, changed metadata formatting, or failed to retrieve metadata. The two metadata formats that we considered, LTER-LIFE and Croissant, extract partially overlapping sets of metadata fields (Table 1). Where these overlap, performance is similar (Fig. 4c, $p = 0.91$, two-way likelihood-ratio test controlling for the random effect of all shared metadata fields), with (insignificant) variability caused by differences in metadata field definitions between the formats (that are used in the prompt).

3.2 Filling in the Blanks: Recognising Unstructured Metadata

The metadata harvester was able to recognise unstructured metadata with the same accuracy as structured metadata (Fig. 5, $p = 0.88$, two-way likelihood-ratio test controlling for the random effect of all shared metadata fields). Still, unstructured metadata scored lower on average for a number of metadata fields (Fig. 5), in particular; *Distribution access URL*, *Metadata date* and *Spatial coverage*. Unsurprisingly, these metadata fields are typically difficult to contextualise without structure: for example, while GBIF distribution access URLs are clearly structured by labelling them as "Endpoint: <URL>" in a metadata table (and as such, these are 'structured' and were all retrieved perfectly), Datahuis Wadden URLs are listed without standardised labels, which could include the data endpoint, related data, reports, online data viewers etc. (as such, these are 'unstructured' and scored 0.39 on average).

We further evaluated the fuzzy match accuracy of the *Description* and *Keywords* fields, using LLM metrics Faithfulness and Relevancy (Fig. 6). Keywords

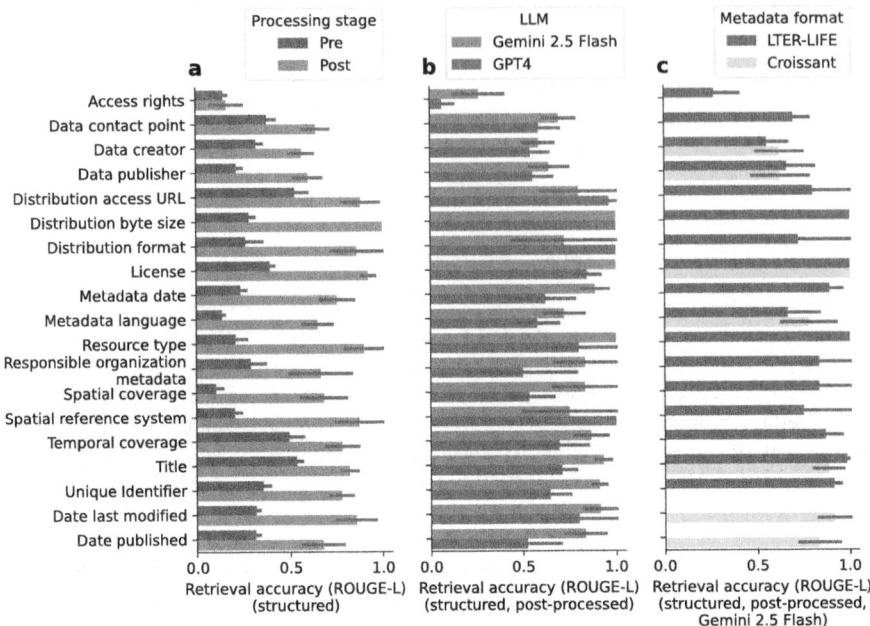

Fig. 4. Retrieval accuracy of present, structured metadata, split by processing stage (a), LLM (b) and metadata format (c).

can be generated (especially if originally absent) and descriptions can be summarised, which prevent evaluation using the deterministic ROUGE metric. We found that generally Faithfulness was very high, meaning that the metadata was accurately describing the datasets.

While retrieval accuracy does not differ significantly between structured and unstructured metadata, unstructured metadata is more often reported as 'not available' than structured metadata (Table 3). Importantly, this retrieval rate differs considerably between the two LLMs, which partly explains their difference in accuracy (Table 3, Fig. 4). In general, Gemini 2.5 Flash has a higher retrieval rate, including for unavailable metadata. We manually examined the 70 instances where Gemini 2.5 Flash 'retrieved' unavailable metadata, and found that these were generally sensible and none were totally unfounded (hallucinations). Examples include; access rights labelled as 'open access' based on open licenses, authors listed as contact points, (sensible) keywords generated where none were listed, non-specific answers (such as "Contact owner" as data contact point), or loosely inferred spatial and temporal resolutions (such as 'municipalities' or 'event-based'). Still, some of these answers were verifiably wrong when the contexts of different metadata were mixed (for example for dates), but most were ambiguous and difficult to score objectively.

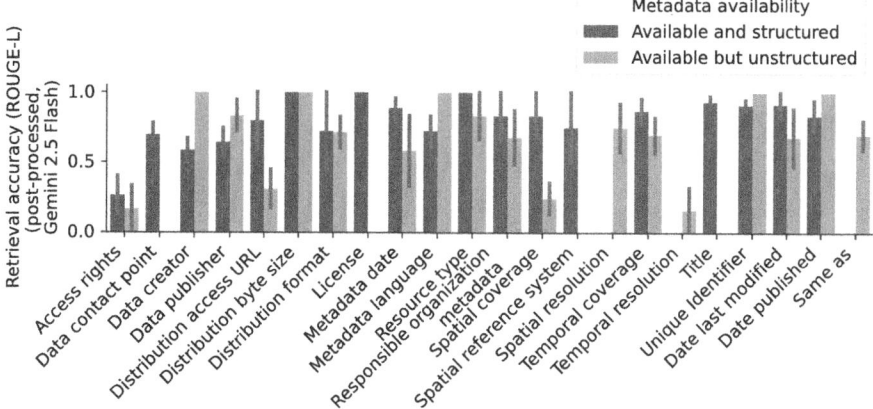

Fig. 5. Retrieval accuracy of structured vs unstructured metadata using Gemini 2.5 Flash. Please note that for some metadata fields all metadata (across datasets) was either structured or unstructured (see Fig. 2).

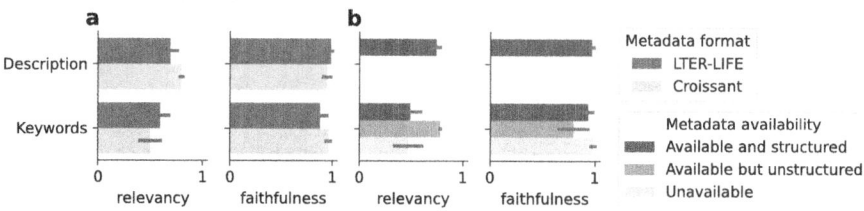

Fig. 6. LLM-evaluated accuracy of *Description* and *Keywords* metadata. Only post-processed, Gemini 2.5 Flash results for *Description* and *Keywords* metadata was evaluated.

3.3 Establishing Links Between Datasets

In this section we aim to demonstrate how the successfully retrieved metadata can be used to create a knowledge base that links datasets from different providers. We trial two methods; first, by directly computing similarity between datasets using LLM embeddings, and second, by using LLMs to convert metadata into a unified format, which can then be used for establishing rule-based knowledge graphs. To demonstrate the former, we converted all dataset descriptions into embeddings using the SBERT sentence embeddings [24], and then calculated pairwise cosine similarity between embeddings (Fig. 7a). This similarity matrix successfully identifies clusters of similar datasets – which we purposefully included in the evaluation dataset (Fig. 7a, Table 2). Next, we used an LLM to unify the formatting of extracted *Temporal coverage* metadata (Table 4), such that they could be processed using rule-based logic, and as an example, we calculated the temporal overlap between datasets (Fig. 7b). Together, these examples

Table 3. Fraction of metadata fields that were not identified by the LLMs. For available metadata, this includes structured fields that were not retrieved and unstructured fields that were not recognised (false negatives (FN)). For unavailable metadata, this includes fields that were reported as unavailable (true negatives (TN)). Post-processed results for both LTER-LIFE and Croissant formats were used.

Metadata availability	GPT4	Gemini 2.5 Flash
Available and structured metadata not retrieved (FN, %)	12.5	0.0
Available but unstructured metadata not recognised (FN, %)	21.2	6.2
Unavailable metadata reported as unavailable (TN, %)	56.8	34.7

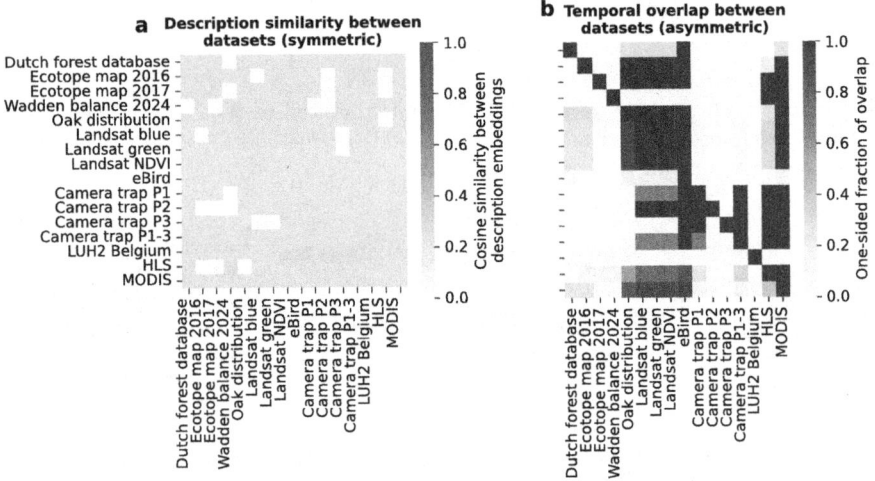

Fig. 7. a) Cosine similarity matrix of dataset description embeddings, computed with SBERT sentence embeddings [24]. b) Fraction of temporal overlap, computed one-sided using fraction$_{ij}$ = overlap$_{ij}$/duration$_i$ for data sets i (y-axis) and j (x-axis).

illustrate how the extracted metadata can be used to connect datasets for subsequent graph-based RAG and knowledge graph applications.

4 Discussion

Searching for datasets remains a major obstacle for researchers [6], and while the introduction of metadata standards has improved data FAIRness, differences in metadata standards and their variable uptake require an adaptive solution to efficiently search for datasets across providers [16]. Here, we have addressed this challenge by using LLMs to flexibly retrieve and convert both structured and unstructured metadata, which achieve equivalent retrieval accuracy (Fig. 5). We found that LLM post-processing was key to achieving good performance, followed by choice of LLM (Fig. 4). We then demonstrated how LLMs can link

Table 4. After the LLM metadata harvester retrieved the *Temporal coverage* of each dataset, another LLM (Gemini 2.5 Flash) call was made to convert these into a consistent format (YYYY-MM-DD-YYYY-MM-DD), where 'Present' was instructed to be converted to 2025-06-7.

Dataset	LLM-retrieved temporal coverage	LLM-formatted temporal coverage
Dutch forest database	1982-2005 (Measurements), 1983-2000 (Designation)	1982-01-01-2005-12-31
Ecotope map 2016	2010-12-08 to 2016-11-01	2010-12-08-2016-11-01
Ecotope map 2017	2017	2017-01-01-2017-12-31
Wadden balance 2024	2024	2024-01-01-2024-12-31
Oak distribution	2000-01-01 00:00:00 UTC – 2020-12-31 00:00:00 UTC	2000-01-01-2020-12-31
Landsat blue	2000-01-01 00:00:00 UTC – 2022-12-31 00:00:00 UTC	2000-01-01-2022-12-31
Landsat green	2000-01-01 00:00:00 UTC – 2022-12-31 00:00:00 UTC	2000-01-01-2022-12-31
Landsat NDVI	2000-01-01 00:00:00 UTC – 2022-12-31 00:00:00 UTC	2000-01-01-2022-12-31
eBird	January 1, 1800 - December 31, 2023	1800-01-01-2023-12-31
Camera trap P1	August 13th 2021 - August 2023	2021-08-13-2023-08-31
Camera trap P2	August 14, 2021 - September 24, 2021	2021-08-14-2021-09-24
Camera trap P3	March 1, 2023 - March 31, 2023	2023-03-01-2023-03-31
Camera trap P1-3	2021–2023	2021-01-01-2023-12-31
LUH2 Belgium	Present to 2050	2025-06-07-2050-12-31
HLS	2015-11-28T00:00:00Z–2025-05-31T23:38:19Z	2015-11-28-2025-05-31
MODIS	2000-02-18 to Present	2000-02-18-2025-06-07

datasets using either LLM-based embeddings or by unifying formats for rule-based processing (Fig. 7).

We manually annotated 24 metadata fields for 16 diverse datasets across 7 data providers to validate our approach. Most metadata fields could be evaluated using the deterministic natural language processing metric ROUGE [15], and additionally we used LLM metrics Faithfulness and Relevancy to evaluate the free-form fields *Description* and *Keywords*. When metadata field definitions do not include strict formatting rules, ROUGE can underestimate the accuracy if the correct information is formatted differently than the ground-truth annotations (as exemplified for *Temporal coverage*, Table 4). The most challenging LLM results to validate were instances where metadata was absent (Table 3), where results were often ambiguous. Ideally, LLM behaviour in these cases should follow user preference, specifying whether to report these metadata as missing or to provide a 'best guess' if possible.

While retrieving metadata solves part of the challenge of searching for datasets across providers, another challenge is linking datasets to create a knowledge base. To address this, we prompted an LLM to convert all *Temporal coverage* metadata into a unified format, which then enabled rule-based processing (such as calculating temporal overlap between datasets, Fig. 7b). Alternatively, we used embedding similarity to quantify connections between datasets for free-form text such as the *Description* field [9,27]. In our analysis, this successfully identified clusters of similar datasets that we purposefully included (Fig. 7a). This is an important feature, because this can enable researchers to find all datasets similar to one that matches their query, for example via a graph-based RAG system [7]. Here, we constrained the output to contain a single entity per metadata field. While we found that this generally improved performance, a future direction would be to let go of this constraint to enable more flexible links between datasets (*e.g.*, by splitting up data creators into separate entities).

LLMs are revolutionising science, and promise to have wide-ranging impacts in ecology [23,25]. We have developed an LLM application that aids ecological data discovery by flexibly harvesting and organising metadata. We selected a set of 16 diverse datasets to demonstrate and validate our tool, with which a larger, structured knowledge base of datasets can now be constructed. More annotated datasets, including from more languages, would help to validate a broader application of our tool in the future. With different research communities adopting varying metadata standards, we opted for a user-centric design where researchers can specify their desired set of metadata fields and definitions. Our tool hence yields metadata in a unified an standardised format, and a promising future direction is to use this to create formal ontologies or a (graph-based) RAG system to efficiently aid researchers with their data discovery queries [2,9]. For example, by specifying metadata fields using the DCAT definitions, extracted metadata could be converted to DCAT ontologies using LLMs or rule-based processing [2,10]. Further, our tool can be integrated into virtual research environments and ecological research infrastructures, for example for automating metadata generation, ensuring compliance to metadata standards or for data discovery. This would reduce the metadata annotation workload for researchers, while enhancing data FAIRness.

Acknowledgments. We acknowledge funding from the Dutch Research Council (NWO) Large-Scale Research Infrastructures (LSRI) programme for the LTER-LIFE (http://www.lter-life.nl) infrastructure (grant 184.036.014).

Author Contributions.. Conceptualization: all authors. Data curation: PR and TvdP. Formal analysis: ZL and TvdP. Funding acquisition: IA and WDK. Methodology: ZL and TvdP. Software: ZL and TvdP. Supervision: IA and WDK. Validation: ZL and TvdP. Visualization: TvdP. Writing – original draft: TvdP. Writing – review & editing: all authors.

Disclosure of Interests. The authors have no competing interests to declare that are relevant to the content of this article.

References

1. Akhtar, M., et al.: Croissant: a metadata format for ml-ready datasets. Adv. Neural. Inf. Process. Syst. **37**, 82133–82148 (2024)
2. Caufield, J.H., et al.: Structured prompt interrogation and recursive extraction of semantics (spires): a method for populating knowledge bases using zero-shot learning. Bioinformatics **40**(3), btae104 (2024)
3. Culina, A., Baglioni, M., Crowther, T.W., Visser, M.E., Woutersen-Windhouwer, S., Manghi, P.: Navigating the unfolding open data landscape in ecology and evolution. Nat. Ecol. Evol. **2**(3), 420–426 (2018)
4. Farley, S.S., Dawson, A., Goring, S.J., Williams, J.W.: Situating ecology as a big-data science: current advances, challenges, and solutions. Bioscience **68**(8), 563–576 (2018)
5. Google: Gemini 2.5 flash preview model card (2025). https://storage.googleapis.com/model-cards/documents/gemini-2.5-flash-preview.pdf. Accessed 12 Jun 2025
6. Gregory, K., Groth, P., Scharnhorst, A., Wyatt, S.: Lost or found? discovering data needed for research. Harvard Data Sci. Rev. **2**(2) (2020)
7. Guo, Z., Xia, L., Yu, Y., Ao, T., Huang, C.: LightRAG: simple and fast retrieval-augmented generation. arXiv preprint arXiv:2410.05779 (2025)
8. Hampton, S.E., et al.: Big data and the future of ecology. Front. Ecol. Environ. **11**(3), 156–162 (2013)
9. Hayashi, T., Sakaji, H., Dai, J., Goebel, R.: Metadata-based data exploration with retrieval-augmented generation for large language models. In: International Conference on Big Data, pp. 6574–6583. IEEE (2024)
10. Jackson, R.C., Balhoff, J.P., Douglass, E., Harris, N.L., Mungall, C.J., Overton, J.A.: Robot: a tool for automating ontology workflows. BMC Bioinform. **20**(1), 407 (2019)
11. Johnston, A., et al.: North American bird declines are greatest where species are most abundant. Science **388**(6746), 532–537 (2025)
12. Keck, F., Peller, T., Alther, R., Barouillet, C., Blackman, R., Capo, E., et al.: The global human impact on biodiversity. Nature **641**(8062), 395–400 (2025)
13. Kissling, W.D., Walls, R., Bowser, A., Jones, M.O., Kattge, J., Agosti, D., et al.: Towards global data products of essential biodiversity variables on species traits. Nat. Ecol. Evol. **2**(10), 1531–1540 (2018)
14. Langhammer, P.F., et al.: The positive impact of conservation action. Science **384**(6694), 453–458 (2024)
15. Lin, C.Y.: Rouge: a package for automatic evaluation of summaries. In: Text Summarization Branches Out, pp. 74–81 (2004)
16. Löffler, F., Wesp, V., König-Ries, B., Klan, F.: Dataset search in biodiversity research: do metadata in data repositories reflect scholarly information needs? PLoS ONE **16**(3), e0246099 (2021)
17. MacKenzie, D.I., Nichols, J.D., Royle, J.A., Pollock, K.H., Bailey, L.L., Hines, J.E.: Chapter 3 - fundamental principals of statistical inference. In: Occupancy Estimation and Modeling, 2nd edn., pp. 71–111. Academic Press, Boston (2018)
18. Nathan, R., et al.: Big-data approaches lead to an increased understanding of the ecology of animal movement. Science **375**(6582), eabg1780 (2022)

19. Noy, N., Burgess, M., Brickley, D.: Google dataset search: Building a search engine for datasets in an open web ecosystem. In: Proceedings of the 2019 World Wide Web Conference, pp. 1365–1375 (2019)
20. OpenAI: GPT-4 technical report. arXiv preprint arXiv:2303.08774 (2023)
21. Papoutsoglou, E.A., Athanasiadis, I.N., Visser, R.G.F., Finkers, R.: The benefits and struggles of fair data: the case of reusing plant phenotyping data. Sci. Data **10**(1), 457 (2023)
22. Van der Plas, T.L., Alexander, D.G., Pocock, M.J.: Monitoring protected areas by integrating machine learning, remote sensing and citizen science. Ecol. Solut. Eviden. **6**(2), e70040 (2025)
23. Rafiq, K., Beery, S., Palmer, M.S., Harchaoui, Z., Abrahms, B.: Generative AI as a tool to accelerate the field of ecology. Nature Ecol. Evol. **9**, 378–385 (2025)
24. Reimers, N., Gurevych, I.: Sentence-Bert: sentence embeddings using SIAMESE Bert-networks. In: Proceedings of the 2019 Conference on Empirical Methods in Natural Language Processing. Association for Computational Linguistics (2019)
25. Reynolds, S.A., et al.: The potential for AI to revolutionize conservation: a horizon scan. Trends Ecol. Evol. **40**(2), 191–207 (2025)
26. Runting, R.K., Phinn, S., Xie, Z., Venter, O., Watson, J.E.: Opportunities for big data in conservation and sustainability. Nat. Commun. **11**(1), 2003 (2020)
27. Sundaram, S.S., Musen, M.A.: Making metadata more fair using large language models. arXiv preprint arXiv:2307.13085 (2023)
28. Wang, D.Y.B., Shen, Z., Mishra, S.S., Xu, Z., Teng, Y., Ding, H.: Slot: structuring the output of large language models. arXiv preprint arXiv:2505.04016 (2025)
29. Watanabe, Y., Ito, K., Matsubara, S.: Capabilities and challenges of LLMs in metadata extraction from scholarly papers. In: International Conference on Asian Digital Libraries, pp. 280–287. Springer (2025)
30. Wilkinson, M.D., et al.: The fair guiding principles for scientific data management and stewardship. Sci. Data **3**(1), 1–9 (2016)
31. Zhang, S., Wu, M., Zhang, X.: Utilising a large language model to annotate subject metadata: a case study in an Australian national research data catalogue. arXiv preprint arXiv:2310.11318 (2023)

Open Access This chapter is licensed under the terms of the Creative Commons Attribution 4.0 International License (http://creativecommons.org/licenses/by/4.0/), which permits use, sharing, adaptation, distribution and reproduction in any medium or format, as long as you give appropriate credit to the original author(s) and the source, provide a link to the Creative Commons license and indicate if changes were made.

The images or other third party material in this chapter are included in the chapter's Creative Commons license, unless indicated otherwise in a credit line to the material. If material is not included in the chapter's Creative Commons license and your intended use is not permitted by statutory regulation or exceeds the permitted use, you will need to obtain permission directly from the copyright holder.

Ecolink: Towards a Knowledge Graph Schema for Complex Environmental Systems

Tim Alamenciak[1](✉)[iD], Carlos Alberto Arnillas[2][iD], Harry Caufield[3][iD], Katherine Compton[4][iD], Kian Drew[5][iD], Robert Frühstückl[6][iD], Tina Heger[7][iD], Birgitta König-Ries[8][iD], Chris Mungall[3][iD], Sierra Moxon[3][iD], Justin Reese[3][iD], Jordan Tardif[9], and Lars Vogt[10][iD]

[1] Carleton University, Ottawa, ON K1S 5B6, Canada
TimAlamenciak@cunet.carleton.ca
[2] Department of Physical and Environmental Sciences, University of Toronto at Scarborough, Toronto, ON M1C 1A4, Canada
[3] Division of Environmental Genomics and Systems Biology, Lawrence Berkeley National Laboratory, Berkeley, CA 94720, USA
[4] H. G. Thode Library of Science and Engineering, McMaster University, Hamilton, ON L8S 4L8, Canada
[5] School of Environment, Resources and Sustainability, University of Waterloo, Waterloo, ON N2L 3G1, Canada
[6] Johannes Kepler University Linz, Linz, Austria
[7] Leibniz Institute of Freshwater Ecology and Inland Fisheries (IGB), Berlin, Germany
[8] Faculty of Mathematics and Computer Science, University of Jena, Jena, Germany
[9] University of Waterloo, Waterloo, ON N2L 3G1, Canada
[10] TIB Leibniz Information Centre for Science and Technology University Library, Hannover, Germany
http://timalamenciak.github.io

Abstract. Research findings in ecology have the potential to drive evidence-based actions that could reverse biodiversity decline, inspire nature-based solutions to climate change and enhance restoration of severely degraded waters and lands. However, publishing findings in peer-reviewed papers alone is not sufficient to turn ecological research into action, as evidenced by the burgeoning field of translational ecology. Scholarly literature remains inaccessible to many conservation and restoration practitioners. While the open access publishing movement has increased the availability of research, the knowledge is still poorly indexed and unstructured, leading to inadequate findability.

We present a solution to these challenges in the form of the Ecolink Model (ELM) – an open-source schema for creating knowledge graphs that describe environmental variables, ecological processes and the relationships between them. Drawing on core concepts from ecological modeling and advances in biomedical knowledge synthesis, we outline a model written in LinkML – a domain-agnostic data modeling language – that captures the relationships at the heart of complex systems, thereby providing a structure for knowledge graphs. ELM establishes a consistent and reusable format that enables the discovery of new connections and presents knowledge in an easily searchable, intuitive way. Knowledge graphs that are constructed using ELM have the potential to enable restoration and conservation practitioners to easily access relevant research findings, to unveil new insights using graph data science techniques and drive an AI interface to provide plain-language access to ecological knowledge as described in the graph.

Keywords: ecology · restoration ecology · conservation · knowledge graph · knowledge representation · semantic modeling

1 Introduction

Ecological research can contribute valuable knowledge to restoration ecology and conservation practitioners who are working at the frontline of global ecosystem collapse, but the research is often buried in journals or scattered across multiple, inaccessible sources. Scientific data and knowledge should be findable, accessible, interoperable, and reusable (FAIR) [35], but ecological research is unstructured and poorly indexed, hampering findability and its usefulness. As a result, knowledge synthesis in restoration and conservation ecology is a resource-intensive undertaking.

A graph representation of scientific findings in ecology that utilizes ontologies and semantic data schemata has the potential to facilitate data discovery, enable novel theoretical insights through connections between nodes and enable the application of artificial intelligence to ecology broadly. Findings in ecology emerge from the study of complex systems in which heterogeneity is a core characteristic [1,10]. This heterogeneity frustrates syntheses as the expressed knowledge can be difficult to compare across studies. While some tools exist for documenting scientific findings in the Resource Description Framework (RDF), including nanopublications [9] and the super pattern ontology [3], a schema specific to ecology does not yet exist. In this paper we outline Ecolink Model (ELM) - a schema for describing the findings of ecological research. This schema provides a structure to graph databases that seek to describe the relationships between environmental variables and processes, providing insights about complex environmental systems.

ELM applies existing best practices in biological data to ecology, including the use of ontologies (i.e. machine-interpretable knowledge bases of terms, links between them and definitions), structured templates and semantic data schemata (i.e. specifications for the structure of datasets) [8]. These practices are implemented in biology through the Biolink Model - an open-source schema that formalizes the associations between types of biological entities (e.g. genes and diseases; phenotypes and diseases; etc.) [34]. The Biolink Model characterizes relationships between entities in a nested structure. The Biolink Model emerged from an interoperability challenge in biomedicine: many separate labs were producing knowledge graphs, but there was no central structure allowing them to be combined, potentially missing out on insights from synthesis [34]. Much like in ecology, the research findings and data on which they were based were heterogeneous, frustrating synthesis. The Biolink Model has allowed researchers to produce multiple knowledge graphs with diverse focuses such as the synthesis of Covid-19 research [27] and phenotype-genotype relationships to support precision medicine and disease modeling [24]. The model has also led to the creation of a central hub for the construction and use of such knowledge graphs [6].

ELM applies the association form of the Biolink Model to the relationships among environmental variables and environmental processes. By building on existing technologies, we are able to integrate ELM with a software stack that includes a flexible knowledge graph depiction format[1], ontology-driven text extraction[2], and programmatic access to the schema along with validation using LinkML [23][3]. ELM taps into a network of scientists, practitioners and data curators already using the Biolink Model software stack, creating interdisciplinary linkages that will help broadly advance knowledge representation.

ELM can be used to specify graph data models, which allow for the representation of knowledge and empirical data using triples – subject, predicate, object [30]. ELM is most suited for a labeled property graph-style database (e.g. Neo4j). ELM is also paired with its own project ontology, Ecolink Model Ontology (ELMO), which imports terms from well-developed domain ontologies like the environment ontology (ENVO), an ontological representation of NCBI's taxon database (NCBITaxon) and the relation ontology (RO). A significant portion of the work of constructing ELM has involved updating ontologies that may be used to describe ecological processes, such as adding ecosystem management processes to ENVO, as well as gathering terminology for environmental variables and incorporating the IUCN's ecosystem functional group typology into ENVO [16]. While the primary subject of this paper is ELM itself, we will briefly discuss ELMO as well.

1.1 Use-Cases

The quality of a schema is determined by how effectively it can meet the needs of its users. ELM is primarily a tool for modeling findings – it does not attempt to model reality, but rather the findings as depicted in journal articles. The literature we are aiming to capture using the ELM schema focuses on observational or experimental studies in real ecosystems, or on greenhouse studies in which some ecosystem condition is simulated. While ELM can be applied broadly in ecology, to illustrate its usefulness we focus on restoration ecology, for which we describe three possible use-cases:

1. **ELM as building blocks for a knowledge organization system.** ELM and the ontologies it uses can enable restoration practitioners and researchers

---

[1] https://github.com/biolink/kgx.
[2] https://github.com/monarch-initiative/ontogpt.
[3] https://github.com/linkml/linkml.

to easily search for findings in similar contexts to their own that are relevant to taxa, techniques and processes they are interested in.
2. **ELM as graph data schema.** ELM enables the use of graph data science techniques to discover new linkages between and among environmental variables and processes.
3. **ELM for retrieval-augmented generation.** We intend to power an LLM interface to provide plain-language access to ecological knowledge as described by a graph based on ELM.

1.2 Assumptions and Constraints

ELM is best understood as a schema that can provide the basis for useful interfaces, such as a knowledge organization system [22]. Its goal is to depict the research on complex environmental systems in such a way as to facilitate knowledge discovery. It seeks to model knowledge in academic articles, not to reproduce it entirely in a new form or model the world. Therefore, some assumptions are required to scope the schema.

We draw inspiration from the practice of ecological modeling - creating representations of ecological processes using state variables (i.e. environmental variables) and flows [15]. Such models are very useful as they are able to answer questions about the anticipated behaviour of complex systems. However, they must necessarily include assumptions in order to allow for the depiction of these systems. Such assumptions limit the scope of what can be modeled, but increase the explanatory power within the scope covered [13].

ELM focuses on links among environmental processes and environmental variables [25]. In an ecological model, links between environmental variables (called "state variables") take the form of mathematical equations that either limit or enhance flows. Broadly speaking, the structure of ecological process associations in ELM take basic flow rate equations from ecological modeling as inspiration for the structure. Specifically, ELM allows for the expression of a second-order flow rate, where the flow rate between two environmental variables is conditioned by up to two other environmental variables C_1 and C_2:

$$rate = \frac{dC}{dt} = k \times C_1 \times C_2$$

In this basic equation, dC refers to the degree of change at each time step dt. That rate is said to be equal to k which can be interpreted as the coefficient of correlation between two environmental variables in a given model. In modeling, these parameters represent environmental variables that have some impact on the direct flow expressed by k. Palmeri et al. [25] write that this expression, and modified versions of it, are at the core of many ecological models. In ELM, the core association (i.e. subject-predicate-object) corresponds to the flow rate k and the slot `conditioned by qualifier` corresponds to C_1 and C_2. However, the correspondences are conceptual only and contain no numerical values.

ELM is a schema that models research findings as published rather than the ecosystems in which those findings occur – an important distinction. A complete ELM entry cannot be directly translated into equations, or mathematically verified. It can, however, provide vital evidence for the construction of ecological models by linking findings across contexts. For instance, a modeler working in the wetland ecosystem and modeling *Phragmites australis* could draw all entries with *Phragmites australis* as the subject or object of an association documented in that ecosystem. As a semantic artifact, ELM's expressiveness is somewhere between metadata (i.e. descriptions of the article including keywords, title, author, etc.) and the full text in terms of level of complexity.

2 ELM Specification and Core Example

ELM is specified in LinkML and submitted on GitHub for integration with the Biolink Model. ELM inherits classes from Biolink, specifically the core association class and qualifiers (see Fig. 1). Qualifier slots combine with other slots to form compound statements. For example, the `direction qualifier` slot combines with the `subject value` slot to form a subject qualified with the direction of change. This allows ELM to specify the nature and direction of the association.

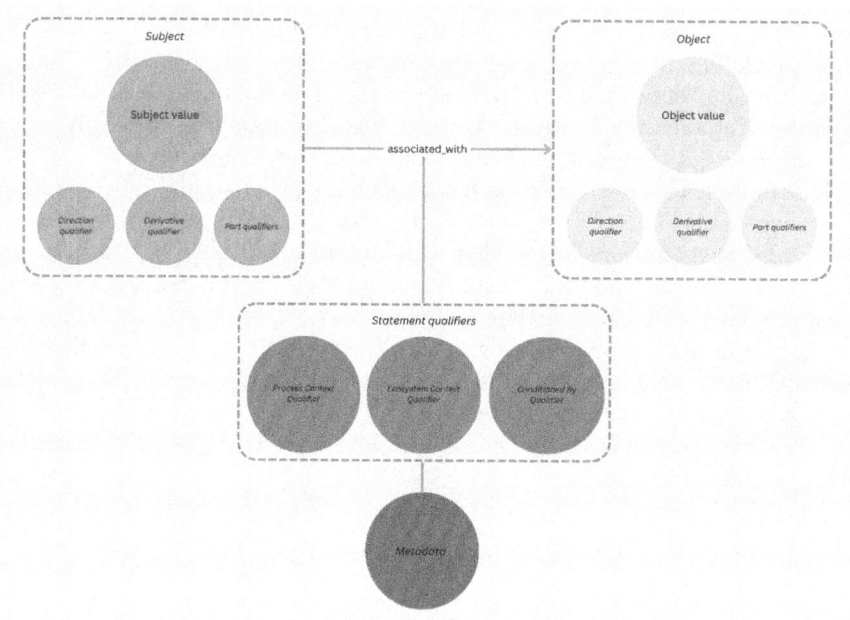

Fig. 1. The overall structure of ELM's association schema. Each circle represents a "slot" in LinkML. This representation shows all possible slots in the schema. Note that the statement qualifiers and metadata apply to the entire association and not simply the edge. It is represented here as attached to the edge because a Neo4j database would model it as such.

Other qualifiers, such as statement qualifiers, apply to the entire statement, providing context in which the statement holds true. In short, qualifier slots allow for the combination of individual ontology terms, increasing the expressivity of ELM. We have placed additional constraints around certain slots in ELM to constrain the possible entries to ones rooted in an ontology. For instance, any values in the `ecosystem context qualifier` slot must have a value that is a subclass of *ecosystem functional group* in the ELM ontology in order for validation to be successful. This combination of a defined graph pattern with slots that restrict the value to instances of specific ontology classes ensures that all data that is modeled using this schema will be semantically interoperable, which facilitates data integration, findability, and reusability. However, this also increases the importance of ensuring that depictions of ecosystem types in the ontology is consistent with current best practices. We will break down the individual slots in the coming sections with reference to an ongoing example, outlined below.

2.1 Core Example: Bare Soil Cover and *Myrmica Scabrinodis* Population

We provide an example that uses ELM to depict one part of the findings from a paper that investigated the effect of sod translocation on the population of *Myrmica scabrinodis*, a species of ant that was the target of a restoration intervention [29]. The paper itself uses a generalized linear mixed model to analyze the relationship between the responses of several environmental variables to a restoration intervention. Bare soil cover is found to have a statistically significant, inverse relationship with the population of *Myrmica scabrinodis*.

This finding means that as bare soil increases, the population of *Myrmica scabrinodis* tends to decrease. The authors suggest this is because *Myrmica scabrinodis* needs the shade provided by plants to survive [29], but for our purposes the relationship and its attribution are sufficient. You can see a representation of the Ecolink entry for [29] in Fig. 2.

The graphical representation shows how the layers of meaning are affected by the structure of ELM. A completed representation of [29] would contain several iterations on the association depicted in Fig. 2 describing the relationships among other variables in the study. There is a representation of the core example in YAML contained in Fig. 3.

2.2 Environmental Variables and Environmental Processes

ELM specifies that each association's subject and object should consist of environmental variables and/or environmental processes. Environmental variables represent some aspect of the state or condition of an ecosystem at a given point in time [15]. Examples of environmental variables include bare soil cover, the population abundance of a particular taxon, or the phylogenetic distance between two taxa. Some environmental variables may be represented using a term from an ontology, while others may have to be post-composed in ELM relating multiple ontology terms to each other. For instance, an ontology could specify a term

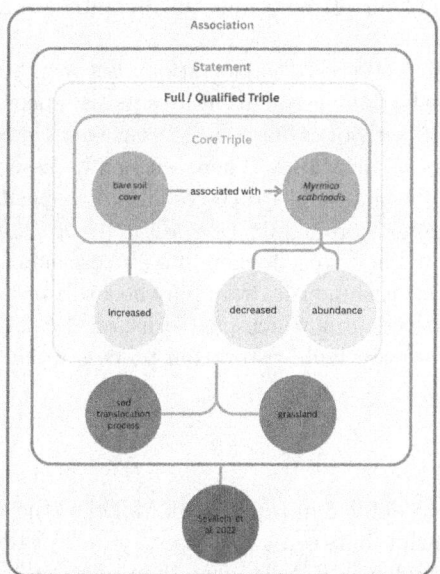

Fig. 2. Biolink Model is based on a nested structure with a core triple in the centre. The subject and object in the triple can be qualified. The whole statement can also receive qualifiers. Everything is wrapped in metadata that provides provenance for the statement. This graphical representation shows the values that would be included in a single ELM entry that is representing one association discovered in Sevilleja et al. 2022.

for *bare soil cover* as "the amount of bare soil in a given area," in which case that term could be used in the subject or object. *Species abundance*, however, would have to be post-composed in ELM as referring to the abundance of a specific taxon by using the `derivative qualifier` slot (Fig. 1). Some terms may be relative and require additional information to have meaning. For instance, *phylogenetic distance* is a measure that only has meaning when that distance is between two or more taxa. In that case, those taxa could be included in the `part qualifier` slots.

Qualifiers combine with the core subject or object and become attached to that element in the graph database. For example, the direction qualifier (Fig. 1) indicates the direction of change that the variable experiences as part of the association (i.e. increase or decrease), as is the case with increased *bare soil cover* in the core example.

The `derivative qualifier` signifies that the full subject should be interpreted as "*qualifier* of *subject*" – for instance, "abundance of *Myrmica scabrinodis*". This enables rich semantic searching, where users could search for the taxon they are interested in, or the qualifier of some taxa, or a combination of both.

Processes are represented in ELM as a series of associations between state variables, where the process in which that association occurs is specified through the `process context qualifier` slot. One process (e.g. *sod translocation process*) can involve numerous associations. These elemental associations may or may not be linked to one another. Processes may be specified as subject or object in the association's core triple (see Fig. 2), or as the `process context qualifier`. That qualifier is used when one process acts as a sub-process of a larger one. For instance, crushing tile drain may be a sub-process of some specific wetland restoration process, in which case crushing tile drain would be either the subject or object and wetland restoration process would be the `process context qualifier`.

2.3 Edge Type: Associated With

ELM uses the `associated_with` edge as defined in the Biolink Model as the sole edge type. This is defined as a relationship between two things, typically statistical in nature, that is weaker than correlation but stronger than relation [34].

The use-cases described in Sect. 1.1 point to a need to gather a wide variety of literature, rather than to deeply and thoroughly model each study. There is a trade-off inherent in this practice: a more detailed graph will take more resources to assemble. By simplifying the edge type in this association, the syntax of the model language is clear and replicable across numerous studies. A more complex edge type that accounted for coefficients may be beneficial, but would also require significantly more time in which to extract information.

2.4 Context and Conditioning Qualifiers

ELM provides three slots for qualifiers that apply to the entire association: `process context qualifier`, `ecosystem context qualifier` and `conditioned-by qualifiers` (Fig. 1). The two context qualifiers describe the conditions in which the association was observed or studied.

An environmental variable or a process can condition the association, which indicates it has some meaningful impact on the association. For instance, in a predator-prey relationship, the association may be conditioned by the population of the predator. This property mimics the concept of "forcing functions" from environmental modeling [15] in that the `conditioned-by qualifier` can be said to have either a dampening or enhancing effect on the association. The direction of that effect is not specified in ELM.

2.5 Ecolink Model Ontology (ELMO)

The Ecolink Model Ontology (ELMO[4]) is a project ontology that imports terms from environment domain ontologies in three main areas: environmental vari-

---

[4] https://github.com/timalamenciak/elmo.

ables, ecosystem types and environmental processes. Its primary and sole usecase is to power the Ecolink Model. We created the ontology repository in compliance with best practices for ontologies established by OBO Foundry[5], using the Ontology Development Kit [21]. The project ontology consists largely of imported classes from existing mature domain ontologies like ENVO [4,5], the Ontology for Biomedical Investigations (OBI) [2], the Relations Ontology (RO) and other OBO Foundry sources [11].

As a project ontology, ELMO may introduce new terms, but should aim to incorporate those terms into a relevant domain ontology where possible. We used the Simple Standard for Sharing Ontological Mappings [20] to specify entity mappings between modified terms in ELMO and their corresponding terms in existing ontologies to support their semantic (terminological) interoperability, and created comprehensive new term requests for relevant additions (e.g. 204 ecosystem management process terms are under review for inclusion in ENVO).

3 Applications of ELM

3.1 ELM as Building Blocks for a Knowledge Organization System

There are millions of scholarly publications and more being published every year [17]. While paper production increases year over year, the capacity of people to find, read and integrate new science does not keep pace, leading to a growing pool of "dark knowledge" that goes underutilized [12]. Librarians are at the forefront of knowledge organization, but there is great variety in the systems used to organize research and the efficacy of those systems [28]. Rather than proposing a completely novel system, we build upon best practices in digital libraries by using a data schema, linked datasets, ontologies and structured entries to create ELM [31].

The data that is gathered in the format of ELM's schema can be converted into RDF or JSON and used directly by popular search and database technologies. The flexibility of LinkML allows ELM to be used by virtually any repository management software. For instance, a public-facing digital repository could be created using Islandora [14] and made navigable using ELM entries associated with journal DOIs. Alternatively, ELM data could be incorporated into the discovery layer of a library using ExLibris Alma[6], Koha[7] or other integrated library software that supports RDF. It could be incorporated into smaller, project-based repositories built using Islandora[8] or CollectionBuilder[9]. A user could then query for variables they are interested in and associations that occur in study areas similar to their own, providing immediate relevant results (Fig. 3c). Incorporating ELM into ILS discovery layers actively encourages the iterative process of

---

[5] https://obofoundry.org/.
[6] https://exlibrisgroup.com/.
[7] https://koha-community.org/.
[8] https://islandora.github.io/.
[9] https://collectionbuilder.github.io/.

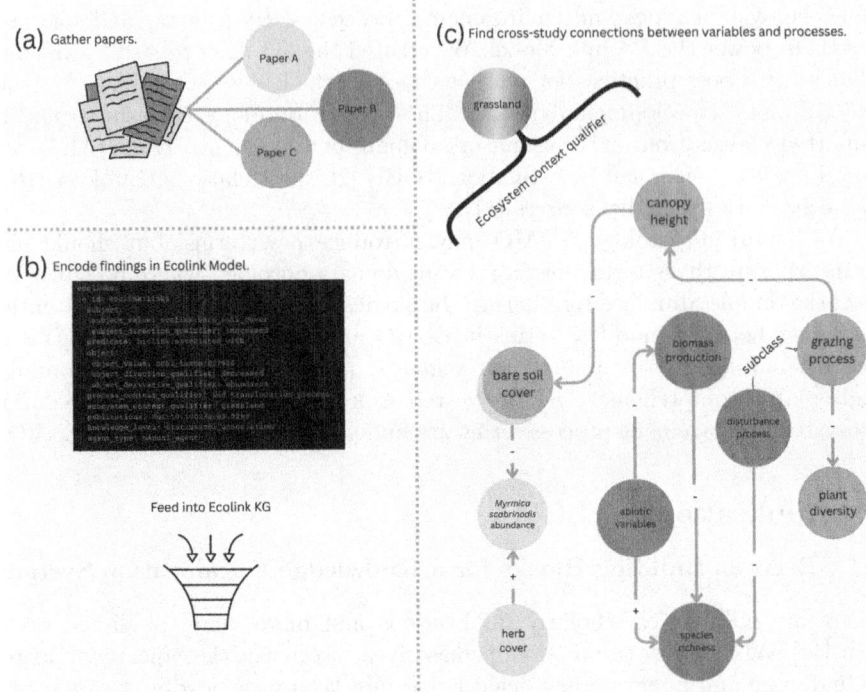

Fig. 3. This diagram shows how the process of encoding papers using the Ecolink Model would function when feeding those papers into a knowledge graph (KG). First, studies are gathered using systematic searching protocols (a). Second, the data is manually or automatically extracted and fitted to the ELM schema in a "semantic parsing" process in which natural language text is translated into an RDF-based syntax using ontology terms, following the structure and constraints in the ELM schema (b). Third, links are established between common node classes (c). Note that (c) is simplified to represent links as + or - for graphical ease. The formal representation would specify whether each node increases or decreases as part of the association.

research, diversifies scholarly conversation, and champions the strategic exploration of sources [7]. In this way, ELM can become the basis for a knowledge organization system that better captures ecological knowledge.

3.2 ELM for Retrieval-Augmented Generation

ELM provides a schema for the creation of structured datasets that describe findings from ecological research, enabling the wider application of artificial intelligence methods. These methods require data that can be collated across ecological gradients, with well-articulated meta-data [18]. Synthesis across ecosystems can improve ecological restoration outcomes and the predictive capacity of restoration ecologists [19]. However, there is a widespread lack of standardization across ecology which hampers interoperability [32]. The combination of ELM and the use of ELMO (and other ontologies) increases the semantic interoperability of knowledge that is represented using the ELM schema, and allows for findings to be collated across ecological gradients.

For instance, retrieval-augmented generation – an artificial intelligence protocol where a large-language model consults a corpus of knowledge to refine its answers – using ecological knowledge may be broadly relevant to the field. This technique may also be useful for building out an ELM knowledge graph based on existing literature [33]. A knowledge graph has the potential to provide information for such an application [26]. ELM would provide a structure for such a graph and could underlie future artificial intelligence research. Additionally, approaches should be explored to add formal semantics to property graphs based on ELM, such as using *OWLStar*[10].

4 Future Research

ELM's model of associations between environmental variables and processes is a powerful, flexible tool for cataloguing ecological knowledge. However, there may be other elements around which core associations could form (e.g. ecosystem types; landscape attributes; climatic regimes). The Biolink Model contains many such associations – gene to gene, phenotype to disease, gene to disease, and so on. Another approach may be making a more precise association type that is focused on containing correlation values, P-values and statistical methods. We provide ELM as a proof of concept to support mobilization of skills and knowledge to use semantic data schema in ecology.

ELM's usefulness will be greatly enhanced by a user interface layer that allows users to query, contribute and edit datasets based on ELM without a significant burden of technical knowledge. The sufficiency and usefulness of ELM should be evaluated by testing with users who need to access the knowledge, such as practitioners of restoration ecology or ecology researchers.

We plan to gather published systematic reviews of ecological literature that document interventions and synthesize them using ELM. This work will also feed the expansion of ELMO – the project ontology – which will in turn improve the comprehensiveness and accuracy of domain ontologies that feed into it.

Finally, we seek to mobilize ELM datasets specifically among conservation and restoration practitioners globally through the establishment of a community of practice. The development of ELM will prioritize accessibility, and we will conduct outreach to communities who may be able to use the data contained within ELM knowledge graphs to justify ecological interventions, manage landscapes and protect biodiversity. Our goal is that ELM, and the knowledge graphs it underpins, will provide an invaluable open knowledge resource globally.

Acknowledgments. We thank Nico Matentzoglu for an abundance of technical support in developing this project, and Nancy Shackelford, Meike Wittmann, Eric Higgs and Stephen Murphy for providing comments.

---

[10] https://github.com/linkml/owlstar.

Disclosure of Interests. The authors have no competing interests to declare that are relevant to the content of this article.

References

1. Alamenciak, T., et al.: Ecological restoration research in Canada: who, what, where, when, why, and how? FACETS **8**, 1–11 (2023). https://doi.org/10.1139/facets-2022-0157
2. Bandrowski, A., et al.: The ontology for biomedical investigations. PLoS ONE **11**(4), e0154556 (2016). https://doi.org/10.1371/journal.pone.0154556
3. Bucur, C.I., Kuhn, T., Ceolin, D., Van Ossenbruggen, J.: Expressing high-level scientific claims with formal semantics. In: Proceedings of the 11th Knowledge Capture Conference, Virtual Event USA, pp. 233–240. ACM (2021). https://doi.org/10.1145/3460210.3493561
4. Buttigieg, P., Morrison, N., Smith, B., Mungall, C.J., Lewis, S.E.: The Envo consortium: the environment ontology: contextualising biological and biomedical entities. J. Biomed. Semant. **4**(1), 43 (2013). https://doi.org/10.1186/2041-1480-4-43
5. Buttigieg, P.L., Pafilis, E., Lewis, S.E., Schildhauer, M.P., Walls, R.L., Mungall, C.J.: The environment ontology in 2016: bridging domains with increased scope, semantic density, and interoperation. J. Biomed. Semant. **7**(1), 57 (2016). https://doi.org/10.1186/s13326-016-0097-6
6. Caufield, J.H., et al.: KG-Hub—building and exchanging biological knowledge graphs. Bioinformatics **39**(7), btad418 (2023). https://doi.org/10.1093/bioinformatics/btad418
7. of College & Research Libraries, A.: Framework for Information Literacy for Higher Education (2016). https://www.ala.org/acrl/standards/ilframework
8. Cunha-Oliveira, T., Ioannidis, J.P.A., Oliveira, P.J.: Best practices for data management and sharing in experimental biomedical research. Physiol. Rev. **104**(3), 1387–1408 (2024). https://doi.org/10.1152/physrev.00043.2023
9. Groth, P., Gibson, A., Velterop, J.: The anatomy of a nanopublication. Inf. Serv. Use **30**(1–2), 51–56 (2010). https://doi.org/10.3233/ISU-2010-0613
10. Heger, T., et al.: Mapping and assessing the knowledge base of ecological restoration. Restor. Ecol. **32**(8), e13676 (2024). https://doi.org/10.1111/rec.13676
11. Jackson, R., et al.: OBO Foundry in 2021: operationalizing open data principles to evaluate ontologies. Database **2021**, baab069 (2021). https://doi.org/10.1093/database/baab069
12. Jeschke, J.M., Lokatis, S., Bartram, I., Tockner, K.: Knowledge in the dark: scientific challenges and ways forward. FACETS **4**(1), 423–441 (2019). https://doi.org/10.1139/facets-2019-0007
13. Jhanwar, M.: Role of assumptions in models: a study. Int. J. Multidisciplinary Innovative Res. (2021)
14. Jones, S., Lampert, C., Lapworth, E., Shaw, S.: Islandora for archival access and discovery. Code4Lib Journal (2023)
15. Jørgensen, S.E., Fath, B.D.: Concepts of modelling. In: Developments in Environmental Modelling, vol. 23, pp. 19–93. Elsevier (2011). https://doi.org/10.1016/B978-0-444-53567-2.00002-8

16. Keith, D.A., et al.: A function-based typology for Earth's ecosystems. Nature **610**(7932), 513–518 (2022). https://doi.org/10.1038/s41586-022-05318-4
17. Khabsa, M., Giles, C.L.: The number of scholarly documents on the public web. PLoS ONE **9**(5), e93949 (2014). https://doi.org/10.1371/journal.pone.0093949
18. Ladouceur, E., Shackelford, N.: The power of data synthesis to shape the future of the restoration community and capacity. Restor. Ecol. **29**(1), e13251 (2021). https://doi.org/10.1111/rec.13251
19. Ladouceur, E., et al.: Knowledge sharing for shared success in the decade on ecosystem restoration. Ecol. Sol. Evid. **3**(1), e12117 (2022). https://doi.org/10.1002/2688-8319.12117
20. Matentzoglu, N., et al.: A Simple Standard for Sharing Ontological Mappings (SSSOM). Database **2022**, baac035 (2022). https://doi.org/10.1093/database/baac035
21. Matentzoglu, N., et al.: Ontology development Kit: a toolkit for building, maintaining and standardizing biomedical ontologies. Database **2022**, baac087 (2022). https://doi.org/10.1093/database/baac087
22. Mazzocchi, F.: Knowledge organization system (kos): an introductory critical account. Knowl. Organ. **45**(1), 54–78 (2018). https://doi.org/10.5771/0943-7444-2018-1-54
23. Moxon, S., et al.: The linked data modeling language (linkml): a general-purpose data modeling framework grounded in machine-readable semantics. CEUR Workshop Proceedings **3073**, 148–151 (2021)
24. Mungall, C.J., et al.: The monarch initiative: an integrative data and analytic platform connecting phenotypes to genotypes across species. Nucleic Acids Res. **45**(D1), D712–D722 (2017). https://doi.org/10.1093/nar/gkw1128
25. Palmeri, L., Barausse, A., Jorgensen, S.E.: Ecological Processes Handbook. CRC Press, 0 edn. (2013). https://doi.org/10.1201/b15380
26. Procko, T.T., Ochoa, O.: Graph retrieval-augmented generation for large language models: a survey. In: 2024 Conference on AI, Science, Engineering, and Technology (AIxSET), pp. 166–169. IEEE, Laguna Hills, CA, USA (2024). https://doi.org/10.1109/AIxSET62544.2024.00030
27. Reese, J., et al.: KG-COVID-19: a framework to produce customized knowledge graphs for COVID-19 response (2020). https://doi.org/10.1101/2020.08.17.254839
28. Salatino, A., Aggarwal, T., Mannocci, A., Osborne, F., Motta, E.: A survey on knowledge organization systems of research fields: resources and challenges. Quant. Sci. Stud. 1–37 (2025). https://doi.org/10.1162/qss_a_00363
29. Soergel, D.: Digital libraries and knowledge organization. In: Kruk, S.R., McDaniel, B. (eds.) Semantic Digital Libraries, pp. 9–39. Springer, Heidelberg (2009). https://doi.org/10.1007/978-3-540-85434-0_2
30. Sikos, L.F.: Description Logics in Multimedia Reasoning. Springer, Cham (2017). https://doi.org/10.1007/978-3-319-54066-5
31. Soergel, D.: Digital Libraries and Knowledge Organization. In: Kruk, S.R., McDaniel, B. (eds.) Semantic Digital Libraries, pp. 9–39. Springer, Heidelberg (2009). https://doi.org/10.1007/978-3-540-85434-0_2
32. Thessen, A.: Adoption of machine learning techniques in ecology and earth science. One Ecosyst. **1**, e8621 (2016). https://doi.org/10.3897/oneeco.1.e8621
33. Toro, S., et al.: Dynamic retrieval augmented generation of ontologies using artificial intelligence (DRAGON-AI). J. Biomed. Semant. **15**(1), 19 (2024). https://doi.org/10.1186/s13326-024-00320-3, https://jbiomedsem.biomedcentral.com/articles/10.1186/s13326-024-00320-3

34. Unni, D.R., et al.: The biomedical data translator consortium: biolink model: a universal schema for knowledge graphs in clinical, biomedical, and translational science. Clin. Transl. Sci. **15**(8), 1848–1855 (2022). https://doi.org/10.1111/cts.13302
35. Wilkinson, M.D., et al.: The FAIR guiding principles for scientific data management and stewardship. Sci. Data **3**(1), 160018 (2016). https://doi.org/10.1038/sdata.2016.18

Monitoring and Modeling the Dynamics of *Halophila Stipulacea* Meadows Using Satellite Imagery and Machine Learning Techniques

Tom Avikasis Cohen[1], Gil Rilov[2], Gidon Winters[3,4], and Anna Brook[1(✉)]

[1] Spectroscopy and Remote Sensing Laboratory, School of Environmental Sciences, University of Haifa, Abba Khoushy Ave 199, Mt. Carmel, 3498838 Haifa, Israel
abrook@geo.haifa.ac.il
[2] National Institute of Oceanography, Israel Oceanographic and Limnological Research, Tel-Shikmona, 3108000 Haifa, Israel
[3] The Dead-Sea and Arava Science Center (ADSSC), Tamar Regional Council, 8691000 Neve Zohar, Israel
[4] Eilat Campus, Ben-Gurion University of the Negev, 8499000 Eilat, Israel

Abstract. *Halophila stipulacea*, a small-leaved, fast-spreading seagrass, dominates subtidal meadows in the northern Gulf of Aqaba (GoA), where its distribution is affected by seasonal flash floods and climate-related stressors. Accurate monitoring of such meadows remains challenging due to their fine-scale structure and growth in optically complex, turbid waters. Traditional field-based mapping is logistically limited in scope, while many remote sensing approaches underperform in deeper or noisy marine environments.

In this study, we present an AI-powered, reproducible workflow for subtidal seagrass mapping, integrating multi-source satellite reflectance data (VENμS and Sentinel-2) with field-validated machine learning models. Five regression algorithms (RT, RF, GBRT, SVR, and XGBR) were trained and tested using in situ data and satellite-derived spectral inputs, including raw bands and vegetation indices. XGBR models trained on VENμS imagery outperformed all others ($R2 = 0.97$; $RMSE = 0.21$), demonstrating strong predictive performance even in dynamic coastal zones. We further examined the influence of episodic disturbances such as floods on spatial patterns of vegetation loss and regrowth.

Beyond performance benchmarking, the workflow contributes to ecological informatics by producing spatially explicit, scalable predictions designed with transparency and interoperability in mind. The pipeline supports standardized data ingestion, flexible ML configuration, and modular visualization of outputs, enabling integration into digital libraries, semantic search tools, and spatial decision-support systems.

This work illustrates how combining remote sensing, structured ecological data, and AI-based inference can improve knowledge synthesis in marine ecology. It offers a transferable methodology for monitoring invasive species, supporting conservation planning, and evaluating ecosystem resilience under climate-driven pressures.

Keywords: Subtidal Seagrass Mapping · Super-Resolution Imagery · Machine Learning · Remote Sensing · Gulf of Aqaba · *Halophila Stipulacea*

1 Introduction

Seagrasses are a unique group of marine flowering plants (angiosperms) that thrive worldwide in shallow sedimentary coastal shorelines, in both tropical and temperate regions, where they can form dense meadows (Les et al. 1997, Bertelli et al., 2021). With an estimated value of US$2.8 million km^{-2} yr^{-1} in terms of ecosystem services and functions (Costanza et al. 2014, Dewsbury et al. 2016), seagrass meadows represent one of the most productive ecosystems on earth. Seagrass meadows are important primary producers that enrich their surrounding water with oxygen, enhancing local biodiversity (Bloomfield and Gillanders 2005, Duffy 2006). They take up and sequester large amounts of atmospheric carbon (termed "blue carbon") and for longer periods compared with the "green" carbon sequestered by terrestrial ecosystems (Duarte et al. 2005, Fourqurean et al. 2012). Coastal blue carbon ecosystems (including seagrass meadows) are included in the "Coastal and marine ecosystems in the 2030 Agenda: SDG14 – Life below water", which calls on countries to conserve and sustainably use the oceans, seas and marine resources" (Leal Filho et al. 2020). Seagrass meadows also act as nurseries for juvenile fish and invertebrates and protect shorelines through wave attenuation and sediment stabilization (Potouroglou et al., 2017, James et al. 2019). Tropical seagrass meadows close to coral reefs, as is the case in the northern Gulf of Aqaba (GoA), also enable trophic exchanges between the two habitats, improve water quality, and have the potential to buffer ocean acidification for nearby corals (Heck et al. 2008; Lamb et al. 2017; Unsworth et al. 2012).

Despite their high ecological and economic value, accurate, high-resolution mapping of subtidal small-leaved seagrass species such as *Halophila stipulacea* remains rare, especially in regions with optically complex waters like the Red Sea. Remote sensing has been applied to seagrass mapping for nearly four decades (Mederos-Barrera et al. 2022; McKenzie et al. 2022). However, previous work focused on large-leaved or intertidal species that are visible during low tide or in clear shallow waters. Newer studies suggest integrating remote sensing with machine learning and spectral indices to better map subtidal seagrass (Chand and Bollard, 2021; Veettil et al. 2020).

The focus of this study is the northern GoA, where *Halophila stipulacea*, a Red Sea native is the most widespread (and sometimes only) seagrass species (Angel et al., 1995; Al-Rousan et al., 2011). H. stipulacea is a small, tropical seagrass with 4–6 cm leaves that forms subtidal meadows down to 51 m. It has spread invasively to the Mediterranean and the Caribbean, often forming dense monocultures and altering benthic habitats. In the GoA, H. stipulacea is affected by episodic flash floods from ephemeral rivers ("wadis") that deliver pulses of sediment and nutrients to nearshore zones (Winters et al. 2017). These events, coupled with climate-driven sea surface warming in the Red Sea (Wolfe et al. 2020), present mounting stressors for seagrass populations.

Traditional snorkeling-based mapping (Winters et al. 2017) provided key insights into seagrass distributions, but such efforts are labor-intensive, limited in spatial scale, and infrequent. Satellite platforms like Sentinel-2 (10 m) and VENμS (5 m, high temporal resolution) offer promising alternatives for regular, large-scale seagrass monitoring. The use of super-resolution space-borne imagery (VENμS), which revisits the region every two days, is particularly promising for tracking temporal changes and short-term disturbances. This enables automated, objective assessments of seagrass dynamics and recovery from stress events like flash floods.

This study contributes to the growing body of literature on seagrass remote sensing by focusing on a small-leaved, subtidal species in optically complex waters—conditions underrepresented in previous machine learning studies. While ensemble models such as XGBR have been widely applied in terrestrial mapping, their application to dynamic marine environments using super-resolution imagery (e.g., VENµS) remains limited. By integrating satellite data with flood disturbance timelines and optimizing models via Particle Swarm Optimization, this study offers a transferable and scalable methodology tailored to submerged vegetation dynamics in the Gulf of Aqaba.

2 Methods

To examine the spatial distribution and temporal dynamics of *Halophila stipulacea* meadows, an integrated methodology was developed that combines field-based observations, satellite remote sensing, and supervised machine learning. This approach was designed to address the challenges of mapping small-leaved subtidal seagrasses in optically complex marine environments, while enabling scalable and reproducible predictions of vegetation cover. High-resolution imagery from the VENµS and Sentinel-2 satellites was preprocessed and linked with in situ snorkeling surveys. Reflectance data and spectral indices were used as predictors in regression-based models trained to estimate seagrass cover across three coastal sites subjected to different levels of disturbance. The methodological workflow incorporated standardized preprocessing, multivariate dataset construction, model optimization, and time-series analysis to support both predictive performance and ecological interpretation.

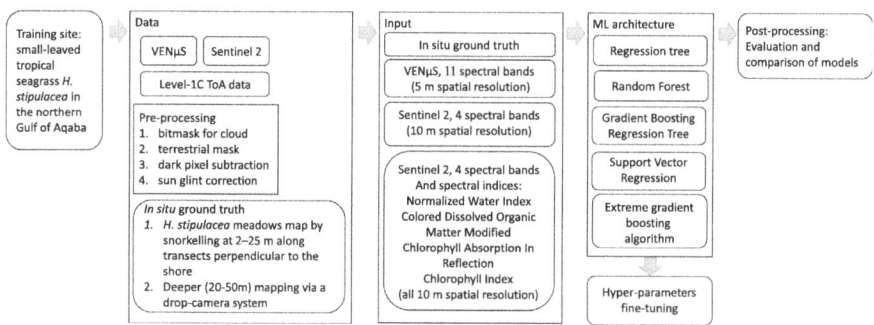

Fig. 1. The overall workflow diagram.

The workflow was structured to support transparency, modularity, and reproducibility. While no public repository is currently provided, the methodology was designed using standardized input formats and interoperable components, facilitating future sharing and integration into ecological information systems. The complete workflow is summarized in Fig. 1, outlining the sequence of preprocessing, modeling, and validation steps.

2.1 Study Area

The study focuses on *Halophila stipulacea* meadows along the western shore of the northern Gulf of Aqaba (GoA), adjacent to Eilat, Israel. Due to high year-round water clarity, snorkeling-based surveys have proven effective in mapping these subtidal meadows at depths of 15–25 m (Winters et al., 2017). The area includes three distinct beach zones differing in slope, substrate, and anthropogenic disturbance: [1] North Beach: high anthropogenic influence, extensive meadows (~343,000 m2) beginning at 2 m depth on a 2.5° sandy slope, reaching 30 m depth. [2] South Beach: lower disturbance, smaller meadows (~61,900 m2) starting at 5–7 m on a 17.5° gravel and coral slope, reaching 50 m depth. [3] Katzaa Beach: intermediate exposure to single-source flash floods.

2.2 Field Survey and Ground Truth

In situ seagrass data were collected via snorkeling and drop-camera surveys, following Winters et al. (2017). Snorkeling transects were perpendicular to the shoreline at depths of 2–25 m, with seagrass percent cover recorded every 5–15 m across ~ 9.7 km of coastline. Drop-camera surveys covered an additional 283 deeper points (20–50 m). Overall, ~ 3,100 observations were interpolated using linear triangulation to create continuous vector layers of depth and percent cover. Field surveys were stratified across the three beach zones (North, Katzaa, and Taba), ensuring representative sampling within each site's specific depth range, substrate type, and disturbance level. Transects and drop-camera points were spatially distributed to capture within-site variability and support zone-specific model validation. The spatial layout of these field observations is shown in Fig. 2.

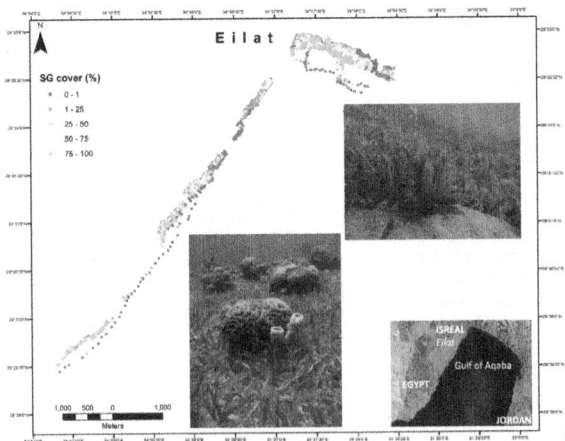

Fig. 2. The tropical *Halophila stipulacea* meadows (% seagrass cover; "SG cover (%)") mapped by snorkelling along transects in GoA with examples of *Halophila stipulacea* meadows in the north and south beaches of Eilat.

2.3 Satellite Data Acquisition and Preprocessing

VENµS and Sentinel-2 imagery were used to derive surface reflectance values in the study area for two key periods: 2018 and 2020. VENµS imagery provided 11 spectral bands at 5.3-m resolution, while Sentinel-2 imagery offered 13 bands with spatial resolution ranging from 10 to 60 m. Level 1 top-of-atmosphere data were obtained and processed to surface reflectance using ESA's SNAP toolbox.

To ensure high-quality inputs, imagery was visually inspected and selected for minimal cloud coverage, with preference given to acquisitions aligned with field surveys and flash flood events. Cloud and land areas were masked using band-specific QA flags and supervised classification based on vegetation and water indices. Sun-glint was corrected using the Hedley et al. (2005) method, which applies a linear regression between visible and NIR bands to remove specular reflections. Additionally, deep-water dark pixel subtraction (Armstrong, 1993) was performed to reduce atmospheric bias in submerged areas. This preprocessing chain was designed to minimize optical noise and improve feature separability for model input. It reflects recommendations from prior seagrass mapping efforts and addresses reviewer comments on sun-glint correction and mask accuracy.

2.4 Spectral Indices and Dataset Composition

To enhance model sensitivity to biophysical vegetation features, several spectral indices were calculated from Sentinel-2 imagery: the Normalized Difference Water Index (NDWI by Gao, 1996), the Colored Dissolved Organic Matter index (CDOM by Kowalczuk et al. 2005), the Modified Chlorophyll Absorption in Reflectance Index (MCARI), and the Chlorophyll Index (CI by Zoffoli et al. 2020). These indices were chosen based on previous applications in submerged vegetation monitoring and were computed alongside standard reflectance bands.

Three datasets were prepared for training and testing the models: [a] Dataset 1: VENµS reflectance bands only (11 bands, 5.3 m resolution); [b] Dataset 2: Sentinel-2 bands only (4 key bands, 10 m resolution); [c] Dataset 3: Sentinel-2 bands + 4 spectral indices (total of 8 variables).

All datasets were co-registered to the ground truth vector layers generated from field surveys, using spatial alignment at sub-pixel accuracy. Spectral values were extracted from georeferenced locations of snorkeling and camera-based observations.

2.5 Machine Learning Model Implementation

Five supervised regression models were implemented using Scikit-learn in Python: Regression Tree (RT), Random Forest (RF, Breiman, 2001), Gradient Boosting Regression Tree (GBRT, Friedman, 2001), Support Vector Regression (SVR), and eXtreme Gradient Boosting Regression (XGBR). These models were selected to represent both linear and nonlinear approaches (e.g., Ashphaq et al., 2022), and to account for spatial autocorrelation and the high dimensionality of spectral inputs.

2.6 Hyperparameter Tuning and Validation

Hyperparameters were optimized using Particle Swarm Optimization (PSO) to maximize R2 scores on the training set. A 70/30 train-test split was used, and 5-fold cross-validation was applied to estimate generalization error. Each model was tuned independently across 200 PSO iterations, with convergence evaluated based on performance stability. The full list of hyperparameters and their value ranges for each algorithm is provided in Table 1.

Table 1. Fine-tuning of hyper-parameters. Optimized hyper-parameters of the five machine-learning (ML) algorithms used in the study. Shown are the values range of each hyper-parameter.

Hyper-parameter	Description	ML algorithm	Val Range
Max_depth	Max depth of RT	RT, RF, Ensemble GBRT, Ensemble XGBR	3–10
Min_sample_split	Min number of samples for the split	RT, Ensemble GBRT, Ensemble XGBR	2–10
Min_sample_leaf	Min number of samples at the leaf node	RT, RF, Ensemble GBRT, Ensemble XGBR	1–10
Max_RT	Max number of RT models in the ensemble	RF, Ensemble GBRT, Ensemble XGBR	20–1000
Learning rate	Shrinks the contribution of each RT	Ensemble GBRT, Ensemble XGBR, SVR	0.01 - 1

2.7 Temporal Composites and Flood Analysis

Time-series composites were generated from monthly VENμS imagery for 2018 and 2020. These composites were created by averaging reflectance values after cloud and land masking, using pixels corresponding to seagrass meadows. Sequences were analyzed for each of the three coastal sites and interpreted alongside known flash flood occurrences provided by the Arava Institute database.

By aligning modeled SG cover with the timing of flood events, the workflow enabled a visual and statistical analysis of disturbance impacts and post-disturbance recovery patterns.

3 Results

The performance results for the five ML regression models using Dataset_1 (VENμS), which contains 11 variables, are shown in Fig. 3 and Table 2. The average R2 on the training set increased from 0.78 to 0.91 when the training set size increased from 50% to 70%. A similar trend was observed on the testing set. This confirmed that the training dataset size significantly influenced model generalization performance, with diminishing returns beyond 70%.

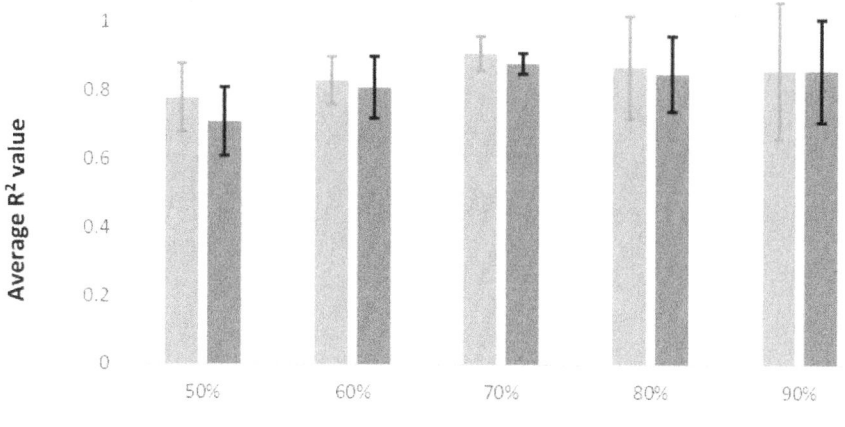

Fig. 3. The influence of training set size (50–90%) on ensemble XGBR performance (in terms of R^2 values) with hyper-parameters from Scikit-learn hyper-parameters. Shown in light grey are performances in the training phase, and in dark grey are performances in the testing phase.

Table 2. Accuracy comparison results of machine learning (ML) algorithms used to predict seagrass cover (SG in %) from Dataset_1 (test phase data using VENμS with 11 spectral bands, 5 m resolution after pre-processing in reflectance). Highlighted in bold are the best results both R^2 and RMSE.

ML algorithm	R2 Training (70%)	R2 Testing (30%)	RMSE (SG%)
RT	0.8230	0.7668	2.9055
RF	0.7925	0.7264	3.1712
ensemble GBRT	0.8750	0.8466	2.1051
SVR	0.9080	0.8887	1.5193
ensemble XGBR	**0.9890**	**0.9718**	**0.2124**

In this study, Particle Swarm Optimization (PSO) was used for hyper-parameter optimization. For each ML model, five random splits of the training data (70%) were used. The average R2 from 5-fold cross-validation was recorded for each PSO iteration (Figs. 4 and 5), showing consistent performance improvements. For example, XGBR improved from R2 = 0.93 to 0.98.

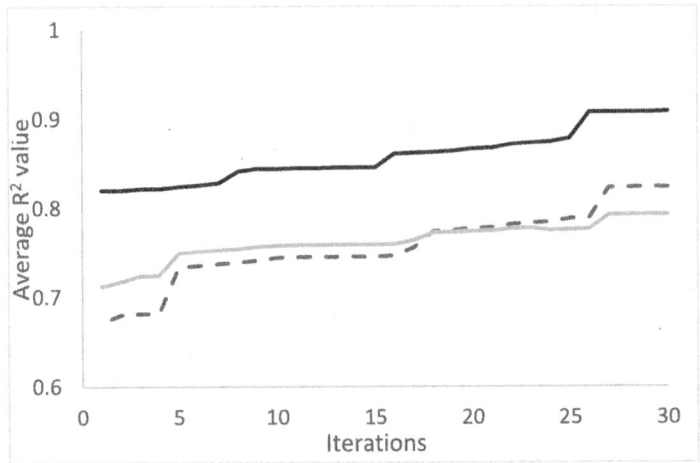

Fig. 4. Fine-tuning of hyper-parameters. Effects of increasing particle swarm optimization (PSO) iterations on the average R^2 value for RT (dashed line), RF (solid grey line), and SVR (solid black line) ML algorithms.

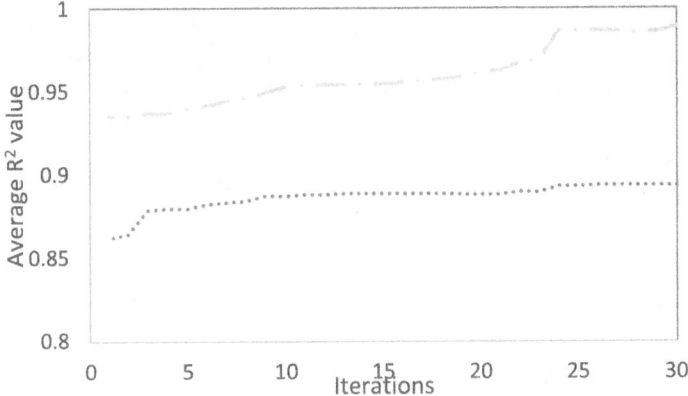

Fig. 5. Fine-tuning of hyper-parameters. Effects of increasing particle swarm optimization (PSO) iterations on the average R^2 value for ensemble GBRT (dotted line) and ensemble XGBR (long-dashed dotted light grey line) ML algorithms.

Figure 6 presents the predicted vs. measured seagrass cover (%) on Dataset 1. The ensemble XGBR model achieved $R2 = 0.97$ on the testing set ($RMSE = 0.2$), which was the highest among all tested models. SVR was second-best with $R2 = 0.88$. Confidence intervals (95%) are shown as dashed lines.

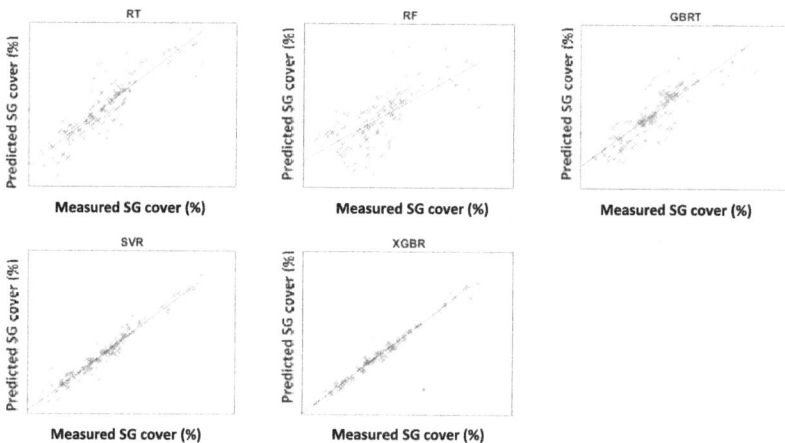

Fig. 6. Performance comparisons among the optimum individual regressors on the testing set (124 samples). Scatter plots of the field-measured versus predicted percent of seagrass (SG cover %) where grey solids are 124 tested inputs, the solid line is the fit line, and the dashed lines are the 95% confidence bounds.

The most important spectral bands identified by XGBR are presented in Fig. 7. Green (555 nm), red (660 nm), and red-edge bands (740–783 nm) contributed most to prediction accuracy. These bands relate to chlorophyll and canopy structure.

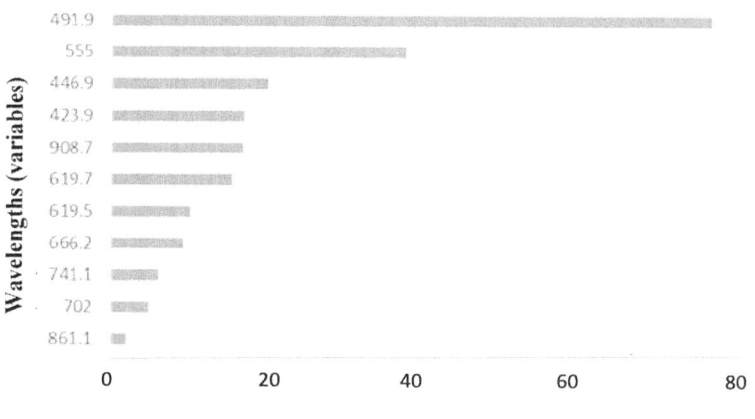

Feature importance ranked by F-score (0-100%)

Fig. 7. Order of Dataset_1 variable importance to SG cover (%). Y-axis are wavelengths (variables), X-axis is the feature importance ranked by F-score (0–100%).

Figure 8 presents visual similarity between the in situ mapping and the predicted SG cover % by the ensemble_XGBR model.

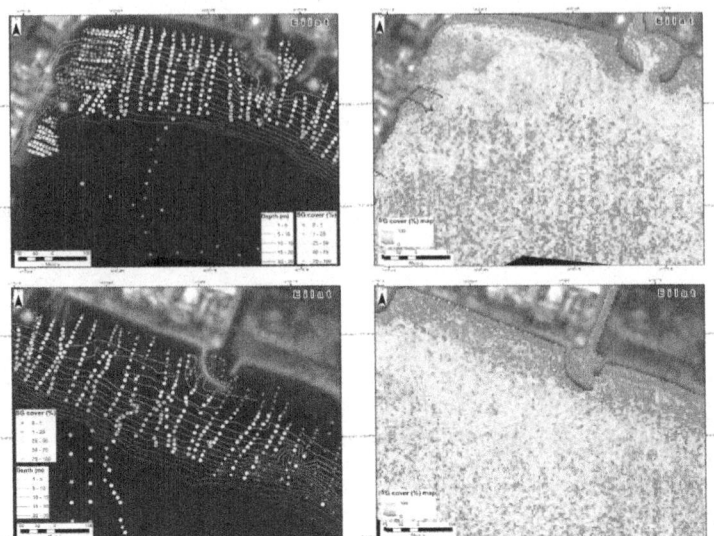

Fig. 8. Spatial distribution of SC cover (%) found in the *in situ* surveys (left) and retrieved by the ensemble_XGBR model (right).

Accuracy of predictions varied by depth and percent cover. Figure 9 shows that RMSE was lowest (< 0.3) in depths < 15 m and increased at depths > 25 m. Figure 10 demonstrates that model performance was best for moderate SG cover (25–75%) and worse for low (<25%) or very high (>75%) cover, where RMSE reached ~0.4.

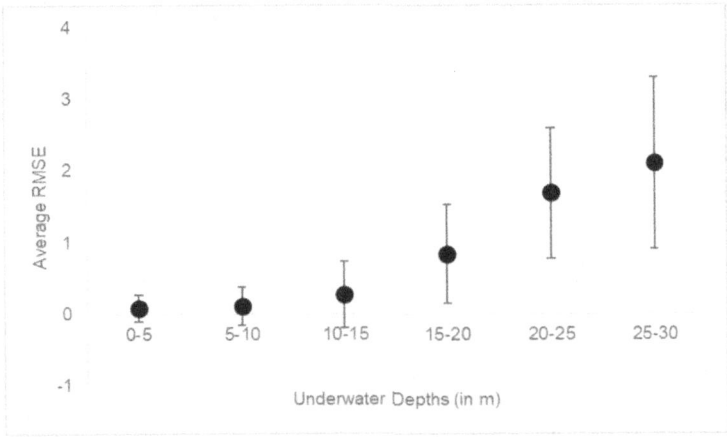

Fig. 9. The ensemble_XGBR model average RMSE (black dots) and its standard deviation (error bars) for Dataset_1 in predicting SG cover (%) at different depths.

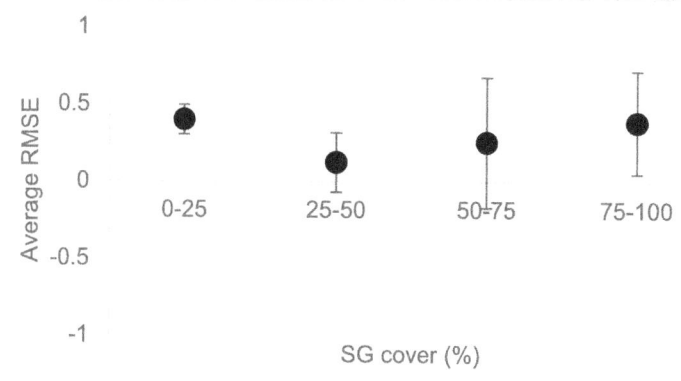

Fig. 10. The ensemble_XGBR model average RMSE (black dots) and its standard deviation (error bars) for Dataset_1 in predicting SG cover in four different cover categories. SG cover, 0–100%, categorized into 4 groups (low coverage < 25%, mid coverage (25–50%), high coverage (50–75%) and very high coverage (>75%)).

The spatial and temporal effect of flash floods is visualized in Fig. 11. In 2018, SG cover at the north beach dropped from ~40% to <10% within ~2 months. In 2020, cover dropped from ~90% to <10% within 1 month. Recovery was slower in 2020, starting only after 5–6 months. Katzaa showed similar but milder patterns. Taba, the most distant site, showed no detectable flood-related impact.

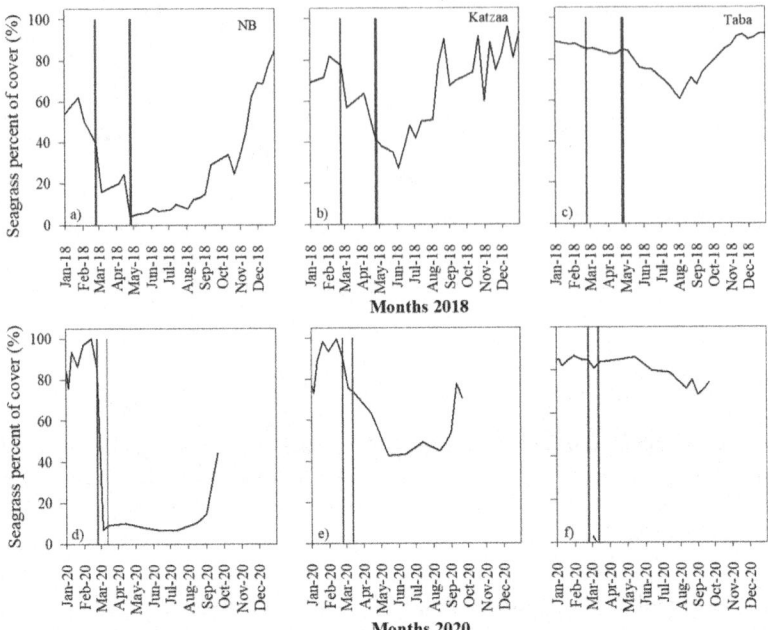

Fig. 11. Predicted SC cover (%) derived from the ensemble XGBR model, showing the temporal effect of flash floods on three sites: 1) North Beach, 2) Katzaa Beach, and 3) Taba Beach, between January 2018 and October 2020. Flood events are marked by blue vertical lines. These data are model outputs, not field observations.

4 Discussion

The results of the present study demonstrate that regression models based on ensemble learning, when applied to high-resolution VENμS imagery, can accurately estimate the percent cover of subtidal *Halophila stipulacea* meadows. This level of performance is notable given the optical complexity of the Gulf of Aqaba and the relatively small, patchy morphology of the species.

These findings are consistent with recent developments in aquatic vegetation mapping, which indicate that combining spectral, temporal, and contextual information improves accuracy in dynamic coastal environments (e.g., Chand and Bollard, 2021). Unlike previous studies that focused on large-leaved or intertidal seagrasses, the current analysis addresses a longstanding challenge—the spatial prediction of small-leaved subtidal meadows in oligotrophic waters.

While high model accuracies were obtained, post-classification validation using independent datasets is recommended as a future step, in order to ensure that the performance is not solely attributable to interpolation or spatial overfitting (Rodriguez-Galiano et al., 2012).

The appearance of "salt and pepper" noise in shallow water zones may be attributed to spectral confusion, mixed pixel effects, or depth-driven variability in reflectance. Incorporating bathymetric data and water quality parameters in future modeling efforts could reduce such misclassifications.

Flash floods were shown to exert significant, site-specific effects on seagrass cover. For instance, North Beach—being closest to multiple wadi outflows—experienced a near-complete loss of vegetation following the March 2020 flood. In contrast, Taba Beach remained relatively stable, while Katzaa Beach exhibited intermediate disturbance and partial recovery. The observed regrowth by late summer at North and Katzaa may suggest the presence of viable seed banks buried in flood-deposited sediments, particularly as H. stipulacea typically flowers and fruits between May and August (Malm, 2006; Nguyen et al., 2018). However, this remains a hypothesis requiring confirmation through direct sediment core analysis.

The ability to monitor monthly changes in seagrass cover was essential for distinguishing abrupt flood-driven disturbances from gradual seasonal dynamics, such as natural senescence in summer. This capability, based entirely on model-generated outputs, underscores the potential of remote sensing workflows for tracking mid-term ecological changes without the need for continuous field monitoring. This highlights the advantage of combining high-temporal-resolution satellite data with ecological field context in subtidal monitoring.

5 Conclusion

This study presents a novel methodology for mapping and monitoring subtidal seagrass dynamics using super-resolution satellite imagery in combination with AI-based regression modeling techniques. By integrating VENµS imagery with validated field data, a scalable and robust workflow was developed for quantifying spatial and temporal variation in *Halophila stipulacea* cover.

The results successfully captured spatial heterogeneity, detected vegetation loss due to flash floods, and documented regrowth patterns over time.

The proposed methodology follows FAIR data principles, offering a reproducible, modular framework that can be integrated into digital libraries, ecological databases, and spatial decision-support systems. The approach contributes to ecosystem-based management and represents a transferable model for monitoring marine vegetation in other environmentally sensitive regions.

Acknowledgments. This research was supported by Grant #SIS70021GR3019 from the Middle East Regional Cooperation (MERC).

References

Al-Rousan, S., Al-Horani, F., Eid, E., Khalaf, M.: Assessment of seagrass communities along the Jordanian coast of the Gulf of Aqaba, Red Sea. Mar. Biol. Res. **7**, 93–99 (2011)

Angel, D.L., Eden, N., Susel, L.: The influence of environmental variables on *Halophila stipulacea* growth. Improving the Knowledge Base in Modern Aquaculture. In: Rosenthal, H., Moav, B., Gordin, H. (eds.) (Ghent: European Aquaculture Society Special Publication), pp.103–128 (1995)

Armstrong, R.A.: Remote sensing of submerged vegetation canopies for biomass estimation. Int. J. Remote Sens. **14**(3), 621–627 (1993)

Ashphaq, M., Srivastava, P.K., Mitra, D.: Analysis of univariate linear, robust-linear, and nonlinear machine learning algorithms for satellite-derived bathymetry in complex coastal terrain. Reg. Stud. Mar. Sci. **56**, 102678 (2022)

Bertelli, C.M., Bull, J.C., Cullen-Unsworth, L.C., Unsworth, R.K.F.: Unravelling the spatial and temporal plasticity of eelgrass meadows. Front. Plant Sci. 12 (2021)

Bloomfield, A.L., Gillanders, B.M.: Fish and invertebrate assemblages in seagrass, mangrove, saltmarsh, and nonvegetated habitats. Estuaries **28**, 63–77 (2005). https://doi.org/10.1007/BF02732754

Breiman, L.,: Random forests. Mach. Learn. **45**(1), 5–32 (2001). https://doi.org/10.1023/A:1010933404324

Chand, S., Bollard, B.: Detecting the spatial variability of seagrass meadows and their consequences on associated macrofauna benthic activity using novel drone technology. Remote Sens. **14**(1), 160 (2021)

Costanza, R., et al.: Changes in the global value of ecosystem services. Glob. Environ. Chang. **26**, 152–158 (2014)

Dewsbury, B.M., Bhat, M., Fourqurean, J.W.: A review of seagrass economic valuations: gaps and progress in valuation approaches. Ecosyst. Serv. **18**, 68–77 (2016)

Duarte, C., Middleburg, J., Caraco, N.: Major role of marine vegetation on the ocean carbon cycle. Biogeosciences **2**, 1–8. https://doi.org/10.5194/bg-2-1-2005 (2005)

Duffy, J. E.: Biodiversity and the functioning of seagrass ecosystems. Mar. Ecol. Prog. Ser. **311**, 233–250 (2006). https://doi.org/10.3354/meps311233

Fourqurean, J.W., et al.: Seagrass ecosystems as a globally significant carbon stock. Nat. Geosci. **5**, 505–509 (2012)

Friedman, J.H.,: Greedy function approximation: a gradient boosting machine. Ann. Stat. 1189–1232 (2001)

Gao, B.C.: NDWI—a normalized difference water index for remote sensing of vegetation liquid water from space. Remote Sens. Environ. **58**(3), 257–266 (1996)

Heck, K.L., et al.: Trophic transfers from seagrass meadows subsidize diverse marine and terrestrial consumers. Ecosystems **11**, 1198–1210 (2008)

Hedley, J.D., Harborne, A.R., Mumby, P.J.: Simple and robust removal of sun glint for mapping shallow-water benthos. Int. J. Remote Sens. **26**(10), 2107–2112 (2005)

James, R.K., et al.: Maintaining tropical beaches with seagrass and algae: a promising alternative to engineering solutions. Bioscience **69**, 136–142 (2019)

Kowalczuk, P., Stoń-Egiert, J., Cooper, W.J., Whitehead, R.F., Durako, M.J.: Characterization of chromophoric dissolved organic matter (CDOM) in the Baltic Sea by excitation emission matrix fluorescence spectroscopy. Mar. Chem. **96**(3–4), 273–292 (2005)

Lamb, J.B., et al.: Seagrass ecosystems reduce exposure to bacterial pathogens of humans, fishes, and invertebrates. Science **355**, 731–733 (2017)

Leal Filho, W., Azul, A.M., Brandli, L., Lange Salvia, A., Wall, T. (eds.): Life Below Water. Springer, Cham (202). https://doi.org/10.1007/978-3-319-98536-7

Les, D.H., Cleland, M.A., Waycott, M.: Phylogenetic studies in Alismatidae, II: evolution of marine angiosperms (seagrasses) and hydrophily. Syst. Bot. **22**, 443–463 (1997). https://doi.org/10.2307/2419820

Malm, T.: Reproduction and recruitment of the seagrass *Halophila stipulacea*. Aquat. Bot. **85**(4), 345–349 (2006)

McKenzie, L.J., Langlois, L.A., Roelfsema, C.M.: Improving approaches to mapping seagrass within the great barrier reef: from field to spaceborne earth observation. Remote Sens. **14**(11), 2604 (2022). https://doi.org/10.3390/rs14112604

Mederos-Barrera, A., Marcello, J., Eugenio, F., Hernández, E.: Seagrass mapping using high resolution multispectral satellite imagery: a comparison of water column correction models.

Int. J. Appl. Earth Observat. Geoinform. **113**, 102990 (2022). https://doi.org/10.1016/j.jag.2022.102990

Nguyen, H.M., Kleitou, P., Kletou, D., Sapir, Y., Winters, G.: Differences in flowering sex ratios between native and invasive populations of the seagrass *Halophila stipulacea*. Bot. Mar. **61**(4), 337–342 (2018)

Potouroglou, M., et al.: Measuring the role of seagrasses in regulating sediment surface elevation. Sci. Rep. **7**, 11917. https://doi-org.ezproxy.haifa.ac.il/https://doi.org/10.1038/s41598-017-12354-y (2017)

Rodriguez-Galiano, V.F., Ghimire, B., Rogan, J., Chica-Olmo, M., Rigol-Sanchez, J.P.: An assessment of the effectiveness of a random forest classifier for land-cover classification. ISPRS J. Photogramm. Remote. Sens. **67**, 93–104 (2012)

Unsworth, R.K.F., Collier, C.J., Henderson, G.M., McKenzie, L.J.: Tropical seagrass meadows modify seawater carbon chemistry: implications for coral reefs impacted by ocean acidification. Environ. Res. Lett. **7**, 024026 (2012). https://doi.org/10.1088/1748-9326/7/2/024026

Veettil, B.K., Ward, R.D., Lima, M.D.A.C., Stankovic, M., Hoai, P.N., Quang, N.X.: Opportunities for seagrass research derived from remote sensing: a review of current methods. Ecol. Ind. **117**, 106560 (2020)

Winters, G., et al.: The tropical seagrass *Halophila stipulacea*: reviewing what we know from its native and invasive habitats, alongside identifying knowledge gaps. Front. Mar. Sci. **7** (2020)

Winters, G., Edelist, D., Shem-Tov, R., Beer, S., Rilov, G.: A low cost field-survey method for mapping seagrasses and their potential threats: an example from the northern Gulf of Aqaba, Red Sea. Aquat. Conserv. Mar. Freshwat. Ecosyst. **27**, 324–339 (2017)

Wolfe, K., Nguyen, H.D., Davey, M., Byrne, M.: Characterizing biogeochemical fluctuations in a world of extremes: a synthesis for temperate intertidal habitats in the face of global change. Glob. Change Biol. **26**(7), 3858–3879 (2020)

Zoffoli, M.L., et al.: Sentinel-2 remote sensing of Zostera noltei-dominated intertidal seagrass meadows. Remote Sens. Environ. **251**, 112020 (2020)

Compressed Species Classification Models for Biodiversity Monitoring

Katriona Goldmann[1]([✉]), Oliver Strickson[1], Tom A. August[2],
Jonas Beuchert[2], Dylan Carbone[2], Mariya Iqbal[1], Jenna L. Lawson[2],
Grace Skinner[2], and David Roy[2]

[1] The Alan Turing Institute, London, UK
kgoldmann@turing.ac.uk
[2] UK Centre for Ecology and Hydrology, Wallingford, UK

Abstract. Scalable biodiversity monitoring remains a critical challenge for global conservation, particularly in ecologically rich but underrepresented regions with limited data infrastructure. The AMBER project (Automated Monitoring of Biodiversity using Edge and Remote Sensing) addresses this gap by integrating lightweight, compressed machine learning models with the AMI insect-monitoring system to enable on-device species identification.

We focus on moth classification as a tractable use case and evaluate two end-to-end inference pipelines: a full-featured, server-based baseline and a compressed, edge-optimised alternative. To support field deployment on low-power devices, we apply quantisation, and model distillation techniques and evaluate trade-offs between full-featured server-based inference and resource-efficient edge deployment strategies.

Our results show that compressed models retain strong classification performance while drastically reducing computation and bandwidth needs, enabling scalable, real-time monitoring in remote settings. This work lays the foundation for scalable, real-time ecological monitoring through trustworthy edge AI systems.

Keywords: Biodiversity Monitoring · Machine Learning · Edge ML · Remote Sensing

1 Introduction

Biodiversity is declining at unprecedented rates, prompting urgent global efforts in ecosystem restoration and conservation [4]. These initiatives depend on timely, high-quality ecological data, such as species distributions, population trends, and environmental change indicators. However, large-scale biodiversity monitoring faces major challenges, notably a shortage of taxonomic expertise and a lack of standardised data collection. Sensors for biodiversity data collection are often deployed in remote, ecologically important regions where infrastructure, power, and connectivity are limited.

Processing large volumes of image data under such constraints is difficult. Traditional approaches that rely on transmitting raw data to central servers are often infeasible in remote or bandwidth-limited environments. Edge computing offers a solution: performing inference directly on the device prioritises relevant ecological information at the source [12]. This reduces transmission costs, enables real-time species detection, and supports timely ecological responses. Edge methods are especially valuable for continuous, unmonitored deployments in inaccessible areas.

The AMBER (Automated Monitoring of Biodiversity using Edge and Remote Sensing) project addresses these challenges with a scalable system that combines automated insect-sensing hardware from the AMI (Automated Monitoring of Insects) system and lightweight edge machine learning (ML) models trained on open biodiversity datasets [10]. The system enables real-time inference, reduces bandwidth via data summarisation, and produces structured evidence to inform conservation decisions.

In its initial deployment, AMBER targets moth identification, a tractable case due to moths' sensitivity to environmental change, wide distribution, and attraction to light-based image capture systems. Prior work [6] introduced the AMI system and highlighted ML challenges in ecology, including class imbalance, noisy data, and few-shot learning.

Historically, global biodiversity datasets are often biased: image and occurrence records are concentrated in well-sampled areas like Europe and North America [8], while tropical, biodiverse regions remain underrepresented [2,7]. AMBER helps address this by enabling local inference and data collection in understudied areas using efficient edge ML.

Our long-term goal is real-time, autonomous biodiversity monitoring via on-device inference and data prioritisation. This work focuses on developing and validating compressed ML models for edge deployment. Although the AMI sensors have collected over 7 million images, these are not yet labelled and were not used in training or evaluation. Instead, models were trained and validated on open-source images, from GBIF [5], based on species lists from our target regions. Active deployment of inference models is a future step. First, we aim to assess model accuracy and reliability to ensure ecological trust and avoid bias in conservation workflows. This paper lays the groundwork by evaluating edge-optimised pipelines using representative ecological image data from AMI deployments in the UK and Costa Rica.

Our specific contributions are:

1. Applying model compression techniques (e.g., quantisation, distillation) for species classification.
2. Design and benchmarking of lightweight inference pipelines (including TensorFlow Lite models [1]) for low-power hardware.
3. Comparison of trade-offs in accuracy, latency, and memory usage between compressed and baseline pipelines on real-world ecological data.

By adapting ecological ML pipelines to resource-constrained settings, we advance scalable and equitable biodiversity monitoring and contribute new digital resources to ecological data libraries.

2 Methodology

2.1 Datasets and Use Case

We used two primary datasets for model development and evaluation, chosen to reflect taxonomic coverage, and real-world deployment conditions, respectively:

- GBIF Training Data: Annotated species images from GBIF, filtered to match expected species in monitoring regions. This dataset was used for all model development, including training, validation, and evaluation, ensuring broad taxonomic and visual coverage.
- Images captured by AMI systems deployed in field locations, as described in [10], were used solely to test real-world model feasibility. These high-resolution images were triggered by motion or periodic snapshots, enabling performance assessment during edge deployment.

GBIF Training Data: Species occurrence records were obtained from the GBIF using code repository[1]. GBIF is a globally recognised biodiversity data repository, adhering to high standards of expert curation. We curated a target species list based on expert input and regional literature, mapping names to GBIF taxon keys. Records were filtered to retain images from human observations with precise coordinates, excluding non-adults. Cleaned images and metadata were organised for model training, with CSVs storing species, location, image URL, and GBIF ID. Up to 1,000 adult images per moth species were gathered, though availability varied, introducing inherent species bias.

AMI Experiment Images: AMI systems, developed by UKCEH and Aarhus University [11], comprise of cameras, UV/white light sources, high-capacity storage, and autonomous power. These devices enable standardised image acquisition in remote areas, reducing sampling bias and improving data quality.

AMI systems have been deployed in Costa Rica, Japan, Kenya, Singapore, Thailand, and other countries through AMBER and related projects. Over 7 million images have been captured across diverse ecosystems. This provides a rigorous testbed for evaluating the generalisability of baseline and edge-optimised ML pipelines. This study focuses on UK and Costa Rica models. These countries were selected as showcase regions due to their contrasting ecological environments and the differing availability and coverage of species data. Figure 1 shows some example snapshots captured in Costa Rica.

---

[1] https://github.com/AMI-system/gbif_download_standalone.

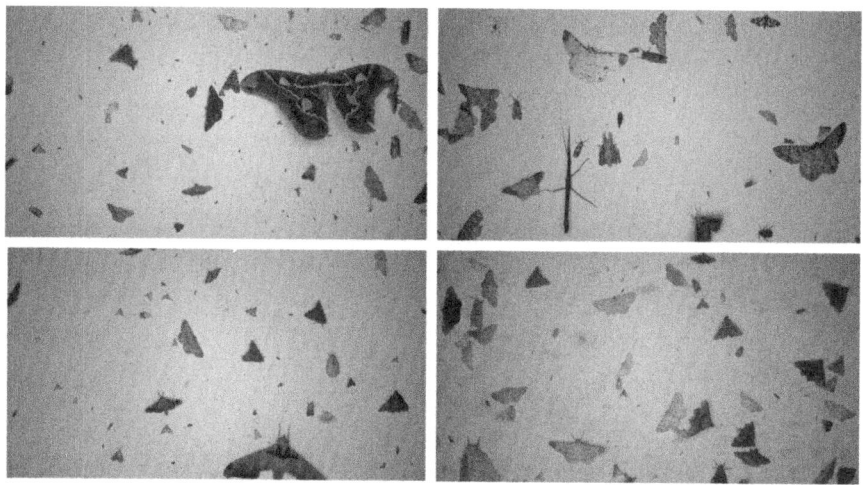

Fig. 1. Four example images, showing many moths and other insects, captured during a night-time AMI deployment in Costa Rica.

2.2 Baseline and Model Compression Techniques

We developed two inference pipelines (Fig. 2) to evaluate trade-offs between server-based and edge-based inference:

1. Baseline Pipeline. This pipeline follows the architecture, models, and methods previously described in [6]:
   - Object Detection: A model to identify all objects within each image.
   - Binary Moth Classifier: Classifies detected crops as moths or non-moths.
   - Species Classifier: A PyTorch [9] classifier trained on region-specific species lists, applied to moth crops.
2. Edge Pipeline.
   - Moth Detection: A lightweight object detector optimised for edge performance.
   - Compressed Species Classifier: A quantised TensorFlow Lite model for moth-positive crops.

Baseline Pipeline Details: We adapted the multi-stage insect monitoring pipeline from Jain et al. [6] originally designed for server-side processing. It integrates detection, binary filtering, species classification and tracking using high-resolution images and large CNNs. In this work, we preserve the pipeline logic (detecting objects, filtering moths, and classifying species using GBIF-trained models) but adapt components for edge deployment. Tracking was omitted for simplicity.

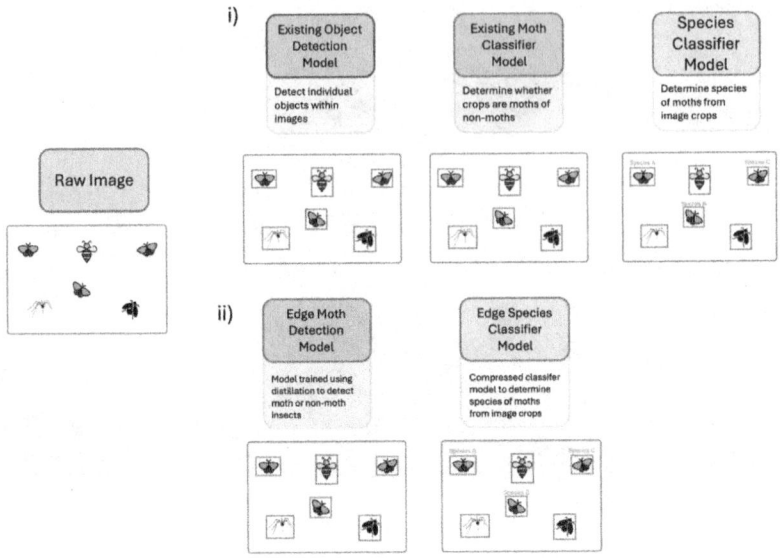

Fig. 2. Inference pipelines for (i) server-based and (ii) edge-device deployment.

Species classifiers were tailored per region using expert species lists (2,660 UK; 5,951 Costa Rica). These lists were created through consultation with local entomologists, reference to regional biodiversity records, and review of relevant literature. Taxa were validated through cross-referencing with GBIF occurrence data and taxonomic databases to ensure consistency and reproducibility. GBIF-sourced data showed regional imbalance, with the UK offering richer coverage.

Images were resized to 300 × 300 px, and normalised using ImageNet mean and standard deviation statistics[2]. Data were split into 75:10:15 train/val/test. Inference followed the detection; moth classification; and species classification sequence.

Edge Pipeline Details: A lightweight binary moth classifier was developed using EfficientDet-Lite4 and TensorFlow Lite Model Maker. Training data were generated by applying MegaDetector [3] to GBIF images. Bounding boxes were matched to species names to identify moths, creating a distillation-style dataset.

Baseline PyTorch classifiers were compressed using 8-bit quantisation via TensorFlow's QAT. We selected QAT (quantisation-aware training) over other compression methods because it typically results in higher accuracy retention compared to post-training quantisation. This makes it well-suited for deployment in accuracy-sensitive ecological monitoring applications on constrained devices. Models were trained with quantisation-aware layers, exported with ONNX, and converted to TFLite.

---

[2] mean = [0.485, 0.456, 0.406], std = [0.229, 0.224, 0.225].

2.3 Edge Deployment Setup and Benchmarking

Pipelines were deployed on Raspberry Pi 4 Model B (8GB RAM) running Debian 12 (bookworm) and Python 3.9. Object detection used TensorFlow Lite models via the TFLite Task Library. For species classification, we benchmarked both PyTorch and TFLite models using torch v1.9.0 and tflite_runtime v2.14.0.

Preprocessing was optimised for speed. Inference ran on a single thread without EdgeTPU acceleration to simulate field conditions. A directory was continuously monitored for new images, which were processed and logged in CSV or JSON. Performance was benchmarked post-warm-up by recording model size, average latency, and peak memory usage.

3 Results

The discrepancy in training image availability on GBIF for different regions is evident in Fig. 3, which shows that most Costa Rican species had fewer than 10 images, while many UK species reached the 1,000-image threshold. This long-tailed distribution of training images across species, with a small number of taxa represented by many images and the majority by relatively few, led to notable differences in model performance and presents challenges for generalisation in regions underrepresented in research.

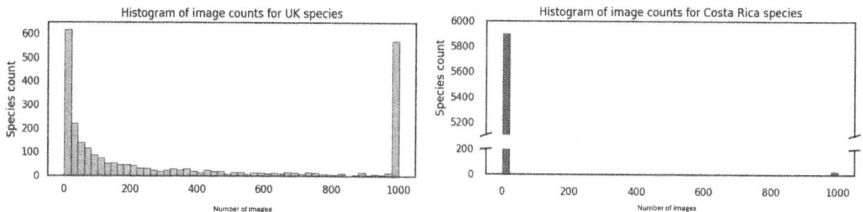

Fig. 3. Histogram showing the number of images available for species.

As shown in Fig. 4, species classification accuracy strongly correlated with the number of training images per species, with UK classifiers consistently outperforming those for Costa Rica (Table 1). Quantisation had minimal effect on accuracy: post-quantisation performance remained within 1% of the original models and, in some cases, even exceeded it, likely due to minor regularisation effects or training noise, demonstrating that lightweight deployment can preserve core classification capabilities.

3.1 Deployment Feasibility

Quantised and lightweight models enabled inference on the Raspberry Pi 4 in real-time or near-real-time conditions. Table 2 compares the performance of

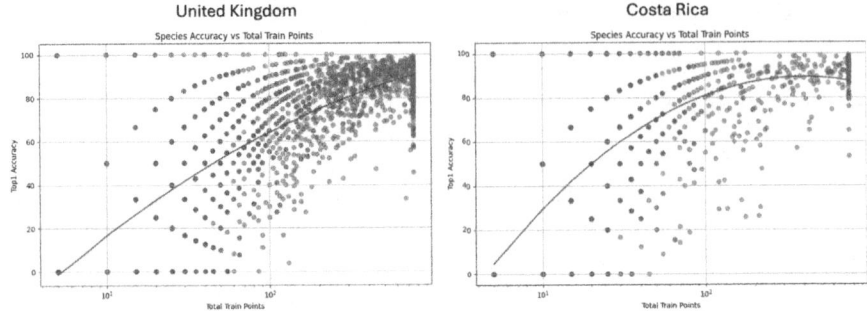

Fig. 4. Test species accuracy versus number of available species training images in the United Kingdom, left, and Costa Rica, right, with the best fit shown in red. (Color figure online)

Table 1. Accuracy and balanced accuracy for species classifier models at each taxon level.

		UK		Costa Rica	
		PyTorch	TFLite	PyTorch	TFLite
Taxon Accuracy (%)	Species	85.4	85.5	82.3	82.1
	Genus	89.6	89.6	85.5	85.3
	Family	95.1	95.1	91.8	91.7
Balanced Accuracy (%)	Species	59.7	59.8	29.5	29.4
	Genus	76.9	77.1	42.5	42.4
	Family	82.0	82.0	66.9	66.6

PyTorch and TensorFlow Lite species classifier models, operating on the Raspberry Pi, demonstrating a significant reduction in latency (approximately one-eighth the runtime) and model size (approximately one-quarter the size) when using compressed models. This performance gain supports their use in field deployments, where snapshots are typically taken every 10 s.

3.2 Bandwidth Reduction

Performing inference at the edge substantially reduces the volume of data that needs to be transmitted. For instance, a single night of operation in Costa Rica generates a large volume of image data, yet the corresponding inference summary can be stored in a compact text file. For example, for one deployment in Costa Rica on 21st June 2024, there were 3420 snapshot images captured resulting in 8.8GB of data, each image on average 2.8MB, whereas the inference CSV for the entire night is only 218kB. Overall, this summary data is small enough to be transmitted via wireless networks with low data rates, making it feasible to extract actionable information even in bandwidth-constrained environments. This reduction is also significant from a cost perspective: transmitting gigabytes

Table 2. Comparison between Pytorch and TFLite species classifier models for the UK and Costa Rica run on Raspberry Pi 4.

	UK		Costa Rica	
	PyTorch	TFLite	PyTorch	TFLite
Model Size (MB)	111.03	28.00	136.74	34.43
Average Latency (ms/frame)	24,665.49	2,944.61	24,740.43	3,025.44
Peak Memory Usage (MB)	323.75	191.69	350.28	276.47

of data over mobile or satellite networks can be expensive, whereas transmitting kilobyte-scale summaries incurs minimal to negligible cost. While data transmission methods are beyond the scope of this paper, they are the focus of ongoing work within AMBER.

4 Discussion and Conclusion

The AMBER project has collected over 7 million images across diverse environmental conditions, with more being added daily. These images, and the corresponding species inferences captured by AMI devices, form a growing data resource for long-term biodiversity monitoring. Collected from deployments in tropical and underrepresented regions globally, this dataset supports expanding the geographical and taxonomic scope of automated biodiversity monitoring. While we focused on deployments in Costa Rica and the UK, the broader AMBER network includes systems in Kenya, Nigeria, Thailand, and beyond.

A key contribution of this work is showing that edge-optimised models can offer near-baseline accuracy while drastically reducing processing time, transmission costs, and infrastructure demands, making minor performance trade-offs worthwhile. Running inference on-device enables immediate species detection.

On-site processing means data can be prioritised or filtered before transmission, enabling collection of much larger volumes of ecologically relevant information. This is especially beneficial in remote or logistically challenging regions with limited bandwidth.

No additional pruning or structural compression techniques were applied in this iteration, though such methods could further reduce model size and inference cost in future versions.

Deploying AI systems in the field reveals key lessons. Model performance depends heavily on the quality and diversity of training data, highlighting the need for better image coverage in tropical and global South regions. AMI systems can help fill these gaps by capturing in-situ images that feed back into the modelling pipeline. This iterative process improves model accuracy and ensures future systems are more attuned to the environments in which they operate. Each deployment thereby strengthens the global biodiversity monitoring ecosystem.

Automated species identification in the field also raises important questions of transparency and trust. To gain confidence from ecologists, compressed models must be interpretable and verifiable. This involves validating model accuracy, surfacing uncertainty, and enabling domain expert oversight. Our models provide predicted labels with confidence scores, allowing low-confidence outputs to be flagged for review. Future iterations will explore lightweight out-of-distribution detection to highlight novel or unexpected inputs. Post-hoc interpretability techniques such as Grad-CAM may help users understand model decisions and detect failures. Automatically flagging uncertain outputs may support detection of rare or invasive species, while tracking commonly confused classes could guide retraining or annotation.

Such strategies are essential for transparent and accountable AI. Interpretability and feedback loops are as critical as accuracy. Experts may review edge-generated summaries, especially edge cases or rare observations, and contest results where ambiguity exists. Supporting uncertainty visualisation and expert-in-the-loop workflows helps ensure ML complements taxonomic expertise.

Developing lightweight models for edge deployment involves epistemological trade-offs. Techniques like pruning and quantisation reduce computational load but may also reduce representational complexity, limiting the model's capacity to capture ecological nuance. This risks losing fine-grained distinctions, especially in rare or similar species. Yet in remote, under-observed regions, edge ML can provide otherwise unobtainable observations. Responsible use involves acknowledging these limitations, incorporating expert validation, and retraining with local data. Systems designed to be transparent, updateable, and uncertainty-aware can help mitigate trade-offs and support fine-scale, inclusive biodiversity monitoring.

As Fig. 3 shows, there is a substantial imbalance in training images per species, reflecting biases in GBIF imagery and species visibility. While current models prioritise coverage, future evaluations should use more balanced test sets or stratified metrics to ensure performance across common and rare taxa. As more imagery becomes available models can be retrained to improve class balance.

Overall, this work represents a first iteration of a lightweight species classification model optimised for edge deployment. With continued image collection and annotation from diverse environments, classification performance will improve. Retraining on local data will ensure models remain ecologically relevant and robust across regions. By enabling ML at the point of data collection, AMBER provides a practical path to responsive, efficient, and scalable ecological monitoring.

Acknowledgments. We would like to thank the AMI consortium for their invaluable support and contributions to the development of the initial model pipelines. We are also grateful to Aberdeen Group Charitable Foundation for funding the project and making the AMBER deployments and research possible. Parts of this work were also supported by the Natural Environment Research Council programmes delivering National Capability [NE/X006247/1; NE/Y006208/1; NE/W005069/1], and by the MAMBO project under the European Union's research and innovation programme No. 101060639. And by Darwin Plus project DPLUS203 funded by Defra. We further acknowledge the support of our deployment partners, whose collaboration and dedication to uploading data have been instrumental to the project's success.

Disclosure of Interests. The authors have no competing interests to declare that are relevant to the content of this article.

References

1. Abadi, M., et al.: TensorFlow: large-scale machine learning on heterogeneous systems (2015). https://www.tensorflow.org/, software available from tensorflow.org
2. Beck, J., Böller, M., Erhardt, A., Schwanghart, W.: Spatial bias in the gbif database and its effect on modeling species' geographic distributions. Eco. Inform. **19**, 10–15 (2014)
3. Beery, S., Morris, D., Yang, S.: Efficient pipeline for camera trap image review. arXiv preprint arXiv:1907.06772 (2019)
4. Butchart, S.H., et al.: Global biodiversity: indicators of recent declines. Science **328**(5982), 1164–1168 (2010)
5. GBIF.org: Gbif home page (2025). https://www.gbif.org. Accessed 28 May 2025
6. Jain, A., et al.: A machine learning pipeline for automated insect monitoring. arXiv preprint arXiv:2406.13031 (2024)
7. Joppa, L., et al.: Filling in biodiversity threat gaps. Science **352**(6284), 416–418 (2016)
8. Meyer, C., Kreft, H., Guralnick, R., Jetz, W.: Global priorities for an effective information basis of biodiversity distributions. Nat. Commun. **6**(1), 1–8 (2015)
9. Paszke, A., et al.: Pytorch: an imperative style, high-performance deep learning library. Advances in neural information processing systems **32** (2019)
10. Roy, D., et al.: Towards a standardized framework for ai-assisted, image-based monitoring of nocturnal insects. Philosophical Trans. Roy. Soc. B **379**(1904), 20230108 (2024)
11. UKCEH: Ukceh ami system (2025). https://www.ceh.ac.uk/solutions/equipment/automated-monitoring-insects-trap. Accessed 2 June 2025
12. Zhu, G., Liu, D., Du, Y., You, C., Zhang, J., Huang, K.: Toward an intelligent edge: wireless communication meets machine learning. IEEE Commun. Mag. **58**(1), 19–25 (2020)

Creating Datasets of Moth Morphology and Behaviour from Textual Sources with Large Language Models

Bartolome Ortiz-Viso[1,2] 🖂 ⓘ, Jenna L. Lawson[2] ⓘ, and Tom August[2] ⓘ

[1] Department of Computer Science and Artificial Intelligence, CITIC-UGR (Research Center for Information and Communication Technologies), Granada, Spain
[2] UK Centre for Ecology and Hydrology, Wallingford, UK
bortiz@ugr.es, {jenlaw,tomaug}@ceh.ca.uk

Abstract. The integration of language models into ecological workflows is opening new possibilities for automated species monitoring. Classification systems are especially relevant in this context, as the high volume of data generated by automated systems requires efficient tools to support expert curators. Multimodal approaches, which incorporate textual information alongside visual or acoustic data, have shown potential to improve classification performance and interpretability. However, for many insect taxa, structured and usable textual descriptions remain scarce or difficult to access. In this work, we present a tool for retrieving and merging textual information about moth species from official repositories and citable sources. The resulting descriptions can be used to enrich multimodal classification models across different taxonomic levels or to build structured databases for species comparison and discovery.

Keywords: Computational Entomology · Automated insect monitoring · Multimodal category discovery · Large Language Models · Biodiversity

1 Introduction

In recent years, there has been significant growth in the development of automated insect monitoring systems [10]. These technologies are made possible by recent advances in image-based machine learning models and low-power electronics, which together enable the construction of specialised devices designed specifically for this task [13]. This trend reflects the growing need to understand the dynamics of insect populations and how they are being affected by multiple environmental factors, including climate change [31], as most studies suggest a declining on populations has been a clear pattern each year (see [5] for specific UK data across multiple years and [31] for overall discussion).

Camera-based automated systems for monitoring insects have proven to be highly effective in generating large volumes of insect monitoring data, which has in turn sparked a wide range of questions and applications in the field of computer science [11,14,25]. These range from how we collect and store ecological data to how we design robust algorithms for species classification or detecting rare species within datasets.

The vast amount of data collected by such systems presents a considerable workload in terms of identifying the species in each image. This highlights the urgent need for machine learning tools that can alleviate the burden on taxonomists—experts who are already in short supply [15]—by identifying species where the model is able, and referring others that require expert attention.

In this context, classification systems play a crucial role in helping us to make sense of complex datasets. Among these, multimodal systems are particularly promising, as they enable the integration of multiple types of data, such as text and images, within a shared feature space. This not only facilitates the interpretation of machine decisions but also supports clustering and labelling processes, even when the exact taxonomic classification of a specimen is unknown.

Deploying multimodal classification systems in entomology requires the creation of high-quality multimodal datasets—a task that presents unique challenges. Despite the availability of trait and abundance data, textual descriptions of insects —covering features such as colour, shape, and size—remain scarce, fragmented, and complex to process automatically. This contrasts with domains such as ornithology, where rich textual data resources are already available [20]. In addition to the value of trait data for supporting multimodal classification models, trait data are also crucial for understanding the role of species in ecological systems. The notable lack of trait data for insects is highlighted [16,32].

In this work, we present our experience building a pipeline that leverages large language models (LLMs) to guide the extraction, standardisation, and formatting of species descriptions into usable forms for moth species. This contribution closes the gap between the potential of computational methods and the current limitations of available entomological data.

This paper is structured as follows: After the Introduction, Sect. 2 provides an overview of related work from a computational perspective, highlighting how textual information can support multimodal approaches in tasks such as classification and novel category discovery. In Sect. 3, we present our work on UK moths. Some experiments derived from the created dataset are given in Sect. 4, along with a brief discussion. Finally, we conclude the paper in Sect. 5 by reflecting on the outcomes of our work and outlining the next steps.

2 Related Works

Image classification models continue to advance rapidly, with increasing capabilities being integrated into everyday applications. These models have recently been enhanced by the development of new multimodal architectures—a branch of machine learning that enables the joint representation of visual and textual data within a shared latent space. This shared space not only facilitates explainability but also supports cross-modal applications, such as image-to-text and text-to-image generation [9].

One of the most widely used models in this area is CLIP [23], which employs a contrastive learning framework. In this architecture, the model learns to align images and their corresponding textual descriptions by bringing similar pairs closer in the latent space and pushing dissimilar ones apart. This approach has led to significant improvements, particularly in the task of novel category discovery [28,30], where the goal is to identify previously unseen categories in an open-world setting. This discovery-type scenario has clear implications in ecology, although it is not widely known and therefore not integrated into the automatic insect monitoring studies.

A multimodal perspective offers several advantages: it enables more targeted and guided training, improves generalisation, and enhances the interpretability of resulting clusters. While CLIP includes a relatively small text transformer by default, longer and more informative descriptions can be utilised through extensions such as LongCLIP [34], which is better suited to handling detailed textual data. In addition, there are now CLIP models trained on natural data as BIO-CLIP [27] and InsectFoundation [29] that have shown the considerable potential these models have in the taxonomic/nature domain, creating a good starting point for fine-tuning tasks and other modalities alignment [33]. The trade-off, however, is that these models require a reliable source of textual descriptions corresponding to the images, so that a rich semantic latent space can be learned—linking the words used to describe insects with their visual representations. While such descriptions often exist in the form of trait annotations and identification keys, they are rarely available in structured datasets suitable for machine learning. Nevertheless, they represent a valuable resource in their own right, enabling applications such as natural language search and classification. One example is shown in [21], which presents a natural language classifier for insects based on Spanish descriptions. This problem becomes even more pronounced in biodiversity hotspots, such as Costa Rica. For this reason, studies like the present one contribute by proposing methods to generate and curate such datasets, serving as a foundation for the development of more accurate and practically useful multimodal resources.

3 Methodology

Our workflow is designed to extract, normalise, and synthesise textual descriptions of moth species from various online sources, supporting multimodal classification and structured trait extraction. The process involves several steps described below. A summary is presented in Fig. 1. We began with a specific list of species based on a particular location (in this case, the United Kingdom), primarily to test our approach with a scenario that should contain a reasonable amount of textual descriptions and be well-documented. Based on that, we searched for databases of descriptions for UK and northern European species, as the overlap between those could offer a good complement. This is a key step that may vary between different countries and is also the main challenge to overcome, as we will discuss in Sect. 5.

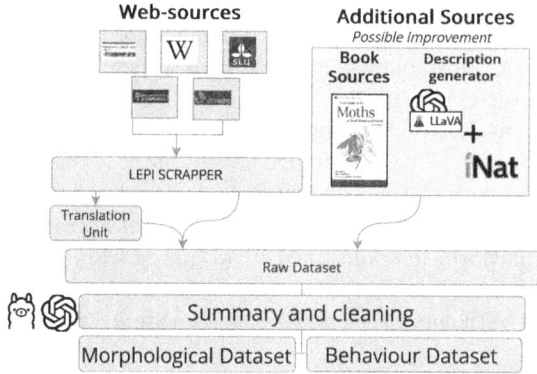

Fig. 1. Overview of the proposed workflow for textual data extraction, processing, and trait structuring.

3.1 Selection of Web Sources

We identified six web-based sources containing textual information about moth species/families/genus descriptions. These services include both official repositories and citable biodiversity platforms. The selected sources are:

- **Wikipedia** [4]: Wikipedia is a widely accessible and citable source that contains a substantial amount of biological information. It offers broad taxonomic coverage and is often the first point of reference for many users. However, its content is contributed by volunteers, and thus, the accuracy of descriptions can vary. While many pages do include cited references, there is a clear bias toward more popular or well-known species. Moreover, the textual information on species pages is typically unstructured, making it difficult to extract relevant data in a consistent manner. At higher taxonomic levels (e.g., genus or family), Wikipedia provides a high number of positives in terms of species coverage. However, the quality of this information tends to be low, as these pages often consist of long enumerations of species names without any accompanying morphological or behavioural descriptions.
- **Butterflies and Moths of North America** [2]: BAMONA is a curated online resource providing species information, distribution data, and user-submitted observations of Lepidoptera across North America. One of its strengths is the availability of concise species-level descriptions, often accompanied by high-quality images and confirmed locality records. Additionally, when species-level descriptions are not available, it is often possible to retrieve

general information at the genus or family level. The data is curated by several volunteers mentioned in the acknowledgements [1], and some of the identification keys come from three specific manuals that need to be cited [3,7] [22]
- **UKMoths** [12]: UKMoths is a reference website for moths in the United Kingdom. It provides species profiles that include a variety of information such as life cycle, host plants, and physical appearance. However, the content is unstructured and not all entries contain the same fields, making text processing essential for extracting relevant data.
- **Animal Diversity** [17]: Animal Diversity offers species-level content with structured sections including descriptions and various biological data. Since much of the content is created by students, it is not always curated by domain experts. The platform is maintained by volunteers and is based in the USA, which introduces both geographical and popularity-related biases. Nevertheless, for species with complete entries, the site offers a wealth of well-organised information.
- **Swedish Museum of Natural History (NRM)** [6]: The NRM provides a repository containing textual and specimen-level information for species housed in the museum's collections. For some species, general descriptive information is also available. We discovered this resource by following citation links from other biodiversity and abundance databases, where records of these specimens are maintained. There is an obvious geographic bias, but it has an insightful description of a wide selection of species.
- **Artfakta – SLU: Swedish Species Information Centre** [26]: Artfakta is another Swedish biodiversity repository frequently referenced in Scandinavian specimen abundance databases. The platform offers robust services and provides an API through which textual information, primarily written in Swedish, can be accessed. This facilitates automated extraction, and since experts curate the content, it is well-structured and organised. When descriptive text is available, it is typically easy to locate.

In summary, the selected sources, despite their value, obviously exhibit biases such as uneven geographic coverage, with underrepresentation of species outside the UK, North America, and Scandinavia. Some rely on user- or student-generated content, leading to inconsistencies in taxonomy or descriptive detail. When multiple descriptions exist, minor discrepancies (e.g., in colour or size) may arise; in such cases, our summarisation favours the more structured source. To ensure transparency, the dataset includes all original texts used, enabling verification. These limitations are further discussed in Sect. 5, and we advise verifying content before using descriptions for model training or trait analysis.

3.2 LLM-Guided Summarization

In this section, we explain our pipeline step by step, highlighting the key aspects of each step. A diagram of this is shown in Fig. 2 for a specific species.

1. **Grouping and Translation** The collected texts are grouped by species, genus, or family to facilitate subsequent processing. Descriptions written in languages other than English are translated using a machine translation system[1] that is based on the DeepTranslator Python library[2].
2. **Merging**
   The translated descriptions are merged and cleaned to remove formatted content (such as species lists, which are commonly found in Wikipedia) and special characters. From webpages that have a fixed schema, description fields are extracted. For those which do not have it, regular expressions are used to search for the most similar header to the description. This step ensures that most irrelevant information is discarded for subsequent summarisation, reducing the text size.
3. **Summarisation** We employ a LLM with tailored prompts (see source code 5 for a full description of the prompts used[3]) to generate three types of descriptions:
   - **Morphological description**: covering antennae, body structure, colouration, and other visual features.
   - **Behavioural description**: including months of activity, larval behaviour, and host plant preferences.
   - **Visual-only morphological description**: a refined version of the morphological description, restricted to strictly visual traits, intended for use in downstream multimodal models.

   The model is guided by structured prompts that were carefully designed depending on the type of summarisation task—morphological, behavioural, or visual-only. Each prompt included: (i) a specific framing or role context for the model (e.g., "You are an entomologist writing short scientific summaries"), (ii) a list of target traits or guide words (e.g., wingspan, forewings, antennae, colouration, host plants, flight period), and (iii) concrete examples of input-output pairs illustrating the expected format and content.

   Importantly, the prompts were explicitly crafted to discourage hallucination and ensure that the output remains grounded in the available source information. This was achieved by instructing the model to state when information was unavailable or insufficient (e.g., returning "Sorry, information missing" or similar variants). This behaviour proved particularly useful when processing rare or poorly documented species, for which textual sources were incomplete or highly variable. These cases were primarily observed when applying the pipeline to the full dataset, where particular species yielded short or empty summaries, which were straightforward to detect and filter during post-processing.

   To test performance, we implemented the summarisation pipeline using two

---

[1] We avoided using LLMs for translation due to inconsistent performance on technical entomological vocabulary, though they remain a possible alternative.
[2] https://github.com/nidhaloff/deep-translator.
[3] Latest updated prompts applied in our research can be found in a specific txt file in the *code* directory.

large language models, including *gpt4-o-mini* [18,19] and LLaMA 3 [8]. We used LLaMA 3 via the Hugging Face Transformers pipeline. All generations were performed with the following parameters: *do sample* set to *False* (i.e., deterministic decoding), *max new tokens* set to 512. OpenAI models used the following generation parameters: *temperature=1.0*, *top_p=1.0*, *max_tokens* set by default (up to the model's context limit), and both *frequency_penalty* and *presence_penalty* set to *0.0*. Due to its smaller size and the lack of sampling, LLaMA 3 exhibited lower performance in our summarisation task compared to *gpt4-o-mini*. Therefore, subsequent analysis will primarily focus on results from *gpt4-o-mini*.

To verify the factual accuracy of the generated summaries, we applied the *faithfulness* metric from the RAGAS evaluation framework[4]. This metric estimates how well the generated text is grounded in the provided sources by using a reference LLM (in this case, *GPT4-o* [18,19]), larger than the one used in the summarisation, to check whether each factual statement in the summary can be traced back to the source material. This serves as an initial, indicative metric that helps confirm the system is not introducing hallucinations or noise, and that it remains faithful to the original content. Nevertheless, human expert validation would still be necessary to cross-check that there are no errors in the original sources.

The full implementation of the summarisation process with each model, along with the evaluation results of each step and examples, are available in the public repository.

4. **Dual Textual Datasets**

 The output of the LLM is assembled into a dataset containing cleaned and standardised descriptions per species, one for the morphological traits and the other for the behavioural characteristics (more broadly, including larval behaviour, eating patterns, and months). The result is a dataset that could be suitable for training multimodal classification systems or conducting ecological trait analysis via unsupervised trait extraction from the data, an example of this can be seen in Sect. 4.

5. **Structured Trait Extraction**

 In a final step, we optionally guide the LLM to transform the descriptive data into structured tables capturing individual traits (e.g., wing span, colouration patterns, activity periods). This structured dataset enables several downstream applications, such as:

 – Trait-based species comparison;
 – Integration with existing ecological trait databases;
 – Semi-automated validation of extracted descriptions through comparison with known trait values.

This dual use—as both a reference and a validation tool—enhances the robustness of the overall workflow and facilitates its integration into ecological monitoring pipelines. One example of this application could utilise

---

[4] https://docs.ragas.io/en/latest/.

models trained in works like [21] with descriptions, along with vision models via contrastive learning, as in [33]. This model enabled natural language search within a set of pictures and zero-shot, few-shot classification of images, which can be potentially helpful in discovering novel categories.

3.3 Description Generation

We could complement textual sources with a visual approach using a pipeline that crops moth specimens from iNaturalist images. These can be processed by multimodal large language models (MLLMs), such as LLaVA and GPT-4-V, to generate captions emphasising traits like colouration, wing shape, and other morphological features.

This method could be useful when textual data is scarce, such as in hyperdiverse ecosystems or museum collections lacking detailed annotations, but it still needs to learn from the datasets that combine both images and tests, as the one we are creating here.

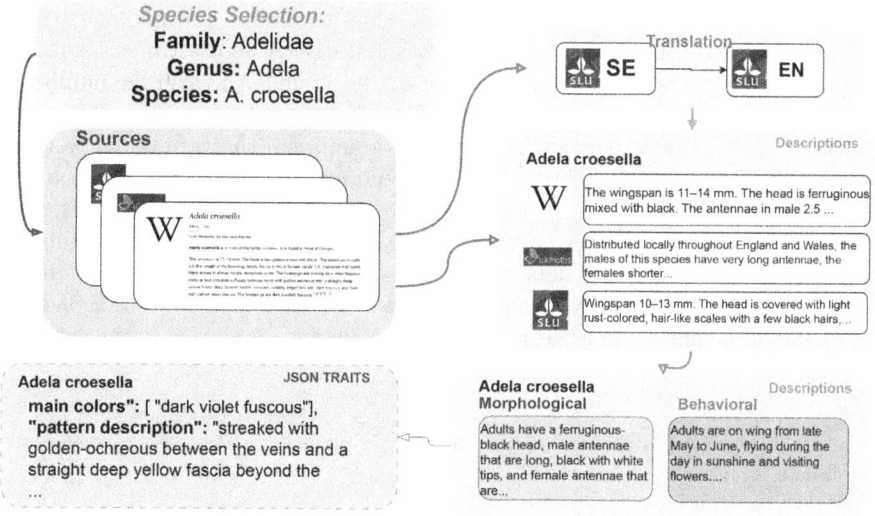

Fig. 2. Example of the pipeline for Adela croesella.

4 Results

In this section, we present the first results of our approach from the UK dataset. First, we will describe the species coverage that can be obtained from the dataset. We start with a dataset that contains 2682 species from 213 genus and 57 families of moths, with a variable length and distribution (see Table 1 and Fig. 3

for additional details). This species list was extracted from the master list used in the AMI project for automatic moth monitoring[5]. It comprises moth species recorded and counted in GBIF for the United Kingdom for which we have photographic records, making them suitable for automatic visual recognition. The genus and family information is derived directly from these species, and the released dataset includes the scientific name, common name, and the *GBIF taxon ID*[6] to link these names with any other nomenclature used in the sources or by other databases.

This coverage can be generalised to some extent to other northern regions, as many of the same resources and species overlap; therefore, we expect a comparable number of descriptions to be obtainable for those areas as well. In the results, we present insights into the species coverage and demonstrate how textual models can be applied to the morphological descriptions for tasks such as similarity search. We discuss both aspects further after the results are presented. Section 5 will outline the next steps based on the data presented here.

4.1 Species Coverage

To assess the quality and richness of the generated morphological and behavioural descriptions, we computed basic statistics across three taxonomic levels: species, genus and family. These statistics include the average number of words, standard deviation, the number of descriptions with fewer than 20 words, and the corresponding percentage. Table 1 summarises the results. In terms of coverage, based on GBIF records[7], we achieved morphological descriptions longer than 20 words for 79.9% of species and behavioural descriptions longer than 20 words for 89.7%. The average coverage across families is 84.8% for morphological descriptions and 92.6% for behavioural ones. Notably, the families *Tortricidae* (only 62% morphology, 89% behaviour) and *Noctuidae* (only 85% morphology, 85% behaviour) show the largest absolute gaps in the number of species not yet described in the dataset.

Table 1. Descriptive statistics of morphological and behavioural descriptions across taxonomic levels.

Level	Type	Mean	Std.	Less than 20 words
Species	Morphological	57.56	38.47	19.35%
	Behavioral	42.36	18.55	9.26%
Family	Morphological	42.82	25.78	24.56%
	Behavioral	48.75	27.07	15.79%
Genus	Morphological	48.72	30.08	14.55%
	Behavioral	36.40	19.38	21.60%

---

[5] https://github.com/AMI-system.
[6] https://www.gbif.org/dataset/d7dddbf4-2cf0-4f39-9b2a-bb099caae36c.
[7] https://doi.org/10.15468/dl.b9nhv6.

Overall, morphological descriptions tend to be longer than behavioural ones across all taxonomic levels. The species-level descriptions exhibit the highest average word count for morphology, while the genus-level behavioural descriptions show the highest proportion of short texts (less than 20 words).

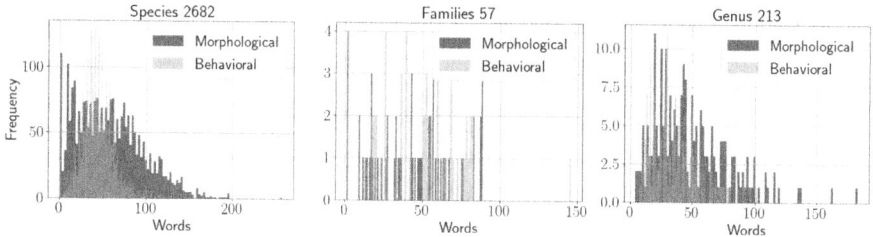

Fig. 3. Histogram of descriptions lengths for species, genus and families from the UK dataset.

4.2 Textual Similarity

In addition to descriptive statistics, we evaluated the semantic similarity among the morphological and behavioural descriptions using a pretrained language model. Specifically, we employed the *all-MiniLM-L6-v2*[8] model from the *sentence-transformers* library [24], which provides a lightweight transformer-based architecture for computing sentence embeddings.

Each description was embedded into a high-dimensional semantic space, and cosine similarity was used to measure pairwise similarities between descriptions within the species range. Results showed that morphological descriptions exhibit a similarity $mean = 0.6147$, $std = 0.1271$, while behaviour similarity $mean = 0.6258$ with $std = 0.125$. Some examples are shown in Fig. 4, where a random species was selected and its similarity to all other species was computed. We then selected the top 3 most similar, the bottom 3 least similar, and 3 examples with mid-range similarity.

4.3 Results' Discussions

It is important to note that this analysis was conducted using a pretrained language model that was not specifically trained on insect-related descriptions. Therefore, this represents only a preliminary exploration of how general-purpose language models interpret and compare the semantic content of these descriptions.

From the results, we observe that species with similar description structures tend to be marked as highly similar. For instance, the top three most similar descriptions often follow a standard descriptive scheme, highlighting comparable traits such as metallic colouration, head patterning, or wing texture.

---
[8] https://huggingface.co/sentence-transformers/all-MiniLM-L6-v2

In contrast, the least similar descriptions are often brief and lack detail; they frequently refer to general information, such as size or resemblance to other species, without elaborating on specific morphological features. This hypothesis was tested by comparing morphological descriptions in short texts (less than 20 words), which exhibited a significantly lower mean similarity to other descriptions ($\mu_{short} = 0.5286$) compared to longer ones ($\mu_{long} = 0.6309$). A similar pattern was observed for behavioural descriptions, where short texts averaged $\mu_{short} = 0.4923$ in similarity versus $\mu_{long} = 0.6340$ for long ones. These differences were statistically significant, as shown by the results of independent t-tests: Morphological descriptions: $t = -20.19$, $p < 0.05$ and Behavioral descriptions: $t = -11.98$, $p < 0.05$.

These findings suggest that shorter descriptions tend to be less semantically aligned with the rest of the dataset. This may be due to reduced lexical richness, a lack of detailed traits, or template-like phrasing, which limits their usefulness in tasks that require semantic comparison.

Descriptions with mid-range similarity are typically more detailed and offer a more nuanced comparison. While not identical in content, they tend to share semantically rich elements, such as references to colours and textures commonly used in moth descriptions, which result in moderate similarity scores. These findings suggest that semantic similarity scores can reflect both structural and content-based resemblance, particularly when the descriptions are sufficiently informative and detailed. These models will enhance their discriminative power when trained alongside images in multimodal approaches, or we could further fine-tune them for a specific classification task, for example. This will improve the model's performance for those with complete descriptions, as well as for others that require further completion. At the same time, the question of a standardised or at least similar description pattern arises, and that's an interesting application of a structured trait/descriptive database, from which we can create those.

As part of this work, we publish an open partial dataset comprising the 100 most common moth species in the UK, selected based on occurrence data from iNaturalist in the United Kingdom, along with family and genus. This dataset includes the original textual sources used for summarisation, allowing for detailed evaluation and reproducibility. The *faithfulness* metric was applied to this subset as a preliminary indicator of its validation and standardisation. These scores provide insight into the alignment between generated summaries and their source materials, serving as a first step toward ensuring data reliability in downstream applications. The average *faithfulness* score for morphological descriptions was 0.956 ($\sigma = 0.112$), while behavioural descriptions scored slightly higher, with a mean of 0.978 ($\sigma = 0.081$). These values suggest a strong factual alignment between the generated summaries and their corresponding source texts, supporting the reliability of the summarisation pipeline in preserving original content. We detected some differences between descriptions, as well as additional descriptions (pages where moths and larvae are described simultaneously) in cases where faithfulness was below 1.0, highlighting this approach as a first step in analysing the initial data. The Families dataset also showed similar performance, whereas

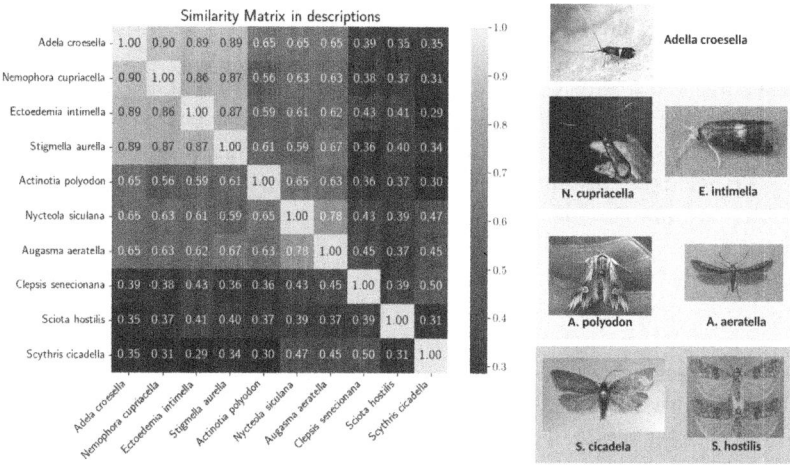

Fig. 4. Similarity matrix from Adela croesella selecting top three, mid three and bottom three matching descriptions. Some photos of the species are highlighted in green (top 3), orange (mid-similarity), and red (low-similarity). (Color figure online)

the Genus dataset was the only one with notably lower scores. Upon analysis, these lower scores were attributed to the model providing characteristics of specific species within the genus, likely because most of the source materials consisted of species lists. This remains the only detected example of hallucination in the model.

5 Conclusions and Future Works

The workflow presented in this work demonstrates a comprehensive pipeline that can retrieve data from textual sources and summarise it in a manner that is beneficial for multimodal approaches, as well as the creation of new resources (both structured and unstructured). One of the main aspects that is still an open issue is the validation of the final data. At any point in the pipeline, the descriptions remain perfectly traceable from the sources, allowing for any check to be made to assess the summarisation performance. Additionally, the trait database can also serve as a double-check system, where previously known traits are cross-referenced with extracted ones to verify accuracy. Another relevant issue we detected using the similarity approach is the need for a standardised and structured collection of descriptions, as length and content may affect the similarities.

A significant challenge is the lack of accessible, digitised taxonomic records. Outside Europe, structured species descriptions are scarce and often trapped in non-digital or paywalled formats. Even in the UK, unified collections of morphological or behavioural text data are limited. Historically, text descriptions were not considered machine-readable, but this is changing: digitalisation and semantic structuring now enable both the extraction and generation of coherent taxonomic descriptions.

Crucially, biodiversity monitoring and taxonomy remain deeply tied to domain expertise. While AI can assist and accelerate specific tasks, it must not overshadow the core issue: the chronic underfunding and fragmentation of taxonomic knowledge. Any models developed from this data should remain open, shareable, and built in close collaboration with entomologists and taxonomists.

Future work will involve expanding the current approach to incorporate more structured data and taxonomic nomenclature, particularly from underrepresented regions. We also plan to benchmark multimodal models against fine-tuned models with this data to assess their performance across ecological contexts (images vs text vs images + text). Ultimately, our goal is to develop adaptable, lightweight tools that serve entomologists and strengthen computational support for biodiversity conservation.

Acknowledgments. The research reported in this paper is partially funded by the European Union (BAG-INTEL project, grant agreement no. 101121309)

This publication is based upon work from COST action InsectAI CA22129, supported by COST (European Cooperation in Science and Technology)

The authors would also like to acknowledge the support from:
– University of Granada Mobility plans programme.
– UK Centre for Ecology and Hydrology
– Alan Turing Institute

Disclosure of Interests. *The authors have no competing interests to declare that are relevant to the content of this article.*

Source Code. Source code, prompts and other supplementary material can be found at https://thebooort.github.io/ecodl2025-paper/

References

1. Acknowledgments | Butterflies and Moths of North America. https://www.butterfliesandmoths.org/acknowledgments
2. Butterflies and Moths of North America | collecting and sharing data about Lepidoptera. https://www.butterfliesandmoths.org/
3. Western Butterflies (Peterson Field Guide) by Opler, P.a.; Wright, A.b. https://www.pemberleybooks.com/product/western-butterflies-peterson-field-guide/35828/
4. Wikipedia, the free encyclopedia. https://www.wikipedia.org/
5. Ball, L., Still, R., Riggs, A., Skilbeck, A., Shardlow, M., Whitehouse, A., Tinsley-Marshall, P.: The bugs matter citizen science survey (2021). https://cdn.buglife.org.uk/2022/05/Bugs-Matter-2021-National-Report.pdf
6. Bert Gustafsson, T.M.: Lepidoptera - Svenska fjärilar - Naturhistoriska riksmuseet. http://www3.nrm.se/en/svenska_fjarilar/svenska_fjarilar.html
7. Charles V Covell, J.: A Field Guide to Moths of Eastern North America. https://www.nhbs.com/a-field-guide-to-moths-of-eastern-north-america-book

8. Grattafiori, A., et al.: The llama 3 herd of models (2024). https://arxiv.org/abs/2407.21783
9. Guo, R., et al.: A survey on advancements in image–text multimodal models: from general techniques to biomedical implementations. Comput. Biol. Med. **178**, 108709 (2024). https://doi.org/10.1016/j.compbiomed.2024.108709, https://linkinghub.elsevier.com/retrieve/pii/S0010482524007947
10. Høye, T.T., et al.: Deep learning and computer vision will transform entomology. Proc. Natl. Acad. Sci. **118**(2), e2002545117 (2021). https://doi.org/10.1073/pnas.2002545117, https://www.pnas.org/doi/full/10.1073/pnas.2002545117, publisher: Proceedings of the National Academy of Sciences Proceedings of the National Academy of Sciences Proceedings of the National Academy of Sciences
11. Jain, A., Cunha, F., Bunsen, M., Pasi, L., Viklund, A., Larrivée, M., Rolnick, D.: A machine learning pipeline for automated insect monitoring, June 2024. https://doi.org/10.48550/arXiv.2406.13031, http://arxiv.org/abs/2406.13031, arXiv:2406.13031 [cs]
12. Kimber, I.: UKMoths | Guide to the moths of Great Britain and Ireland. https://www.ukmoths.org.uk/
13. van Klink, R., et al.: Emerging technologies revolutionise insect ecology and monitoring. Trends Ecol. Evol. **37**(10), 872–885 (2022). https://doi.org/10.1016/j.tree.2022.06.001, https://www.sciencedirect.com/science/article/pii/S0169534722001343
14. Korsch, D., Bodesheim, P., Brehm, G., Denzler, J.: Automated Visual Monitoring of Nocturnal Insects with Light-based Camera Traps, July 2023. https://doi.org/10.48550/arXiv.2307.15433, http://arxiv.org/abs/2307.15433, arXiv:2307.15433 [cs]
15. Löbl, I., Klausnitzer, B., Hartmann, M., Krell, F.T.: The Silent Extinction of Species and Taxonomists—An Appeal to Science Policymakers and Legislators. Diversity **15**(10), 1053 (2023). https://doi.org/10.3390/d15101053, https://www.mdpi.com/1424-2818/15/10/1053, number: 10 Publisher: Multidisciplinary Digital Publishing Institute Multidisciplinary Digital Publishing Institute
16. Meier, R., Hartop, E., Pylatiuk, C., Srivathsan, A.: Towards holistic insect monitoring: species discovery, description, identification and traits for all insects. Philosophical Trans. Roy. Soc. B: Biol. Sci. **379**(1904), 20230120 (2024). https://doi.org/10.1098/rstb.2023.0120, https://royalsocietypublishing.org/doi/10.1098/rstb.2023.0120, publisher: Royal Society publisher: Royal Society publisher: Royal Society publisher: Royal Society
17. Myers, P., Espinosa, R., Parr, C.S., Jones, T., Hammond, G.S., Dewey, T.A.: The animal diversity web (online) (2025). https://animaldiversity.org. Accessed 06 June 2025
18. OpenAI, et al.: Gpt-4 technical report (2024). https://arxiv.org/abs/2303.08774
19. OpenAI, et al.: Gpt-4o system card (2024). https://arxiv.org/abs/2410.21276
20. of Ornithology, C.L.: Search, All About Birds, Cornell Lab of Ornithology. https://www.allaboutbirds.org/guide/search
21. Ortiz-Viso, B., Martin-Bautista, M.J.: "Let It BEE": natural language classification of arthropod specimens based on their spanish description. In: Larsen, H.L., Martin-Bautista, M.J., Ruiz, M.D., Andreasen, T., Bordogna, G., De Tré, G. (eds.) Flexible Query Answering Systems, pp. 118–128. LNCS, Springer, Cham (2023). https://doi.org/10.1007/978-3-031-42935-4_10
22. Powell, J.A., Opler, P.A.: Moths of Western North America. Univ of California Press (May 2009), google-Books-ID: USoWEQAAQBAJ

23. Radford, A., et al.: Learning Transferable Visual Models From Natural Language Supervision, February 2021. https://arxiv.org/abs/2103.00020v1
24. Reimers, N., Gurevych, I.: Sentence-BERT: Sentence Embeddings using Siamese BERT-Networks, August 2019. https://doi.org/10.48550/arXiv.1908.10084, http://arxiv.org/abs/1908.10084, arXiv:1908.10084 [cs]
25. Roy, D.B., et al.: Towards a standardized framework for AI-assisted, image-based monitoring of nocturnal insects. Philosophical Trans. Roy. Soc. B: Biol. Sci. **379**(1904), 20230108 (2024). https://doi.org/10.1098/rstb.2023.0108, https://royalsocietypublishing.org/doi/10.1098/rstb.2023.0108, publisher: Royal Society
26. SLU Artdatabanken: Artfakta (2024). https://www.artfakta.se. Accessed 06 June 2025
27. Stevens, S., et al.: BioCLIP: a vision foundation model for the tree of life, May 2024. https://doi.org/10.48550/arXiv.2311.18803, http://arxiv.org/abs/2311.18803, arXiv:2311.18803 [cs]
28. Troisemaine, C., Lemaire, V., Gosselin, S., Reiffers-Masson, A., Flocon-Cholet, J., Vaton, S.: Novel Class Discovery: an Introduction and Key Concepts, February 2023. https://doi.org/10.48550/arXiv.2302.12028, http://arxiv.org/abs/2302.12028, arXiv:2302.12028 [cs]
29. Truong, T.D., Nguyen, H.Q., Nguyen, X.B., Dowling, A., Li, X., Luu, K.: Insect-Foundation: A Foundation Model and Large Multimodal Dataset for Vision-Language Insect Understanding, February 2025. https://doi.org/10.48550/arXiv.2502.09906, http://arxiv.org/abs/2502.09906, arXiv:2502.09906 [cs]
30. Vaze, S., Han, K., Vedaldi, A., Zisserman, A.: Generalized Category Discovery, June 2022. https://doi.org/10.48550/arXiv.2201.02609, http://arxiv.org/abs/2201.02609, arXiv:2201.02609 [cs]
31. Wagner, D.L., Grames, E.M., Forister, M.L., Berenbaum, M.R., Stopak, D.: Insect decline in the Anthropocene: death by a thousand cuts. Proceedings of the National Academy of Sciences **118**(2), e2023989118 (2021). https://doi.org/10.1073/pnas.2023989118, https://www.pnas.org/doi/full/10.1073/pnas.2023989118, publisher: Proceedings of the National Academy of Sciences Proceedings of the National Academy of Sciences
32. Wong, M.K.L., Guénard, B., Lewis, O.T.: Trait-based ecology of terrestrial arthropods. Biological Reviews **94**(3), 999–1022 (2019). https://doi.org/10.1111/brv.12488, https://onlinelibrary.wiley.com/doi/abs/10.1111/brv.12488, _eprint: https://onlinelibrary.wiley.com/doi/pdf/10.1111/brv.12488
33. Zhai, X., Wang, X., Mustafa, B., Steiner, A., Keysers, D., Kolesnikov, A., Beyer, L.: LiT: Zero-Shot Transfer with Locked-image text Tuning, November 2021. https://arxiv.org/abs/2111.07991v3
34. Zhang, B., Zhang, P., Dong, X., Zang, Y., Wang, J.: Long-CLIP: Unlocking the Long-Text Capability of CLIP, July 2024. https://doi.org/10.48550/arXiv.2403.15378, http://arxiv.org/abs/2403.15378, arXiv:2403.15378 [cs]

Augmenting Geospatial Data With Large Language Models Using Compositional Attention for Improved Avian Mobility Tasks Prediction

Kehinde Owoeye(✉)

TÜV SÜD, National Engineering Laboratory Scottish Enterprise Technology Park, Napier Building, Glasgow G75 0QF, UK
kehinde.owoeye@tuvsud.com

Abstract. Several sustainable development goals, such as life on land, sustainable cities and communities, as well as good health and well-being, are heavily dependent on the migration of avian species from one end of the Earth to another. Machine learning tasks in this space rely on a supervised approach where a categorical output corresponding to a certain movement phenomenon is estimated leveraging geospatial and weather covariates. Although these covariates are sufficient for some tasks, they have limitations for some other tasks. We argue that some of these tasks can benefit from more expressive data, such as those generated by Large Language Models (LLMs). In this work therefore, we consider the task of augmenting spatio-temporal geospatial data with the output from an LLM for improved animal mobility prediction tasks. More specifically, first, we prompt an LLM and show it can be used to generate text data that can be used on its own for predicting animal movement phenomena, surpassing the performance of spatio-temporal geospatial data on some experiments. Second, we propose an algorithm to eliminate redundancies in LLM queries and reduce carbon footprints by finding coordinates in a mobility dataset that maximizes entropy. Third, we show that when these two data modalities are used together, the performance on the aforementioned prediction tasks is significantly higher than when each modality is used on its own. Finally, we propose a novel compositional attention framework to combine the two data modalities and select relevant features by alternating between geospatial covariates and LLM embeddings. Experiments on two tasks for reducing biodiversity loss via the forecast of migration states and another task for managing future global health risks via the one-health paradigm by estimating stop-over duration show that the proposed approach outperforms competing baselines.

Keywords: Sustainability · Language Models · Attention · Ecology

1 Introduction

A wide range of sustainable development goals (SDGs) are highly dependent on the migration of animals, especially avian species, from one end of the Earth to another. For example, to reduce future biodiversity loss, given that 6% of avian life is functionally extinct and 21% currently threatened [28], it is important to ensure modern cities are sustainable by incorporating sustainability into critical infrastructures such as wind turbines using artificial intelligence. This can be achieved, for example, by forecasting the migration states of migrating avian species in and around a city [21], so that these critical infrastructures can behave intelligently given the likelihood of a migration state for endangered species.

Furthermore, considering the one health initiative, it is important to jointly optimize the health of animals, humans, and the environment to minimize future global health risks given the increasing interdependency in the complex relationships between these three entities due to human development activities and climate change [19]. Major human infectious diseases such as Ebola and avian flu have been shown to have animal origin with 20% of this coming from primates alone [36]. One way to achieve this is to be in a position to estimate stop-over duration of wild migratory birds that are vectors of infectious diseases, as well as map their stop-over sites to minimize interaction with humans [20]. This can potentially help in the area of disease outbreak management, prevention, and containment.

These two machine learning tasks described above are few examples of tasks related to animal mobility [22, 25–27] that affect one or more of the SDGs such as life on land, climate action, sustainable cities and communities, good health and well-being [18], as well as affordable and clean energy, with direct or indirect relationships existing between these goals [24]. It is therefore important to ensure the performance of the models designed for these tasks are optimized for the best possible outcomes where applicable to ensure we are able to meet the related SDGs come 2030.

In recent times, Large Language Models (LLMs) that can comprehend and generate human language texts have proven to be important foundation models that can be prompted or fine-tuned to perform tasks across several domains such as finance [14] for portfolio management, law [13] for processing large volumes of legal text, education [16] to create interactive games and educational activities by leveraging the huge corpus of data available on the web. These LLMs can be prompted to output geographical, weather, and rather expressive features about a location that can be used to augment existing spatio-temporal geospatial data towards boosting the performance of models on animal mobility prediction related tasks (see Fig. 1). As seen in Fig. 1, expressive geospatial knowledge and information relating to economic activities can be obtained from an LLM via carefully engineered prompts containing the relevant coordinates.

In this work, therefore, we consider the task of using LLM output as augmented input for several animal mobility prediction-related tasks. First, we show that LLMs can be used to generate more expressive features regarding location coordinates and mobility of migrating avian species when the prompts are carefully engineered. Second, we propose an algorithm with connections to information theory to ensure sustainability by reducing the number of LLM prompts and queries so that the overall carbon footprints of our method can be reduced.

> User: Rural and Urban features of the coordinates 34.05166667, -116.5726667 and of nearby places.
>
> GPT-4o: The coordinates 34.05166667, -116.5726667 point to a location in Southern California in the United States. Specifically, this location is near the town of Joshua Tree, which is part of San Bernardino County. The area encompasses both rural and urban features, adding a unique character to the region. Here's a look at these features in the vicinity:### Rural Features:1. **Joshua Tree National Park**: This national park is a major rural attraction, known for its stunning desert landscapes, rock formations, and the famous Joshua Trees. The area offers numerous outdoor activities such as hiking, rock climbing, and bird watching.2. **Mojave Desert**: The surrounding environment is largely desert, characterized by arid landscapes and native wildlife. The open spaces and clear skies are ideal for stargazing.3. **Rural Communities**: There are small communities and unincorporated territories with a rural feel, featuring wide open spaces, ranches, and homesteads. **Conservation Areas**: Numerous conservation efforts focus on preserving the natural desert habitat, promoting biodiversity, and studying native plant and animal species.### Urban Features:1. **Joshua Tree Town**: Despite its small size, the town serves as a cultural and economic hub with a mix of local businesses, art galleries, music venues, and eateries that cater to both residents and tourists.2. **Twentynine Palms**: Nearby, this city offers more urban amenities, including shops, restaurants, schools, and healthcare facilities. It's also known for its connection to the US Marine Corps Air Ground Combat Center. **Tourism Industry**: Tourism greatly influences the local economy, with numerous businesses and services tailored to visitors, including guided tours, accommodations, and recreational activities.4. **Cultural Events and Festivals**: The area hosts various events and festivals, drawing urban influence and visitors from cities like Los Angeles and Palm Springs.### Nearby Places:- **Yucca Valley**: Just west of Joshua Tree, Yucca Valley offers more extensive services and suburban developments, including shopping centers and chain stores.\n- **Palm Springs**: A well-known urban center located southwest of Joshua Tree, known for its resorts, golf courses, and vibrant arts scene. **Coachella Valley**: Known for agricultural production and home to the famous Coachella. Valley Music and Arts Festival.These features, combining the tranquility and isolation of rural life with the conveniences and cultural attractions associated with urban settings, make the area around Joshua Tree unique and attractive to residents and visitors alike

Fig. 1. Prompt and corresponding output from GPT-4o. Useful geospatial, weather information and economic activities related information can be generated with the right prompt.

Finally, we propose a compositional attention framework to optimize the selection of the two data modalities for downstream animal mobility prediction tasks. Results on several experiments show that the proposed approach outperform competing baselines on two major tasks with ablations showing the effectiveness of the proposed approach.

2 Related Work

We discuss related literature under four broad themes of modelling of animal movement phenomena, mining knowledge from LLMs, use of Natural Language Processing (NLP) in geospatial tasks, and attention mechanism. While these themes are not exhaustive, they provide a good foundation for the work carried out in this paper.

2.1 Modelling of Animal Movement Phenomena

Previously, using the dataset of white-fronted Geese collected over multiple years, an attempt was made to forecast the stopover sites of these birds with the aid of Markov chain using historical information [2]. In a related work, [3] used random forest to determine important variables such as roads, ecotone, agricultural land among others relevant for stop-over in migratory whooping crane (Grus americana) for conservation purpose, and [11] reviewed various methods for estimating stop-over duration in birds. While [21] proposed a recurrent neural network for forecasting avian migration at a finer spatio-temporal granularity, [32] used dataset of bird densities from radar in the Netherlands to predict their migration intensities for applications in the area of improved aviation security. To reduce the deaths of some aquatic animals due to their collision with hydroelectric power plants, [31] proposed a seasonal autoregressive method to forecast their migration intensities in advance using datasets of silver eel migration. While

these previous works have tried to predict the migration states/intensities, our emphasis is on
investigating how LLMs can be used to augment the features used for these tasks. To model collective animal movement activities for application in conservation, [25] proposed a recurrent neural network to classify the different collective activities of a flock. A wide range of methods with foundation in information theory was also proposed in [26] to model different animal movement phenomena, including abnormal movement activities in animals with neurological conditions, and [27] used unsupervised machine learning methods to quantify unusual movement activities of sheep in a flock with applications in assessing the efficacy of therapeutic interventions during preclinical trials.

2.2 Mining Knowledge from LLMs

Knowledge can be extracted from LLMs either by prompt engineering, fine tuning or prompt tuning. Most of the work described here are mainly based on fine-tuning LLMs, although some work have been carried out in the area of prompt tuning. Recently, [34] fine-tuned the LLaMA-2-7b model on a set of geospatial data to improve their ability to generate tool-use solutions for geospatial tasks. In a similar vein, [15] proposed a few-shot approach leveraging data pruning for efficient LLM-based recommendation. To ensure efficient fine-tuning, a parameter-efficient fine-tuning was proposed by [1] in a few-shot settings leveraging meta-learning, while [10] introduced multiple adapters, with each adapter bespoke to the task of interest. To get the best output from LLM, [35] described a series of prompt engineering techniques towards solving a variety of problems. For efficient prompt engineering in our work, we propose a novel algorithm to eliminate redundancies and reduce cost to ensure overall sustainability of our approach.

2.3 NLP for Geospatial Tasks

Natural Language Processing (NLP) has been used in the past for various geospatial tasks. We discuss a few of them below. Semantic relationships between cities were extracted and used for the downstream task of identifying the main topics of news articles [9]. In an attempt to increase the efficiency of developing workflows for handling geo-processing tasks by integrating the semantic understanding ability inherent in LLMs with mature tools within the GIS community, [38] proposed a framework that can conduct geospatial data collection, processing, and analysis in an autonomous fashion. Using several methods for automated classification of text expressions leveraging features for machine learning, [29] attempted to detect geospatial location descriptions in natural language text. Similarly, [8] proposed a computational framework for harvesting local place names from geo-tagged housing advertisements using textual content of housing advertisements and clustering. Recently, [17] demonstrated the usefulness of foundation models on seven geospatial tasks across domains including geospatial semantics, health geography, urban geography, and remote sensing.

2.4 Attention Mechanism

To improve the performance on language translation tasks [23], compositional attention was used in a few shot setting to accommodate both syntactic and semantic components of language. A compositional attention networks (CAN) with two-stream fusion for video question answering was also proposed in [37] to improve the performance of video question answering models. Lastly, [30] proposed a compositional de-attention network that learns whether to add, subtract or nullify a certain vector when learning representations with approach showing state of the art results on a variety of language tasks. We aim to use a variant of the compositional attention framework in this work to allow the use of both geospatial spatio-temporal data and embeddings from LLMs in the right framework.

3 Methodology

We show a schematic of the proposed approach in Fig. 2 and a description of the problem setting and the steps involved in detail below.

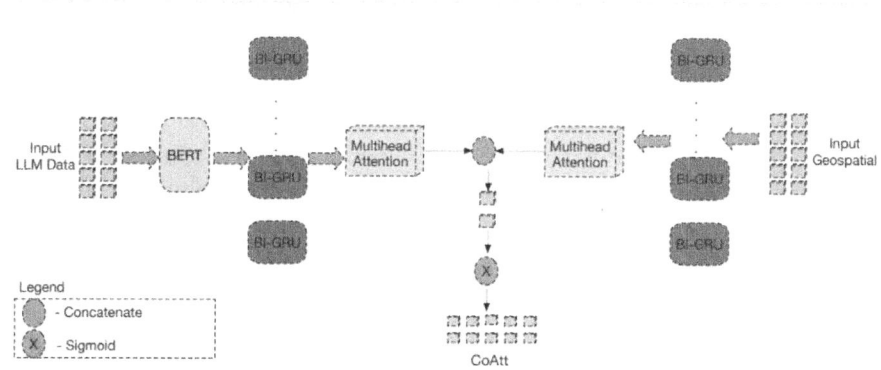

Fig. 2. Compositional attention framework. There is a multi-head attention module for each data modality. The output of each multi-head attention network are concatenated via a sigmoid layer to get a weighted output from both attention networks and passed through a linear layer for downstream prediction tasks.

3.1 Problem Statement

Given a time series $\{X_{\leq t}, y_{mt}\}_{t=n}^{T}$ where $X_{\leq t} \in \mathbb{R}^d$ and y_{mt} is a multi-dimensional vector representing input features ($X_{\leq t} = X_{t-d}, ..., X_t$, d is the duration of the temporal context relevant for the prediction task) and discrete migration states respectively at each time-step t where $m \geq 2$, the goal is to estimate $\{y_{m(t+k)}\}_{t=n}^{T}$ given $\{X_{\leq t}\}_{t=n}^{T-k}$ where k is the temporal period in advance with respect to the movement phenomena of interest, in this case, migration states and stop-over decisions (duration of stop-over).

3.2 Geospatial Prompt

Several factors are known to influence the movement directions and stop-over decisions of migrating avian species. These factors, though not exhaustive, are summarized in three broad themes discussed below.

1. **Urban, Rural Infrastructures and Activities:** It has been shown that avian species are more likely to breed in areas with little urban activity, and population density [21] as urban developments can easily lead to loss of biodiversity, stemming from habitat loss and, by extension, species displacement. Urbanization can also directly or indirectly create barriers that hinder avian species from easily finding food, mating partners, and shelter.
2. **Weather and Geographical Information:** Migrating birds are known to start their autumn migration journey when the temperature drops in their breeding grounds while seeking warmer climates. In addition, wind has been shown to have an impact on migration [5], with very strong wind impacting the orientation of young birds. Migration intensities have also been shown to increase when there are no precipitations, as well as periods of increased atmospheric pressure [5].
3. **Nearby Places:** While information about a coordinate can carry useful knowledge about a location, surrounding places and their features can be useful most especially when a coordinate corresponds to a location in a remote place with little to no human activities.

We combine all of this information in a single prompt and send it to the LLM as input. See Fig. 1 for example of prompt and the corresponding output.

Efficiency of Queries. To reduce the number of queries for the LLM of choice and, by extension the carbon footprints of the proposed approach for the purpose of overall sustainability, first, we compute the contiguous haversine distance in kilometers for all coordinates in the dataset. We then use the Jenks natural break mechanism to minimize the within-group variance and maximize the between-group variance of the distances covered in the dataset. The distances covered are further assigned labels using the approach described above. These labels are later used to determine the change points in the distances covered such that only the coordinates at the change points are queried using the LLM (see Algorithm 1 for more details).

Connections to Maximum Entropy: The proposed algorithm (Algorithm 1) is related to information theory via maximum entropy. Given that Shannon entropy $H(X)$ is defined as:

$$\mathcal{H}(X) = - \sum_{x \in X} p(x) \, log \, p(x) \qquad (1)$$

where $p(x)$ is the discrete probability distribution of a random variable x in this case the labels assigned by the Jenks natural break algorithm, the goal is to

Algorithm 1. Efficient Prompts

Input: Dataset $\mathcal{D}$ of coordinates, $\mathcal{M}$ representing LLM.
Output: Dataset $\mathcal{D}'$ with LLM Data.

1: **for** each d_i in $\mathcal{D}$ **do**
2:     **COMPUTE** Haversine Distances $\mathcal{H}_{d_i}$ using (d_i, d_{i+1}).
3: **end for**
4: **ASSIGN** $\mathcal{H}_d$ into groups using Jenks natural break algorithm.
5: **ATTACH** group Labels $\mathcal{L}$ to each d_i.
6: **EXTRACT** $\mathcal{L}$ change-points $\mathcal{L}_{ch}$.
7: **for** each $L_{ch,i}$ in $\mathcal{L}_{ch}$ **do**
8:     **RUN** $\mathcal{M}(f(context, instruction))$.
9:     **PROPAGATE** $\mathcal{M}(f(context, instruction))$ FORWARDS till another change point is detected.
10: **end for**
11: **return** $\mathcal{D}'$

find coordinates in the dataset $\mathcal{D}$ where $H(X)$ is maximized given the Haversine distance covered. These coordinates ensure that there is the highest possible homogeneity in the two regimes on either side of these coordinates, resulting in the maximum reduction of entropy between these two regimes.

More formally, our objective is to maximize $\mathcal{H}(X)$ subject to: $\sum_{x \in X} p(x) = 1$ and $\sum_{x \in X} \Gamma_x p(x) = \mathcal{A}$, where $\mathcal{A}$ is the average value or expectation $\mathcal{A}$ with values Γ_x. The overall objective function $\mathcal{L}$ where λ_1 and λ_2 are Lagrange multipliers can therefore be defined as:

$$\mathcal{L}(X, \alpha, \beta) = \mathcal{H}(X) - \lambda_1 \left(\sum_{x \in X} p(x) - 1 \right) - \lambda_2 \left(\sum_{x \in X} \Gamma_x p(x) - \mathcal{A} \right) \quad (2)$$

3.3 Attention Mechanism

We introduce the standard multi-head attention and then describe the compositional attention proposed in this work.

Scaled Dot-Product Attention: In key-value attention [33], for a given set of queries and key-value pairs, a scaled cosine similarity is computed between each query and the set of keys. This similarity score then determines how much each value contributes to the output corresponding to that query. More formally, given a set of input elements represented by the matrix $X \in \mathbb{R}^{N \times d}$, we first derive the queries Q, keys K, and values V by applying linear transformations to $\mathcal{X}$ using learnable projection matrices such that $Q = XW_q$, $K = XW_k$ and $V = XW_v$ where $W_k \in R^{d \times d_k}$, $W_q \in R^{d \times d_k}$ and $W_v \in R^{d \times d_v}$. For each query, a similarity score is calculated with each key using a scaled cosine similarity, where the scaling factor is the inverse of the square root of the dimension of the keys d_k. These scores serve as attention weights that are then multiplied by the values as follows:

$$Attention(Q, K, V) = Softmax\left(\frac{QK^T}{\sqrt{d_k}}\right)V \qquad (3)$$

Multi-head Attention: To increase the representational capacity of a model, multiple scaled dot-product attention mechanisms are used in parallel called multi-head attention to attend to different positions. The outputs from these multiple heads are then concatenated and projected via a linear layer as follows:

$$MultiHead(Q, K, V) = Concat(head_1, ..., head_h)W^O$$
$$where\ head_i = Attention(Q_i, K_i, V_i) \qquad (4)$$

3.4 Compositional Attention

We construct two networks, one for each data modality. A multi-head attention mechanism is applied to each of these networks, and then a compositional attention is applied to the outputs of these two networks. Given that the multi-head attention networks for the geospatial and LLM data are defined respectively as $MultiHead(Q, K, V)_{geo}$, and $MultiHead(Q, K, V)_{LLM}$. These two outputs are then concatenated to derive a new output $CoAtt$:

$$MH_{geoLLM} = Concat(MultiHead(Q, K, V)_{geo},$$
$$MultiHead(Q, K, V)_{LLM}) \qquad (5)$$

The compositional attention is then defined as:

$$CoAtt = Sigmoid(MH_{geoLLM})W^O \qquad (6)$$

where $W^O \in R^{d \times d_{MH_{geoLLM}}}$.

A sigmoid function is used to add compositional weights to the outputs of the attention networks for the reason that, compared to softmax, sigmoid probabilities do not add up to one. This ensures that each dimension of the output from each attention network is assigned a weight that would otherwise have been lower if softmax was used, guaranteeing that each dimension of the attention network outputs make some contributions towards the downstream task.

4 Datasets and Preprocessing

We evaluate the proposed method and baselines using both geospatial and LLM data as described below.

4.1 Data

Geospatial Data: The geospatial data include the environmental and weather data as obtained in [21] where the movement trajectories of the Turkey vulture were annotated with weather and environmental data with the aid of the Env-DATA Track Annotation Service [7]. Features include sunshine duration, snow temperature, population density, atmospheric water, albedo, downward ultraviolet radiation at the surface, plant canopy surface water at surface, incident solar radiation, elevation. dew point temperature, snow evaporation, soil water content, water vapour concentration, snow albedo among others. See [21] for a complete list.

LLM Data: GPT-4o is used as the representative LLM in this work, where prompts as described above are used to generate text data via its API.

5 Experiments and Procedures

5.1 Model Architecture, Parameters and Metrics

We pass the LLM data via BERT [6] and into a deep bidirectional recurrent neural networks using GRU modules [4]. The geospatial data is also passed through another deep bidirectional network. The hyperparameters for this network include the Adam optimizer [12], cell units = 60, time step = 60, batch size = 100 learning rate = 1e−2. The outputs of each of these two networks are fed into different multi-head attention modules, each with a head size of 256, 10 heads and a dropout of 0.2. The outputs of these two networks are further concatenated, and compositional weights applied via a sigmoid layer before it is passed through a dense layer and then a Softmax at the output. We evaluate all models based on the accuracy for the entire dataset and F1 scores computed for the migration window alone. For the second task, we use the original model proposed for this task as the base model before using compositional attention. We carry out all evaluations using the migration window alone. Each deep learning model is trained three times and evaluated on the test set for the same number of times. The reported results include the mean and standard deviations of these evaluations.

5.2 Tasks

Two tasks are considered in this work as described below.

1. **Forecast Migration States:** This task involves forecasting the migration states of certain avian species [21] more specifically the Turkey Vulture. This has application, for example, in minimizing biodiversity loss by incorporating sustainability via artificial intelligence into critical infrastructures such as wind turbines that are causing these deaths. There are four movement or migration states in this task, representing the autumn, winter, spring, and summer seasons.

2. **Forecast Stop-Over Decisions (Duration):** The goal of this second task is to forecast stop-over decisions and, by extension, stop-over duration of migrating avian species for the purpose of disease containment, prevention, and management for species that are vectors of zoonotic diseases.

5.3 Experiments

To answer multiple questions about the proposed approach, we design several experiments including ablations described below.

1) Are LLM outputs sufficient for the kind of tasks considered in this work? To answer this question, we use just the embeddings of the LLM outputs and train our model end-to-end without adding the geospatial data.
2) How does the performance of LLM output alone compare with geospatial data alone? To answer this question, we compare the performance of the baseline models when used with geospatial data alone to when used with only LLM data.
3) How does the proposed compositional framework compare with methods using geospatial data alone and LLM data alone? To answer this question, we compare the results of the proposed approach with other algorithms using each data modality only.
4) How does the proposed compositional framework compare with other methods when a naive combination of each data modality is used? We compare the proposed framework with other baselines in the literature where the two data modalities are combined naively.
5) How does the proposed architecture compare with baselines in the literature? We compare the proposed approach with other baselines described in the literature, ensuring that the parameters are the same as much as possible.

5.4 Baselines

We compare our approach with several baselines including deep and classical learning methods as well as ablations.

1) Markov chain (MC): Markov chain was used in [2] to forecast stop-over sites. Here, we use only the labels (the decision to move or not) as input to the model. We use this as a baseline for the task of predicting stop-over duration.
2) Deep Bidirectional Recurrent Neural Network with Auxiliary Task (DBi-RNN 2-L, A. Task): A deep bidirectional recurrent network to forecast migration states augmented with a mean square error loss by forecasting longitude [21]. We use this baseline for both tasks.
3) Deep Neural Network (DNN): With two layers and 256 neurons each, dropout = 0.2, Softmax layer and Adam optimizer [12]. We train all neural networks given similar procedures described for our approach above. We use this for both tasks.

4) **Recurrent Neural Network (RNN):** A GRU network and also a bidirectional GRU network with 1 layer, 2 layers, and 3 layers, 50 cells, dropout = 0.2, Softmax layer and Adam optimizer [12]. We use this baseline and its variants for both tasks.
5) **Deep RNN with Pseudo Loss Objective (DBRPLO):** A four layer bidirectional recurrent neural network with a pseudo-objective scanning in both directions implemented using the gated recurrent unit [4]. The hyperparameters used include the Adam optimizer [12], cell units = 60, time step = 60, batch size = 100 learning rate = 1e-2 and a Softmax at the output layer. We use this baseline for the task of forecasting stop over decisions.
6) **Logistic Regression (LR):** We use a multinomial variant with lbfgs solver for logistic regression. We use this baseline for both tasks.
7) **Support Vector Machine (SVM), Random Forest (RF), Adaboost (AB):** We use a one-versus-one strategy for SVM and also use other tree-based method such as random forest and Adaboost as used in [21]. We use these baselines for both tasks.

Table 1. Performance comparison. Proposed approach can be seen to outperform all baselines across the three experiments. We report only the F1 scores for the onset of fall and spring migration in that order for brevity. The strong performance of the proposed approach demonstrates the utility of using the two data modalities as well as the proposed compositional attention mechanism.

We use the LLM output with BERT embeddings as input to the baselines described above as well as in combination with traditional geospatial data.

Table 2. Performance comparison for the forecast of stop-over decisions task. The proposed architecture can be seen to outperform the other baselines when the two data modalities are used with performance decreasing as forecast horizons increases.

No of hours in advance	Data	Performance Metric	MC	LR	RF	AB	SVM	DNN	RNN (1-L)	Bi-RNN (1-L)	DBRPLO	Bi-RNN (2-L, A task)	CoAtt
1	geo	acc. (%)	74.11±0.98	83.11	85.11	85.22	68.11	73.40±7.40	32.09±0.4	55.58±1.1	**86.74±0.47**	78.55±0.87	
		F1	(0.87, 0.58±0.02)	(0.88, 0.72)	(0.86, 0.77)	(0.80, 0.75)	(0.81, 0)	(0.83±0.03, 0.26)	(0, 0.48±0.01)	(0.35±0.22, 0.54±0.03)	**(0.91, 0.79)**	(0.86±0.02, 0.51±0.15)	
	llm	acc. (%)	74.11±0.98	29.78	30.33	66.96	60.88	71.26±0.4	69.49	69.49	71.9±1.34	69.49	
		F1	(0.87, 0.58±0.02)	(0.1, 0.42)	(0.12, 0.42)	(0.72, 0.4)	(0.82, 0)	(0.79±0.05, 0.13±0.05)	(0.82, 0)	(0.82, 0)	(0.8±0.01, 0.54±0.01)	(0.82, 0)	
	geo-llm	acc. (%)	74.11±0.98	83.11	84.66	86.22	68.11	75.33±4.13	69.49	74.16±0.44	82.10±1.92	88.25±0.9	**92.21±0.78**
		F1	(0.87, 0.58±0.02)	(0.88, 0.72)	(0.86, 0.77)	(0.9, 0.77)	(0.81, 0)	(0.84±0.02, 0.45±0.14)	(0.82, 0)	(0.82, 0.61±0.15)	(0.87±0.02, 0.71±0.03)	(0.92, 0.80±0.02)	**(0.94, 0.87±0.01)**
6	geo	acc. (%)	33.44±1.43	55.28	53.61	76.41	68.96	68.96	34.5±1.9	55.78±2.46	**79.67±0.2**	73.79±3.4	
		F1	(0.49±0.01, 0.24±0.02)	(0.56, 0.52)	(0.51, 0.56)	(0.84, 0.53)	(0.82,0)	(0.82, 0)	(0, 0.49)	(0.55±0.05, 0.56±0.01)	**(0.86, 0.36±0.07)**	(0.83±0.01, 0.34±0.17)	
	llm	acc. (%)	33.44±1.43	31.48	34.93	66.96	70.86	70.97	69.49	69.46	**73.07±1.52**	69.46	
		F1	(0.49±0.01, 0.24±0.02)	(0.22, 0.43)	(0.21, 0.45)	(0.79, 0.16)	(0.83, 0)	(0.83, 0)	(0.82, 0)	(0.82, 0)	**(0.81±0.01, 0.54±0.02)**	(0.82, 0)	
	geo-llm	acc. (%)	33.44±1.43	55.28	50.44	75.08	69.96	66.18±2.11	69.46	67.53	78.73±0.31	89.22±0.55	**90.83±0.16**
		F1	(0.49±0.01, 0.24±0.02)	(0.58, 0.52)	(0.52, 0.48)	(0.83, 0.53)	(0.81, 0)	(0.79±0.02, 0.15±0.19)	(0.82, 0)	(0.81,0)	(0.84, 0.67±0.02)	(0.92, 0.82±0.01)	**(0.93, 0.85)**
18	geo	acc. (%)	19.03±0.9	67.41	65.96	72.88	69.31	68.27±1.47	32.92±0.4	48.77±11.75	**75.07**	67.42	
		F1	(0.29, 0.24±0.02)	(0.75, 0.52)	(0.73, 0.53)	(0.82, 0.39)	(0.82, 0)	(0.81±0.01, 0)	(0, 0.49)	(0.31±0.28, 0.52±0.03)	**(0.83, 0.55)**	(0.8, 0)	
	llm	acc. (%)	19.03±0.9	36.94	34.05	66.40	71.54	71.39±0.05	69.35	69.35	**70.67±1.26**	69.35	
		F1	(0.29, 0.24±0.02)	(0.28, 0.43)	(0.21, 0.45)	(0.79, 0.17)	(0.83, 0)	(0.82±0.01, 0.02±0.03)	(0.82, 0)	(0.82, 0)	**(0.79±0.01, 0.5±0.03)**	(0.82, 0)	
	geo-llm	acc. (%)	19.03±0.9	65.4	50.44	73.21	69.31	65.33±3.4	69.35	67.42	69.24±1.45	**87.21±0.12**	86.38±1.32
		F1	(0.29, 0.24±0.02)	(0.73, 0.51)	(0.52, 0.48)	(0.82, 0.45)	(0.82, 0)	(0.76±0.02, 0.39±0.03)	(0.82, 0)	(0.82, 0)	(0.7±0.1, 0.58±0.12)	**(0.91, 0.78)**	(0.86±0.06, 0.82±0.06)
24	geo	acc. (%)	16.27±0.6	70.95	72.18	71.17	68.82	68.82	32.61±0.4	33.41±1.07	**73.37±0.18**	67.35	
		F1	(0.23, 0.26)	(0.75, 0.55)	(0.79, 0.57)	(0.81, 0.37)	(0.81, 0)	(0.81, 0)	(0, 0.49)	(0, 0.48±0.02)	**(0.82, 0.47±0.04)**	(0.8, 0)	
	llm	acc. (%)	16.27±0.6	36.76	31.28	57.54	**71.17**	68.38±2.56	69.28	69.28	60.86±3.18	69.28	
		F1	(0.23, 0.26)	(0.45, 0.13)	(0.43, 0.71)	(0.20, 0.83)	(0.81±0.02, 0.08±0.05)	(0.82, 0)	(0.82, 0)	(0.64±0.12, 0.44±0.17)	(0.82, 0)		
	geo-llm	acc. (%)	16.27±0.6	70.95	54.86	68.04	68.82	56.27±19.02	69.28	67.35	68.58±1.46	64.22±1.41	**84.68±0.02**
		F1	(0.23, 0.26)	(0.78, 0.55)	(0.56, 0.51)	(0.77, 0.46)	(0.81, 0)	(0.58±0.32, 0.3±0.09)	(0.82, 0)	(0.82, 0.02±0.02)	(0.77±0.02, 0.5±0.04)	(0.89±0.01, 0.71±0.03)	**(0.89, 0.73±0.01)**

6 Results and Discussion

We discuss the results in this section focusing on the answers to the questions asked above in the experiments section.

LLMs Data are on Their Own Sufficient for Modelling Avian Movement Phenomena: The results in Tables 1 and 2 show the LLM outputs are sufficient for the two tasks considered in this work, demonstrating that they contain valuable geospatial and economic knowledge that can help predict a variety of animal movement phenomena. The performance can be seen to surpass that of geospatial when used alone sometimes.

Performance Using LLMs Data Stronger on First Task: Performance using just the LLM data appears to be stronger on the first task of forecasting migration states for reasons we attribute to the static nature of this data compared to the more dynamic geospatial data where real time weather and environmental conditions are collected which helps when modelling more dynamic movement phenomena as in the second task.

Each Data Modality has Its Strengths: Results in Tables 1 and 2 show that with geospatial data alone, the performance can be stronger sometimes and weaker some other times and vice versa for LLM data. This demonstrates that each data modality has its strengths and that the combination of the two modalities should be able to leverage individual strengths towards producing superior results compared to when each modality is used alone.

LLM and Geospatial Data Combined Together Can Improve Performance: The proposed approach can be seen to outperform methods using each data modality alone (Tables 1 and 2), suggesting that with the right architecture, both categories of data can be leveraged towards forecasting various animal movement phenomema. Not only are the accuracies better, the F1 scores are also good, implying that even when certain phenomena are underrepresented, they can still be modelled given the right data modalities.

Naive Combination of Data Modalities Can Negatively Impact Performance: From results in Tables 1 and 2, we are able to demonstrate that special care must be taken when combining several data modalities as a naive approach as used in the baselines will not be able to maximize the utilities inherent in the combination of multiple data modalities. This can be seen, for example, where the performance with each data modality is no different compared to when they are combined together in some cases.

Performance When Both Data Modalities are Used is Stronger at Shorter Horizons: As seen in Tables 1 and 2, the performance when both data modalities are used is stronger at shorter horizons compared to longer horizons, and the results appear to parallel those of other baselines if the forecast horizon is increased enough. This suggests that a special architecture may be needed to capture the requisite dependencies the combination of the two data modalities needs to produce superior performance at longer horizons.

Neural Network Models are Better, the Deeper They are, the Better: The results in both Tables 1 and 2 also show that as before, neural network models are able to better model the animal movement phenomena of interest in this work compared to non-deep learning models, suggesting that their ability to model sequences gives them a superior advantage for these kinds of tasks, especially for the sequence-based models. Also, from the results of experiments carried out, it can be seen on average that the deeper networks are better than shallow ones and also that bidirectional networks are in general better than unidirectional ones.

7 Conclusion

In this work, we have proposed a compositional attention framework using LLM data for augmenting geospatial data towards improving the performance on animal mobility prediction related tasks. First, we show that LLMs can be mined for not just expressive geospatial knowledge regarding location of any avian species but also for economic features regarding a particular coordinate or location. Second, we demonstrate that these information are rich and on their own predictive of several animal movement phenomena, which when combined with traditional geospatial data can produce even better results. While the data from LLMs can be static, the attention mechanism allows us to use this data modality when important to improve the performance on the relevant animal mobility prediction related tasks. In the future, we will investigate other prompt strategies to obtain more informative features from LLMs. We will also explore other architectures that can better combine the two data modalities in a single architecture trained end-to-end towards boosting the performance over longer forecast horizons.

References

1. Bansal, T., Alzubi, S., Wang, T., Lee, J.Y., McCallum, A.: Meta-adapters: parameter efficient few-shot fine-tuning through meta-learning. In: International Conference on Automated Machine Learning, pp. 19–1. PMLR (2022)
2. Bayram, U., Sun, R., Lee, W.: Modeling stopover sites of migratory birds' routes for conservation of population and prevention of
3. Belaire, J.A., Kreakie, B.J., Keitt, T., Minor, E.: Predicting and mapping potential whooping crane stopover habitat to guide site selection for wind energy projects. Conserv. Biol. **28**(2), 541–550 (2014)
4. Cho, K., et al.: Learning phrase representations using rnn encoder-decoder for statistical machine translation. arXiv preprint arXiv:1406.1078 (2014)
5. Cooper, N.W., et al.: Atmospheric pressure predicts probability of departure for migratory songbirds. Mov. Ecol. **11**(1), 23 (2023)
6. Devlin, J.: Bert: Pre-training of deep bidirectional transformers for language understanding. arXiv preprint arXiv:1810.04805 (2018)
7. Dodge, S., et al.: The environmental-data automated track annotation (env-data) system: linking animal tracks with environmental data. Mov. Ecol. **1**, 1–14 (2013)
8. Hu, Y., Mao, H., McKenzie, G.: A natural language processing and geospatial clustering framework for harvesting local place names from geotagged housing advertisements. Int. J. Geogr. Inf. Sci. **33**(4), 714–738 (2019)
9. Hu, Y., Ye, X., Shaw, S.L.: Extracting and analyzing semantic relatedness between cities using news articles. Int. J. Geogr. Inf. Sci. **31**(12), 2427–2451 (2017)
10. Hu, Z., et al.: Llm-adapters: an adapter family for parameter-efficient fine-tuning of large language models. arXiv preprint arXiv:2304.01933 (2023)
11. Kaiser, A.: Stopover strategies in birds: a review of methods for estimating stopover length. Bird Study **46**(sup1), S299–S308 (1999)
12. Kingma, D.P.: Adam: A method for stochastic optimization. arXiv preprint arXiv:1412.6980 (2014)
13. Lai, J., Gan, W., Wu, J., Qi, Z., Philip, S.Y.: Large language models in law: a survey. AI Open (2024)
14. Li, Y., Wang, S., Ding, H., Chen, H.: Large language models in finance: a survey. In: Proceedings of the Fourth ACM International Conference on AI in Finance, pp. 374–382 (2023)
15. Lin, X., Wang, W., Li, Y., Yang, S., Feng, F., Wei, Y., Chua, T.S.: Data-efficient fine-tuning for llm-based recommendation. In: Proceedings of the 47th International ACM SIGIR Conference on Research and Development in Information Retrieval, pp. 365–374 (2024)
16. Lyu, W., Wang, Y., Chung, T., Sun, Y., Zhang, Y.: Evaluating the effectiveness of llms in introductory computer science education: A semester-long field study. In: Proceedings of the Eleventh ACM Conference on Learning@ Scale. pp. 63–74 (2024)
17. Mai, G., et al.: On the opportunities and challenges of foundation models for geospatial artificial intelligence. arXiv preprint arXiv:2304.06798 (2023)
18. Owoeye, K.: Learning to smell for wellness. arXiv preprint arXiv:1912.00895 (2019)

19. Owoeye, K.: Preventing future outbreaks: A case for global surveillance of wild migratory birds. In: Workshop on Machine Learning for Global Health, ICML (2020)
20. Owoeye, K.: Deep rnn with pseudo loss objective for forecasting stop-over decisions of wild migratory birds. In: 2021 International Joint Conference on Neural Networks (IJCNN), pp. 1–8. IEEE (2021)
21. Owoeye, K.: Forecasting avian migration patterns using a deep bidirectional rnn augmented with an auxiliary task. In: Proceedings of the Twenty-Ninth International Joint Conference on Artificial Intelligence, pp. 4382–4388. IJCAI International Joint Conferences on Artificial Intelligence Organization (2021)
22. Owoeye, K.: On computational models of animal movement behaviour. Ph.D. thesis, UCL (University College London) (2021)
23. Owoeye, K.: Curriculum compositional continual learning for neural machine translation. Procedia Comput. Sci. **222**, 167–176 (2023)
24. Owoeye, K.: Graph neural network with quasi-data augmentation for modelling food web relationships. In: 2024 IEEE Congress on Evolutionary Computation (CEC), pp. 1–8. IEEE (2024)
25. Owoeye, K., Hailes, S.: Online collective animal movement activity recognition. arXiv preprint arXiv:1811.09067 (2018)
26. Owoeye, K., Musolesi, M., Hailes, S.: Characterizing animal movement patterns across different scales and habitats using information theory. BioRxiv, p. 311241 (2018)
27. Owoeye, K., Musolesi, M., Hailes, S.: Quantifying unusual neurological movement phenotypes in collective movement phenotypes. bioRxiv pp. 2021–07 (2021)
28. Şekercioğlu, Ç.H., Daily, G.C., Ehrlich, P.R.: Ecosystem consequences of bird declines. Proc. Natl. Acad. Sci. **101**(52), 18042–18047 (2004)
29. Stock, K., Jones, C.B., Russell, S., Radke, M., Das, P., Aflaki, N.: Detecting geospatial location descriptions in natural language text. Int. J. Geogr. Inf. Sci. **36**(3), 547–584 (2022)
30. Tay, Y., Luu, A.T., Zhang, A., Wang, S., Hui, S.C.: Compositional de-attention networks. Advances in Neural Information Processing Systems **32** (2019)
31. Trancart, T., Acou, A., Oliveira, E., Feunteun, E.: Forecasting animal migration using sarimax: an efficient means of reducing silver eel mortality caused by turbines. Endangered Species Res. **21**(2), 181–190 (2013)
32. Van Belle, J., Shamoun-Baranes, J., Van Loon, E., Bouten, W.: An operational model predicting autumn bird migration intensities for flight safety. J. Appl. Ecol. **44**(4), 864–874 (2007)
33. Vaswani, A., et al.: Attention is all you need. Advances in neural information processing systems **30** (2017)
34. Wei, C., et al.: Geotool-gpt: a trainable method for facilitating large language models to master gis tools. Int. J. Geograph. Inf. Sci., 1–25 (2024)
35. White, J., et al.: A prompt pattern catalog to enhance prompt engineering with chatgpt. arXiv preprint arXiv:2302.11382 (2023)
36. Wolfe, N.D., Dunavan, C.P., Diamond, J.: Origins of major human infectious diseases. Nature **447**(7142), 279–283 (2007)
37. Yu, T., Yu, J., Yu, Z., Tao, D.: Compositional attention networks with two-stream fusion for video question answering. IEEE Trans. Image Process. **29**, 1204–1218 (2019)
38. Zhang, Y., Wei, C., He, Z., Yu, W.: Geogpt: an assistant for understanding and processing geospatial tasks. Int. J. Appl. Earth Obs. Geoinf. **131**, 103976 (2024)

Author Index

A

Ahokas, Minna 35
Alamenciak, Tim 353
Almohaishi, Moayad 90
Arnillas, Carlos Alberto 353
Arnold, Caroline 311
Arnold, Frederik 135
Ateia, Samy 90
Athanasiadis, Ioannis N. 338
August, Tom A. 382
August, Tom 392
Azaïs, Marc-Alexis 110, 146

B

Balke, Wolf-Tilo 258
Ballatore, Andrea 80
Banerjee, Bipasha 57
Basset, Alberto 324
Bastien, Marie 219
Bergamaschi, Sonia 124
Beuchert, Jonas 382
Boros, Emanuela 14
Bos, Floris 70
Broise, Jean-Baptiste de la 25
Brook, Anna 367
Bruno, Carole 219

C

Carbone, Dylan 382
Caufield, Harry 353
Christopoulou, Aikaterini 100
Cochin, Gregory 219
Cohen, Tom Avikasis 367
Compton, Katherine 353
Correia, Ricardo A. 299
Coustaty, Mickaël 110
Cuculovic, Milos 25

D

Dadic, Petra 287
Dam, Arpan 156

De Leo, Francesco 324
de Viron, Olivier 146
Delaunay, Julien 146
Di Muri, Cristina 324
Dimitropoulos, Harry 185, 276
Doucet, Antoine 146
Drew, Kian 353
Dupiat, Anne 219

E

Ermakova, Liana 287
Eto, Masaki 207
Evangelatos, Andreas 100

F

Fafalios, Pavlos 229
Foufoulas, Yannis 185, 276
Frühstückl, Robert 353

G

Gatos, Basilis 100
German, Fausto 57
Ghafourian, Yasin 166
Goldmann, Katriona 382
Guillaume, Jean-Loup 110
Gupta, Sharad Kumar 311

H

Hanbury, Allan 166
Heger, Tina 353

I

Ikejiri, Ryohei 46
Ingram, William A. 57
Ioannidis, Yannis 185, 276
Iqbal, Mariya 382
Isaac, Maxim C. 299

J

Jäschke, Robert 135

K

Kaddas, Panagiotis 100
Kafle, Dipendra Sharma 146
Kakridis, Andreas 100
Katsouros, Vassilis 100
Khan, Taimur 311
Kissling, W Daniel 338
Klair, Hajra 57
Knoth, Petr 166
Kong, Beibei 196
König-Ries, Birgitta 353
Koschmider, Agnes 90
Krebs, Jasmin 311
Kreutz, Christin Katharina 258
Kroll, Hermann 258
Kruschwitz, Udo 90
Kumpulainen, Sanna 35

L

La Marra, Mariantonietta 324
Lawson, Jenna L. 382, 392
Li, Qian 196
Lu, Zehao 338

M

Machizawa, Daisuke 46
Maeda, Akira 3
Manola, Natalia 185, 276
Marx, Maarten 70, 176
Meijere, Sanita 25
Mitkousis, Efthimios 238
Mitra, Bivas 156
Mountantonakis, Michalis 248
Moxon, Sierra 353
Mungall, Chris 353

N

Nölke, Nils 311

O

Opijnen, Marc van 70
Ortiz-Viso, Bartolome 392
Owoeye, Kehinde 407

P

Palaiologos, Konstantinos 100
Pathak, Sayan 156
Poulovassilis, Alexandra 80

Przerwa, Karolina 267
Pulieri, Martina 324

R

Raho, Davide 324
Rashidi, Parinaz 338
Reese, Justin 353
Renkel, Jonathan 311
Rilov, Gil 367
Rohr, Salomé 267
Rosati, Ilaria 324
Roy, David 382

S

Sackhoff, Pascal 258
Sala, Luca 124
Sapidis, Iordanis 248
Sauerburger, Frank 25
Sawahata, Naoki 46
Sayas, Enric 25
Scholz, Melanie 90
Sedoud, Morgane 219
Sendra, Anna 35
Sidere, Nicolas 146
Skinner, Grace 382
Slager, Gregory 176
Strickson, Oliver 382
Sullutrone, Giovanni 124
Sumikawa, Yasunobu 46

T

Tarallo, Andrea 324
Tardif, Jordan 353
Tecu, Dan-Marin 25
Thang, Bill Matthias 258
Tzitzikas, Yannis 238, 248
Tzortzakakis, Elias 229

V

van der Plas, Thijs L. 338
Vigliermo, Riccardo Amerigo 124
Vogt, Lars 353

W

Wang, Lu 196
Winters, Gidon 367

Wood, Peter T. 80
Wright, George A. 80
Wu, Bohao 3
Wu, Zhenxin 196

Z
Zacharia, Eleni 185, 276
Zervos, Valantis 248
Zhang, Zhixiong 196

Made in the USA
Monee, IL
03 May 2026

49438493R00247